THE BRUMBACK LIBRARY

IN MEMORY OF:

Ransom and Ann Oetzel

PRESENTED BY:

Mr. and Mrs. Terry Oetzel
and
Family

From Suffrage to the Senate

From Suffrage to the Senate

An Encyclopedia of American Women in Politics
Volume 2: N–Z

Suzanne O'Dea Schenken

Foreword by Ann W. Richards

ABC-CLIO

Santa Barbara, California
Denver, Colorado
Oxford, England

Library of Congress Cataloging-in-Publication Data

Schenken, Suzanne O'Dea
    From suffrage to the Senate : an encyclopedia of American women in
  politics / Suzanne O'Dea Schenken.
      p. cm.
    Includes bibliographical references and index.
    ISBN 0-87436-960-6 (acid-free paper)
    1. Women in politics—United States—Encyclopedias.   I. Title.
    HQ1236.5.U6S32   1999
    320'.082—dc21   99-048951
                                                                        CIP

ABC-CLIO, Inc.
130 Cremona Drive, P.O. Box 1911
Santa Barbara, California 93116-1911

This book is printed on acid-free paper ∞.

Manufactured in the United States of America

Contents

From Suffrage to the Senate

Volume 2: N–Z

Appendix 1: Documents, 729

Setting Political Agendas

Woman Suffrage

Equal Rights Amendment

Women, Campaigns, and Political Parties

Women of Sovereign Nations

Entries by Category

Activists and Authors

Abbott, Grace (1878–1939)

Addams, Jane (1860–1935)

Alexander, Sadie Tanner Mosell (1898–1989)

Allred, Gloria Rachel (b. 1941)

Ames, Jessie Harriet Daniel (1883–1972)

Anderson, Marian (1902–1993)

Angelou, Maya (b. 1928)

Anthony, Susan Brownell (1820–1906)

Atkinson, Ti-Grace (b. 1939)

Baker, Ella Josephine (1903–1986)

Balch, Emily Greene (1867–1961)

Barnard, Catherine (Kate) Ann (1875–1930)

Bass, Charlotta Spears (1880–1969)

Bates, Daisy Lee Gatson (b. 1920)

Beauvoir, Simone Lucie Ernestine Marie Bertrand de (1908–1986)

Belmont, Alva Erskine Smith Vanderbilt (1853–1933)

Bethune, Mary Jane McLeod (1875–1955)

Blackwell, Alice Stone (1857–1950)

Blatch, Harriot Eaton Stanton (1856–1940)

Bloomer, Amelia Jenks (1818–1894)

Bloor, Ella Reeve Ware Cohen Omholt (Mother Bloor) (1862–1951)

Bonney, Mary Lucinda (1816–1900)

Bradwell, Myra Colby (1831–1894)

Brady, Sarah Jane Kemp (b. 1942)

Bravo, Ellen (b. 1944)

Brent, Margaret (ca. 1607–ca. 1671)

Brown, Elaine (b. 1943)

Brown, Judie (b. 1944)

Brown, Rita Mae (b. 1944)

Byrne, Jane Margaret Burke (b. 1934)

Caldicott, Helen Broinowski (b. 1938)

Cammermeyer, Margrethe (b. 1942)

Carpenter, Mary Elizabeth (Liz) Sutherland (b. 1920)

Carson, Rachel Louise (1907–1964)

Catt, Carrie Clinton Lane Chapman (1859–1947)

Chavez, Linda (b. 1947)

Chavez-Thompson, Linda (b. 1944)

Child, Lydia Maria Francis (1802–1880)

Clark, Septima Poinsette (1898–1987)

Cleaver, Kathleen Neal (b. 1945)

Croly, Jane Cunningham (1829–1901)

Davis, Angela Yvonne (b. 1944)

Day, Dorothy (1897–1980)

Decter, Midge Rosenthal (b. 1927)

Dennett, Mary Coffin Ware (1872–1947)

Dix, Dorothea Lynde (1802–1887)

Douglass, Frederick (1817–1895)

Duniway, Abigail Jane Scott (1834–1915)

Dworkin, Andrea (b. 1946)

Eastman, Crystal (1881–1928)

Edelman, Marian Wright (b. 1939)

Eisenhuth, Alming, Laura J. Kelly (1858–1937)

Estrich, Susan (b. 1953)

Evers-Williams, Myrlie Louise Beasley (b. 1933)

Farenthold, Frances (Sissy) Talton (b. 1926)

Fauset, Crystal Dreda Bird (1894–1965)

Fonda, Jane Seymour (b. 1937)

Friedan, Betty Naomi Goldstein (b. 1921)

Fuller, Margaret (1810–1850)

Futrell, Mary Alice Franklin Hatwood (b. 1940)

Gage, Matilda Joslyn (1826–1898)

Gilman, Charlotte Perkins (1860–1935)

Goldman, Emma (1869–1940)

Grimké, Angelina Emily (1805–1879) and Sarah Moore (1792–1873)

Guinier, Lani (b. 1950)

Hamer, Fannie Lou Townsend (1917–1977)

Height, Dorothy Irene (b. 1912)

Hill, Anita Faye (b. 1956)

hooks, bell (b. 1952)

Howe, Julia Ward (1819–1910)

Huerta, Dolores (b. 1930)

Hurley, Ruby (1909–1980)

Hutchinson, Anne Marbury (1591–1643)

Ireland, Patricia (b. 1945)

Kelley, Florence (1859–1932)

Kennedy, Florynce Rae (b. 1916)

King, Coretta Scott (b. 1927)

King, Mary (b. 1940)

Kissling, Frances (b. 1943)

Kuhn, Margaret (Maggie) E. (1905–1995)

La Flesche, Susette (1854–1903)

Lampkin, Daisy Elizabeth Adams (ca. 1884–1965)

Landes, Bertha Ethel Knight (1868–1943)

Lease, Mary Elizabeth Clyens (1850–1933)

Lockwood, Belva Ann Bennett McNall (1830–1917)

Lyon, Phyllis (b. 1924)

MacKinnon, Catharine Alice (b. 1946)

Madar, Olga Marie (1916–1996)

Malcolm, Ellen Reighley (b. 1947)

Martin, Del (b. 1921)

Matalin, Mary Joe (b. 1953)

McCabe, Jewell Jackson (b. 1945)

McCormack, Ellen (b. 1926)

Millett, Katherine (Kate) Murray (b. 1934)

Mott, Lucretia Coffin (1793–1880)

Murray, Pauli (1910–1985)

Natividad, Irene (b. 1948)

Nussbaum, Karen (b. 1950)

O'Hare, Kathleen Richards (1876–1948)

Park, Maud Wood (1871–1955)

Parks, Rosa Louise McCauley (b. 1913)

Paul, Alice (1885–1977)

Quinton, Amelia Stone (1833–1926)

Robinson, Ruby Doris Smith (1941–1967)

Ruffin, Josephine St. Pierre (1842–1924)

Sanger, Margaret Louise Higgins (1879–1966)

Schlafly, Phyllis Stewart (b. 1924)

Shabazz, Hajj Bahiyah (Betty) (1936–1997)

Shaw, Anna Howard (1847–1919)

Simmons, Althea T. L. (1924–1990)

Smeal, Eleanor Cutri (b. 1939)

Stanton, Elizabeth Cady (1815–1902)

Steinem, Gloria Marie (b. 1934)

Stewart, Maria W. (1803–1879)

Stone, Lucy (1818–1893)

Stowe, Harriet Elizabeth Beecher (1811–1896)

Talbert, Mary Morris Burnett (1866–1923)

Terrell, Mary Eliza Church (1863–1954)

Truth, Sojourner (ca. 1797–1883)

Tubman, Harriet (ca. 1820–1913)

Wald, Lillian D. (1867–1940)

Wattleton, Alyce Faye (b. 1943)

Weddington, Sarah Ragle (b. 1945)

Wells-Barnett, Ida Bell (1862–1931)

Willard, Frances Elizabeth Caroline (1839–1898)

Wollstonecraft, Mary (1759–1797)

Woodhull, Victoria Claflin (1838–1927)

Wright, Frances (Fanny) (1795–1852)

Administrative Appointments

Adams, Annette Abbott (Justice Department)

Adkins, Bertha Sheppard (Health, Education, and Welfare)

Anderson, Eugenie Moore (Ambassador)

Anderson, Mary (Women's Bureau)

Armstrong, Anne Legendre (Ambassador)

Baca, Pauline Celia (Polly) (Office of Consumer Affairs; General Services Administration)

Banuelos, Romana Acosta (Treasurer)

Bellamy, Carol (Peace Corps)

Bentley, Helen Delich (Federal Maritime Commission)

Berry, Mary Frances (Commission on Civil Rights)

Campbell, Bonnie Jean Pierce (Violence Against Women Office)

Clark Gray, Georgia Neese (Treasurer)

Costanza, Margaret (Midge) (White House Public Liaison)

East, Catherine Shipe (Department of Labor)

Echaveste, Maria (Deputy White House Chief of Staff)

Elders, Joycelyn (Surgeon General)

Harriman, Pamela Beryl Digby Churchill Hayward (Ambassador)

Hernandez, Aileen Clarke (Equal Employment Opportunity Commission)

Koontz, Elizabeth Duncan (Women's Bureau)

Lathrop, Julia (Children's Bureau)

Lewis, Ann Frank (White House Director of Communications; Counselor to the President)

Louchheim, Kathleen (Katie) Scofield (Ambassador)

Meissner, Doris Marie (Immigration and Naturalization Service)

Motley, Constance Baker (Federal Judge)

Myers, Margaret Jane (Dee Dee) (White House Press Secretary)

Ortega, Katherine Davalos (Treasurer)

Novello, Antonia Coello (Surgeon General)

Peterson, Esther (Women's Bureau)

Priest, Ivy Maude Baker (Treasurer)

Smith, Mary Louise (Commission on Civil Rights)

Watson, Barbara Mae (State Department)

Wexler, Anne Levy (White House Public Liaison)

Widnall, Sheila Evans (Secretary of the Air Force)

Willebrandt, Mabel Walker (Department of Justice)

Agencies and Organizations

Alpha Kappa Alpha Sorority

Alpha Suffrage Club

American Association of University Women

American Civil Liberties Union

American Life League, Inc.

American Woman Suffrage Association

Association of Southern Women for the Prevention of Lynching

Business and Professional Women/USA

Catholics for a Free Choice

Center for the American Woman and Politics

Children's Bureau

Children's Defense Fund

Christian Coalition

Citizens' Advisory Council on the Status of Women

Coalition for Women's Appointments

Coalition of Labor Union Women

Colored Women's League

Comisión Femenil Mexicana Nacional, Inc.

Commissions on the Status of Women

Communist Party, USA

Concerned Women for America

Congressional Caucus for Women's Issues

Congressional Union

Council of Presidents

Daughters of Bilitis

Daughters of Liberty

Day Care Council of America

Delta Sigma Theta Sorority

Democratic Party, Women in the

Eagle Forum

EMILY's List

Equal Employment Opportunity Commission

Barshefsky, Charlene, 1997–

Browner, Carol, 1993–

Dole, (Mary) Elizabeth Hanford, 1983–1987, 1989–1991

Franklin, Barbara Hackman, 1992–1993

Harris, Patricia Roberts, 1977–1979, 1979–1981

Heckler, Margaret Mary O'Shaughnessy, 1983–1985

Herman, Alexis Margaret, 1997–

Hills, Carla Helen Anderson, 1975–1977, 1989–1993

Hobby, Oveta Culp, 1953–1955

Hufstedler, Shirley Ann Mount, 1979–1981

Kirkpatrick, Jeane Duane Jordan, 1981–1985

Kreps, Juanita Morris, 1977–1979

Martin, Judith Lynn Morley, 1991–1993

McLaughlin, Ann Dore Lauenstein, 1987–1989

O'Leary, Hazel Rollins, 1993–1997

Perkins, Frances (Fanny) Corlie, 1933–1945

Reno, Janet, 1993–

Rivlin, Alice Mitchell, 1994–1996

Shalala, Donna Edna, 1993–

Tyson, Laura D'Andrea, 1995–1997

Yellen, Janet, 1997–

Court Cases

Adkins v. Children's Hospital (1923)

Akron v. Akron Center for Reproductive Health (1983)

Bachur v. Democratic National Committee (1987)

Beal v. Doe (1977)

Bellotti v. Baird (1976, 1979)

Bowe v. Colgate-Palmolive Company (1969)

Bowers v. Hardwick (1986)

Bradwell v. Illinois (1873)

Bray v. Alexandria Clinic (1993)

California Federal Savings and Loan v. Guerra (1987)

Carey v. Population Services International (1977)

Cleveland Board of Education v. LaFleur (1974)

Clinton v. Jones (1997)

Colautti v. Franklin (1979)

Corning Glass Works v. Brennan (1974)

County of Washington, Oregon v. Gunther (1981)

Craig v. Boren (1976)

Diaz v. Pan American World Airways, Inc. (1971)

Doe v. Bolton (1973)

Dothard v. Rawlinson (1977)

Eisenstadt v. Baird (1972)

Frontiero v. Richardson (1973)

Geduldig v. Aiello (1974)

General Electric v. Gilbert (1976)

Goesaert v. Cleary (1948)

Griswold v. Connecticut (1965)

Grove City College v. Bell (1984)

H. L. v. Matheson (1984)

Harris v. Forklift Systems (1993)

Harris v. McRae (1980)

Hishon v. King and Spalding (1984)

Hodgson v. Minnesota (1990)

Hoyt v. Florida (1961)

Johnson v. Transportation Agency of Santa Clara County (1987)

Kirchberg v. Feenstra (1981)

Maher v. Roe (1977)

McCarty v. McCarty (1980)

Orr, Kay Avonne Stark (R-NE), 1987–1991

Ray, Dixy Lee (D-WA), 1977–1981

Richards, Ann Willis (D-TX), 1991–1995

Roberts, Barbara Hughey (D-OR), 1991–1995

Ross, Nellie Tayloe (D-WY), 1925–1927

Roy, Vesta M. (R-NH), 1982–1983

Shaheen, Jeanne (D-NH), 1997–

Wallace, Lurleen Burns (D-AL), 1967–1968

Whitman, Christine Todd (R-NJ), 1994–

Issues and Movements

Abolitionist Movement, Women in the

Abortion

Affirmative Action

Antilynching Movement

Child Day Care

Child Support Enforcement

Civil Rights Movement, Women in the

Consciousness Raising

Conservatism

Displaced Homemakers

Divorce Law Reform

Domestic Violence

Education, Women and

Employment Discrimination

The Feminine Mystique

Feminist Movement

Feminization of Poverty

Flint Auto Workers' Strike

Gender Gap

Health Care, Women and

Lawrence Textile Mill Strike

Lesbian Rights

Liberalism

Military, Women in the

News Media, Women Politicians and

Pay Equity

Peace Movement

Pornography

Protective Legislation

Public Speaking

Quaker Women

Racial Discrimination

Rape

Reproductive Rights

RU-486 (Mifepristone)

Seneca Falls Convention

Separate Spheres

Sex Discrimination

Sexual Harassment

Shirtwaist Workers Strike

Social Security

Socialism

Stalking

Suffrage

Temperance Movement, Women in the

Triangle Shirtwaist Company Fire

Welfare

Women's Liberation Movement

Year of the Woman

Political Party Leaders

Adkins, Bertha Sheppard (Republican National Committee)

Blair, Emily Newell (Democratic National Committee)

Crisp, Mary Dent (Republican National Committee)

Dewson, Mary (Molly) Williams (Democratic National Committee)

Edwards, India Moffett (Democratic National Committee)

Flynn, Elizabeth Gurley (Communist Party)

Martin, Marion E. (Republican National Committee)

Moskowitz, Belle Lindner Israels (Democratic National Committee)

Smith, Mary Louise (Republican National Committee)

Upton, Harriet Taylor (Republican National Committee)

Westwood, Frances Jean Miles (Democratic National Committee)

Willebrandt, Mabel Walker (Republican National Committee)

U.S. House Representatives and Years They Served

Abzug, Bella Savitzky (D-NY), 1971–1977

Andrews, (Leslie) Elizabeth Bullock (D-AL), 1972–1973

Ashbrook, (Emily) Jean Spencer (R-OH), 1982–1983

Baker, Irene Bailey (R-TN), 1964–1965

Baldwin, Tammy (D-WI), 1999–

Bentley, Helen Delich (R-MD), 1985–1995

Berkley, Shelley (D-NV), 1999–

Biggert, Judith Borg (R-IL), 1999–

Blitch, Iris Faircloth (D-GA), 1955–1963

Boggs, Marie Corinne Morrison Claiborne (Lindy) (D-LA), 1973–1991

Boland, Veronica Grace (D-PA), 1942–1943

Bolton, Frances Payne Bingham (R-OH), 1940–1969

Bono, Mary Whitaker (R-CA), 1998–

Bosone, Reva Zilpha Beck (D-UT), 1949–1953

Boxer, Barbara Levy (D-CA), 1983–1993

Brown, Corrine (D-FL), 1993–

Buchanan, Vera Daerr (D-PA), 1951–1955

Burke, Perle Yvonne Watson Brathwaite (D-CA), 1973–1979

Burton, Sala Galante (D-CA), 1983–1987

Byrne, Leslie Larkin (D-VA), 1993–1995

Byron, Beverly Barton Butcher (D-MD), 1979–1993

Byron, Katharine Edgar (D-MD), 1941–1943

Cantwell, Maria (D-WA), 1993–1995

Capps, Lois (D-CA), 1998–

Carson, Julia May Porter (D-IN), 1997–

Chenoweth, Helen Palmer (R-ID), 1995–

Chisholm, Shirley Anita St. Hill (D-NY), 1969–1983

Christian-Green, Donna (D-VI), 1997–

Church, Marguerite Stitt (R-IL), 1951–1963

Clarke, Marian Williams (R-NY), 1933–1935

Clayton, Eva McPherson (D-NC), 1992–

Collins, Barbara-Rose (D-MI), 1991–1997

Collins, Cardiss Hortense Robertson (D-IL), 1973–1997

Cubin, Barbara Lynn (R-WY), 1995–

Danner, Patsy Ann (D-MO), 1993–

DeGette, Diana (D-CO), 1997–

DeLauro, Rosa L. (D-CT), 1991–

Douglas, Emily Taft (D-IL), 1945–1947

Douglas, Helen Mary Gahagan (D-CA), 1945–1951

Dunn, Jennifer (R-WA), 1993–

Dwyer, Florence Price (R-NJ), 1957–1973

Emerson, Jo Ann (R-MO), 1996–

English, Karan (D-AZ), 1993–1995

Eshoo, Anna G. (D-CA), 1993–

Eslick, Willa McCord Blake (D-TN), 1932–1933

Farrington, Mary Elizabeth Pruett (R-HI), 1954–1957

Fenwick, Millicent Hammond (R-NJ), 1975–1983

Ferraro, Geraldine Anne (D-NY), 1979–1985

Fiedler, Roberta (Bobbi) Frances Horowitz (R-CA), 1981–1987

Fowler, Tillie Kidd (R-FL), 1993–

Fulmer, Willa Lybrand (D-SC), 1944–1945

Furse, Elizabeth (D-OR), 1993–1999

Gasque Van Exem, Elizabeth Mills Hawley (D-SC), 1938–1939

Gibbs, Florence Reville (D-GA), 1940–1941

Granahan, Kathryn Elizabeth O'Hay (D-PA), 1956–1963

Granger, Kay (R-TX), 1997–

Grasso, Ella Rosa Giovanna Oliva Tambussi (D-CT), 1971–1975

Green, Edith Louise Starrett (D-OR), 1955–1975

Greene, Enid (R-UT), 1995–1997

Greenway King, Isabella Selmes (D-AZ), 1933–1937

Griffiths, Martha Edna Wright (D-MI), 1955–1974

Hall, Katie Beatrice Green (D-IN), 1982–1985

Hansen, Julia Caroline Butler (D-WA), 1960–1974

Harden, Cecil Murray (R-IN), 1949–1959

Harman, Jane Frank (D-CA), 1993–1999

Heckler, Margaret Mary O'Shaughnessy (R-MA), 1967–1983

Hicks, (Anna) Louise Day (D-MA), 1971–1973

Holt, Marjorie Sewell (R-MD), 1973–1987

Holtzman, Elizabeth (D-NY), 1973–1981

Honeyman, Nan Wood (D-OR), 1937–1939

Hooley, Darlene (D-OR), 1997–

Horn, Joan Kelly (D-MO), 1991–1993

Huck, Winifred Sprague Mason (R-IL), 1922–1923

Hyde, Henry John (R-IL), 1975–

Jackson Lee, Sheila (D-TX), 1995–

Jenckes, Virginia Ellis (D-IN), 1933–1939

Johnson, Eddie Bernice (D-TX), 1993–

Johnson, Nancy Lee (R-CT), 1983–

Jones, Stephanie Tubbs (D-OH), 1999–

Jordan, Barbara Charline (D-TX), 1973–1979

Kahn, Florence Prag (R-CA), 1925–1937

Kaptur, Marcia (Marcy) Carolyn (D-OH), 1983–

Kee, Maude Elizabeth Simpkins (D-WV), 1951–1965

Kelly, Edna Patricia Kathleen
Flannery (D-NY), 1949–1969
Kelly, Sue W. (R-NY), 1995–
Kennelly, Barbara Bailey (D-CT),
1982–1999
Keys, Martha Elizabeth Ludwig
(D-KS), 1975–1979
Kilpatrick, Carolyn Cheeks
(D-MI), 1997–
Knutson, Coya Gjesdal (D-MN),
1955–1959
Langley, Katherine Gudger
(R-KY), 1927–1931
Lee, Barbara (D-CA), 1998–
Lincoln, Blanche Lambert (D-AR),
1993–1997
Lloyd Bouquard, Rachel Marilyn
Laird (D-TN), 1975–1995
Lofgren, Zoe (D-CA), 1995–
Long, Catherine Small (D-LA),
1985–1987
Long Thompson, Jill Lynnette
(D-IN), 1989–1995
Lowey, Nita Melnikoff (D-NY),
1989–
Luce, Clare Boothe (R-CT),
1943–1947
Lusk, Georgia Lee Witt (D-NM),
1947–1949
Maloney, Carolyn Bosher (D-NY),
1993–
Mankin, Helen Douglas (D-GA),
1946–1947
Margolies-Mezvinsky, Marjorie
(D-PA), 1993–1995
Martin, Judith Lynn Morley
(R-IL), 1981–1991
May Bedell, Catherine Dean
Barnes (R-WA), 1959–1971
McCarthy, Carolyn (D-NY),
1997–
McCarthy, Karen (D-MO), 1995–

McCormick Simms, Ruth Hanna
(R-IL), 1929–1931
McKinney, Cynthia Ann (D-GA),
1993–
McMillan, Clara Gooding (D-SC),
1939–1941
Meek, Carrie Pittman (D-FL),
1993–
Meyers, Jan (R-KS), 1985–1997
Meyner, Helen Day Stevenson
(D-NJ), 1975–1979
Mikulski, Barbara Ann (D-MD),
1977–1987
Millender-McDonald, Juanita
(D-CA), 1996–
Mink, Patsy Matsu Takemoto
(D-HI), 1965–1977, 1990–
Molinari, Susan (R-NY),
1990–1997
Morella, Constance Albanese
(R-MD), 1987–
Myrick, Sue (R-NC), 1995–
Napolitano, Grace Flores (D-CA),
1999–
Nolan, Mae Ella Hunt (R-CA),
1923–1925
Norrell, Catherine Dorris (D-AR),
1961–1963
Northrup, Anne Meagher (R-KY),
1997–
Norton, Eleanor Holmes (D-DC),
1991–
Norton, Mary Teresa Hopkins
(D-NJ), 1925–1951
Oakar, Mary Rose (D-OH),
1977–1993
O'Day, Caroline Love Goodwin
(D-NY), 1935–1943
O'Laughlin, Kathryn Ellen Mc-
Carthy (D-KS), 1933–1935
Oldfield, Pearl Peden (D-AR),
1929–1931

Owen Rohde, Ruth Bryan (D-FL), 1929–1933

Patterson, Elizabeth Johnston (D-SC), 1987–1993

Pelosi, Nancy B. (D-CA), 1987–

Pettis Roberson, Shirley Neil McCumber (R-CA), 1975–1979

Pfost, Gracie Bowers (D-ID), 1953–1963

Pratt, Eliza Jane (D-NC), 1946–1947

Pratt, Ruth Sears Baker (R-NY), 1929–1933

Pryce, Deborah (R-OH), 1993–

Rankin, Jeannette Pickering (R-MT), 1917–1919, 1941–1943

Reece, Louise Goff (R-TN), 1961–1963

Reid, Charlotte Thompson (R-IL), 1963–1971

Riley, Corrine Boyd (D-SC), 1962–1963

Rivers, Lynn Nancy (D-MI), 1995–

Robertson, Alice Mary (R-OK), 1921–1923

Rogers, Edith Frances Nourse (R-MA), 1925–1960

Ros-Lehtinen, Ileana (R-FL), 1989–

Roukema, Margaret Scafati (R-NJ), 1981–

Roybal-Allard, Lucille (D-CA), 1993–

Saiki, Patricia Fukuda (R-HI), 1987–1991

St. George, Katharine Delano Price Collier (R-NY), 1947–1965

Sanchez, Loretta (D-CA), 1997–

Schakowsky, Janice D. (D-IL), 1999–

Schenk, Lynn (D-CA), 1993–1995

Schneider, Claudine Cmarada (R-RI), 1981–1991

Schroeder, Patricia Nell Scott (D-CO), 1973–1997

Seastrand, Andrea Ciszek (R-CA), 1995–1997

Shepherd, Karen (D-UT), 1993–1995

Simpson, Edna Oakes (R-IL), 1959–1961

Slaughter, Louise McIntosh (D-NY), 1987–

Smith, Howard Worth (D-VA), 1931–1967

Smith, Linda A. (R-WA), 1995–1999

Smith, Margaret Madeline Chase (R-ME), 1940–1949

Smith, Virginia Dodd (R-NE), 1975–1991

Snowe, Olympia Jean Bouchles (R-ME), 1979–1995

Spellman, Gladys Blossom Noon (D-MD), 1975–1981

Stabenow, Deborah Ann (D-MI), 1997–

Stanley, Winifred Claire (R-NY), 1943–1945

Sullivan, Leonor Kretzer (D-MO), 1953–1977

Sumner, Jessie (R-IL), 1939–1947

Tauscher, Ellen (D-CA), 1997–

Thomas, Lera Millard (D-TX), 1966–1967

Thompson, Ruth (R-MI), 1951–1957

Thurman, Karen L. (D-FL), 1993–

Unsoeld, Jolene Bishoprick (D-WA), 1989–1995

Velázquez, Nydia Margarita (D-NY), 1993–

Vucanovich, Barbara Farrell (R-NV), 1983–1997

Waters, Maxine Moore (D-CA), 1991–

Weis, Jessica McCullough (R-NY), 1959–1963

Wilson, Heather (R-NM), 1998–

Wingo, Effiegene Locke (D-AR), 1930–1933

Woodhouse, Chase Going (D-CT), 1945–1947, 1949–1951

Woolsey, Lynn (D-CA), 1993–

U.S. Senators and Years They Served

Abel, Hazel Pearl Hempel (R-NE), 1954

Allen, Maryon Pittman (D-AL), 1978

Bowring, Eva Kelly (R-NE), 1954

Boxer, Barbara Levy (D-CA), 1993–

Burdick, Jocelyn Birch (D-ND), 1992–

Bushfield, Vera Cahalan (R-SD), 1948

Caraway, Hattie Ophelia Wyatt (D-AR), 1931–1945

Collins, Susan Margaret (R-ME), 1997–

Edwards, Elaine Lucille Schwartzenburg (D-LA), 1972

Feinstein, Dianne Goldman (D-CA), 1992–

Felton, Rebecca Ann Latimer (D-GA), 1922

Frahm, Sheila Sloan (R-KS), 1996

Graves, Dixie Bibb (D-AL), 1937–1938

Hawkins, Paula Fickes (R-FL), 1981–1987

Humphrey Brown, Muriel Fay Buck (D-MN), 1978

Hutchison, Kathryn (Kay) Ann Bailey (R-TX), 1993–

Kassebaum Baker, Nancy Landon (R-KS), 1979–1997

Landrieu, Mary (D-LA), 1997–

Lincoln, Blanche Lambert (D-AR), 1999–

Long, Rose McConnell (D-LA), 1936–1937

Mikulski, Barbara Ann (D-MD), 1987–

Moseley-Braun, Carol (D-IL), 1993–1999

Murray, Patty Johns (D-WA), 1993–

Neuberger, Maurine Brown (D-OR), 1960–1967

Pyle, Gladys (R-SD), 1938–1939

Smith, Margaret Madeline Chase (R-ME), 1949–1973

Snowe, Olympia Jean Bouchles (R-ME), 1995–

U.S. Supreme Court Justices

Ginsburg, Ruth Joan Bader, 1993–
O'Connor, Sandra Day, 1981–

Women of Sovereign Nations

Bonnin, Gertrude Simmons (a.k.a. Zitkala-Ša and Red Bird) (1876–1938)

Deer, Ada Elizabeth (b. 1935)

Harris, LaDonna (b. 1931)

Jumper, Betty Mae (b. 1923)

LaDuke, Winona (b. 1959)

Liliuokalani (1838–1917)

Mankiller, Wilma P. (b. 1945)

From Suffrage to the Senate

N

Napolitano, Grace Flores (b. 1936)

Democrat Grace Napolitano of California entered the U.S. House of Representatives on 3 January 1999, the fifth Latina elected to Congress. She began her political career as the first Latina member of the Norwalk, California, city council, serving from 1986 to 1992. Elected to the California State Assembly in 1992, she led the effort to preserve 1,400 acres of open land for parks and wilderness, one of the largest new areas of its kind in Southern California, and sought to enhance California's international trade by promoting the state in China, Thailand, Mexico, and other countries. She served in the assembly until her election to Congress in 1998. As a member of Congress, Napolitano has focused on helping small businesses to participate in international markets, obtaining federal assistance for environmental cleanup projects in her district, and identifying new water resources for the Los Angeles area.

Born in Brownsville, Texas, Napolitano completed her formal education at Brownsville High School in 1954.

See also Congress, Women in; State Legislatures, Women in

References "Grace F. Napolitano" (1998).

Nashville Gas Co. v. Satty (1977)

In *Nashville Gas Co. v. Satty,* the U.S. Supreme Court considered two of the company's employment policies related to pregnant women. Nashville Gas Company required pregnant women to take a leave of absence without receiving sick pay, even though the company provided it for nonoccupational disabilities other than pregnancy. In addition, when women returned to work, they lost their seniority, even though employees who took sick leave for other nonoccupational disabilities retained their seniority.

The Court decided that denying sick pay for pregnancy did not violate Title VII of the Civil Rights Act of 1964, unless it was a pretext for discriminating against one sex or the other, and remanded the case for consideration of that point. The Court decided that denying seniority to employees returning from pregnancy leave violated Title VII, saying that the policy imposed a substantial burden on women.

See also *Geduldig v. Aiello; General Electric v. Gilbert;* Pregnancy Discrimination Act of 1978

References *Nashville Gas Co. v. Satty,* 434 U.S. 136 (1977).

National Abortion and Reproductive Rights Action League

Founded in 1969, the National Abortion and Reproductive Rights Action League (NARAL) promotes reproductive freedom through its 500,000 members and thirty-six state affiliates. Initially known as the National Association for the Repeal of Abortion Laws, the organization changed its name to National Abortion Rights Action League in 1973 after the U.S. Supreme Court's decision in *Roe v. Wade* legalizing abortion. Its second name change came in 1994, when NARAL expanded its mission to include the prevention of unwanted pregnancies and advocacy for healthy pregnancies and children.

NARAL is a nonprofit organization that develops political strategies, organizes grassroots campaigns, and lobbies Congress and state legislatures. Through its political action committee, NARAL supports prochoice candidates with paid media advertising, financial contributions, and get-out-the-vote projects on election days. The NARAL Foundation supports research and legal work, publishes policy reports, conducts public education campaigns, and provides leadership training.

NARAL successfully worked with other groups to remove the gag rule that prevented abortion counseling at federally funded family planning clinics, to lift the ban on federally funded medical research on fetal tissue transplants, and to permit abortions at military hospitals. It also helped pass the Freedom of Access to Clinic Entrances Act of 1994. NARAL supports testing and marketing the abortifacient RU-486, health reform that includes a full range of reproductive health services for women, and the proposed Freedom of Choice Act.

See also Abortion; Freedom of Access to Clinic Entrances Act of 1994; *Roe v. Wade;* RU-486 (Mifepristone)

References www.naral.org.

National Advisory Committee for Women

Created in 1978 by President Jimmy Carter's Executive Order 12050, the National Advisory Committee for Women (NACW) was established to monitor the progress of the National Plan of Action passed at the 1977 National Women's Conference. Carter appointed thirty-eight women and men to the commission and designated former congresswoman Bella Abzug and Carmen Delgado Votaw to be its cochairs. The executive order also created an interdepartmental task force and directed it to review the impact of agency programs and regulations on women. Before it had completed its work, the committee issued a press release criticizing Carter's economic policies, saying the policies placed a disproportionately unfair burden on women. The White House fired Abzug from the committee, and several committee members then resigned in protest. The President's Advisory Committee for Women replaced the NACW in mid-1979 and operated until December 1980.

See also Abzug, Bella Savitzky; National Women's Conference

References East, *American Women: 1963 1983 2003* (1983).

National American Woman Suffrage Association

The National American Woman Suffrage Association (NAWSA) was created in 1890, when the National Woman Suffrage Association (NWSA) and the American Woman Suffrage Association (AWSA) merged. For thirty years the organization served as the primary advocate for woman suffrage, educating the public, seeking congressional support, and assisting in campaigns for state amendments. It was the largest suffrage association in the nation when the Nineteenth Amendment was ratified in 1920.

Veteran women's rights advocate Elizabeth Cady Stanton was NAWSA's first president, serving from 1890 to 1892. Her longtime political partner Susan B. Anthony followed her in the presidency, guiding the organization until 1900. By that year, four western states had granted women full suffrage: Wyoming, Colorado, Idaho, and Utah. Anthony chose Carrie Chapman Catt, a less well-known suffrage leader who was a generation younger than her predecessors, to succeed her. During the four years that Catt served as NAWSA president, several states conducted campaigns, but none of the amendments passed. The federal suffrage amendment had even less success. Congressional supporters of the amendment regularly introduced the amendment but were unable to obtain significant action on it.

Under Anna Howard Shaw's presidency, from 1904 to 1915, seven states adopted constitutional amendments granting women suffrage rights, and one state, Illinois, gave women presidential suffrage through

The National American Woman Suffrage Association organized parades like this one in New York City to advance their cause, 1908 (Library of Congress)

legislation, but lobbying efforts at the congressional level failed to result in substantive action. A new force entered the campaign in 1913 when Alice Paul, who had worked with British suffragists, brought new energy and ideas to the association. As chair of NAWSA's congressional committee, she organized a suffrage parade in Washington, D.C., that competed with President-elect Woodrow Wilson's arrival for his inauguration. The parade and other actions she orchestrated attracted publicity, provoked debate, and gained her the reputation of being a militant. Paul proved to be too controversial for the more staid and conservative NAWSA leadership, who objected to her strategies. Paul formed the Congressional Union, left NAWSA, and remained a visible force in the suffrage effort, frustrating NAWSA leaders with her actions, which they believed hindered the amendment's progress.

Catt returned to NAWSA's presidency in 1915 with a new strategy, called the "Winning Plan." The plan had three aspects to it. Women living in suffrage states were to work for political candidates who supported woman suffrage. NAWSA would no longer participate in every state campaign but would limit itself to working only in those campaigns that leaders thought could be won. Every available resource would be devoted to congressional passage of a federal amendment. The plan was a political strategy that contrasted with the educational campaigns that NAWSA had traditionally conducted. Catt presented it to NAWSA's 1915 convention and obtained the convention's approval of it. She also worked to gain President Woodrow Wilson's support for the amendment, keeping communications open between them.

When the United States entered World War I, NAWSA financed several hospitals in Europe and at home, and NAWSA leaders held visible roles in federal war agencies. NAWSA members volunteered for the Red Cross, canvassed their neighborhoods for food conservation programs, participated in the war service census, and worked on the Liberty Loan drives. President Woodrow Wilson rewarded these patriotic efforts in 1918 with his announcement that the war could not have been conducted without women's contributions and that he supported woman suffrage.

The U.S. House of Representatives passed the amendment in January 1918, but the Senate defeated it in February 1919. The House again passed the amendment in May 1919, and the Senate followed in June 1919. NAWSA turned its focus to ratifying the amendment, reaching the goal on 20 August 1920, when Tennessee became the last state needed to add the Nineteenth Amendment to the U.S. Constitution.

At NAWSA's 1920 convention, Catt had suggested the creation of an educational organization to provide newly enfranchised women with information about citizenship, voting, and related matters. The League of Women Voters emerged from her proposal.

> **See also** American Woman Suffrage Association; Anthony, Susan Brownell; Catt, Carrie Clinton Lane Chapman; Congressional Union; League of Women Voters; National Woman Suffrage Association; Paul, Alice; Shaw, Anna Howard; Stanton, Elizabeth Cady; Suffrage
>
> **References** Flexner and Fitzpatrick, *Century of Struggle: The Woman's Rights Movement in the United States* (1996).

National Association for the Advancement of Colored People, Women in the

Founded in 1909, the National Association for the Advancement of Colored People (NAACP) is the oldest and largest civil rights organization in the United States, with more than 500,000 members in 2,200 branches located in every state, the District of Columbia, Japan, and Germany. The NAACP has used legal actions as its primary strategy to end discrimination and to gain full citizenship for African Americans. The organization also lobbies state legislatures and Congress to ensure and protect the rights of minority citizens.

A 1908 race riot in Springfield, Illinois, prompted black and white Americans to join together to fight racism. W. E. B. Du Bois, Ida B. Wells-Barnett, Henry Moscowitz, Oswald Garrison Villard, William English

Women members of the planning committee for the National Association for the Advancement of Colored People standing by tables loaded with membership information, ca. 1910–1940 (Corbis)

Walling, and Mary White Ovington issued a call to form the organization. In its early years, several women, including Ida B. Wells-Barnett, Mary McLeod Bethune, and Mary Church Terrell, made significant contributions to the development and effectiveness of the organization, especially in its antilynching campaigns and its attempts, though unsuccessful, to pass antilynching legislation.

The NAACP worked against racial discrimination in New Deal programs and in the military during World War II. During the civil rights movement of the 1950s and 1960s, Daisy Lampkin, Ella Baker, Ruby Hurley, and Daisy Bates were among the notable activists in the organization. The NAACP provided leadership in developing coalitions for civil rights legislation, including the Civil Rights Acts of 1957, 1960, and 1964; the Voting Rights Act of 1965; and the Fair Housing Rights Act of 1968.

In addition to its leadership in Congress, the NAACP has developed numerous court cases and provided legal support to civil rights activists. In 1954, the NAACP's lawyers argued *Brown v. Board of Education of Topeka, Kansas,* the landmark case that ended legal racial segregation in public education. The next year, the organization's Montgomery Branch secretary, Rosa Parks, refused to surrender her bus seat to a white man, prompting the city's bus boycott. Among the many lawyers working for the NAACP, Constance Baker Motley assisted in and argued several of the civil rights cases of the 1950s and 1960s, including defending Martin Luther King, Jr., and other notable civil rights leaders.

See also Baker, Ella Josephine; Bates, Daisy Lee Gatson; Bethune, Mary Jane

McLeod; Civil Rights Movement, Women in the; Hurley, Ruby; Lampkin, Daisy Elizabeth Adams; Motley, Constance Baker; Simmons, Althea T. L.; Terrell, Mary Eliza Church; Wells-Barnett, Ida Bell

References www.naacp.org.

National Association of Colored Women

Founded in 1896, the National Association of Colored Women (NACW) brought together black women's clubs across the country into the first national communications network among African American women. As the Progressive reform movement emerged in the 1890s, African American women began to form local service and education clubs in several cities. When the General Federation of Women's Clubs refused to accept the Woman's Era Club, an organization of African American women, black women's clubs became affiliated with either the National Federation of Afro-American Women (NFAAW) or the National Colored Women's League (NCWL). In 1896, the NFAAW and NCWL merged to form the NACW. The organizing committee elected Mary Church Terrell the group's first president.

With the motto "Lifting as We Climb," NACW members participated in local projects including kindergartens, day nurseries, orphanages, jail and settlement work, and girls' homes. Mothers' clubs, hospitals, and the needs of black women domestic workers were other areas in which members worked. The NACW also supported equal rights for

A delegation representing the National Association of Colored Women picketed the White House in protest of the quadruple lynching at Monroe, Georgia, 1946 (Corbis/Bettmann)

blacks, work opportunities for black women, and changes in the criminal justice system. These areas of concern represented the priorities of members who sought racial uplift as NACW's primary focus. NACW also worked for woman suffrage, particularly to include provisions in the woman suffrage amendment to protect southern black women's suffrage rights.

After World War I, the number of lynchings increased dramatically, and NACW responded by mobilizing women to distribute information about the crime and to raise money for the National Association for the Advancement of Colored People's national campaign to end it. In 1922, Mary Talbert formed the Antilynching Crusaders in an effort to unite 1 million women against lynching and to pass a federal antilynching bill. NACW published reports on the crime that refuted the myths surrounding it, particularly that white men lynched black men in retribution for black men raping white women. Antilynching legislation did not pass, but the publicity and other organizational efforts to end the crime contributed to a reduction in the number of instances of it.

By 1920, NACW had 300,000 members and had paid the $5,000 mortgage on abolitionist Frederick Douglass's home in Anacostia, which it continues to maintain. When Mary McLeod Bethune became president in 1924, she led efforts to purchase a building for the organization's national headquarters. When she founded the National Council of Negro Women in 1935 to work for national policy changes, NACW became less politically involved and more social. By the 1980s, the association's membership had dropped to 45,000, where it has remained relatively stable.

See also Bethune, Mary Jane McLeod; Civil Rights Movement, Women in the; National Council of Negro Women; National Federation of Afro-American Women; Ruffin, Josephine St. Pierre; Suffrage; Talbert, Mary Morris Burnett; Terrell, Mary Eliza Church

References Kendrick, "'They Also Serve': The National Association of Colored Women, Inc." (1990); Slavin, ed., *U.S. Women's Public Interest Groups* (1995).

National Association of Commissions for Women

Founded in 1969, the National Association of Commissions for Women (NACW) is a nonpartisan membership organization of government-created regional, state, and local commissions that work to improve the status of women. With equality and justice for all women as its mission, NACW provides leadership on the national level, taking policy positions on national issues. NACW provides its more than 270 state and local commissions for women with technical advice and support.

See also Commissions on the Status of Women; President's Commission on the Status of Women

References www.nacw.org.

National Coalition Against Domestic Violence

Founded in 1978, the National Coalition Against Domestic Violence (NCADV) seeks to end violence in the lives of women and children through a national network of state coalitions and local organizations serving battered women and their children. The coalition provides technical assistance to member groups, conducts community awareness campaigns, and develops public policy recommendations. NCADV sponsors Domestic Violence Awareness Month every October to focus attention on the problem and a national registry called "Remember My Name" of women killed as a result of domestic violence.

See also Domestic Violence

References www.ncadv.org.

National Coalition of 100 Black Women

Founded in 1981, the National Coalition of 100 Black Women (NCBW) develops programs to empower African American women. The organization has sixty-two chapters in twenty-three states and the District of Columbia. The organization's roots are in a 1970 gathering of African American women in New York City to address the needs of black women, including the black family, career advancement, and political and economic empowerment. Through the coalition's programs, members developed leadership skills and sought ways to use them. The membership grew beyond the 100 in its name, and through the leadership of president Jewell Jackson McCabe, it expanded into a national organization in 1981.

The coalition's areas of interest in public policy include affirmative action, pay equity, equal opportunity, foreign aid, reproductive health rights, welfare reform, and support for federal appointees. Among the projects NCBW has sponsored are a program to match pregnant teenagers with role models, a career exploration program for high school students, and a model mentoring program. In 1986, NCBW held a colloquy examining the leadership values of prominent black women, and in 1989 it launched a health rights education program.

See also Abortion; Affirmative Action; McCabe, Jewell Jackson; Pay Equity

References www.womenconnect.com/ncbw/history.htm.

National Commission on the Observance of International Women's Year, 1975

Created by President Gerald Ford's Executive Order 11832 on 9 January 1975, the National Commission on the Observance of International Women's Year, 1975 was later charged by Congress with organizing and convening a National Women's Conference (NWC). The congressional action, signed by the president on 24 December 1975, was sponsored by Congresswoman Bella Abzug (D-NY) and constituted U.S. recognition of the United Nations' project to focus attention on the problems of women throughout the world.

Among those appointed to the commission were presiding officer Jill Ruckelshaus, actor Jean Stapleton, former congresswoman Clare Boothe Luce, and Republican National Committee chair Mary Louise Smith, all active feminists. The commissioners appointed committees to review the progress women had made since the issuance of the 1963 report by the President's Commission on the Status of Women and to make recommendations. In addition, an interdepartmental task force was created to ensure that agencies prepared analyses of the impact of federal programs on women. The commission made its report in "*To Form a More Perfect Union . . . ,*" which included 115 recommendations for policy changes to improve women's status. The report became an integral part of the planning for the 1977 National Women's Conference.

After the passage of Abzug's bill, the commission's tasks changed from performing research and making recommendations to developing plans for a national convention, organizing fifty-six state and territorial preliminary conventions, and providing support to them. In addition, with the election of President Jimmy Carter, several of the commission members were replaced with his appointees.

Congress gave the commission a feminist mandate, directing it to involve groups "which work to advance the rights of women," to "recognize the contributions of women to the development of our country," and to "assess the progress that has been made to date by both the private and public sectors in promoting equality between men and women in all aspects of life in the United States." The women and men appointed to the commission generally had strong feminist credentials, and some of them were feminist leaders, including commission cochair Abzug, *Ms.* magazine editor Gloria Steinem, Liz Carpenter, National Women's Political Caucus chair Audrey Rowe Colom, former congresswoman Martha Griffiths, former first lady Betty Ford, and others. The topical areas that the commission drafted for the conference's attention reflected feminist priorities: child care, reproductive rights, employment, the Equal Rights Amendment, and related issues.

The commission's duties included appointing state coordinating committees to organize and convene a state meeting. At the state meetings, the public participated by choosing delegates to the national conference, commenting on draft resolutions prepared by the national commission, and proposing resolutions for the national commission's consideration.

Although the state meetings were free to select delegates of their choice, Congress specifically directed the commission to ensure that low-income women; members of diverse racial, ethnic, and religious groups; and women of all ages were represented in the delegations. The commission accomplished the goal by reserving some delegate assignments to itself and creating the required balance after the states had selected their delegates.

Congress appropriated $5 million to fund the commission. Some of the funds were allocated to the states for their meetings, and the balance was used to provide financial assistance to delegates who could not pay their own expenses, to prepare and distribute background information and the final report, to hire staff, and to pay for the conference and its related expenses.

The National Women's Conference was held in November 1977, and the commission submitted its report, *The Spirit of Houston,* to President Jimmy Carter on 22 March 1978. The commission dissolved on 31 March 1978 as mandated by Congress. Carter established the National Advisory Committee for Women in April 1978, but its effectiveness was limited by a disagreement between Abzug, its chair, and Carter. Ultimately, a group of volunteers formed the National Women's Conference Committee to continue the NWC's work.

See also Abortion; Abzug, Bella Savitzky; Carpenter, Mary Elizabeth (Liz) Sutherland; Employment Discrimination; Equal Rights Amendment; Ford, Elizabeth Ann (Betty) Bloomer; Griffiths, Martha Edna Wright; Luce, Clare Boothe; National Advisory Committee for Women; National Women's Conference; National Women's Conference Committee; Smith, Mary Louise; Steinem, Gloria Marie

References Bird, *What Women Want* (1979); East, *American Women: 1963 1983 2003* (1983).

National Committee on Pay Equity

The National Committee on Pay Equity is a coalition of more than 180 organizations working to end sex-based and race-based wage discrimination. The organization provides leadership, information, and technical assistance to pay equity advocates, public officials, employers, the media, and the public. The organization supports the proposed Paycheck Fairness Act and the proposed Fair Pay Act.

See also Pay Equity
References http://feminist.com.

National Committee to Defeat the UnEqual Rights Amendment

Organized in 1944, the National Committee to Defeat the UnEqual Rights Amendment (NCDURA) was a coalition of twenty-seven groups, including labor unions, the National Consumers League, the League of Women

Voters, the National Council of Catholic Women, and the National Council of Negro Women. The organization emerged as the Equal Rights Amendment (ERA) and attracted increasingly favorable attention during World War II. NCDURA advocated "specific bills for specific ills" instead of the ERA because the ERA would invalidate protective labor legislation for women. The organization first proposed an equal pay act as an alternative to the ERA but was unable to gain congressional approval for the measure.

In 1947, under the leadership of Women's Bureau director Mary Anderson, NCDURA changed its name to the National Committee on the Status of Women and proposed the Status Bill. The bill stated that "no distinctions on the basis of sex shall be made except such as are reasonably based on differences in physical structure, biological or social function." The measure also included a provision to create a Commission on the Legal Status of Women to study sex discrimination, but Congress did not pass it. The committee dissolved without passing legislation. President John F. Kennedy, however, created the President's Commission on the Status of Women in 1961 by executive order.

See also Anderson, Mary; Equal Rights Amendment; League of Women Voters; National Consumers League; National Council of Negro Women; President's Commission on the Status of Women

References Freeman, "From Protection to Equal Opportunity: The Revolution in Women's Legal Status" (1990).

National Consumers League

Formed in 1899, the National Consumers League (NCL) sought to improve women's and children's working conditions through consumer pressure and protective labor legislation. At the end of the twentieth century, the NCL stated that its mission was "to protect and promote the economic and social interests of America's consumers." It operates the National Fraud Information Center and the Internet Fraud Watch and manages the Alliance Against Fraud in Telemarketing, the Child Labor Coalition, and a public service campaign to teach young children what to do in case of a fire.

The NCL began as a local effort in New York to help retail saleswomen obtain relief from long hours and low wages. In 1890, a group of philanthropists, social reformers, and settlement house leaders established the Consumers League of New York (CLNY). The group developed a list of minimum working conditions, including minimum pay at $6 per week, a ten-hour day, a six-day week, a locker room, a lunch room, and no children under the age of fourteen. CLNY investigated local retailers, identified those that met the minimum conditions, and published the results as its White List. Only eight stores made the first White List, but CLNY leaders encouraged consumers to limit their purchases to merchants on its list. In addition, the CLNY encouraged and helped women retail workers organize unions despite the resistance of male union leaders. As the league expanded into other cities, it identified sweatshops and the products they made and encouraged consumers to avoid purchasing items produced by them.

As more cities organized consumers' leagues, they joined together as the National Consumers League in 1899. By that time, it had become apparent that voluntary efforts had only limited success, and the organization entered a period of professionalization. A key part of the transformation was the decision to hire Florence Kelley as the first general secretary. Kelley organized leagues in sixty cities in twenty states and launched a series of investigations and reports. First, the league investigated workplaces where women's and children's stitched cotton underwear was produced and documented low wages, long hours, forced speed-ups, and poor working conditions. The second investigation probed home work and revealed filthy tenements, people with contagious diseases working on clothing, starvation wages, and child labor. The third researched child labor, disclosing the 1.7 million children under sixteen years old working in New England and southern textile mills.

Kelley kept the NCL's focus on child labor for the rest of her tenure as the organization's executive secretary. In 1904, NCL published a handbook on child labor that included a state-by-state report on child labor laws. She helped organize the National Child Labor Committee and, with Lillian Wald, proposed the creation of a federal commission on children. President Theodore Roosevelt's 1909 White House Conference on Child Health and Welfare provided a forum for the two women to advocate their proposal. In 1912, Congress created the Children's Bureau, and NCL provided the bureau with information that guided the formation of its legislative agenda. NCL advocated passing federal child labor laws and twice succeeded, but the U.S. Supreme Court found both of them unconstitutional. Proponents next gained congressional approval of a child labor amendment, but the states did not ratify it. New Deal legislation, however, prohibited most child labor.

NCL's 1907 study of self-supporting women's wages and standards of living led to the organization's effort to pass minimum wage laws. Kelley drafted a model minimum wage law that Massachusetts passed in 1912, and she traveled the country, speaking on the law and playing a significant role in nine additional states' passing similar policies within the year.

NCL also played significant roles in defending protective labor legislation in the courts. The most visible case was *Muller v. Oregon* (1908), a challenge to the state's law limiting women's workday to ten hours. Kelley persuaded Louis D. Brandeis, who donated his services, to defend the law before the U.S. Supreme Court. NCL gathered much of the research for what became known as the Brandeis brief, an innovation that presented more than 100 pages of social and economic research to support the defense. NCL raised funds to print the brief and to pay other expenses. The court decided in favor of Oregon's law limiting women's workday. NCL took thirteen more cases to the courts, and eight of them went to the U.S. Supreme Court.

In the 1930s, New Deal legislation addressed many of the issues that NCL had raised, including minimum wage legislation that covered both women and men, maximum working hours, and child labor. During World War II, NCL turned its attention to advocacy in state legislatures, and in the 1950s and 1960s, NCL worked to include migrant workers under state and federal employment laws. Consumer protection and efforts to reduce child labor were NCL's focus in the 1990s.

See also Employment Discrimination; Kelley, Florence; *Muller v. Oregon;* Protective Legislation

References National Consumers League, *Roots of the Consumer Movement. A Chronicle of Consumer History in the Twentieth Century* (1979); www.nclnet.org.

National Council of Jewish Women

Founded in 1893, the National Council of Jewish Women (NCJW) emerged from the desire to preserve Judaism by teaching Jewish women their religious duties. It soon became an advocacy organization addressing a wide range of social, health, environmental, and peace issues. Its more than 90,000 members in more than 500 affiliates seek to ensure individual and civil rights, improve the status of women, further the quality of Jewish life, improve day care and public schooling, and promote the well-being of children and families.

Early projects included founding a religious school for Jewish immigrant girls in Chicago and a synagogue in Indiana. Described as a "conduit through which Progressive ideology entered the Jewish community," NCJW provided aid to single immigrant women, meeting them as they entered the country, offering them housing, and providing other services to help prevent them from becoming prostitutes. The success of the programs caused the federal government to seek NCJW's assistance with immigrants. In 1904, NCJW established a permanent immigrant aid station at Ellis Island to receive Jewish women. Other early programs included programs for the blind and assistance to delinquent children.

In the early 1900s, NCJW's advocacy work began with its support for the 1906 Pure Food and Drug Act and Meat Inspection Act and continued with advocacy for child labor laws and protective labor legislation for women. In 1920, NCJW joined the Women's Joint Congressional Committee and helped pass the Sheppard-Towner Maternity and Infancy Protection Act of 1921 and the Cable Acts, among other measures. NCJW supported civil rights legislation, beginning with the antilynching bill in 1938; continuing through the Civil Rights Acts of 1957, 1964, and 1985; and placing particular emphasis on the Voting Rights Act of 1965. The organization supports the Equal Rights Amendment, reproductive rights, an end to domestic violence, and development of safe, affordable, quality child day care.

See also Abortion; Cable Acts; Civil Rights Act of 1964, Title VII; Domestic Violence; Equal Rights Amendment; Protective Legislation; Sheppard-Towner Maternity and Infancy Protection Act of 1921; Voting Rights Act of 1965; Women's Joint Congressional Committee

References Rogow, *Gone to Another Meeting: The National Council of Jewish Women, 1893–1993* (1993); www.ncjw.org.

National Council of Negro Women

Founded in 1935 by Mary McLeod Bethune, the National Council of Negro Women (NCNW) was the first national coalition of black women's organizations. The National Association of Colored Women (NACW), founded in 1896, had brought together women's clubs and national associations of women's clubs, and the NCNW created an umbrella organization that included the NACW, African American women's college-based professional sororities, and other professional, religious, and political organizations. NCNW's mission is "to advance opportunities and the quality of life for African American women, their families and communities," and it seeks to "extend the collective power and leadership of African American women."

When she organized NCNW, Bethune believed that bringing black women's organizations together would "harness the great power of nearly a million women into a force for constructive action." After serving as president of the National Association of Colored Women from 1924 to 1928, Bethune was convinced that a national coalition of women's groups was needed to gain the full representation of African American women in national public affairs. By bringing national African American women's organizations together, Bethune believed that coordination of the organizations' efforts would reduce duplication among them and increase their effectiveness.

Ending segregation and other forms of racism has been an NCNW priority since its beginning. In the 1940s, the organization exposed discriminatory practices that excluded African Americans from government training programs and employment opportunities at plants producing materials for World War II. NCNW worked for the admission of black women into the women's divisions of the Army, Navy, and Air Force, and Bethune recruited many of the first black women to join the Women's Army Corps. Through NCNW's advocacy, African American women gained positions in the War Manpower Commission, the Women's and Children's Bureaus, the Department of Labor, and other federal agencies. By the end of Bethune's tenure as president of NCNW in 1949, the organization was recognized as the major advocate for black women.

Another African American woman with strong leadership ability, Dorothy Irene Height, became president in 1957. Height had served NCNW in several posts and brought a strong understanding of the issues before the organization, particularly the emerging civil rights movement. In the 1960s, NCNW worked with the Student Nonviolent Coordinating Committee on voter registration projects by sending volunteers, money, and other resources. In 1965, NCNW recruited northern white female professionals to work in Freedom Schools that offered classes in voting and other related areas.

Under Height's leadership, NCNW focused attention on youth, employment opportunities, housing, health, hunger, civil rights, women's issues, family issues, and related areas. With a grant from the U.S. Agency for International Development, NCNW established an international division to work with women in Africa, the Caribbean, and other areas of the world. NCNW dedicated the Mary McLeod Bethune Memorial in 1974, the first monument to an African American or to a woman of any race on public land in Washington, D.C., and the Mary McLeod Bethune Museum and National Archives for Black Women's History was also dedicated in 1974.

In 1986, Height began the Black Family Reunion celebrations, annual cultural events that focus on the strengths and values of the African American family. The *Black Family Reunion Cookbook* was published in 1992, the first of three volumes that document the diversity and heritage of African American cuisine.

The Dorothy I. Height Leadership Institute held its first programs in 1997. The institute provides three kinds of leadership training—for affiliate organizations' members, community volunteers, and college students. The fourth component of the institute is the African American Women's Critical Issues Research and Development, a think-tank approach to developing positions on current issues and the subsequent dissemination of the information to members and affiliates.

NCNW's membership includes thirty-seven affiliated national organizations, 250 community groups in forty-two states, and 45,000 individuals. The national affiliates include sororities, professional associations, and civic and social clubs.

See also Alpha Kappa Alpha Sorority; Baker, Ella Josephine; Bethune, Mary Jane McLeod; Civil Rights Movement, Women in the; Height, Dorothy Irene; National Association of Colored Women; Tubman, Harriet

References Fitzgerald, *The National Council of Negro Women* (1985); Hine, *Black Women in America* (1993); www.ncnw.com.

National Federation of Afro-American Women

Formed in 1895, the National Federation of Afro-American Women (NFAAW) was organized "to teach an ignorant and suspicious world that our [black women's] aims are identical with those of all good aspiring women." African American leader Josephine Ruffin wrote those words as part of her call to create a group to counter a journalist's assertion that black women were "prostitutes, thieves, and liars." Ruffin called on African American women to work together to teach the world the truth. Twenty clubs founded the NFAAW, a number that grew to thirty-six clubs from twelve states. NFAAW merged with the Colored Women's League in 1896 to form the National Association of Colored Women.

See also Colored Women's League; National Association of Colored Women

References Hine and Thompson, *A Shining Thread of Hope: The History of Black Women in America* (1998).

National Federation of Republican Women

Founded in 1938, the National Federation of Republican Women (NFRW) is the largest women's partisan organization in the United States, with more than 115,000 members in 2,100 local groups based in every state, the District of Columbia, Puerto Rico, and the Virgin Islands. NFRW members work to elect Republicans to every level of public office through educational programs, fund-raising efforts, and volunteer work.

Republican women had begun forming local groups in the 1870s to support the party's efforts, particularly in election years. Often, these groups organized on an ad hoc basis and dissolved after the election. Hundreds of clubs existed by the late 1930s; Indiana, for example, had more than 100 Republican women's organizations. Some of the groups caused Republican Party leaders concern because they tried to establish party policy, endorsed candidates in the primary elections, or worked for Democratic candidates. In addition, by the 1930s the Democratic Party had developed a national network of women volunteers and held firm majorities in Congress; a majority of the nation's governors were Democrats; and Democratic President Franklin D. Roosevelt was in the White House.

Party leaders decided that they could impose discipline on the groups, coordinate their programs, and utilize the volunteer resources by

The National Federation of Republican Women sponsored a get-out-the-vote rally (left to right): Representative Sue Myrick (R-NC); Senator Sheila Frahm (R-KS); Representative Enid Greene (R-UT); Republican National Committee chair Haley Barbour (at the podium); Senator Kay Bailey Hutchison (R-TX); Marilyn Thayer, president of the federation; and Representative Constance Morella (R-MD), 1996 (Associated Press AP)

bringing them together under an umbrella. In 1938, Republican National Committee (RNC) assistant chairperson and director of women's activities Marion E. Martin called a meeting to unite the groups into a national organization. Eleven states joined as charter members, representing eighty-five clubs and 95,000 members. Martin became executive director of NFRW and developed political education programs, organized affiliates, and provided leadership. By 1940, NFRW had 350,000 members.

At the 1967 NFRW biennial convention, a controversy developed over the election of the group's leadership. Generally, the organization's vice president is elected president for the next two-year term. Phyllis Schlafly had held the vice presidency for the 1965–1967 term, but some NFRW and Republican Party leaders believed that she was too conservative for the good of the party and influenced the nominating committee to endorse NFRW board member Gladys O'Donnell and leave Schlafly off the ballot. Amid charges of unfair voting procedures, O'Donnell won the presidency. Outraged, Schlafly called for the creation of a conservative women's organization and launched the *Phyllis Schlafly Report,* a monthly newsletter.

NFRW seeks to advance the power of women through political access and participation and to develop leaders for the future. NFRW's current programs include recruiting women candidates for local and state office, lobbying, training women in campaign management, and organizing leadership development seminars.

See also Eagle Forum; Martin, Marion E.; National League of Republican Colored Women; Republican Party, Women in the; Schlafly, Phyllis Stewart

References Rymph, "Marion Martin and the Problem of Republican Feminism" (1996); Williams, comp., *The History of the Founding and Development of the National Federation of Republican Women* (1963); www.nfrw.org.

National Gender Balance Project USA

Founded in 1988, the National Gender Balance Project USA (NGBP) works to increase the number of women serving on state boards and commissions by passing legislation requiring governors to appoint women to the positions. In 1988, Iowa became the first state in the nation to require gender balance on all state boards and commissions, committees, and councils. Iowa feminist Kappie Spencer founded NGBP to encourage replication of Iowa's law in other states. By bringing the concept to the attention of other feminist groups, NGBP has enlisted the support of several groups, including the American Association of University Women, the Women's Agenda Conference, the National Association of Commissions for Women, and the National Women's Political Caucus. Several states have adopted variations of Iowa's law, with Florida expanding it to include ethnic representation. NGBP argues that attaining gender balance better utilizes women's talents and provides a broader perspective for developing policy. In addition, serving on policymaking bodies provides a route to elective office for women and men.

See also American Association of University Women; National Association of Commissions for Women; National Women's Political Caucus

National League of Republican Colored Women

The National League of Republican Colored Women (NLRCW) developed from the National Association of Colored Women (NACW) in 1924, when Republican national committeewomen Mamie Williams of Georgia and Mary Booze of Mississippi united black women's Republican clubs. Among the group's officers was treasurer Mary Church Terrell, the first president of NACW. With the slogan "We are in politics to stay and we shall be a stay in politics," the group worked to gain African American women's support for the Republican ticket in the 1924 elections.

In 1928, NLRCW president Nannie Burroughs of Washington, D.C., was appointed to the Republican National Committee's Speakers Bureau and was a popular and sought-after speaker. The group celebrated Republican presidential candidate Herbert Hoover's success, and several NLRCW members went to Washington for his inauguration. When they arrived, however, Burroughs was asked to retrieve inauguration tickets accidentally sent to the African American women who had worked in the campaign. In addition, the inaugural ball was segregated.

Over the next four years, an accumulation of racial offenses and the Hoover administration's inaction on civil rights prompted many African American women to leave the Republican Party and give their allegiance to the Democratic Party. By 1932, the NLRCW had dissolved.

See also National Federation of Republican Women; Republican Party, Women in the; Terrell, Mary Eliza Church

References Higginbotham, "In Politics to Stay: Black Women Leaders and Party Politics in the 1920s" (1990).

National Organization for Women

Founded in 1966, the National Organization for Women (NOW) has 250,000 members and 450 chapters, making it the largest organization of feminist activists in the United States. NOW was founded out of frustration with the Equal Employment Opportunity Commission's (EEOC) resistance to enforcing the prohibitions against sex discrimination in Title VII of the Civil Rights Act of 1964. Feminist leaders Betty Friedan, Pauli Murray, EEOC commissioner Aileen Hernandez, Catherine East, and others concluded that a civil rights organization for women was needed to advocate for women's concerns. Their idea was to create a group for women comparable to the National Association for the Advancement of Colored People. Twenty-eight women each contributed $5, and NOW was born. The founders stated NOW's purpose as follows: "To take action to bring women into full participation in the mainstream of American society *now*, assuming all the privileges and responsibilities thereof in truly equal partnership with men." NOW's first action was sending a telegram to the EEOC, urging the commissioners to end sex-segregated help-wanted newspaper ads. Challenging the EEOC was a primary focus of NOW's efforts for several years.

In late October 1966, an organizing conference elected Friedan president, Karen Clarenbach chair of the board, and Hernandez executive vice president. In 1967, task forces on women in poverty, legal and political rights, equal opportunity in employment, the image of women in mass media, and other groups gathered information and stated NOW's position on the issues. NOW's first priorities included federal aid for child care centers and full income tax deductions for child care services. In addition that year, support for the Equal Rights Amendment (ERA) and the repeal of all abortion laws became and continue to be the group's most publicized, most ardently supported, and most controversial issues.

Support for the ERA had a divisive effect on NOW. Several of its leaders and followers came from organized labor, particularly the United

Auto Workers (UAW). In 1967, UAW opposed the ERA, and although the UAW members active in NOW supported the amendment, they felt that they had to withdraw from NOW when the organization endorsed it. Two years later, after the UAW decided to support the ERA, women UAW members rejoined NOW and resumed their active participation.

NOW's support for the repeal of abortion laws also caused division. Some feminists who supported the Equal Rights Amendment believed that adding abortion to the organization's agenda made it unnecessarily controversial and held the potential for alienating feminists who did not want abortion decriminalized. In 1968, one of NOW's founding members left and organized the Women's Equity Action League. Despite the controversy, NOW continued its work for reproductive rights by organizing clinic defense, lobbying Congress for the Freedom of Access to Clinic Entrances Act, and winning a major lawsuit against Operation Rescue under the Racketeer Influenced and Corrupt Organizations (RICO) statute.

Attracting and effectively using press attention were among the leadership's greatest strengths. Members picketed men-only restaurants, demonstrated on Mother's Day for "Rights, Not Roses," and protested laws against abortion. NOW initiated and largely organized the Women's Strike for Equality on 26 August 1970, an event that included demonstrations in more than ninety major cities in forty-two states and involved more than 100,000 women nationwide. In another demonstration supporting child care tax deductions, a baby carriage brigade included signs asking: "Are children as important as martinis?" referring to the tax deductions allowed for business entertaining. Other examples of NOW-sponsored marches include the 1978 march for the Equal Rights Amendment, which drew more than 100,000 people to Washington, D.C., and the March for Women's Lives in 1992, which drew 750,000 abortion rights supporters to Washington, D.C., the largest protest ever in the nation's capital.

Through the NOW Legal Defense and Education Fund (LDEF), founded in 1970, NOW also gained publicity for the lawsuits it filed. For example, in 1970 NOW filed a sex discrimination complaint under Executive Order 11375 against 1,300 corporations that had failed to file affirmative action plans for hiring women. Beginning in 1971, NOW protested the discriminatory practices of AT&T in hiring, promotions, fringe benefits, and executive appointments. In the agreement reached between the Department of Labor, EEOC, and AT&T, the corporation agreed to a lump-sum payment of $15 million to 15,000 workers, wage adjustments, and new hiring practices, including giving more women craft jobs and broadened management opportunities. In the 1990s, NOW LDEF won major settlements in sex discrimination lawsuits against the Mitsubishi Corporation and Smith-Barney.

In addition to its controversial stands on abortion and equal rights, NOW added a third issue: lesbianism as a concern of feminism. Initially, Friedan had rejected including lesbian issues in NOW's agenda and had referred to lesbians as the "lavender menace." At its 1971 convention, however, NOW passed a resolution stating that lesbianism was a concern of feminism.

After congressional approval of the Equal Rights Amendment in 1972, NOW committed much of its resources to its ratification. The early successes of the amendment in 1972—twenty-two states ratified that year—lulled some leaders into believing that the amendment would easily be ratified by the necessary thirty-eight states. After Phyllis Schlafly organized Stop ERA in 1973 and defeated ratification attempts in several states, it became clear that a more organized and better-funded effort would be required for ratification. In 1978, NOW announced a boycott of unratified states, an effort that other organizations joined. NOW helped extend the ratification deadline and intensified its efforts, but the amendment failed in 1982.

Although the ERA consumed many of the organization's resources for several years and remains one of the organization's platforms, it continued to support and develop other issues related to obtaining women's equality. NOW works to end sexual harassment and sexual and physical violence against women, elect feminists to public office, end racism, protect abortion rights and reproductive freedom, and secure civil rights for lesbians.

See also Abortion; Affirmative Action; Civil Rights Act of 1964, Title VII; Equal Employment Opportunity Commission; Equal Rights Amendment; Feminist Movement; Friedan, Betty Naomi Goldstein; Hernandez, Aileen Clarke; Murray, Pauli; National Association for the Advancement of Colored People, Women in the; *NOW v. Scheidler;* Suffrage; Women's Equity Action League

References Carabillo, Meuli, and Csida, *Feminist Chronicles 1953–1993* (1993); Freeman, *The Politics of Women's Liberation* (1975); www.now.org.

National Organization of Black Elected Legislative Women

Founded in 1985, the National Organization of Black Elected Legislative Women (NOBEL) trains African American women to prepare them for elective and appointive office. Founded by former state legislator Diane Watson, NOBEL works to increase the number of African American women serving at every level of government by sponsoring forums and other educational programs. NOBEL focuses on public policy issues, promotes black women's participation in the development of public policy, and develops policy proposals.

NOBEL has lobbied for programs to help black youth, pressed for the rights of political refugees in South Africa, and sponsored a symposium on the black community and diseases affecting women.

See also National Political Congress of Black Women; National Women's Political Caucus

References Hine, ed., *Black Women in America* (1993).

National Political Congress of Black Women

Founded in 1984, the National Political Congress of Black Women (NPCBW) provides a political forum for African American women. Shirley Chisholm, the first black woman to run for president of the United States and a former member of Congress, founded the organization to encourage African American women to become active in elective politics. Educating women about all levels of the political process and bringing black women into political leadership are the goals of the organization. NPCBW has identified and recommended African American women for

C. Delores Tucker, chair of the National Political Congress of Black Women, spoke out against gangsta rap at the National Press Club in Washington, D.C., 1995 (Associated Press AP)

appointment to high-level policy positions within President Bill Clinton's administration, contributing to the greater number of African American women serving in his administration than in any previous administration.

NPCBW has worked for affirmative action, access to nontraditional jobs, economic development, housing and urban development, and other issues. Through its hearings on housing market discrimination against African Americans, it has prompted legislative action. NPCBW continues to work on job discrimination, health care, drug abuse, single parenting, education, and the availability of child day care.

See also Chisholm, Shirley Anita St. Hill

References www.npcbw.org.

National Right to Life Committee

Founded in 1973 by the Roman Catholic Church, the National Right to Life Committee (NRLC) later became a nonsectarian group. The largest prolife organization in the United States, NRLC was organized after the 1973 U.S. Supreme Court decision in *Roe v. Wade* legalized abortions. NRLC coordinates lobbying efforts at the state and federal levels, involves its membership in letter-writing campaigns and other forms of citizen advocacy to enact restrictions on abortions and to end legal abortions, and employs professional lobbyists.

NRLC has supported a human life amendment to declare the personhood of the fetus from the moment of conception. Although NRLC and other prolife groups have not succeeded in passing the amendment, they have helped to pass restrictive laws in most states, including measures that required parental notification before a minor could obtain an abortion and mandatory waiting periods.

See also Abortion

References Blanchard, *The Anti-Abortion Movement and the Rise of the Religious Right: From Polite to Fiery Protest* (1994).

National Welfare Rights Organization

Founded in 1967, the National Welfare Rights Organization (NWRO) educated welfare recipients about their rights and lobbied Congress. In the 1960s, the presence of poverty in the midst of affluence led President Lyndon Johnson to discuss the possibility of eliminating poverty in the United States. As Congress passed several antipoverty measures, welfare recipients created networks to educate themselves and others about the programs and their rights within them.

Initially, local groups used protest strategies such as occupying welfare offices and demanding resolution to their grievances. Later, NWRO lobbied Congress for a guaranteed national income and for resources to allow welfare recipients to manage their own lives, and they protested policies that invaded welfare recipients' privacy. The organization's successes included an increase in the benefit level of the food stamp program and the addition of a cost-of-living provision in the program. NWRO also won cases in the U.S. Supreme Court, including one that gave welfare recipients the right to a hearing before the termination of their benefits. Bankruptcy in 1975 forced the closing of the national headquarters.

References Slavin, ed., *U.S. Women's Interest Groups* (1995).

National Woman Suffrage Association

Founded in 1869 by Elizabeth Cady Stanton and Susan B. Anthony, the National Woman Suffrage Association (NWSA) resulted from a conflict between the abolitionist and women's rights movements over the Fifteenth Amendment. Conflicts had first emerged over the Fourteenth Amendment's inclusion of the word *male* in its identification of citizens. When the Fifteenth Amendment was proposed, it limited its guarantees for voting rights to former slaves and did not include women. Suffragists Anthony and Stanton supported providing voting rights to former slaves, but they wanted the amendment to also include women. They appealed to the abolitionists and Republicans with whom they had long been allied but to no avail, and the amendment was introduced and ratified without including women in its provisions. To organize opposition against the amendment and to organize support for a woman suffrage amendment, Anthony and Stanton formed NWSA. In response, women's rights advocates who supported the Fifteenth Amendment, even though it did not include women, organized the American Woman Suffrage Association. The two groups merged into the National American Woman Suffrage Association in 1890.

See also American Woman Suffrage Association; Anthony, Susan Brownell; Fifteenth Amendment; National American Woman Suffrage Association; Nineteenth Amendment; Stanton, Elizabeth Cady

References Flexner and Fitzpatrick, *Century of Struggle: The Woman's Rights Movement in the United States,* enlarged edition (1996).

National Woman's Loyal League

See **Woman's National Loyal League**

National Woman's Party

The National Woman's Party (NWP), founded by Alice Paul, initiated the concept of the Equal Rights Amendment in the early 1920s and continues to support passage and ratification of it. For decades, the NWP was the

Amelia Earhart joined members of the National Woman's Party in support of the Equal Rights Amendment, 1932 (Archive Photos)

only active advocate of the amendment and was regularly in conflict with many women's organizations, leaving it isolated from them. In addition, the NWP membership was an elite group of women, and its leaders made no attempt to become a mass membership organization.

The NWP has its roots in two organizations founded to further the suffrage cause. The first, the Congressional Union, sought to obtain congressional approval of a suffrage amendment. In 1916, Paul began organizing the second organization, the Woman's Party, in states that had granted women suffrage. Through the Woman's Party, Paul hoped to elect congressional candidates who would support the suffrage amendment. After passage of the Nineteenth Amendment granting women suffrage, the Woman's Party and the Congressional Union dissolved, and the NWP emerged in its place.

NWP viewed woman suffrage as the first step in women achieving full equality, noting that the vote had not eliminated sex discrimination. NWP conducted a survey of state laws and identified policies that discriminated against women, including limits on women's rights to their earnings, to own property, to serve on juries, and to hold public office. In addition, child custody and divorce laws favored men. Based upon its research, the NWP announced its goal to gain complete equality for women.

In 1923, on the seventy-fifth anniversary of the Seneca Falls, New York, women's rights convention, the NWP approved the Lucretia Mott Amendment, also known as the Equal Rights Amendment. The amendment stated: "Men and women shall have equal rights throughout the United States and every place subject to its jurisdiction."

Social feminists and several women's organizations, including the National Women's Trade Union League, the League of Women Voters, the American Association of University Women, and the General Federation of Women's Clubs, opposed the amendment, fearing that it would make protective labor laws for women unconstitutional. They proposed the alternative of passing laws that removed the discriminatory policies, one law at a time, one state at a time. The NWP acknowledged that the ERA would likely outlaw protective labor legislation. In addition, some members believed that the protective legislation kept women out of higher-paying jobs and generally reduced their opportunities. They rejected the alternative, saying that it would take too long. By insisting on the amendment, NWP became alienated from other women's organizations.

Through the efforts of the NWP, the ERA was introduced in the U.S. Congress every session beginning in 1923. Occasionally, hearings were held on it, but there was no substantial action on it. With the advent of World War II, NWP launched a massive publicity campaign to pass the ERA. It obtained endorsements for the ERA from celebrities, including novelist Pearl Buck, artist Georgia O'Keeffe, and actresses Helen Hayes and Katharine Hepburn, but the NWP remained unable to overcome labor and women's groups' objections to the amendment. After World War II, organizational turmoil and disputes diminished the group's effectiveness, and by the mid-1950s, its membership had declined from old age and death.

Although the NWP was able to have the amendment introduced in Congress, it was unable to move it beyond that initial step. In the 1960s, as the modern feminist movement developed and the ERA gained the support of the newly formed women's political organizations, NWP participated in congressional hearings. However, leadership in the ratification campaign that followed congressional approval of the ERA came from the National Organization for Women, the National Women's Political Caucus, and other groups.

See also American Association of University Women; Congressional Union; Equal Rights Amendment; General Federation of Women's Clubs; Juries, Women on; League of Women Voters; National American Woman Suffrage Association; National Organization for Women; National Women's Political Caucus; Nineteenth Amendment; Paul, Alice; Suffrage; Women's Trade Union League

References Cott, "Feminist Politics in the 1920s: The National Woman's Party" (1984); Freeman, "From Protection to Equal Opportunity: The Revolution in Women's Legal Status" (1990); Lemon, *The Woman Citizen* (1973).

National Women's Conference

Held in Houston, Texas, from 19 to 21 November 1977, the National Women's Conference (NWC) brought together thousands of U.S. women delegates and observers to debate and approve the National Plan of Action. The NWC was the brainchild of Congresswoman Bella Abzug (D-NY), who successfully sponsored legislation authorizing the National Commission on the Observance of International Women's Year, 1975 to call the conference and to provide federal funding for it.

Congress provided the commission with clear directions regarding conference delegates, purposes, and processes. Public Law 94-167, which mandated the conference, overtly stated feminist goals, including recognition of "the contributions of women to the development of our country"; an assessment of "the progress that has been made to date by both the private and public sectors in promoting equality between men and women in all aspects of life in the United States"; an identification of "the barriers that prevent women from participating fully and equally in all aspects of national life"; and development of "recommendations for means by which such barriers can be removed." The feminist predisposition of the commission becomes apparent from some of those appointed to it: commission cochair Abzug, *Ms.* magazine editor Gloria Steinem, former congresswoman Martha Griffiths (D-MI), California assemblywoman and later congresswoman Maxine Waters (D-CA), National Organization for Women president Eleanor Smeal, and other feminist leaders. Although the law also called for racial, ethnic, age, and religious diversity and the purposeful inclusion of low-income women, it did not require political diversity.

Congress mandated state meetings in every state and the six territories (the District of Columbia, the Commonwealth of Puerto Rico, Guam, American Samoa, the Virgin Islands, and the Trust Territory of the Pacific Islands), and in compliance fifty-six state conferences were held before the November NWC. At the state meetings, which were open to the public, attendees debated the draft resolutions proposed by the commission and proposed their own resolutions. Attendees also selected delegates to the NWC, an open process that resulted in considerable consternation among conference organizers when conservative groups such as the Eagle Forum, the John Birch Society, the Ku Klux Klan, and the Mormon Church began packing state meetings to elect sympathetic delegates. After Utah, Mississippi, and other states elected conservative delegates, NWC organizers began to fear confrontations between feminists and conservatives and the ultimate defeat of their agenda.

After states had chosen their delegations, 1,403 women had been selected. In addition, 186 alternates, forty-seven commissioners, and 370

delegates-at-large had official standing at the NWC. The status of delegate-at-large had been created as a way for the commission to establish the required diversity. The states, however, had successfully reached out to groups that had historically been underrepresented, resulting in 64.5 percent of the delegates being white, compared to 84.4 percent of the general female population, leaving some of the delegate-at-large positions to be filled by white, middle-class women.

The NWC opened on 19 November 1977, featuring the presentation of a lighted torch that more than 2,000 women runners had relayed 2,610 miles from Seneca Falls, New York, the site of the first women's rights convention, to Houston. After First Lady Rosalynn Carter and former first ladies Betty Ford and Lady Bird Johnson spoke to the convention, deliberations on the resolutions began. Using microphones placed throughout the convention hall, delegates addressed the convention, supporting, attempting to amend, and speaking against the proposed resolutions. The confrontations between feminists and conservatives did not develop in any significant way. Delegates held signs and wore buttons that announced their support of or opposition to issues such as abortion and the Equal Rights Amendment.

The NWC approved twenty-six resolutions that became the National Plan of Action. The resolutions called for the end of violence in the home, prevention of child abuse and treatment for abused children, expanded legislation recognizing the needs of disabled women, an increase in the

Notable women rallied for the Equal Rights Amendment at the National Women's Conference in Houston (left to right): Betty Friedan, Elizabeth Carpenter, First Lady Rosalynn Carter, First Lady Betty Ford, Esther Peterson, Jill Ruckelshaus, and Representative Bella Abzug (D-NY), 1977 (Corbis/Bettmann)

number of women in elective and appointive public offices, ratification of the Equal Rights Amendment, support for displaced homemaker programs, improved services for older women, and changes in criminal codes to correct inequities against rape victims. Among the other topical areas were arts and humanities, business, child care, credit, education, minority women, offenders, rural women, and welfare and poverty.

NWC organizers had known that the two most controversial resolutions were on reproductive freedom and sexual preference. As debate began on the reproductive freedom resolution, which included abortion rights, supporters stepped to the microphones and made their points, but there were only a few brief comments from the opposition to the resolution, despite the chair's request that an opponent comment. Delegates approved the resolution.

The resolution to eliminate discrimination on the basis of sexual preferences had not been among the recommendations drafted by the commission, but thirty state meetings had approved the issue in their agendas. The commission responded by adding a resolution barring discrimination on the basis of sexual preferences for consideration by the NWC. Both feminists and conservatives struggled with the resolution, with one feminist calling it "an albatross" for the feminist agenda and saying that it would make ratification of the Equal Rights Amendment more difficult. Feminist Betty Friedan told the convention: "I am known to be violently opposed to the lesbian issue" but added: "I believe we must help the women who are lesbians" and supported the resolution. After the conference approved the resolution, delegates from Mississippi turned their backs to the podium, bent their heads as if praying, and held signs saying "Keep Them in the Closet."

The last resolution approved by the conference related to establishing a committee of the conference with the responsibility to call another NWC, as required by Public Law 94-167. In April 1978, President Jimmy Carter established the National Advisory Committee for Women (NACW), appointed forty people to it, and named Bella Abzug and Carmen Delgado Votaw its cochairs. The NACW's effectiveness was interrupted by a dispute between Abzug and Carter, resulting in Carter's dismissal of Abzug and several committee members' resignations in protest.

Ultimately, a group of volunteers formed the National Women's Conference Committee, which coordinated efforts to implement the National Plan of Action.

See also Abortion; Abzug, Bella Savitzky; Domestic Violence; Education, Women and; Equal Rights Amendment; Friedan, Betty Naomi Goldstein; Griffiths, Martha Edna Wright; Lesbian Rights; National Advisory Committee for Women; National Commission on the Observance of International

Women's Year, 1975; National Women's Conference Committee; Rape; Schlafly, Phyllis Stewart; Smeal, Eleanor Cutri; Steinem, Gloria Marie; Waters, Maxine Moore

References Bird, *What Women Want* (1979); East, *American Women: 1963 1983 2003* (1983).

National Women's Conference Committee

The National Women's Conference Committee (NWCC) works through existing organizations to implement the National Plan of Action approved by the National Women's Conference in 1977. Created in 1978 as the International Women's Year Continuing Committee, the NWCC is a private, nonprofit corporation that is supported by paid memberships and a volunteer corps.

The NWCC has its roots in the 1977 National Women's Conference held in Houston, Texas. The National Commission on the Observance of International Women's Year, 1975, which had planned and organized the conference, dissolved in early 1978 as required by the law that had authorized the conference. Among the resolutions in the National Plan of Action was one for a continuing committee, which had also been a provision of the legislation authorizing the conference. Within a short time, President Jimmy Carter had created the National Advisory Committee for Women, but its work was abandoned after Carter and committee cochair Abzug disagreed and Carter fired her, prompting several committee members to resign. Carter appointed another committee, but it dissolved at the end of his administration in 1980.

A group of women who had been involved in the National Women's Conference organized the NWCC to pursue the goals it had outlined. NWCC has helped organize advocacy networks in thirty-four states, developed strategies for international networks of women, and convened annual national meetings to assess progress on the National Plan of Action. It has published materials on the Equal Rights Amendment and on the National Plan of Action.

See also Abzug, Bella Savitzky; National Advisory Committee for Women; National Commission on the Observance of International Women's Year, 1975; National Women's Conference

References Bird, *What Women Want* (1979); East, *American Women: 1963 1983 2003* (1983).

National Women's Political Caucus

Founded in 1971, the National Women's Political Caucus (NWPC) is a national grassroots organization dedicated to increasing the number of prochoice women in elected and appointed positions at every level of government. Through its work, NWPC has helped raise women's awareness of themselves as a political interest group and has helped gain politicians' recognition of women as a constituency.

Feminist leader Betty Friedan conceived the idea of forming the NWPC and founded the organization with some of modern feminism's most notable leaders, including Gloria Steinem, Fannie Lou Hamer, Olga Madar, LaDonna Harris, Liz Carpenter, Dorothy Height, and Congresswomen Shirley Chisholm and Bella Abzug, among many others. They shared a belief that a multipartisan women's organization was needed to promote the election and appointment of women to political offices.

At the time, the number of women serving in political leadership roles and public office had not become an issue in the public consciousness. There were no national campaign funds for women candidates and only random efforts to obtain political appointments for women. In the year NWPC was founded, less than 3 percent of the members of Congress were women, and 4.5 percent of the members of state legislatures were women. Caucus members believed that increasing the number of women would enhance the potential for passage of the Equal Rights Amendment and other feminist legislative priorities.

NWPC identifies, recruits, trains, and supports women seeking elected and appointed office. In one campaign cycle in the 1990s, NWPC trained more than 2,500 women, teaching them how to raise money, develop a campaign message and strategy, motivate volunteers, and work with the news media. It also endorses candidates and raises money for endorsed candidates.

Increasing the numbers of women delegates to the Democratic National Convention and the Republican National Convention was an early priority for NWPC. In 1972, NWPC established training programs to assist women interested in becoming delegates and to teach them the process of becoming delegates. NWPC also sent representatives to both parties' conventions, meeting with women delegates, explaining NWPC's priorities, organizing networks, and providing support in the forms of information and strategy suggestions. The Republican Women's Task Force and the Democratic Women's Task Force emerged from the 1972 efforts and continued to work for feminist platform proposals at subsequent national conventions.

NWPC's legislative priorities have included the Equal Rights Amendment, abortion rights, child care, economic equity, welfare reform, fair housing, and the Pregnancy Discrimination Act of 1978. NWPC organizes and works with coalitions for the appointment of women to policymaking positions.

See also Abzug, Bella Savitzky; Carpenter, Mary Elizabeth (Liz) Sutherland;

Chisholm, Shirley Anita St. Hill; Congress, Women in; Democratic Party, Women in the; Equal Rights Amendment; Friedan, Betty Naomi Goldstein; Hamer, Fannie Lou Townsend; Height, Dorothy Irene; Madar, Olga Marie; Meissner, Doris Marie; Pregnancy Discrimination Act of 1978; Republican Party, Women in the; State Legislatures, Women in; Steinem, Gloria Marie

References Feit, "Organizing for Political Power: The National Women's Political Caucus" (1979); www.feminist.com/nwpc.htm.

Natividad, Irene (b. 1948)

Irene Natividad was chair of the National Women's Political Caucus from 1985 to 1989. Under Natividad's leadership, the NWPC established the Minority Women Candidates' Training Program, analyzed factors affecting success and defeat in women's congressional races, and held training workshops for political candidates and their staffs. In addition, Natividad explained: "One of our missions [at the NWPC] is to transfer the political experience we have developed on a national level to the state and local level. We want to train women to run for local offices because if we don't feed that pipeline we won't have winners." Interested in helping women obtain federal appointments, she met with President George Bush to discuss potential women appointees in his administration.

After the end of her second term as chair of NWPC in 1989, Natividad's interests turned to international issues. She worked on the 1992 Global Forum of Women and the 1994 Taiwan Forum for Women.

Born in Manila, the Philippines, Irene Natividad moved with her family to Okinawa, Japan, Iran, Greece, and India because of her father's work. Natividad graduated from high school in Greece. She earned her bachelor's degree in 1971 from Long Island University and a master's degree in American literature in 1973 and another master's degree in philosophy in 1976, both from Columbia University. She completed the course requirements for a doctoral degree but has yet to complete her dissertation for it.

Natividad became involved in politics during Eugene McCarthy's unsuccessful campaign for president in 1968. She held college faculty and administrative positions from 1974 to 1985. Founder and president of Asian American Professional Women in 1980, she also founded the National Network of Asian-Pacific American Women and the Child Care Action Campaign. From 1982 to 1984, Natividad chaired the New York state Asian Pacific Caucus of the Democratic Party and was deputy vice chair of the Asian Pacific Caucus of the Democratic National Committee. During Democratic vice presidential nominee Geraldine Ferraro's 1984 campaign, Natividad served as Asian American liaison for it.

See also National Women's Political Caucus

References *New York Times*, 18 November 1987; Zia and Gall, eds., *Notable Asian Americans* (1995).

Neuberger, Maurine Brown (b. 1907)

Democrat Maurine Neuberger of Oregon served in the U.S. Senate from 9 November 1960 to 3 January 1967. Her political career began shortly after she married Richard L. Neuberger in 1945. In 1948 Richard Neuberger won a seat in the Oregon state Senate, and in 1950 Maurine Neuberger won a seat in the Oregon House of Representatives. When the session began in 1951, Maurine and Richard Neuberger were the first married couple in the nation to serve simultaneously in both houses of a state legislature. They wrote *Adventures in Politics: We Go to the Legislature* (1954) about their experiences, in addition to other published work.

While in the legislature, Maurine Neuberger cosponsored the bill that created the Oregon Fair Employment Practices Act. She contributed to the passage of bills that made it unlawful to discriminate in employment, housing, public accommodations, and education based upon race, color, national origin, religion, sex, marital status, handicap, or age. Maurine Neuberger served in the Oregon House of Representatives through the 1955 session, when she decided to join her husband in Washington, D.C. In 1954, Richard Neuberger had won election to the U.S. Senate.

In Washington, Neuberger became her husband's political partner, worked in his office, researched bills, wrote a monthly constituent newsletter, and prepared a weekly radio program. When Richard Neuberger unexpectedly died on 9 March 1960, two days before the filing deadline for the primary elections, Maurine Neuberger became a candidate to fill the vacancy and to serve for the full term beginning in 1961. She won both contests.

As a member of the U.S. Senate, Maurine Neuberger supported the regulation of billboards along federal highways, higher soybean price supports, reform of immigration laws to end national origins quota systems, and stronger controls on cigarette advertising and warning labels on cigarette packages. She declined to run for a second full term. She later taught at Boston University, Radcliffe Institute, and Reed College.

Born in Multnomah County, Oregon, Maurine Neuberger graduated from high school in 1923 and two years later earned a teaching certificate from Oregon College of Education. After teaching in public schools for a few years, she returned to college and earned a bachelor's degree in English and physical education from the University of Oregon. She later attended graduate school at the University of California at Los Angeles.

See also Congress, Women in; State Legislatures, Women in

References H. W. Wilson, *Current Biography Yearbook, 1961;* Office of the Historian, U.S. House of Representatives, *Women in Congress, 1917–1991* (1991).

New York Radical Women

Formed by Pam Allen and Shulamith Firestone in 1967, New York Radical Women (NYRW) was one of the earliest radical women's liberation groups. The group's most publicized demonstration occurred outside the 1968 Miss America beauty pageant in Atlantic City, New Jersey. Two hundred women carried picket signs saying: "Women are people, not livestock" and "Can makeup cover the wounds of our oppression?" They designated a large container "the freedom trash can" and invited participants to toss items of "female torture" into it. Hair curlers, girdles, bras, and high heels went into the can, acts that attracted media attention. Reports that women burned their bras at the event are untrue, but from those reports feminists were given the derogatory appellation of "bra burners." The media attention alerted the nation that a new feminist movement was emerging in this country. The group dissolved in 1969.

References Echols, *Daring to Be Bad: Radical Feminism in America, 1967–1975* (1989)

News Media, Women Politicians and

The U.S. news media plays a substantial role in shaping the public's appraisals of political candidates and politicians, female and male. The media has a long tradition of reporting on political women differently than it has reported on political men, encouraging the perception that women do not belong in the political arena and perpetuating stereotypes of women. The information news outlets offer about female candidates may be accurate, but it also may emphasize matters of little consequence or use prejudicial language.

Women's physical appearance and attire have attracted undue attention, with descriptions of a woman's height, weight, and hairstyle appearing regularly. In 1982, for example, the *Des Moines Register* concluded that Iowa Democratic gubernatorial nominee Roxanne Conlin's changing hairstyles over several years deserved space in its news section and displayed several photos of her with different hairstyles. Other political women have objected when their clothing received more space than their accomplishments. In 1974, after President Richard Nixon resigned as a result of the Watergate scandal, Mary Louise Smith became chair of the Republican National Committee (RNC). At a time when the Republican Party was mired in controversy, reporters asked Smith if she planned to dye her hair and if she purchased her clothes from designers or off the rack. Such practices trivialize political women and minimize their accomplishments.

The adjectives used to describe political women provide an example of the news media's tendency to stereotype women. Female members of

Congress have been described as "plucky," "perky," "spunky," and "feisty," words that would not be used to describe a male member of Congress. U.S. Senator Kay Bailey Hutchison (R-TX) was once described as an "aging cheerleader" and U.S. Representative Bella Abzug (D-NY) was called "aggressive" and "abrasive." Abzug noted that if she were a man, the words *courageous* and *dynamic* would more likely have been used. RNC chair Smith was consistently referred to as a gray-haired grandmother from Iowa, which was true, but reporters did not characterize Democratic National Committee chairman Robert Strauss as a gray-haired grandfather from Texas.

Sex-role stereotyping in the news media takes several forms. Political women are asked about their homemaking, sewing, and cooking skills, questions that political men are spared. In addition, men are not asked about their abilities to repair an automobile, build a house, or mow a lawn. Reporters frequently question political women about how it feels to be a woman officeholder, a question that men are not asked to address.

See also Abzug, Bella Savitzky; Hutchison, Kathryn (Kay) Ann Bailey; Public Offices, Women Elected to; Smith, Mary Louise

References Braden, *Women Politicians and the Media* (1996).

9to5, National Association of Working Women

Founded in 1973 by Karen Nussbaum and nine other women, 9to5, National Association of Working Women seeks to end workplace discrimination and to help women make the transition from welfare to work. The organization and its 15,000 members work on several levels, from providing information to working women seeking advice to lobbying state legislatures and Congress. Its bill of rights for working women includes fair pay, family-friendly policies, prorated benefits for part-time work, a voice in job design, job security, safe and healthful workplaces, and workplaces free from all forms of discrimination and harassment.

Through its Job Survival Hotline, staff members answer as many as 25,000 phone calls a year from women wanting advice on job security, sexual harassment, workers' rights, maternity leave, and discrimination. Because ending sexual harassment in the workplace is a priority for 9to5, the association's director, Ellen Bravo, and Ellen Cassedy wrote *The 9to5 Guide to Combating Sexual Harassment: Candid Advice from 9to5, the National Association of Working Women* in 1992. The book defines sexual harassment, provides statistics about it, offers advice on how to deal with harassers, and includes information on filing complaints.

9to5's public policy priorities include tax benefits for family-friendly companies, withholding government contracts from those companies that are not family-friendly, increasing the minimum wage, increasing

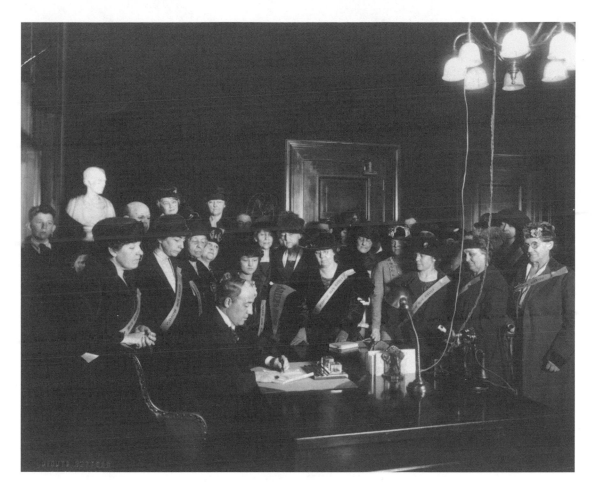

child care options, and requiring benefits for part-time employees. The organization supported the Family and Medical Leave Act of 1993, the Civil Rights Act of 1991, the 1990 child care legislation, and state laws on workplace health and safety and sexual harassment.

The organization inspired the 1980 movie and song *Nine to Five*.

> **See also** Bravo, Ellen; Child Day Care; Civil Rights Act of 1991; Family and Medical Leave Act of 1993; Nussbaum, Karen; Pay Equity; Sexual Harassment
>
> **References** www.feminist.com.

Suffragists looked on as Governor Edwin P. Morrow of Kentucky signed the Anthony Amendment; Kentucky was the thirty-sixth state to ratify the Nineteenth Amendment, which passed in 1920 (Library of Congress)

Nineteenth Amendment

The Nineteenth Amendment guarantees women the right to vote. Passed by Congress on 4 June 1919, it was ratified and added to the U.S. Constitution on 26 August 1920 after more than seventy years of lobbying, organizing, and campaigning for it.

The text of the Nineteenth Amendment reads:

> The right of citizens of the United States to vote shall not be denied or abridged by the United States or by any State on account of sex.

Congress shall have power to enforce this article by appropriate legislation.

See also American Woman Suffrage Association; Anthony, Susan Brownell; Catt, Carrie Clinton Lane Chapman; Mott, Lucretia Coffin; National American Woman Suffrage Association; National Woman Suffrage Association; National Woman's Party; Paul, Alice; Seneca Falls Convention; Stone, Lucy; Suffrage

Nixon, Pat Ryan (1912–1993)

Pat Nixon was first lady from 1969 to 1974, the years her husband Richard Nixon was president of the United States. Her life as a politician's wife began in 1946, the year her husband ran for Congress, and continued until he resigned from office as a result of the Watergate scandal. Throughout Richard Nixon's political career, Pat Nixon steadfastly stood by her husband, campaigning for him, entertaining political supporters and other guests, and traveling with him on international trips, especially during the years he was vice president and president. During Richard Nixon's first term as president, she sought but did not identify a special project by which she would become known. Although she continued to explore possibilities during his second term, the turmoil created by the Watergate scandal overwhelmed her search. After Richard Nixon resigned from the presidency, the couple returned to California.

First Lady Pat Nixon witnessed her husband's inauguration ceremony, 1969 (Archive Photos)

Born in Ely, Nevada, Pat Nixon was named Thelma Catherine Ryan, which she changed to Pat Ryan in 1931. After graduating from the University of Southern California in 1937, she taught school in Whittier, California, and met Richard Nixon when they both had roles in a community theater production. They married in 1941, and she ended her teaching career.

References Eisenhower, *Pat Nixon* (1986).

Nolan, Mae Ella Hunt (1886–1973)

Republican Mae Nolan of California served in the U.S. House of Representatives from 23 January 1923 to 3 March 1925. She won the election to fill the vacancy created by the death of her husband, John Nolan. As chair of the Committee on Expenditures in the Post Office Department, Mae Nolan was the first woman to chair a House committee. She introduced a measure for a minimum daily wage of $3 for federal employees, which passed the House but failed in the Senate. She passed legislation that transferred the Palace of Fine Arts from the federal government to the City of San Francisco and that authorized the construction of a federal building. She declined to run for a second term, saying politics was "entirely too masculine to have any attraction for feminine responsibilities."

Born in San Francisco, California, Mae Ella Nolan attended Ayres Business College in San Francisco.

See also Congress, Women in

References Chamberlin, *A Minority of Members* (1973); Engelbarts, *Women in the United States Congress, 1917–1972* (1974).

Norrell, Catherine Dorris (1901–1981)

Democrat Catherine Norrell of Arkansas served in the U.S. House of Representatives from 18 April 1961 to 3 January 1963. She entered politics through her husband, Congressman William Norrell, serving as his staff assistant. After her husband died in office, she won the election to fill the vacancy. Congresswoman Norrell sought to protect Arkansas's clay, textile, and lumber industries through tariffs and other government regulation. She declined to run for a second term.

Born in Camden, Arkansas, Catherine Norrell attended Ouachita Baptist College and the University of Arkansas. She then taught music and was director of the Arkansas A&M music department.

After leaving Congress, Norrell was appointed deputy assistant secretary of state for educational and cultural affairs by President John Kennedy and served from 1963 to 1965. She was director of the State Department's reception center in Honolulu from 1965 to 1969.

See also Congress, Women in

References Office of the Historian, U.S. House of Representatives, *Women in Congress, 1917–1990* (1991).

Northrup, Anne Meagher (b. 1948)

Republican Anne Meagher Northrup of Kentucky entered the U.S. House of Representatives on 3 January 1997. Among her congressional priorities is the construction of a bridge over the Ohio River near Louisville. Northrup has worked to increase accountability in federal programs and seeks local government control of programs and the reduction of government regulations to help small businesses. Northrup has also worked on health care reform, focusing on making health care both affordable and accessible. She founded the House Reading Caucus in 1998, a bipartisan group that seeks to raise awareness of the problems of illiteracy.

Born in Louisville, Kentucky, Anne Northrup earned her bachelor's degree in economics and business from St. Mary's College in 1970. Northrup served in the Kentucky House of Representatives from 1987 to 1996.

See also Congress, Women in; State Legislatures, Women in

References Congressional Quarterly, *Politics in America 1998* (1997); www.house.gov/northrup/bio.htm.

Norton, Eleanor Holmes (b. 1937)

Democrat Eleanor Holmes Norton of the District of Columbia entered the U.S. House of Representatives on 3 January 1991. As representative for the district, Norton is a delegate and does not have a vote in House business. She is the first African American woman elected to Congress from the District of Columbia.

Born in Washington, D.C., Eleanor Holmes Norton earned her bachelor of arts degree from Antioch College in 1959 and her master of arts degree in 1963 and her law degree in 1964 from Yale Law School. Norton clerked for a federal judge following law school and then was assistant legal director of the American Civil Liberties Union (ACLU). Representing a white supremacist group that had been denied permission to hold a rally in Maryland, she argued and won her first case before the U.S. Supreme Court in 1968.

Norton headed the New York City Human Rights Commission from 1971 to 1977. She convinced several companies to provide maternity benefits, helped change workers' compensation policies, and won a woman sportswriter the right to sit in the press box at hockey games, in addition to other successes. From 1977 to 1981, Norton chaired the Equal Employment Opportunity Commission (EEOC). When she began her work

there, the commission had a backlog of almost 100,000 worker complaints. Norton changed the arbitration system and reduced the backlog to 32,000 cases. Her work with the EEOC contributed to her decision in 1991 to urge the Senate to hold hearings after Anita Hill alleged that she had been sexually harassed by U.S. Supreme Court nominee Clarence Thomas. One of the women who marched to the U.S. Senate in October 1991, Norton explained: "As a black woman I identified with Anita Hill, as the former chair of the EEOC and because I wrote the guidelines, I had a special obligation and I believe if we didn't walk the hearing would not have been held." She walked for "black women who have had their sexuality trivialized and scandalized; black women who have had their sexuality demeaned just as Clarence Thomas had done to Anita Hill."

Congresswoman Norton has worked for civil rights, women's rights, law enforcement, education, and economic development and political independence for the District of Columbia. A unique situation exists in the district. Residents pay taxes, but their congressional representative does not have a constitutional right to vote on the floor of the House. In 1993, Norton persuaded her colleagues to grant the district's representative that privilege, but when Republicans gained the majority for the 104th Congress in 1995, the privilege was withdrawn. Norton relies on her persuasive abilities perhaps more than other members of Congress as she works to represent the district's needs for infrastructure maintenance and improvements, additional federal funds, and an adequate tax system.

See also Congress, Women in; Equal Employment Opportunity Commission; Hill, Anita Faye; Sexual Harassment

References Boxer, *Strangers in the Senate* (1994); www.house.gov/norton/bio.htm.

Norton, Mary Teresa Hopkins (1875–1959)

Democrat Mary Teresa Norton of New Jersey served in the U.S. House of Representatives from 4 March 1925 to 3 January 1951, making her the dean of congresswomen at the time of her retirement. Norton's political careers emerged from her efforts to assist working women through a day nursery she founded. Seeking financial support from Jersey City, she appealed to Mayor Frank Hague, who facilitated the city government's making a financial commitment to the nursery. In return, Norton permitted Hague and the state Democratic committee to use her name on its list of members.

After the woman suffrage amendment was ratified in 1920, both Democrats and Republicans sought women's votes and organizational skills. Democrat Hague, one of the most powerful political bosses in U.S. history, enlisted Norton's help attracting women to the party and helped her develop her political skills. For three years, she recruited and organized women voters. In 1923, Hague persuaded Norton to run for the Hudson County Board of Freeholders. On the county board, she worked for the construction of a maternity hospital that the county would build and support, an effort that resulted in the only facility in the country financed that way. Her experience on the board exposed her to the inadequate services and assistance available for disabled, old, or elderly people.

At Hague's urging, Norton resigned from the board in 1924 to run for the U.S. House of Representatives. With the help of Hague and the mothers who had known Norton through the day nursery, she won the election. She was the first Democratic woman elected to Congress who had not followed her husband into the office and the first woman elected from the East. After her election, a reporter asked her to pose for photographs: one hanging clothes on the line and the other cooking in her kitchen. She refused, saying: "I do not expect to cook, and I do not expect to wash any clothes in Congress."

In 1925, Congresswoman Norton sponsored legislation that funded construction of the first veterans' hospital in New Jersey. By 1928, Norton had become part of a circle of Democratic women activists that included Eleanor Roosevelt, Belle Moskowitz, and Molly Dewson, all of whom worked to involve more women in party politics. During the 1930s, Norton worked with Dewson to enhance the status of women working for the party at the local level and sought to highlight their contributions to the party and reward them.

When Democrats gained the majority in Congress in 1931, Norton became the second woman to chair a congressional committee, the District of Columbia Committee. At the time, Congress governed the district. Norton worked for home rule for the district, to improve slum areas in the city, to give women the right to serve on juries, and to permit women to be police officers. She helped improved the district's public transportation, made progress in improving its slums, passed the district's first old-age pension, and obtained an appropriation to build a hospital for tubercular children. Her diligent attention to the district earned Norton the nickname "Mayor of Washington." She chaired the committee until 1937.

She next chaired the Labor Committee, making her the first woman to chair a major legislative committee, beginning in 1937 and holding the post until 1946. A strong supporter of President Franklin D. Roosevelt's New Deal legislation, she had been instrumental in the passage of the National Labor Relations Act of 1935. As chair of the Labor Committee, her most outstanding work was the Fair Labor Standards Act of 1938, which took a full year to pass. Secretary of Labor Frances Perkins and Norton shared a commitment to establish a minimum pay provision based upon occupation and not sex, but the American Federation of Labor (AFL) opposed the wages and hours sections of the bill and wanted it killed. At the request of the AFL, Hague asked Norton to kill the bill, a power she had as committee chair, but she refused and took the bill to the House floor, where it failed. In 1938, Norton negotiated a compromise with AFL and brought out a new bill, but the Rules Committee buried it. Norton obtained the necessary 218 signatures on a discharge petition to move the bill out of the Rules Committee and onto the floor for debate. The bill passed with its provision that maximum hours and minimum wages be the same for men and women. The act established a minimum wage of twenty-five cents an hour, a forty-hour workweek, and overtime wages at time and a half. In addition, it prohibited child labor. After the bill's passage, Norton said: "I am prouder of getting that bill through the House than anything else I've ever done in my life."

Her interest in the area of pay continued, and she was instrumental in raising the minimum wage, eventually to seventy-five cents an hour. In 1945, she introduced the Women's Equal Pay Act, but a measure enacting the policy did not pass until 1963. As committee chair, Norton encountered the resentment of some of her male colleagues, who sabotaged some legislation originating in her committee. In addition, important labor legislation that was within the purview of her committee sometimes went to other committees because a woman chaired the Labor Committee.

In 1941, Norton enlisted the help of eight of the nine women in Congress to develop bipartisan support for a $6 million appropriation for federal nursery schools for the children of women working in war industries. During the years of World War II, the appropriation rose to $75 million.

Since the 1920s, when Norton had recruited women to join the ranks of the Democratic Party, she had continued her efforts to encourage women to become politically active. Her interests included displaced homemakers, maternity leave, and equal pay for equal work for women. She wrote: "I think women should first of all be interested in other women, interested in other women's projects, their dreams, and their ambitions. It's up to women to stand for each other." She had intended to run for another term in 1950, but while she was in the hospital with pneumonia, she decided against it. She served as a consultant to the Labor Department until 1953.

Born in Jersey City, New Jersey, Norton's formal education ended when she was fourteen years old.

See also Congress, Women in; Displaced Homemakers; Equal Pay Act of 1963; Family and Medical Leave Act of 1993

References Kaptur, *Women of Congress* (1996); Mitchell, "Women Standing for Women: The Early Political Career of Mary T. Norton" (1978); Tomlinson, "Making Their Way: A Study of New Jersey Congresswomen, 1924–1994" (1996).

Novello, Antonia Coello (b. 1944)

Antonia Novello was the first woman, the first Puerto Rican, and the first Hispanic surgeon general of the United States, serving from 1990 to 1993. Before appointing her surgeon general, President George Bush confirmed that Novello shared the administration's opposition to abortion. Novello, who was born with an abnormally large and malfunctioning colon that required several surgical operations, explained: "Having been born with a congenital defect makes me think that everything has a chance to live." She added: "Women have to move a little bit away from abortion as the only issue to tackle."

As surgeon general, Novello campaigned against teen smoking and called on R. J. Reynolds Tobacco Company to stop using ads featuring Joe Camel, a cartoon character that had more appeal to children than to adults. She also asked beer and wine companies to end advertising campaigns directed at children and teenagers, saying: "The ads have youth believing that instead of getting up early, exercising, going to school, playing a sport or learning to be a team player, all they have to do to fit in is learn to drink the right alcohol." Novello also focused attention on domestic violence, the number of children not vaccinated against common infectious diseases, and the high rates of injury and death experienced by farm families.

Born in Fajardo, Puerto Rico, Novello earned her bachelor of science degree in 1965 and her medical degree in 1970, both from the University of Puerto Rico. She completed her internship in pediatrics at the University of Michigan and subspecialty training in pediatric nephrology at the University of Michigan Medical Center from 1973 to 1974 and at Georgetown University Hospital from 1974 to 1975. She earned her master's degree in public health from Johns Hopkins University in 1982.

Novello opened a private practice in Springfield, Virginia, in 1976, but left it two years later, saying, "when the pediatrician cries as much as the parents [of the patients] do, then you know it's time to get out." She joined the U.S. Public Health Service and was a project officer in the artificial kidney and chronic uremia program at the National Institutes of Health (NIH). A staff physician at NIH in 1979 and 1980, she was executive secretary of the Division of Grants at NIH from 1981 to 1986 and deputy director of the National Institute of Child Health and Human Development from 1986 until 1989. While at NIH, Novello also held a legislative fellowship and worked with the Senate Committee on Labor and Human Resources. During her fellowship, she made significant contributions to the drafting and enactment of the National Organ Transplant Act of 1984 and helped draft the warning used on cigarette packages.

Former U.S. surgeon general Antonia Novello talked with Arthur Roth in the New York state Senate chamber as she waited to be confirmed as state health commissioner, 1999 (Associated Press AP)

References H. W. Wilson, *Current Biography Yearbook, 1992* (1992).

NOW v. Scheidler (1994)

In *NOW v. Scheidler* (1994), the U.S. Supreme Court found that the Racketeer Influenced and Corrupt Organizations Act (RICO) applied to a coalition of antiabortion groups. The case arose from a lawsuit brought by the National Organization for Women (NOW) and abortion clinics, alleging that the Pro-Life Action League Network (PLAN); Operation Rescue; and several individuals, including Joseph Scheidler, who was named in the lawsuit, were part of a nationwide conspiracy that sought to close abortion clinics. NOW contended that the violence that had occurred at abortion clinics, including trespass, threats, physical attacks, arson, theft of fetuses, and other actions, was coordinated events. The question that the Court had to decide was whether RICO applied only to enterprises with an economic motive, and the Supreme Court concluded that the law could be applied more broadly.

See also Abortion; National Organization for Women; Operation Rescue; Pro-Life Action League

References Bradley, "*NOW v. Scheidler:* RICO Meets the First Amendment" (1995).

Nussbaum, Karen (b. 1950)

Karen Nussbaum was a cofounder of 9to5, National Association of Working Women and served as its first executive director from 1973 to 1993. She was director of the Women's Bureau of the Department of Labor from 1993 to 1996.

When she worked as a clerk-typist at Harvard University, Nussbaum found the low pay and lack of benefits and vacation time unacceptable and resented the lack of respect with which secretaries were treated. Discussing the issues with other women secretaries, she found several of them shared her grievances. With a few of her colleagues, Nussbaum called a meeting that about fifty women attended. The group expanded from Harvard University to include Boston in 1973. The Boston group joined similar groups that had formed in other cities to create 9to5, National Association of Working Women.

The organization seeks to improve its members' working conditions, wages, and promotion opportunities. Nussbaum led the formation of a national union in 1982, District 925 of the Service Employees International Union, a sister organization for those workers who want to belong to a union.

In 1993, President Bill Clinton appointed Nussbaum director of the Women's Bureau. She focused the bureau's attention on average working women and initiated the Working Women Count! survey of working women and the challenges they face in the workplace. She created programs to inform working women of their rights regarding sexual harassment, pregnancy discrimination, and the Family and Medical Leave Act of 1993. In 1996, Nussbaum became the first head of the Working Women's Department of the American Federation of Labor–Congress of Industrial Organizations.

Born in Chicago, Illinois, Karen Nussbaum attended the University of Chicago.

See also Family and Medical Leave Act of 1993; 9to5, National Association of Working Women; Women's Bureau

References http://dol.gov/dol/opa/public/media/press/wb/wb96066.htm; www.dol.gov/dol/wb/public/edu/gallery.htm.

O

Oakar, Mary Rose (b. 1940)

Democrat Mary Rose Oakar of Ohio served in the U.S. House of Representatives from 3 January 1977 to 3 January 1993. Oakar entered politics by serving on the Cleveland City Council from 1973 to 1976. In her 1976 congressional campaign, Oakar was one of twelve candidates in the Democratic primary and the only woman, a point that she highlighted and that helped her win. As a member of Congress, Oakar worked to protect retirement benefits for federal retirees and to expand health care coverage for elderly Americans.

An early advocate of Medicare coverage for mammograms, she succeeded in getting the coverage included in a 1988 act, but it was repealed the next year, along with several other programs. In 1990, Oakar again sought to have Medicare coverage for mammograms, but Republicans fought it because of the cost. After assuming that this benefit had been included in the 1991 budget bill, Oakar said: "When I found out they left it out, I just lost it." She went to the media to develop public support for it, and she raised the issue on the House floor, during caucus meetings and whip meetings. She explained her crusade "as just day after day of badgering." Her most influential convert was House Ways and Means Committee chairman Dan Rostenkowski (D-IL), who helped her convince others in leadership that the coverage was necessary. Medicare coverage of mammograms was included in the 1991 budget bill. Oakar served as secretary of the House Democratic Caucus in the 99th Congress (1985–1987) and as vice chair of the House Democratic Caucus in the 100th Congress (1987–1989).

Oakar came under investigation for having 213 overdrafts in the 1991 House bank scandal. Even though she was defeated in 1992, the probe continued and revealed that she had transferred $16,000 in campaign contributions from her House bank account to her campaign. She had also filed false information with the Federal Election Commission in an effort to camouflage the sources of campaign donations. In 1997, Oakar admitted committing both offenses. She was fined and sentenced to two years of probation and ordered to perform 200 hours of community service.

Oakar is chief executive officer and president of Oakar and Associates, Inc., a consulting and public relations firm working on both the domestic and international levels. She also hosts radio broadcasts and a television talk show.

Born in Cleveland, Ohio, Oakar earned her bachelor of arts degree at Ursuline College in 1962, completed her master of arts degree at John Carroll University in 1966, and studied acting at the Royal Academy of Dramatic Arts in London. She taught English and drama in a high school from 1963 to 1967 and was a college professor from 1967 to 1975.

See also Congress, Women in

References Congressional Quarterly, *Politics in America 1994* (1993); *Politics in America: The 98th Congress* (1983); *Congressional Quarterly Almanac, 102nd Congress, 2nd Session . . . 1992* (1993); "Former Rep. Oakar Sentenced in Campaign Finance Case" (1998).

O'Connor, Sandra Day (b. 1930)

Appointed by President Ronald Reagan in 1981, Republican Sandra Day O'Connor is the first woman to serve on the U.S. Supreme Court. As an associate justice, O'Connor's work has been categorized as restrained. She has been called a leader of the new center on the court and has regularly cast the deciding vote in cases.

Born in El Paso, Texas, O'Connor earned her bachelor of arts degree in 1950 and her law degree in 1952, both from Stanford University. Even though O'Connor graduated third in her law school class, she encountered sex discrimination when she began her job search. Employers refused to hire a woman lawyer, but one firm offered her a job as a legal secretary that she declined.

O'Connor began her professional career as deputy county attorney for San Mateo County, California, in 1952. A civil attorney for the U.S. Army in Frankfurt, West Germany, from 1954 to 1957, O'Connor opened a private practice in 1959 in Phoenix, Arizona, and was assistant attorney general for the State of Arizona from 1965 to 1969. She served in the Arizona state Senate from 1969 to 1975. Elected majority leader in 1973, she was the first woman in the nation to hold that leadership position. Her legislative achievements included regular reviews for people committed to mental institutions, probate code reform, establishment of no-fault divorce laws, and repeal of a law that limited women to an eight-hour workday.

In 1975, O'Connor won election to become a superior court judge in Maricopa County, Arizona. She served on the Arizona Court of Appeals from 1979 to 1981, when President Ronald Reagan appointed her to the U.S. Supreme Court.

See also Divorce Law Reform; Ginsburg, Ruth Joan Bader; Protective Legislation; State Legislatures, Women in

References *New York Times*, 8 July 1981; Van Sickel, *Not a Particularly Different Voice: The Jurisprudence of Sandra Day O'Connor* (1998).

Supreme Court Justice Sandra Day O'Connor was the first woman to be appointed to the Supreme Court, 1983 (Library of Congress)

O'Day, Caroline Love Goodwin (1875–1943)

Democrat Caroline O'Day of New York served in the U.S. House of Representatives from 3 January 1935 to 3 January 1943. A social reformer, O'Day was involved in the suffrage movement, the New York Consumers League, the Women's International League for Peace and Freedom, and the League of Women Voters. She also worked at a maternity center and a social settlement house in New York. After serving as commissioner of the New York State Board of Social Welfare from 1923 to 1935, she chaired the Women's Division of the Democratic state committee in 1923 and worked with Eleanor Roosevelt recruiting and organizing women for the party. When O'Day ran for a seat in the U.S. House of Representatives, Eleanor Roosevelt made personal appearances for her, and the Roosevelt administration supported her candidacy.

Congresswoman O'Day supported President Franklin D. Roosevelt's New Deal proposals and helped pass child labor amendments to a 1936 act that set employment standards for government contractors and to an act setting minimum ages for employment. O'Day declined to run for a fifth term. She died the day following the end of her congressional service.

Born on her grandfather's plantation near Perry, Georgia, O'Day studied art at the Cooper Union and in Paris, Munich, and Holland. She supported herself by doing magazine illustrations but ended her painting career following her marriage in 1901. Her husband died in 1916.

See also Child Labor Amendment; Congress, Women in; League of Women Voters; National Consumers League; Suffrage; Women's International League for Peace and Freedom

References Engelbarts, *Women in the United States Congress, 1917–1972* (1974); James, ed., *Notable American Women 1607–1950* (1971); Office of the Historian, U.S. House of Representatives, *Women in Congress, 1917–1990* (1991).

O'Hare, Kathleen Richards (1876–1948)

Noted orator and Socialist Party leader Kathleen Richards O'Hare traveled the country in the 1900s and 1910s calling for protective legislation for all workers, shorter workdays, and the end of child labor. Committed to the working masses of the United States, she believed that the exploitation of the proletariat would help undermine the capitalist structure so that socialism could replace it and improve workers' lives through reform.

Opposed to U.S. entry into World War I, O'Hare spoke against the draft and advised men to resist it. Charged under the Espionage Act of 1917 for allegedly saying in 1917 that U.S. women were "nothing more or less than brood sows to raise children to get into the army and be made into fertilizer," she insisted she did not make that statement. The prosecution said that she made the statement to discourage enlistment and to undermine Americans' patriotism. Found guilty and sentenced to five years in prison, she appealed to the U.S. Supreme Court, but the Court refused to hear her case. She served fourteen months of the sentence before President Woodrow Wilson commuted it in 1920.

When she left prison, she found that the Socialist Party had lost much of its vitality and turned her attention to seeking political amnesty for people convicted under the Espionage Act of 1917 and Sedition Act of 1918 and ending convict labor in the prison system. After 1930, she retreated from public life.

Born in a sod-walled cabin in Kansas, O'Hare attended a school for Socialist organizers in 1901.

See also Addams, Jane; Communist Party, USA; Socialism

References Miller, *From Prairie to Prison: The Life of Social Activist Kate Richards O'Hare* (1993).

Ohio v. Akron Center (1990)

In 1985, the Ohio legislature enacted a measure making it a criminal offense for a physician or other person to perform an abortion on an unmarried, unemancipated woman under eighteen years of age, with several exceptions. The exceptions included the physician giving one of the woman's parents, guardians, or custodians twenty-four-hour notice of the intention to perform the procedure. If the attempts to notify a parent failed, then the physician could give forty-eight hours' notice by mail. Another option involved the minor and the woman's adult brother, sister, stepparent, or grandparent filing affidavits that the minor feared physical, sexual, or severe emotional abuse from one of her parents. In addition, a parent, guardian, or custodian could consent in writing. Two judicial bypass procedures provided other options.

The U.S. Supreme Court decided that Ohio's law did not place an undue or unconstitutional burden on a minor seeking an abortion. The Court wrote: "It would deny all dignity to the family to say that the State cannot take this reasonable step in regulating its health professions to ensure that, in most cases, a young woman will receive guidance and understanding from a parent."

See also Abortion; *Akron v. Akron Center for Reproductive Health*; *Bellotti v. Baird*; *Planned Parenthood Association of Kansas City, Mo. v. Ashcroft*

References *Ohio v. Akron Center,* 497 U.S. 502 (1990).

O'Laughlin, Kathryn Ellen McCarthy (1894–1952)

Democrat Kathryn McCarthy of Kansas served in the U.S. House of Representatives from 4 March 1933 to 3 January 1935. In Congress, McCarthy supported New Deal legislation, particularly the Agriculture Adjustment Act, which she hoped would help Kansas farmers. Seeking reelection in 1934, she found farmers frustrated with the bureaucratic requirements of the program and lost the race. McCarthy returned to her Kansas law practice.

Born in Ellis County, Kansas, McCarthy graduated from Kansas State Teachers College in 1917 and the University of Chicago's law school in 1920. She practiced law in Chicago, returning to Kansas to practice law in 1928. McCarthy became involved in the Democratic Party in 1930 and won a seat in the Kansas House of Representatives, serving from 1931 to 1933.

See also Congress, Women in; State Legislatures, Women in

References Office of the Historian, U.S. House of Representatives, *Women in Congress, 1917–1990* (1991).

Oldfield, Pearl Peden (1876–1962)

Democrat Pearl Oldfield of Arkansas served in the U.S. House of Representatives from 9 January 1929 to 3 March 1931. Following her husband's death in office, Oldfield won the special election to fill the vacancy and election to a full term. Congresswoman Oldfield worked to continue federal aid to rehabilitate farmland damaged by the 1927 Mississippi River floods. She also sought $15 million to alleviate malnutrition in areas affected by drought. In 1929, she explained: "I shall advance no strange or exceptional feminine governmental ideas, as I entertain none. I believe that a government if properly administered in behalf of our husbands, our sons, our fathers, and our brothers is equally safe and sound for our women." Oldfield did not run in 1932 because she said that a woman's place was at home.

Born in Cotton Plant, Arkansas, Oldfield attended Arkansas College.

See also Congress, Women in

References http://clerkweb.house.gov.; Office of the Historian, U.S. House of Representatives, *Women in Congress, 1917–1990* (1991); "Representative Pearl Peden Oldfield" (1929).

O'Leary, Hazel Rollins (b. 1937)

African American Hazel O'Leary was the first woman to serve as U.S. secretary of energy, a position she held from 1993 to 1997. O'Leary reorganized the department, made the lines of authority clearer, and reduced the duplication of effort within it. She lifted the veil of secrecy that had surrounded the government's nuclear armaments by declassifying more than 32 million documents. She revealed the federal government's radiation experiments on uninformed citizens in the 1940s, 1950s, and as late as the 1980s. In at least forty-eight experiments, Americans were given radioactive isotopes to explore the effects of radiation on the human body. In other tests, radiation was deliberately released over populated areas. O'Leary offered a public apology for the government's role to the families involved in the experiments. She sought to protect nuclear plant employees who revealed rules infractions and laws broken by their employers.

Born in Newport News, Virginia, Hazel O'Leary attended racially segregated schools for her first eight years and then lived with an aunt in New Jersey, where she attended Arts High School for artistically gifted students. She earned her bachelor of arts degree from Fisk University in 1959 and her law degree from Rutgers University School of Law in 1966.

O'Leary began her work in public service as assistant prosecutor in Essex County, New Jersey, in 1967 and later was an assistant attorney general for the state. In President Gerald Ford's administration, she worked in the Federal Energy Administration's (FEA) Office of Consumer Affairs as director of several antipoverty programs. Through her work there, O'Leary became known as an advocate for the poor. General counsel for the Community Services Administration in 1976 and 1977, she was assistant administrator for conservation and environment with the FEA. During President Jimmy Carter's administration, O'Leary was chief of the Department of Energy's Economic Regulatory Commission from 1978 to 1980.

References H. W. Wilson, *Current Biography Yearbook, 1994* (1994); *New York Times*, 24 November 1997.

Onassis, Jacqueline Bouvier Kennedy (1929–1994)

First lady from 1961 to 1963, Jacqueline Kennedy Onassis charmed Americans with her elegance, style, and grace. Following the November 1963 assassination of her husband, President John F. Kennedy, the nation mourned with her.

Born in Southampton, New York, Onassis attended Vassar College for two years, spent her junior year in Paris, and graduated from George Washington University in 1951. She married Representative John Kennedy in 1953.

As first lady, Onassis led the restoration of the White House and helped create the White House Historical Association in 1961 to assist with the restoration of the dwelling. In early 1962, she conducted a tour of the White House for television crews that brought additional support to the effort.

After President Kennedy's assassination, she arranged his funeral, modeling it after President Abraham Lincoln's funeral. She married Aristotle Onassis in 1968. Following his death in 1975, she was an editor for Viking Press and then Doubleday.

References Caroli, "Jacqueline Kennedy" (1996).

Operation Rescue

Founded in 1986 by Randall Terry, Operation Rescue protests abortion by holding demonstrations at abortion clinics and practicing civil disobedience with the intention of preventing abortions from being performed during the protest. A demonstration at a specific clinic might be scheduled for one day or for several weeks, depending upon the site and members' willingness to continue the protest. Protest organizers often inform law enforcement officers of their plans, the number of protesters expected, and the number prepared to be arrested for civil disobedience, usually blockading the clinic entrance. Blockade participants have chained themselves to clinic entrances or in other ways attempted to hinder access to clinics.

Operation Rescue's goals include closing all clinics in the area of the demonstration because of the threat created by the demonstration at the selected clinic, placing prochoice groups on the defensive, and providing inspiration to the prolife movement. Operation Rescue succeeded in temporarily closing several clinics, but the fines, injunctions, and other actions taken against the organizations and its members in the 1990s limited its ability to continue. In addition, the Freedom of Access to Clinic Entrances Act of 1994 created greater penalties for the actions Operation Rescue had characteristically conducted.

In the early 1990s, the National Organization for Women (NOW) sued Operation Rescue, the Pro-Life Action League, other groups, and Joseph Scheidler, alleging the defendants were part of a nationwide conspiracy that sought to close abortion clinics. In 1994, the U.S. Supreme Court found that the Racketeer Influenced and Corrupt Organizations Act applied to the coalition of antiabortion groups, but it did not decide the merits of the case.

See also Abortion; National Organization for Women; *NOW v. Scheidler;* Pro-Life Action League

References Bell, "Operation Rescue" (1988); Blanchard, *The Anti-Abortion Movement and the Rise of the Religious Right: From Polite to Fiery Protest* (1994); Bradley, "*NOW v. Scheidler:* RICO Meets the First Amendment" (1995).

Orr, Kay Avonne Stark (b. 1939)

Governor Kay Orr (R-NE) was the first woman governor of Nebraska, 1988 (Associated Press AP)

The first elected Republican woman governor in U.S. history, Kay Orr served as governor of Nebraska from 1987 to 1991. Her gubernatorial campaign was the first in the nation in which two women ran against each other. Throughout her campaign, Orr promised that she would not increase taxes in the state. As governor, Orr created benefits for business and reduced income taxes for the highest and lowest ends of the scale. Lower- and middle-income taxpayers, however, paid higher taxes and believed that Orr had broken her promise. In addition, her support for creating a nuclear waste dump in the state was so controversial that she received threats on her life, and she refused to campaign in the area of the dump site when she ran for reelection. She lost her bid for reelection in 1990.

Born in Burlington, Iowa, Kay Orr attended the University of Iowa from 1956 to 1957. Her political career began when she worked for Barry Goldwater's 1964 presidential campaign. She held offices at the county, state, and national levels of the Federation of Young Republicans in the 1960s. Nebraska governor Charles Thone's chief of staff from 1979 to 1981, she was appointed state treasurer to fill a vacancy in 1981, was elected to the position in 1982, and served until 1986.

See also Governors, Women

References Mullaney, ed., *Biographical Directory of the Governors of the United States 1988–1994* (1994).

Orr v. Orr (1979)

Orr v. Orr challenged Alabama divorce laws that provided that husbands, but not wives, may be required to pay alimony. The U.S. Supreme Court wrote that "even statutes purportedly designed to compensate for and ameliorate the effects of past discrimination must be carefully tailored." The Court found the Alabama statutes unconstitutional under the equal protection clause of the Fourteenth Amendment.

See also Fourteenth Amendment

References *Orr v. Orr*, 440 U.S. 268 (1979).

Ortega, Katherine Davalos (b. 1934)

Appointed treasurer of the United States by President Ronald Reagan, Hispanic American Katherine D. Ortega served from September 1983 to June 1989. She first served in the Reagan administration as a member of the Presidential Advisory Committee on Small and Minority Business Ownership.

Born in Tularosa, New Mexico, Ortega earned her bachelor's degree at Eastern New Mexico State University in 1957. She became a certified public accountant in 1979. Ortega worked in accounting and banking in the 1960s and 1970s. In 1975, she became the first woman president of a California bank.

References Telgen and Kamp, eds., *Notable Hispanic American Women* (1993).

Owen Rohde, Ruth Bryan (1885–1954)

Democrat Ruth Owen of Florida served in the U.S. House of Representatives from 15 April 1929 to 4 March 1933. The daughter of William Jennings Bryan, who had run for president three times and who was renowned for his oratory, Owen shared her father's oratorical skills. In the 1920s she was a professional lecturer with the Chautauqua, which traveled the country offering education and entertainment. Her abilities as a speaker helped her win a congressional seat in 1928 after a failed attempt for Congress in 1926. Her opponent, however, challenged her success by claiming that her citizenship status was uncertain. Owen had married a British subject in 1910, and under the laws of the time, she had forfeited her U.S. citizenship. The Cable Act of 1922 had given women independent citizenship, but legal technicalities left her citizenship in doubt. The

Elections Committee, however, decided in her favor. As a member of Congress, Owen clarified married women's status as citizens by amending the Cable Act, one of her most significant achievements in Congress. The first woman since Jeannette Rankin (R-MT) to work for women's issues, Owen proposed the creation of a federal Department of Home and Child and supported the creation of a mothers' pension.

Owen sought to make the Everglades a national park and worked for other conservation and wildlife preservation issues. She also supported Prohibition, a position that likely contributed to her defeat in the 1932 primary election. President Franklin Roosevelt appointed her to head a U.S. diplomatic mission to Denmark in 1933, making her the first woman to hold the position of envoy extraordinary and minister plenipotentiary. She resigned in 1936 after marrying a Danish citizen. She held other appointments in the State Department and to the United Nations.

Born in Jacksonville, Illinois, Owen lived in Jamaica, West Indies, from 1910 to 1912 and in London, England, from 1912 to 1915. A war nurse in the Voluntary Aid Detachment in the Egypt-Palestine campaign from 1915 to 1918, she returned to the United States in 1919. She lectured regularly on the Chautauqua and Lyceum series from 1918 to 1928 and was a member of the University of Miami faculty from 1926 to 1928.

See also Cable Acts; Congress, Women in

References Breckenridge, *Women in the Twentieth Century* (1933); H. W. Wilson, *Current Biography: Who's News and Why, 1944* (1944); Tolchin, *Women in Congress: 1917–1976* (1976).

P

Park, Maud Wood (1871–1955)

First president of the League of Women Voters, Maud Wood Park led the congressional lobbying effort of the National American Woman Suffrage Association (NAWSA) from 1917 to 1919. As chair of NAWSA's Congressional Committee, Park's task was to obtain congressional approval of the woman suffrage amendment. She trained volunteers who visited Washington, D.C., to lobby their congressional representatives, coordinated the lobbying effort, managed an extensive set of biographical and personal information about each member of Congress, and developed strategies for the amendment's passage. Because the United States had entered World War I and Congress had decided to debate only war-related measures, Parks sought to have a special committee on woman suffrage created as a way to circumvent the limit. Using social contacts and the political network she had developed, Parks got her committee, which favorably reported a woman suffrage amendment. The U.S. House of Representatives approved it in 1918, but the Senate did not approve it that session. In 1919 both chambers passed the amendment, and it was ratified in 1920.

In 1919, Park agreed to accept the presidency of the League of Women Voters (LWV), the organization that NAWSA president Carrie Chapman Catt had proposed to succeed NAWSA. Park traveled the country lecturing and recruiting members for the league, helped develop its legislative agenda, and led the organization during its formative years, serving as president from 1920 to 1924. In addition to her league responsibilities,

Park helped organize and was head of the Women's Joint Congressional Committee, a lobbying coalition that passed the Sheppard-Towner Maternity and Infancy Protection Act of 1921 and the Cable Act of 1922.

Born in Boston, Massachusetts, Park graduated from Radcliffe College in 1898.

See also Cable Acts; Catt, Carrie Clinton Lane Chapman; League of Women Voters; National American Woman Suffrage Association; Nineteenth Amendment; Sheppard-Towner Maternity and Infancy Protection Act of 1921; Suffrage; Women's Joint Congressional Committee

References Park, *The Front Door Lobby* (1960); Sicherman and Green, eds., *Notable American Women: The Modern Period* (1980).

Rosa Parks, the woman who sparked the civil rights movement for refusing to give up her seat on a bus in Montgomery, Alabama, in 1955, received the Congressional Medal of Honor in 1999 (Courtesy: National Archives)

Parks, Rosa Louise McCauley (b. 1913)

Called "the first lady of civil rights" and "the mother of the freedom movement," Rosa Parks helped launch the modern civil rights movement in the 1950s by refusing to relinquish her seat on a Montgomery, Alabama, city bus to a white man. Her refusal to comply with the city's bus segregation laws provided a catalyst for a bus boycott that lasted 381 days and a U.S. Supreme Court decision that bus segregation was illegal.

Parks's visible work in civil rights began in 1943, when she became secretary of the Montgomery affiliate of the National Association for the Advancement of Colored People (NAACP). She attempted to register to vote in 1943, but her application was denied, as it was in 1944. She received her certificate to vote in 1945. In addition to her NAACP work, Parks belonged to the Montgomery (Alabama) Voters League, and in the summer of 1955 she had attended civil rights workshops. Acutely aware of segregation and offended by it, she avoided using segregated facilities whenever she could.

On 1 December 1955, she was riding home from her job as an assistant tailor and was seated in the first row of seats designated for blacks. When the white section filled and another white rider got on the bus, the bus driver asked the four black people sitting in that first row of the black section to move to give the seat to the white man. Three of them submitted. Parks refused. She later recollected:

> After so many years of oppression and being a victim of the mistreatment that my people suffered, not giving up my seat—and whatever I had to face after not giving it up—was not important. I did not feel any fear at sitting in the seat I was sitting in. All I felt was tired. Tired of being pushed around. . . . Tired of the Jim Crow laws. Tired of being oppressed. I was just plain tired.

Arrested, jailed, convicted, and fined $10, Parks refused to pay the fine and appealed her case.

The Women's Political Council, a local civil rights organization, had been looking for an opportunity to challenge bus segregation, and Parks's arrest provided the opportunity. On 2 December, the council distributed more than 52,000 flyers calling for a one-day bus boycott on the day of Parks's trial. More than 7,000 African Americans responded by gathering at the Holt Street Baptist Church, which led to the formation of the Montgomery Improvement Association, the group that helped launch Martin Luther King, Jr.'s national leadership. The bus boycott that followed helped galvanize the civil rights movement and ended when the U.S. Supreme Court upheld a lower court decision that segregated bus seating was unconstitutional.

By that time, Parks had lost her job, but she has said that she had no proof that she lost her job because of the boycott. She moved to Detroit, remained involved in the civil rights movement, and continued to support herself by working as a seamstress. In 1965, she joined Congressman John Conyers's staff.

Born in Tuskegee, Alabama, Rosa Parks left high school to care for her seriously ill mother and worked as a housekeeper and a seamstress. She received her high school diploma in 1934. She wrote her autobiography, *Rosa Parks: My Story,* in 1992. She continues to speak around the country and to raise money for the National Association for the Advancement of Colored People.

See also Civil Rights Movement, Women in the; National Association for the Advancement of Colored People, Women in the

References H. W. Wilson, *Current Biography Yearbook, 1989* (1989); Parks, *Quiet Strength* (1994).

Patterson, Elizabeth Johnston (b. 1939)

Democrat Elizabeth Patterson of South Carolina served in the U.S. House of Representatives from 3 January 1987 to 3 January 1993. Patterson's political experience began when she was a young girl working on her father Olin D. Johnston's campaign for the U.S. Senate in 1945 and continued through 1965. Patterson's first political office was on the Spartanburg

County Council, where she served from 1975 to 1976. She then served in the South Carolina Senate from 1979 to 1986.

A fiscal conservative, Patterson worked to reduce the federal budget deficit, supported a constitutional amendment to ban desecration of the American flag, worked for veterans' concerns, and opposed the Family and Medical Leave Act of 1993. She chaired the Congressional Textile Caucus and the Conservative Democratic Forum's Budget Reform Task Force. Defeated in 1992, she became director of continuing education for Converse College and an adjunct professor at Spartanburg Methodist College.

Born in Columbia, South Carolina, Patterson graduated from Columbia College in 1961 and attended graduate school at the University of South Carolina for a year. She worked for the Peace Corps from 1962 to 1964 and for VISTA from 1965 to 1967, was a Head Start coordinator from 1967 to 1968, and held a job as a congressional staff assistant from 1969 to 1970.

See also Congress, Women in; Family and Medical Leave Act of 1993; State Legislatures, Women in

References Congressional Quarterly, *Politics in America 1992* (1991); Office of the Historian, U.S. House of Representatives, *Women in Congress, 1917–1990* (1991).

Paul, Alice (1885–1977)

American militant suffrage leader Alice Paul introduced controversial and confrontational strategies to the U.S. campaign for woman suffrage, founded the National Woman's Party, and proposed the first Equal Rights Amendment. She began her political activism in England and Scotland, where she lived from 1907 to 1910, working with mother-and-daughter British suffragists Emmeline and Christabel Pankhurst. From them, she learned the strategies that characterized her efforts in the U.S. woman suffrage campaign, including the use of civil disobedience to generate publicity for a cause. Arrested seven times and jailed three times for her suffrage activities, she went on hunger strikes each time she was incarcerated. During one of the hunger strikes, officials force-fed her using a nasal tube twice a day for four weeks, a painful and bloody process.

When Paul returned to the United States in 1910, she joined the National American Woman Suffrage Association (NAWSA). From the time that Paul became involved in the U.S. suffrage movement, she and NAWSA's leaders differed in their perceptions of effective strategies to pass the woman suffrage amendment. NAWSA focused on passing state constitutional amendments and placed less emphasis on its Congressional Committee, a group that was allotted a budget of only $10 a year. NAWSA was successful in gaining the introduction of the amendment every ses-

Alice Paul, radical leader of the National Woman's Party and tireless advocate of the Equal Rights Amendment, 1920 (Library of Congress)

sion but was unable to move it out of committee. In addition, NAWSA leaders resisted public demonstrations, believing in a more reserved approach. Paul believed that state campaigns would take too long and were an inefficient use of resources. She firmly believed in a federal amendment and organized demonstrations, parades, and other events to attract publicity and place the amendment before the public.

In 1912, Paul accepted the chair of NAWSA's Congressional Committee with the understanding that NAWSA would not allocate any funds to the committee. She planned a massive suffrage parade in Washington, D.C., raised funds to pay for it, and invited women across the country to participate. She scheduled the event for 3 March 1913, the day President-elect Woodrow Wilson was to arrive in the city and the day before his inauguration. Twenty-six floats, ten bands, five squadrons of cavalry, six chariots, and approximately 8,000 women marched by 500,000 spectators, who chose to watch the suffragists instead of Wilson's arrival in the city. When the crowd became unruly and moved into the parade route, the police did not protect the marchers, and 200 people were treated for injuries. Press coverage of the parade and the subsequent Senate investigation of the police superintendent renewed interest in the Congressional Committee and the amendment.

A month after the parade, conflicts between Paul and NAWSA developed over money. Paul's success raising money led some NAWSA leaders to suggest that Paul should give some of it to the larger organization because they felt that donors were confused about which group they had contributed to. Paul solved the problem by creating the Congressional Union (CU), a separate organization that was affiliated with NAWSA, to raise money for the Congressional Committee's projects. She continued to chair the Congressional Committee, and conflict persisted. Late in 1913, NAWSA leaders told Paul she could chair the Congressional Committee or the CU but not both. Paul chose the Congressional Union. Because NAWSA president Anna Howard Shaw viewed the CU as a threat to her organization, the CU was not permitted to remain a NAWSA auxiliary. In 1914, Paul left NAWSA and continued to lead the CU.

Paul had brought the idea of marches and parades to the United States from her experience in England. She also used the British suffragists' strategy of placing responsibility on the political party in power, regardless of individual members' support for suffrage. By organizing women voters in suffrage states to oppose Democratic candidates in the 1914 elections, she made suffrage an issue in several states. The CU took credit for defeating five Democrats and contributing to the defeat of twenty-three more. In 1916, Paul formed the Woman's Party and repeated the strategy.

As the United States prepared to enter World War I, Paul and her followers remained steadfast in their focus on suffrage. Although many suffragists opposed the war, only Paul supported Wyoming congresswoman Jeannette Rankin's vote against declaring war. Early in 1917, Paul and her followers started picketing outside the White House. After several months, police began to arrest the pickets for obstructing traffic but would then release them. As the pickets continued, they were arrested, tried, found guilty, and fined. Those who refused to pay the fines were jailed for a few days. When Paul was arrested in an October 1917 demonstration, however, she was sentenced to seven months at a women's prison, where she went on a hunger strike. Force-fed, she was separated from other prisoners and placed in a psychiatric ward and denied visitors, mail, and messages. Protests over her treatment led to her release within a month.

The Nineteenth Amendment granting woman suffrage became part of the U.S. Constitution on 26 August 1920. Paul's contributions to the suffrage campaign include attracting publicity to the amendment through the marches, parades, and pickets she organized and by making the amendment an issue in the 1914 and 1916 elections. President of NAWSA Carrie Chapman Catt, however, has generally received primary credit for the amendment's passage in Congress and its ratification by the states, with Paul's role receiving considerably less attention.

In 1921, Paul transformed the Woman's Party into the National Woman's Party (NWP), which had as its sole purpose the passage and ratification of a federal equal rights amendment. Sometimes referred to as the Lucretia Mott Amendment, it read: "Men and women shall have equal rights throughout the United States and every place subject to its jurisdiction." Initially, the amendment was opposed by virtually every women's organization in the country. Paul and the NWP, however, worked for the amendment for the next fifty years. They succeeded in getting the amendment introduced in every session of Congress beginning in 1923. When Congress passed the amendment in 1972, it was the result of work done by the modern feminist movement. Paul worked for its ratification until 1974, when ill health prevented her from continuing. The amendment failed because it was three states short of the thirty-eight needed for ratification when the final deadline arrived in 1982.

Paul also worked on the international level. She led the creation of the World Woman's Party in 1938 and served as its founding president. Intended to unite American, Asian, and European feminists, the potential for the World Woman's Party was lost when World II began. She later fought for the inclusion of sex equality in the preamble to the United Nations Charter. In 1977, Paul said: "The thing I think that was the most useful I ever did was having a part in getting the vote for all the women, because that was a big transformation for the country to have one-half the country enfranchised."

Born in Moorestown, New Jersey, Alice Paul graduated from Swarthmore College in 1905 and earned her master of arts degree in 1907 and her doctoral degree in 1912, both from the University of Pennsylvania. She also held three law degrees.

See also Catt, Carrie Clinton Lane Chapman; Congressional Union; Equal Rights Amendment; National American Woman Suffrage Association; National Consumers League; National Woman's Party; Nineteenth Amendment; Protective Legislation; Rankin, Jeannette Pickering; Shaw, Anna Howard; Suffrage; Women's Bureau; Women's Trade Union League

References Lunardini, *From Equal Suffrage to Equal Rights: Alice Paul and the National Woman's Party* (1986); *New York Times,* 4 November 1975, 10 January 1977.

Pay Equity

Pay equity, sometimes called "comparable worth" or "fair pay," is a method for determining wages so as to overcome traditional gender and racial biases that result, on average, in female workers earning less than male workers and minority workers earning less than white workers. The wage gap for women has ranged from 56.6 percent of men's earnings in 1973 to 73.8 percent in 1996, although there has not been a steady increase. In 1997, white women earned about 75 percent of men's earnings, African American women earned about 67 percent, Asian American women earned about 80 percent, and Latinas earned about 58 percent. In a 1994 survey conducted by the Women's Bureau, over a quarter of a million U.S. women said that their top priority was "improving pay scales."

Following the passage of the 1963 Equal Pay Act, many thought that the differences between women's and men's pay would significantly diminish. When it became clear that the act would not close the wage gap, other reasons for its persistence were examined. Pay discrimination continues despite state and federal policies against it, and women tend to work in traditionally undervalued jobs and cluster in a few job categories: clerical, teaching, service work, and nursing. The more that an occupation is dominated by women or people of color, the greater the wage gap between people in that occupation and men in general.

One approach used to achieve pay equity is comparable worth, a method for evaluating jobs that uses a point system to rate the skill, effort, responsibility, and working conditions of each job; totals the points; and establishes the job's relative worth. Seniority, merit, quantity of work, and quality of work continue to differentiate individuals' wages within equivalent job classifications. Some states and municipalities have implemented comparable worth programs, even though the approach has not received support at the federal level. The Equal Employment Opportunity Commission concluded that Congress had not authorized it to implement comparable worth programs, and the courts have not made a definitive decision on the issue.

In the 1990s, pay equity or fair pay proposals gained renewed vitality as groups supporting the issue began to identify pay equity as a working family issue instead of exclusively a women's issue. Several organizations made pay equity a legislative priority, including the Coalition of Labor Union Women, National Committee on Pay Equity, and American Federation of Labor–Congress of Industrial Organizations. In addition, the

Women's Bureau of the Department of Labor has established the Fair Pay Clearinghouse, offering resources and information about fair pay. Conservative groups, including Concerned Women for America, have generally opposed the idea of pay equity.

> **See also** Civil Rights Act of 1964, Title VII; Coalition of Labor Union Women; Concerned Women for America; *County of Washington, Oregon v. Gunther;* Employment Discrimination; Equal Employment Opportunity Commission; National Committee on Pay Equity; Women's Bureau
>
> **References** Baer, *Women in American Law,* 2nd ed. (1996); www.cwfa.org; www.dol.gov/dol/wb/public/programs.

Peace Movement

Women's leadership in the peace movement gained visibility and formal organization in 1914 as war raged in Europe. The Woman's Peace Party has its roots in the Civil War era and developed in response to World War I, later becoming the U.S. section of the Women's International League for Peace and Freedom (WILPF). Jane Addams, Emily Greene Balch, and Carrie Chapman Catt were among the most notable leaders in the two organizations. During the interwar years, peace activists sought disarmament and mediation for international disputes. The peace movement languished during World War II and gained limited momentum in the 1950s as activists opposed the proliferation of nuclear weapons and intervention by the U.S. military in conflicts.

Concern about radioactive fallout from aboveground nuclear bomb threats prompted the formation of Women Strike for Peace (WSP) in 1961. Along with other women and men who were not part of established organizations, WSP and WILPF opposed the Vietnam War and publicly demonstrated against U.S. involvement in it. In the 1980s and 1990s, peace activists advocated a range of alternatives to war to resolve international conflicts, including educational programs, economic development, and increased power for women.

> **See also** Addams, Jane; Balch, Emily Greene; Catt, Carrie Clinton Lane Chapman; Woman's Peace Party; Women Strike for Peace; Women's International League for Peace and Freedom
>
> **References** Alonso, *Peace as a Women's Issue: A History of the U.S. Movement for World Peace and Women's Rights* (1993).

Pelosi, Nancy B. (b. 1940)

Democrat Nancy Pelosi of California entered the U.S. House of Representatives on 2 June 1987. The daughter of Thomas D'Alesandro, a former member of Congress and a former mayor of Baltimore, Pelosi grew up in a powerful political family. Democratic national committeewoman for

California from 1976 to 1996, Pelosi chaired the Northern California Democratic Party from 1977 to 1981 and was state party chair from 1981 to 1983. She was financial chairperson of the Democratic Senatorial Campaign Committee from 1985 to 1986.

Early in 1987, Sala Burton, the incumbent member of Congress for the district, was stricken ill with cancer and endorsed Pelosi to succeed her. Although well known among party leaders, Pelosi was not familiar to voters, and Burton's support helped her win the election.

When the Presidio, a military base in San Francisco, was scheduled to be closed, Congresswoman Pelosi worked to have it converted to national park land. To ease the financial burden on the National Park Service, which was already underfunded, she proposed leasing the grounds for five years and putting the proceeds in a trust fund to maintain the buildings and grounds.

Congresswoman Pelosi has written and passed legislation relating to health insurance coverage, programs for people stricken with acquired immunodeficiency syndrome (AIDS), and perinatal care for low-income families. Pelosi has also authored and passed bills to prevent homelessness among people with AIDS, to preserve housing for low-income people, and to promote human rights and environmental protection.

Born in Baltimore, Maryland, Nancy Pelosi received her bachelor of arts degree from Trinity College in 1962.

See also Congress, Women in

References Congressional Quarterly, *Politics in America 1996* (1995); Office of the Historian, U.S. House of Representatives, *Women in Congress, 1917–1990* (1991); www.house.gov/pelosi.bio_pel.htm.

Perkins, Frances (Fanny) Corlie (1882–1965)

Appointed secretary of labor in 1933 by President Franklin D. Roosevelt, Frances Perkins was the first woman to hold a cabinet position. A social reformer, Perkins entered politics through her work as a researcher and lobbyist for the New York Consumers League. She found a supporter for the league's agenda in assemblyman Al Smith, who helped her pass a bill limiting women's and children's workweeks to fifty-four hours. In 1919, when Smith was governor of New York, he asked Perkins to serve on the state's Industrial Commission, a position she held until 1921, when Smith lost his bid for reelection. After Smith won his 1923 bid for the governorship, he appointed Perkins to the New York Industrial Board. In 1928, Franklin D. Roosevelt was elected governor of New York. Through the efforts of Democratic Party leader Molly Dewson, who had organized women to help Roosevelt win the election, Governor Roosevelt appointed Perkins to serve again on the New York Industrial Commission. After

Roosevelt was elected president in 1932, Dewson again served as Perkins's advocate and persuaded him to appoint Perkins to the position of secretary of labor.

Perkins had several ideas for the Department of Labor's role in relieving the problems created by the Depression. She believed in public works to stimulate the economy, advocated passing federal minimum wage legislation, and argued for unemployment insurance. She reorganized the Bureau of Immigration, the Bureau of Labor Statistics, and the federal employment office and developed the Civilian Conservation Corps. She organized a conference that brought together union representatives and the Department of Labor to plan strategies to respond to the Depression. They developed a package of recommendations that included establishing a federal employment relief fund that the states would distribute, creating public works to stimulate basic industries, abolishing child labor, and placing limits on the number of hours employees worked per week.

Frances Perkins, appointed as secretary of labor by President Franklin D. Roosevelt, was the first woman to serve in the U.S. Cabinet, 1941 (Courtesy: National Archives)

In 1934, Perkins chaired the Committee on Economic Security, the group that drafted the framework for Social Security, unemployment insurance, and assistance for the elderly. The next year, Perkins drafted the Public Contracts Act to replace the National Industrial Recovery Act (NRA). Perkins helped pass the Fair Labor Standards Act of 1938, which instituted a minimum wage, set maximum hours people could work, and prohibited child labor in products sold in interstate commerce, policies that reformers had advocated for decades.

As the nation began preparations for involvement in World War II, the Depression eased, and the focus moved from economic recovery to producing military materials and machinery. Perkins's role changed as many of the new programs and projects were designed and administered by military and war boards and commissions. Following Roosevelt's death in 1945, Perkins resigned at President Harry Truman's request. Truman later appointed her to the Social Security Commission.

In 1955, she became a visiting professor at Cornell University. She wrote *People at Work* (1934), a history of labor from the colonial era to the

Depression and a description of the Department of Labor's responsibilities, and *The Roosevelt I Knew* (1946).

Born in Boston, Frances Perkins earned her undergraduate degree from Mount Holyoke in 1902 and her master's degree from Columbia University in 1910.

See also Cabinets, Women in Presidential; Child Labor Amendment; Democratic Party, Women in the; Dewson, Mary (Molly) Williams; Protective Legislation; Roosevelt, Eleanor

References Martin, *Madam Secretary Frances Perkins* (1976); Roosevelt and Hickok, *Ladies of Courage* (1954).

Personal Responsibility and Work Opportunity Reconciliation Act of 1996

The Personal Responsibility and Work Opportunity Reconciliation Act of 1996 made the most dramatic changes in welfare in the United States since the Great Society programs of the 1960s by replacing the federal welfare program with block grants to states that provided financial incentives for moving welfare recipients into the workforce. The measure initiated work requirements, limiting benefits to two years, at which time recipients would have to show "work activity," with a lifetime cap of five years. The act also provided support for families moving from welfare to work through child care funding and guaranteed medical coverage for a year after leaving welfare.

The law strengthened child support enforcement measures by creating new tools for identifying parents delinquent in their child support and simplifying the legal process for establishing paternity. New provisions related to minors include the development of programs to prevent teen pregnancy and the requirement that unmarried minor parents live with a responsible adult or in a setting with adult supervision and participate in educational and training activities.

Two years after the measure was enacted, the Children's Defense Fund (CDF) reported that welfare rolls had declined, that an increased number of recipients had found employment, and that there was a slight decline in the child poverty rate. CDF also reported that there was an increase in extreme childhood poverty, that most of the new jobs paid salaries below the poverty line (about $16,000 for a family of four in 1999), and that many former welfare recipients had not found steady jobs.

See also Children's Defense Fund

References www.acf.dhhs.gov; www.childrensdefense.org.

Personnel Administrator of the Commonwealth of Massachusetts v. Feeney (1979)

In *Personnel Administrator of the Commonwealth of Massachusetts v. Feeney,* Massachusetts state employee Helen B. Feeney challenged the constitutionality of Massachusetts's veterans preference law on the grounds that it discriminated against women in violation of the equal protection clause of the Fourteenth Amendment. The Massachusetts law states that all veterans who qualify for state civil service positions must be considered for appointment before any qualifying nonveterans. Feeney, who was not a veteran, had been a state employee for twelve years and had passed several qualifying civil service exams for higher-paying positions, but she had not been appointed to them because veterans had to be considered before nonveterans. Feeney argued that because until 1975 the military had quotas limiting the number of women who could serve in it to 2 percent, the policy violated her Fourteenth Amendment rights.

The Court wrote: "Absolute and permanent preferences . . . have always been subject to the objection that they give the veteran more than a square deal. But the Fourteenth Amendment cannot be made a refuge from ill-advised . . . laws. The substantial edge granted to veterans [by the Massachusetts law] may reflect unwise policy." The Court found the Massachusetts veterans preference law constitutional.

See also Fourteenth Amendment

References *Personnel Administrator of the Commonwealth of Massachusetts v. Feeney,* 442 U.S. 256 (1979).

Peterson, Esther (1906–1997)

The highest-ranking woman in President John F. Kennedy's administration, Esther Peterson was director of the Women's Bureau of the U.S. Department of Labor from 1961 to 1964 and assistant secretary of labor for labor standards from 1961 to 1969. Peterson's work in labor issues began in the 1930s, when she taught at the Bryn Mawr Summer School for Women Workers in Industry. Assistant director of education for the Amalgamated Clothing Workers of America, she was the organization's lobbyist in the 1940s. From 1958 to 1961, she lobbied for the American Federation of Labor–Congress of Industrial Organizations (AFL-CIO).

From her years in the labor movement, Peterson strongly supported protective labor legislation for women and adamantly opposed the Equal Rights Amendment (ERA) because it would make such protective measures unconstitutional. In the hopes of proving the ERA unnecessary, Peterson lobbied Kennedy to create a commission to study state and federal laws and policies related to women. With the added encouragement of

Eleanor Roosevelt, Kennedy established the President's Commission on the Status of Women in 1961 and made Peterson its executive vice chairperson.

Another priority of Peterson's was to get Congress to pass the equal pay for equal work bill that had languished since 1945; she believed that its passage would also help reduce interest in the ERA. In 1961, Peterson hired a lobbyist to coordinate congressional work for the equal pay bill and enlisted the help of Congresswoman Edith Green and others. The Equal Pay Act became law in 1963.

When President Lyndon Johnson appointed Peterson to be a special assistant for consumer affairs in 1964, one trade group called her "the most pernicious threat to advertising today." Peterson worked for uniform packaging, unit pricing, truth in advertising, and nutrition information labeling. At one time, manufacturers used codes for the expiration dates on perishable items; she successfully pressed for "sell by" or "use by" dates. She resigned from the Johnson administration because of the pressure from business. She said: "Industry hated me, but you've got to say what you've got to say."

Peterson returned to the Amalgamated Clothing Workers of America from 1969 to 1970. She was chair of the Consumer Affairs Council from 1970 to 1980, and during President Jimmy Carter's administration, she again served as special assistant to the president for consumer affairs from 1977 to 1980. President Bill Clinton appointed her to the U.S. delegation to the United Nations in the mid-1990s.

Born in Provo, Utah, Peterson earned her bachelor of arts degree from Brigham Young University in 1927 and her master of arts degree from Columbia Teachers College in 1930. She began her teaching career in 1927 at the Branch Agricultural College in Cedar City, Utah, in 1927. She also taught at Utah State University, Windsor School in Boston, and the Bryn Mawr Summer School for Women Workers in Industry from 1932 to 1939.

See also Equal Pay Act of 1963; Equal Rights Amendment; National Organization for Women; President's Commission on the Status of Women; Women's Bureau

References Harrison, *On Account of Sex: The Politics of Women's Issues, 1945–1968* (1988); *New York Times,* 18 December 1996, 22 December 1997.

Pettis Roberson, Shirley Neil McCumber (b. 1924)

Republican Shirley Pettis of California served in the U.S. House of Representatives from 29 April 1975 to 3 January 1979. Following the death of her husband, Congressman Jerry Pettis, Shirley Pettis won the special election to fill the vacancy. She passed legislation that established the California Desert Conservation Area and gave wilderness status to almost 500,000 acres in the Joshua Tree National Monument. She won a full term in 1976 but did not seek a second full term.

Born in Mountain View, California, Shirley Pettis attended Andrews University in Michigan from 1942 to 1943 and the University of California at Berkeley from 1944 to 1945.

See also Congress, Women in

References Office of the Historian, U.S. House of Representatives, *Women in Congress, 1917–1990* (1991).

Pfost, Gracie Bowers (1906–1965)

Democrat Gracie Pfost of Idaho served in the U.S. House of Representatives from 3 January 1953 to 3 January 1963. Pfost first ran for Congress in 1950 but lost. When she ran in 1952, she designed her campaign slogan to let voters know how to pronounce her name: "Tie Your Vote to a Solid Post—Gracie Pfost for Congress." As a member of Congress, Pfost supported irrigation, flood control, and power projects on the Snake River, and she wanted the federal government to build them. Nicknamed "Hell's Belle" for her fight against private construction of a dam in Hell's Canyon, she lost the battle in 1957. She is credited with passing the Wilderness Act that preserved areas in the far West. She unsuccessfully ran for the U.S. Senate in 1962. From 1963 until her death, Pfost served as special assistant for the elderly in the Federal Housing Administration.

Born in Harrison, Arkansas, Gracie Pfost graduated from Link's Business College and Secretarial School in Boise, Idaho, in 1929. Over the next ten years, she held several offices in the Canyon County, Idaho, government. From 1941 to 1951, she was the county's treasurer.

See also Congress, Women in

References Engelbarts, *Women in the United States Congress, 1917–1972* (1974); Office of the Historian, U.S. House of Representatives, *Women in Congress, 1917–1990* (1991); Tolchin, *Women in Congress: 1917–1976* (1976).

Phillips v. Martin Marietta Corporation (1971)

Phillips v. Martin Marietta Corporation was the first case to reach the U.S. Supreme Court that dealt with gender discrimination under Title VII of the Civil Rights Act of 1964. In the case, Ida Phillips, a mother with two young children, applied for an assembly trainee position with Martin Marietta, but the company's hiring policy excluded mothers with preschool children. The company, however, did hire men with preschool children. The Court decided that the company's policy discriminated against women based on Title VII.

See also Civil Rights Act of 1964, Title VII; Employment Discrimination; Sex Discrimination

References *Phillips v. Martin Marietta Corporation*, 400 U.S. 542 (1971).

Planned Parenthood Association of Kansas City, Mo. v. Ashcroft (1983)

In *Planned Parenthood Association of Kansas City, Mo. v. Ashcroft,* the U.S. Supreme Court considered four questions regarding Missouri laws related to abortion. The Court rejected the state's requirement that abortions after twelve weeks of pregnancy had to be performed in a hospital because it "unreasonably infringes upon a woman's constitutional right to obtain an abortion," as the Court noted in *Akron v. Akron Center for Reproductive Health* (1983). The Court found that the state's requirement of a pathology report after an abortion was reasonable and constitutional. The Court also accepted the state's requirement that a second physician be present during abortions because the state has a compelling interest in fetal life. In addition, the Court accepted the state's requirement that minors obtain parental consent or consent from the juvenile court for an abortion, saying that by providing the judicial alternative to parental consent, the state had met the legal standards.

> **See also** Abortion; *Akron v. Akron Center for Reproductive Health*
>
> **References**: Congressional Quarterly, *Congressional Quarterly Almanac, 98th Congress, 1st Session . . . 1983* (1984); *Planned Parenthood Association of Kansas City, Mo. v. Ashcroft,* 462 U.S. 476 (1983).

Planned Parenthood Federation of America

Founded in 1939 as the Birth Control Federation of America, Planned Parenthood Federation of America (PPFA) provides reproductive health care, offers educational programs on human sexuality, promotes research on reproductive health, and advocates public policies that guarantee reproductive rights. PPFA and its affiliates have challenged several state and federal laws in the courts and have participated in cases initiated by others that relate to reproductive rights. PPFA has over 150 affiliates in forty-nine states and the District of Columbia and serves more than 5 million Americans.

The Birth Control Federation of America was formed when the American Birth Control League and the Clinical Research Bureau merged in 1939. Birth control advocate Margaret Sanger had founded both groups in her quest to overturn the portions of the 1873 Comstock laws that classified contraceptive information as obscene and made its dissemination illegal. In 1936, the U.S. Circuit Court of Appeals decided in *United States v. One Package of Japanese Pessaries* (a pessary is a contraceptive device) that birth control could no longer be classified as obscene, but the decision applied only to New York, Connecticut, and Vermont. In 1965 the U.S. Supreme Court found unconstitutional state laws prohibiting married couples from using contraceptives in *Griswold v. Connecticut,* and in

1972 the Court found unconstitutional a state law forbidding the distribution of contraceptives to unmarried people in *Eisenstadt v. Baird.*

After the U.S. Supreme Court legalized abortion in *Roe v. Wade,* PPFA affiliates began offering abortion counseling and services in their clinics as well as continuing to offer family planning counseling and distributing contraceptives. As the states and the federal government enacted restrictions on abortions, such as informed consent, parental notification or consent, and other regulations, PPFA and its affiliates challenged these policies in the courts.

As the acquired immunodeficiency syndrome (AIDS) epidemic struck the nation in the 1980s, PPFA affiliates worked to educate the public about the disease and other sexually transmitted diseases as part of their mission to provide a wide range of reproductive health services, including screening. The organization has also worked to address the problem of teen pregnancy through its educational programs.

See also Abortion; Dennett, Mary Coffin Ware; *Eisenstadt v. Baird; Griswold v. Connecticut; Roe v. Wade;* Sanger, Margaret Louise Higgins

References www.plannedparenthood.org.

Planned Parenthood of Central Missouri v. Danforth (1976)

In *Planned Parenthood of Central Missouri v. Danforth,* the U.S. Supreme Court considered several aspects of a Missouri abortion law. The Court accepted the state's requirement that a woman seeking an abortion sign a form asserting that she had freely given her consent to the procedure as well as the requirement that health facilities and physicians performing abortions maintain records on the abortions they perform and report them to the state. The Court rejected the stipulation that a married woman obtain the written consent of her spouse before obtaining an abortion, saying that the state cannot give a husband power that the state is forbidden to exercise. The Court also found unconstitutional the requirement that an unmarried woman under the age of eighteen obtain written consent from a parent before being able to have an abortion, although the Court would revisit this issue several times over the next two decades. It rejected the prohibition against using the abortion procedure known as saline amniocentesis after the first twelve weeks of the pregnancy. The Court said that it was the most commonly used and safest procedure and that the policy was designed to prevent the majority of abortions after the first twelve weeks, thus making it unconstitutional. Finally, the Court found unconstitutional the requirement that physicians preserve the fetus's life and health regardless of the stage of the pregnancy.

See also Abortion

References *Planned Parenthood of Central Missouri v. Danforth,* 428 U.S. 52 (1976).

Planned Parenthood of Southeastern Pennsylvania v. Casey (1992)

The U.S. Supreme Court affirmed a woman's right to end a pregnancy in its early stages, discarded the trimester framework it had established in *Roe v. Wade,* adopted a less rigorous standard for review of abortion restrictions, and approved new restrictions on the procedure in *Planned Parenthood of Southeastern Pennsylvania v. Casey.* The new standard for evaluating abortion laws became "undue burden test," meaning that state regulations can survive constitutional review as long as they do not place a "substantial obstacle in the path of a woman seeking an abortion of a nonviable fetus."

The Court upheld a Pennsylvania law mandating a twenty-four-hour waiting period before an abortion may be performed, overturning its 1983 decision in *City of Akron v. Akron Center for Reproductive Health.* It also upheld a provision requiring physicians to provide patients with information about fetal development in an effort to discourage abortion, overturning its 1986 decision in *Thornburgh v. American College of Obstetrics and Gynecology.* A provision requiring reports on abortions, including the name and location of facilities performing abortions that receive state funds, was also upheld. The Court struck down a provision that required a married woman seeking an abortion to notify her husband before the procedure could be performed.

> **See also** Abortion; *Akron v. Akron Center for Reproductive Health; Roe v. Wade; Thornburgh v. American College of Obstetrics and Gynecology*
>
> **References** Congressional Quarterly, *Congressional Quarterly Almanac, 102nd Congress, 2nd Session . . . 1992* (1993); *Planned Parenthood of Southeastern Pennsylvania v. Casey,* 505 U.S. 833 (1992); www.aclu.org.

Poelker v. Doe (1977)

The public hospitals owned by the City of St. Louis provided publicly financed hospital services for childbirth and abortions when there was a threat of grave physiological injury or death to the mother. The hospitals did not provide nontherapeutic abortions. The question before the U.S. Supreme Court was whether the policy violated any constitutional rights. The Court concluded that the constitutional question involved was the same as that involved in *Maher v. Roe* (1977), which concerned a state's refusal to provide Medicaid benefits for abortions while providing them for childbirth. As in *Maher,* the Court found that the City of St. Louis did not violate the Constitution by providing publicly financed hospital services for childbirth and for certain abortions but not for nontherapeutic abortions.

> **See also** Abortion; *Maher v. Roe*
>
> **References** *Poelker v. Doe,* 432 U.S. 519 (1977).

Pornography

In 1985, Andrea Dworkin and Catharine MacKinnon proposed an ordinance that defined pornography as sex discrimination and an infringement on women's civil rights. They argue that pornography promotes misogynist attitudes and behaviors and that it constitutes an evil comparable to racism because both pornography and racism represent one person's or group's power over another person or group.

Dworkin and MacKinnon's antipornography ordinances to protect women's liberties, however, clash with First Amendment rights to free speech. To overcome this obstacle, they point out that pornography resembles other categories of speech that the courts have decided are not protected under the First Amendment, and some feminists agree with them. Women Against Pornography was organized to support antipornography ordinances as women's route to freedom from harm, pain, and humiliation. The group contends that pornography degrades women and that a society that tolerates it also accepts women's inferiority. The Feminists Against Censorship Task Force (FACT), in contrast, argues that the antipornography measures pose a threat to First Amendment rights. FACT also seeks to protect women's rights to earn their living as models or stars in pornographic productions.

Minneapolis, Minnesota, adopted versions of the ordinance in 1983 and 1984, but the mayor vetoed it both times. Indianapolis, Indiana, also adopted a version of it, but the U.S. Supreme Court found it unconstitutional in 1986, saying that the definition of pornography was too broad. Versions of the measure have been adopted in Western Europe, Australia, New Zealand, Tasmania, and the Philippines. In 1992, Canada's Supreme Court permitted a definition of obscenity that included materials that degrade or dehumanize women.

> **See also** Dworkin, Andrea; MacKinnon, Catharine Alice
>
> **References** Brill, "Freedom, Fantasy, Foes, and Feminism: The Debate around Pornography" (1990); Cowan, "Pornography: Conflict among Feminists" (1995).

Poverty
See **Feminization of Poverty**

Pratt, Eliza Jane (1902–1981)

Democrat Eliza Jane Pratt of North Carolina served in the U.S. House of Representatives from 25 May 1946 to 3 January 1947. From 1924 to 1946, Pratt worked as administrative assistant to the members of Congress who represented the Eighth Congressional District. When the incumbent died in 1946, she won the special election to fill the vacancy. She concluded that

Representative Ruth Pratt (R-NY) demonstrated how a voting machine works during her campaign, 1928 (Corbis/Bettmann)

she could not afford the costs of a campaign for a full term and declined to run. Between 1947 and 1956, she worked for several federal agencies, and from 1957 to 1962, she was again secretary to the congressional representative for the Eighth Congressional District.

Born in Morven, North Carolina, Pratt attended Queens College in North Carolina.

See also Congress, Women in

References Office of the Historian, U.S. House of Representatives, *Women in Congress, 1917–1990* (1991).

Pratt, Ruth Sears Baker (1877–1965)

Republican Ruth Pratt of New York served in the U.S. House of Representatives from 4 March 1929 to 3 March 1933. In Congress, she worked for appropriations to publish books for the blind, opposed the Eighteenth Amendment establishing Prohibition, and supported President Herbert Hoover's policy to avoid public financing of programs to relieve the unemployment created by the Depression. She lost her bid for a third term.

Born in Ware, Massachusetts, Pratt attended Wellesley College. A woman suffrage leader, she was active in Republican Party politics, serving as a committee vice chair for the Republican National Committee in 1918. In 1925, Pratt became the first female alderman in New York City, a post she held until 1929, when she ran for Congress. She was Republican national committeewoman for New York from 1929 to 1943.

See also Congress, Women in; Suffrage

References Office of the Historian, U.S. House of Representatives, *Women in Congress, 1917–1990* (1991).

Pregnancy Discrimination Act of 1978

The Pregnancy Discrimination Act of 1978 amends Title VII of the Civil Rights Act of 1964 by prohibiting discrimination on the basis of pregnancy, childbirth, or related medical conditions. Under the Pregnancy Discrimination Act, employers are not allowed to refuse to hire a pregnant woman if she can perform the major tasks of the job. Employers must treat pregnancy the same as any other temporary disability, which means they must provide disability benefits and accrued sick leave for hospitalization and recovery from childbirth.

The U.S. Supreme Court's decision in *General Electric v. Gilbert* (1976), that pregnancy was a unique condition that did not have to be treated by employers as an ensured disability and that the exclusion did not violate Title VII, led women's rights groups, labor organizations, and civil rights groups to draft legislation to reverse the decision. Among the more than fifty organizations involved in lobbying for the bill were the National Organization for Women, the American Federation of Labor–Congress of Industrial Organizations, and an antiabortion group.

After introducing the bill in 1977, its supporters argued that discrimination based on pregnancy was a central women's employment issue. They insisted that employers had used pregnancy as a way to place women on the margins of the workforce. Supporters believed that the bill would enhance women's equal employment opportunities. Opponents of the bill argued that it would be expensive and that pregnancy was not an equal employment issue. The Chamber of Commerce of the United States and the National Association of Manufacturers worried that women would abuse the system. They insisted that pregnancy was a voluntary condition and should not be considered a disability.

See also Civil Rights Act of 1964, Title VII; Fourteenth Amendment; *Geduldig v. Aiello*; *General Electric v. Gilbert*

References *Congressional Quarterly Almanac, 95th Congress, 1st Session . . . 1977* (1977), *Congressional Quarterly Almanac, 95th Congress, 2nd Session . . . 1978* (1979); *Geduldig v. Aiello*, 417 U.S. 484 (1974); www.eeoc.gov/facts/fs-preg. html.

President and Vice President, Women Candidates for

More than twenty women have sought the presidency of the United States, but none of them have won the nomination of the Democratic Party or the Republican Party. In 1964, Republican senator Margaret Chase Smith was the first woman to run for the nomination of a major party and to secure nomination for president by a major party. Smith ran in primaries in several states, received twenty-seven votes at the convention, and then withdrew her name. Congresswoman Shirley Chisholm of New York became the first African American woman to enter a presidential race when she ran for the Democratic Party's nomination in 1972. Chisholm entered twelve primaries and campaigned across the country in an effort to educate the public on a wide array of issues. When the party met to choose its candidate, Chisholm received 151.25 votes. Congresswoman Patricia Schroeder of Colorado considered entering the Democratic primaries for president but abandoned the attempt before entering any primaries. She concluded that she could not raise enough money to be a serious contender.

In 1952, Charlotta Spears Bass was the first African American woman to run for vice president when she was the Progressive Party's candidate. LaDonna Harris was the Citizens Party's 1980 vice presidential candidate. Congresswoman Geraldine Ferraro of New York became the first, and to date the only, woman to receive a major party's nomination for vice president in 1984, when Democratic Party presidential candidate Walter Mondale named her as his running mate. Twelve years earlier, Gloria Steinem had orchestrated an effort to place Frances "Sissy" Farenthold's name in nomination for vice president on the Democratic Party ticket in 1972. Farenthold received 400 votes.

In 1872, before women could vote, Victoria Claflin Woodhull ran on the Equal Rights Party ticket. Lawyer Belva Lockwood followed her in 1884 and 1888 on that party's ticket. Women have run on other third-party tickets, including the New Alliance Party, Communist Party, Socialist Party, Workers World Party, and Reform Party.

In 1998, a group of women organized the White House Project to create a climate of opinion that would make voters more amenable to a woman president by the year 2008.

> **See also** Bass, Charlotta Spears; Chisholm, Shirley Anita St. Hill; Democratic Party, Women in the; Farenthold, Frances (Sissy) Talton; Ferraro, Geraldine Anne; Harris, LaDonna; Lockwood, Belva Ann Bennett McNall; Republican Party, Women in the; Schroeder, Patricia Nell Scott; Smith, Margaret Madeline Chase; Steinem, Gloria Marie; Woodhull, Victoria Claflin
>
> **References** Center for the American Woman and Politics, Eagleton Institute of Politics, Rutgers University.

President's Commission on the Status of Women

With Executive Order 10980, President John F. Kennedy created the President's Commission on the Status of Women on 14 December 1961. He appointed fifteen women and eleven men to serve on the commission, which published its report in October 1963. Formed in part to halt congressional passage of the Equal Rights Amendment (ERA), the commission instead renewed interest in it.

The American Association of University Women and Business and Professional Women/USA (BPW/USA) had worked for the creation of a commission since the 1940s but failed to obtain congressional approval for it. In 1957, the National Manpower Commission at Columbia University recommended that the Department of Labor review state and federal laws related to women's employment, but the Women's Bureau rejected the idea. The concept gained momentum in 1961 with Esther Peterson's appointment to head the Women's Bureau. With the creation of a commission on the status of women, Peterson saw an opportunity to stop congressional action on the ERA, a measure she opposed because she believed it would end protective labor legislation for women. Peterson believed that the more appropriate way to end women's legal disabilities was through "specific bills for specific ills" and that a panel to identify legal barriers confronting women would serve that purpose. Peterson obtained the support of Eleanor Roosevelt, who in turn discussed it with Kennedy. The idea appealed to Kennedy, the first president since Herbert Hoover who did not have a woman in his cabinet, because it provided him with a program for women.

Kennedy appointed Roosevelt to chair the commission, which included U.S. senators Maurine Neuberger and George D. Aiken; Congresswomen Edith Green and Jessica M. Weis; National Council of Negro Women president Dorothy Height; Margaret Hickey, public affairs editor for *Ladies Home Journal*; cabinet members; labor representatives; and others. In addition to the commission members, more than 100 people served on the commission's committees and consulting groups. Fifty organizations contributed to the commission's work, some of them by preparing papers. Absent from those recruited to serve on the commission or to contribute to the reports were members of the National Woman's Party, an organization that had first conceptualized the ERA and had advocated its passage since 1923. The only commission member who supported the amendment was Marguerite Rawalt, a former BPW/USA president.

The commission established seven study committees: education and counseling, home and community services, women in employment, labor standards, security of basic income, women under the law, and women as citizens. Two additional committees addressed the specific problems that African American women confronted and the portrayal of women in the mass media. In its report, the commission made several recommendations for enhancing women's status and opportunities. The educational recommendations included vocational education at all levels, continuing education for adult women, and increased guidance counseling. In the area of home and community, the commission pointed to the need for child care services and called for fewer restrictions on tax deductions for child care and for equal opportunity in employment. Under labor standards, the commission sought the extension of the Fair Labor Standards Act of 1938 to categories of employment not covered, including retail establishments, agriculture, and nonprofit organizations. Other recommendations included passage of state laws to establish the principle of equal pay for comparable work and to protect the right of all workers to join unions of their choice and to bargain collectively.

In the area of equal rights, the panel suggested three routes for securing them: litigating to test sex discrimination in the courts, filing court cases arguing that the Fifth and Fourteenth Amendments provided women with constitutional equality, passing the ERA, and pressing for state legislative action. The panel preferred court and state action over the ERA but did not reject it as a possibility. Encouraging women to serve in elective and appointive offices, the commission said that positions at every level of government should be filled without regard to sex.

The commission's last recommendation called for the appointment of a cabinet officer to direct implementation of the report. On 1 November 1963, President Kennedy issued Executive Order 11126, creating the Interdepartmental Committee on the Status of Women and the Citizens' Advisory Council on the Status of Women to ensure the continuation of the work begun by the commission. Among the other implemented recommendations were the equalization of civil service health benefits, revisions in the Departments of State and Defense regulations for dependency allowances, and amendments in the Department of Labor's eligibility rules to end sex bias in federal apprenticeship programs.

In 1963, the governor of Washington appointed the first state commission, and by 1967 every state except one had some form of panel on women's status. The President's Commission on the Status of Women and the state commissions that followed can be credited, at least in part, with influencing several changes, beginning in the mid-1960s. Three states repealed laws limiting the hours women could work, and eleven states made them less restrictive; nine states enacted equal pay laws; four states changed their policies regarding women and jury service; six states enacted minimum wage laws that applied to both women and men, and nine states extended the coverage to men; and three states amended laws that restricted women's rights to dispose of their own property. Throughout the country, state reports created an agenda for change, and panel members became advocates for it.

In 1964, the Citizens' Advisory Council on the Status of Women and the Interdepartmental Committee on the Status of Women held the first of several annual, national conferences of the state commissions. At the third conference in 1966, a small group of attendees created the National Organization for Women, which became a leading advocate for the ERA.

See also American Association of University Women; Business and Professional Women/USA; Civil Rights Act of 1964, Title VII; Equal Pay Act of 1963; Equal Rights Amendment; Executive Order 10980; Executive Order 11126; Fourteenth Amendment; Green, Edith Louise Starrett; Height, Dorothy Irene; Juries, Women on; National Association of Commissions for Women; National Committee to Defeat the UnEqual Rights Amendment; National Council of Negro Women; National Organization for Women; Neuberger, Maurine Brown; Peterson, Esther; Protective Legislation; Roosevelt, Eleanor; Weis, Jessica McCullough; Women's Bureau

References Harrison, *On Account of Sex: The Politics of Women's Issues, 1945–1968* (1988); Mead and Kaplan, eds., *American Women: The Report of the President's Commission on the Status of Women and Other Publications of the Commission* (1965).

President's Interagency Council on Women

Established by President Bill Clinton in 1995, the President's Interagency Council on Women seeks to implement the Platform for Action adopted at the United Nations Fourth World Conference on Women held that year. Through interagency groups, the council develops policy, organizes events, promotes dialogue on issues, holds quarterly public briefings and discussions, and publishes updates on its progress and priorities.

The six working groups focus on women and the global economy, mentoring, women and prisons, rural women, trafficking in women and girls, and gender and institutional change, with each group establishing its own agenda. For example, the agenda for the group on women and the global economy includes developing a bibliography on the effects of globalization on women and producing an overview of federal government activities relating to the global economy and women. The council also sponsors events that involve the public, including the Ms. Foundation for Women's Take Our Daughters to Work Day.

See also Ms. Foundation for Women

References http://secretary.state.gov/www/iacw/.

President's Task Force on Women's Rights and Responsibilities

Established by President Richard Nixon on 1 October 1969, the President's Task Force on Women's Rights and Responsibilities was charged with reviewing women's status and making recommendations to advance women's opportunities. The task force dissolved on 15 December 1969 after presenting its report.

The task force resulted from the intense lobbying by four Republican congresswomen, Florence Dwyer of New Jersey, Margaret Heckler of Massachusetts, Catherine Barnes May of Washington, and Charlotte Reid of Illinois, who believed that Republicans needed to demonstrate an interest in and concern for women's issues. Nixon agreed to create the task force and asked it to collect information for his 1970 State of the Union Address. The ten women and two men appointed to it detailed discrimination against women and recommended steps to alleviate it. Nixon, however, did not mention women in his address.

The task force's guidelines stated that the report was for the president's information and guidance and that its contents were not to be revealed to the public by the task force. Completed and delivered on 15 December 1969, it was not released to the public until bootlegged copies appeared in the *Miami Herald* and other newspapers in mid-1970. After Elizabeth Koontz, head of the Women's Bureau, and several women's organizations protested the administration's continued resistance to making the report public, it was officially released.

The report, titled "A Matter of Simple Justice," recommended that Nixon establish an Office of Women's Rights and Responsibilities, convene a White House Conference on Women's Rights and Responsibilities, and urge passage of the Equal Rights Amendment, a measure he endorsed. Other recommendations included granting the Equal Employment Opportunity Commission enforcement powers, amending the Civil Rights Act of 1964 to prohibit discrimination on the basis of sex in public accommodations, and expanding the Civil Rights Act of 1957 to grant the Civil Rights Commission jurisdiction in cases involving denial of rights because of sex. Examples of recommendations to the executive branch included appointing more women to the cabinet and other high-level positions and directives to federal department heads to establish women's units to end discrimination within the departments. A total of twenty-two recommendations were made in the report.

Few of the recommendations were implemented; however, Nixon appointed Barbara Hackman Franklin to identify and recruit women to high-level federal appointments, and Congress passed the Equal Employment Opportunity Act of 1972 empowering the Equal Employment Opportunity Commission to file lawsuits against employers that discriminated against women.

See also Dwyer, Florence Price; Equal Employment Opportunity Commission; Franklin, Barbara Hackman; Heckler, Margaret Mary O'Shaughnessy; Koontz,

Elizabeth Duncan; May Bedell, Catherine Dean Barnes; Reid, Charlotte Thompson; Women's Bureau

References Linden-Ward and Green, *American Women in the 1960s: Changing the Future* (1993).

Price Waterhouse v. Hopkins (1989)

In *Price Waterhouse v. Hopkins,* the U.S. Supreme Court decided whether an employer's consideration of sex in employment decisions violated Title VII of the Civil Rights Act of 1964. Ann Hopkins had worked for the accounting firm of Price Waterhouse for five years by 1982, when she was a proposed candidate for partner in the company. At the time, Price Waterhouse had 662 partners, seven of whom were women; that year, of the eighty-eight candidates for partner, only Hopkins was a woman. The firm admitted forty-seven new partners, rejected twenty-one candidates, and held twenty over for recommendation the next year. Hopkins was among those whose candidacy was held over, but the partners refused to propose her again. Hopkins sued Price Waterhouse, accusing the company of sex discrimination under Title VII of the Civil Rights Act of 1964.

Price Waterhouse partners praised Hopkins's accomplishments, character, and professional skills, but in criticism of her interpersonal skills they also said that she could be abrasive, impatient, and unduly harsh. Some of the partners reacted negatively to Hopkins's personality because she was a woman. One partner described her as macho, another said that she "overcompensated for being a woman," and another suggested she take a charm school course. Yet another partner said that she should learn to "walk more femininely, talk more femininely, dress more femininely, wear make-up, have her hair styled, and wear jewelry." Lower courts concluded that the sex stereotyping and the sex-based evaluations constituted discrimination based on sex in violation of Title VII. The courts said that when an employer allowed discrimination to play a role in an employment decision, it had to prove by clear and convincing evidence that it would have made the same decision if the discrimination had not been part of the decision.

The U.S. Supreme Court disagreed with the lower courts, saying that the level of proof (clear and convincing evidence) that the lower courts had used was too high and that the employer only had to prove that it would have made the same decision with a preponderance of the evidence. Congress disagreed with the Court, and in the Civil Rights Act of 1991, it prohibited the consideration of race, color, religion, sex, or national origin in employment decisions, even if the decision would have been the same without consideration of those factors.

See also Civil Rights Act of 1991; Employment Discrimination

References *Price Waterhouse v. Hopkins,* 490 U.S. 228 (1989).

Priest, Ivy Maude Baker (1905–1975)

Head of the Women's Division of the Republican National Committee (RNC) in 1952 and 1953, Ivy Baker Priest served as treasurer of the United States from 1953 to 1961. Priest became active in politics in 1932 doing organizational work for the Young Republicans. After an unsuccessful candidacy for the Utah legislature, she was president of Utah Young Republicans from 1934 to 1936, Republican cochairperson for eleven western states, and Republican national committeewoman for Utah from 1944 to 1952. In 1950, she unsuccessfully ran for Congress, losing to Reva Beck Bosone.

An early supporter of Dwight D. Eisenhower's presidential candidacy in 1952, she was the only Utah delegate to the Republican National Convention committed to him. Following his nomination by the Republican Party that year, Priest was appointed assistant chair of the RNC and head of the Women's Division, holding primary responsibility for organizing women's support for Eisenhower.

After his election, President Eisenhower appointed Priest treasurer of the United States, the second woman to hold the position. At the end of Eisenhower's second term, Priest moved to California. In 1966, she successfully ran for state treasurer, serving from 1967 to 1975.

Born in Kimberly, Utah, Ivy Baker Priest took extension courses at the University of Utah. She abandoned her studies when her father's ill health made it necessary for her to find employment. Priest worked as a telephone operator, sales clerk, and department store buyer. Her autobiography, *Green Grows Ivy,* was published in 1958.

See also Bosone, Reva Zilpha Beck; Clark Gray, Georgia Neese; Republican Party, Women in the

References Layton, "Ivy Baker Priest" (1996); *New York Times,* 25 June 1975.

Progressive Party, Women in the

Before women had voting rights, women reformers worked for and with Progressive Party candidates at the local, state, and national levels. When the Progressive Party organized on the national level in 1912, women held seats on its national committee, recognition that Democrats did not give their female members until 1920 and Republicans until 1924. Women delegates to the 1912 Progressive Party convention helped write the party platform, which included support for woman suffrage, minimum wage insurance, child labor reform, and old age insurance, all priorities of women reformers. Women joined Bull Moose Clubs to work for Theodore

Roosevelt's election, held offices in them, and ran for statewide offices themselves on the party's ticket.

Among the more notable women involved in the party were Jane Addams and Ruth Hanna McCormick. Addams became the first woman to nominate a major political candidate when she gave her speech for Theodore Roosevelt at the 1912 convention. McCormick served as an important member of the party's campaign committee. Women promoted the Progressive Party as the one most likely to help women gain suffrage and as the party that offered women the opportunity to have a national voice in politics.

See also Addams, Jane; Democratic Party, Women in the; McCormick Simms, Ruth Hanna; Republican Party, Women in the

References Dinkin, *Before Equal Suffrage: Women in Partisan Politics from Colonial Times to 1920* (1995).

Pro-Life Action League

Founded in 1980 by Joseph M. Scheidler, the Pro-Life Action League (PLAL) seeks to prevent abortion through direct action, including picketing, closing abortion clinics, and sidewalk counseling. Sidewalk counseling, which PLAL considers one of its more effective strategies, involves approaching women going into abortion clinics and attempting to persuade them not to proceed with their abortions. PLAL demonstrates at abortion clinics, offices of prochoice organizations, and homes of physicians who perform abortions. In addition, PLAL leaders take pride in their ability to infiltrate prochoice conventions and monitor prochoice activities. PLAL lobbies Congress and state legislatures and takes credit for Illinois's restrictive abortion laws. In addition, the organization opposes birth control and sex education in public schools.

PLAL has been the target of several lawsuits, including *NOW v. Scheidler,* a case that went to the U.S. Supreme Court. In the case, the National Organization for Women (NOW) sued Operation Rescue, the Pro-Life Action League, other groups, and Joseph Scheidler, alleging the defendants were part of a nationwide conspiracy that sought to close abortion clinics. In 1994, the U.S. Supreme Court found that the Racketeer Influenced and Corrupt Organizations Act applied to the coalition of antiabortion groups, but it did not decide the merits of the lawsuit.

See also Abortion; National Organization for Women; *NOW v Scheidler;* Operation Rescue

References Blanchard, *The Anti-Abortion Movement and the Rise of the Religious Right: From Polite to Fiery Protest* (1994); Bradley, "*NOW v. Scheidler:* RICO Meets the First Amendment" (1995).

Protective Legislation

Protective legislation emerged as a social reform issue in the last decades of the nineteenth century. Through it, advocates sought to shield workers from the harshest abuses and the health and safety hazards of factory work, mining, and other industries. The U.S. Supreme Court's rejection of the laws that covered women and men led social reformers to limit legislation to women and children. The Women's Trade Union League, the National Consumers League, and other groups worked for the passage of legislation that limited the number of hours per day and the number of days per week that women and children could work, prohibited them from working at night, established minimum pay, limited the amount of weight they could lift, and excluded them from certain occupations. Massachusetts passed the first effective protective legislation in 1874, a measure that limited women and children to working ten hours per day. By 1900, fourteen states had passed comparable measures. The U.S. Supreme Court accepted measures that were limited to women in *Muller v. Oregon* (1908), and by 1960, every state had some form of protective legislation.

When Congress passed Title VII of the Civil Rights Act of 1964, the measure made discrimination on the basis of sex illegal. The law did not specifically address protective legislation, but the Equal Employment Opportunity Commission concluded that protective legislation discriminated on the basis of sex and that the federal policy overruled state laws.

See also Civil Rights Act of 1964, Title VII; Equal Rights Amendment; *Muller v. Oregon;* National Consumers League; Women's Trade Union League

References Baer, *The Chains of Protection: The Judicial Response to Women's Labor Legislation* (1978); Lehrer, *Origins of Protective Labor Legislation for Women, 1905–1925* (1987).

Pryce, Deborah (b. 1951)

Republican Deborah Pryce of Ohio entered the U.S. House of Representatives on 3 January 1993. Pryce held the leadership position of House conference secretary in the 105th and 106th Congresses (1997–2001). A fiscal conservative, Pryce told the House: "For the Democrats, it is the American people who have too much money. For us Republicans, it is the government that has too much." She has been a leader in efforts to fight congressional spending, win passage of national term limits legislation, and enact a constitutional amendment to balance the budget. A member of the Decorum and Civility Task Force, which works to improve relations between parties and foster civil conduct in the House of Representatives, she has also worked to improve deliberations and accountability in the House.

Representative Deborah Pryce (R-OH) with Representative Jennifer Dunn (R-WA) supported the short-lived election of Representative Bob Livingston (R-LA) as speaker of the House, 1998 (Associated Press AP)

Born in Warren, Ohio, Pryce received her bachelor of arts degree from Ohio State University in 1973 and her law degree from Capital University in 1976. A prosecutor for eight years, her first elected post was to the Franklin County Municipal Court as a judge, where she served from 1985 to 1992.

See also Congress, Women in

References Congressional Quarterly, *Politics in America 1996* (1995); www.house.gov/pryce/prycebio.htm.

Public Offices, Women Elected to

Women have been elected to public offices since the late nineteenth century. Laura J. Eisenhuth, North Dakota superintendent of public instruction from 1893 to 1895, was the first woman elected to a statewide public office. Susannah Medora Salter of Argonia, Kansas, was the first woman mayor in the United States, serving from 1887 to 1889. Colorado was the first state to elect women to its state legislature, sending three women to its House of Representatives in 1894. Republican Jeannette Rankin of Montana was the first woman elected to Congress, entering the House of Representatives in 1917. The first woman governor was Democrat Nellie Tayloe Ross of Wyoming, who served from 1925 to 1927. By 1969, however, only twenty-three women held statewide elective executive offices, or

6.6 percent of the 346 offices in the nation. Over the next thirty years, the number grew to ninety-one women in statewide elective executive offices, or 28.2 percent of 323 offices. (In the meantime, states had eliminated certain offices, combined them with other offices, or made them appointed positions.)

Several factors account for the small number of women who have served in public offices. Although women in some states, including Montana, had voting rights when Rankin was elected to Congress, U.S. women did not gain full suffrage rights until the ratification of the Nineteenth Amendment in 1920. Of the women who developed political experience as leaders in the suffrage movement, few sought public office, and fewer succeeded.

Women found that the Democratic and Republican Parties did not welcome them into their decisionmaking circles, appoint them to party positions, or recommend them for appointive positions in government. Seeking equality in the parties has been a long struggle for women, one that has received significant attention from women and from party leaders. The parties also resisted nominating women for public office unless it appeared that that party's candidate had virtually no chance of winning the general election. For example, in 1924, of the five Democratic women running for Congress, four of them ran in Republican districts, and the lone Republican woman ran in the South. Only Democrat Mary T. Norton of New Jersey won that year because of the backing of the party's machine.

Women have also found it difficult to raise the money needed to adequately finance their campaigns, in part because so many ran as sacrificial lambs for offices that they had little chance of winning. In the 1970s, the National Women's Political Caucus was founded to recruit women to pursue public office and train candidates to run effective campaigns, as well as help fund the campaigns. In the 1980s, EMILY's List, the WISH List, and other political action committees (PACs) formed to raise money for female candidates' campaigns. These groups have educated potential donors about the necessity of candidates having adequate financing for their campaigns and have raised substantial amounts of money, but money remains a significant barrier to women's candidacies and women's successes.

Another factor for women seeking office is incumbency, which both benefits women in office and poses a barrier to women challenging incumbents. In the 1998 elections, all fifty women seeking reelection to the U.S. House of Representatives won. Of the seventeen women nominated by a major party who ran for open seats, six won, but none of the fifty-four women challenging House incumbents won. In the U.S. Senate, three of the four women seeking reelection won, one of the two women running for open seats won, and none of the four women challengers won. Both women governors who ran for reelection won, and thirty-four of the thirty-six women incumbents seeking statewide offices won.

Arizona made history in the 1998 elections when voters elected women to all five statewide executive positions in the line of constitutional succession. The governor, secretary of state, attorney general, state treasurer, and state superintendent of schools in Arizona are all women, the first time any state has selected women for all its top offices.

See also Congress, Women in; Democratic Party, Women in the; EMILY's List; Landes, Bertha Ethel Knight; Republican Party, Women in the; State Legislatures, Women in; WISH List

References Center for the American Woman and Politics, National Information Bank on Women in Public Office, Rutgers University.

Public Speaking

In the early nineteenth century, several barriers stood between women and their participation in society. One of the first obstacles that women overcame was the social and religious prohibition against their speaking in public before audiences of women and men. Women's public silence had its roots in St. Paul's admonition that women should not be permitted to speak, a rule that the dominant Protestant churches heeded. In addition, it was considered unseemly for women to be heard in public. The exception was women of the Quaker religion, who were permitted to speak in meetings.

The first few women who broke through the barrier suffered the outrage of ministers and the public. In 1828 and 1829, Frances Wright, probably the first female public speaker in the United States, advocated equal education for women and men. Notorious for speaking in public and for her ideas, she attracted both large audiences and condemnation from the pulpit and the press. African American Maria Stewart was likely the next female public speaker, lecturing in Boston in 1832 and 1833 on abolition and educational opportunities for girls.

The two women who truly opened the public lecture stage to women were Angelina and Sarah Grimké, the first female agents of the American Anti-Slavery Society. These two sisters went on several speaking tours between 1837 and 1839. Attacked by churches for speaking in public, the Grimké sisters responded to their critics by articulating the connection between slavery and women's rights and arguing that women needed equality in order to take their places in the fight against slavery. In 1838, Angelina Grimké entered new territory for women when she spoke to the Massachusetts legislature on the need to end the slave trade in Washington, D.C. She was the first woman to speak to a legislative body. The Grimké sisters broke the public speaking barrier, and other women soon followed them, first calling for the end of slavery and then calling for women's rights.

See also Abolitionist Movement, Women in the; Grimké, Angelina Emily and Sarah Moore; Stewart, Maria W.; Wright, Frances (Fanny)

References Flexner and Fitzpatrick, *Century of Struggle: The Woman's Rights Movement in the United States* (1996).

Pyle, Gladys (1890–1989)

Republican Gladys Pyle of South Dakota served in the U.S. Senate from 9 November 1938 to 3 January 1939 but was never sworn into office. She was elected to the Senate following the death of the incumbent, but Congress had adjourned before her election and did not convene until the new Congress was organized following the 1938 general elections.

Pyle entered public service as the first woman elected to the South Dakota House of Representatives, an office she held from 1923 to 1927. She orchestrated the state's ratification of the Child Labor Amendment in 1923 and worked to give women the right to serve on juries, a right women gained in 1947. South Dakota secretary of state from 1927 to 1931, Pyle was the first woman in the state elected to hold a constitutional office. As secretary of state, Pyle sponsored legislation for a safety code for motor vehicles. In 1930, she lost in her attempt to become the Republican Party's candidate for governor, even though she received the most votes of the five Republican candidates. To win the nomination, a candidate needed at least 35 percent of the votes cast, which neither Pyle nor the other candidates accomplished, and the decision went to the state Republican convention. The candidate who had received the fewest votes in the election became the nominee. Appointed to the state's securities commission, Pyle served from 1931 to 1933, again the first woman to serve on a state commission. She was also a member of the South Dakota Board of Charities and Corrections from 1943 to 1957.

Born in Huron, South Dakota, Gladys Pyle earned her bachelor of arts degree from Huron College in 1911 and also studied at the American Conservatory of Music for one year. She taught in public high schools from 1912 to 1920.

See also Congress, Women in; State Legislatures, Women in

References Kinyon and Walz, *The Incredible Gladys Pyle* (1985); Office of the Historian, U.S. House of Representatives, *Women in Congress, 1917–1990* (1991).

Quaker Women

Quaker women emerged as the first group of European women in America to have public lives, a status that developed from their roles as preachers and one that led them to take active and public roles in the temperance, abolitionist, and suffrage movements. The tenets of the Quaker faith provided the unusual independence Quaker women had from male authority. Quakers believe that the "inner light" reveals the way to truth and salvation and that it is available to both women and men, empowering women and men and giving both authority. Among the nineteenth-century Quaker women leaders were suffragists Susan B. Anthony and Lucretia Mott.

> **See also** Abolitionist Movement, Women in the; Anthony, Susan Brownell; Mott, Lucretia Coffin; Suffrage; Temperance Movement, Women in the
>
> **References** Matthews, *The Rise of Public Woman: Woman's Power and Woman's Place in the United States, 1630–1970* (1992).

Quinton, Amelia Stone (1833–1926)

Native American rights advocate Amelia Stone Quinton joined Mary L. Bonney's crusade in 1879 to protect the Oklahoma Territory from white settlers and to save it for the Native Americans to whom it belonged. Working with Bonney in the Central Indian Committee, which eventually became the Women's National Indian Association (WNIA), Quinton planned and organized the efforts, and Bonney provided the financial support. The WNIA advocated doing away with reservations, allotting private plots of land to individuals, and assimilating Native Americans into white culture.

Quinton prepared research, drafted petitions, and organized other groups to help with the petition effort. In 1882, Quinton and five others presented President Chester A. Arthur with more than 100,000 signatures on petitions for Native American land allotment, education, and citizenship. She also made speeches, lobbied members of Congress, persuaded others to send letters to Congress, and wrote articles. Quinton's work significantly contributed to the passage of the Dawes Act of 1887. Under the measure's provisions, Native Americans could exchange their participation in tribal holdings for an individual land grant and American citizenship.

Quinton served as president of WNIA from 1887 to 1905. During those years, the organization grew, expanding into the South and West and from eighty-six auxiliaries to 120. She continued to lobby Congress, particularly to improve conditions on reservations. With her health declining, Quinton refused reelection to the presidency of WNIA in 1905. She continued, however, to work for Native Americans until 1910.

Born in Jamesville, New York, Quinton received her education at Cortland Academy in Homer, New York, and taught in girls' seminaries and academies. One of the earliest members of the Woman's Christian Temperance Union, she represented the organization and helped establish new chapters from 1874 to 1877.

See also Bonney, Mary Lucinda; Woman's Christian Temperance Union

References Hardy, *American Women Civil Rights Activists* (1993).

R

Racial Discrimination

Racial discrimination in the United States has its roots in the enslavement of Africans beginning in the seventeenth century. With the passage and ratification of the Thirteenth Amendment to the U.S. Constitution, slavery ended in the United States, but the amendment did not end discrimination on the basis of race. Throughout the nation, local and state laws and policies as well as local customs authorized or permitted racial discrimination at every level.

The U.S. Supreme Court's 1954 decision in *Brown v. Board of Education of Topeka, Kansas,* provided the first substantial federal policy to end some discriminatory practices by ordering the end of segregated public schools. Laws and policies requiring or permitting discrimination on the basis of race in employment, housing, public accommodations, and higher education, however, persisted until passage of the Civil Rights Act of 1964, which prohibited those forms of discrimination. The Voting Rights Act of 1965 provided the legal basis and enforcement for ending policies that discriminated against African Americans seeking to register to vote.

The first significant law restricting immigration into the United States discriminated against the Chinese. The Chinese Exclusion Act of 1882 prohibited Chinese immigration for ten years and was renewed in 1892 for another ten years. Congress made Chinese immigration permanently illegal in 1902. In addition, citizenship was denied to Chinese until 1943.

Official discrimination against Japanese immigrants was based upon a "gentleman's agreement" between President Theodore Roosevelt and

Japan made in 1907, prohibiting immigration from that country. Following Japan's bombing of Pearl Harbor in December 1941, the U.S. federal government forced all Japanese Americans, citizens and noncitizens, to leave the West Coast. Forced to quickly dispose of their property, deprived of the opportunity to continue their occupations, and placed into internment camps, 100,000 people of Japanese descent were denied their constitutional civil rights. The United States was also at war with Germany and Italy, but people of those descents were not deprived of their freedoms. In addition, the U.S. Supreme Court upheld the internment of Japanese immigrants and people of Japanese descent. President Franklin Roosevelt withdrew the internment order in 1945 and the camps closed later that year. Japanese Americans were reimbursed for lost property in 1968 and Congress gave $20,000 to each of the 60,000 surviving internees in 1988.

Native Americans and Latinos have also endured racial discrimination that limited their access to education, housing, and employment. Like the groups mentioned above, they have been denied their constitutional civil rights, and often their pleas to obtain those rights have been rejected. While the Civil Rights Act of 1964, affirmative action programs, and other measures have attempted to address racial discrimination, the legacy of racial discrimination continues to haunt American society and to limit the full realization of the fundamental ideals of the U.S. Constitution.

See also Civil Rights Act of 1964, Title VII; Voting Rights Act of 1965

References Crawford, Rouse, and Woods, eds., *Women in the Civil Rights Movement: Trailblazers and Torchbearers, 1941–1965* (1990); Foner and Garraty, *The Reader's Companion to American History* (1991).

Radicalesbians

Founded in 1970, Radicalesbians resulted from attempts to purge lesbians from the feminist movement. Labeled the "lavender menace" by feminist and National Organization for Women (NOW) president Betty Friedan, Rita Mae Brown and other lesbians left NOW to form a lesbian feminist movement. At the second Congress to Unite Women, the lights went out in the meeting hall, and when the lights came back on, they revealed several lesbians wearing lavender T-shirts stenciled with the words "lavender menace." The women described their experiences as lesbians in a heterosexual culture and distributed copies of the "The Woman-Identified Woman," a paper intended to assuage feminists' fears of lesbianism. The paper described lesbianism as a political choice that aligned women with other women and not solely as a matter of sexual expression.

See also Brown, Rita Mae; Friedan, Betty Naomi Goldstein; Lesbian Rights; National Organization for Women

References Wandersee, *American Women in the 1970s: On the Move* (1988).

Rambaut, Mary Lucinda Bonney

See **Bonney, Mary Lucinda**

Rankin, Jeannette Pickering (1880–1973)

Republican Jeannette Rankin of Montana was the first woman to serve in the U.S. Congress. When Rankin won the race for the U.S. House of Representatives in 1916, women in three-fourths of the states still did not have full suffrage rights. She served from 4 March 1917 to 3 March 1919 and from 3 January 1941 to 3 January 1943. A devoted peace advocate, she was the only person to vote against U.S. entry into both World War I and World War II.

Born near Missoula, Montana, Jeannette Rankin was the eldest daughter in a prosperous ranching family. Early in her life, Rankin wrote in her journal: "Go! Go! Go! It makes no difference where just so you go!" and she did. She entered the University of Montana in 1898, graduated with a degree in biology in 1902, and began teaching school. She soon decided that teaching was not for her and began traveling across the country looking for her life's work.

A trip to Boston exposed her to urban poverty and the squalor in which poor families lived, especially women and children. From 1904 until 1908, Rankin sought to help remedy the problems of poverty through social work in several cities, including New York and San Francisco. By 1913, she had concluded that without the vote women could not make substantial societal change and had turned her efforts toward woman suffrage. She worked in a number of states, including her home state of Montana, which passed a state constitutional amendment for woman suffrage in 1914.

A Progressive Republican, she decided to run for the U.S. Congress in 1916. She began her campaign with an important advantage. Through her travels for the suffrage amendment, Rankin had developed a wide base of supporters who worked on her campaign.

Her primary campaign theme was the need for attention to children's well-being, which was consistent with her earlier social work. One example she used to demonstrate the lack of interest in children was that the federal government spent $300,000 a year for research on pig fodder but only $30,000 a year to study children's needs. She promised to work for an amendment to the U.S. Constitution for full woman suffrage. Another campaign issue involved the war raging in Europe. Americans were not yet involved in World War I, but the possibility of it appeared increasingly great. Rankin pledged that she would not vote to send Montana boys to war.

Rankin took her seat in Congress on 2 April 1917, and on 6 April Congress voted on a declaration of war. Rankin carefully deliberated

Representative Jeannette Rankin (R-MT) was the only member of Congress to vote against both world wars, for which she had to have a police escort to ensure her safety (Library of Congress)

about how she would vote. Because she was the first woman to serve in Congress, some people regarded her as a test of whether or not women should be there. If she voted against war, it might be interpreted as proof that women were weak and could not make difficult decisions. If she voted for war, she would be breaking her campaign pledge to stay out of it. She voted against war, along with fifty-five male members of the House of Representatives. She later said being the first woman elected to Congress was less significant than being "the first woman who was ever asked what she thought about war [and] said 'no!'"

Rankin supported several measures that addressed women's concerns. She passed a bill to regulate the hours and conditions for women workers at the U.S. Mint, protective labor legislation that social reformers of the time favored. She developed support for woman suffrage and introduced a bill to end child labor. Her bill to provide health care and instruction for mothers became the Sheppard-Towner Maternity and Infancy Protection Act of 1921, and she helped build support for the Cable Act of 1922, giving women citizenship rights regardless of their marital status or the citizenship of their husband.

She decided to run for the U.S. Senate in 1918 but lost in the Republican primary. Her vote against war had turned voters against her. Rankin's commitment to peace became clear in her work over the next twenty years. She devoted herself to lobbying Congress and organizing people to work for peace.

Her work in peace issues once again attracted Montana voters' support in 1940, when she ran for the U.S. House of Representatives the second time. As in 1916, Europe was at war, and Americans were debating whether or not to enter World War II. Rankin campaigned on peace themes and won her seat in Congress. True to her beliefs, when Congress voted on whether or not to enter the war, she voted no. She was the only person in the House or the Senate to cast a no vote and the only person in the United States to vote against both world wars. Widely ridiculed for having kept her campaign promises, she did not run again in 1942.

During the Vietnam War, she joined the peace protests against it. As the leader of the Jeannette Rankin Brigade, she marched in Washington,

D.C., with other protesters in an antiwar rally in 1968. That same year, she considered running for Congress for the third time, but poor health made her abandon those plans. She was eighty-eight years old. She died five years later, in 1973, in Carmel, California.

See also Congress, Women in; Suffrage

References Anderson, "Steps to Political Equality: Woman Suffrage and Electoral Politics in the Lives of Emily Newell Blair, Anne Henrietta Martin, and Jeannette Rankin" (1997); Kaptur, *Women of Congress: A Twentieth Century Odyssey* (1996).

Rape

With the emergence of the modern feminist movement in the 1960s, women focused attention on rape, reports on it, prosecutions of it, and laws relating to it. The topic began to receive serious attention through the efforts of Susan Brownmiller, who was a leader in the New York Radical Women's decisions to hold a speak-out and a conference in 1971 on the topic. These events contributed to raising women's consciousness about rape, served as forums for analyzing societal assumptions about it, and provided some of the inspiration for Brownmiller's landmark study of it. In *Against Our Will* (1975), Brownmiller traced the social and legal history of rape, arguing that rape "is an exercise in power" and not an act of passion. She explained that rape "is nothing more or less than a conscious process of intimidation by which *all men* keep *all women* in a state of fear." The fear affected the dailiness of women's lives, including their willingness to live alone, walk outside alone at night, or leave their windows open.

Rape is one of the most underreported of crimes—approximately 132,000 women report that they have been victims of rape or of attempted rape every year, but it is estimated that two to six times that number of women are raped but do not report it. The crime is generally not reported for several reasons, including women's fear and embarrassment and their knowledge that prosecutors are often reluctant to file charges and that prosecutions are difficult to obtain.

Women often find the experience of dealing with law enforcement officials degrading and traumatic, contributing to their resistance to continuing with the reporting process. Because women had so few options at the time the feminist movement began, feminists opened rape crisis hotlines and rape crisis centers, with the first hotline opening in Washington, D.C., in 1972 and hundreds more opening over the next four years. The centers generally provide assistance to rape victims, accompany them to police stations, and serve as advocates for them after the attack. Centers also offer self-defense classes, rape prevention seminars, support groups, and training for professionals.

In the 1970s, feminists also began to change state laws related to rape. Several states had special rules of evidence in rape trials, including requiring corroborating evidence in addition to the woman's testimony. To prove that force was involved and that the woman had resisted, the evidence could include a weapon, bruises, or torn clothing. To prove that penetration had occurred, possible evidence included vaginal tears, bruises, and sperm. The courts permitted testimony about the woman's prior sexual history as relevant to the issue of consent, and the victim's attire could be part of the defense, which could assert that revealing or sexy clothing constituted an invitation to be assaulted, the "she asked for it" defense. In addition, judges' instructions to juries included the caution articulated by a seventeenth-century jurist: "Rape is an accusation easily to be made and hard to be proved, and harder to be defended."

Since the 1970s, every state in the country has revised its rape laws, with some of the states amending them several times to move the emphasis from the victim's behavior and clothing to the defendant's actions. The requirement that women resist the attack and examinations of victims' behavior and prior sexual activity, with some exceptions, and the seventeenth-century instructions to the jury have been dropped in most states. As states changed their laws, they also renamed the offense sexual assault and made it gender-neutral.

In the 1970s, because rape was defined as "forcible penetration of an act of sexual intercourse on the body of a woman not the man's wife," forced sex between a husband and wife was legal, and even if she was injured, no law had been broken. Whether a state labeled forcible sex as rape or as sexual assault, there was often a marital exemption, but by the 1990s, that exemption had been eliminated in almost every state. In addition, sexual assault laws covered cohabitants and people on dates.

In the 1990s, an increasing number of women reported that they had been raped after they had been drugged. An odorless, colorless, tasteless drug, Rohypnol relaxes people so that resistance is almost impossible and it may lead to memory loss. By secretly placing the drug in a drink, rapists disarmed their intended victims. In 1996, Congress increased the penalties for giving drugs, especially Rohypnol, to a person without the person's knowledge and with the intent to commit a violent crime. In addition, college safety groups and other organizations produced warnings to alert women of the potential danger.

See also Feminist Movement; New York Radical Women

References Baer, *Women in American Law: The Struggle toward Equality from the New Deal to the Present* (1996); Brownmiller, *Against Our Will: Men, Women, and Rape* (1975); *Congressional Quarterly Almanac, 104th Congress,*

2nd Session . . . 1996 (1997); Wandersee, *On the Move: American Women in the 1970s* (1988).

Ray, Dixy Lee (1914–1994)

Democrat Dixy Lee Ray was governor of Washington from 1977 to 1981. President Richard Nixon appointed her to the Atomic Energy Commission in 1972, and she chaired it from 1973 to 1975. A strong supporter of nuclear power, she believed that nuclear power plants were safe and that mass destruction from an accident was unlikely. When the Atomic Energy Commission's responsibilities were transferred to another agency, President Gerald Ford appointed Ray assistant secretary of state for oceans, international environmental, and scientific affairs. After leaving the federal government, Ray ran for governor of the state of Washington. Governor Ray was viewed as friendly to business and was criticized by environmentalists for her support of nuclear power and its development. Ray ran for a second term but lost in the primary election.

Born in Tacoma, Washington, Dixy Lee Ray earned her bachelor's degree from Mills College in 1937 and her doctorate from Stanford University in 1945. Ray taught in Oakland, California, from 1938 to 1942. She was an associate professor of zoology at the University of Washington from 1945 to 1976.

See also Governors, Women

References *New York Times*, 3 January 1994.

Reagan, Nancy Robins (b. 1923?)

Nancy Reagan served as first lady from 1981 to 1989, when her husband Ronald Reagan was president of the United States. Nancy Reagan began her years in the White House supervising a major restoration of the residence and its furnishings, a project that became one of the first controversies she encountered. The drug abuse prevention program she developed, "Just Say No," was criticized for its seemingly simplistic approach to a complex social problem. Her influence on the president in the areas of his staff and policy was questioned and criticized. She acknowledged that she did not like White House chief of staff Donald Regan, but she insisted that she did not stage a coup to get rid of him, despite his assertions that she had managed his dismissal and those of other officials in the administration. Nancy Reagan explained her perspective on a president's wife's duties: "Don't be afraid to look after your husband or to voice your opinions, either to him or his staff. In spite of a White House full of people taking care of various aspects of a President's life, you're the one who knows him best."

First Lady Nancy Reagan spoke out against drugs during her "Just Say No" campaign at a conference at the White House, 1986 (Corbis/Bettmann)

While President Reagan was in office, in 1987, Nancy Reagan learned that she had breast cancer. She, like Betty Ford before her, permitted the information to be made public. Following the announcement, the number of women obtaining mammograms increased substantially.

Born in New York City, Nancy Reagan was christened Anne Frances Robins but was called Nancy throughout her life. An actress, she performed on Broadway, television, and in movies. She married Ronald Reagan in 1952 and soon left her acting career in favor of homemaking and raising her family.

References *New York Times*, 25 May 1988; Reagan, *My Turn* (1989).

Redstockings

Founded in New York City in 1969 by Shulamith Firestone and Ellen Willis, the Redstockings were a group of women's liberationists who viewed themselves as radical and militant. The group's name derived from the term *bluestocking*, a nineteenth-century derogatory term used to describe feminist theorists and writers, and the symbolism of the revolutionary color red.

Redstockings' members argued in their manifesto that women's submission to male domination "was not the result of brainwashing, stupidity, or mental illness but of continual, daily pressure from men." They also argued that women marry because of the difficulties of being single and working at a "boring and alienating job." One member suggested that women worked to make themselves attractive to men as a survival strategy.

Committed to action, they chose the New York legislature's hearing on abortion reform as the stage for their first public protest and disrupted the hearing by speaking from the audience and calling for the repeal of abortion laws, not reform. The Redstockings later held a public speak-out on abortion, at which a dozen women who had had illegal abortions described their experiences to an audience of 300 people. The group disbanded in 1970.

> **See also** Women's Liberation Movement
>
> **References** Echols, *Daring to Be Bad: Radical Feminism in America, 1967–1975* (1989).

Reece, Louise Goff (1898–1970)

Republican Louise Reece of Tennessee served in the U.S. House of Representatives from 16 May 1961 to 3 January 1963. Following the death of her husband Brazilla Reece, Louise Reece won the special election to fill the vacancy. In Congress, Louise Reece worked to protect her district's glass industry. She did not run for reelection.

Born in Milwaukee, Wisconsin, Louise Reece was the daughter and granddaughter of U.S. senators. An active businesswoman, she chaired the boards of two banks and managed Goff Properties.

> **See also** Congress, Women in
>
> **References** Office of the Historian, U.S. House of Representatives, *Women in Congress, 1917–1990* (1991).

Reed v. Reed (1971)

In *Reed v. Reed,* the U.S. Supreme Court decided that the equal protection clause of the Fourteenth Amendment applied to sex discrimination and invalidated a state law on that basis. In addition, the Court established an intermediate level of scrutiny that applied only to sex discrimination cases.

The Idaho law in question designated the classes of people eligible to administer a deceased person's estate. Under the law, when a man and a woman of the same relationship to the deceased filed to be appointed the estate administrator, the state gave mandatory preferences to the man. The Court decided that mandatory preferences to members of either sex "merely to accomplish the elimination of hearings on the merits, is to make the very kind of arbitrary legislative choice forbidden by the equal protection clause of the Fourteenth Amendment" and found the law unconstitutional.

Reed v. Reed was the first case litigated by the American Civil Liberties Union's Women's Rights Project. Supreme Court Justice Ruth Bader Ginsburg, then a law professor and head of the Women's Rights Project, directed the project and argued the case.

See also Fourteenth Amendment; Ginsburg, Ruth Joan Bader

References Getman, "The Emerging Constitutional Principle of Sexual Equality" (1973); *Reed v. Reed*, 404 U.S. 71 (1971).

Reid, Charlotte Thompson (b. 1913)

Republican Charlotte Reid of Illinois served in the U.S. House of Representatives from 3 January 1963 to 7 October 1971. Charlotte Reid's husband Frank Reid was running for Congress in 1962 when he died. Republican political leaders chose Charlotte Reid to replace him on the ticket, and she won the election. Congresswoman Reid worked to protect agricultural interests through price supports, favored building a National Cultural Center, and introduced a constitutional amendment to permit prayer in public schools. She opposed much of President Lyndon Johnson's Great Society programs but supported Johnson's and President Richard Nixon's conduct of the Vietnam War. Reid resigned her congressional seat to accept an appointment to the Federal Communications Commission in 1971, serving until 1976. She served on the President's Task Force on International Private Enterprise from 1983 to 1985.

Born in Kankakee, Illinois, Charlotte Reid attended Illinois College. She sang professionally for NBC using the name Annette King. Following her marriage to Frank Reid, she became involved in civic, community, and political groups.

See also Congress, Women in

References Office of the Historian, U.S. House of Representatives, *Women in Congress, 1917–1990* (1991).

Religious Coalition for Reproductive Choice

The Religious Coalition for Reproductive Choice (RCRC) was founded in 1973 to protect women's right to an abortion and to offer an interpretation of abortion based on religious faith that was an alternative to the Roman Catholic Church's opposition to abortion. Although all of the forty member organizations support reproductive rights, they represent a spectrum of specific views on abortion, but none of them intend to have their denominational stance written into law.

Initially called the Religious Coalition for Abortion Rights (RCAR), the organization was established to counter the U.S. Catholic Conference's commitment to reverse *Roe v. Wade* (1973), the U.S. Supreme Court decision that legalized abortion. Twenty major Christian, Jewish, and other religious organizations were brought together by the United Methodist General Board of Church and Society as a temporary group to respond to the antichoice movement, but when it became apparent that a sustained effort was necessary, RCAR was independently incorporated in 1981. It later changed its name to Religious Coalition for Reproductive Choice.

RCRC works through forty member organizations, fifty-five grassroots organizations, and a network of prochoice clergy to advocate its position on the local, state, and federal levels. It supported the Freedom of Access to Clinic Entrances Act of 1994 and opposed cuts in family planning appropriations and efforts to outlaw partial birth abortion. Other priorities include medical care for all children, sexuality education, and teen pregnancy prevention programs.

Another facet of RCRC's work is its Women of Color Partnership, a program that focuses on including Latinas and African American women, poor women, and underrepresented women in its policymaking and programs. Through the Women of Color Partnership, RCRC seeks to counter racism and related prejudices that contribute to the formulation of punitive public policies and practices.

RCRC's membership includes boards and committees of the United Methodist Church, Presbyterian Church USA, United Church of Christ, Episcopal Church, and Moravian Church in America. In addition, several federations and associations within the conservative, reconstructionist, and reform movement of the Jewish faith belong, as well as those in the Unitarian Universalist denomination and the Ethical Culture Movement.

See also Abortion; *Roe v. Wade*

References Wood, "The Religious Coalition for Abortion Rights: An Analysis of Its Role in the Pro-Choice Movement" (1990); www.rcrc.org.

Reno, Janet (b. 1938)

Janet Reno became the first female attorney general of the United States in 1993. She was President Bill Clinton's third choice. His first choice had withdrawn because she had hired an illegal immigrant as a nanny and had not paid Social Security taxes for her. A second woman's nomination was planned but was not made because she had also employed an undocumented worker as a nanny. Although the practice had been legal at the time, it was enough to make Clinton reconsider her nomination. The longest-serving attorney general, Reno has also been one of the most visible and popular officials in President Bill Clinton's administration. Known for her ability to speak her mind, Reno once told a convention of juvenile court judges that they were "dunderheads" and walked out.

Born in Miami, Florida, Janet Reno earned her bachelor of arts degree from Cornell University in 1960 and her law degree from Harvard University in 1963. When Reno began looking for a job after receiving her law degree, she encountered sex discrimination but eventually found a job in private practice. One of the law firms that refused to hire her at that time made her a partner fourteen years later.

In 1971 and 1972, Reno served as staff director for the Judicial Committee of the Florida House of Representatives. In 1973, she was consultant to the Florida Senate's Criminal Justice Committee for Revision of Florida's Criminal Code. Administrative assistant to the state prosecutor for Dade County from 1973 to 1976, Reno was a partner in a private law practice from 1976 to 1978. When the state attorney resigned before the end of his term, Florida governor Reubin Askew appointed Reno state attorney for Dade County. She was elected to the office of state attorney in November 1978, where she served until 1993.

As state attorney, Reno was responsible for an annual budget of $30 million and 940 employees. Her office prosecuted cases involving homicide, child abuse, rape, drug trafficking, and white-collar crimes. She helped reform the juvenile justice system and pursued parents who were delinquent on their child support payments. She also established a special court for drug offenses. During her tenure, she dealt with race riots, waves of immigrants, political corruption, and police brutality.

Reno's priorities as U.S. attorney general include reducing crime and violence by incarcerating serious, repeat offenders and finding alternative forms of punishment for first-time offenders. By focusing on prevention and early intervention, she hopes to keep children away from gangs, drugs, and violence. Other priorities include protecting the environment and making integrity, excellence, and professionalism the hallmarks of the Department of Justice.

Shortly after becoming attorney general and head of the U.S. Department of Justice, Reno was faced with several crises: she was responsible for the investigation of the terrorist bombing of the New York World Trade Center; allegations were made that the director of the Federal Bureau of Investigation (FBI) had been involved in misconduct; and the Bureau of Alcohol, Tobacco, and Firearms was engaged in a standoff with the Branch Davidians, a religious group in Waco, Texas. After two months, Reno authorized the FBI to use nonlethal tear gas to end the siege, but a fire erupted that killed eighty-five people. Reno took full responsibility for the tragedy. A Department of Justice inquiry challenged some of the statements she had made regarding the reasons for using the tear gas and criticized her for not being more directly involved in the siege.

Reno has traveled across the country, speaking to bar associations, elementary school students, and rehabilitation clinics and visiting police stations to inspect crime-fighting programs.

See also Cabinets, Women in Presidential

References Congressional Quarterly, *Cabinets and Counselors: The President and the Executive Branch* (1997); *New York Times,* 12 February 1993, 15 May 1994; www.usdoj.gov/bios/jreno.html.

Reproductive Rights

Reproductive rights are based upon the premise that human dignity and equality grant each person the right and the responsibility to make reproductive decisions for herself or himself. Information about human sexuality and reproduction is fundamental to making those decisions, as is access to the services necessary to act upon the decisions. Among the areas encompassed by reproductive rights are good personal health practices, fertility, family planning, pregnancy, fetal development, childbirth, contraception, and abortion. Reproductive rights include fertility services for infertile couples, prenatal care that enhances the health of mother and fetus, delivery and postnatal procedures that contribute to the health of mother and baby, safe abortion procedures, freedom from forced sterilization, and many other reproductive options.

In the United States, a range of obstacles inhibit women's exercise of their reproductive rights. Financial barriers prevent many poor and low-income women, especially women of color, from having adequate health insurance. Even women who have health insurance may find that their insurance company discriminates against them by refusing to cover birth control prescriptions while covering prescriptions for male erectile dysfunction like Viagra. Medicaid, the government health insurance program for poor people, does not cover most abortions, further limiting low-income women's options. Economic considerations are also a barrier to women having regular gynecological exams and mammograms. Inadequate or nonexistent prenatal care contributes to infant mortality rates being nearly twice as high for Native American and African American infants as they are for white infants. Another economic factor that limits the full exercise of reproductive rights appears in welfare programs. For example, some states cap benefits to families that have additional children while receiving welfare, a policy known as a "family cap." Forced sterilizations, forced use of contraceptives, and unneeded surgical procedures during childbirth (Cesarean section deliveries) are violations of reproductive health rights that are imposed upon women of color and low-income women more frequently than upon wealthier white women. The uneven distribution of health care providers across the country also limits reproductive rights. Twenty-six percent of the counties in the United States do not have a hospital or clinic that provides prenatal care, and more than half of the counties do not have an abortion provider. Inner-city health facilities may be understaffed and often have inadequate funding.

See also Abortion

References www.crlp.org.

Republican Party, Women in the

Women's relationship with the Republican Party has ranged from trying to find their place in it to strong party allegiance to their growing dissatisfaction with it in the 1990s, as evidenced by the gender gap. For many women, the National Federation of Republican Women, an auxiliary, has provided an avenue for them to develop their skills and make their con-

tributions. Other women have worked to created places for themselves and other women in the party itself.

At the 1876 Republican National Convention, a Massachusetts woman became the first woman to address a convention committee when she made a presentation to the Resolutions Committee on woman suffrage. Women were first officially seated at the 1892 convention, when two women from Wyoming were alternate delegates. Also at that convention, for the first time a woman addressed an entire convention, saying that women were there to help the party and were there to stay. The first woman delegate to a Republican National Convention was also a Wyoming woman, who was seated in 1900.

The Republican Party reluctantly endorsed woman suffrage at its 1916 national convention, but it endorsed state amendments only, not the federal amendment that suffrage leaders sought. As states granted women suffrage rights, the party sought to gain their support and their votes by establishing the Women's Division of the Republican National Committee (RNC) in 1919. After women gained suffrage rights nationwide in 1920, the party created the position of associate member, one for each state, to give women a voice but not a vote in the party's decisionmaking body.

Republican women gathered for a tribute from the Republican National Committee (left to right): Republican National Committee cochair Evelyn McPhail, Elizabeth Dole, Maureen Reagan, and Representative Barbara Vucanovich (R-NV), 1996 (Associated Press AP)

Delegates to the 1924 Republican National Convention discarded the classification of associate members and created the office of national committeewoman, parallel to the existing national committeeman, again one for each state.

The years between 1932 and 1952 were difficult for the party. Democrats held the presidency, and they gained significant attention for the number of women appointed to posts in the party and in government. In addition, Democratic women had the tremendous benefit of Eleanor Roosevelt's advocacy for their inclusion in party leadership. Republican women, however, had formed local women's clubs for decades, and although many of them existed only through an election cycle and then disbanded, some of them had become semipermanent by the 1930s. To impose discipline on them, develop members' skills, and organize their efforts, RNC assistant chairperson Marion Martin brought the clubs together under an umbrella organization, the National Federation of Republican Women, in 1937. The clubs proved to be a significant resource during elections, but for most women, the clubs did not advance their status or power in the party machinery.

In 1940, the Republican National Convention endorsed the Equal Rights Amendment, the first major party to include the amendment in its platform. That year, women gained equal representation on all RNC committees. Equal representation on the convention committees took significantly longer, but the process started in 1944 when women gained equal representation on the resolutions committee.

The 1952 presidential campaign was the party's first organized effort to mobilize American women's vote, a strategy developed Ivy Baker Priest for Dwight D. Eisenhower. The 1952 campaign was also the first time that the gender gap appeared, with a greater proportion of female than male voters supporting Republican Eisenhower. The next gender gap would not appear until the 1980s. President Eisenhower appointed Oveta Culp Hobby secretary of the Department of Health, Education, and Welfare in 1953, the first Republican woman to serve in a Republican president's cabinet.

Women's status and power in the party, however, changed little between 1924 and the late 1960s. Margaret Chase Smith ran for the party's presidential nomination in 1964, and the next year Elly Peterson of Michigan was the first woman to chair a state party in either major party, but most women continued to be excluded from positions of power and status in the Republican Party. Partly to increase the number of women delegates to the 1972 national convention, a group of women convinced the party to establish the Delegates and Organization Committee (DOC) to review the party's rules and make recommendations. Chaired by Rosemary Ginn of Missouri, the DOC could only make suggestions to states about selecting delegates to the 1972 Republican National Convention, but the committee called on each state to "endeavor to have equal representation of men and women in its delegation." Seventeen percent of the 1968 convention delegates had been women, but by 1972 almost 30 percent of the delegates were women.

One of the groups that had worked with Ginn and her committee was the newly formed National Women's Political Caucus (NWPC), an organization that sought to increase women's power in the political parties and to encourage and help women gain election or appointment to public offices. The NWPC established an office at the 1972 Republican National Convention to organize delegates to support the Equal Rights Amendment and reproductive rights. NWPC executive director Doris Meissner invited women delegates to daily meetings to explain the caucus's purpose, goals, and strategies. The convention strengthened the party's statement supporting the ERA, passed two rules calling on state parties to increase their efforts to broaden the diversity of their delegations to the 1976 convention, and ignored reproductive rights.

In 1974, at the recommendation of President Gerald Ford, the RNC elected Mary Louise Smith as chair. The first woman to hold the position in the Republican Party, Smith became chair during one of the party's most difficult times, only a few weeks after President Richard Nixon resigned in the midst of the Watergate scandal. Throughout the more than two years Smith chaired the party, her primary focus centered on rebuilding the party, which at times could claim the allegiance of as few as 17 percent of Americans.

The Republican Women's Task Force (RWTF) of the National Women's Political Caucus led the campaign to keep the Equal Rights Amendment in the party's 1976 platform. President Ford and RNC chairperson Mary Louise Smith both strongly supported the amendment, and Smith was a strong advocate for abortion rights. By 1976, however, Republican leader Phyllis Schlafly had organized Stop ERA, and Ronald Reagan was challenging Ford for the party's nomination. Ford's intercession kept the amendment in the platform. Instead of feminists adding a reproductive rights plank to the platform, the party added an antiabortion plank to the platform, despite valiant efforts by Representative Millicent Fenwick of New Jersey to keep it out.

At the 1980 convention, former RNC chairperson Smith represented feminists at the platform hearings, and she met with likely presidential nominee Ronald Reagan to discuss abortion rights and the ERA. The convention expressed strong prolife sentiments and removed the ERA from the platform. Moderate Republicans, both women and men, found themselves increasingly distanced from the party, whereas conservative Republicans on the religious right were nurturing their constituencies into dominance in the party. Party cochair, moderate Mary Dent Crisp, was pushed out of the party in 1980 because of her prochoice views. The fissures that had appeared between feminists and the party in 1976 became chasms by 1984. In addition, women, regardless of their views on abortion and the ERA, increasingly receded into the background, with the exception of Schlafly, who did not have an office in the party but did have power.

The party's conservative views served it well in many ways. After Ronald Reagan's 1980 election to the presidency and his reelection in 1984, his vice president, George Bush, succeeded him in 1988. The gender gap that had first appeared in the 1980 race between Jimmy Carter and Reagan expanded throughout the 1980s: women voters increasingly favored the Democratic Party and its candidates more than men did, and men increasingly favored the Republican Party and its candidates. In the 1992 presidential contest between President Bush and Democratic nominee Bill Clinton, women provided Clinton with the winning margin of votes, as they did again in 1996. Republican women have tried to convince the party to address the gender gap by developing programs that will attract women voters. At the end of the twentieth century, however, the Republican Party continued to lose women voters' support.

See also Abortion; Adkins, Bertha Sheppard; Democratic Party, Women in the; Equal Rights Amendment; Fenwick, Millicent Hammond; National Federation of Republican Women; National Women's Political Caucus; Schlafly, Phyllis Stewart; Smith, Margaret Madeline Chase; Smith, Mary Louise; Stop ERA

References Feit, "Organizing for Political Power: The National Women's Political Caucus" (1979); Freeman, "Feminism vs. Family Values: Women at the 1992 Democratic and Republican Conventions" (1995), "Who You Know vs. Who You Represent: Feminist Influence in the Democratic and Republican Parties" (1987); "NFRW: Fifty Years of Leadership, 1938–1988" (1987).

Republicans for Choice

Founded in 1989 by Republican activist Ann E. W. Stone, Republicans for Choice (RFC) seeks to build a prochoice movement within the Republican Party, remove the party's antichoice platform plank, and elect prochoice Republicans. RFC contends that historically the Republican Party has been prochoice, and that in the 1990s, more than 70 percent of the party membership is prochoice. RFC opposes a constitutional amendment prohibiting abortions, arguing that opposing governmental interference in private lives is a tenet of the Republican Party.

See also Abortion; Republican Party, Women in the

References www.rfc-pac.org.

Richards, Ann Willis (b. 1933)

Democrat Ann W. Richards was governor of Texas from 1991 to 1995 and was treasurer of Texas from 1983 to 1991. She gave a keynote address to the 1988 Democratic National Convention, during which she said that Vice President George Bush was "born with a silver foot in his mouth." The speech and its humor gained her national celebrity.

Richards became active in politics in the 1950s, working on local and statewide campaigns and for civil rights and economic justice issues. She worked in John F. Kennedy's 1960 presidential campaign, and in 1962 she helped form the groups North Dallas Democratic Women and the Dallas Committee for Peaceful Integration. Richards responded to Sarah Weddington's pleas for help in her 1972 campaign for a seat in the Texas House of Representatives and later managed Weddington's legislative office for a session. She also helped other women win legislative races.

In 1976, Richards ran for and won a seat on the Travis County Commissioners Court, where she helped create the state's first juvenile probation system. She explained that at the time, "Texas was not noticeably hospitable to the notion that a woman could handle that kind of responsibility." She served until 1982.

In 1983, Richards became treasurer of Texas and was reelected to a second four-year term in 1986. As treasurer, Richards modernized the office's procedures and initiated innovations in banking and investment that earned unprecedented returns for the state. She helped formulate plans to provide water and sewers to impoverished areas of the state and guided the state through a fiscal crisis. Richards, who had gone through an alcoholism treatment program in 1980, obtained health insurance coverage for substance abuse treatment for state employees.

In 1989, Richards published her autobiography, *Straight from the Heart: My Life in Politics and Other Places.* She also entered Texas's race for governor that year. During her campaign for governor, Richards pledged that there would be no new taxes, called for a "new Texas," and asked voters to help her "take back the government."

Elected governor of Texas in 1990, Richards stressed education, public safety, economic development, and efficiency during her administration. As governor, Richards increased the amount of prison space, reduced the number of violent offenders released from prison, and introduced a new substance abuse program in the prisons. She also attracted new and expanded manufacturing facilities to the state. After losing her bid for re-election in 1994, she joined a law firm as a senior adviser.

Born in Lakeview, Texas, Richards earned her bachelor of arts degree from Baylor University in 1954 and attended the University of Texas at Austin, where she earned her teaching certificate. Richards taught social studies and history from 1955 to 1956.

See also Governors, Women

References Mullaney, *Biographical Directory of the Governors of the United States 1988–1994* (1994); *New York Times,* 18 July 1988; Richards, *Straight from the Heart: My Life in Politics and Other Places* (1989).

Riley, Corrine Boyd (1893–1979)

Democrat Corrine Riley of South Carolina served in the U.S. House of Representatives from 10 April 1962 to 3 January 1963. After her husband, Congressman John Jacob Riley, died in office, she won the special election to fill the vacancy. Congresswoman Riley introduced a bill to have the General Services Administration transfer surplus property to the South Carolina State Historical Society and another to require television to be equipped with both ultra high– and very high–frequency channels. She was not a candidate for another term.

Born in Piedmont, South Carolina, Corinne Riley graduated from Converse College in 1915. She taught high school from 1915 to 1937. A field representative for the South Carolina State Text Book Commission from 1938 to 1942, she worked for the Civilian Personnel Office at Shaw Air Force Base from 1942 to 1944.

See also Congress, Women in

References Office of the Historian, U.S. House of Representatives, *Women in Congress, 1917–1990* (1991).

Rivers, Lynn Nancy (b. 1956)

Democrat Lynn Rivers of Michigan entered the U.S. House of Representatives on 3 January 1995. Rivers entered politics, she said, "as a mom who got mad at the system." She served on the Ann Arbor school board from 1984 to 1992 and in the Michigan House of Representatives from 1993 to 1995. Rivers brought her experiences as a teen mother, the wife of an auto worker, an adult student, and a school board member to her work as a congresswoman. She has said, "I understand what families are struggling with. I know what it's like to go without health insurance, not to be able to buy a home, and to have more bills than money."

Rivers sees education as the key to improving the economy, advocates investing in vocational and school-to-work programs, and favors developing private-public ventures to create high-wage, high-skill jobs for workers. She sponsored legislation banning gifts to members of Congress and another measure to end congressional benefits such as pensions and automatic pay raises.

Born in Au Grey, Michigan, Rivers attended the Bay-Arenac Skills Center and trained in commercial food preparation. She earned her bachelor of arts degree from the University of Michigan in 1987 and her law degree from Wayne State University in 1992.

See also Congress, Women in; State Legislatures, Women in

References Congressional Quarterly, *Politics in America 1996* (1995); www.house.gov/rivers/bio.htm.

Rivlin, Alice Mitchell (b. 1931)

The first head of the Congressional Budget Office, Alice Rivlin became deputy director of the Office of Management and Budget in 1993 and director of it in 1994 and served as vice chair of the Board of Governors of the Federal Reserve Board from 1996 to 1999. An economist, Rivlin began her public service career as consultant to the House Committee on Education and Labor from 1961 to 1962 and to the secretary of the treasury from 1964 to 1966, when she became deputy assistant secretary for the Department of Health, Education, and Welfare. Two years later, President Lyndon Johnson appointed her assistant secretary for planning and evaluation in the department.

In 1974, Congress created the Congressional Budget Office (CBO), part of landmark federal budget reform legislation. The CBO, a nonpartisan agency, assists Congress in analyzing and forming policy on the federal budget. During her tenure, Rivlin insisted that the CBO had "taken no policy position, nor will we ever." Appointed jointly by the speaker of the House of Representatives and the president pro tempore of the Senate,

Rivlin took office in 1975 and served two four-year terms. She left the CBO in 1983 when she became director of economic studies at the Brookings Institution. In 1993 Rivlin joined President Bill Clinton's administration as deputy budget director. Known for her strong support for reducing the federal deficit, Rivlin held an important role in developing the annual federal budget.

Born in Philadelphia, Pennsylvania, Rivlin graduated from Bryn Mawr in 1952 and earned her master of arts degree in 1955 and her doctoral degree in 1958, both from Radcliffe College. Rivlin became a research fellow at the Brookings Institution in 1957 and by 1969 was a senior fellow. During those years, she wrote and coauthored several studies in economics and related areas.

References H. W. Wilson, *Current Biography Yearbook, 1982* (1982); *New York Times,* 28 June 1994; www.bog.frb.fed.us.

Roberts, Barbara Hughey (b. 1936)

Democrat Barbara Roberts was governor of Oregon from 1991 to 1995. The first woman governor of the state, Roberts reorganized elementary and secondary schools and provided state employees with unpaid family leave. She also worked to diversify the state's economy to reduce its reliance on the logging industry.

Roberts began her political career as an unpaid lobbyist seeking help for her autistic son. In the late 1960s, she succeeded in getting the Oregon legislature to pass the nation's first education rights law for emotionally handicapped children. Her legislation also created the State Advisory Committee for Emotionally Handicapped Children. Roberts applied for and received an appointment on the committee. In 1980, she won a seat in the Oregon House of Representatives, served in the body from 1981 to 1985, and became the state's first woman majority leader in 1983. Elected secretary of state in 1984, she won reelection in 1988. As secretary of state, Roberts sponsored election reform legislation, policies to ensure polling places' accessibility to people with disabilities, and construction of a new state archives building.

Born in Corvallis, Oregon, Roberts attended Portland State University, Marylhurst College, and the John F. Kennedy School of Government at Harvard University.

See also Governors, Women; State Legislatures, Women in

References Mullaney, *Biographical Directory of the Governors of the United States 1988–1994* (1994); Roberts, "Coloring Outside the Lines" (1998).

Robertson, Alice Mary (1854–1931)

Republican Alice Robertson of Oklahoma served in the U.S. House of Representatives from 4 March 1921 to 3 March 1923. She campaigned with the slogan "Christianity, Americanism, Standpattism."

Even though she had opposed woman suffrage and had served as vice president of the state antisuffrage league, she ran for Congress in the first election following the ratification of the Nineteenth Amendment. Robertson pledged to help farmers, women, and soldiers during her 1920 campaign.

In Congress, she opposed the Sheppard-Towner Maternity and Infancy Protection Act of 1921, a measure that funded maternity and infant care and was a key piece of legislation advocated by suffragists. Robertson attacked the measure, describing it as paternalistic, a threat to the American family, and Bolshevistic. She argued that it provided only instruction, which she interpreted as propaganda. Robertson supported limiting immigration, saying: "We are taking in foreign people so rapidly that we cannot Americanize them. Too many are here already who do not appreciate American liberties and are doing their best to tear the nation down." Despite a campaign promise to support veterans, Robertson opposed the veterans' bonus bill, saying the nation could not afford it. Her constituents protested her opposition to the bill by defeating her in the 1922 general elections.

After her defeat, Robertson said that politics was too rough and immoral for women, and she willingly retired. President Warren Harding appointed her a social worker at the Veterans Hospital in Muskogee, Oklahoma, in 1923. She left after a few months and became the Washington correspondent for the *Muskogee News* and then worked for the Oklahoma Historical Society.

The daughter of missionaries, Robertson was born at Tullahassee Mission, Creek Nation, Indian Territory (now Oklahoma). After attending Elmira College from 1871 to 1873, she was a clerk in the Office of Indian Affairs from 1873 to 1879, and she taught school at Tullahassee and then at Carlisle Indian School. From 1885 to 1899, Robertson was the administrator of the Oklahoma Indian Territory Girls' School, a Presbyterian boarding school for girls. It became the Henry Kendall College, a coeducational facility, in 1894. She supervised Creek Indian schools from 1900 to 1905 and then became a postmaster until 1913. She wrote *Alice Mary Robertson of Oklahoma* (1912).

See also Congress, Women in; Sheppard-Towner Maternity and Infancy Protection Act of 1921; Suffrage

References Office of the Historian, U.S. House of Representatives, *Women in Congress, 1917–1990* (1991); Stanley, "Alice M. Robertson, Oklahoma's First Congresswoman" (1967).

Representative Alice Mary Robertson (R-OK) who opposed woman suffrage, ran for Congress the same year women got the vote, 1920 (UPI/ Corbis)

Robinson, Ruby Doris Smith (1941–1967)

A founding member of the Student Nonviolent Coordinating Committee, Ruby Robinson served as its executive secretary from 1966 to 1967. She began her civil rights activism as a college sophomore, participating in a lunch-counter sit-in in Greensboro, North Carolina, and in other demonstrations at restaurants to protest segregation. In April 1960, she attended the meeting at Shaw University that led to the formation of the Student Nonviolent Coordinating Committee (SNCC).

In 1961, Robinson joined other SNCC members in Rock Hill, South Carolina, where she sat at a segregated lunch counter and was arrested with three of her companions. Sentenced to thirty days in jail, she refused bail in order to further focus attention on segregation and served her term. It was the first time that civil rights workers arrested for this violation chose to serve the full sentence rather than post bail. She was arrested in Jackson, Mississippi, for attempting to use a white restroom. Charged with breaching the peace, she was given a suspended sentence and fined $200, but refused to pay the fine. She spent two weeks in a county jail with as many as twenty-three others and then was sent to the maximum security area of the Parchman State Penitentiary for forty-five days.

During the summer of 1961, Robinson participated in a voter registration drive in McComb, Mississippi, and attended a training seminar at Fisk University. The next summer, she worked with the SNCC project in Cairo, Illinois, and in the fall joined SNCC as a full-time administrative assistant to the executive secretary. She organized student volunteers, assisted the field staff, and handled emergencies. By 1962, she had also become one of the organization's intellectual leaders and one of its most dedicated administrators. Elected executive secretary of SNCC in 1966, she had come to believe that the movement needed to alter its focus from civil rights legislation to fundamental socioeconomic change. Early in 1967, Robinson became terminally ill with a form of blood cancer. She died in October 1967.

Born in Atlanta, Georgia, Robinson enrolled in Spelman College in 1959 and received her bachelor of science degree from that institution in 1965.

See also Civil Rights Movement, Women in the

References Hardy, *American Women Civil Rights Activists* (1993).

Roe v. Wade (1973)

In *Roe v. Wade,* the U.S. Supreme Court declared invalid all state laws restricting abortion in the first three months of pregnancy, using the right of privacy as the basis for the decision. In this case, Jane Roe, later identified as Norma McCorvey, a single, pregnant woman living in Texas, wanted a legal abortion, but Texas law at the time permitted legal abortions only if the life of the mother was endangered by the pregnancy. Roe's pregnancy did not appear to endanger her life, so if she had obtained an abortion in Texas, it would have been a criminal act. Roe argued that the law was unconstitutionally vague and infringed on her right of privacy, a right that she asserted was protected by the First, Fourth, Fifth, Ninth, and Fourteenth Amendments.

The decision, written by Justice Harry Blackmun, reviewed English common law, early abortion legislation from the colonial period to the time of the decision, the American Medical Association's involvement in abortion, the American Bar Association's positions on abortion law, and other historical considerations. He noted three explanations for the criminalization of abortion: (1) the laws were an attempt by nineteenth-century Victorians to discourage illicit sexual conduct; (2) the laws attempted to protect women from the dangers of abortion that existed during the nineteenth century when most of the laws were enacted; and (3) the state had an interest in protecting maternal and fetal life. On the first point, he accepted the argument that the Texas law was too broad and was not a proper state purpose. On the second point, he noted improved medical practices that reduced the dangers of infection but indicated that the state has a role to play in protecting women's health and safety. On the third point, he wrote that the state may have interests beyond the protection of the woman that include protecting fetal life after viability (sometime during the third trimester).

Blackmun pointed out that the U.S. Constitution does not explicitly mention a right of privacy but that the Court had recognized certain areas of privacy. He suggested that it might be found in the Fourteenth Amendment's statements on personal liberty and its restrictions on state action or in the Ninth Amendment's reservation of rights to the people. Regardless of its constitutional basis, Blackmun wrote that it "is broad enough to encompass a woman's decision whether or not to terminate her pregnancy."

Limitations on the right existed, however. During the first trimester, abortions could be performed without state interference. After the first trimester, a state could regulate abortion to protect the woman. After fetal viability, the state had permission to regulate or prohibit abortion, except when the mother's health or life was endangered by her pregnancy. The decision invalidated the Texas abortion statutes as well as those in other states that limited women's access to the procedure.

In a companion case, *Doe v. Bolton,* the Court struck down portions of a Georgia law relating to the requirements that abortions must be performed in accredited hospitals, that abortions must be approved by medical committees, and that only residents of the state could obtain abortions. The Court did not address the question of when life begins but did note that the Fourteenth Amendment's use of the word *person* does not include the unborn.

See also Abortion; *Akron v. Akron Center for Reproductive Health; Beal v. Doe; Bellotti v. Baird; Bray v. Alexandria Clinic; Colautti v. Franklin; Doe v. Bolton; Harris v. McRae; Hodgson v. Minnesota; Ohio v. Akron Center; Planned Parenthood Association of Kansas City, Mo. v. Ashcroft; Planned Parenthood of Central Missouri v. Danforth; Poelker v. Doe; Rust v. Sullivan; Thornburgh v. American College of Obstetrics and Gynecology; Webster v. Reproductive Health Services; Williams v. Zbaraz*

References Harrison and Gilbert, eds., *Abortion Decisions of the United States Supreme Court: The 1970s* (1993).

Rogers, Edith Frances Nourse (1881–1960)

Republican Edith Rogers of Massachusetts served in the U.S. House of Representatives from 30 June 1925 to 10 September 1960. Rogers began her

Representative Edith Nourse Rogers (R-MA) served for thirty-five years in Congress, 1953 (UPI/Corbis)

public life through her husband John Rogers, who entered Congress in 1913. When he went to Britain and France on a congressional mission during World War I, Edith Rogers accompanied him. In England, Edith Rogers volunteered for the Young Men's Christian Association, and in Europe she went to battle zones as a member of a Red Cross party, visiting base and field hospitals. When she returned to the United States, she worked seven days a week at Walter Reed Hospital. In 1922, President Warren G. Harding appointed her a dollar-a-year veterans' hospital inspector, an appointment renewed by Presidents Calvin Coolidge and Herbert Hoover.

In March 1925, John Rogers died in office following an operation. At the requests of veterans, family members, and Republican leaders, Edith

Rogers became a candidate to fill the vacancy. Congresswoman Rogers warned Americans about the threat that Hitler posed, argued for military preparedness, and supported U.S. entry into World War II. In 1942, she sponsored the legislation that created the Women's Army Auxiliary Corps (WAACs), which eventually had 150,000 members, the legal limit. Later, the word *auxiliary* was dropped, and the acronym became WAC.

Throughout her political career, Rogers served on the Veterans Affairs Committee, chairing it in 1947. She once said that helping veterans was her "greatest interest in life." She cosponsored the GI Bill of Rights and sponsored the Korean Veterans Benefits bill, as well as passing measures to develop prosthetic appliances and appropriating funds for automobiles for amputees. She was affectionately called the "mother of veterans."

Rogers also supported legislation to protect her district's textile and shoe manufacturing and food processing industries. She advocated protective tariffs for cotton mill owners and benefits for laborers, again reflecting issues important to her district. Rogers died two days before the 1960 Massachusetts primary, in which she was a candidate for a nineteenth term.

Born in Saco, Maine, Edith Rogers attended a finishing school near Paris and traveled in Europe before marrying John Jacob Rogers in 1907.

See also Congress, Women in; Equal Rights Amendment

References Kaptur, *Women of Congress: A Twentieth-Century Odyssey* (1996).

Roosevelt, Eleanor (1884–1962)

First lady from 1933 to 1945, Eleanor Roosevelt established herself as a leader in her own right and became one of the most beloved women in the country. Shy and self-conscious as a child, she matured into a force on the national and international stages, respected by heads of state and blue-collar workers. Her tenure as first lady was unlike that of any first lady before or since.

Born in New York City, she was the daughter of socially prestigious families on both her mother's side and her father's side. After her mother died when Roosevelt was eight, her maternal grandmother raised her. Isolated and lonely, tutored at home until she was fifteen years old, she found companionship when she attended a private girls' school in England for three years. After returning to the United States, she taught at a settlement house. She married her fifth cousin Franklin Delano Roosevelt in 1905 in a ceremony officiated by her uncle, President Theodore Roosevelt. Over the next eleven years, she bore six children, one of whom died in infancy, and managed her household.

Franklin Roosevelt's 1921 bout with poliomyelitis left him unable to walk and led Eleanor Roosevelt to her reluctant involvement in politics.

After a family friend told her that her husband needed politics to help him recuperate, she became the means for his return to political life. She became increasingly active in women's activities in the Democratic Party and at one time knew every Democratic Party county chairperson in New York. When Franklin Roosevelt ran for governor of New York in 1928, she played a pivotal role in gaining women's support for his candidacy. She also headed the women's organization for Democratic presidential nominee Al Smith's candidacy and recruited Molly Dewson to work on the campaigns. The two women worked together to reelect Franklin Roosevelt governor of New York in 1930 and to elect him president in 1932. In the 1930s and 1940s, Eleanor Roosevelt played significant roles in expanding women's opportunities and enhancing women's status in the Democratic Party.

After Franklin Roosevelt became president, Eleanor Roosevelt resigned herself to a life limited to social activities, but she soon had a more diverse schedule. Because of her husband's limited mobility, she traveled in his place and reported her observations to him. She called them "go-and-see journeys" and went to places and events that no one from the White House had ever visited. She went down into coal mines, visited the cardboard shacks of people living in Oklahoma, walked along the irrigation ditches in California, and traveled through the Dust Bowl. She visited wartime Great Britain and Guadalcanal. She also reported her experiences through her speeches and her writings, including a column entitled "My Day."

First Lady and Ambassador Eleanor Roosevelt dedicated her life to the human rights of all people and helped pass the United Nations Universal Declaration of Human Rights in 1948 (Courtesy: Corel Corporation)

Eleanor Roosevelt was the first president's wife to hold a press conference. Limited to women reporters, Roosevelt used the forum to introduce women in the administration to the public, to discuss the administration's programs, and to comment on the effect that the Depression and later World War II had on women.

Her stands on civil rights attracted publicity, criticism, and goodwill. When the Daughters of the American Revolution refused the use of Constitution Hall to African American singer Marian Anderson in 1939, Roosevelt resigned from the organization. The same year, she attended the Southern Conference on Human Welfare meeting in Birmingham, Alabama. Resisting the South's segregation policies, she placed her chair so that half of it was on each side of the color line. During World War II, Roosevelt was one of the few voices calling for the United States to assist Jewish refugees.

After her husband died in 1945, President Harry Truman appointed her to the U.S. delegation to the United Nations, the only woman in the delegation. She chaired the preliminary Commission on Human Rights in 1946 and was elected chair of the commission after it became permanent in 1947. She shaped much of the Universal Declaration of Human Rights that the UN General Assembly passed in 1948. When Truman left office in 1953, she left the United Nations at the same time. President John Kennedy reappointed her to the U.S. delegation to the United Nations in 1961.

President John F. Kennedy appointed her chair of the President's Commission on the Status of Women in 1961. She died before the commission completed its work.

See also Anderson, Marian; Democratic Party, Women in the; Dewson, Mary (Molly) Williams; President's Commission on the Status of Women

References Cook, *Eleanor Roosevelt*, vol. 1: *1884–1933* (1992); Lash, *Eleanor: The Years Alone* (1972); Roosevelt and Hickok, *Ladies of Courage* (1954).

Ros-Lehtinen, Ileana (b. 1952)

Republican Ileana Ros-Lehtinen of Florida entered the U.S. House of Representatives on 29 August 1989. She is the first Hispanic woman and the first Cuban American elected to Congress. The first Hispanic elected to the Florida legislature, Ros-Lehtinen served in the Florida House of Representatives from 1982 to 1986 and the Florida Senate from 1986 to 1989. She played key roles in the passage of victim rights' legislation, drug-free workplace measures, and tuition assistance programs. She left the state Senate after winning the special election to fill the vacancy created by the death of incumbent Claude Pepper.

A conservative, Ros-Lehtinen opposes reproductive rights and supports a constitutional amendment banning flag desecration. She has, however, objected to her party's anti-immigrant stand and defended immigrants, saying they have "contributed greatly to all facets of life in the economic, cultural, and political fields." A former Cuban refugee, Ros-Lehtinen has called Fidel Castro an "inhuman tyrant" and has advocated policies to end his leadership in Cuba and replace it with a democracy. She has also taken strong stands in support of Israel.

Born in Havana, Cuba, Ileana Ros-Lehtinen fled with her parents to Miami in 1960, a year after Fidel Castro's revolution. She earned her associate of arts degree from Miami-Dade Community College in 1972. She completed her bachelor of arts degree in 1975 and master of science degree in 1986 from Florida International University. A schoolteacher, Ros-Lehtinen is the founder and former owner of a private elementary school.

See also Congress, Women in; State Legislatures, Women in

References Congressional Quarterly, *Politics in America 1994* (1993), *Politics in America 1998* (1997); www.house.gov/ros-lehtinen/bio.htm.

Representative Ileana Ros-Lehtinen (R-FL) spoke on the floor during the House debate on the four articles of impeachment against President Bill Clinton (Associated Press/APTN)

Ross, Nellie Tayloe (1876–1977)

Democrat Nellie Tayloe Ross was the first woman governor in the United States, serving from 1925 to 1927, and she was the first woman director of the U.S. Mint. After her husband, Wyoming governor William Bradford Ross, died in 1924 with two years left in his term, Nellie Tayloe Ross won the special election to complete the term. As governor, she changed law enforcement commissioners three times in attempts to place a person in office who would enforce Prohibition laws. Protecting water for irrigation was another priority, as was protecting bank deposits threatened by bank closures. Ross ran for reelection in 1926 but lost.

In 1928, she became vice chair of the Democratic National Committee. For the next four years, she directed women's activities within the party. She also became a friend and colleague of Eleanor Roosevelt. When Franklin D. Roosevelt ran for president, Ross directed women's efforts during his 1932 campaign.

Roosevelt named Ross director of the U.S. Mint in 1933. With the first signs of economic recovery in the mid-1930s, demand for coins increased steadily and with it the need for increased facilities, equipment, and staff. Three new mints were constructed, and the number of personnel more than trebled. In addition, the U.S. Bullion Depository at Fort Knox, Kentucky, the U.S. Bullion Depository at West Point, New York, the Mint building in San Francisco, and the Denver Mint were constructed during her tenure.

During World War II, metal shortages led to the use of substitute metals for coins, including the steel penny, which looked so much like dimes that Ross ended the use of them in 1943. She said: "That awful 'war penney' almost ruined our reputation, but nobody disliked it more than we did at the Mint." Ross oversaw the development of the Roosevelt dime and the replacement of the buffalo nickel with the Jefferson nickel.

Born in St. Joseph, Missouri, Ross obtained her education in private schools in Omaha, Nebraska.

See also Governors, Women

References Donaldson, "The First Woman Governor" (1926); H. W. Wilson, *Current Biography: Who's News and Why, 1940* (1940); *New York Times,* 21 December 1977.

Roukema, Margaret Scafati (b. 1929)

Republican Margaret Roukema of New Jersey entered the U.S. House of Representatives on 3 January 1981. She lost her first attempt to win a seat in Congress in 1978 and then won on her second attempt in 1980. Congresswoman Roukema was a stalwart supporter of the Family and Medical Leave Act of 1993. Calling it a "bedrock family issue," she worked on it for eight years, despite President George Bush's veto of the bill on two occasions, in 1990 and 1992. Some of her commitment to the measure arose from personal experience. She had left her academic pursuits in 1976 to care for her seventeen-year-old son who was dying of leukemia. She posed the question: "What would I have done if not only did I have the tragedy of and trauma of caring for my child, but also had to worry about losing a job and the roof over my head?" The bill passed a third time in 1993, and President Bill Clinton signed it.

Roukema was a key leader in the development and passage of the Family Support Act of 1988 and the Child Support Enforcement Amendments of 1984. She served on the U.S. Commission on Interstate Child Support, incorporating legislation resulting from the commission's work into the Personal Responsibility and Work Opportunity Reconciliation Act of 1996.

She has proposed bills to permit banks to act as stockbrokers and to allow stockbrokers to offer banking services. Another measure would end the distinction between banks and savings and loans. Roukema supports a balanced budget amendment to the Constitution and reductions in spending. Her other policy priorities include reproductive rights, child support enforcement, education and student loans, pension reform, job training, and famine relief.

Born in West Orange, New Jersey, Roukema received her bachelor of arts degree from Montclair State College in 1951, did graduate work in secondary school guidance there, and also studied urban and regional planning at the graduate level at Rutgers University. She taught American history and government in secondary school.

Roukema served on the Ridgewood Board of Education from 1970 to 1973. In 1970, she cofounded the Ridgewood Senior Citizens Housing Corporation. She became active in the Ridgewood Republican Club in the 1970s, serving as its president in 1977.

See also Abortion; Child Support Enforcement; Congress, Women in; Family and Medical Leave Act of 1993; Personal Responsibility and Work Opportunity Reconciliation Act of 1996

References Congressional Quarterly, *Politics in America 1994* (1993), *Politics in America: The 100th Congress* (1987).

Roy, Vesta M. (b. 1925)

Republican Vesta M. Roy was acting governor of New Hampshire from December 1982 to January 1983. On 1 December 1982, Roy was elected Senate president in an organizational meeting of the legislature. Shortly thereafter, incumbent governor Hugh Gallen was hospitalized and became incapacitated. Under New Hampshire's constitution, the Senate president serves as acting governor when the governor is unable to carry out his or her duties. In January 1983, John Sununu, who had been elected governor in the November general elections, was inaugurated, and Roy returned to her seat in the state Senate.

Born in Detroit, Michigan, Vesta Roy graduated from Wayne State University. She served in the Royal Canadian Air Force during World War II and was named Leading Air Woman.

Roy was the first woman commissioner for Rockingham County, New Hampshire. She served in the state House of Representatives from 1973 to 1974 and in the state Senate from 1975 to 1984. She served as the assistant Senate whip and the assistant Senate majority leader. Her legislative priorities included reorganizing the executive department, balancing the state budget, and opposing off-track betting and the nuclear weapons freeze.

See also Governors, Women; State Legislatures, Women in

References Raimo, ed., *Biographical Directory of the Governors of the United States 1978–1983* (1985).

Roybal-Allard, Lucille (b. 1941)

Democrat Lucille Roybal-Allard of California entered the U.S. House of Representatives on 3 January 1993. She is the first Mexican American woman elected to Congress. The daughter of Edward Roybal, who served in Congress for thirty years, Roybal-Allard began folding, stuffing, and stamping campaign materials when she was a child. Later, she helped with voter registration for her father's campaigns. When her father retired from Congress, Roybal-Allard won his seat. While in Congress, Roybal-Allard has worked to help low- and moderate-income families buy homes and to protect federal funds for bilingual education, a reflection of the large Spanish-speaking immigrant population in her district. Her priorities include economic and environmental issues, sexual assault, domestic violence, and protection for children and consumers. She believes that one of

Representative Lucille Roybal-Allard (D-CA) talked with Representatives Christopher Cox (R-CA) and Bobby Scott (D-VA) at a press conference about Chinese possession of classified U.S. nuclear information, 1999 (Associated Press AP)

the most critical issues facing Latinos is a fair and accurate census in the year 2000.

At first reluctant to enter politics, Roybal-Allard was drawn into her first candidacy by frustrations with the barriers created by policymakers. She served in the California Assembly from 1987 to 1992. During her years in the assembly, she worked to stop the construction of a prison in East Los Angeles and helped organize Mothers of East Los Angeles to help. She also fought the construction of a toxic waste incinerator and was again supported by Mothers of East Los Angeles.

Born in Los Angeles, Lucille Roybal-Allard received her bachelor of arts degree from California State University in 1965.

See also Congress, Women in; State Legislatures, Women in

References Congressional Quarterly, *Politics in America 1994* (1993); www.house.gov/royball-allard/biography.htm.

RU-486 (Mifepristone)

RU-486 (mifepristone) is a nonsurgical abortion pharmaceutical developed by a French company in 1980. Used in Great Britain, France, and Sweden, it was banned for personal use in the United States in 1989 at the urging of prolife groups and prolife members of Congress. Studies of it proceeded in the United States, however, and researchers concluded that it was a safe and effective emergency contraceptive and also useful as a method for early abortions. Scientists also encouraged further research on RU-486 as a possible treatment for endometriosis, some types of breast cancer, uterine fibroids, and other medical conditions. In 1995, the pharmaceutical company that developed RU-486 donated the U.S. patent rights for the drug to the Population Council, which began clinical trials. In 1996, the Food and Drug Administration gave limited approval for the use of RU-486, but in 1997 the drug manufacturer ended its relationship with the Population Council, and the search for a new manufacturer began.

See also Abortion

References www.naral.org.

Ruffin, Josephine St. Pierre (1842–1924)

Josephine St. Pierre Ruffin was active in women's clubs and the suffrage movement. In 1894, she founded the Woman's Era Club, the first black women's civic organization in Boston. She served as president of the group and edited its monthly periodical, *Woman's Era,* which was the first paper published by African American women. She organized the first national conference of Colored Women in 1895. At the meeting, the National Federation of Afro-American Women was formed, uniting twenty clubs in ten states. In 1896, the organization merged with the Colored Women's League and became the National Association of Colored Women.

Ruffin worked throughout her life to create bridges between black and white women, but her efforts were repeatedly rebuffed. The most notorious occurrence was in 1900, when the General Federation of Women's Clubs refused to permit her to represent the Woman's Era Club at its convention. Ruffin, who also represented white women's groups, was told that she could attend as a delegate for the white groups but not for the dominantly black Woman's Era Club. She refused, and the General Federation of Women's Clubs maintained its segregationist position for several more decades.

Born free in Boston, Massachusetts, African American Josephine Ruffin went to school in Salem because her parents did not want her in Boston's segregated school system. After Boston schools were integrated in 1855, she attended school there until 1858. She married George Lewis Ruffin when she was sixteen years old and moved to England with him in 1858. The couple returned to Boston during the Civil War. Josephine Ruffin became active in the black rights, woman suffrage, and other social movements. In 1879, Josephine Ruffin helped establish the Boston Kansas Relief Association to help southern African Americans settling in Kansas.

See also General Federation of Women's Clubs; National Association of Colored Women; Suffrage

References Hardy, *American Women Civil Rights Activists* (1993).

Rust v. Sullivan (1991)

In 1988, the secretary of health and human services issued regulations that prohibited federally funded (Title X) family planning centers from counseling clients about abortion, making abortion referrals, or advocating abortion as a family planning method. The regulation, known as the "gag rule" by its opponents, required that abortion services and family planning services have separate facilities, personnel, and accounting records. The regulations were challenged on the basis that they violated the First Amendment right of a woman to receive unimpeded information from her physician and her constitutional right to choose abortion.

In *Rust v. Sullivan,* the U.S. Supreme Court found the regulations permissible. The Court said that they did not violate First Amendment rights because the government can make value judgments, favor childbirth over abortion, and fund one procedure and not the other. In addition, the regulations did not prohibit counselors or providers from discussing abortion; instead the requirement stated that there had to be a separation between counseling provided through Title X funds and counseling that discussed abortion. The Court also said that a woman's Fifth Amendment rights were not violated because the government does not have a constitutional duty to subsidize an activity simply because it is protected by the Constitution.

In 1993, President Bill Clinton issued an executive order that ended enforcement of the regulations.

See also Abortion

References *Rust v. Sullivan,* 500 U.S. 173 (1991).

S

Saiki, Patricia Fukuda (b. 1930)

Republican Patricia Saiki of Hawaii served in the U.S. House of Representatives from 3 January 1987 to 3 January 1991. In Congress, Saiki cosponsored a bill to compensate Japanese Americans interned during World War II. She also helped add land to the Kilauea National Wildlife Refuge. Saiki unsuccessfully ran for the U.S. Senate in 1990. President George Bush appointed Saiki head of the U.S. Small Business Administration in 1991, where she served until late in 1992. She unsuccessfully ran for governor of Hawaii in 1994.

Born in Hilo, Hawaii, Saiki received her bachelor of arts degree from the University of Hawaii in 1952 and became a junior and senior high school teacher. A delegate to Hawaii's 1968 Constitutional Convention, she also won a seat in the Hawaii House of Representatives that year. In the House, Saiki helped establish Hawaii's community college system and its emergency medical services system. She served in the House until 1974, the year she entered the state Senate. An unsuccessful candidate for lieutenant governor in 1982, she chaired the Republican Party of Hawaii from 1983 to 1985.

> **See also** Congress, Women in; State Legislatures, Women in
>
> **References** Office of the Historian, U.S. House of Representatives, *Women in Congress, 1917–1990* (1991); Zia and Gall, eds., *Notable Asian Americans* (1995).

St. George, Katharine Delano Price Collier (1894–1983)

Republican Katharine St. George of New York served in the U.S. House of Representatives from 3 January 1947 to 3 January 1965. She entered politics as a member of the Tuxedo Park, New York, town board from 1926 to 1949 and was a member of the Tuxedo Park Board of Education from 1926 to 1946. She held offices in the Orange County Republican Party from 1942 to 1948.

As a member of Congress, St. George sought to negotiate a compromise that would permit passage of the Equal Rights Amendment in 1950 but failed. In 1959, she proposed making the equal pay for comparable work bill, which had stalled over definitions of comparable work, into an equal pay for equal work measure. In 1963, Congress passed the Equal Pay Act. St. George also attempted to expand the provisions of the Veterans Administration law to include Women's Army Auxiliary Corps personnel. She lost her attempt for a tenth term in Congress.

Born in Bridgenorth, England, she moved to the United States with her parents when she was two years old. When she was eleven years old, she returned to Europe; received her education in England, France, and Germany; and moved back to the United States in 1914.

See also Congress, Women in; Equal Pay Act of 1963; Equal Rights Amendment; Military, Women in the

References Freeman, "From Protection to Equal Opportunity: The Revolution in Women's Legal Status" (1990); Office of the Historian, U.S. House of Representatives, *Women in Congress, 1917–1990* (1991).

Sanchez, Loretta (b. 1960)

Democrat Loretta Sanchez of California entered the U.S. House of Representatives on 3 January 1997. After an unsuccessful campaign for the Anaheim City Council in 1994, Sanchez was not favored to win the primary election or the general election for Congress in 1996. When she defeated incumbent Republican Robert Dornan by only 984 votes in the general election, Dornan challenged the election results, charging that the election was rigged using votes by Hispanic noncitizens. The House of Representatives investigated the issue for thirteen months before concluding that 748 votes were illegally cast by noncitizens, but that was not enough to negate Sanchez's victory. When the House voted to end the investigation in February 1998, Democrats accused Republicans of trying to intimidate Hispanic voters. Sanchez added: "Racism is as real and persistent today as it was 100 years ago."

Sanchez opposes flat tax plans and reductions in the student loan program. She wants to improve public schools but rejects the use of private school vouchers to do so. She supports affirmative action programs, gay rights, reproductive rights, and gun control.

Born in Lynwood, California, Sanchez earned her bachelor of arts degree from Chapman University in 1982 and her master's degree in business

Representative Loretta Sanchez (D-CA), second from right, got support from other Democratic congresswomen (left to right): Representative Ellen Tauscher (D-CA), Representative Karen McCarthy (D-MO), Representative Carolyn Maloney (D-NY), Sanchez, and Representative Debbie Stabenow (D-MI), during her contested election, 1997 (Associated Press AP)

administration from American University in 1984. She was a financial adviser and strategic management consultant before entering Congress.

See also Abortion; Affirmative Action; Congress, Women in; Lesbian Rights; Reproductive Rights

References Congressional Quarterly, ed., *Politics in America 1998* (1997); "House Ends Investigation of Sanchez's Election" (1998).

Sanger, Margaret Louise Higgins (1879–1966)

Margaret Sanger was a leader in the effort to make the distribution of birth control information legal by removing it from the list of obscene materials prohibited by the Comstock law of 1873. Sanger told audiences that she began her crusade after nursing Sadie Sachs, a tenement mother who died after attempting a self-induced abortion. Although the story may be a myth that Sanger created, it encapsulated her frustration that knowledge of birth control methods existed but was denied to women.

Because so little birth control information was available in the United States, Sanger went to Scotland and France in 1913 to study the methods used in those countries. When she returned to the United States in 1914, Sanger started publishing *The Woman Rebel,* a magazine with the slogan "No gods; no masters." Although she did not publish information on contraceptive methods in *The Woman Rebel,* the U.S. government indicted her

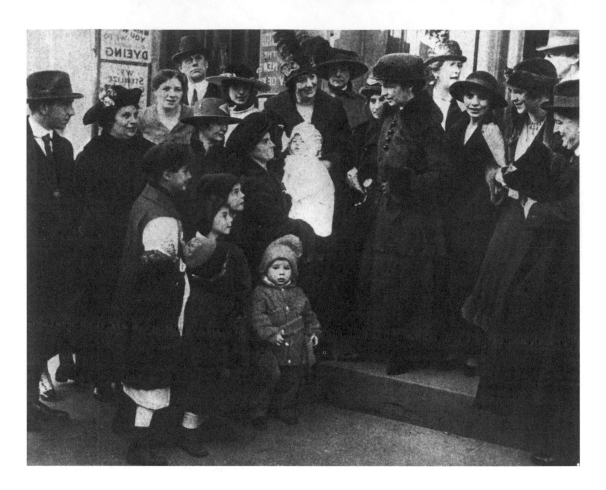

Margaret Sanger, founder of the organization that became the Planned Parenthood Federation of America, talked with a crowd of supporters during her trial for distributing illegal birth control information through the U.S. mail, 1914 (Library of Congress)

in 1914 for sending birth control information through the mails. To test the Comstock law, she refused to plead guilty but then decided that she had not been given enough time to prepare her case and left the country the day before she was to go to trial. She went to Europe, visited Holland's birth control clinics, the first in the world, and returned to the United States in 1915. The indictment against her was dropped in 1916, and the case did not go to trial.

Before she left the country, Sanger had written and printed "Family Limitation," a pamphlet describing birth control methods, but she did not distribute it. In Sanger's absence, her husband William Sanger mistakenly gave a copy to Anthony Comstock, author of the Comstock law. William Sanger was arrested and convicted of distributing obscene material and was sentenced to a jail term.

In 1916, Sanger, one of her sisters, and a friend opened a birth control clinic in Brooklyn, New York. Nine days after it opened, authorities closed the clinic, and Sanger and her sister were given thirty-day prison terms. Upon appeal, the U.S. Court of Appeals decided in their favor in 1918, and the dissemination of birth control became legal in that jurisdiction. The women, however, had already served their time in prison.

While in prison, Sanger concluded that she needed a different strategy, one based on education, organization, and legislation. In 1921, Sanger founded the American Birth Control League, in her words, to "build up public opinion so that women should demand instruction from doctors, to assemble the findings of scientists, to remove hampering Federal statutes, to send out field workers into those states where laws did not prevent clinics, to cooperate with similar bodies in studying population problems, food supplies, and world peace."

An international personality in the 1920s, Sanger organized the 1927 World Population Conference, held in Geneva, Switzerland, and in 1931, she organized the National Committee on Federal Legislation for Birth Control (NCFLBC) to lobby Congress for changes in birth control laws. NCFLBC developed regional, state, and local organizations with trained lobbyists, organizers, and fieldworkers. By working with and through local women's clubs, religious denominations, and medical organizations, these groups intended to pressure Congress and the states to permit physicians to dispense birth control information and devices.

By 1936, Sanger concluded that the legislative route was not going to be successful and decided to seek the changes she wanted through a court decision. After fighting a series of court battles, NCFLBC initiated *United States v. One Package of Japanese Pessaries*. In the 1936 case, a federal court concluded that the Comstock law could not stop the importation of diaphragms for legitimate medical use and created a distinction between legal and illegal use of contraceptives. The next year, the American Medical Association resolved that contraception was a valid health practice and that it should be taught in medical schools. Government agencies began incorporating birth control services into their programs in 1938.

The Birth Control Clinical Research Bureau, which collected information on the reliability of contraceptives, and the American Birth Control League merged in 1939 to form the Planned Parenthood Federation of America.

Sanger wrote *The Pivot of Civilization* (1922), *Woman and the New Race* (1923), *Happiness in a Marriage* (1926), and her autobiographies, *My Fight for Birth Control* (1931) and *Margaret Sanger: An Autobiography* (1938).

Born in Corning, New York, Margaret Sanger attended Claverack College, a preparatory school. She completed her nursing training at White Plains Hospital in 1902.

See also Abortion; Dennett, Mary Coffin Ware; Planned Parenthood Federation of America; Reproductive Rights

References Kennedy, *Birth Control in America: The Career of Margaret Sanger* (1970).

Schakowsky, Janice D. (b. 1944)

Democrat Jan Schakowsky of Illinois entered the U.S. House of Representatives on 3 January 1999. Schakowsky believes that Medicare is a "spectacular success" and wants to expand its coverage to all Americans. She thinks that Social Security is "one of the most successful government initiatives in our history" and wants to extend its benefits. Her congressional priorities include federal programs to rebuild public schools and full funding for Head Start, prenatal care, affordable housing, and environmental cleanup. Maintaining affirmative action programs, banning employment discrimination based on sexual orientation, and promoting alternative sentencing for nonviolent criminals are also among her priorities.

A member of the Illinois House of Representatives from 1991 to 1998, she passed legislation that increased support for day care centers, libraries, and Meals on Wheels and that strengthened the Hate Crimes Act. She also worked for union rights, expanded family leave benefits, and changes in medical insurance laws that consumer groups sought.

Born in Chicago, Illinois, Schakowsky earned her bachelor of science degree from the University of Illinois in 1965. A consumer and senior citizens' advocate, Schakowsky helped lead the successful campaign in the 1970s to require freshness dating on food products. She became executive director of the Illinois State Council of Senior Citizens in 1985, where she worked for lower-cost prescription drugs and property tax relief for seniors.

See also Affirmative Action; Child Day Care; Congress, Women in; Lesbian Rights

References "Jan Schakowsky" (1998); www.medill.nwu.edu/people/cook.

Schenk, Lynn (b. 1945)

Democrat Lynn Schenk of California served in the U.S. House of Representatives from 3 January 1993 to 3 January 1995. Schenk's policy interests included the environment, the line-item veto, and deficit reduction. She lost her attempt for a second term in 1994.

The daughter of Hungarian Holocaust survivors, Schenk was born in New York shortly after her parents' immigration to the United States. She received her bachelor of arts degree from the University of California in 1967, completed her law degree from the University of San Diego in 1970, and attended the London School of Economics from 1970 to 1971. California secretary of business, transportation, and housing from 1980 to 1983, Schenk later served on the San Diego Port Commission from 1990 to 1993. In 1998, she unsuccessfully ran for attorney general of California.

See also Congress, Women in

References Congressional Quarterly, *Politics in America 1994* (1993).

Schlafly, Phyllis Stewart (b. 1924)

Conservative leader Phyllis Schlafly founded Stop ERA and Eagle Forum and emerged as the primary opponent of and most powerful leader against state and federal Equal Rights Amendments. Schlafly became a national celebrity in 1964 with the publication of her best-selling book, *A Choice, Not an Echo,* in support of Republican Barry Goldwater's candidacy for his party's presidential nomination. In it, she argued that eastern liberal Republicans had conspired to keep the party from choosing conservative presidential nominees since 1936, even though the majority of Republicans had preferred more conservative candidates.

Schlafly entered politics in the 1950s through the Illinois Federation of Republican Women, ran for Congress in 1952, and served as the federation's president from 1960 to 1964. She moved to the national level in 1965 when she became vice president of the National Federation of Republican Women (NFRW), serving from 1965 to 1967. She ran for the presidency of the NFRW in 1967 but lost in a divisive contest. After losing, she wrote to the 500,000 members of the NFRW and asked them to send part of the dues to a war chest to promote conservative candidates and issues. She established the Eagle Forum Trust Fund and began publishing *The Phyllis Schlafly Report* in 1967. In 1970, Schlafly again ran for Congress and lost.

After Congress passed the Equal Rights Amendment in 1972, Schlafly began voicing her objections to it, although she had not objected to it during Congress's consideration of it. The next year, she formed Stop ERA and began presenting her arguments against the ERA across the nation. Schlafly's objections to the amendment included her belief that it would destroy families, force women into combat, and require unisex public toilet facilities. She began an odyssey of testifying before state legislatures, organizing state lobbying groups, and appearing on national television shows. Schlafly claimed credit for slowing the ratification and for the failure of more than twenty-six ratification attempts.

She founded and became president of Eagle Forum in 1975. She organized a profamily rally at the Houston Astro Arena to protest the National Women's Conference (NWC) in 1977 because she said that the NWC did not represent her constituency. Schlafly has written several books, including *Who Will Rock the Cradle* (1989) and *Meddlesome Mandate: Rethinking Family Leave* (1991).

Born in St. Louis, Missouri, Phyllis Schlafly earned her bachelor of arts degree at Washington University in 1944, her master of arts degree from Harvard University in 1945, her doctor of laws degree from Niagara University in 1976, and her juris doctor degree from Washington University in 1978.

See also Eagle Forum; Equal Rights Amendment; National Federation of Republican Women; National Women's Conference

References Felsenthal, *The Biography of Phyllis Schlafly* (1982); Schoenebaum, ed., *Political Profiles: The Nixon/Ford Years* (1979).

Schneider, Claudine Cmarada (b. 1947)

Republican Claudine Schneider of Rhode Island served in the U.S. House of Representatives from 3 January 1981 to 3 January 1991. Schneider entered politics out of her concern for the environment. She founded the Rhode Island Committee on Energy in 1973, served as executive director of the Conservation Law Foundation in 1974, and was federal coordinator of the Rhode Island Coastal Management Program in 1978. She was also a television producer and talk show host.

Schneider ran unsuccessfully for the U.S. House in 1978 and then won her first term in 1980. As a member of Congress, Schneider was instrumental in stopping the construction of the Clinch River Nuclear Reactor, a project she called "a notorious white elephant," and was a leader in the effort to ban dumping sludge and medical waste in the ocean. She helped pass the Civil Rights Restoration Act of 1988. Schneider left the House to run for the Senate in 1990 but lost.

Born in Clairton, Pennsylvania, Schneider attended the University of Barcelona and Rosemont College, receiving her bachelor of arts degree from Windham College in 1969. She also attended the University of Rhode Island School of Community Planning.

See also Civil Rights Restoration Act of 1988; Congress, Women in

References Congressional Quarterly, *Politics in America: The 98th Congress* (1983); Office of the Historian, U.S. House of Representatives, *Women in Congress, 1917–1990* (1991).

Schroeder, Patricia Nell Scott (b. 1940)

Democrat Patricia Schroeder served in the U.S. House of Representatives from 3 January 1973 to 3 January 1997. Throughout her congressional career, Schroeder fought for equity for women, sought to reduce military spending, and worked for policies that she believed would benefit families. In the summer of 1987, she explored the possibility of a presidential candidacy but decided against pursuing it.

Schroeder based her 1972 campaign for Congress on her opposition to the Vietnam War and her support for children and elderly people. Married and the mother of two children, Schroeder was asked after her election how she could be a mother and a congresswoman. She explained: "I have a brain and a uterus and they both work."

When she entered Congress, Schroeder asked to be on the Armed Forces Committee because of her opposition to the Vietnam War, but committee chair F. Edward Hébert (D-LA) refused her request, saying that she had not been in combat. Learning that several committee members had not been in combat, she pursued the matter and received the committee assignment. In addition to Schroeder, Hébert had objected to Ronald Dellums (D-CA) serving on the committee. To demonstrate his displeasure with their appointments, Hébert provided only one chair for Schroeder and Dellums in the committee room. They sat on the same chair until the Congressional Black Caucus pressured the leadership to convince Hébert to provide a second chair.

Three broad themes characterize Schroeder's congressional career—women's rights, families, and the military—and her legislative proposals often included some aspect of all three. A leader in the passage of the

Representative Patricia Schroeder (D-CO) led a pro-choice rally on the Capitol steps against the Hyde Amendment, which banned the use of federal funds for abortion, 1977 (Corbis/Bettmann)

Pregnancy Discrimination Act of 1978, she supported ratification of the Equal Rights Amendment, advocated federal funding of abortions, and fought to grant military personnel the right to have abortions in military hospitals. In 1984, Schroeder began working on the Family and Medical Leave Act. She held hearings on it, modified it, and in 1993 finally saw it enacted. The law provides for unpaid leave to care for a newborn, newly adopted child, or seriously ill child or parent. After President George Bush vetoed it twice, President Bill Clinton signed it in 1993.

Schroeder advocated improved child support enforcement, enhanced services for child abuse victims, and, as cochair of the Congressional Caucus for Women's Issues, helped develop the Economic Equity Act. In addition to supporting cuts in the defense budget, she opposed the MX missile system and led an effort to ban nuclear testing. She worked to improve family housing and facilities for military service members and persuaded the Armed Services Committee to permit women to fly combat missions. She helped expose cases of sexual harassment within the armed services and called on the military to end its discriminatory policies toward women and gays.

When Anita Hill accused U.S. Supreme Court nominee Clarence Thomas of sexually harassing her, Schroeder and other congresswomen sought to have the charges heard before the Senate confirmed Thomas. In her remarks to the House of Representatives, Schroeder said: "Mr. Speaker, we are at a very critical time in which a woman has come forward and made very serious allegations, and there is an attempt to brush them under the rug in the speed to have an adjournment for the Columbus Day recess. Columbus, I think, would even be appalled that we could be hurrying home to celebrate this great Nation, and also tainting this great Nation's reputation for justice." With six other Democratic congresswomen, her image was captured as they walked up the steps to the Senate to convince the Senate Judiciary Committee to investigate the charges before voting on Thomas's nomination.

Schroeder also called for an investigation of another incident of sexual harassment and assault. At the September 1991 national convention of the Tailhook Association, whose members are Marine and Navy aviators, more than twenty-five women, some of them naval officers, were sexually abused and assaulted. When the Navy attempted to minimize the incident, Schroeder pressed for further inquiries into it. She connected the Tailhook events with limits imposed upon women in the military and pressed for policies that would permit women to fly in combat. She noted: "If women can qualify . . . it would be silly to deny ourselves half the brain power of this country, just because they have the wrong chromosomes." Schroeder retired from Congress in 1997.

Born in Portland, Oregon, Schroeder learned to fly an airplane when she was fifteen years old and worked her way through college by running her own flying service. She received her bachelor of arts degree from the University of Minnesota in 1961 and her law degree from Harvard University in 1964. A field attorney for the National Labor Relations Board with responsibilities in Colorado, Utah, and Wyoming, she did pro bono work for Planned Parenthood in Colorado and taught law at the Community College of Denver and the University of Denver. Schroeder is the author of *Champion of the Great American Family* (1989) and *24 Years of House Work . . . and the Place Is Still a Mess: My Life in Politics* (1998).

See also Congress, Women in; Equal Rights Amendment; Family and Medical Leave Act of 1993; Hill, Anita Faye; Pregnancy Discrimination Act of 1978; Reproductive Rights; Sexual Harassment

References Boxer, *Strangers in the Senate* (1994); Doherty, "Surface Racial Harmony on Hill Hides Simmering Tensions" (1998); Kaptur, *Women of Congress: A Twentieth Century Odyssey* (1996); Schroeder, *Champion of the Great American Family* (1989), *24 Years of House Work . . . and the Place Is Still a Mess: My Life in Politics* (1998).

Seastrand, Andrea Ciszek (b. 1941)

Republican Andrea Seastrand of California served in the U.S. House of Representatives from 3 January 1995 to 3 January 1997. Seastrand worked to lower taxes for working families, saying: "I oppose higher taxes, period.

Our national budget problems do not exist because we send too little money to Washington. The problem is that politicians and special interest groups never run out of ways to spend our money." Opposed to reproductive rights and gay rights, she worked to stop illegal immigration and to prohibit welfare payments to minor mothers. She sought to create a national spaceport agency that would convert defunct military bases into facilities for commercial space projects.

Born in Chicago, Andrea Seastrand earned her bachelor of arts degree from DePaul University in 1963. A teacher, Seastrand entered politics when she managed her husband's state legislative campaigns. After his death, she won the seat that he had held and served in the California Assembly from 1991 to 1995.

See also Abortion; Congress, Women in; Lesbian Rights; State Legislatures, Women in

References Congressional Quarterly, *Politics in America 1996* (1995).

Seneca Falls Convention

In July 1848, Elizabeth Cady Stanton, Lucretia Coffin Mott, and three other women issued a call for the nation's first women's rights convention. Held in Seneca Falls, New York, on 19 and 20 July 1848 at Wesleyan Church, the convention attracted about 100 women and men, who discussed, amended, and adopted a *Declaration of Sentiments and Resolutions*. Modeled after the American Declaration of Independence, the Seneca Falls declaration stated in part:

> The history of mankind is a history of repeated injuries and usurpations on the part of man toward woman, having in direct object the establishment of an absolute tyranny over her. To prove this, let facts be submitted to a candid world.
>
> He has never permitted her to exercise her inalienable right to the elective franchise.
>
> He has compelled her to submit to laws, in the formation of which she had no voice.
>
> He has withheld from her rights which are given to the most ignorant and degraded men—both natives and foreigners.
>
> Having deprived her of this first right of a citizen, the elective franchise, thereby leaving her without representation in the halls of legislation, he has oppressed her on all sides.
>
> He has made her, if married, in the eye of the law, civilly dead.

Other grievances listed include divorce laws, property laws, tax laws, employment and educational opportunities, and exclusion from the ministry. Of the resolutions that the convention considered, the most controversial was proposed by Stanton and called for woman suffrage, and it was the only resolution that did not pass unanimously. When the discussion ended, sixty-eight women and thirty-two men signed the declaration. Of the women who signed the declaration, only Charlotte Woodward lived long enough to vote after the Nineteenth Amendment was ratified in 1920.

Over the next decade, women's rights conventions were held in Albany and Rochester, New York; Salem and Worcester, Massachusetts; Cleveland, Ohio; and other communities. Conventions were not held during the Civil War, and afterward, they generally took place under the auspices of a suffrage organization.

References Flexner and Fitzpatrick, *Century of Struggle: The Woman's Rights Movement in the United States*, enlarged edition (1996); Ravitch, ed., *The American Reader* (1990).

Separate Spheres

"Separate spheres" was a nineteenth-century phrase that articulated the belief that men belonged in the public world and women in the private world. Based on the assumption that men had greater physical strength and intellectual and mental abilities than women, it was believed that men were better suited for war, politics, work, the professions, and art. Women, with their presumed greater morality, nurturing skills, and self-sacrificing natures, were believed to be created for motherhood, domestic duties, and marriage.

The concept of separate spheres did not extend to women in slavery. Fieldwork and heavy labor were more likely their plight than even domestic service. In addition, poor women, including those once married but widowed and those whose husbands did not support them, did not have the luxury of confining their lives to domestic activities.

See also Coverture

Sex Discrimination

Discriminating on the basis of sex was the policy in the United States until women began challenging it in the 1840s in the first wave of the women's rights movement and continued to challenge it in the second wave of the movement that began in the 1960s. The areas in which women were legally discriminated against included education, employment, pay, jury service, and credit. In addition, women could not vote, hold public office in many states, or serve in the military, and married women could not conduct business in their own names, sue, or be sued.

In the mid–nineteenth century, states began to pass married women's property acts, but until passage of the Nineteenth Amendment in 1920, little action was taken to remove discriminatory laws against women. In the 1920s, some states eliminated prohibitions against women holding public office and serving on juries. Until passage of the Equal Pay Act in 1963, it was legal to pay different rates to women and men performing the same job, and until passage of the Civil Rights Act of 1964, it was legal to refuse to hire a woman for a job based on her sex.

The emergence of the feminist movement in the 1960s brought demands for the elimination of other forms of sex discrimination. Title IX of the Education Amendments of 1972 ended sex discrimination in education at institutions that received federal funds, and the Equal Credit Opportunity Act of 1974 prohibited discrimination in financing on the basis of sex or marital status. Also in the 1970s, the U.S. Supreme Court began to decide that sex discrimination violated the Fourteenth Amendment. Feminists, however, found that the progress was inadequate and too slow and began a campaign for passage of the Equal Rights Amendment. Congress passed the amendment, but it failed in 1982 because only thirty-five out of the necessary thirty-eight states had ratified it.

> **See also** Cable Acts; Civil Rights Act of 1964, Title VII; Education Amendments of 1972, Title IX; Equal Credit Opportunity Act of 1974; Equal Pay Act of 1963; Equal Rights Amendment; Married Women's Property Acts; Nineteenth Amendment; Suffrage

Sexual Harassment

The Equal Employment Opportunity Commission (EEOC) defines sexual harassment as follows: "Unwelcome sexual advances, requests for sexual favors, and other verbal or physical conduct of a sexual nature . . . when submission to or rejection of this conduct explicitly or implicitly affects an individual's employment, unreasonably interferes with an individual's work performance or creates an intimidating, hostile, or offensive work environment."

Harassers can be women or men, and victims can be women or men. The harasser could be a supervisor, an agent of the employer, a coworker, or not an employee. The victim does not have to be the person harassed and could be anyone affected by the offensive conduct. In addition, the victim does not have to suffer economic injury or be discharged to have a complaint.

The EEOC has defined two kinds of sexual harassment, quid pro quo and hostile environment. Quid pro quo harassment is committed when a person submits to being harassed out of concern for her or his job, potential promotion, job assignment, or other conditions of work. Only a supervisor or manager can commit quid pro quo harassment because a coworker or someone without supervisory authority cannot affect the victim's job. There only needs to be one event of this form of harassment for it to be illegal.

Hostile work environment harassment has been defined by the EEOC and accepted by the U.S. Supreme Court in *Meritor Savings Bank v. Vinson* (1986) as unwelcome conduct that "has the purpose or effect of unreasonably interfering with an individual's work performance or creating an intimidating, hostile, or offensive working environment." Sexual slurs and comments, sexually offensive images, and unwanted touching of intimate body areas are all forms of hostile environment harassment. Unlike quid pro quo harassment, hostile environment harassment does not require that the person's job is threatened by the harasser. Frequency and severity are key to this form of harassment—the more often it occurs, the less severe it must be to constitute harassment.

In *Harris v. Forklift Systems* (1993), the U.S. Supreme Court ruled that employees do not need to show that the offensive sexual behavior left them psychologically damaged or unable to perform their jobs. The Court wrote: "So long as the environment would reasonably be perceived, and is perceived, as hostile or abusive, there is no need for it also to be psychologically injurious." Although *Meritor* expanded the definition of sexual harassment and *Harris* made a hostile environment easier to prove, women who initiate legal remedies for workplace sexual harassment often face public scorn and lengthy and expensive legal obstacles.

Sexual harassment gained national attention in 1991 when law professor Anita Hill alleged that U.S. Supreme Court nominee Clarence Thomas had sexually harassed her. In her testimony before the U.S. Senate Judiciary Committee, Hill described the humiliation and embarrassment of being sexually harassed. The televised hearings prompted women who had suffered experiences of sexual harassment to file complaints and take other actions to stop the exploitation.

Two other sexual harassment cases also gained national attention in the 1990s. Sexual harassment of women in the military gained national attention following revelations in 1992 that women had been assaulted at the 1991 convention of the Tailhook Association, a private association of naval aviators. On one night, more than 100 association members were involved in assaults that included the men grabbing or removing the clothing of twenty-six women, half of them Navy officers, as they tried to pass through a hallway. In the course of the weekend convention, eighty-three women and seven men were assaulted. Navy lieutenant Paula Coughlin, an admiral's aide and helicopter pilot, feared that she would be gang-raped, but she escaped after biting one of the men. Coughlin filed a formal complaint, which resulted in two internal Navy investigations, but only two suspects were identified. The Department of Defense inspector general conducted another investigation that resulted in several officers being disciplined and others facing court martial proceedings, but all of the cases were dismissed. No one involved was convicted of a crime.

The second sexual harassment case that gained national attention involved Republican senator Bob Packwood of Oregon. Packwood, who had long supported women's issues and abortion rights, was accused of making unwanted sexual advances toward women beginning in 1969. Twenty-six women accused him of sexual misconduct, which he originally denied. While the Senate Ethics Committee began investigating the allegations, Packwood attempted to defend himself through references to his personal diaries, leading the Senate to subpoena them. The revelations in his diaries led to his resignation in 1995.

See also Civil Rights Act of 1964, Title VII; Employment Discrimination; Equal Employment Opportunity Commission; *Harris v. Forklift Systems;* Hill, Anita Faye; *Meritor Savings Bank v. Vinson*

References Bingham, *Women on the Hill: Challenging the Culture of Congress* (1997); Fallon, "Sexual Harassment, Content, Neutrality, and the First Amendment Dog That Didn't Bark" (1995); Hoff, *Law, Gender, and Injustice* (1991); Levy and Paludi, *Workplace Sexual Harassment* (1997); www.eeoc.gov/ facts/ fs-sex.html.

Shabazz, Hajj Bahiyah (Betty) (1936–1997)

Betty Shabazz, widow of slain civil rights leader Malcolm X, reconciled her differences with Islam leader Louis Farrakhan, 1995 (Corbis/Robert Maass)

Widow of civil rights leader Malcolm X, Betty Shabazz also became a national figure in the civil rights movement. Born in Detroit, Michigan, Shabazz attended Tuskegee Institute, where she met Malcolm X during her junior year. They married and had four daughters. Shabazz was pregnant with twins when she witnessed Malcolm X's assassination on 21 February 1965 in New York City's Audubon Ballroom. Shabazz then focused her attention on raising their daughters and completing her own education. She earned a registered nursing degree from Brooklyn State Hospital School of Nursing and her doctoral degree from the University of Massachusetts in 1975.

A professor of health administration at Medgar Evers College, she also served as the school's director of institutional advancement and public relations. Shabazz became a national figure through her public speaking on education and issues of race relations.

See also Civil Rights Movement; Evers-Williams, Myrlie Louise Beasley

References Smith, ed., *Powerful Black Women* (1996).

Shaheen, Jeanne (b. 1947)

Democrat Jeanne Shaheen became governor of New Hampshire in 1997. A member of the New Hampshire Senate from 1991 to 1996, Shaheen passed health care reform legislation providing guarantees for adequate hospital stays for women after childbirth, stabilizing health insurance rates, and ending discrimination against people with preexisting conditions. She helped open the electric utility industry to competition to help lower the state's electric rates and helped create the first state-sponsored industrial research center.

In her campaign for governor, Shaheen pledged to apply for federal grants for Goals 2000, a federal program that provides grants to states that meet certain educational goals. She proposed raising the state's cigarette tax and permitting video poker machines at the state's racetracks to help fund public kindergarten classes, which were not universally available in New Hampshire.

Born in St. Charles, Missouri, Jeanne Shaheen earned her bachelor's degree from Shippensburg University in 1969 and her master's degree from the University of Mississippi in 1973.

See also Governors, Women; State Legislatures, Women in

References *Congressional Quarterly Almanac, 104th Congress, 2nd Session . . . 1996* (1997); www.state.nh.us/governor/bio.html.

Shalala, Donna Edna (b. 1941)

Democrat Donna Shalala became secretary of the U.S. Department of Health and Human Services in 1993. She is the longest-serving secretary of health and human services in U.S. history. Shalala began her political career as treasurer and a director of New York City's Municipal Assistance Corporation, which worked to restore the city's financial stability in the mid-1970s. Assistant secretary for policy development and research at the Department of Housing and Urban Development from 1977 to 1980, she discovered that only 18 percent of the owner-occupied homes in the United States were owned by women and began a "Women and Mortgage Credit" program. The project held workshops that taught women the advantages and disadvantages of home ownership. She developed a women's policy and program staff, funded battered women's shelters, and commissioned studies of the housing needs of families headed by women. Shalala explained: "Sex discrimination existed in rental housing, against families with children, against elderly single women, against black and minority women. We began to review all federal housing policies to assess their impact on women."

As secretary of health and human services, Shalala participated in reforming welfare and implemented the changes, gained approval of the Children's Health Insurance Program, and raised child immunization rates to the highest in history. She campaigned against tobacco use and sought to end the association between smokeless tobacco and professional baseball, a project that included her throwing the first pitch (the full 60 feet, 6 inches) for the Orioles 1998 season. In addition to developing national initiatives to fight breast cancer and violence against women, she worked for improved medications to treat acquired immunodeficiency syndrome (AIDS) and tried to increase access to them.

Born in Cleveland, Ohio, Shalala earned her bachelor of arts degree from Western College for Women in 1962. She volunteered for the Peace Corps from 1962 to 1964, teaching at the University of Ahwaz in Iran. After returning to the United States, Shalala taught at Syracuse University while working on her doctoral degree, which she received in 1970 from Syracuse University. Shalala taught at Bernard M. Baruch College from 1970 to 1972, when she began teaching at Teachers College at Columbia University. She became president of Hunter College in 1980 and held the position until 1988, when she became chancellor of the University of Wisconsin at Madison, the first woman to head a Big Ten university.

See also Cabinets, Women in Presidential

References H. W. Wilson, *Current Biography Yearbook, 1991* (1991); *New York Times,* 15 January 1976; www.hhs.gov/about/bios/dhhssec.html.

Shaw, Anna Howard (1847–1919)

Anna Howard Shaw was president of the National American Woman Suffrage Association from 1904 to 1915, a period considered the doldrums for the woman suffrage movement. The first woman ordained in the Methodist Protestant Church as well as a physician, Shaw began her political career as a lecturer for woman suffrage in 1883.

Born in Newcastle upon Tyne, England, Shaw moved to the United States in 1851 with her parents, settling in Lawrence, Massachusetts. An education was a priority for Shaw, but she was unable to attend high school until she was twenty-three years old. Her ability to preach soon came to the attention of a Methodist minister who invited her to join him in his circuit, and she began her career as an itinerant preacher.

In 1873, Shaw entered Albion College, and while she continued to preach, she also began lecturing on temperance. Three years later, she left Albion before graduating and moved to Boston to attend Boston Univer-

sity Theological Seminary. After graduating in 1878, she received a call to a church on Cape Cod. She applied to the Methodist Episcopal Conference for ordination in 1880, but the bishop refused to ordain her because of her sex. Later that year, the Methodist Protestant Church ordained her.

Shaw decided that a medical degree would be useful in her ministries and entered Boston University School of Medicine in 1882, graduating in 1886. She resigned her pastorate and earned her living as a lecturer on suffrage, temperance, and social purity. In 1887, the American Woman Suffrage Association hired her as its national lecturer. Shaw met Susan B. Anthony when both women were lecturing in Kansas, leading Anthony to hire her as the National American Woman Suffrage Association's

(NAWSA) national lecturer in 1890. Two years later, Shaw became NAWSA's vice president–at–large.

When Anthony resigned the presidency of NAWSA in 1900, Carrie Chapman Catt became the group's president, serving until 1904. Following Catt's resignation, Shaw became NAWSA president. During her tenure from 1904 to 1915, Shaw increased the organization's membership from 17,000 to 183,000 and its annual budget from $5,000 to almost $50,000. In addition, the number of states with full woman suffrage grew from four to eleven. Shaw also moved NAWSA's headquarters from Warren, Ohio, the home of NAWSA treasurer Harriet Taylor Upton, to New York. Despite these improvements in the organization and the increase in the number of suffrage states, some suffrage leaders were dissatisfied with the progress being made. They felt that with a more active and energetic campaign, success would come more quickly.

Shaw's approach to the presidency may have contributed to the campaign's pace. She used a democratic approach, seeking the opinions of the board members before acting. She wrote long letters updating and consulting them on an almost weekly basis, but with board members located around the country, it was a slow process and an inefficient way to manage the association and conduct the campaign. NAWSA's structure impaired quick action because it limited the president's freedom to act by requiring board or convention approval in many situations. In addition, Shaw faced regional conflicts in the use of resources such as speakers and money, as well as in the underlying goal of suffrage. Southern women, in particular, wanted suffrage for whites only, resisting universal suffrage out of racism. Another limit arose from Shaw's personal situation: she could not devote all of her time to NAWSA because she had to support herself by lecturing around the country.

The overall strategy pursued by NAWSA at the time also created problems. By attempting to conduct state campaigns across the country, often supporting several efforts in one election year, NAWSA's resources were constantly drained. For those who believed passing a federal amendment provided the best opportunity, the sometimes futile state amendments appeared to be an unwise use of funds.

By 1912, dissatisfaction with the slow progress led to criticism of Shaw and NAWSA. That year, NAWSA executive secretary Mary Ware Dennett sought to change the association's constitution and to reorganize it, but her effort failed. Dennett then joined others in openly criticizing Shaw, eventually leaving the organization out of frustration. In 1915, Shaw resigned the presidency, at least in part as a result of the increased and persistent criticism she faced.

Shaw chaired the Woman's Committee of the Council of National

Defense from 1916 to 1918. Following the end of World War I, she lectured on peace. In 1915 she wrote her autobiography, *A Story of a Pioneer.*

> **See also** American Woman Suffrage Association; Anthony, Susan Brownell; Catt, Carrie Clinton Lane Chapman; Dennett, Mary Coffin Ware; National American Woman Suffrage Association; Suffrage
>
> **References** Linkugel and Solomon, *Anna Howard Shaw: Suffrage Orator and Social Reformer* (1991).

Shepherd, Karen (b. 1940)

Democrat Karen Shepherd of Utah served in the U.S. House of Representatives from 5 January 1993 to 3 January 1995. Shepherd entered electoral politics through the state legislature, serving in the Utah Senate from 1991 to 1993. During her congressional campaign, Shepherd proposed a ten-point plan for children, including fully funding Head Start and improving the collection of child support payments. After losing her bid for a second term to Enid Greene Waldholtz, Shepherd was a fellow at the Institute of Politics at the John F. Kennedy School of Government at Harvard University. In 1996, President Bill Clinton appointed her to the International Bank for Reconstruction and Development.

Born in Silver City, New Mexico, Karen Shepherd earned her bachelor of arts degree from the University of Utah in 1962 and her master of arts degree from Brigham Young University in 1963. A former English teacher, Shepherd was assistant director for Salt Lake County social services from 1975 to 1976 and director from 1976 to 1978. Shepherd published and edited *Network* magazine for working women from 1978 to 1984.

> **See also** Congress, Women in; State Legislatures, Women in; Greene, Enid
>
> **References** Congressional Quarterly, *Politics in America 1994* (1993).

Sheppard-Towner Maternity and Infancy Protection Act of 1921

The first goal of newly enfranchised women following the passage of the Nineteenth Amendment, the Sheppard-Towner Maternity and Infancy Protection Act allocated federal money to states to reduce maternal and infant mortality. In a 1917 study conducted by the Children's Bureau, the United States ranked seventeenth among twenty nations in maternal mortality and eleventh in infant mortality.

In 1917, Julia Lathrop, head of the Children's Bureau, recommended federal aid to states to protect pregnant women and their infants. The next year, Congresswoman Jeannette Rankin (R-MT) introduced a bill to provide education for pregnant women through pre- and postnatal care as well as federal aid to states for hospital care, medical care, and visiting nurses for new mothers and their infants. Rankin did not return to Congress in 1919, but that year Congressman Horace Mann Towner (R-IA) and Senator Morris Sheppard (D-TX) introduced a comparable measure. In 1921, the Women's Joint Congressional Committee developed grassroots support for a maternal and infant health bill by distributing pamphlets and by deluging members of Congress with letters and telegrams in support of the Sheppard-Towner Act. The lobbying campaign included *Good Housekeeping* magazine, which also encouraged women to lobby Congress. Criticized by conservatives as a Bolshevik plan, the Sheppard-Towner Act was opposed by the American Medical Association because its members wanted to maintain control over medical care delivery. The Women Patriots opposed the measure, also labeling it a Communist plan.

The U.S. Senate passed the Sheppard-Towner Act in 1921, but the chairman of the House committee handling the bill tried to kill it. Republican National Committee vice chair Harriet Taylor Upton, however, interceded on behalf of the bill, telling President Warren G. Harding that delaying it alienated women. Wanting to please the new women voters, Harding intervened on the bill's behalf on two occasions at Upton's request. Members of Congress supported the bill for the same reason: to please women voters, whose strength as a voting bloc was unknown. When the House passed the bill 279 to 39, the only woman in Congress, Alice Robertson, voted against it.

The Sheppard-Towner Act offered each state $5,000, with another $5,000 available to those states providing matching funds. Under the act, child care conferences trained public health and visiting nurses, as did the literature developed and distributed by the Children's Bureau, which administered the act's provisions. In addition, nurses provided instruction in hygiene to pregnant women and new mothers. By 1922, forty-one states participated in the program, and eventually only Connecticut, Illinois, and Massachusetts remained out of it. The program did make a difference in infant mortality: in 1921 the infant death rate was 75 per 1,000 births; after Sheppard-Towner, it was 64 per 1,000. The maternal death rate also dropped.

In 1926, Congress extended the appropriation but included a sunset clause for the program on 30 June 1929, and the program ended. Some states continued to provide the services after the federal appropriations ended. With the passage of the Social Security Act of 1935, the programs were restored.

See also Abbott, Grace; Children's Bureau; Lathrop, Julia; Rankin, Jeannette Pickering; Robertson, Alice Mary; Upton, Harriet Taylor; Women's Joint Congressional Committee

References Lemons, *The Woman Citizen: Social Feminism in the 1920s* (1973); Lindenmeyer, *"A Right to Childhood": The U.S. Children's Bureau and Child Welfare, 1912–1946* (1997).

Shirtwaist Workers Strike

The Shirtwaist Workers Strike, also known as the Uprising of the 20,000, began on 24 November 1909, when 18,000 garment workers walked out of almost 500 shops in Manhattan and Brooklyn. Eventually, about 20,000 garment workers were on strike. The strikers, who made the blouses that female clerical workers wore at the time, primarily worked in dirty, poorly lit, unsafe factories for long hours at starvation wages. Required to purchase their sewing needles and thread from the employer, they were fined for making errors, arriving late at work, and other infringements of company rules. Generally young women ages sixteen to twenty-five, the waist makers were mostly Russian Jewish immigrants. The strikers wanted a 10 percent wage increase and recognition of their union in contract negotiations.

Local 25 of the International Ladies' Garment Workers' Union led the strike, and the Women's Trade Union League (WTUL) provided support to the strikers. The WTUL, whose leaders included some of New York's wealthy socialites, offered its offices for a strike headquarters, stood in picket lines with the strikers, and generated publicity for the cause. The WTUL also helped raise money for food and for bail for the more than 700 strikers who were arrested. After strikers realized that New York garment makers were subcontracting work to Philadelphia factories, the strike spread to that city.

Several small manufacturers relented and signed agreements that included a fifty-two-hour workweek, limitations on overtime, and provision of needles, thread, and other equipment and supplies. In addition, union officials were given access to payroll records on a weekly basis. The agreements covered about 10,000 workers, who returned to work. Larger manufacturers, however, hired strikebreakers.

In late December, New York employers offered strikers a fifty-two-hour workweek, four paid holidays, and sewing supplies. They agreed to rehire strikers and pledged that they would not discriminate against union members. The strikers rejected the offer because the employers did not agree to recognize the union.

In early February 1910, the Philadelphia strike ended in an arbitrated agreement that did not include the union shop. Ten thousand garment workers, however, joined Local 15 of the International Ladies' Garment Workers' Union.

The New York socialites who had supported the strike began to lose interest in it, particularly after the strikers had rejected the December offer. Without the WTUL's support, the strikers increasingly suffered. The union signed an agreement that included time-and-a-half pay for overtime hours and a fifty-two-hour workweek and did not include union recognition. Twenty thousand workers joined Local 25.

The largest strike of women workers at the time, the Shirtwaist Workers Strike demonstrated that women could be organized into unions and laid the foundation for the development of a strong union for women garment workers.

See also Women's Trade Union League

References Foner, *Women and the American Labor Movement: From the First Trade Unions to the Present* (1982); Wertheimer, *We Were There: The Story of Working Women in America* (1977).

Simmons, Althea T. L. (1924–1990)

Chief lobbyist for the National Association for the Advancement of Colored People (NAACP) from 1979 until her death in 1990, Althea Simmons began her career with the organization as volunteer executive secretary for the Texas State Conference of NAACP and joined the staff in 1961 as field secretary. Director of the NAACP's 1964 voter registration drive, she also served as the organization's director for training from 1964 until 1974. As NAACP national education director from 1974 to 1977, Simmons developed handbooks, pamphlets, and programs designed for black youth. When she served as associate director of branch and field services from 1977 to 1979, her responsibilities included the network of local and state branches, field staff, and other divisions.

NAACP's chief lobbyist during the Reagan administration, Simmons worked to prevent erosion of the 1964 Civil Rights Act and helped pass the extension of the Voting Rights Act in 1982, considered the most important civil rights legislation in nearly two decades. Simmons successfully lobbied for sanctions against South Africa to protest apartheid, and after President Ronald Reagan vetoed the measure, she successfully lobbied for Congress's override of the veto. She also worked for the bill making Martin Luther King, Jr.'s birthday a national holiday.

Born in Shreveport, Louisiana, Althea Simmons earned her bachelor of science degree from Southern University in 1945, her master's degree from the University of Illinois in 1951, and her law degree from Howard University in 1956. She also studied at the University of California at Los Angeles and the New School for Social Work, among other schools.

See also National Association for the Advancement of Colored People, Women in the

References *New York Times*, 30 June 1987, 17 September 1990.

Simpson, Edna Oakes (1891–1984)

Republican Edna Simpson of Illinois served in the U.S. House of Representatives from 3 January 1959 to 3 January 1961. Nine days after the death of her husband, Representative Sidney Simpson, Edna Simpson was elected to the seat he had held. She did not make any campaign appearances but easily won the contest. Simpson never spoke on the House floor. She announced in December 1959 that she would not be a candidate for reelection.

Edna Simpson was born in Carrollton, Illinois.

See also Congress, Women in

References Office of the Historian, U.S. House of Representatives, *Women in Congress, 1917–1990* (1991).

Slaughter, Louise McIntosh (b. 1929)

Democrat Louise Slaughter of New York entered the U.S. House of Representatives on 3 January 1987. Slaughter held the leadership position of minority whip–at–large in the 106th Congress (1999–2001). Congresswoman Slaughter has passed legislation that created the first federal research and education program on DES, a drug that was erroneously thought to prevent miscarriage but that can cause birth defects and other problems in subsequent generations. She helped increase appropriations for breast cancer research and was responsible for the creation of a permanent Office of Women's Health at the National Institutes of Health (NIH) and for guaranteeing that women and minorities are included in all health trials at the NIH. An author of the Violence Against Women Act of 1994, she succeeded in including immigrant spouses in it. She passed a measure that gives states an incentive to make it easier for homeless children to attend school. Slaughter also passed legislation to establish a Women's Rights National Historic Trail.

Slaughter was one of the seven Democratic congresswomen who marched to the Senate to register their concerns about the sexual harassment charges against U.S. Supreme Court nominee Clarence Thomas. Their goal was to convince the Senate Judiciary Committee to investigate the charges before voting on his nomination.

Slaughter passed an amendment for a special tax break that allows small manufacturers and farmers to issue tax-exempt bonds through local governments and has worked for the development of a high-speed railroad. In other areas, Slaughter helped pass a measure to end the dumping of sewage sludge in the ocean and another to help older women attend college by expanding financial aid to part-time and other nontraditional students.

Eleanor Smeal, president of the National Organization for Women, led thousands of prochoice activists in a march on Washington, D.C., 1986 (Corbis/Bettmann)

Born in Harlan County, Kentucky, Louise Slaughter received her bachelor of science degree in 1951 and her master of science degree in 1953, both from the University of Kentucky. Slaughter was a Monroe County legislator from 1975 to 1979 and served in the New York Assembly from 1983 to 1987.

See also Congress, Women in; Health Care, Women and; Hill, Anita Faye; Sexual Harassment; State Legislatures, Women in; Violence Against Women Act of 1994; Women's Health, Office of Research on

References Congressional Quarterly, *Politics in America 1994* (1993); Office of the Historian, U.S. House of Representatives, *Women in Congress, 1917–1990* (1991); www.house.gov/slaughter/bio.htm.

Smeal, Eleanor Cutri (b. 1939)

President of the National Organization for Women (NOW) from 1977 to 1982 and from 1985 to 1987, Eleanor Smeal was a cofounder and founding president of the Fund for the Feminist Majority in 1987. Smeal entered politics out of frustration. After completing her master's degree, she had intended to pursue a doctorate, but the lack of child care prevented her from continuing. Later, when she suffered a back ailment that required her to take a year of complete bed rest, she again found there were no child care services available. Through the experience, she also became aware of the need for disability insurance for wives and mothers. Smeal and her husband, who had performed many household tasks during that year, became confirmed feminists, opened a day care center, and in 1970, joined NOW.

From 1971 to 1973, Smeal convened and served as the first president of a NOW chapter in suburban Pittsburgh, Pennsylvania, and was elected president of Pennsylvania NOW in 1972. She made educational injustice her priority and worked for equal opportunity for girls in physical education and sports programs. Smeal joined NOW's national board of directors and its legal defense and education board of directors in 1973 and was elected national president four years later. Smeal led efforts to ratify the Equal Rights Amendment (ERA), including a boycott of states that had not yet ratified the ERA. She was appointed to the National Commission on the Observance of International Women's Year, 1975, by President Jimmy Carter and was a visible leader at the National Women's Conference held in Houston, Texas, in 1977. When she became president, the organization had 55,000 members and a deficit of $120,000. At the end of her first tenure as president in 1982, NOW had 225,000 members and a budget of more than $9 million.

Born in Ashtabula, Ohio, Smeal earned her bachelor of arts degree from Duke University in 1961 and her master of arts degree from the University of Florida in 1963.

See also Equal Rights Amendment; The Feminist Majority; National Organization for Women; National Women's Conference

References H. W. Wilson, *Current Biography Yearbook, 1980* (1980).

Smith, Howard Worth (1883–1976)

Democrat Howard Worth Smith of Virginia served in the U.S. House of Representatives from 1931 to 1967. Although he was opposed to civil rights legislation, he played a crucial role in expanding Title VII of the Civil Rights Act of 1964 to include women. As the House debated Title VII, Smith introduced a one-word amendment, "sex," to the section related to employment discrimination. Some observers have attributed his motives for introducing the amendment to a desire to kill the entire bill. Others have suggested that he introduced it at the request of the National Woman's Party. Regardless of his motives, congresswomen and others who supported the amendment also supported Smith's introduction of it, correctly believing that other southern congressmen would follow Smith's lead and vote for it. When the amendment and the bill passed, employment discrimination on the basis of sex, race, color, and national origin became illegal.

Born in Broad Run, Virginia, Smith graduated from Bethel Military Academy in 1901 and earned his bachelor of laws degree from the University of Virginia in 1903. He entered private practice in Alexandria, Virginia, the next year. Smith served as commonwealth attorney of Alexandria from 1918 to 1922, judge in Alexandria's Corporation Court from

Representative Linda Smith (R-WA) ran unsuccessfully against Senator Patty Murray for the U.S. Senate in 1998 (Associated Press AP)

1922 to 1928, and judge in the 16th Judicial Circuit of Virginia from 1928 to 1932.

See also Civil Rights Act of 1964, Title VII; National Woman's Party

References Freeman, "How 'Sex' Got into Title VII: Persistent Opportunism as a Maker of Public Policy" (1991); *New York Times,* 4 October 1976.

Smith, Linda A. (b. 1950)

Republican Linda Smith of Washington served in the U.S. House of Representatives from 3 January 1995 to 3 January 1999. Her strong antiabortion beliefs and anger over a state tax increase motivated Smith to enter politics. She served in the Washington House of Representatives from 1983 to 1987 and in the state Senate from 1987 to 1995. She authored two state initiatives, one for campaign and ethics reform and one to limit state expenditures and taxes, both approved by voters. Smith won her place on the 1994 general election ballot through a write-in petition drive for the Republican primary, the first person in Washington state history to qualify through that route. The work she had done on the ballot initiatives and her strong support among Christian activists gave her the grassroots base she needed. The all-volunteer Smith organization called 40,000 households and mailed write-in instructions to 150,000 households.

Congresswoman Smith concentrated on campaign finance reform, and worked to ban political action committees (PACs), create voluntary campaign spending limits, and ban certain kinds of political contributions. Smith explained her motives: "You're elected as an idealist and thrown into the sewer. People believe [Congress] is a sewer, and they elected a bunch of cleaners to go in and clean it up." Smith's other priorities include a balanced budget, elimination of corporate welfare, Social Security reform, tax reform, breast cancer research, and natural resources management. She was an unsuccessful candidate for the U.S. Senate in 1998, having lost to the Democratic incumbent, Patty Murray.

Born in La Junta, Colorado, Smith managed tax consulting centers and was a tax consultant.

See also Congress, Women in; State Legislatures, Women in

References Congressional Quarterly, *Politics in America 1994* (1993), *Politics in America 1996* (1995), *Politics in America 1998* (1997); www.house.gov/linda-smith/bio.htm.

Smith, Margaret Madeline Chase (1897–1995)

Republican Margaret Chase Smith of Maine served in the U.S. House of Representatives from 3 June 1940 to 3 January 1949 and served in the U.S. Senate from 3 January 1949 to 3 January 1973. She is the first woman to win election to both houses of Congress and the first woman nominated for the presidency at a major national party convention. In 1930, she married Clyde Smith and through him entered politics. When Clyde Smith won a seat in the U.S. House of Representatives in 1936, his wife joined his staff. When he died in 1940, she won the race to fill the vacancy.

Congresswoman Smith did not view herself as a feminist or an advocate for women, saying: "I definitely resent being called a feminist." Women assumed that she would be sympathetic to them, however, and Smith responded to several gender-based difficulties, including ending barriers to women's employment, securing maternity and infant care for military dependents at base hospitals, and developing support for public nurseries and day care centers. She also introduced and passed a measure that granted permanent regular status for women who served in auxiliary units of the military and worked for passage of the 1948 Women's Armed Services Integration Act.

When Maine's senior senator announced in 1948 that he would not run for reelection, Smith entered a three-way primary, running on the slogan "Don't trade a record for a promise." National security was the issue she considered most important, also noting that the housing shortage the nation faced was a disgrace. She won both the primary and the general elections.

On 1 June 1950, Senator Smith and six other Republican senators wrote a speech titled "A Declaration of Conscience," which Smith delivered. Aiming at Senator Joseph McCarthy's anti-Communist excesses without saying his name, she accused her colleagues of permitting individual senators to abuse their power by making unproven charges that defamed innocent Americans. She told the Senate: "I do not like the way the

Margaret Chase Smith (R-ME), the first woman to serve in both the House and the Senate, fought for child care and integration of women into the military, 1950 (Corbis/Bettmann)

Senate has been made a rendezvous for vilification, for selfish political gain at the sacrifice of individual reputations and national unity. . . . I do not want to see a party ride to political victory on the Four Horsemen of Calumny—fear, ignorance, bigotry, and smear." After she had read the statement, five of the six male cosponsors withdrew their names, fearing retribution from McCarthy. McCarthy punished Smith for criticizing him by having her removed from an important subcommittee and from the Republican Policy Committee. In 1954, he recruited a primary opponent to run against Smith, but she won the primary and general elections. A strong anti-Communist herself, Smith voted to censure McCarthy in 1954.

In 1964, Smith announced her candidacy for the Republican presidential nomination but received only a few votes at the Republican National Convention later that year. Smith lost her attempt for a fifth Senate term in 1972. In retirement, she was a college lecturer.

Born in Skohegan, Maine, she was a primary schoolteacher following graduation from high school. She was also a telephone operator and commercial manager of a telephone company, circulation manager of a weekly newspaper, office manager of a woolen mill, and treasurer of a waste process company.

See also Congress, Women in

References Boxer, *Strangers in the Senate* (1994); Wallace, *Politics of Conscience: A Biography of Margaret Chase Smith* (1995).

Smith, Mary Louise (1914–1997)

Elected chairperson of the Republican National Committee (RNC) on 16 September 1974, she was the first and only woman to hold the position. Smith began her political career in Eagle Grove, Iowa, in the late 1940s. Like many women of the time, she entered the political arena at the precinct level, knocking on doors during campaigns, and recruiting and organizing women for the Republican Party. Although she held a number of local and county offices in the party, she devoted most of her attention to the National Federation of Republican Women, holding local and state offices in it. She once explained that in those early days, "If someone told me that I would be party chairman, I don't know if I would have known what they were talking about."

In the early 1960s, having worked for the party for almost two decades, she concluded that she wanted to be among those making the party's policy decisions. When the incumbent Republican national committeewoman for Iowa retired, Smith saw an opportunity and took it. Elected Republican national committeewoman for Iowa in 1964, she won reelection four more times, retiring in 1984. She served on the RNC Committee on Convention Reforms in 1966; was a member of the U.S. delegation to the Fifteenth Session of the Population Commission of the Economic and Social Council of the United Nations in 1969; and was a member of the U.S. Delegation to the Third Extraordinary Session of the General Conference of the United Nations Educational, Scientific, and Cultural Organization in Paris in 1973.

In February 1974, George Bush, then RNC chairman, appointed Smith cochair of the RNC. At the time, the party's image was being badly damaged by President Richard Nixon's involvement in the Watergate scandal. Smith's grassroots organizational skills, her notable speaking skills, and her extensive knowledge of party organization were viewed as important assets in sustaining party members' loyalty and commitment as the scandal continued to unfold. In a clearly hopeless quest, Smith traveled the country that summer, attempting to motivate Republicans to rally around their party and support candidates in the fall elections.

After Nixon resigned in August 1974, President Gerald Ford granted George Bush's request to leave the RNC and become U.S. envoy to China. At the same time, Bush recommended that Smith become chair of the RNC. Her election to the office by the Republican National Committee, based upon Ford's recommendation, was received with mixed reactions. Feminists lauded it as an important step forward for women, whereas conservatives questioned whether she was tough enough and objected to her feminist beliefs. Political observers and party conservatives speculated that she would hold the office for only a short time before being replaced, probably after the fall elections.

Despite Smith's efforts, the fall elections were a disaster for the party. Republican candidates at every level of government lost their races as voters expressed their outrage over Watergate. Following the elections, Smith believed that her primary objective was to rebuild the party. Her efforts included an ambitious, innovative, and controversial public relations, advertising, and fund-raising program. She also began planning the 1976 Republican Convention. When she gaveled the convention to order, she became the first woman of either major party to organize and convene a presidential nominating convention. Gerald Ford, the party's presidential nominee, lost that November, and Smith resigned the chairmanship in January 1977.

Throughout those years, Smith's identity as a feminist had evolved, and she had become a strong advocate of the Iowa and the federal Equal Rights Amendments, civil rights, and reproductive rights. President Ronald Reagan appointed Smith to the U.S. Commission on Civil Rights in March 1982. She served as its vice chair until November 1983, when it was reorganized. Despite agreements that Smith would be appointed to the new commission, her outspoken advocacy for strengthening civil rights enforcement did not coincide with the Reagan administration's views, and she was not appointed to the new commission. The public's protests over the decision to leave her off the commission provided Smith with a forum to discuss the history, significance, and imperatives of civil rights enforcement in this country. As the Republican Party became increasingly more conservative in the 1980s and 1990s, she publicly criticized it for abandoning its support for reproductive rights and the Equal Rights Amendment.

She was a founder of the Iowa Peace Institute and a member of its board from 1986 to 1990, the year she resigned to accept an appointment to the board of the U.S. Institute of Peace, where she served until her death in 1997.

Born in Eddyville, Iowa, on 6 October 1914, she received a bachelor's degree in social work administration from the University of Iowa in 1935. She met and married Elmer Smith while studying there.

See also National Federation of Republican Women; Republican Party, Women in the

Smith, Virginia Dodd (b. 1911)

Republican Virginia Smith of Nebraska served in the U.S. House of Representatives from 3 January 1975 to 3 January 1991. Smith and her husband farmed in Nebraska, where she became involved in educational and agricultural associations. She entered public life as a member of the state's school board association in 1949 and served until 1960. National president of the American Country Life Association from 1951 to 1954 and national chair of American Farm Bureau Women from 1954 to 1974, she also served on the National Cattle and Livestock Board from 1955 to 1958. Secretary of Agriculture Ezra Taft Benson appointed her to the Home Economics Research Advisory Committee in 1955. She was also a Republican county chair and a delegate to national party conventions. In 1971 and 1972, Smith chaired the Presidential Task Force on Rural Development, and from 1972 to 1974 she served on an advisory board for the Department of Health, Education, and Welfare.

Smith's success in her 1974 candidacy for the U.S. House of Representatives was notable because it was the first public office she sought, but more notably it was the year in which President Richard Nixon resigned in the wake of the Watergate scandal, and few Republicans won their races. Smith's interests in Congress reflected her agricultural and rural background and that of her district. She worked on water development programs that were important to wheat growers in her area. She fought for one program for more than a decade but lost to environmentalists and spending cuts during the Reagan administration. She obtained funding for agricultural research centers in Nebraska and kept rural post offices and rural weather stations open in Nebraska when comparable facilities were closed around the country. In addition, she defended and preserved appropriations for the Rural Electrification Administration, an important source of inexpensive electricity for rural residents. She also worked to protect the interests of cattle and wheat producers and supported farm exports.

Born near Randolph, Iowa, Virginia Smith attended Missouri State Teachers College for two years before transferring to the University of Nebraska at Lincoln in 1929. Unable to afford to complete her undergraduate studies at the time, she completed her bachelor's degree in education at the University of Nebraska in 1936.

See also Congress, Women in

References Congressional Quarterly, *Politics in America 1984* (1983); Süllwold, "Nebraska's Virginia" (1993).

Snowe, Olympia Jean Bouchles (b. 1947)

The first Greek American woman elected to Congress, Republican Olympia Snowe of Maine served in the U.S. House of Representatives from 3 January 1979 to 3 January 1995, and she entered the U.S. Senate on 4 January 1995. She held the leadership position of vice chair of the Senate Republican Conference in the 105th and 106th Congresses (1997–2001).

Snowe entered politics while still in college, working as a summer intern for a Democratic governor. After changing her party registration in the late 1960s, she joined the district staff of a Republican member of Congress in 1972. Following the death of her first husband, a state representative, she won the election to fill the vacancy in 1973. She served in the Maine House of Representatives until 1977 and then served in the Maine Senate from 1977 to 1979. While in the state Senate, she became known for her work on health care legislation.

In the U.S. House of Representatives, Snowe worked to change the federal funding formula to give less populous states, like Maine, a larger portion of federal grants. Particularly concerned with energy assistance to low-income families and energy conservation, she successfully fought for the restoration of some of these funds in 1981 and 1982. She also succeeded in pushing for duty-free transportation of steam energy across the Canadian border, supporting it as a form of alternative energy.

Cochair of the Congressional Caucus for Women's Issues, Snowe helped develop the Economic Equity Act and helped pass portions of it. She supports federal funding for family planning and reproductive rights and has worked for employer tax credits for child care. She has sought funding for a local Job Corps center and attempted to keep the Portsmouth Naval Shipyard in Maine open.

Born in Augusta, Maine, Olympia Snowe was the daughter of Greek immigrants. When she was eight years old, her mother died, and then her father died the next year. An aunt and uncle raised her. Snowe earned her bachelor of arts degree from the University of Maine in 1969.

See also Abortion; Child Day Care; Congress, Women in; Congressional Caucus for Women's Issues; Economic Equity Act; State Legislatures, Women in

References www.senate.gov/~snowe/bio.htm.

Social Security

Enacted in 1935, the Social Security Act created a federal old-age assistance program for retired workers and a federal and state program of unemployment insurance, among other programs. Since its creation, Social Security has been amended several times, with some programs moved to other agencies and other programs added to it. These amendments created the Medicare and Medicaid programs and established assistance programs for disabled people and children of disabled or deceased people. The creation of Medicare in 1965, providing for the medical needs of persons ages sixty-five and older, was one of the more important additions to the program. Social Security is financed by employees who pay 7.65 percent of their earnings to the fund, an amount that employers match, and by self-employed people who pay the full 15.3 percent.

For about two-thirds of the nation's elderly population, Social Security provides 50 percent or more of their retirement income. Of the 44 million people receiving Social Security, almost 60 percent are women; the program provides about 90 percent of elderly women's income. This assistance is especially important to women because only 38 percent of women receive pension benefits provided by their employers, whereas 57 percent of men receive them. Between 1965 and 1996, Social Security reduced the percentage of elderly people living below the poverty level from 35.2 percent to 10.8 percent.

Social Security programs also benefit younger Americans. The Social Security Supplemental Income (SSI) program contributes to the support of 3 million children and their sole-caretaker parents. Four million disabled workers under the age of sixty-five and their 1.6 million dependents receive benefits.

References www.ssa.gov; www.now.org.

Socialism

In the last decades of the nineteenth century and the early decades of the twentieth century, socialism appealed to people living with the harshness of factory labor, poverty, and hunger. Women activists like Ella Reeve

Bloor, Dorothy Day, Elizabeth Gurley Flynn, Emma Goldman, and Kate Richards O'Hare believed that capitalism had enslaved the American laborer and that a Socialist economic system would end the inequities inherent in capitalism. Each of these women as well as others sought to unify laborers through unions or other organizations and use the resulting power to end the abuses of capitalism.

The contemporary meaning of socialism is based upon the writings of Karl Marx, who theorized that history is determined by economic systems. The economic systems dictate society's political, social, and intellectual life. Marx argued that the exploitation of the working class in capitalist society would result in revolution and predicted that a classless society based on communism would replace capitalism. Regarding history through the perspective of class struggle, socialism rejects the primacy of private property and advocates making it into public property and distributing the wealth throughout the population.

In the United States, the Industrial Workers of the World (IWW), formed in 1905, sought to organize industrial employees into one all-encompassing union that would lead a mass strike and end capitalism. The IWW participated in numerous strikes across the country, provided leadership during the strikes, and organized workers. In the 1910s, Socialist Party candidates won over 1,000 local elections, including dozens of mayors. When Eugene V. Debs ran on the Socialist ticket for president in 1912, he received 6 percent of the vote, the greatest strength the party had demonstrated.

When the United States entered World War I, Socialists became the target of government harassment and attacks, including beatings, arrests, and deportations. Socialist movements gained marginal public support during the Depression years in the 1930s and again during the unrest of the 1960s.

See also Bloor, Ella Reeve Ware Cohen Omholt; Communist Party, USA; Day, Dorothy; Flynn, Elizabeth Gurley; Goldman, Emma; O'Hare, Kathleen Richards

Spellman, Gladys Blossom Noon (1918–1988)

Democrat Gladys Spellman of Maryland served in the U.S. House of Representatives from 3 January 1975 to 24 February 1981. Spellman began her political career as a member of the Prince George's County Board of County Commissioners from 1961 to 1975. The first woman member elected to the commission, she was also the first woman elected president of the National Association of Counties. As a member of Congress, Spellman worked to protect the interests of federal employees and supported cost-of-living increases for military retirees. She proposed a measure to provide support for pregnant teens through life support centers.

Spellman suffered a heart attack on 31 October 1980 while she was campaigning for another term in the House of Representatives. She won the election but was in a semiconscious state. On 24 February 1981, the House declared her seat vacant because she was unable to discharge the duties of her office. Her husband entered the race to fill the vacancy but did not win the election.

Born in New York, New York, Spellman attended George Washington University and the graduate school of the U.S. Department of Agriculture. She was a public schoolteacher.

See also Congress, Women in; Congressional Caucus for Women's Issues

References Lamson, *In the Vanguard: Six American Women in Public Life* (1979); Office of the Historian, U.S. House of Representatives, *Women in Congress, 1917–1990* (1991).

Spider Web

An attempt to discredit feminists, the spider web chart was assembled in 1923 by a secretary working in the War Department to demonstrate that women activists had created a network to disarm the United States and promote a Bolshevik takeover of the country. The alleged network included members of the boards of directors of the Women's Trade Union League, the League of Women Voters, the American Association of University Women, the Woman's Christian Temperance Union, and other reform organizations. The spider web showed that some women served on more than one board and alleged that their service on multiple boards constituted an interlocking directorate.

Accusations that activist women had unpatriotic goals had emerged before World War I, when suffragists were accused of being Socialists. During the war, suffrage opponents argued that the suffrage effort was a German plot, and after Bolsheviks took over Russia, opponents labeled suffrage a Bolshevik strategy. The Woman Patriots, formerly the National Association Opposed to Woman Suffrage, linked the Sheppard-Towner Maternity and Infancy Protection Act of 1921 to Bolshevism and argued in a 1922 pamphlet that the Women's Bureau and its allies were trying to Bolshevize the United States by destroying the family.

After the spider web chart appeared in 1923, the Women's Joint Congressional Committee responded to the allegations, the charts were destroyed, and an apology was given. In 1924, however, an expanded version of the chart appeared in a Dearborn, Michigan, newspaper and was accompanied by articles that were reprinted as pamphlets. The conspiracy theory that developed then argued that the proposed Child Labor Amendment was inspired by Communists, an accusation that became an important factor in the amendment's defeat. In addition, the spider web created dissent within the accused organizations, weakened them, and significantly contributed to the dissolution of the Women's Joint Congressional Committee.

See also American Association of University Women; Child Labor Amendment; League of Women Voters; Sheppard-Towner Maternity and Infancy Protection Act of 1921; Woman's Christian Temperance Union; Women's Joint Congressional Committee

References Lemons, *The Woman Citizen: Social Feminism in the 1920s* (1973).

Stabenow, Deborah Ann (b. 1950)

Democrat Debbie Stabenow of Michigan entered the U.S. House of Representatives on 3 January 1997. A leadership training consultant, Stabenow was an Ingham County commissioner from 1975 to 1978 and the commission's chair from 1977 to 1978. She served in the Michigan House of Representatives from 1979 to 1991 and the state Senate from 1991 to 1995. In the legislature, Stabenow worked on child abuse prevention, mental health care, and domestic violence. Her work on state school financing reduced property taxes for Michigan's residents and gained her statewide recognition. She sought the Democratic Party's nomination for governor in 1994 and was the party's unsuccessful candidate for lieutenant governor that year.

Congresswoman Stabenow cosponsored the Computer Donation Incentive Act that provides enhanced tax deductions to businesses that donate computer equipment to schools or tax-exempt charitable organizations. The measure passed as part of a 1997 tax bill. Her priorities include connecting schools to the Internet, training teachers to use computers, tax relief for older citizens, and health insurance for children of low-income families.

Born in Clare, Michigan, Debbie Stabenow received her bachelor of arts degree in 1972 and her master of social work degree in 1975 from Michigan State University.

See also Congress, Women in; State Legislatures, Women in

References Congressional Quarterly, *Politics in America 1998* (1997); www.house.gov/stabenow/about.

Stalking

The first federal law making it a crime to cross state lines to stalk, that is, to follow a person with the intention of harming or harassing that person, was passed in 1994. Senator Kay Bailey Hutchison amended the law in 1996 to address situations in which the victim and the stalker are not related and to make restraining orders issued in any state valid in all states.

Hutchison explained: "For years, women have been threatened and harassed by stalkers who could not be stopped because there was no prosecutable crime. Most states have stalking laws, but until now, stalkers could not be charged if they went to another state."

See also Hutchison, Kathryn (Kay) Ann Bailey; Violence Against Women Act of 1994

References *Congressional Quarterly Almanac, 104th Congress, 2nd Session . . . 1996* (1997).

Stanley, Winifred Claire (1909–1996)

Republican Winifred Stanley of New York served in the U.S. House of Representatives from 3 January 1943 to 3 January 1945. When Stanley accepted the Republican nomination for Congress, she did it with the understanding that it would be for only one term. New York Republican Party leaders wanted to eliminate the party's two at-large seats and sought candidates willing to retire after one term. Stanley campaigned for Congress on a twelve-point program for winning World War II. She believed that Washington dignitaries should make the same sacrifices for the war as the rest of the nation, and she pledged to seek further protection against sabotage. Congresswoman Stanley proposed a measure for equal pay for equal work and an Equal Rights Amendment.

Following her term in Congress, Stanley served as chief counsel of the New York State Employees' Retirement System from 1945 to 1955. She was assistant attorney general with the New York State Law Department from 1955 to 1979, when she went into private law practice. She retired in 1986.

Born in the Bronx, New York, Winifred Stanley received her bachelor of arts degree in 1930 and her law degree in 1933, both from the University of Buffalo. She worked for a private law firm until 1938, when she became an assistant district attorney in Erie County, New York, serving there until 1943.

See also Congress, Women in

References H. W. Wilson, *Current Biography: Who's News and Why, 1943* (1943); Office of the Historian, U.S. House of Representatives, *Women in Congress, 1917–1990* (1991).

Stanton, Elizabeth Cady (1815–1902)

Elizabeth Cady Stanton was one of the primary organizers of the 1848 Seneca Falls Convention, an early proponent of woman suffrage, and among the foremost leaders of the nineteenth-century women's rights movement. With her friend Susan B. Anthony, Stanton launched the

Elizabeth Cady Stanton (center) with the International Council of Women Executive Committee, 1888 (Library of Congress)

National Woman Suffrage Association in 1869 and through it campaigned across the nation for various state ballot measures for woman suffrage.

Born in Johnston, New York, Stanton graduated from the community's academy in 1830 and wanted to attend college, but no college in the nation admitted women. In 1831, she entered Troy Female Seminary, a school that sought to provide a classical and scientific curriculum to women. After graduating two years later, Stanton returned to her family's home in Johnston.

Stanton married abolitionist agent Henry Stanton 1840, and twelve days after their wedding the couple left for the World Anti-Slavery Convention in London. Henry Stanton was a delegate to the convention, and Elizabeth Cady Stanton attended as an observer. Two American female antislavery societies also sent delegates, among them Lucretia Mott. When the convention opened, some male delegates protested seating the female delegates, leading to an extended debate and the convention's refusal to seat the women on the convention floor. Instead, they were relegated to a balcony with other women, among them Elizabeth Stanton.

After spending hours together, Stanton and Mott, a Quaker minister, abolitionist, and feminist, became friends. They discussed women's status and resolved to hold a women's convention as soon as they returned to the United States. Eight years later, the Stantons lived in Seneca Falls, New York, and when Lucretia Mott visited a nearby town, the two women renewed their friendship and finally planned a women's rights convention for the following week. Stanton and Mott drafted the *Declaration of Rights and Sentiments,* based upon the Declaration of Independence, to present to the attendees. As the convention date approached, Stanton questioned whether anyone would attend a meeting on women's civil, social, and religious status, but on the day of the convention, the sight of women and men making their way to the meeting place reassured her. Because it was considered unseemly for women even to speak in public, Lucretia Mott's husband, James Mott, presided over the convention, held on 19 and 20 July 1848. The declaration created only minimal controversy until the point on woman suffrage was presented. After some debate, it was also accepted. Sixty-eight women and thirty-two men signed the declaration.

The convention placed Stanton in the vanguard of the women's rights movement, even though she essentially remained a housewife in a small town. She did not attend another women's rights convention until 1860. She did, however, begin writing for Amelia Bloomer's *The Lily,* a reform publication; and in 1851, she began wearing the shorter skirt over pants that Bloomer advocated, although she later abandoned it because of the controversy it created.

A partnership that lasted more than fifty years began in 1851, when Susan B. Anthony attended an antislavery meeting in Seneca Falls and met Stanton. A single woman who never married, Anthony had the freedom to travel that Stanton, with her growing family and household, did not have. As their partnership in the women's rights movement developed, Stanton provided ideas, rhetoric, and strategies, and Anthony delivered the speeches, circulated petitions, and organized women's rights groups.

Of the reforms Stanton advocated, one of the most controversial appeared in the 1850s and was a continuing theme: the need to make divorce an option to married women. She believed married women needed to be able to protect themselves by divorcing their husbands because husbands legally owned their wives, their children, and even their wives' clothing. In February 1854, Stanton addressed the New York legislature on the subject. She concluded by saying:

> Now, do you candidly think these wives do not wish to control the wages they earn—to own the land they buy—the houses they build? to have at their disposal their own children, without being subject to the constant interference and tyranny of an idle, worthless, profligate? Do you suppose that any woman is such a pattern of devotion and submission that she willingly stitches all day for the small sum of fifty cents, that she may enjoy the unspeakable privilege, in obedience to your laws, of paying for her husband's tobacco and rum? Think you the wife of the confirmed, beastly drunkard would consent to share with him her home and bed, if law and public sentiment would release her from such gross companionship? Verily, no!

During the Civil War, work on women's rights became secondary to efforts supporting emancipation and the war effort. Stanton believed that if women supported the Civil War, they would be granted equal citizenship and equal suffrage as rewards for their patriotism. Stanton spoke and wrote for emancipation and with Anthony formed the Woman's National Loyal League, which collected 400,000 signatures on petitions supporting the Thirteenth Amendment. In 1865, when the Fourteenth Amendment was drafted using the word *male* to define citizens and legal voters, Stanton was outraged and felt betrayed by the abolitionists with whom she had worked and who supported the amendment. She demanded that women as well as former male slaves gain voting rights, but reformers insisted it was "the Negro's hour" and rejected her pleas.

Feeling abandoned by the Republicans who had supported woman suffrage along with emancipation of the slaves, Stanton accepted the help of two people who brought controversy and scorn to her. George Train, a racist Democrat who opposed suffrage for African Americans, was the first. Stanton met him while campaigning for woman suffrage in Kansas in 1867 and accepted his offer to finance a woman's rights publication that they named *The Revolution*. Stanton edited and wrote it, and Anthony managed it. After the first issue, Train left for London and provided no further financial assistance. The other person was Victoria Woodhull, whose presidential candidacy and free love advocacy, arguing that women should have unqualified control over their own reproductive and sexual lives, also created controversies that haunted the women's rights movement for several years.

In 1869, Stanton and Anthony formed the National Woman Suffrage Association (NWSA), with Stanton as president and Anthony as vice president. Their decision formalized the break between them and many abolitionists and women's rights supporters. NWSA supported a woman suffrage amendment, opposed the Fifteenth Amendment unless woman suffrage was included, and did not permit male members. NWSA's agenda included a broad range of women's rights issues, including divorce. The same year, Lucy Stone organized the American Woman Suffrage Association (AWSA), a group that advocated a state-by-state approach to gain woman suffrage and did not endorse any other issue. The two groups battled for members and for financial support for more than twenty years.

With her children older and less dependent upon her, Stanton expanded her work to include speaking on the lyceum tour from 1871 to 1880. She wrote the first volumes of *The History of Woman Suffrage* with Anthony and Matilda Joslyn Gage; the first volume was published in 1881 and the second the next year. When the NWSA and AWSA merged in 1890, Stanton was elected president of the newly formed National American Woman Suffrage Association (NAWSA). She served one term and refused to serve a second.

Stanton created the greatest controversy of her career in 1895, when *The Woman's Bible* was published. In it, Stanton attacked the use of Scripture to justify maintaining women's secondary status and questioned the Bible's authority, which some considered a heretical stance. When NAWSA met in 1896, the convention censured Stanton and distanced itself from her.

Stanton continued to write and publish about woman suffrage, religion, divorce, and related topics the rest of her life. She died before passage of the Nineteenth Amendment in 1920.

> **See also** American Woman Suffrage Association; Anthony, Susan Brownell; Coverture; Fourteenth Amendment; Gage, Matilda Joslyn; Mott, Lucretia Coffin; National American Woman Suffrage Association; National Woman Suffrage Association; Nineteenth Amendment; Seneca Falls Convention; Stone, Lucy; Suffrage; Woodhull, Victoria Claflin
>
> **References** Dubois, *Woman Suffrage and Women's Rights* (1998); Griffith, *In Her Own Right: The Life of Elizabeth Cady Stanton* (1984); Ravitch, ed., *The American Reader* (1990).

State Legislatures, Women in

More than 6,000 women have served in American territorial and state legislatures. Colorado was the first state to elect women to a state legislature in the United States. In 1893, Colorado passed a referendum granting women voting rights, and the next year, the Democratic, Republican, and Prohibitionist Parties each nominated three women for the legislature in an effort to gain the favor of the newly enfranchised women. Three Republican women, Carrie Clyde Holling, Frances S. Klock, and Clara Clessingham, won their races to serve in the Colorado House of Representatives. When Holling gained passage of a bill to raise the age of consent for girls from sixteen to eighteen, she became the first woman in American history to pass a bill in an American legislative body. None of the women ran for a second term, but other women followed them. The first woman to serve in a state Senate was Martha Hughes Cannon, a Democrat, of Salt Lake City, Utah, who served from 1897 to 1901.

The first eleven states that elected women to their legislatures were all west of the Mississippi River. In 1919, New York became the first state east of it to have women in its legislature. The year after women gained suffrage rights through the Nineteenth Amendment in 1920, women began serving in nine additional state legislatures, among them New Hampshire. The attorney general of New Hampshire had stated that under common law, women could not hold public office, but the two women elected to the New Hampshire legislature that year were permitted to take their seats.

Louisiana was the last state of the forty-eight states that were in the Union in 1920 to have women in its legislature. Democrat Doris Lindsey Holland succeeded her deceased husband in 1936 and then won a full term.

Women began serving in the territorial legislatures of Hawaii and Alaska in 1925 and 1937, respectively. In 1959, when Alaska and Hawaii became states, both had women in their legislative bodies. For other U.S. territories the dates are as follows: Puerto Rico, 1933; Guam, 1947; American Samoa, 1953; Virgin Islands, 1953; and the Northern Mariana Islands, 1979.

In 1991, for the first time in American history, women served in every state legislature in the nation. In 1993, every state except Nebraska, which is unicameral, had at least one woman in the House and at least one woman in the Senate.

The first African American woman to serve in a state legislature was Republican Minnie Buckingham Harper, who was appointed to the West Virginia legislature in 1929. She succeeded her deceased husband. The first African American woman elected to a state legislature was Crystal Dreda Bird Fauset, who entered the Pennsylvania legislature in 1938. The first Asian American woman to serve was Democrat Patsy Takemoto Mink, who served in Hawaii's Territorial House of Representatives in 1957, Territorial Senate in 1959, and the Hawaii state Senate from 1963 to 1964. The first Hispanic American women, Republican Fedelina Lucero Gallegos and Democrat Porfirria Hidalgo Saiz, entered the New Mexico House of Representatives in 1931. The first Native American woman to serve in a state legislature, Republican Cora Belle Reynolds Anderson, a La Pointe Band Chippewa, was a member of the Michigan House of Representatives from 1925 to 1926.

From the time women entered legislative service, they have served in leadership positions, some of which are listed below:

- Caucus secretary: Republican Clara Clessingham, Colorado, 1895

- Caucus chair: Populist Mary A. Wright, Idaho, 1899

- Majority leader: Democrat Reva Beck Bosone, Utah, 1935

- Majority whip: Democrat Concha De Ortiz y Pino, New Mexico, 1941

- Speaker: Non Partisan League member Minnie D. Craig, North Dakota, 1933

- Senate president pro tempore: Democrat Louise Holland Coe, New Mexico, 1931

- Senate president: Republican Consuelo Northrop Bailey, Vermont, 1955

Between 1895 and 1921, the number of women serving in state legislatures was uneven, declining to no women in 1905 and 1907, until 1923, when small increases became a weak pattern. In the years from 1923 to 1971, growth was steady but again slow. It was not until 1971 that women made up 4.5 percent of all legislatures. Significant growth in the number of women in state legislatures appeared in the mid-1970s, suggesting that the modern feminist movement influenced the number of women running for and winning seats.

Even with the growth, however, only 22.3 percent of all state legislators (1,652 female state legislators out of 7,424 total state legislators) were women in 1999, more than seventy-five years after women gained suffrage rights. In 1999, the state of Washington had the highest percentage of women (40.8 percent) in its legislature, followed by Nevada with 36.5 percent and Arizona with 35.6 percent. Alabama had the lowest percentage of women, with 7.9 percent; Oklahoma had the next lowest percentage, with 10.1 percent; and Kentucky had 11.6 percent. In 1999, Arkansas's state Senate was the only legislative body that had no women serving in it. Of the women serving in state legislatures in 1999, African American women held 166 seats, Asian American/Pacific Islander women held seventeen seats, Latinas held forty-eight, and Native American women held eleven.

The significance of women serving in state legislatures rests in the additional perspectives that women bring to decisionmaking and the differences in priorities between women and men, regardless of party affiliation. For example, women's top-priority bills more frequently deal with health and welfare issues than men's top-priority bills. Women tend to develop expertise in the areas of health and welfare, whereas men tend to develop expertise in fiscal matters. In addition, the higher the proportion of women legislators, the more likely that women's priority bills will deal with women, children, and families and the more likely that they will win passage. Women legislators have worked for and won changes in rape legislation and social welfare, child care, family violence, divorce, and education policies. Women have also offered and advocated changes in other areas, including tax policy, the environment, economic development, transportation, and agriculture. By adding to the pool of ideas and knowledge, women alter the legislative agenda and expand the options for solving identified problems and for initiating legislative action.

In addition, state legislatures often provide the base from which both female and male candidates for higher office begin their political careers. For example, of the fifty-six women serving in the 106th Congress (1999–2001), twenty-nine had first served in state legislatures.

See also Bosone, Reva Zilpha Beck; Fauset, Crystal Dreda Bird; Mink, Patsy Matsu Takemoto

References Center for the American Woman and Politics, National Information Bank on Women in Public Office, Eagleton Institute of Politics, Rutgers University; Cox, *Women State and Territorial Legislators, 1895–1995* (1996); Thomas, *How Women Legislate* (1994).

Steinem, Gloria Marie (b. 1934)

Feminist, journalist, author, and founder of *Ms.* magazine Gloria Steinem's involvement in feminist activities began in the early 1960s. A dynamic speaker, Steinem quickly emerged as a media celebrity and a leading publicist for feminism. She has argued that sexism and racism are related caste systems and that heterosexism is a form of patriarchy, and she has sought unity with African Americans and lesbians.

One of the ironies of Steinem's ascendancy as a feminist leader involves her physical attractiveness. At a time when women were demanding to be judged on their abilities, intelligence, and skills and not on their physical appearance, Steinem's physical appeal provided reassurance to some women that feminists can be attractive and enjoy the company of men, in addition to having power. This combination of power and sexuality threatened some men while giving her access to other male decision-makers. A late arrival to the feminist movement, Steinem became an instant celebrity within it and in the media.

Born in Toledo, Ohio, Gloria Steinem graduated from Smith College in 1956 after spending her junior year in Geneva, Switzerland, and a summer at Oxford University in England. She went to India on a fellowship for almost two years beginning in 1957. While there, she traveled throughout the country, wrote travel pamphlets and other material, and studied Mahatma Gandhi's strategies of nonviolence. Gandhi's teachings influenced the rest of Steinem's life, including her later involvement with Dolores Huerta's, Cesar Chavez's, and the United Farm Workers' organizational campaigns. She returned to the United States in 1958 and began looking for work in New York but was unsuccessful.

Steinem moved to Cambridge, Massachusetts, in 1959 to direct a nonprofit educational foundation that encouraged American youth to attend International Communist Youth Festivals in an attempt to counter Communist influence. Steinem did not know that the foundation was partially funded by the Central Intelligence Agency, but in the 1970s the connection was the basis for an attack on Steinem by radical feminists.

In the early 1960s, Steinem was a freelance journalist, writing for *Esquire, Glamour, Vogue, Ladies' Home Journal, New York Times Magazine,* and other publications. In 1963, she went underground and applied for a job as a Playboy bunny. She held the job long enough to write an article about the experience. Published in *Show* magazine, the article made her an instant celebrity. In it she exposed the poor working conditions and low wages paid women at the Playboy Club. In 1968, she was a founding editor of *New York* magazine and became one of the country's first female political commentators. During the late 1960s, Steinem also began her career as a political activist when she became involved with Democratic Party politics and worked with Dolores Huerta and Cesar Chavez for United Farm Workers and their table grape boycott.

Gloria Steinem, founder of Ms. *magazine, whose name became synonymous with the "second wave" of feminism (Courtesy:* Ms. *magazine)*

While covering a 1969 abortion hearing organized by Redstockings leader Kathie Sarachild in New York, Steinem became aware of her feminist beliefs, describing the event as "the great blinding light bulb" that led to her identifying herself as a feminist. Speaking on behalf of feminism became her next goal, but she was terrified of public speaking and recruited a partner. In 1970, Steinem and African American activist Dorothy Pitman Hughes began addressing groups on the topics of women's rights and civil rights. Later, one of the people with whom Steinem spoke and traveled was Florynce Kennedy. During a cab ride, the two women were discussing abortion, when the driver said: "Honey, if men could get pregnant, abortion would be a sacrament," a quote that Steinem and Kennedy often used and one that became part of the movement's most effective consciousness-raising tools.

In 1971, Steinem joined several veteran feminists to found the National Women's Political Caucus (NWPC), one of her earlier cooperative efforts with some of the established leaders of the feminist movement. Steinem's response to Congresswoman Bella Abzug, another NWPC founding member, provides an indication of Steinem's development as a feminist at the time. She found Abzug's style too loud and too brash, until Steinem came to realize that she was using a patriarchal definition of appropriate behavior for women. As Steinem's feminism matured, she admired Abzug for her courage and strength and worked on her subsequent campaigns.

In 1971, Steinem and Brenda Feigen founded the Women's Action Alliance to help women overcome the barriers they encountered at the local level, including marital abuse and desertion, sexist textbooks, and lack of job opportunities. Enthusiasm for the alliance led to the idea of a newsletter, which Feigen argued should be in a magazine format. *Ms.* magazine evolved from these discussions.

A sample issue of *Ms.* appeared in the 1971 year-end edition of *New York* magazine, and a preview issue was published in the spring of 1972, selling out in eight days despite the skepticism of publishing industry experts. The first regular issue appeared in mid-1972. Steinem brought together a talented staff, including publisher Pat Carbine. Carbine and Steinem attempted to avoid creating a hierarchy in the magazine's organization, but Steinem was and remained the publication's dominant figure, even though she was regularly absent lecturing and raising money to keep it going. Steinem planned to shepherd *Ms.* for a few years and then move to other projects, but its ongoing financial instability kept Steinem at its head for fifteen years.

With high hopes for the magazine's success, Steinem created the Ms. Foundation for Women in 1972 to be the beneficiary of its profits. Steinem believed the foundation would fill a philanthropic gap because at the time there were no foundations that gave money to women as a group or a category. The magazine did not enjoy the financial success that Steinem had hoped for, but the foundation developed its own resources and by the late 1990s had an annual budget of $6.2 million and an endowment fund of $10 million.

After the Equal Rights Amendment passed Congress in 1972 and went to the states for ratification, Steinem joined other feminists in traveling the country to develop support for it. Also that year, at the Democratic National Convention, the NWPC chose Steinem for its spokeswoman. Steinem gained further attention at the convention when she and Fannie Lou Hamer nominated Frances "Sissy" Farenthold for vice president of the United States, but Farenthold did not succeed.

Through her work and *Ms.* magazine, Steinem developed a loyal constituency of feminists, but others criticized her. Feminist author Betty Friedan, who had helped launch the modern feminist movement with the publication of *The Feminine Mystique* in 1963, viewed Steinem as a competitor for the leadership of the movement and worked to undermine and discredit her. The two women disagreed on the issues, particularly the movement's responsibility to lesbians. Friedan regarded lesbians as a menace, but Steinem believed that lesbians were an important part of the feminist movement. In 1975, the Redstockings, a radical feminist group, accused Steinem of having a ten-year-long association with the Central

Intelligence Agency, referring to her foundation work in the late 1950s. The Redstockings questioned her loyalty to feminism and implied that she might be an informant. The group also questioned the motives of the Women's Action Alliance and asserted that *Ms.* magazine hurt the feminist movement because it was inadequately radical. The allegations did not have merit, but they did reveal some of the fragmentation within the feminist movement.

In 1977, President Jimmy Carter appointed Steinem to the National Commission on the Observation of the International Women's Year, 1975. The next year, she was a Woodrow Wilson Fellow at the Smithsonian Institution. In 1979, Steinem was a founder of Voters for Choice, an independent political committee organized to support prochoice congressional candidates.

Steinem continued her work with *Ms.* magazine, writing for it and raising money to keep it in business. The readership was stable, but costs had escalated, and the advertising revenue had been a constant disappointment. After she discovered that she had breast cancer in 1986, Steinem felt the need to have fewer responsibilities and wanted the freedom to write. When the opportunity to sell *Ms.* appeared in 1987, she took it and sold the magazine to an Australian communications conglomerate. Steinem remained as a consultant for five years.

Steinem has written *Outrageous Acts and Everyday Rebellions* (1983); *Marilyn,* a biography of Marilyn Monroe (1986); *Revolution from Within: A Book of Self-Esteem* (1992); and *Moving beyond Words* (1994).

> **See also** Abzug, Bella Savitzky; Equal Rights Amendment; *The Feminine Mystique;* Feminist Movement; Friedan, Betty Naomi Goldstein; Huerta, Dolores; Kennedy, Florynce Rae; Ms. Foundation for Women; *Ms.* Magazine; National Women's Political Caucus; Redstockings
>
> **References** H. W. Wilson, ed., *Current Biography Yearbook, 1988* (1988); Heilbrun, *The Education of a Woman* (1996).

Stewart, Maria W. (1803–1879)

The first woman in the United States to stand on a lecture platform and raise a political issue before an audience of women and men, African American Maria Stewart spoke against a plan to repatriate black Americans to Africa during her lecture on 21 September 1832 in Boston, Massachusetts. An abolitionist and women's rights champion, Stewart urged blacks to demand their human rights from their oppressors and called on women to develop their intellects and participate in the community. According to Stewart, a religious conversion experience had made her a "warrior" obedient to God's will, leading her to protest tyranny, victimization, injustice, and political and economic injustice. In four years, from

1831 to 1835, she wrote the first political manifesto by a black woman, wrote a collection of religious meditations, delivered four public lectures, and compiled her work into a volume of collected works.

Born in Hartford, Connecticut, Stewart was a household servant during her young adolescence and a domestic servant from the time she was fifteen until she married in 1826. Widowed in 1829, she underwent a religious experience that led to her brief public life. She moved to New York in 1834 and taught school there as well as in Baltimore and the District of Columbia. After the Civil War, Stewart was matron of the Freedmen's Hospital.

See also Abolitionist Movement, Women in the; Public Speaking

References Richardson, ed., *Maria W. Stewart, America's First Black Woman Political Writer: Essays and Speeches* (1987).

Stone, Lucy (1818–1893)

Abolitionist lecturer and suffrage leader Lucy Stone and her husband Henry Blackwell founded the American Woman Suffrage Association (AWSA) in 1869. Stone gained notoriety for retaining her family name after her marriage, and other women who did the same became known as Lucy Stoners.

Born near Brookfield, Massachusetts, Stone yearned for a formal education, for which her father refused her financial assistance. She began teaching when she was sixteen years old, saving her earnings to attend academies and seminaries that would prepare her for a college education. When she entered Oberlin College in 1843, Stone believed that women should vote and run for office, study the professions, and become public speakers for reform causes, philosophies that Oberlin College did not share. Chosen to prepare a graduation essay during her senior year, Stone objected to the college's traditions that permitted male students to read their essays in public but prohibited women from reading theirs, instead having professors present the women's essays. Stone refused to have a professor read her work, and it was not presented. She received her bachelor of arts degree from Oberlin College in 1847, the same year she made her first public speech on women's rights.

After graduating, Stone became an agent for the American Anti-Slavery Society and an independent women's rights lecturer. An accomplished orator, she attracted audiences as large as 3,000 people. Her public speeches also created controversy because it was considered scandalous for a woman to speak before audiences of men and women. The hostility she evoked appeared when people tore down posters announcing her speeches, burned pepper in the audience while she spoke, and threw prayer books and other items at her. At other times, angry mobs prevented her from speaking.

In 1850, Stone and other suffragists called a national convention on women's rights in Worcester, Massachusetts, which more than 1,000 people attended. In her speeches on women's rights, Stone discarded the notion of "separate spheres" and called for women to define their spheres of work and influence. With equal educational opportunities, she argued, women would find their appropriate sphere. Stone criticized the church, which she believed was committed to the continued subjugation of women, and her outspokenness contributed to her being expelled from the Congregational Church.

Lucy Stone, well-known abolitionist and suffragist, founded the American Woman Suffrage Association in 1869 (Library of Congress)

Stone also attacked the concept of women losing their personhood in marriage under the laws of coverture. In her lectures, she condemned marriage as little better than chattel slavery for women, but she reserved her greatest criticism for the economic relationship between a woman and a man that marriage laws defined. With other activists of the time, she worked for revisions in married women's property laws that would give women power over their property and earnings. Stone also believed that women should be able to control the number and spacing of their children through male restraint and that women should be able to refuse sex with their husbands. In cases of drunkenness or loveless marriages, she believed that divorce needed to be an option.

Despite her strong views against marriage, Stone married Henry Blackwell in 1855, after years of persistence on Blackwell's part. An abolitionist and feminist, Blackwell shared Stone's views, including her refusal to take his name. During their wedding ceremony, they publicly declared their distaste for the unjust marriage laws of the period, including their objections to laws giving a husband control of his wife's person, of their children, and of her property and earnings and the loss of the wife's legal existence.

Stone continued to lecture until the birth of their daughter in 1857, when she found it difficult to maintain her career and raise a child. After the Civil War, she returned to suffrage work, especially focusing on efforts to remove the word *male* from the proposed Fourteenth Amendment, but she was unsuccessful. In 1867, Stone and Blackwell went to

Kansas to campaign for the state's proposed amendments to grant African Americans and women suffrage rights. Upon her return to New York, she learned that Susan B. Anthony, who was also campaigning in Kansas, had used Stone's name in connection with lectures that Anthony and George Train were giving. Stone and many other abolitionists viewed Train, a racist Democrat, with disdain and saw him as a threat to their work because although he supported woman suffrage, he opposed suffrage for African Americans. When both amendments failed, Stone held Train accountable for the losses. She also publicly distanced herself from Anthony and Elizabeth Cady Stanton, who had also aligned herself with Train.

The schism in the woman suffrage movement was formalized in 1869 when Anthony and Stanton formed the National Woman Suffrage Association (NWSA), and in response Stone organized the AWSA. The next year, Stone and Blackwell began publishing *The Woman's Journal*, which existed for forty-seven years. In the mid-1870s, with the suffrage movement needing new energy, Stone organized local suffrage clubs, which supported both federal and state constitutional amendments.

In 1887, Stone presented a resolution to the AWSA convention to negotiate a merger with the NWSA, and in 1890, the first National American Woman Suffrage Association meeting was held. Stone, too ill to attend, was elected chair of the executive committee. She died three years later.

See also American Woman Suffrage Association; Anthony, Susan Brownell; Coverture; Fourteenth Amendment; Married Women's Property Acts; National American Woman Suffrage Association; National Woman Suffrage Association; Separate Spheres; Stanton, Elizabeth Cady; Suffrage

References Kerr, *Lucy Stone: Speaking Out for Equality* (1992); Matthews, *Women's Struggle for Equality* (1997); Ravitch, ed., *The American Reader* (1990); Spender, *Feminist Theorists* (1983).

Stop ERA

Founded by Phyllis Schlafly in 1972, Stop ERA worked to defeat state and federal Equal Rights Amendments. During the campaign for ratification of the federal Equal Rights Amendment, members effectively lobbied state legislators to vote against ratification. Through its strong grassroots network, members used the media in innovative ways; for example, they gave legislators loaves of bread with notes saying: "I was bred to be a lady and like it that way." Following defeat of the Equal Rights Amendment in 1982, Stop ERA disbanded.

See also Eagle Forum; Equal Rights Amendment; Schlafly, Phyllis Stewart

Stowe, Harriet Elizabeth Beecher (1811–1896)

Considered a profoundly political writer, Harriet Beecher Stowe wrote the 1852 novel *Uncle Tom's Cabin,* which deepened antislavery sentiment in the North. Serialized in a magazine beginning in June 1851 and continuing through March 1852, *Uncle Tom's Cabin* exposed tens of thousands of Americans to the human horror of slavery. The characters Stowe created resonated with readers who appreciated a story and who did not read the political tracts and other antislavery material of the time.

Harriet Beecher Stowe garnered sympathy for the abolitionist cause with her novel Uncle Tom's Cabin, *which was far more political than women's literature of the day (Library of Congress)*

Passage of the 1850 Fugitive Slave Act prompted Beecher to write a series of sketches about slavery, and they evolved into *Uncle Tom's Cabin.* By writing a political and dramatic piece, Beecher moved beyond the kind of novel women generally wrote in the mid–nineteenth century. When she met President Abraham Lincoln during the Civil War, he reportedly said, "So this is the woman who started the big war."

Born in Litchfield, Connecticut, Stowe was the daughter of Presbyterian minister Lyman Beecher and the sister of Congregational clergyman Henry Ward Beecher and educator Catharine Beecher. She attended Connecticut Female Seminary in 1824.

See also Abolitionist Movement, Women in the

References Scott, *Woman against Slavery: The Story of Harriet Beecher Stowe* (1978).

Suffrage

U.S. women gained the vote in 1920 with the passage of the Nineteenth Amendment to the U.S. Constitution. The woman suffrage movement had its origins at the 1848 Seneca Falls, New York, convention for women's rights. For the next seventy-two years, women organized, petitioned, marched, and passed state referenda measures in their efforts to become fully enfranchised voters.

For a brief time, New Jersey did not have restrictions against women voting after 1776. If a person owned at least 50 pounds worth of property, had been a resident for at least one year, and was over twenty-one years of

age, the person was qualified to vote, whether male or female. Because the U.S. Constitution stipulated that anyone who could vote for the most numerous branch of state government could also vote in federal elections, it meant that women could also vote for members of Congress and the president. In 1806, New Jersey changed its constitution, and no woman in the United States could vote because New Jersey women had been the only female voters in the country. The New Jersey experience was an anomaly and did not precipitate the suffrage movement.

The suffrage movement emerged from the abolitionist movement, in which women found their actions limited and their efforts constrained. Frustrated with the social and political restraints placed upon them, some women leaders in the abolitionist movement came to believe that unless they had full citizenship rights, their ability to effectively work for the end of slavery would remain marginal.

The 1840 World Anti-Slavery Convention in London highlighted the limits of women's effectiveness for two women in particular. Lucretia Mott, a U.S. delegate to the convention, and Elizabeth Cady Stanton, who had recently married and had accompanied her husband to the convention, found themselves and other women banished from the meeting floor and relegated to a balcony. While in their forced seclusion, Mott and Stanton resolved to hold a convention on women's rights, but it took eight years for them to act on their decision. The meeting finally took place in

Seneca Falls, New York, in 1848 and concluded with acceptance of the *Declaration of Rights and Sentiments,* which included a controversial demand for woman suffrage. The idea of women voting was so radical that some of those who had voted for it during the convention soon reconsidered and asked that their names be removed as signers of the declaration. At a time when married women had virtually no civil, legal, or political rights, the demand for woman suffrage became the basis for ridicule that was intolerable for women less courageous than Stanton.

Stanton, however, persevered, even though her freedom to lecture on women's rights was limited by her responsibilities to her husband and her family, which was young and growing. Although her family responsibilities did not lessen, her effectiveness was greatly enhanced when Susan B. Anthony joined her crusade. A single woman, Anthony had become involved in the temperance movement and the abolitionist movement, lecturing and organizing on behalf of the two reforms. When the two women combined their skills, Stanton developing strategies and writing speeches and articles and Anthony organizing and occasionally delivering the speeches, they made a formidable team for woman suffrage. Of the suffrage leaders in the nineteenth century, Stanton and Anthony became the most notable.

During the years of the Civil War, the women's rights movement moved into the background as the emancipation of slaves and the abolition of slavery moved to the forefront. When Congress considered the proposed Fourteenth Amendment after the war, however, Anthony and Stanton renewed their organizational efforts and began working to change the proposal. The amendment included the word *male* in its definition of citizens, which Anthony and Stanton protested, arguing that abolitionists and suffragists had pledged to support citizenship for women and freed slaves. After Congress approved the amendment with the word *male* in it, Anthony and Stanton opposed its ratification. The two women were further outraged when Congress passed the Fifteenth Amendment guaranteeing suffrage for freed slaves and did not include women.

Republican leaders insisted that including women in either amendment would have jeopardized its passage, probably because Republicans, the party in power, knew that they could rely on the freed slaves to support them at the polls out of gratitude for ending slavery. Adding women to the voting lists, however, would have increased the numbers of Democrats as well as Republicans. Abolitionist leader Wendell Phillips and others argued that African Americans needed the protections offered by the amendments more than did women. Describing the time as "the Negro's hour," they argued that women needed to be patient and wait.

Instead, Stanton and Anthony formed the National Woman Suffrage Association (NWSA) in 1869 to work for women's rights, including woman suffrage. Suffragist Lucy Stone, who did not agree with Anthony and Stanton, responded by organizing the American Woman Suffrage Association (AWSA) the same year. The AWSA accepted the argument that African American men faced a greater and more urgent need for the guarantees of citizenship and enfranchisement. It supported state constitutional amendments for woman suffrage.

The woman suffrage amendment was first introduced in the U.S. Senate in 1868, in both chambers in 1869, and a dozen more times between 1875 and 1888. In 1887, the Senate voted on it but defeated it. Also on the federal level, in 1875 the U.S. Supreme Court decided that the Fourteenth Amendment did not apply to state laws preventing women from voting in *Minor v. Happersett.*

Women first gained voting rights in the West. In 1869, the Wyoming territorial legislature debated a bill introduced by a member who believed in women's right to vote as a part of citizenship. Without a suffrage campaign, the legislature approved the measure as well as others permitting women to serve on juries and hold public offices. Anthony responded to women's enfranchisement by encouraging women to move to the territory. When Wyoming applied for statehood, Congress considered rejecting it because members feared it would encourage woman suffrage elsewhere. The territorial legislature responded with a telegram telling Congress that it would stay out of the Union for 100 years before it would join without woman suffrage. Wyoming entered the Union as a suffrage state.

Utah's territorial legislature enfranchised women in 1870 in the hope that doing so would help preserve and protect Mormon traditions. Legislators also hoped that it would counter some of the bad publicity the territory had received about polygamy, which the Mormon church officially rejected in 1890. When Utah became a state in 1896, its constitution included voting rights for women.

In Colorado, male voters considered woman suffrage in 1877 in the first general election after statehood. Susan B. Anthony and others campaigned in mining towns, saloons, and hotel dining rooms, anyplace they could find an audience. The opposition, however, insisted that if women could vote, married women would argue with their husbands, and single women would never marry. The measure was defeated. Colorado women gained voting rights in 1893.

By 1890, the National Woman Suffrage Association and the American Woman Suffrage Association had merged into the National American Woman Suffrage Association (NAWSA), with Elizabeth Cady Stanton serving as its first president. Despite the successes in the West, the suffrage movement entered a period of stagnation between 1896 and 1910—no new states granted women suffrage, and the federal amendment was dormant in Congress.

Opposition to the amendment, however, was developing. Opponents argued that the concept of women voting threatened the sanctity of home, marriage, and family; could alter the structure of society; and defied nature. Contending that women's role was to mold children and that men's role was to protect women and children, they asserted that women had a different but equal status in the family with men. The arguments against suffrage also included racism, with antisuffragists stating that black suffrage posed dangers to society and that adding African American women as voters increased the threat. Some proposed limiting suffrage to exceptional citizens, basing the definition on race and class. Another approach expressed concern that if women were voters, they would be less involved in charitable work.

Suffrage leaders worked to invigorate the movement by experimenting with new techniques, organizing at the precinct level, and developing the support of society women with the expectation they would bring increased acceptability to it. In addition, the movement gained an organizational ally when Frances Willard became president of the Woman's Christian Temperance Union (WCTU).

In 1912, Alice Paul, who had been active in the British suffrage movement, joined NAWSA and chaired its Congressional Committee. Paul brought a more militant approach to the U.S. suffrage movement, attracted publicity to it, and raised large sums of money for it. She organized a suffrage parade in Washington, D.C., timed to coincide with President-elect Woodrow Wilson's arrival for his inauguration on 3 March 1913. Instead of greeting Wilson at the train station, the crowds that had been anticipated watched the spectacle of thousands of women marching through the capital. Later that year, Paul separated from NAWSA and formed the Congressional Union, which in 1917 became the National Woman's Party. In 1914, Paul used another strategy from her British experience: vote against the party in power to punish them for not passing the amendment. She told women living in states where they had voting rights to vote against Democrats, regardless of whether the individual candidate supported woman suffrage or not. Fewer Democrats than had been expected won that year. However, in 1916, when she used the same strategy and called upon women to vote against Democratic president Woodrow Wilson, he won in ten of the twelve suffrage states.

When Carrie Chapman Catt, who had been president of NAWSA from 1900 to 1904, accepted the presidency for a second time in 1915, she reorganized the association, introduced the "Winning Plan," and reinvigorated the suffrage movement at the national level. Catt changed the focus of NAWSA from educating the public to convincing state and federal politicians that suffrage was inevitable. She formed a national press bureau and a publicity council, recruited campaign directors, and established a professional congressional lobby. In two years, NAWSA grew from 100,000 members to 2 million members. In part, the ambitious program Catt developed was possible because a wealthy benefactor had willed $900,000 to Catt to use for suffrage.

U.S. entry into World War I in 1917, however, created new challenges for suffrage leaders, most of whom were pacifists. Despite their opposition to war in general, Catt and other suffrage leaders pledged their support for the U.S. effort in World War I and served on federal war-related agency boards. NAWSA financially supported several hospitals in Europe, and its members worked for the Red Cross, took nontraditional jobs to free men for fighting, and sold war bonds. The lobbyists suspended their congressional work and toured the states, lecturing on suffrage.

The Woman's Party began picketing the White House in 1917, carrying signs with messages such as "Mr. President, how long must women wait for liberty?" On one day, a riot erupted in which bystanders attacked the pickets and tore their banner, and two of the pickets were arrested for blocking the sidewalk. Catt opposed the attempts to embarrass President Wilson into supporting woman suffrage, but the pickets indirectly helped her by casting her and NAWSA as moderate and giving her increased access to the president.

In January 1918, the House of Representatives voted 274 to 136 in favor of the suffrage amendment, but when the Senate voted on it in October, it failed to pass by two votes. In response to the defeat, NAWSA initiated a campaign to defeat four senators who had voted against it. That November, two of the senators NAWSA had targeted lost their reelection bids as women voters demonstrated their political clout.

In early 1919, the Senate again defeated the suffrage amendment, but in the spring the House again passed it, and less than a month later the Senate passed it and sent the amendment to the states for ratification. By September 1919, seventeen states had ratified the amendment, but thirty-six states were needed before the amendment could be added to the Constitution. NAWSA conducted ratification campaigns in several states, and by August 1920, thirty-five states had ratified. They needed only one more state.

Tennessee seemed an unlikely choice to target for ratification but appeared to be the best option of the states that had not ratified the amendment. The governor called the Tennessee legislature into a special session beginning 9 August 1920. The Tennessee state Senate quickly passed the amendment, but the Tennessee House of Representatives was divided and became the focus of intense lobbying. After two weeks of debate, the voting in the House began with every indication that the amendment would be defeated with a tie vote. Earlier in the day, the youngest member of the House, Harry Burn, had voted for a motion to table the amendment, which would have killed it. Burn had told his mother, a suffragist, that if ratification needed only one vote, he would vote yes. When the speaker of the Tennessee House of Representatives called his name, Harry Burn voted yes. By that one vote on 18 August 1920, seventy-two years of campaigning came to an end. On 26 August, the secretary of state signed the proclamation certifying final adoption of the Nineteenth Amendment, and 26 million U.S. women gained suffrage rights.

For African American women in the South, however, ratification of the Nineteenth Amendment meant far less than it did for women of European descent. Racism had haunted the suffrage movement since the late 1860s, when the controversies over the Fourteenth and Fifteenth Amendments had erupted. NAWSA shunned African American women who supported the amendment, fearing that association with them would make it more difficult to gain congressional passage and ratification of it, even though black women and men supported woman suffrage more than white women and men. In addition, NAWSA leaders believed that if black women were admitted to the organization, white women in every region of the country would object, hurting NAWSA fund-raising efforts and public image and causing dissension among members.

In 1916, both the Democratic and the Republican platforms called for state action on suffrage, in deference to southern racists. Several southern states had passed laws that denied African Americans their right to vote, and they wanted to continue that exclusion. They feared a federal amendment would involve federal enforcement and result in both African American women and men gaining full suffrage rights. Northern suffrage leaders, including Carrie Chapman Catt, used racist rhetoric in their speeches, especially to southern audiences. She claimed that white women needed the vote to overcome the votes of African American and immigrant men.

For example, in 1919, an affiliate of the National Association of Colored Women (NACW) attempted to join NAWSA and through its membership demand suffrage protection for African American women. They sought protection by adding congressional enforcement of the suffrage amendment in an effort to subvert southern states' intentions to disenfranchise black women. NAWSA refused to admit NACW, fearing that the enforcement provisions it wanted would hamper ratification of the suffrage amendment. The suffrage amendment passed without the protections NACW had sought. Between 1920 and 1940, southern states disenfranchised black women, comprising 75 percent of all African American women. Southern black women did not gain full suffrage rights until the civil rights movement of the 1960s and the passage of the Voting Rights Act and other measures in that decade.

For African American women living in the South, passage of the Nineteenth Amendment accomplished far less than for white women. African American women and men continued to be disenfranchised by state laws, including literacy tests, that acted as barriers to voter registration. As early as 1921, black women appealed to the League of Women Voters and the National Woman's Party for assistance in eliminating these barriers. Those groups responded by insisting that the problems were race issues and not women's issues and did nothing to help remedy the problems.

African American women continued to work for voting rights, attempting to register themselves and their families, neighbors, and friends. Although often threatened with violence and frequently the targets of violence and despite their persistence and dedication, African American women were generally overshadowed by the greater visibility given to African American men.

See also American Woman Suffrage Association; Anthony, Susan Brownell; Catt, Carrie Clinton Lane Chapman; Fifteenth Amendment; Fourteenth Amendment; *Minor v. Happersett;* National American Woman Suffrage Association; National Association of Colored Women; National Woman Suffrage Association; National Woman's Party; Nineteenth Amendment; Paul, Alice; Stanton, Elizabeth Cady; Stone, Lucy

References Berry, *Why ERA Failed* (1986); Flexner and Fitzpatrick, *Century of Struggle: The Woman's Rights Movement in the United States* (1996); Graham, *Woman Suffrage and the New Democracy* (1996).

Sullivan, Leonor Kretzer (1902–1988)

Democrat Leonor Sullivan of Missouri served in the U.S. House of Representatives from 3 January 1953 to 3 January 1977. Married to Representative John Sullivan, Leonor Sullivan was active in the Democratic Party, served on his staff, and was his campaign manager. When he died in office, Leonor Sullivan wanted to run for his seat, but Democratic Party leaders would not support her candidacy and gave the nomination to a man who lost the election. In 1952, Sullivan won the seat.

Sullivan believed that women were deeply concerned about consumer issues. She successfully initiated and passed the Poultry Products Inspection Act of 1957. She was responsible for passing legislation that banned cancer-inducing agents in food, that required testing of all chemical additives to food, and that tightened controls on the manufacture and distribution of several prescription drugs. She introduced and guided the passage of the Consumer Credit Protection Act of 1968 (known as the truth in lending act) and the Fair Credit Reporting Act. She wrote the first Food Stamp Law in 1959 and the expanded version of it in 1964.

The only woman in Congress to vote against the Equal Rights Amendment, she argued that it would outlaw protective legislation for women and make women subject to the military draft. She explained: "ERA says you are my equal. . . . I think I'm a whole lot better." She held the leadership position of secretary of the Democratic Caucus in the 86th to 93rd Congresses (1959 through 1975). Sullivan retired from Congress in 1977.

Born in St. Louis, Missouri, Sullivan worked at a telephone company and attended night school at Washington University. She taught at a local business school until her marriage to John Sullivan in 1941.

See also Congress, Women in; Equal Pay Act of 1963; Equal Rights Amendment

References Engelbarts, *Women in the United States Congress, 1917–1972* (1974); Kaptur, *Women of Congress: A Twentieth-Century Odyssey* (1996); Schoenebaum, ed., *Political Profiles: The Nixon/Ford Years* (1979).

Sumner, Jessie (1898–1994)

Republican Jessie Sumner of Illinois served in the U.S. House of Representatives from 3 January 1939 to 3 January 1947. Sumner entered politics after her uncle, a county judge, died, and she ran to fill the vacancy. Her opposition to the New Deal and her disapproval of President Franklin D. Roosevelt's other programs led her to run for Congress in 1938. As a member of Congress, Sumner opposed the draft and any U.S. involvement in World War II, arguing that it could be avoided. However, she supported child day care to help mothers working for the war effort. Her isolationist views continued after the war, when she opposed U.S. participation in the United Nations, the International Monetary Fund, and the International Bank for Reconstruction and Development. She also opposed price controls, housing subsidies for veterans, and congressional pensions. Sumner declined to run in 1946 and returned to the family business, becoming president of Sumner National Bank.

Born in Milford, Illinois, Jessie Sumner studied economics at Smith College, taking classes from Chase Going Woodhouse, who would later be a congressional colleague. Sumner graduated from Smith College in 1920 and studied law at the University of Chicago, Oxford University in England, Columbia Law School, and New York University School of Commerce. She was admitted to the Illinois bar in 1923. After working for the Chase National Bank of New York, she returned to Milford in 1932 to practice private law.

See also Congress, Women in; Woodhouse, Chase Going

References Gaer, "A Study of the Activities of Women in Congress with Special References to the Careers of Margaret Chase Smith, Mary T. Norton, and Edith Nourse Rogers" (1952); H. W. Wilson, *Current Biography: Who's News and Why, 1945* (1945).

T

Talbert, Mary Morris Burnett (1866–1923)

An organizer for and leader in the National Association for the Advancement of Colored People (NAACP), Mary Talbert helped organize NAACP branches in Texas and Louisiana, served on the NAACP board, and was NAACP vice president from 1918 to 1923. When lynchings increased after World War I, Talbert organized and was national director of the NAACP's antilynching campaign. The campaign sought to unite 1 million women against lynching, to raise $1 million to support federal legislation against lynching, and to petition the government to pass the measure. Talbert formed a group of women that publicized the effort and obtained endorsements from white women's groups for it. They also asked women to hold meetings with local ministers to convince them to preach antilynching sermons.

Talbert's activism began with her membership in women's clubs and continued with her leadership in the National Association of Colored Women (NACW). She was NACW's parliamentarian from 1910 to 1912, chaired the executive board from 1912 to 1924, was vice president–at–large from 1914 to 1916, and was president from 1916 to 1920. During her presidency, NACW paid the mortgage on Frederick Douglass's home and in 1920 became its owner.

Born in Oberlin, Ohio, Talbert earned her S.P. degree in 1886 from Oberlin College. Recipients of the degree later received a bachelor of arts degree; Talbert received hers in 1896. She taught at Bethel University in Little Rock, Arkansas, and became its assistant principal in 1887. Later in the year, she became principal of Union High School in Little Rock. Following her marriage in 1891, Talbert's teaching career ended because school rules prohibited married women from teaching.

See also Civil Rights Movement, Women in the; National Association for the Advancement of Colored People, Women in the; National Association of Colored Women

References Hardy, *American Women Civil Rights Activists* (1993).

Tauscher, Ellen (b. 1951)

Democrat Ellen Tauscher of California entered the U.S. House of Representatives on 3 January 1997. Congresswoman Tauscher has introduced measures to reform the nation's child care system and to rebuild schools. She obtained more than $2 billion for the San Francisco Bay Area transportation system and $33 million for highway projects in her congressional district. Her other priorities include passing a constitutional amendment for a balanced budget and balancing the federal budget. She supports environmental protection, the assault weapons ban, the Brady gun law, and the death penalty. In her first term, Tauscher was vice chair of the Democratic Congressional Campaign Committee and was one of only two women in the House Democratic leadership.

Born in East Newark, New Jersey, Tauscher received her bachelor of science degree in early childhood education from Seton Hall University in 1974. She began her career working for a financial securities firm on Wall Street. From 1976 to 1989, she held a seat on the New York Stock Exchange, leaving to move to California.

Tauscher founded ChildCare Registry, a national research service to help parents verify the background of child care workers, in 1992 and published *The ChildCare Sourcebook* in 1996. She also became an advocate for children of working families and directed the Tauscher Foundation, which provided funds for computer equipment in elementary schools. She cochaired Dianne Feinstein's campaigns for the 1992 special election to the U.S. Senate from California and for the full term in 1994.

See also Brady, Sarah Jane Kemp; Congress, Women in; Feinstein, Dianne Goldman

References Congressional Quarterly, *Politics in America 1998* (1997); Sample, "California's Newest 'New Democrat'" (1997); www.house.gov/tauscher. biograph.htm.

Taylor v. Louisiana (1975)

In *Taylor v. Louisiana*, the U.S. Supreme Court found that Louisiana's functional exclusion of women from juries violated the Sixth and Fourteenth Amendments. Fourteen years earlier, the Court had ruled in *Hoyt v. Florida* (1961) that gender discrimination in jury selection did not violate constitutional rights and that women had responsibilities in the home that held precedence over jury duty. In *Taylor,* the Court pointed to women's labor force participation as evidence that women's lives and responsibilities were not limited to the home.

At that time in Louisiana, a woman could not be selected for jury duty unless she had filed a written declaration of her desire to be a juror. In this case, Billy Taylor had been indicted for kidnapping, but because there were no women on the jury, he claimed that he would be deprived of "a fair trial by a jury of a representative segment of the community."

Although Louisiana's system did not disqualify women, the Court wrote: "Louisiana's special exemption for women operates to exclude them from petit juries, which in our view is contrary to the commands of the Sixth and Fourteenth Amendments." The decision ended the gender discrimination in jury selection that women had fought since the Seneca Falls Convention in 1848 and more consistently attempted to end since the passage of the Nineteenth Amendment granting women suffrage rights in 1920.

> **See also** Fourteenth Amendment; *Hoyt v. Florida;* Juries, Women on;
> Nineteenth Amendment; Seneca Falls Convention
>
> **References** Ginsburg, "Gender in the Supreme Court: The 1973 and 1974
> Terms" (1976); *Taylor v. Louisiana,* 419 U.S. 522 (1975).

Temperance Movement, Women in the

Women's involvement in the temperance movement began in the 1840s, a time when married women's legal dependence upon their husbands made them financially vulnerable. An alcoholic husband could consume not only his income and financial resources but his wife's as well, leaving her and her children destitute. Several temperance organizers also became women's rights advocates after concluding that without political power they had little hope of accomplishing their goals. The temperance movement prompted the founding of the first newspaper edited and published by a woman in the United States, *The Lily: A Ladies Journal Devoted to Temperance and Literature.* Founded in 1849 by Amelia Bloomer in Seneca Falls, New York, *The Lily* added women's rights to the issues it advocated. Other early temperance leaders who became women's rights leaders include Lucretia Mott, Lucy Stone, Susan B. Anthony, and Elizabeth Cady Stanton.

In the 1870s, the temperance movement entered a new phase with the formation of the Woman's Christian Temperance Union (WCTU). Under the leadership of Frances Willard, WCTU president from 1879 to 1898, the WCTU expanded its agenda to include advocacy for woman suffrage. Women in the WCTU and other organizations significantly contributed to the passage in 1917 and the ratification in 1919 of the Eighteenth Amendment prohibiting alcohol in the United States.

In 1929, Pauline Sabin of New York called together two dozen women and formed the Women's Organization for National Prohibition Reform (WONPR), dedicated to the repeal of the Eighteenth Amendment. WONPR advocated temperance and argued that Prohibition had increased alcohol use, crime, and political corruption in addition to contributing to the general disregard for the law. By the 1932 elections, the organization had more than 1 million members, who through grassroots networks and state and national organizations pressured political candidates to support repeal of the Eighteenth Amendment. WONPR endorsed candidates, generally Democrats, and campaigned for them. After Congress passed the Twenty-first Amendment repealing the Eighteenth Amendment, WONPR members helped organize state ratification conventions. The process was completed in less than a year.

See also Anthony, Susan Brownell; Bloomer, Amelia Jenks; Coverture; Mott, Lucretia Coffin; Stanton, Elizabeth Cady; Stone, Lucy

References Flexner and Fitzpatrick, *Century of Struggle: The Woman's Rights Movement in the United States,* enlarged edition (1996); Kyvig, "Women against Prohibition" (1976).

Terrell, Mary Eliza Church (1863–1954)

Lecturer, political activist, and educator Mary Church Terrell committed herself to improving the lives of African American women. She served as the first president of the National Association of Colored Women (NACW) and led the new organization's development of its programs. In 1909, she helped found the National Association for the Advancement of Colored People. In the 1940s, she provided leadership in a successful effort to desegregate restaurants in Washington, D.C.

Born in Memphis, Tennessee, Mary Church Terrell was born the same year that President Abraham Lincoln signed the Emancipation Proclamation, freeing African Americans from slavery, including Terrell's parents. Wanting a good education for their daughter, her parents sent her from Memphis, Tennessee, with its segregated schools, to an elementary school associated with Antioch College in Ohio. She attended Oberlin Academy during her high school years and earned her bachelor of arts degree in 1884 and her master of arts degree in 1888, both from Oberlin College. She also taught from 1885 to 1888. Traveling in Europe with her father in the late 1880s, Terrell studied languages, learning French and German.

She married Robert H. Terrell in 1891 and became a homemaker because married women could not teach in public schools, although she did teach in the Colored Women's League's night school. In 1895, Terrell received an appointment to the District of Columbia Board of Education, making her one of the first African American women on a U.S. school board. She later served again on the board from 1906 to 1911.

Terrell began her long association with women's clubs in 1891, joining the Colored Women's League of Washington, D.C. (CWL), which sought to improve black women's lives. In 1896, the CWL and the National Federation of Afro-American Women, an association of local black women's clubs, merged into the National Association of Colored Women (NACW) and elected Terrell president. NACW was the first national network of communication among black women, providing them with information about events across the country.

African American women had begun forming women's clubs at about the same time as white women, but African American women had to form their own associations because of the racial prejudice of white women who did not permit them to participate in their clubs. The extent of the prejudice is apparent from an event in 1900. When the General Federation of Women's Clubs held its convention, Terrell was denied the opportunity to offer them greetings on behalf of NACW because of the objections of southern white women.

Mary Church Terrell, first president of the National Association of Colored Women, fought against segregation and lynching, ca. 1890 (Library of Congress)

As president of NACW, Terrell established the organization's monthly newsletter, *National Notes,* organized biennial conventions with art and literature exhibits, and trained women in leadership. She encouraged local clubs to create kindergartens and day nurseries, and she raised the money to hire a kindergarten adviser to motivate and help clubs open them. More than a dozen facilities had opened by 1901. She also led the formation of Mother's Clubs, which taught housekeeping and child-rearing skills. Several clubs also opened homes for girls. Terrell stepped down in 1901 because the NACW constitution prohibited anyone from serving more than two consecutive terms.

By the mid-1890s, Terrell had become a professional lecturer, speaking at Chautauquas, forums, and universities across the nation. In the course of her travels she encountered the South's segregation laws and the inhumanity of them. Those experiences led to her commitment to interracial understanding and her conviction about the importance of communication between the races. She wrote articles about the accomplishments of African Americans, criticized the white press for its stereotypical articles about blacks, and attempted to educate whites about blacks and their lives. She decried lynching and exposed the lies behind the myth that black men were lynched in retaliation for raping white women, and she described the inhumanity of the convict lease system.

During World War I, Terrell helped support the war effort by working at the War Risk Insurance Bureau but was dismissed because of her race. She then went to work at the Census Bureau, but the humiliation of the federal government's segregation policies led her to resign the position.

Terrell was also active in other political movements. She had met suffrage leader Susan B. Anthony in 1898, and the two women had become friends. Even though she was aware of the racism within the suffrage movement, she lectured on the topic and worked for passage of the woman suffrage amendment. After ratification of the Nineteenth Amendment, she worked for the National Republican Committee as the director of black women in the eastern division. From 1929 to 1930, Terrell organized black women for Ruth Hanna McCormick's campaign for the U.S. Senate.

After World War II, Terrell changed the emphasis of her work from racial understanding to a more militant approach. In 1946, she applied to the District of Columbia chapter of the American Association of University Women (AAUW), was rejected on the basis of race, and appealed to the organization's national board, which decided in Terrell's favor. In 1948, AAUW approved a new national bylaw that prohibited discrimination on the basis of race, religion, or politics. Terrell and two other African American women joined the District of Columbia chapter in 1949.

She began another desegregation campaign in 1949. The district had passed laws in the 1870s requiring service in public accommodations regardless of color, but when the district's legal code was written in the 1890s, the laws were disregarded and segregation became the norm. Research showed that the laws had not been repealed, and Terrell formed a committee to enforce the district's antidiscrimination laws. As chair of the Coordinating Committee for the Enforcement of District of Columbia Anti-Discrimination Laws in 1949, she recruited the support of labor, religious, women's, and civic organizations. In 1950, an interracial party of four requested service at Thompson's Restaurant, but the three black people in the group were not permitted to purchase food. They filed a complaint that the municipal court dismissed. The next year, Terrell led a sit-in at Kresge's lunch counter, and after six weeks, the management changed its policy and began serving African Americans. The same year,

Terrell led a boycott and a picket line at Hecht Company, a department store that had segregated lunch counters. After four months, the management capitulated. Terrell was ninety years old when she led these and other demonstrations in the District of Columbia. In 1953, the U.S. Supreme Court decided in *District of Columbia v. John Thompson,* the owner of the first restaurant that had refused Terrell and her party service, that the laws from the 1870s were in force, and the district began to be desegregated.

Terrell wrote *The Progress of Colored Women: An Address Delivered before the National American Woman Suffrage Association* (1898), *Harriet Beecher Stowe: An Appreciation* (1911), *Colored Women and World Peace* (1932), and *A Colored Woman in a White World* (1940).

See also American Association of University Women; Anthony, Susan Brownell; Civil Rights Movement, Women in the; National Association of Colored Women; Suffrage

References Jones, *Quest for Equality: The Life and Writings of Mary Eliza Church Terrell, 1863–1954* (1990).

Thomas, Lera Millard (1900–1993)

Democrat Lera Thomas of Texas served in the U.S. House of Representatives from 26 March 1966 to 3 January 1967. When her husband died in office, Lera Thomas won the special election to fill the vacancy. During her brief tenure in Congress, Thomas sought appropriations for a laboratory in Houston and for the Houston Ship Channel, both projects that her husband had advocated. She did not run for another term.

Born in Nacogdoches, Texas, Lera Thomas attended Brenau College and the University of Alabama. In 1968, Thomas was special liaison for the *Houston Chronicle* to members of the armed forces in Vietnam.

See also Congress, Women in

References Office of the Historian, U.S. House of Representatives, *Women in Congress, 1917–1990* (1991).

Thompson, Ruth (1887–1970)

Republican Ruth Thompson of Michigan served in the U.S. House of Representatives from 3 January 1951 to 3 January 1957. Congresswoman Thompson worked for public library services in rural areas, programs to stimulate the growth of low-cost electric power from a variety of sources, and the establishment of a Department of Peace. Her other interests included flood control and drainage projects. Thompson was defeated in the 1956 primary election.

Born in Whitehall, Michigan, Ruth Thompson graduated from

Muskegon Business College in 1905. From 1918 to 1924, she worked in a law office and studied law at night.

Elected probate judge in Muskegon County, she served from 1925 to 1937. After serving in the Michigan House of Representatives from 1939 to 1941, she worked in the civilian personnel section of the adjutant general's office from 1942 to 1945 and served in the adjutant general's bureau at Headquarters Command in Frankfurt, Germany, and Copenhagen, Denmark, in 1945 and 1946. She returned to private law practice in 1946.

See also Congress, Women in; State Legislatures, Women in

References Office of the Historian, U.S. House of Representatives, *Women in Congress, 1917–1990* (1991).

Thornburgh v. American College of Obstetrics and Gynecology (1986)

In *Thornburgh v. American College of Obstetrics and Gynecology,* the U.S. Supreme Court rejected four provisions of the Pennsylvania Abortion Control Act of 1982 on the basis that they subordinated a woman's privacy interests and concerns in an effort to dissuade her from having an abortion. The invalidated provisions called for a physician to tell a woman seeking an abortion that the father had a financial responsibility for the support of a child and that medical assistance could be available if she chose to continue the pregnancy. The physician was also required to inform the woman of any physical, medical, or psychological risks involved in the abortion. Another rejected provision required the physician to report the identity of the physicians involved in the procedure and information that would permit the ready identification of the woman who had the abortion. The last provision required, in postviability abortions, that two physicians be in attendance; in addition, the physicians had to use the abortion technique most likely to preserve the life of the fetus, even if it placed the woman at risk, and there was no exception for emergency abortions, which also placed the woman's life at risk.

The Court overturned part of *Thornburgh* when it decided *Planned Parenthood of Southeastern Pennsylvania v. Casey* (1992) and permitted states to require informed consent.

See also Abortion; *Akron v. Akron Center for Reproductive Health; Bellotti v. Baird; Bray v. Alexandria Clinic; Colautti v. Franklin; Doe v. Bolton; Harris v. McRae; Hodgson v. Minnesota; Ohio v. Akron Center; Planned Parenthood Association of Kansas City, Mo. v. Ashcroft; Planned Parenthood of Central Missouri v. Danforth; Planned Parenthood of Southeastern Pennsylvania v. Casey; Poelker v. Doe*

References *Thornburgh v. American College of Obstetrics and Gynecology,* 476 U.S. 747 (1986).

Thurman, Karen L. (b. 1951)

Democrat Karen Thurman of Florida entered the U.S. House of Representatives on 3 January 1993. Congresswoman Thurman has worked to apply the concepts of risk assessment and cost benefit analysis to government decisions and to lift the burden of unfunded federal mandates from state and local governments. She has advocated changes in the Medicaid funding formula to better reflect a state's needs and has sought to reimburse Florida for the costs associated with its immigrant population.

Thurman supports reproductive rights and reduction of the budget deficit by cutting outmoded military projects and increasing taxes on foreign corporations. She opposed the North American Free Trade Agreement (NAFTA) because the citrus and peanut crops grown in her area compete with Mexican products, and thus NAFTA created an economic threat to farmers in her district.

Thurman served on the Dunnellson City Council from 1975 to 1983 and was mayor from 1979 to 1981. She served in the Florida Senate from 1983 to 1993, where she worked on environmental issues. She called for greater use of solar energy and worked to clean up leaky underground petroleum tanks, and she sought to protect Florida's drinking water and preserve wetlands. She also worked on consumer protection and education.

Born in Rapid City, South Dakota, Thurman earned her associate's degree from Santa Fe Community College in 1971 and her bachelor of arts degree from the University of Florida in 1973.

See also Congress, Women in; Reproductive Rights; State Legislatures, Women in

References Congressional Quarterly, *Politics in America 1994* (1993); www.house.gov/thurman/about.htm.

Triangle Shirtwaist Company Fire

On 25 March 1911, the muffled sound from an explosion in New York City's Asch Building was the first indication of the fire in which 145 women employees of the Triangle Shirtwaist Company died. After the explosion, smoke billowed from windows on the eighth floor, and flames soon followed. People on the street watched in horror as the only fire escape collapsed with women climbing down it. The fire moved so quickly that some women died at their sewing machines, and other women died trying to escape through an exit door that was locked. Still other women died from jumping out of the building.

The building owners and the owners of the Triangle Shirtwaist Company had been alerted to the many fire hazards that existed at their property. Flammable materials were scattered on the floor, doors opened inward, the stairwells were narrow and drafty, and the building had no sprinklers. The company owners were tried for manslaughter and were found not guilty.

One of those who witnessed the fire was Frances Perkins, who served as a chief investigator for the Factory Investigation Commission that was formed after the fire. The commission's recommendations included passing a fifty-four-hour workweek and a new industrial code, both of which New York enacted.

See also Perkins, Frances (Fanny) Corlie

References Wertheimer, *We Were There: The Story of Working Women in America* (1977).

Truth, Sojourner (ca. 1797–1883)

African American Sojourner Truth made herself a force in nineteenth-century reform movements, denouncing slavery and slavers and advocating freedom, women's rights, woman suffrage, and temperance. An illiterate itinerant preacher, she helped propel the reform movements on which she centered her life.

Sojourner Truth's names reveal much about her. Born a slave in Hurley, New York, and given the name Isabella, she took the name of the Van Wagener family who bought her freedom when she was an adult, as well as her youngest child's freedom. The last shackles of slavery ended when New York abolished it on 4 July 1827. Religious experiences beginning in 1827 endowed her with the power of the Holy Spirit and transformed her into a powerful and moving preacher. In 1843, on the day of Pentecost, she changed her name to Sojourner Truth, which means "itinerant preacher."

While living at a religious commune in Massachusetts, Sojourner Truth met Frederick Douglass, William Lloyd Garrison, and other reform leaders and became part of a network of antislavery activists. She made her first antislavery speech in 1844 and appeared at her first large women's rights meeting in 1850. She helped support herself by selling copies of her autobiography, *Narrative of Sojourner Truth: A Northern Slave Emancipated from Bodily Servitude by the State of New York, in 1828.*

Sojourner Truth's speech at the 1851 Ohio Women's Rights Convention, commonly known as her "Ain't I a Woman" speech, contributed to her growing national celebrity and her stature as a symbol of strength and leadership. Some circumstances on the day of the speech and her words may have been enhanced by the desire to make her an even more dramatic figure than she was in reality. The traditionally accepted version of the speech and its circumstances was written twelve years after the event. It places her in a hostile crowd, has her speaking in dialect, and includes the refrain "and ain't I a woman?" But she may not have used the phrase. An article published in the *Salem Anti-Slavery Bugle* on 21 June 1851 offered

I SELL THE SHADOW TO SUPPORT THE SUBSTANCE.

SOJOURNER TRUTH.

Sojourner Truth, preacher and abolitionist, participated in many suffragist conventions and became famous for her "Ain't I a Woman" speech, ca. 1850s (Library of Congress)

a different account, which was written by the convention secretary and is the one that Sojourner Truth's most recent biographer regards as the more accurate. Although she may have spoken in dialect, the story does not reflect that. In addition, the audience was not hostile, and the article does not include any references to "and ain't I a woman?" In part, the *Anti-Slavery Bugle* report reads:

I have as much muscle as any man, and can so as much works as any man. I have plowed and reaped and husked and chopped and mowed, and can any man do more than that? I have heard much about the sexes being equal; I can carry as much as any man, and can eat as much too, if I can get it. I am as strong as man that is now. As for intellect, all I can say, is a woman have a pint and man a quart—why cant she have her little pint full? You need not be afraid to give us our rights for fear we will take too much,—for we cant take more than our pint'll hold. The poor men seem to be all in confusion, and don't know what to do. Why children, if you have woman's rights give it to her and you will feel better.

The reporter concluded with "The power and wit of this remarkable woman convulsed the audience with laughter."

After the Civil War, a rancorous debate developed over the wording of the Fourteenth Amendment to the U.S. Constitution. It included the word *male*, which white feminists wanted removed. The debate continued when the Fifteenth Amendment guaranteeing suffrage to former slaves was introduced and did not extend the right to women. Most male and black abolitionists, saying it was the "Negro's hour," did not want to imperil black men's suffrage by adding references to woman suffrage. Truth joined white feminists, arguing that if black men could vote, but black women could not, "colored men will be masters over the women, and it will be just as bad as it was before." When the women's rights movement split into two camps, the American Woman Suffrage Association (AWSA) and the National Woman Suffrage Association, however, Truth aligned herself with the more conservative AWSA, which supported the Fourteenth and Fifteenth Amendments.

Until her death, Sojourner Truth remained active in public affairs, primarily serving as an advocate for new arrivals in Washington, D.C., who had been slaves. She worked with the Freedmen's Bureau and with private relief agencies. She also developed a plan to help freed people move to Kansas but was unable to convince Congress to support it. In 1879, however, the state became the destination for many African Americans from the Deep South.

See also Abolitionist Movement, Women in the; Fifteenth Amendment; Fourteenth Amendment

References Painter, *Sojourner Truth: A Life, a Symbol* (1996).

Tubman, Harriet (ca. 1820–1913)

Harriet Tubman escaped slavery and made at least nineteen trips from the North into the southern slave states to conduct more than 300 slaves into freedom. She was called "Moses" for her work freeing slaves. Of her work, Tubman said: "I never ran my train off the track and I never lost a passenger."

Born in Dorchester County near Cambridge, Maryland, Harriet Tubman was named Araminta Ross but adopted her mother's name. Her parents were probably Ashantis, a West African warrior people. From the time Harriet Tubman was about five years old, she was rented to neighboring families to do housekeeping, split fence rails, load timber, nurse children, and perform other tasks. When she was about thirteen years old, Tubman suffered a serious head injury when she attempted to protect another slave and was hit with a two-pound weight. During her long convalescence, she thought about slavery from a philosophical perspective. She prayed for her master to free her and her family but learned that he planned to send them to a chain gang in the Deep South.

Through her philosophy and prayer, she developed self-reliance, courage, and strength of purpose. Two events helped shape her future: she married a free black man, and she learned that her mother should have been freed upon the death of her former owner. Tubman escaped to freedom in Pennsylvania in 1849 and worked as a cook and domestic.

The Fugitive Slave Law of 1850 significantly increased the risks for African Americans who had found freedom in the North because they had legally become fugitive slaves. After passage of the law, Tubman became involved with the Philadelphia Vigilance Committee, a group that assisted fugitive slaves. Through this group, Tubman organized her first return to the South and learned that the slaves she was to accompany included her sister and her children. In the spring of 1851, she made the trip and took them to freedom in Canada. By 1857, she had freed her entire family, including her parents.

Tubman's excursions to the South involved constant danger. The threat to her safety was made greater because she could neither read nor write, but she was creative and could quickly develop alternative strategies. For example, while in a small southern town accompanying some slaves to freedom, she purchased railway tickets to a destination further south. She hoped that observers would dismiss them, believing that slaves would not go south to escape. The ruse worked. A reward of $12,000 was offered for her capture at one point, and in 1858 it reached $40,000.

During the Civil War, Tubman went to South Carolina and Florida to nurse sick and wounded soldiers and to teach newly freed blacks the skills to take care of themselves. She organized African American men to scout the inland waterway of South Carolina for Union raids and assisted in a raid in the Combahee area.

After the war, she went to her home in Auburn, New York, the place that had been her base for several years. She helped the poor and disabled and worked with the black churches that had supported her career on the Underground Railroad. She purchased land for the Harriet Tubman Home for Aged and Indigent Colored People in 1896 and opened it in 1908.

During World War II, a liberty ship was christened the *Harriet Tubman.*

See also Abolitionist Movement, Women in the; Anthony, Susan Brownell

References Mabunda, ed., *Contemporary Black Biography,* vol. 9 (1995); Smith, ed., *Epic Lives* (1993).

Chair of the Council of Economic Advisors Laura D'Andrea Tyson talked to the press about the budget impasse, 1996 (Associated Press AP)

Tyson, Laura D'Andrea (b. 1947)

Laura D'Andrea Tyson served as chair of the Council of Economic Advisers from 1993 to 1995 and chair of the National Economic Council from 1995 to 1997. Tyson began her professional life as a staff economist at the World Bank and then taught at Princeton University. In 1978, she began teaching at the University of California at Berkeley, where she became known for her ability to explain complex economic concepts in interesting and comprehensible ways. She became a full professor in 1988. While at Berkeley, she also served as research director of the Berkeley Roundtable on International Economics.

Tyson met then Democratic presidential candidate Bill Clinton in August 1992. Clinton had gathered a group of economists to explore ways to slow the decline in U.S. manufacturing. Tyson offered ideas for providing seed money to companies with promising technologies and other approaches that appealed to Clinton. After his election, Clinton invited Tyson to serve as chair on the three-member Council of Economic Advisers.

Tyson described her view of the government's role in the market: "The market does many things very well, but there is a rationale for the government doing things that the market doesn't do very well. The role of the Council of Economic Advisers is to help evaluate when there is a defensible role for a government policy and whether government policy in pursuit of that objective is efficient."

As a council member, Tyson and others convinced President Bill Clinton to limit his plans for reducing the federal deficit in order to protect the nation's economic recovery. She also advocated a $16 billion economic stimulus package, but the U.S. Senate killed it. An expert in foreign trade, Tyson was instrumental in articulating the administration's "demand that our trading partners open their market to their exports as ours are open to them."

In 1995, Clinton appointed Tyson chair of the National Economic Council, a group that includes the president, vice president, and members of the cabinet. As chair, Tyson was responsible for managing economic policymaking throughout the executive branch. She also sat on the National Security Council and the Domestic Policy Council.

Born in Bayonne, New Jersey, Tyson earned her bachelor of arts degree from Smith College in 1969 and her doctoral degree from Massachusetts Institute of Technology in 1974.

See also Cabinets, Women in Presidential

References H. W. Wilson, *Current Biography Yearbook, 1996* (1996); *New York Times,* 15 March 1993.

U

UAW v. Johnson Controls (1991)

In *UAW v. Johnson Controls,* the U.S. Supreme Court decided that Johnson Controls's policy of refusing to hire women for certain jobs in order to protect them from workplace hazards violated the Pregnancy Discrimination Act of 1978. A battery manufacturer, Johnson Controls prohibited pregnant women and women capable of bearing children from holding jobs that involved exposure to lead, one of the materials used in batteries and one that poses risks to fetuses. The policy offered fertile men but not fertile women the option of working in the restricted areas and required only women to produce proof that they could not bear children.

The Court noted that unless pregnant employees differ from others "in their ability or inability" to work, "they must be treated the same" as other employees under the Pregnancy Discrimination Act. In its decision, the Court wrote: "It is no more appropriate for the courts than it is for individual employers to decided whether a woman's reproductive role is more important to herself and her family than her economic role. Congress has left this choice to the woman as hers to make."

> **See also** Employment Discrimination; Pregnancy Discrimination Act of 1978
> **References** *UAW v. Johnson Controls,* 499 U.S. 187 (1991).

United States v. Virginia (1996)

In *United States v. Virginia,* the Commonwealth of Virginia defended the single-sex policy at Virginia Military Institute (VMI), an all-male college, on the basis that its mission was to produce citizen-soldiers, that is, men who were trained to be leaders in civilian life and military service. The U.S. Supreme Court restated its earlier opinion in *Mississippi University v. Hogan* that gender-based government actions must have an "exceedingly persuasive justification" and decided that Virginia had not met the standard and that it had violated the equal protection clause of the Fourteenth Amendment. In addition, the Court did not accept Virginia's establishment of a parallel program for women at another institution as an alternative to admitting women to VMI.

The case began when a female high school student seeking admission to VMI filed a complaint with the attorney general, resulting in the United States suing the Commonwealth. As the case progressed through the courts, Virginia developed a plan that left VMI an all-male institution and created a parallel program, the Virginia Women's Institute for Leadership (VWIL). Although a lower court approved the VWIL alternative, the U.S. Supreme Court did not, noting substantive differences between the course offerings, faculty, endowments, policies, and opportunities for military training and scientific specialization at VMI and VWIL.

Justice Ruth Bader Ginsburg wrote the decision, noting in it: "Neither the goal of producing citizen-soldiers nor VMI's implementing methodology is inherently unsuitable to women. And the school's impressive record in producing leaders had made admission desirable to some women." Ginsburg concluded: "There is no reason to believe that the admission of women capable of all the activities required of VMI cadets would destroy the Institute rather than enhance its capacity to serve the 'more perfect Union.'"

See also Education, Women and; Fourteenth Amendment; Ginsburg, Ruth Joan Bader

References *United States v. Virginia*, 518 U.S. 515 (1996).

Unsoeld, Jolene Bishoprick (b. 1931)

Democrat Jolene Unsoeld of Washington served in the U.S. House of Representatives from 3 January 1989 to 3 January 1995. Congresswoman Unsoeld passed bills to impose sanctions against drift-net fishing and to ban oil and gas drilling within the Olympic Coast National Marine Sanctuary. She was one of the seven female House members who marched to the Senate in October 1991 to urge a full hearing of Anita Hill's sexual harassment charges against U.S. Supreme Court nominee Clarence Thomas. Unsoeld was defeated in an attempt for a fourth term.

Born in Corvallis, Oregon, Unsoeld attended Oregon State University from 1950 to 1951. From 1962 to 1967, she lived with her husband, an educator, in Kathmandu, Nepal, where she was director of the English Language Institute for two years. She entered politics as a citizen-lobbyist working on campaign reform in Washington state in the 1970s. A mountain climber, she added environmental concerns to her lobbying agenda. Democratic national committeewoman for Washington from 1983 to 1988, she also served in the Washington House of Representatives from 1985 to 1989. Her environmental efforts there included more stringent requirements for cleaning toxic waste sites.

See also Congress, Women in; Hill, Anita Faye; Sexual Harassment; State Legislatures, Women in

References Congressional Quarterly, *Politics in America 1994* (1993); Office of the Historian, U.S. House of Representatives, *Women in Congress, 1917–1990* (1991).

Upton, Harriet Taylor (1853–1945)

Republican Harriet Taylor Upton worked for woman suffrage from 1899 to 1920, when the Nineteenth Amendment became part of the U.S. Constitution. She then turned her attention to helping women find their place in the Republican Party.

Until the late 1880s, Upton opposed woman suffrage, even though her father, a member of Congress, had been president of the Ohio Woman Suffrage Association. She had met Susan B. Anthony in the 1870s and again in 1888, when she had also met Elizabeth Cady Stanton and Lucy Stone, but none had been able to convince her to support their cause. It was while she was researching material for an antisuffrage article that Upton became convinced of the importance of woman suffrage and turned into an active supporter of it.

In 1890, Upton joined the National American Woman Suffrage Association (NAWSA) and in 1893 served as acting chair of its Congressional Committee. She served as NAWSA treasurer from 1898 to 1910 and president of the Ohio Woman Suffrage Association from 1898 to 1908. Working out of the national headquarters in Warren, Ohio, she administered the daily work of NAWSA, distributing literature, making speeches, and testifying before Congress. Following congressional approval of the woman suffrage amendment to the U.S. Constitution, Upton successfully worked in Ohio and Tennessee for its ratification by those states.

After the Nineteenth Amendment was ratified in 1920, Upton served as vice chair of the Republican National Committee's executive committee and as head of women's activities. She commented that "women today are not on the same political basis as men; they still come in the role of the pleader" and compared women to "hired girls" who must "cook whatever political menu their men order them to prepare." Upton also accurately forecast that women would not vote as a bloc for a candidate based upon gender.

Using the political contacts she had developed over the years, Upton worked to obtain appointments to government agencies and departments for women. Through her efforts, women gained admittance to the diplomatic service and appointment to the Conference for Limitation of Arms. She testified before Congress on women in the civil service, issues related to maternity and child health, and the Child Labor Amendment.

Upton unsuccessfully ran in the 1924 Republican primary for her father's former congressional seat. From 1928 to 1931, she was the assistant state campaign manager for the Ohio Republican Party and served as the governor's liaison to the Ohio Department of Public Welfare. She retired from public life and moved to California in 1931.

Born in Ravenna, Ohio, Upton completed her education in public schools. She did not attend college because her father objected; instead she joined him on his circuit as a judge.

See also National American Woman Suffrage Association; Suffrage

References Hardy *American Women Civil Rights Activists* (1993); Upton, "The Machine and the Woman" (1922).

V

Velázquez, Nydia Margarita (b. 1953)

Democrat Nydia Velázquez of New York entered the U.S. House of Representatives on 3 January 1993. She is the first Puerto Rican woman to serve in Congress. Velázquez was special assistant to a member of Congress in 1983. Appointed to serve on the New York City Council in 1984, she ran for reelection to the city council but lost. From 1986 until 1992, she served as the director of the Department of Puerto Rican Community Affairs in the United States, a cabinet-level position in the Puerto Rican government.

Representative Nydia Velázquez (D-NY) celebrated her election to Congress in New York, 1992 (Associated Press AP)

Velázquez has been an advocate for immigrants, Hispanics, women, and poor people. She has fought legislation that would require employers to ascertain that their employees were in the country legally and legislation that would make English the official language.

Born in Yabucoa, Puerto Rico, Velázquez was the first person in her family to earn a high school diploma. She earned her bachelor of arts degree in political science from the University of Puerto Rico in 1974 and her master of arts degree in political science from New York University in 1976. On the faculty of the University of Puerto Rico from 1976 to 1981, she joined the faculty of Hunter College at the City University of New York in 1981 as an adjunct professor of Puerto Rican studies.

See also Congress, Women in

References Congressional Quarterly, *Politics in America 1996* (1995); www.house.gov/velazquez/bio.htm.

Veterans Preference

Veterans preference gives military veterans seeking state or federal employment advantages in hiring. Most states and the federal government offer some form of veterans preference: some offer absolute preference to veterans who qualify for a position, and some award points to veterans' scores. The federal government gave preference to disabled Civil War veterans, several states enacted veterans preference laws in the nineteenth century, and the federal Veterans Preference Act was enacted in 1944. The Civil Rights Act of 1964, Title VII, protects veterans preference statutes, and the U.S. Supreme Court has found that the policies do not violate the equal protection clause of the Fourteenth Amendment.

Women have objected to veterans preference policies because such policies have excluded many women from civil service jobs and advancement. They have argued that the policies perpetuate discrimination against women because the military had quotas limiting the number of women who could serve until the 1970s. The impact of veterans preference laws can be seen from a few statistics. Women constitute 41 percent of those who pass the entry-level professional and administrative exam but only 27 percent of those who are hired. Male veterans compose 20 percent of those who pass the exams and 34 percent of those hired. Women make up 41 percent of the civilian labor force but only 30 percent of civil service employees. Veterans constitute 25 percent of the labor force and hold 48 percent of all federal civil service jobs.

See also *Personnel Administrator of the Commonwealth of Massachusetts v. Feeney*

References Freeman, "Women and Public Policy: An Overview" (1982); *Personnel Administrator of the Commonwealth of Massachusetts v. Feeney,* 442 U.S. 256 (1979).

Violence Against Women Act of 1994

Passed by Congress and signed by President Bill Clinton as part of the Violent Crime Control and Law Enforcement Act of 1994, the Violence Against Women Act (VAWA) takes a comprehensive approach to domestic violence and sexual assault. The law provides penalties for stalking, allows rape victims to demand that their assailant be tested for human immunodeficiency virus (HIV), and enables victims to file a civil suit for violent crimes motivated by gender. It allows immigrant spouses or children who are victims of domestic violence to petition for legal residency and obtain work permits, changing the policy that required immigrants to stay with the abuser or risk deportation. The measure created the Violence Against Women Office, established a toll-free national hotline, and provided funds to encourage states to implement mandatory arrest policies for domestic abuse or violation of a restraining order.

The National Domestic Violence Hotline provides local referral information to victims. The callers, 89 percent women and 11 percent men, include victims of domestic violence, family and friends of victims, batterers, professional service providers, and members of the press and public.

See also Domestic Violence; Rape; Violence Against Women Office

References *Congressional Quarterly Almanac, 103rd Congress, 2nd Session . . . 1994* (1995); www.usdoj.gov.vawo/vawafct.htm.

Violence Against Women Office

Opened in March 1995, the Violence Against Women Office (VAWO) is part of the Department of Justice. As the primary contact for members of Congress, other federal agencies, state and local governments, and other organizations, VAWO works to reduce domestic violence and other crimes against women.

The first VAWO director, former Iowa attorney general Bonnie Campbell, was appointed in March 1995. Campbell coordinates efforts between the Department of Justice and other agencies and programs, including law enforcement officers, to reduce violence against women. She has also worked to attract attention to the problem through meetings with advocacy groups and others and through public appearances and media interviews.

See also Campbell, Bonnie Jean Pierce; Domestic Violence; Violence Against Women Act of 1994

References www.usdoj.gov/vawo/vawofct.htm.

Voting Rights Act of 1965

Debated and passed as the civil rights movement stormed across the country, the Voting Rights Act of 1965 was the most comprehensive voting rights legislation enacted in ninety-five years. Submitted by President Lyndon Johnson, the act sought to overcome racist laws designed to prevent African Americans from registering to vote and from voting. It suspended literacy tests and comparable voter qualifications; authorized the appointment of federal voting examiners; and introduced federal registration officials into six southern states, specified counties in three other states, and Alaska.

Signed on 6 August 1965, the measure had visible results by the end of the year. The Department of Justice reported that 160,000 African Americans had registered in less than five months, and federal examiners registered almost 80,000 additional African Americans, increasing the number of African American voters by about 40 percent in some areas of the South

See also Civil Rights Movement, Women in the; Delta Sigma Theta Sorority; National Association for the Advancement of Colored People, Women in the; Suffrage

References *Congressional Quarterly, Almanac 89th Congress, 1st Session . . . 1965* (1966).

Vucanovich, Barbara Farrell (b. 1921)

Republican Barbara Vucanovich of Nevada served in the U.S. House of Representatives from 3 January 1983 to 3 January 1997. While in Congress, Vucanovich focused her attention on issues associated with the proposed low-level nuclear waste site in Nevada. She fought several battles over federal land policies, which are important in Nevada because the federal government owns 85 percent of the land in the state. Another battle involved proposed changes in the 1872 Mining Law, also important in a state that produces 60 percent of the nation's gold.

Opposed to the Equal Rights Amendment, comparable worth, reproductive rights, and family and medical leave, Vucanovich has introduced measures to improve child support enforcement, provide tax credits for adoption and elder care, and impose stiffer sentences for crimes against children. She held the leadership position of secretary of the House Republican Caucus in the 104th Congress (1995–1997). Vucanovich did not run for reelection in 1996.

Born in Camp Dix, New Jersey, Barbara Vucanovich attended Manhattanville College from 1938 to 1939. After moving to Nevada in 1949, she owned a travel agency. She became active in the Republican Party in

Representative Barbara Vucanovich (R-NV) talked with master of ceremonies Tom Lorentzen at a luncheon in her honor at the state Republican Convention in Reno, 1996 (Associated Press AP)

the 1950s by working for presidential candidates and also was active in Republican women's groups, including serving as president of the Nevada Federation of Republican Women. She was a grassroots organizer for a member of Congress from 1962 to 1982.

See also Congress, Women in; Equal Rights Amendment; Family and Medical Leave Act of 1993; Pay Equity; Reproductive Rights

References Congressional Quarterly, *Politics in America 1996* (1995), *Politics in America: The 100th Congress* (1987).

W

Wald, Lillian D. (1867–1940)

Nurse and social reformer Lillian Wald founded the Henry Street Settlement in New York City and the visiting nurse service of New York in 1893. In 1896, the settlement had eleven residents, nine of them nurses; by 1929, it had 250 nurses. In 1902, Wald led the effort to create the world's first public school nursing system when she coordinated the efforts of Henry Street nurses and the New York City Board of Health to develop and implement the program. Wald provided the ideas and leadership for several health delivery innovations, including Metropolitan Life Insurance Company's nursing service for industrial policyholders (1909) and the American Red Cross's rural public health nursing service (1912).

Wald's interests extended beyond nursing. With Florence Kelley, she cofounded the National Child Labor Committee to limit child labor in 1904, and the two women planned and worked for a federal agency for children. As a result of Kelley and Wald's work, Congress created the Children's Bureau in 1912. Along with Jane Addams, Wald and Kelley also founded the American Union Against Militarism because of their opposition to World War I. Despite her opposition to war, Wald served on the Committee on Nursing of the General Medical Board of the Council of National Defense, the Committee for Vassar (nurse) Training Camp, and other committees supporting the war effort during World War I.

Born in Cincinnati, Ohio, Wald graduated from New York City's Hospital Training School for Nurses in 1891, enrolled in the Women's Medical College of New York Infirmary in 1892, but left medical school in

Lillian Wald, health care and child labor activist, 1920 (Library of Congress)

1893 and worked as a community health nurse. She wrote *Boarded-Out Babies* (1907), *The House on Henry Street* (1915), and *Windows on Henry Street* (1934).

See also Addams, Jane, Child Labor Amendment; Children's Bureau; Kelley, Florence

References James, ed., *Notable American Women, 1607–1950* (1971); Lindenmeyer, *"A Right to Childhood": The U.S. Children's Bureau and Child Welfare, 1912–1946* (1997).

Waldholtz, Enid Greene
See **Greene, Enid**

Wallace, Lurleen Burns (1926–1968)

Democrat Lurleen Wallace was governor of Alabama from 1967 to 1968, serving as her husband's surrogate because state law prohibited him from succeeding himself. Following World War II, George Wallace began his career as a politician, and Lurleen Wallace began hers as a homemaker. In 1963, George Wallace began his first term as governor of Alabama, gaining national attention when he attempted to stop the integration efforts of the civil rights movement. Even though George Wallace was popular in the state, Alabama's constitution prohibited anyone from serving more than two consecutive terms as governor. After failed attempts to change the policy, he announced that his wife Lurleen Wallace would run for governor in 1966 and continue his policies. During the campaign, Lurleen Wallace told an audience: "My election would enable my husband to carry on his programs for the people of Alabama."

When Lurleen Wallace became governor, George Wallace served as her special adviser and worked out of an office across the hall from her office. Although in many ways her husband's surrogate, Lurleen Wallace obtained passage of measures for a $15 million bond and for a two-cent-per-pack tax on cigarettes, both to finance regional mental hospitals. She also worked for funding for health programs. Her tenure was shortened by her death from cancer.

Born in Tuscaloosa, Alabama, Lurleen Wallace completed her education at Tuscaloosa Business College. When she was sixteen, she worked at a variety store, where she met George Wallace. They married in 1943.

See also Civil Rights Movement, Women in the; Governors, Women

References Yelverton, *They Also Served: Twenty-Five Remarkable Alabama Women* (1993).

Representative Maxine Waters (D-CA) with Bill Clinton, 1992 (Corbis/Joseph Sohm/Ohio Inc.)

Waters, Maxine Moore (b. 1938)

Democrat Maxine Waters of California entered the U.S. House of Representatives on 3 January 1991. Waters explained that it is important to have strong African American women in power: "We have surfaced issues that never got heard or thought about if it weren't here [in the California legislature]. Sometimes we forget that there are still people who have never interacted with blacks."

Born in St. Louis, Missouri, Waters entered the workforce at thirteen years old, busing tables in a segregated restaurant. She married after graduating from high school, and within a short time, the couple had two children and few job prospects. They moved to California, but jobs were scarce there as well: Waters worked in a garment factory, and her husband worked in a printing plant.

In 1966 Waters went to work for Head Start, first as an assistant teacher and then as a supervisor. During that period, she attended college, earning her bachelor of arts degree in sociology from California State University in 1972. She also divorced her husband that year.

After working for a member of the Los Angeles City Council from 1973 to 1976, Waters developed her political skills and ran for the California

Assembly in 1976, serving from 1977 to 1991. While in the assembly, she passed a bill to limit the situations in which law enforcement officers can strip-search (search the body cavities of) the people they arrest and another requiring insurance companies to pay for prosthetic devices after mastectomies. In an effort to combat South Africa's apartheid policy, she passed a bill requiring the State of California to divest itself of investments in companies that conducted business in that country. She was the first woman elected chair of the Democratic Caucus and held the fourth position on the California Assembly leadership team.

Congresswoman Waters has been an advocate for veterans' affairs, improvements in housing in inner cities, and better enforcement of the federal antiredlining law. Waters gained national attention in April 1992, when south-central Los Angeles erupted in violence. Five days of rioting consumed Los Angeles after the acquittal of four white police officers charged with beating Rodney King, a black man. Her district office was among the buildings that burned in the riots. Waters flew to the site of it, attempting to explain to the nation that the riots emerged not only because of the verdict in the trial but out of desperate hopelessness. In the process, she emerged as a spokesperson for the nation's disadvantaged.

See also Congress, Women in; National Political Congress of Black Women

References Congressional Quarterly, *Politics in America 1994* (1993); H. W. Wilson, *Current Biography Yearbook, 1992* (1992); Mills, "Maxine Waters: The Sassy Legislator Who Knows There's More Than One Way to Make a Political Statement" (1988).

Watson, Barbara Mae (1918–1983)

Barbara M. Watson was the first African American and first woman to be assistant secretary of state. Appointed in 1968 by President Lyndon Johnson to be deputy administrator of the Bureau of Security and Consular Affairs, which had the rank of assistant secretary, she oversaw 3,000 federal employees. She supervised the issuance of passports and visas to U.S. citizens and the nation's 250 consuls throughout the world. She has been credited with increasing the efficiency of the bureau through the reduction of duplication of effort. During her administration, Watson negotiated the return of 20,000 American tourists caught during an Arab-Israeli conflict. She also mediated shipping problems encountered in foreign waters and focused on the rights of U.S. citizens arrested in other nations. A private attorney from 1975 to 1976, she returned to public service as assistant secretary of state from 1977 to 1980. In 1980–1981, Watson served as U.S. ambassador to Malaysia.

Born in New York City, Barbara Watson earned her bachelor of arts degree from Barnard College in 1943 and her bachelor of law degree from

New York Law School in 1962. In 1946, Watson founded Barbara Watson Models and Barbara Watson Charm and Modeling Schools. She explained the significance of the modeling agency: "It opened up the whole field for Negro women and men for the benefit of advertisers. Before, Negroes in advertising meant Aunt Jemima and porters carrying luggage." She closed the agency in 1956 and entered law school.

After receiving her law degree in 1962, Watson worked for several New York City agencies as counsel. In 1964, she became executive director of the New York City Commission to the United Nations. She went to Washington, D.C., in 1966 to become special assistant to the deputy undersecretary for administration in the State Department.

References *New York Times,* 7 May 1971, 18 February 1983.

Wattleton, Alyce Faye (b. 1943)

President of the Planned Parenthood Federation of America (PPFA) from 1978 to 1992, Faye Wattleton became one of the most influential leaders in the area of reproductive rights and health care. The first woman, first African American, and youngest person to hold the position in the latter part of the century, Wattleton became the most visible and most persuasive spokeswoman for reproductive rights in the nation. She assumed the post in a difficult time. The strength of anti-abortion groups had become apparent with the passage of the Hyde Amendment in 1977, which limited the use of federal funding for abortions for low-income women. Violence had also become a significant problem. Planned Parenthood clinics in Minnesota, Virginia, Nebraska, Vermont, and Ohio had been burned or bombed. Wattleton explained: "This is not a debate about abortion. This is the defense of the fundamental right to make choices about our sexuality—without the encroachment of the president, the Supreme Court and certainly without the encroachment of politicians!"

President Ronald Reagan advocated policies that limited reproductive choice. His proposals included cutting funding for family planning services to low-income women, requiring parental consent before minors could receive diaphragms, intrauterine devices, or birth control pills in federally funded clinics. Another proposal would prevent clinics that received federal funds from offering abortion counseling. To counter these problems, Wattleton sought to publicize PPFA's role as the largest provider of reproductive health services and to create public support to preserve every person's right to sexual and reproductive choice. Wattleton lobbied Congress to stop conservative measures to restrict abortion, arguing that abortion is a personal decision.

Wattleton first encountered the medical and emotional complications

that women faced with illegal abortions as a nursing instructor. As a graduate student in midwifery, she had watched her patients suffer from unwanted pregnancies and die from illegal abortions and wanted to protect future generations from similar fates. In 1967, she returned to Dayton, Ohio, where she assumed the position of assistant director of Public Health Nursing Services in the city's Department of Health. Invited to join the local Planned Parenthood board, she became its director in 1970. Wattleton moved to the national arena in 1975, when she became chair of the National Executive Directors Council of Planned Parenthood of America.

Born in St. Louis, Missouri, Faye Wattleton earned her nursing degree from Ohio State University in 1964 and her master of science degree in maternal and infant health care and certification as a nurse-midwife at Columbia University in 1967. Wattleton's memoirs, *Life on the Line,* were published in 1996.

See also Abortion; Planned Parenthood Federation of America

References H. W. Wilson, *Current Biography Yearbook, 1990* (1990).

Webster v. Reproductive Health Services (1989)

In *Webster v. Reproductive Health Services,* the U.S. Supreme Court accepted a Missouri abortion law that had several provisions. The law's preamble said that human life begins at conception and that unborn children have rights that must be protected, a statement that the Court permitted. The Court said that until Missouri's courts interpreted it, the federal courts had no reason to address the issue. The Court also accepted the requirement that tests and examinations for fetal viability had to be performed before a physician could perform an abortion on a woman the physician believed to be twenty weeks or more pregnant. The prohibition against using public employees and facilities in abortions was accepted because the Court said it did not violate the due process clause.

See also Abortion; *Roe v. Wade*

References *Webster v. Reproductive Health Services,* 492 U.S. 490 (1989).

Weddington, Sarah Ragle (b. 1945)

As a young Texas lawyer, Sarah Weddington argued *Roe v. Wade* before the U.S. Supreme Court in 1973 and won abortion rights for U.S. women. The case developed when Weddington and an informal network of abortion rights activists, who were providing abortion referral services, decided to try to legalize abortions in Texas by bringing a suit against the state's 1854 law prohibiting the procedure. In 1970, they identified a pregnant woman who wanted an abortion and was willing to participate in a legal challenge to the state's abortion laws. To protect her identity, Weddington gave her the pseudonym "Jane Roe," a name representing all women to Weddington.

Attorney Sarah Weddington won the Roe v. Wade *case, which guaranteed women's right to privacy in their reproductive choices, before the U.S. Supreme Court when she was only twenty-six years old (Archive Photos)*

Weddington argued that the laws were vague and unconstitutionally broad and infringed on the plaintiff's right to safe and adequate medical advice and on her fundamental right to choose whether to bear children. Arguing the case before a three-judge panel in federal court, Weddington won when the court declared the Texas abortion laws unconstitutional. The state appealed the case. Weddington argued the case before the U.S. Supreme Court in 1971.

While the Supreme Court considered *Roe v. Wade,* Weddington and others worked to change Texas's abortion laws but failed, prompting Weddington to run for the Texas legislature in 1972. Her campaign issues included rape law reform, increased access to credit for women, pregnancy leave, and employment equity. Weddington did not believe that she could win the race, but it gave her a platform to bring attention to women's political status. She sought the help of Democratic Party veteran campaigner Ann Richards, pleading with her over a lunch meeting for assistance. Richards agreed to manage the campaign.

Weddington's legislative race encountered an obstacle when she learned that she would have to argue *Roe v. Wade* before the U.S. Supreme Court a second time the month before election day. Even though Weddington had to leave the state to argue the case, in November 1972 she won the legislative race. During her three terms in the Texas House of Representatives, she worked with Kay Bailey Hutchison to pass a bill that reformed Texas rape laws, passed an equal credit bill for women, worked with Eddie Bernice Johnson to pass a pregnancy leave bill for teachers, and prevented passage of antiabortion legislation. In January 1973, Weddington won the landmark U.S. Supreme Court case *Roe v. Wade*. Abortion became a legal option for women wanting to end their pregnancies.

Appointed general counsel of the U.S. Department of Agriculture in 1977, she served as assistant to President Jimmy Carter from 1978 to 1981, identifying women for the federal judiciary and other high-level appointments. Weddington lobbied the U.S. Senate for an extension to ratify the Equal Rights Amendment and received a great deal of credit for the success of the effort. Following the passage of the extension, she helped develop a strategy for ratification of the amendment, but it failed in 1982.

Weddington also helped implement programs to grant women equal treatment in the military, in their attempts to secure loans, and in the delivery of social programs. She was cochair of the U.S. delegation to the 1980 United Nations Mid-Decade Conference on Women in Copenhagen, Denmark.

Born in Abilene, Texas, Weddington earned her bachelor of science degree from McMurry College in 1965 and her law degree from the University of Texas in 1967. She then worked on the American Bar Association's Special Committee on the Reevaluation of Ethical Standards. She is the author of *A Question of Choice* (1992).

See also Abortion; Equal Credit Opportunity Act of 1974; Equal Rights Amendment; Hutchison, Kathryn (Kay) Ann Bailey; Johnson, Eddie Bernice; Richards, Ann Willis; *Roe v. Wade*; State Legislatures, Women in

References *New York Times*, 6 November 1978; Weddington, *A Question of Choice* (1992).

Weeks v. Southern Bell Telephone and Telegraph Company (1969)

In *Weeks v. Southern Bell Telephone and Telegraph Company*, the first sex discrimination case to reach an appellate court, Lorena Weeks challenged Southern Bell's contention that sex was a bona fide occupational qualification for the job of switchman. Southern Bell argued that the job was strenuous, that a switchman was occasionally required to work alone during late-night hours, and that the State of Georgia's protective legislation prevented women from holding jobs that required them to lift more than thirty pounds. Weeks argued that the state's protective policy and Southern Bell's hiring policy violated Title VII of the Civil Rights Act of 1964 by discriminating against her on the basis of sex.

The Fifth Circuit of the U.S. Court of Appeals noted that Georgia had replaced the limit on the amount that women could lift with a broader policy. The appeals court agreed with Weeks, saying: "Labeling a job 'strenuous' does not meet the burden of proving that the job falls within the bona fide occupational qualification exception." It further noted that the company's concerns about women working late at night conflicted with the reality that other women employees were called in to work during emergencies. The court wrote: "Title VII rejects just this type of romantic paternalism as unduly Victorian and instead invests individual women with the power to decide whether or not to take on unromantic tasks." The court found that Southern Bell's refusal to hire women for the job of switchman violated Title VII.

See also Bona Fide Occupational Qualification; Civil Rights Act of 1964, Title VII; Employment Discrimination

References *Weeks v. Southern Bell Telephone and Telegraph Company,* 408 F.2d 228 (1969).

Weinberger v. Wiesenfeld (1975)

In *Weinberger v. Wiesenfeld,* the U.S. Supreme Court decided that a Social Security benefit plan that provided benefits to the widow and children of a deceased male wage earner but that did not provide the same benefits to the widower and children of a deceased female wage earner was unconstitutional.

In the case, Paula Wiesenfeld had died giving birth to her son Jason, who was eligible for Social Security benefits, but her widowed husband Stephen Wiesenfeld was denied benefits that would have been available to a widow. Stephen Wiesenfeld claimed that the policy was a form of illegal discrimination.

The Court agreed with Wiesenfeld's argument as presented by Ruth Bader Ginsburg, writing in response: "Given the purpose of enabling the surviving parent to remain at home to care for a child, the gender-based distinction . . . is entirely irrational. The classification discriminates among surviving children solely on the basis of the sex of the surviving parent." The Court found that the policy violated the due process clause of the Fifth Amendment.

See also Ginsburg, Ruth Joan Bader

References *Weinberger v. Wiesenfeld,* 420 U.S. 636 (1975).

Weis, Jessica McCullough (1901–1963)

Republican Jessica Weis of New York served in the U.S. House of Representatives from 3 January 1959 to 3 January 1963. Weis entered politics in 1936, holding local party offices, and in 1938 she was appointed vice president of the National Federation of Republican Women and was president from 1941 to 1942. She was Republican national committeewoman for New York from 1944 to 1963.

An associate campaign manager in Thomas E. Dewey's 1948 presidential campaign, she worked to gain women's support for him. Appointed to the National Defense Advisory Council in 1953 and reappointed in 1956 and 1960, she was an advisor to the U.S. delegate to the Inter-American Commission on Women in 1954.

A fiscal conservative, Congresswoman Weis opposed federal spending for veterans' housing, airport and power plant construction, and water pollution control. She supported an equal rights amendment and urged an end to wage discrimination against women. Her health prevented her from seeking a third term.

Born in Chicago, Jessica Weis attended Madame Rieffel's French School in New York City from 1916 to 1917.

See also Congress, Women in; Equal Rights Amendment

References H. W. Wilson, *Current Biography Yearbook, 1959* (1959); Office of the Historian, U.S. House of Representatives, *Women in Congress, 1917–1990* (1991).

Welfare

Welfare, or assistance to people in need, emerged as a significant federal program during the Depression in the 1930s. One aspect of a wide array of policies intended to help the U.S. economy recover from the Depression, welfare programs included employment opportunities, assistance to blind persons, maternal and child health grants, and Aid to Families with Dependent Children (AFDC). Over the next six decades, some of the programs were discarded or replaced, and new programs were added.

AFDC, perhaps the most widely recognized welfare program, began as a small program to provide cash assistance to mothers of young children whose fathers had died. Intended to be only a temporary program, AFDC developed into one of the largest of the nation's welfare programs and served approximately 14 million people in 1994. Its purposes were to encourage keeping children in their homes (instead of placing them in orphanages, other facilities, or foster care), to strengthen family life, and to promote self-supporting families. Other federal welfare programs include child support enforcement, child care, food stamps, Medicaid, and Supplemental Security Income.

Critics of welfare programs, especially of AFDC, charged that their financial burden was detrimental to the economy and that they promoted dependency and discouraged employment. Supporters argued that the costs associated with employment, including child care, transportation, and the potential loss of government-supported health insurance, created disincentives to employment and that changes in AFDC would need to include education, employment assistance, and other services. The Personal Responsibility and Work Opportunity Reconciliation Act of 1996 instituted the greatest changes in welfare policy in the United States since the 1960s and addressed many of the issues raised by critics and supporters.

See also Personal Responsibility and Work Opportunity Reconciliation Act of 1996

References "Current Programs" (1995); "Welfare Overview" (1995).

Wells-Barnett, Ida Bell (1862–1931)

Ida Wells-Barnett crusaded against lynching, worked in the black women's club movement, and helped found the Alpha Suffrage Club, the National Association for the Advancement of Colored People, and the National Association of Colored Women. Born a slave in Holly Springs, Mississippi, Wells-Barnett taught school to help support her five brothers and sisters following the deaths of her parents in the 1878 yellow fever epidemic. In 1883 and 1884, she attended Fisk University and the Lemoyne Institute.

Wells-Barnett's protests against segregation began on a train trip from Memphis to Woodstock in 1884, when a railroad conductor ordered her to move to the smoking car. Having purchased a first-class ticket, she refused and was forcibly removed. She sued the railroad and won, but the Tennessee Supreme Court reversed the decision in 1887 and ruled against her.

From 1884 to 1891, she taught school in Memphis, Tennessee. Wells-Barnett became a reporter for and part-owner of the *Memphis Free Speech and Headlight* in 1889 and gained a wide reputation for her militant opinions. She lost her teaching job in 1891 for writing articles critical of the education offered to African American children.

Following the lynching of three African American friends in 1892, Wells-Barnett began an editorial campaign against lynching. In one article she wrote: "Nobody in this section of the country believes the old thread bare lie that Negro men rape white women." After writing the article, Wells-Barnett left for Philadelphia. When the article appeared, a mob broke into the newspaper's building and destroyed the presses. Wells-Barnett was warned not to return to Memphis.

Journalist Ida Wells-Barnett carried out a one-woman crusade in the editorial pages against the lynching practices of the Deep South (Courtesy: University of Chicago)

She moved to New York City and became a staff writer for *New York Age,* where she wrote and lectured about lynching. Wells-Barnett published two pamphlets on lynching, *Southern Horrors* in 1892 and *A Red Record* in 1895, a statistical account of lynchings from 1892 to 1894. She reported that African American men were accused of rape in less than one-third of the cases, and even fewer of the men were found guilty. She revealed that in some situations white women initiated consensual sex with African American men and that white men had raped African American women with apparent impunity. Wells-Barnett found that when African Americans resisted mobs by fighting back, the violence diminished. She wrote: "A Winchester rifle should have a place of honor in every black home. When the white man knows he runs as great a risk biting the dust every time his Afro-American victim does, he will have greater respect for Afro-American life."

Secretary of the National Afro-American Council from 1898 to 1902, Wells-Barnett helped organize a conference on African Americans, helped establish the National Association for the Advancement of Colored People (NAACP) in 1909, and served on its executive committee. She founded in 1910 and was president of the Negro Fellowship League, a settlement house and community center for southern black migrants to Chicago. In 1913 she started the Alpha Suffrage Club, the first African American woman suffrage group, and led the club in the 1916 Chicago suffrage parade to the Republican National Convention. In 1930, she unsuccessfully ran on the Republican ticket for the Illinois Senate.

Wells-Barnett wrote *Mob Rule in New Orleans* (1900), *The Arkansas Race Riot* (1920), and other books.

See also Alpha Suffrage Club; Antilynching Movement; National Association for the Advancement of Colored People, Women in the; National Association of Colored Women

References Giddings, *When and Where I Enter: The Impact of Black Women on Race and Sex in America* (1984); Wells-Barnett, *Crusade for Justice* (1970).

Westwood, Frances Jean Miles (1923–1997)

Jean Westwood was chair of the Democratic National Committee (DNC) in 1972, the first woman to chair either of the major political parties' national committees. Westwood began her political career at the precinct level in the mid-1950s and worked on the staff of a member of Congress from 1964 to 1967. She served as vice chair of the Democratic Party in Utah, cochair of a voter registration campaign, campaign manager for a congressional candidate, and beginning in 1968, national committeewoman for Utah. The first member of the DNC to endorse Senator George McGovern's candidacy for president, she helped him build his organization.

When George McGovern became the Democratic Party's presidential candidate in 1972, he chose Westwood to chair the party. McGovern lost to incumbent president Richard Nixon, and the DNC replaced Westwood shortly after the election. She continued to be active in the party until 1988.

Born in Price, Utah, Westwood attended Carbon College and took classes at other colleges and universities.

References *New York Times*, 15 July 1972, 23 August 1997.

Wexler, Anne Levy (b. 1930)

Democratic Party activist Anne Wexler is considered one of the most powerful lobbyists in Washington, D.C. She began her political career working in congressional and presidential races in the 1960s. She supported Jimmy Carter's 1976 presidential campaign and worked on his transition team following his election. Appointed deputy undersecretary of commerce, she coordinated the department's programs and field operations and chaired the President's Task Force on Women Business Owners. Appointed an assistant to the president in 1978, she was the only woman on President Jimmy Carter's senior staff. As assistant for public liaison, Wexler's responsibilities included working with the business community and other interest groups to build public support for the president's programs and policies. Wexler founded a government relations firm in 1981.

Born in New York City, Wexler earned her bachelor of arts degree from Skidmore College in 1951. She began her political activism while a student, canvassing door-to-door during Harry S. Truman's 1948 presidential campaign.

References *New York Times*, 12 July 1972, 24 November 1978.

Whitman, Christine Todd (b. 1946)

Republican Christine Todd Whitman became governor of New Jersey in 1994, the first woman governor of the state, and was reelected in 1997 for a second four-year term. A fiscal conservative, Whitman promised voters during her first campaign for governor that she would reduce taxes by 30 percent, a pledge she kept and one that helped her when she sought reelection.

Christine Todd Whitman (R-NJ) was elected the first woman governor of New Jersey, 1994 (Corbis/Robert Maass)

Born in New York state, Whitman is the daughter of active and influential Republicans. Her mother Eleanor Todd served on the Republican National Committee for a decade, was the committee's vice chair, and chaired the New Jersey Federation of Republican Women. Her father chaired the New Jersey Republican State Central Committee for eleven years. Whitman's political ventures began when she was a child selling lemonade to benefit Dwight D. Eisenhower's 1952 presidential campaign.

Whitman earned her bachelor of arts degree from Wheaton College in 1968 and worked on Nelson Rockefeller's campaign for the Republican nomination for president. Later that year, she worked at the Republican National Committee, where she developed the Listening Post project and toured the country to learn the reasons why college students were not attracted to the Republican Party. She later worked at the Office of Economic Opportunity. During the 1972 presidential campaign, she worked for the Committee to Reelect the President, organizing support for President Richard Nixon among senior citizens.

Whitman first ran for public office in 1982, when she was elected to the Somerset County Board of Chosen Freeholders, which is comparable to a county board of supervisors. She served on the board for five years, becoming both deputy director and director in that period. She supervised the construction of a new county courthouse, developed an open space program, and helped establish the county's first homeless shelter.

In 1988 Governor Todd Kean appointed Whitman president of the New Jersey Board of Utilities. In response to questionable actions by previous members of the board, Whitman developed a code of ethics for the board. Among her public policy goals for the board was maintaining low utility rates.

Whitman unsuccessfully ran for the U.S. Senate in 1990. Her defeat by only two percentage points convinced her that she could win the governor's seat in 1993. She hosted a biweekly radio talk show, wrote a newspaper column to maintain the name recognition she had developed, and worked for candidates at every level, building a political base for her planned gubernatorial campaign. Her success on election day was marred within a few days by a scandal created by her campaign manager, Ed Rollins. Rollins told a group of reporters that the campaign had spent $500,000 dissuading African American ministers from endorsing incumbent governor Jim Florio and paying Democratic workers to stay home on election day. Whitman immediately responded that she had no knowledge of the activities and began an internal investigation of her campaign. Rollins soon recanted and said that he had not done the things he had said. The New Jersey attorney general and the U.S. attorney general both investigated Whitman's campaign but could find no evidence of the illegal practices.

During her first year in office, Whitman cut income taxes 10 percent, eliminated 400 state jobs, and abolished the Department of Higher Education and the Office of the Public Advocate. The cuts included reductions in contributions to the state pension fund but also made New Jersey more appealing to business. As her first term continued, Whitman reduced income taxes by a total of 30 percent, privatized the Department of Motor Vehicles, and changed the state's Aid to Families with Dependent Children program. Between 1994 and 1999, Whitman helped New Jersey gain a net increase of more than 300,000 jobs through her economic development programs. Whitman also reformed the state's juvenile justice program, establishing a system of preventive programs, sanctions, and aftercare for youthful offenders. The program included a new juvenile boot camp, a facility for female juvenile offenders, and funding for local prevention programs.

A moderate Republican, Whitman supports abortion rights, which has placed her outside the party's prevailing sentiments but not outside the party's favor. In 1995, she became the first woman and the first governor to deliver the Republican Party's response to a presidential State of the Union address.

See also Governors, Women

References Beard, *Growing Up Republican* (1996); McClure, *Christie Whitman* (1996); *New York Times*, 1 July 1994, 5 May 1996.

Widnall, Sheila Evans (b. 1938)

Secretary of the Air Force from 1993 to 1997, Sheila Widnall is the first woman to head a branch of the U.S. military. During her tenure as secretary, Widnall focused attention on quality-of-life issues and scientific and technological development. Before her appointment, Widnall had served on the U.S. Air Force Board of Visitors and several Air Force advisory committees. An internationally recognized authority on fluid dynamics, Widnall began teaching at Massachusetts Institute of Technology (MIT) in 1964 and returned to teaching there after stepping down as secretary of the Air Force.

Born in Tacoma, Washington, Widnall earned her bachelor of science degree in 1960, her master of science degree in 1961, and her doctor of science degree in 1964, all from MIT.

See also Military, Women in the

References www.af.mil.

Willard, Frances Elizabeth Caroline (1839–1898)

Temperance leader and suffragist Frances Willard was president of the Woman's Christian Temperance Union (WCTU) from 1879 until her death. Willard expanded the organization's focus from Prohibition and total abstinence from alcohol to include woman suffrage and other social reform crusades.

Born in Churchville, New York, she grew up in Wisconsin Territory on her family's frontier farm. Her early education was sporadic, but she attended Milwaukee Female College in 1857; transferred to North Western Female College in Evanston, Illinois, and graduated in 1859; and began teaching the next year. From 1871 to 1873, she was president of Evanston College for Ladies, a part of Northwestern University.

Over the next two years, Willard supported herself as a temperance speaker, was elected president of Chicago Woman's Christian Temperance Union, attended her first national WCTU convention, and was elected corresponding secretary of the national group. Elected national WCTU president in 1879, Willard improved the organization's financial condition and decentralized it by giving state and local groups greater autonomy. She also created a variety of departments covering topical areas, including heredity and hygiene, social purity, legislation, and petition.

At the 1881 WCTU convention, Willard told members to "do everything" and pointed out that reforms were interconnected. Over the next decade the WCTU became increasingly politically active by forging an alliance with the Prohibition Party and endorsing presidential candidates. In addition, Willard successfully lobbied the Prohibition Party to include a suffrage plank in its 1888 platform. She led the WCTU in expanding its social reform programs to encompass establishing free kindergartens, reducing the workday to eight hours, passing protective labor legislation, raising the legal age of consent for sex, toughening rape laws, and closing businesses on Sunday.

See also Suffrage; Temperance Movement, Women in the; Woman's Christian Temperance Union

References Lee, *"Do Everything" Reform: The Oratory of Frances E. Willard* (1992).

Frances Willard, president of the Woman's Christian Temperance Union and suffragist leader, between 1880 and 1898 (Library of Congress)

Willebrandt, Mabel Walker (1889–1963)

The first female public defender in the United States, Mabel Walker Willebrandt became an assistant attorney general in 1921, making her the first woman to hold a permanent subcabinet-level appointment. Seven years later, in 1928, she chaired the Credentials Committee of the 1928 Republican National Convention and with that appointment became the first woman to chair an important national convention committee for either party. Throughout her career, she worked to advance the opportunities and careers of other women lawyers.

Born in a sod dugout in southwestern Kansas, Willebrandt attended Park College and Academy in Kansas from 1906 to 1907. She married in 1910 and moved to Arizona because of her husband's poor health. She earned her teaching certificate from Arizona's Tempe Normal School in 1911, and the couple moved to the Los Angeles area, where she taught school during the day and attended law school at night, earning her bachelor of laws degree from the University of Southern California in 1916 and her master of laws degree from the same school the next year. She began her law career as the assistant public defender in Los Angeles, working on more than 2,000 cases brought against women, particularly charges for prostitution. By 1918, she had established herself within the legal profession in Los Angeles, helped organize the Women's Law Club of Los Angeles County, and developed an active private practice.

Willebrandt began her political career by campaigning for candidates and became a member of the California Republican State Central Committee which, combined with her legal skills, led to her appointment in 1921 as a U.S. assistant attorney general by President Warren G. Harding. In charge of Prohibition enforcement, taxes, and the Bureau of Federal Prisons, her responsibilities included coordinating the enforcement programs of the Treasury Department, the Coast Guard, and state and local law enforcement agencies. Willebrandt became most widely known for her prosecution of Prohibition cases, leading New York governor Alfred E. Smith to refer to her as "Prohibition Portia." She responded: "It is not particularly gratifying to be thought of merely as a Nemesis of bootleggers, a chaser of criminals." Her first big cases came in 1922, when she broke two southern rings, one in Savannah, Georgia, and the other in Mobile, Alabama, in which Congressman John W. Langley of Kentucky was found guilty. Willebrandt developed a novel strategy for enforcing the Volstead Act when she decided to use income tax evasion as a way to stop bootleggers. She preferred enforcing tax laws because, as she said: "They require detached and abstract thought, an intellectual exercise of which women were once thought incapable."

Willebrandt aggressively pursued those who broke the law, filing between 49,000 and 55,000 criminal and civil cases annually. In these cases, she helped establish the constitutional validity of the Volstead Act and other laws through U.S. Supreme Court decisions. Of the thirty-nine cases she argued before the Court, she won thirty-seven. By 1929, of all the lawyers who had argued cases before the Court, she ranked fourth in the total number of cases she had presented.

With prisons filling with Volstead violators, the need for additional space in them grew, as did the need to review the related policies. Willebrandt began by calling for a federal women's prison, for which she sought support from the Women's Joint Congressional Committee (WJCC). With the WJCC's help, she found support from the League of Women Voters, the Woman's Christian Temperance Union, the General Federation of Women's Clubs (GFWC), and several other groups. She also believed that young, male, first-time offenders serving their sentences in prison were further corrupted by the exposure to more experienced law violators and that a federal reformatory for them was needed. By enlisting the support of the Young Men's Christian Association, GFWC, American Bar Association, Kiwanis Club International, and other groups, Willebrandt succeeded in creating a federal reformatory. In addition, she sought to improve prison conditions and to provide work within prisons. Her first task, however, was to identify and remove corrupt and incompetent prison officials by planting government agents posing as inmates within the facilities. With the support of GFWC and others interested in prison reform, she then began developing prison industries to provide employment for every prison inmate, engaging in perennial battles for appropriations for the programs.

In 1928, Willebrandt turned some of her attention to the Republican Party and to making Herbert Hoover the party's presidential nominee. She attended the Republican National Convention as a Hoover delegate and was permanent chair of the party's Credentials Committee. As Credentials Committee chair, Willebrandt worked to ensure that the committee decided in favor of delegates pledged to Hoover, which helped him obtain the nomination. A dedicated Hoover supporter, Willebrandt worked for him throughout the campaign and became the center of a national controversy. In a speech to a group of Methodists who supported Prohibition, Willebrandt questioned Democratic presidential nominee Al Smith's commitment to enforcing the Volstead Act and characterized Hoover as ready to provide the necessary leadership in enforcing it. In that and subsequent speeches to other religious groups, she referred to Smith's religion, Catholicism, making it an issue in the campaign. Willebrandt was attacked by the press for injecting religion into the presidential race, and some Republican leaders wanted her silenced. One leading feminist, however, viewed the dispute as testimony that a woman had enough political power to be the center of a disagreement. Commenting on the criticism heaped on Willebrandt, Democratic Party leader Emily Newell Blair said that Willebrandt was the first woman to make a place for herself as a "great figure in politics." After Hoover won the election, Willebrandt concluded that he was not as committed to enforcing Prohibition as she had thought and resigned as assistant attorney general in May 1929.

Willebrandt joined Aviation Corporation as general counsel and began a new career in the emerging field of aviation law, chairing a committee on the topic for the American Bar Association from 1938 to 1942. She also pioneered in the area of radio law, winning a U.S. Supreme Court decision that upheld the Federal Radio Commission's power to regulate broadcasting. In addition, she worked for Louis B. Meyer of MGM Studio and Hollywood stars and other celebrities.

> **See also** General Federation of Women's Clubs; Langley, Katherine Gudger; League of Women Voters; Woman's Christian Temperance Union; Women's Joint Congressional Committee
>
> **References** Brown, *Mabel Walker Willebrandt* (1984); *New York Times*, 9 April 1963; Strakosh, "A Woman in Law" (1927).

Williams v. Zbaraz (1980)

Decided with *Harris v. McRae*, *Williams v. Zbaraz* challenged an Illinois statute prohibiting state medical assistance payments for all abortions except those to save the life of the woman seeking the abortion. Approaching this case as a class action suit, the challengers argued that even though Medicaid funding for medically necessary abortions had ended with the passage of the Hyde Amendment, the state still had an obligation to pay for them under the equal protection clause of the Fourteenth Amendment.

The U.S. Supreme Court rejected the argument, saying that a state was not obligated to pay for medically necessary abortions that were not covered by Medicaid and that the policy did not violate the equal protection clause of the Fourteenth Amendment.

See also Abortion; *Harris v. McRae*

References *Williams v. Zbaraz*, 448 U.S. 358 (1980).

Wilson, Edith Bolling Galt (1872–1961)

First lady from 1915 to 1921, Edith Wilson was the wife of President Woodrow Wilson. After President Wilson suffered a stroke in October 1919, Edith Wilson controlled who could see her husband during the six months of his convalescence, and every document that the president received went first to his wife. Edith Wilson did not attempt to run the presidency, but her control over access to the president determined which matters received his attention and which would languish. Edith Wilson kept the president's condition a secret from all except his doctor and a few intimates; she did not inform the cabinet.

Born in Wytheville, Virginia, Edith Wilson learned to read and write at home and attended Martha Washington College, a girls' preparatory school, from 1887 to 1888 and Powell's School from 1889 to 1890. Her first husband, Norman Galt, died in 1908. Edith Wilson was Woodrow Wilson's second wife; his first wife, Ellen, had died in 1914. Edith Wilson and Woodrow Wilson met at the White House when she was there for tea, and after a brief courtship, they married.

References Weaver, "Edith Bolling Wilson as First Lady: A Study in the Power of Personality, 1919–1920" (1985).

Wilson, Heather (b. 1960)

Republican Heather Wilson of New Mexico was elected to the U.S. House of Representatives on 23 June 1998. Wilson won her seat in a special election to fill the vacancy created by the death of the incumbent. She is the first woman veteran ever elected to Congress.

Born in Keene, New Hampshire, Wilson earned her bachelor of science degree from the U.S. Air Force Academy in 1982. She earned her master's of philosophy in 1984 and her doctor's degree in philosophy in 1985, both from Oxford University. Wilson served as an Air Force officer until 1989, when she became director for European defense policy and arms control on the National Security Council staff. In 1991 she founded a business consulting firm that worked with senior executives in U.S. defense and scientific corporations. She served as cabinet secretary of the New Mexico Children, Youth, and Families Department, leading the development of programs that addressed juvenile crime, abuse and neglect, and child care and early education.

After winning the special election in June 1998, Wilson won reelection to her seat in the November general elections of that year. Her congressional priorities include improving teacher training, strengthening curricula and early childhood education, eliminating the marriage penalty in income taxes, and maintaining the solvency of Social Security. She cast her vote in Congress for a bill to reform the Internal Revenue Service.

See also Congress, Women in

References "Heather Wilson, R-N.M. (1)" (1998); www.house.gov/wilson/biography/index.htm.

Wingo, Effiegene Locke (1883–1962)

Democrat Effiegene Wingo of Arkansas served in the U.S. House of Representatives from 4 November 1930 to 3 March 1933. After the death of her husband, Representative Otis Wingo, Effiegene Wingo was elected to fill the vacancy and then to a full term. She worked to establish a game refuge in Ouachita National Forest, to create Ouachita National Park, and to complete construction of a railroad bridge in her district. Her district had suffered from natural disasters and from the effects of the Depression, problems she attempted to address by seeking various relief measures. She retired from office after serving the full term and in 1934 was a cofounder of the National Institute of Public Affairs, which provided internships in Washington to students.

Born in Lockesburg, Arkansas, Wingo studied music at the Union Female Seminary and graduated from Maddox Seminary in 1901.

See also Congress, Women in

References Office of the Historian, U.S. House of Representatives, *Women in Congress, 1917–1990* (1991).

WISH List

Founded in 1992, the WISH List supports prochoice Republican women for elective offices at every level. The WISH List is an acronym for Women in the Senate and House. In its first seven years, the WISH List raised $1.5 million and supported the successful candidacies of New Jersey governor Christine Todd Whitman; U.S. senators Susan Collins, Kay

Bailey Hutchison, and Olympia Snowe; and ten women members of the U.S. House of Representatives.

The WISH List process for assisting candidates begins with identifying a Republican prochoice woman candidate and investigating her organization, the race, and her likelihood of winning. After selecting candidates, the WISH List recommends them to its members, including a profile of the candidate and her positions on key issues. WISH List members select at least two of the endorsed candidates and send their contributions to WISH List, which bundles them and forwards them to the candidates.

See also Abortion; Collins, Susan Margaret, Hutchison, Kathryn (Kay) Ann Bailey; Republican Party, Women in the; Snowe, Olympia Jean Bouchles; Whitman, Christine Todd

References www.thewishlist.org.

Wollstonecraft, Mary (1759–1797)

Englishwoman Mary Wollstonecraft published *A Vindication of the Rights of Woman* in 1792, a challenge to contemporary philosophers' views of women and their intellectual abilities. She conceded that many women were vain, ignorant, and childish but argued that women were denied the education and opportunity to develop their skills. She advocated education, opportunities to develop physical strength, and equal rights for women. Her book provided some of the philosophical basis for the suffrage movement that developed in the United States in the nineteenth century. Lucretia Mott, a leader of that movement, called it her "pet book," and when suffragists published their history of the movement, Wollstonecraft was among the women to whom they dedicated it.

Born near London, Mary Wollstonecraft rejected becoming dependent upon anyone else when she was fifteen years old. Self-educated, she opened a school and ran it for several years. After the school began to lose money and closed, Wollstonecraft began a career as a writer.

See also Suffrage

References Gurko, *Ladies of Seneca Falls: The Birth of the Woman's Rights Movement* (1974); Matthews, *Women's Struggle for Equality* (1997).

Woman's Christian Temperance Union

Founded in 1874, the Woman's Christian Temperance Union (WCTU) sought to obtain pledges of total abstinence from alcohol and later added tobacco and other drugs. When Frances Willard became WCTU president in 1879, she added a political dimension to the moral suasion used to achieve the goal of abstinence. Using the motto "do everything," the organization expanded its areas of interest to include establishing and managing day care centers, providing housing for homeless people, and setting up medical clinics—any project that members believed would contribute to achieving abstinence. WCTU advocated a range of social reforms, from woman suffrage to equal pay for equal work to federal aid for education. Willard's presidency ended in 1898, and the WCTU narrowed its scope to a stronger focus on temperance. After passage of the Eighteenth Amendment in 1919, which started Prohibition, the WCTU returned to a broader social reform agenda. For example, it worked with the Women's Joint Congressional Committee to establish a federal women's prison in the 1920s. The oldest voluntary, nonsectarian women's organization in continuous existence in the world, the WCTU continues to advocate abstinence from alcohol and tobacco and has added marijuana and other drugs to its agenda.

> **See also** Suffrage; Temperance Movement, Women in the; Willard, Frances Elizabeth Caroline; Willebrandt, Mabel Walker
>
> **References** www.wctu.org.

Woman's National Loyal League

Organized in 1863 by women's rights leaders and abolitionists Elizabeth Cady Stanton and Susan B. Anthony, the Woman's National Loyal League supported the constitutional amendment banning slavery in the United States. At the founding convention, attendees adopted resolutions supporting the government as long as it pursued freedom for slaves and pledged to collect 1 million signatures calling for passage of the Thirteenth Amendment. Stanton served as the organization's president and Anthony as its secretary.

Two thousand women, men, and children circulated the petitions, with Stanton offering honor badges to the children who collected 100 names. The league gathered 100,000 names, presenting them to the U.S. Senate on 9 February 1864. When the league disbanded in August 1864, it had collected 400,000 signatures. The Thirteenth Amendment passed Congress in early 1865 and was ratified by the states that year.

> **See also** Abolitionist Movement, Women in the; Anthony, Susan Brownell; Stanton, Elizabeth Cady
>
> **References** Flexner and Fitzpatrick, *Century of Struggle: The Woman's Rights Movement in the United States*, enlarged edition (1996).

Woman's Peace Party

Founded in 1915 in response to World War I, the Woman's Peace Party (WPP) included delegates from the Daughters of the American Revolution, the Congressional Union, the Woman's Christian Temperance

Union, the General Federation of Women's Clubs, the Women's Trade Union League, and several other women's organizations. At the organizational meeting, the WPP passed planks calling for arms limitations, mediation of the European conflict, the establishment of international laws to prevent war, woman suffrage, and other measures. By 1916, the WPP had 40,000 members, the highest membership it would ever have. In addition to World War I, the WPP protested the presence of U.S. troops in Haiti and the Dominican Republic, U.S. bases in Nicaragua, and the colonial government in Puerto Rico.

As the United States prepared to enter the war, divisions developed within the WPP as leaders and members questioned their responsibilities to their government and as Congress passed measures related to loyalty and treason. Membership declined in some parts of the country, but some WPP members remained steadfast in their advocacy for peace. In 1919, the WPP became the U.S. branch of the Women's International League for Peace and Freedom.

> **See also** Congressional Union; General Federation of Women's Clubs; Woman's Christian Temperance Union; Women's International League for Peace and Freedom; Women's Trade Union League
>
> **References** Alonso, *Peace as a Women's Issue: A History of the U.S. Movement for World Peace and Women's Rights* (1993).

Women in Apprenticeship and Nontraditional Occupations Act of 1992

Introduced by Republican congresswoman Constance A. Morella of Maryland and passed by Congress in 1992, the Women in Apprenticeship and Nontraditional Occupations Act offers grants to community-based organizations to help businesses provide women with apprenticeships in nontraditional occupations. Administered through the Department of Labor, the grants are also used to assist unions and employers in preparing workplaces for women employees. The act seeks to prepare low-income women and welfare recipients for jobs in the skilled trades and technical positions, according to Republican senator Nancy Kassebaum of Kansas.

> **See also** Kassebaum Baker, Nancy Landon; Morella, Constance Albanese
>
> **References** *Congressional Quarterly Almanac, 102nd Congress, 2nd Session . . . 1992* (1993).

Women Strike for Peace

Founded in 1961 to protest atmospheric tests and the danger of radioactive pollution to children's health, Women Strike for Peace (WSP) works for the total elimination of nuclear weapons. As a radioactive cloud from a Russian nuclear test hung over the United States, 50,000 women in more than sixty cities went on strike on 1 November 1961, in the largest women's peace action in the nation to that date. Women lobbied Congress and government offices to "End the Arms Race—Not the Human Race." During the 1962 Cuban missile crisis, more than 20,000 women across the country marched in protest. In 1963, WSP helped convince President John F. Kennedy to complete the limited nuclear test ban treaty with the Soviet Union.

WSP began in book illustrator Dagmar Wilson's home, where she had gathered five women to discuss the nuclear crisis. Through their networks with members of the Women's International League for Peace and Freedom, the League of Women Voters, and other peace activists, they distributed a call for the November 1961 strike. A grassroots movement, WSP has no formal organization, president, board of directors, formal membership, or official policies. Local groups may or may not work together.

In 1962 the House Un-American Activities Committee (HUAC) subpoenaed Wilson and several WSP members as part of its investigation of peace groups and Communist involvement in them. Instead of being fearful of the committee and its interrogation, Wilson and her colleagues belittled the committee with humor and their moral superiority. They acknowledged that Communists could be members but explained they did not know of any. Invoking the Fifth Amendment dozens of times, they also lectured the committee members as they attempted to explain WSP's lack of traditional organization. WSP members received favorable press, and the press ridiculed HUAC, which admitted that WSP was not a subversive organization.

In other areas, WSP has pressured toy manufacturers to stop producing toy guns and war toys and has asked retailers to stop selling them. It issued a Children's Bill of Rights, which called for food, shelter, medical care, and education for all children.

> **See also** League of Women Voters; Women's International League for Peace and Freedom
>
> **References** Linden-Ward and Green, *American Women in the 1960s: Changing the Future* (1993).

Women Work! The National Network for Women's Employment

Women Work! was founded in 1974 to provide advocacy for and assistance to women whose marriage had ended and with it their economic support. Two California women, divorcée Tish Sommers and widow Laurie Shields, created the organization, originally known as the Alliance for Displaced Homemakers and later as the National Displaced Homemakers Network. The organization gained its current name in 1993.

Displaced homemakers are women whose marriage has ended, regardless of the reason. Women Work! contends that for many women, when their marriage is over, their employment also effectively ends, and that those women need job training and other assistance to support themselves. The Displaced Homemakers Self-Sufficiency Assistance Act of 1990 was passed with the support of Women Work!

See also Displaced Homemakers

Women's Bureau

Created in 1920, the Women's Bureau is the single federal government unit exclusively concerned with serving and promoting the interests of working women. The Women's Bureau's mandate states: "It shall be the duty of said bureau to formulate standards and policies which shall promote the welfare of wage-earning women, improve their working conditions, increase their efficiency, and advance their opportunities for profitable employment." The Women's Bureau fulfills its mission by alerting women to their rights in the workplace, proposing legislation that benefits working women, researching and analyzing information about women and work, and reporting its findings to the president, Congress, and the public.

The Women's Bureau began first as the Women's Division of the Ordnance Department during World War I. As increasing numbers of women filled jobs previously held by men who had been called to war, the division was established to monitor the needs of women entering the munitions industry. In 1918, the division was moved to the Labor Department and renamed Women in Industry Service.

When World War I ended and concerns arose that Women in Industry Service would be disbanded and the needs of women workers would be ignored, the New York Women's Trade Union League began lobbying for a permanent government agency. The result was the creation of the Women's Bureau in 1920 as part of the Department of Labor. The first director, Mary Anderson, who served from 1920 to 1944, was an organizer for the Women's Trade Union League.

The relationship between the Women's Trade Union League and the Women's Bureau involved mutual support and a shared agenda. Both groups strongly supported protective legislation for women, including limits on the hours women could work, the amount of weight they could lift, and other matters. A consequence of the Women's Bureau's commitment to protective legislation was its opposition to the Equal Rights Amendment (ERA), proposed in 1923 by Alice Paul of the National Woman's Party. The bureau remained opposed to the amendment until 1969, when under the leadership of Director Elizabeth Duncan Koontz, it came to support the ERA.

Research conducted by the bureau has helped identify problems confronting working women and has been the basis for its advocacy of several public policies and the enactment of federal and state legislation. The Women's Bureau was instrumental in including women in the Fair Labor Standards Act of 1938, which for the first time set minimum wages and maximum hours for women. During World War II, the bureau advocated nontraditional job training and child care, priorities that continue to the present. The bureau played a significant role in the creation of the President's Commission on the Status of Women in 1961 and in the passage of the Equal Pay Act of 1963.

The bureau's 1994 Working Women Count! project involved responses from more than a quarter of a million women. The survey revealed that women continue to seek equitable pay and benefits, a workplace culture that supports and respects families, and equal opportunity. In the 1990s, the bureau also conducted a public education campaign on women's job rights and created programs to help women balance work and family needs and to help women move from welfare to the paid workforce.

See also Equal Pay Act of 1963; President's Commission on the Status of Women; Women's Trade Union League

References Freeman, *The Politics of Women's Liberation* (1975); www.dol.gov.

Women's Campaign Fund

Founded in 1974 by a bipartisan group of women, the Women's Campaign Fund (WCF) was the first organization formed with the specific purpose of providing financial support for women candidates who support the Equal Rights Amendment and other women's issues and are pro-choice, regardless of party affiliation. WCF began raising money for women candidates when many of them could not attract financial support because of their gender. WCF also recruits candidates and provides training for them.

See also EMILY's List; WISH List

References Congressional Quarterly, *Congressional Quarterly's Federal PACs Directory, 1998–1999* (1998).

Women's Educational Equity Act of 1974

Passed in 1974, the Women's Educational Equity Act (WEEA) seeks to provide educational access and opportunities to women and girls. Sponsored by Democratic congresswoman Patsy Takemoto Mink of Hawaii, the WEEA provides funding for the development of nonsexist teaching materials and for model programs. WEEA encourages full educational opportunities for women without the limitations of sex-role stereotypes.

Part of the Department of Education, the WEEA Office funds gender equity research, develops model programs and curricula, and implements policies and programs to address gender bias in schools. WEEA has awarded more than 700 grants and contracts to schools, universities, community organizations, and individuals. Some of the grantees include the National Women's History Project; the National Women's Law Center; the Wichita, Kansas Public Schools; and the National Black Child Development Institute.

In the 1970s, the WEEA focused on awareness of gender equity issues, career counseling for women returning to the workforce and to school, women considering nontraditional occupations, math and science education for women, and displaced homemakers. In the 1980s, WEEA added an emphasis on at-risk populations. By the 1990s, its attention had turned to gender-based violence and school-to-work issues, as well as providing Spanish translations of its publications and publishing works focusing on Native American women.

Since 1977, the WEEA has provided funding for the WEEA Equity Resource Center at the Educational Development Center. The resource center, a nonprofit educational organization, works with schools, community organizations, businesses, and individuals. In these cooperative endeavors, it publishes and markets gender-equitable educational products; fights against discrimination based on gender, race, class, language, and disability; and distributes multicultural, gender-equitable educational resources. The center offers classroom materials, program guides, anthologies of women's voices, and other materials.

See also Education, Women and

References www.edc.org/WomensEquity/weeainfo/index.html.

Women's Equity Action League

The Women's Equity Action League (WEAL) was founded by Elizabeth Boyer in 1968 to advocate feminist issues and to be a moderate alternative to the National Organization for Women (NOW). A founder of NOW, Boyer shared the organization's feminist goals but believed that its militant activities and positions offended moderate Americans. She also thought that NOW's support for abortion rights and gay rights alienated many who supported the equality of women. She left NOW and organized WEAL.

Boyer served as WEAL's first president and recruited a forty-four-member board of directors. Rejecting picketing, demonstrating, and violent or unseemly behavior, WEAL members emphasized working in and with the political structure. They supported the Equal Rights Amendment and tax credits for child care, fought against discrimination in tax laws and sex bias in the Social Security system, and worked for the appointment and election of women on the state and local levels. In 1972, WEAL stopped avoiding the issue of abortion and supported the repeal of laws regulating and prohibiting abortions.

WEAL's initial priorities included the elimination of sex-role stereotyping in elementary and secondary schools, the promotion of women in sports, the analysis of credit and banking practices, and a study of divorce reform. In 1970, WEAL initiated formal complaints against forty-one universities and colleges, charging them with sex discrimination in violation of Executive Orders 11246 and 11375. The orders forbid federal contractors from discriminating on the basis of race, creed, color, national origin, or sex. WEAL contended that the colleges and universities, as federal contractors receiving $3.8 billion per year, were subject to the provisions of the order. The organization pointed to an industry-wide pattern of sex discrimination in the academic community. In 1974, WEAL began a series of lawsuits against the U.S. Department of Health, Education, and Welfare to enforce affirmative action policies, particularly in higher education. The resulting decisions shaped affirmative action policy in education for nearly twenty years. WEAL also helped open Rhodes scholarships to women. By 1975, WEAL had become a primary political pressure group in the feminist movement.

Other groups adopted priorities and tactics similar to WEAL's, and the group disbanded in 1990. The Marguerite Rawalt Legal Defense Fund continues to offer grants to support legal action in the areas that had been WEAL priorities.

> **See also** Affirmative Action; Executive Order 11246; Executive Order 11375; National Organization for Women
>
> **References** Daniels, "W.E.A.L.: The Growth of a Feminist Organization" (1979); Freeman, *The Politics of Women's Liberation* (1975); Slavin, *U.S. Women's Interest Groups* (1995); Stimpson, ed., *Women and the "Equal Rights" Amendment* (1972).

Women's Health Equity Act

First introduced in 1990 by the Congressional Caucus for Women's Issues (CCWI), the Women' Health Equity Act (WHEA) is a package of proposed bills modeled after the Economic Equity Act. It includes provisions to create an Office for Women's Health Research and Development within the National Institutes of Health (NIH), a gynecology research program within NIH, and a Center for Women's Health Research; to require the NIH director to report on progress on women's health and research; to set up a database of research on women's health; and to require the inclusion of women and minorities in NIH clinical trials. New versions of the WHEA are introduced each session of Congress.

The proposed act resulted from a General Accounting Office investigation that CCWI had requested. The report documented women's general exclusion from medical research studies conducted by the NIH. One example of women's exclusion from health research was the 1988 Harvard Medical School study that demonstrated that taking one aspirin a day could help prevent heart attacks. It involved 22,000 subjects, all of them men. Senator Barbara Mikulski noted: "We have no idea whether that technique will help women or not. This is blatant discrimination. It is inexcusable, unforgivable, and we will not allow it to continue."

CCWI helped pass the Breast and Cervical Cancer Mortality Prevention Act in 1990 to make mammograms and Pap smears more accessible to low-income women. Two years later, CCWI succeeded in passing the Mammography Quality Assurance Act, establishing federal standards for mammography facilities and requiring their accreditation. Also in 1992, Congress passed the Infertility Prevention Act, providing screening and treatment for low-income women of chlamydia and other sexually transmitted diseases that can make women infertile. Congress passed three more provisions of the WHEA in 1993, creating the Office of Research on Women's Health, requiring a biennial report on progress in women's health research and treatment, and establishing a clearinghouse on research on women's health.

See also Congressional Caucus for Women's Issues; Economic Equity Act; Health Care, Women and; Mikulski, Barbara Ann; Women's Health, Office of Research on

References Bingham, *Women on the Hill: Challenging the Culture of Congress* (1997).

Women's Health, Office of Research on

The Office of Research on Women's Health (ORWH), authorized by Congress in 1993, serves as a focal point for women's health research at the National Institutes of Health (NIH). ORWH has three general mandates: to increase research into the diseases and other health conditions that affect women, identify gaps in the knowledge about them, and develop research priorities; to ensure that women are included in research studies; and to increase the number of women in biomedical careers.

ORWH works with the scientific and medical community, organizations interested in women's health, Congress, and other relevant constituencies. It conducts workshops and seminars to involve the research community in developing its agenda and priorities. In the late 1990s, its priority research areas included immunologic and arthritic diseases; acute and chronic pain; reproductive health; sexually transmitted diseases; gastrointestinal disorders; and risk factors for women in different racial, ethnic, and socioeconomic groups.

ORWH cosponsors the Women's Health Initiative, one of the largest prevention studies ever conducted in the United States. Focusing on the major causes of death, disability, and frailty in postmenopausal women, it will involve over 164,000 women in a fifteen-year study. When completed, the study will offer information on prevention strategies and risk factors for coronary heart disease, breast and colon cancer, and osteoporosis.

See also Women's Health Equity Act

References Bingham, *Women on the Hill: Challenging the Culture of Congress* (1997); www.od.nih.gov/orwh/overview.html.

A petition on arbitration as a substitute for war was presented to President Calvin Coolidge at the White House by Jane Addams, president of the Women's International League for Peace and Freedom, and other peace activists, 1927 (Corbis/Bettmann)

Women's International League for Peace and Freedom

The Women's International League for Peace and Freedom (WILPF) was founded by women active in the international suffrage movement, who believed that peace required more than treaties between nations and that justice, freedom, nonviolence, opportunity, and equality were essential components of peace. Since its beginnings, WILPF has evolved into an organization that seeks to create an environment of political, economic, social, and psychological freedom for all members of the human community.

As World War I raged across Europe in 1915, European and North American women gathered at The Hague in Holland to register their objections to the use of violence as a response to conflict, to offer suggestions to end it, and to identify strategies to prevent war. They created the International Committee of Women for Permanent Peace, which changed its name to Women's International League for Peace and Freedom after World War I. In the United States, Jane Addams and Carrie Chapman Catt had founded the Woman's Peace Party, which became the U.S. Section of WILPF. In addition, American Emily Greene Balch was the organization's first international secretary. Even though WILPF's American leadership included notable and admired women, in the 1920s and 1930s the organization was suspected of having Communist leanings.

WILPF seeks world disarmament; the end of sexism, racism, classism, and homophobia; and the end of all forms of violence, including rape, battering, exploitation, and war. WILPF's mission also includes promoting sustainable agriculture and economic justice within and among nations. The organization works to fulfill its mission through lobbying, organizing direct action, conducting and publishing research, and supplying members of Congress and state legislatures with information.

See also Addams, Jane; Catt, Carrie Clinton Lane Chapman; Violence Against Women Act of 1994

References www.wilpf.org.

Women's Joint Congressional Committee

Created in 1920 after the passage of the Nineteenth Amendment granting women suffrage rights, the Women's Joint Congressional Committee (WJCC) coordinated the national lobbying efforts of several women's organizations. Its areas of interest were protection for infants, public education, arms reduction, and protective labor legislation in addition to other issues concerning women. The WJCC did not take positions on issues. Instead it served as a clearinghouse for member organizations, and when three or more member organizations shared a position on a bill, they formed a subcommittee to develop and execute a strategy for it. In addition, a standing committee monitored legislation in Congress.

WJCC's charter organizations were the American Association of University Women, American Home Economics Association, Business and Professional Women/USA, General Federation of Women's Clubs, National Congress of Mothers and Parent-Teachers Associations, National Consumers League, National Council of Jewish Women, Women's Trade Union League, and Woman's Christian Temperance Union. For a time, the WJCC had twenty-one member organizations.

Described in 1922 as the most powerful and highly organized lobby in Washington, D.C., the WJCC succeeded in passing several of the measures on its legislative agenda, including the Sheppard-Towner Maternity and Infancy Protection Act in 1921, the Cable Act in 1922, the establishment of the Women's Bureau, and the establishment of a federal prison for women. Research conducted by the WJCC revealed that 60 percent of civil service examinations were closed to women. WJCC worked with a woman on the Civil Service Commission, ended the discrimination, and then passed a measure that reclassified civil service positions to establish pay equity among them. The WJCC's support for the Child Labor Amendment helped gain its approval in Congress, but not enough states ratified it. Because of its support for protective labor legislation, the WJCC opposed the Equal Rights Amendment and succeeded in preventing it from gaining congressional approval. In areas less directly related to women, WJCC also supported the establishment of a coal commission and passage of the 1921 Packers and Stockyards Control Act.

In the mid-1920s, leaders in several of the member organizations were accused of having Communist connections. These and other allegations of a spider web of Communists among women's organizations contributed to the WJCC's loss of influence and its dissolution in the early 1930s.

See also American Association of University Women; Business and Professional Women/USA; Cable Acts; Child Labor Amendment; General Federation of Women's Clubs; National Consumers League; National Council of Jewish Women; Sheppard-Towner Maternity and Infancy Protection Act of 1921; Spider Web; Willebrandt, Mabel Walker; Woman's Christian Temperance Union; Women's Bureau; Women's Trade Union League

References Breckenridge, *Women in the Twentieth Century: A Study of Their Political, Social, and Economic Activities* (1933); Brown, *American Women in the 1920s: Setting a Course* (1987); Lemons, *The Woman Citizen* (1973).

Women's Liberation Movement

In the 1960s, groups of young women in Chicago, Toronto, Seattle, and other cities formed spontaneously and independently of each other. Some of the women had experience in the civil rights movement in the South and others in radical movements in the North, but they shared a common interest in ending male dominance and in fundamentally re-shaping society. For example, after concluding that hierarchies are a male form of organization, they developed nonhierarchical groups with equal relationships. They agreed that no one would be a leader or an achiever, and they would resolve differences through discussion. The groups adopted consciousness raising as a technique for revealing sexism to themselves and each other and developed theories regarding male dominance and sexism.

Women's liberation groups differed from organizations like the National Organization for Women (NOW) in several ways. NOW, for example, works to gain power for women in the existing social, political, and economic systems. Women's liberation adherents rejected those structures and sought to create a new, egalitarian, unstructured society. They rejected men's participation in their groups and explored lesbian relationships as purely feminist relationships. Many of their ideas were initially viewed as radical or undesirable by more staid feminists, but over time the ideas gained acceptance within the larger feminist movement. By the mid-1970s, women's liberation groups had dissolved.

See also Feminist Movement; New York Radical Women; Radicalesbians; Redstockings

References Davis, *Moving the Mountain: The Women's Movement in America Since 1960* (1991).

Women's Policy, Inc.

Founded in 1995, Women's Policy, Inc. (WPI) provides nonpartisan research and information to policymakers, advocates, and the public on issues important to women and children. Through a weekly newsletter, briefing papers, and an annual summary of legislation affecting women and families, WPI reports on abortion, affirmative action, women's health issues, violence against women, and economic equity for women. Other issues covered include workplace fairness, women's entrepreneurship, family-friendly work policies, child care, and child support enforcement.

Two former staff members of the Congressional Caucus on Women's Issues formed WPI after the U.S. House of Representatives abolished dozens of legislative service organizations, including the caucus.

See also Abortion, Affirmative Action; Child Support Enforcement; Economic Equity Act; Health Care,Women and; Pay Equity

References http://orgs.womenconnect.com.

Women's Political Council

Founded in 1946, the Women's Political Council (WPC) played a critical role in the 1955 Montgomery, Alabama, bus boycott and helped launch the civil rights movement of the 1960s. The WPC had threatened a boycott of the city's buses since 1950, and Rosa Parks's refusal to give up her bus seat and subsequent arrest provided the catalyst to spark the boycott. Under the leadership of the WPC, the boycott began four days after her arrest and lasted for more than a year.

A group of well-educated African American women had formed WPC after the Montgomery branch of the League of Women Voters (LWV) refused to admit black women members. About forty women decided to create the WPC to provide themselves with a means to be politically active, focusing their efforts on fighting racial segregation and improving the lives of all African Americans, particularly women and children. To achieve its goals, WPC sponsored a variety of programs, including Negro Youth Day, which sought to inspire African American youth to become leaders and to believe in the possibility of change through electoral politics. Several of the students trained in WPC programs became leaders in the Student Nonviolent Coordinating Committee, registering voters in Mississippi and other states in the Deep South. The organization also organized letter-writing campaigns, taxation protests, and meetings with the mayor.

As the news circulated that Rosa Parks had been arrested on 1 December 1955, WPC leader JoAnn Robinson, head of the English department at Alabama State College in Montgomery, used the college's mimeograph machines to print leaflets calling for a bus boycott. Other WPC members went into action, distributing the leaflets and organizing support for the boycott, which began on 5 December and involved almost all African Americans in the community. Robinson continued to use the college's mimeograph machines throughout the boycott, which provided a vital means of communication, despite the fact that she risked her job and her safety by doing it. Although she attempted to keep her role as invisible as possible, she was among the first arrested as a result of the boycott and later lost her teaching position for her activism.

After members were subpoenaed during the trials relating to the boycott, they destroyed the organization's records out of fear that the information would be subpoenaed and the meeting minutes and membership lists publicized, resulting in retaliation against them. WPC dissolved in 1960 as members lost their jobs, feared being fired or being subjected to other forms of retaliation, and discontinued their activism. The remaining core continued the work through churches.

See also Civil Rights Movement, Women in the; Parks, Rosa Louise McCauley

References Barnett, "Black Women's Collectivist Movement Organizations: Their Struggles during the 'Doldrums'" (1995).

Women's Political Union

Founded by Harriot Stanton Blatch, the Women's Political Union (WPU) began as the Equality League of Self-Supporting Women (ELSSW), a group that Blatch established in 1907 to revitalize the woman suffrage movement. Through the ELSSW, Blatch organized working women from the ranks of doctors, lawyers, milliners, and industrial workers, women

The logo of the Women's Trade Union League, at a convention in New York City, 1924 (Courtesy: University of Florida, Gainesville)

who were generally overlooked by the National American Woman Suffrage Association (NAWSA), the dominant suffrage organization. To help attract working-class women, ELSSW concentrated on their needs; in addition, it did not have membership fees. Through the ELSSW, for example, trade union women testified before the New York legislature in support of woman suffrage, the first time working-class women had done so. ELSSW changed its name in 1910 to the Women's Political Union to include a broader range of women. Considered a radical organization, the WPU held open-air meetings and outdoor parades and sought newspaper publicity, strategies later adopted by the more conservative NAWSA. The WPU merged with the Congressional Union in 1916.

> **See also** Blatch, Harriot Eaton Stanton; Congressional Union; National American Woman Suffrage Association

Women's Trade Union League

Founded in 1903 to help working women organize, the Women's Trade Union League (WTUL) obtained support primarily from wealthy women. The WTUL did not achieve its goal of persuading women to join unions, but it succeeded in other areas. It publicized women's low wages, long working hours, and unhealthy working conditions and helped pass protective legislation. The WTUL held its last national convention in 1947. During the post–World War II years, WTUL's financial support diminished, its leadership aged, and many people feared being associated with unions because they were under attack for alleged connections with communism. WTUL dissolved in 1950.

See also Protective Legislation

References Orleck, *Common Sense and a Little Fire* (1995).

Woodhouse, Chase Going (1890–1984)

Democrat Chase Going Woodhouse of Connecticut served in the U.S. House of Representatives from 3 January 1945 to 3 January 1947 and from 3 January 1949 to 3 January 1951. As secretary of the Democratic Caucus in the 81st Congress (1949–1951), Woodhouse was the first woman to hold a leadership position in Congress. Her term in Congress overlapped that of one of her former students, Jessie Sumner.

A social worker for a brief time, Woodhouse studied economics in Germany and England. She then became a fellow in political economy at the University of Chicago. Between 1918 and 1946, she held teaching and administrative posts. Woodhouse was also involved in women's groups, serving as president of the Connecticut League of Women Voters, Connecticut Federation of Democratic Women's Clubs, and Altrusa Clubs. Connecticut secretary of state from 1941 to 1942, she instituted election law schools in the interest of public information.

In her campaign for Congress, Woodhouse emphasized establishing a world peace organization, maintaining full employment during peacetime, revising the tax system, providing adequate educational facilities, and expanding rural electrification. She worked for congressional approval of the International Monetary Fund and for the International Bank for Reconstruction and Development and has been given credit for the incorporation of these two groups into the United Nations. She fought to maintain wartime price controls to protect consumers and for additional affordable housing for veterans.

After losing her reelection attempt in 1946, Woodhouse was executive director of the women's bureau of the Democratic National Committee from 1947 to 1948. She regained her congressional seat in 1948 but lost again in 1950. Woodhouse was assistant to the director of Price Stabilization from 1951 to 1953.

Born in Victoria, British Columbia, Chase Going Woodhouse graduated in 1912 and received her master of arts degree in 1913, both from McGill University in Montreal, Canada.

See also Congress, Women in

References Center for the American Woman and Politics, Eagleton Institute of Politics, Rutgers University; Engelbarts, *Women in the United States Congress, 1917–1972* (1974); H. W. Wilson, *Current Biography: Who's News and Why, 1945* (1945); Office of the Historian, U.S. House of Representatives, *Women in Congress, 1917–1990* (1991).

Woodhull, Victoria Claflin (1838–1927)

The first woman to run for president of the United States, Victoria Woodhull was a candidate for the office in 1872 and in 1892. A protégée of Cornelius Vanderbilt, Woodhull was also the first woman stockbroker in the United States. Her reform activities and her advocacy for free love created controversies and turmoil within the suffrage movement for more than a decade. To Woodhull, free love meant that women had absolute control over their own sexual and reproductive lives.

Born in Homer, Ohio, Victoria Woodhull received little education. She married when she was fifteen years old and divorced about eleven years later. In 1868, Woodhull and her sister Tennessee Claflin moved to New York City and arranged to meet Cornelius Vanderbilt, reputedly the wealthiest man in the United States. Under his tutelage, the two sisters made a fortune in the gold market in 1869. Vanderbilt sponsored their Wall Street brokerage firm, Woodhull, Claflin, and Company, making Woodhull the country's first woman stockbroker. From 1870 to 1876, the sisters published *Woodhull and Claflin's Weekly,* a financial and reform newspaper that reported on Wall Street fraud, free love, and legalized prostitution in addition to Woodhull's political views.

Woodhull had attended her first women's rights convention in 1869 and heard Susan B. Anthony and Elizabeth Cady Stanton speak on woman suffrage and related topics. In *Woodhull and Claflin's Weekly,* Woodhull advocated education for girls, declared that her experience demonstrated that women could work in many professions, and argued that women should be paid as well as men. A few weeks before *Woodhull and Claflin's Weekly* had begun publication, Woodhull had announced her candidacy for president of the United States in the 1872 elections and promoted it through the newspaper.

Woodhull also became involved in Washington politics in 1870, establishing herself as a lobbyist for woman suffrage. In *Woodhull and Claflin's Weekly,* she wrote that a suffrage amendment was unnecessary if the Constitution were properly interpreted. She argued that women were citizens in the same way that men were and that women paid taxes, as did men. She shared Virginia Minor's belief that the Fourteenth Amendment established women's right to vote, adding that the Fourteenth and Fif-

teenth Amendments nullified state legislation that prohibited women from voting. She concluded that enabling legislation to clarify the point was all that was necessary and lobbied Congress for it as well as meeting with President U.S. Grant to get his support for her interpretation, but he did not provide the endorsement she wanted. She presented a memorial to the House Judiciary Committee asking for the enabling legislation, but it considered and rejected the idea.

Woodhull's presidential candidacy gained the support of Elizabeth Cady Stanton and Susan B. Anthony in 1871. When the 1872 National Woman Suffrage Association (NWSA) convention met, Woodhull attempted to take the leadership away from Stanton and Anthony, but Anthony prevailed in a tumultuous meeting. Woodhull left the NWSA convention, called her own convention, and formed the Equal Rights Party. The party named Woodhull its presidential nominee and Frederick Douglass its vice presidential nominee. Douglass, however, declined. Shortly after the convention, Woodhull's brokerage failed, and she lost her housing and offices.

Scandal erupted shortly before the November 1872 election. After divorcing her first husband in 1865, Woodhull had married Colonel James Harvey Blood in 1868, although no record of the marriage has been found. In 1871, Woodhull's aging and ill first husband had moved in with Woodhull and her second husband, Blood. The revelation of their uncommon arrangement became a scandal. Woodhull responded with a

Victoria Woodhull was the first woman to run for president of the United States in 1872; this woodcut shows her testifying to the House Judiciary Committee regarding woman suffrage, 1871 (Frank Leslie's Illustrated Newspaper)

newspaper article and expounded on her belief in free love "as the only cure for immorality." To justify her lifestyle, Woodhull revealed in the 2 November 1872 edition of *Woodhull and Claflin's Weekly* that powerful Brooklyn preacher Henry Ward Beecher was having an affair with Elizabeth Tilton, a parishioner, who was Theodore Tilton's wife. Beecher had been a mentor to and trusted friend of Theodore Tilton. Woodhull and Claflin were arrested and jailed for publishing the Tilton-Beecher scandal, which authorities deemed obscene. They were both later acquitted, but the scandal effectively ended Woodhull's political career.

The scandal also created a breach within the woman suffrage movement. Anthony and Stanton defended Woodhull, but their defense did little to help Woodhull and generated public criticism of Anthony and Stanton. Woodhull's advocacy of free love was used to attack and discredit woman suffrage and women's rights supporters.

In 1876, Woodhull ended publication of *Woodhull and Claflin's Weekly*, and the next year she moved to England, where she lectured. She returned to the United States for a second presidential campaign in 1892.

> **See also** Anthony, Susan Brownell; National Woman Suffrage Association; Stanton, Elizabeth Cady; Suffrage
>
> **References** Underhill, *The Woman Who Ran for President: The Many Lives of Victoria Woodhull* (1995).

Woolsey, Lynn (b. 1937)

On 3 January 1993, Democrat Lynn Woolsey of California entered the U.S. House of Representatives, where her personal experiences have influenced some aspects of her congressional actions. Divorced in the 1960s, she had three children to support and few economic resources and spent three years on welfare. In 1994, she told her congressional colleagues, "I differ from every mother member of this House because I am the only member of Congress to have been a welfare mother. So my opinions are not based on theory. They are based on real-life experience." The welfare reform bill she introduced included a child support assurance program and guaranteed child support from the federal government.

Believing that education makes a significant difference in people's ability to support themselves, she has made education a top priority. She passed a bill to provide child care, health care, and crime prevention programs to schools. She supports an increase in the minimum wage; tax deductions for college expenses; and expanded pension coverage, portability, and protection.

She has staunchly supported environmental issues, including her proposal for the Point Reyes National Seashore Farmland Protection Act and her efforts to maintain the ban on offshore oil drilling. She has obtained federal funding to extend carpool lanes, construct park-and-ride lots, and complete the purchase of the Northwest Pacific Railroad right-of-way. Other policy priorities include gun control, the solvency of Medicare, reproductive rights, and universal health care coverage. Woolsey held the leadership position of House deputy minority whip in the 106th Congress (1999–2001).

Born in Seattle, Washington, Woolsey attended the University of Washington from 1955 to 1957 and received her bachelor of science degree in human resources and organizational behavior from the University of San Francisco in 1980. Woolsey started Woolsey Personnel Service, a human resources consulting and employment agency, in 1980. She served on the Petaluma City Council from 1985 to 1993.

See also Abortion; Child Support Enforcement; Congress, Women in

References Congressional Quarterly, *Politics in America* 1994 (1993); www.house.gov/woolsey/bio.htm.

Wright, Frances (Fanny) (1795–1852)

Reformer and writer Frances Wright was likely the first woman to speak before a large audience of women and men in the United States when she lectured on 4 July 1828 in New Harmony, Indiana. With a copy of the Declaration of Independence in her hand to remind Americans of their heritage of fighting for natural rights, she called for educational equality for women, arguing that education was the key to equality for both sexes and all economic and social classes. She believed in the fundamental equality of women and men as human beings, advocated free love, and believed miscegenation would solve racial problems. Newspapers and ministers attacked her for speaking in public, calling her the "Whore of Babylon" and "The Red Harlot of Infidelity." Wright responded by denouncing the clergy as opponents to freedom of thought.

Three years earlier, in 1825, Wright had been the first woman in the United States to take action against slavery by establishing Nashoba, a utopian community in Tennessee. Populated by the slaves Wright had purchased as well as by sympathetic white people, Nashoba was to be a model for the gradual abolition of slavery. When reports of sexual activities between unmarried people and between blacks and whites became public, the accompanying scandal along with financial difficulties spelled the end of Nashoba. In 1829, she closed the project and freed her slaves in Haiti.

With Robert Dale Owen, in 1829, she founded and edited the *Free Enquirer*, a newspaper that advocated liberalization of divorce laws, birth control, the rights of working people, and women's rights. She moved to

France in 1830, married, and had a daughter. She returned to the U.S. lecture circuit in 1835, but she did not regain her earlier fame or notoriety.

Born in Dundee, Scotland, Frances Wright inherited adequate funds to pursue an independent life.

See also Grimké, Angelina Emily and Sarah Moore; Public Speaking; Stewart, Maria W.

References Eckhardt, *Fanny Wright: Rebel in America* (1984).

Y

Year of the Woman

Political observers labeled 1992 the "year of the woman" because of the gains women made in winning seats in state legislatures, the U.S. House of Representatives, and the U.S. Senate. The number of women elected to state legislatures increased from 1,369 to 1,527. The number of women serving in the U.S. House of Representatives increased from twenty-eight to forty-seven, and the number in the U.S. Senate went from four to seven. Democratic women dominated the increases, with a net gain of sixteen women in the House and two in the Senate.

More women ran in 1992 than had previously run for Congress in any one election. Many of them said that watching Anita Hill testify before the Senate Judiciary Committee hearings on U.S. Supreme Court nominee Clarence Thomas's confirmation had prompted their candidacies. In addition, several House members had been accused of abusing their privileges in the House's bank and had written hundreds of checks that created overdrafts in their accounts. Another factor that contributed to the increase in the number of women being elected to office was the gender gap.

See also Congress, Women in; Gender Gap; Hill, Anita Faye; State Legislatures, Women in

Yellen, Janet (b. 1946)

Appointed chair of the Council of Economic Advisers (CEA) in 1997 by President Bill Clinton, Janet Yellen had been a member of the Board of

Governors of the Federal Reserve from 1994 to 1997. A cabinet-level position in the Clinton administration, the chair of the three-member council directly advises the president and the senior members of the administration on the economy's trends and developments, recommending policies and helping the public understand economic issues. As chair of the CEA, Yellen questioned the long-term effects of changes in welfare programs made in 1996, concerned that the reductions in programs and program funding could be harmful to children.

Born in Brooklyn, New York, Yellen earned her undergraduate degree from Brown University and her doctoral degree in economics from Yale University in 1971. An assistant professor at Harvard University from 1971 to 1976, she was an economist with the Federal Reserve's Board of Governors from 1977 to 1978, specializing in international trade and finance. A professor at the University of California at Berkeley from 1980 to 1994, she has served on the Panel of Economic Advisers for the Congressional Budget Office and as senior adviser to the Brookings Panel on Economic Activity. Yellen is a recognized scholar in international economics and has written on the causes, mechanisms, and implications of unemployment as well as other related topics.

See also Cabinets, Women in Presidential

References www.businessweek.com/1997/09/b3516111.htm; www.whitehouse.gov/wh/eop/cea/html/yellen.html.

YWCA of the USA

Founded in 1858 as the Young Women's Christian Association, the YWCA of the USA began as a boardinghouse for women and girls in New York City. The organization's mission is to empower women and girls and to end racism. The YWCA began on the local level in several cities, with each group independent from the other, in response to the needs of rural and immigrant women moving into urban areas and needing safe, affordable housing. In 1909, more than 600 local associations coalesced to form the YWCA national organization. Since then the YWCA has grown into more than 400 associations in more than 4,000 locations involving more than 2 million people.

The organization's housing mission evolved into providing shelter and services for victims of violence. Every year about 650,000 women and their children seek services, including emergency shelter, transitional housing, counseling, self-defense training, and legal advocacy. In addition, YWCA sponsors an annual Week Without Violence, an international public awareness campaign.

Racial justice emerged as an early theme for the YWCA. In 1922, the national convention voted to hold national meetings and conferences only

A poster for the Young Women's Christian Association (Library of Congress)

In Service for the Girls of the World

in those places that accepted all members, without segregation or discrimination. As the civil rights movement emerged, the YWCA created its National Office of Racial Justice and initiated the One Imperative program to eliminate racism, first directed by Dorothy Height. One of the first organizations to divest its investments in South Africa, the YWCA encouraged universities to follow suit. Since 1992, the YWCA has sponsored the National Day of Commitment to Eliminate Racism and in 1996 began convening women leaders to discuss institutional forms of racism.

In 1864 the YWCA opened the first day nursery in the United States and now has more than 1,000 sites that serve more than 750,000 children. In addition, the association trains child care providers, has resource and referral services, offers day care for homeless children, and conducts parent education classes. Child care is also one of the areas in which YWCA is a public policy advocate.

Other YWCA programs include leadership training in advocacy, voter participation, and public leadership, as well as employment training, job placement, and sports and physical fitness. Its youth programs include leadership skill development, remedial education, crisis intervention, family violence prevention, and physical and mental health services.

In the 1990s, the YWCA's public policy agenda included advocacy for children, gender equity in sports, increased funding for the National Breast and Cervical Cancer Detection Program, and affirmative action. The organization has worked to increase the number of registered women voters and to get out the vote on election day through the Women's Vote Project. The YWCA has also worked for legislation to end hate crimes, ban assault weapons, implement antidiscrimination policies, and protect abortion rights.

See also Height, Dorothy Irene

References www.ywca.org.

Appendix 1: Documents

Setting Political Agendas

Since the middle of the nineteenth century, women seeking to change their political and social status have gathered together and stated their objections to the status quo and the changes they believed important. Elizabeth Cady Stanton and Lucretia Mott, along with three other women, began the tradition when they organized the first woman's rights convention in 1848 and presented the Declaration of Sentiments and Resolutions to those gathered in Seneca Falls, New York, for their consideration. Modeled after the Declaration of Independence, the Declaration of Sentiments and Resolutions was debated and voted upon with little controversy, except for the resolution on woman suffrage, which passed but with significant dissent.

The Nineteenth Amendment, which granted women in the United States suffrage rights, became part of the Constitution in 1920, but in some parts of the world, women still did not have voting rights in 1953. The United Nations Commission on the Status of Women developed the Convention on the Political Rights of Women declaring the belief that women should be able to vote on equal terms with men and be able to hold public office. The agreement was signed on 31 March 1953.

In the 1960s, U.S. women again focused on their legal, economic, and political status and concluded that the discriminatory state of federal policies and the economic and political discrimination that permeated society needed to end. Organizing in small and large groups across the country, women identified the barriers they perceived and launched the feminist movement. Among these groups, the National Organization for Women (NOW) emerged as the strongest and the largest. At its first national conference, held in 1967, NOW members stated their demands, including passage of the Equal Rights Amendment and the repeal of a law that made abortion illegal, measures so controversial at the time that they even created conflict among the members.

Another national plan of action emerged from the National Women's Conference held in Houston, Texas, in November, 1977. Financed with a congressional appropriation, the conference was held in response to the United Nations Decade for Women (1975–1985). Fifty-six state and territorial conventions elected delegates to the national convention and recommended resolutions to it. By far the most controversial item in the agenda was the call for the elimination of discrimination based on sexual preference.

NOW's 1998 Declaration of Sentiments, passed at the organization's recent national convention celebrating 150 years of the women's rights movement, and signed by more than 700 members, opens by stating a vision of the world it hopes to help create. The organization's resolutions echo more than a century's worth of documents demanding women's emancipation and full equality in all human endeavors.

Declaration of Sentiments and Resolutions, 1848

When, in the course of human events, it becomes necessary for one portion of the family of man to assume among the people of the earth a position different from that which they have hitherto occupied, but one to which the laws of nature and of nature's God entitle them, a decent respect to the opinions of mankind requires that they should declare the causes that impel them to such a course.

We hold these truths to be self-evident: that all men and women are created equal; that they are endowed by their Creator with certain inalienable rights; that among these are life, liberty, and the pursuit of happiness; that to secure these rights governments are instituted, deriving their just powers from the consent of the governed. Whenever any form of government becomes destructive of these ends, it is the right of those who suffer from it to refuse allegiance to it, and to insist upon the institution of a new government, laying its foundation on such principles, and organizing its powers in such form, as to them shall seem most likely to effect their safety and happiness. Prudence, indeed, will dictate that governments long established should not be changed for light and transient causes; and accordingly all experience hath shown that mankind are more disposed to suffer, while evils are sufferable, than to right themselves by abolishing the forms to which they were accustomed. But when a long train of abuses and usurpations, pursuing invariably the same object evinces a design to reduce them under absolute despotism, it is their duty to throw off such government, and to provide new guards for their future security. Such has been the patient sufferance of the women under this government, and such is now the necessity which constrains them to demand the equal station to which they are entitled.

The history of mankind is a history of repeated injuries and usurpations on the part of man toward woman, having in direct object the establishment of an absolute tyranny over her. To prove this, let facts be submitted to a candid world.

He has never permitted her to exercise her inalienable right to the elective franchise.

He has compelled her to submit to laws, in the formation of which she had no voice.

He has withheld from her rights which are given to the most ignorant and degraded men—both natives and foreigners.

Having deprived her of this first right of a citizen, the elective franchise, thereby leaving her without representation in the halls of legislation, he has oppressed her on all sides.

He has made her, if married, in the eye of the law, civilly dead.

He has taken from her all right in property, even to the wages she earns.

He has made her, morally, an irresponsible being, as she can commit many crimes with impunity, provided they be done in the presence of her husband. In the covenant of marriage, she is compelled to promise obedience to her husband, he becoming, to all intents and purposes, her master—the law giving him power to deprive her of her liberty, and to administer chastisement.

He has so framed the laws of divorce, as to what shall be the proper causes, and in case of separation, to whom the guardianship of the children shall be given, as to be wholly regardless of the happiness of women—the law, in all cases, going upon a false supposition of the supremacy of man, and giving all power into his hands.

After depriving her of all rights as a married woman, if single, and the owner of property, he has taxed her to support a government which recognizes her only when her property can be made profitable to it.

He has monopolized nearly all the profitable employments, and from those she is permitted to follow, she receives but a scanty remuneration. He closes against her all the avenues to wealth and distinction which he considers most honorable to himself. As a teacher of theology, medicine, or law, she is not known.

He has denied her the facilities for obtaining a thorough education, all colleges being closed against her.

He allows her in Church, as well as State, but a subordinate position, claiming Apostolic authority for her exclusion from the ministry, and with some exceptions, from any public participation in the affairs of the Church.

He has created a false public sentiment by giving to the world a different code of morals for men and women, by which moral delinquencies which exclude women from society, are not only tolerated, but demand of little account in man.

He has usurped the prerogative of Jehovah himself, claiming it as his right to assign for her a sphere of action, when that belongs to her conscience and her God.

He has endeavored, in every way that he could, to destroy her confidence in her own powers, to lessen her self-respect, and to make her willing to lead a dependent and abject life.

Now, in view of this entire disfranchisement of one-half the people of this country, their social and religious degradation—in view of the unjust laws above mentioned, and because women do feel themselves aggrieved, oppressed, and fraudulently deprived of their most sacred rights, we insist that they have immediate admission to all the rights and privileges which belong to them as citizens of the United States.

In entering upon the great work before us, we anticipate no small amount of misconception, misrepresentation, and ridicule; but we shall use every instrumentality within our power to effect our object. We shall employ agents, circulate tracts, petition the State and National legislatures, and endeavor to enlist the pulpit and the press in our behalf. We hope this Convention will be followed by a series of Conventions in every part of the country.

WHEREAS, The great precept of nature is conceded to be, that "man shall pursue his own true and substantial happiness." Blackstone in his Commentaries remarks, that his law of Nature being coeval with mankind, and dictated by God himself, is of course superior in obligation to any other. It is binding over all the globe, in all countries and at all times; no human laws are of any validity if contrary to this, and such of them as are valid, derive all their force, and all their validity, and all their authority, mediately and immediately, from this original; therefore,

RESOLVED, That such laws as conflict, in any way, with the true and substantial happiness of women, are contrary to the great precept of nature and of no validity, for this is "superior in obligation to any other."

RESOLVED, That all laws which prevent woman from occupying such a station in society as her conscience shall dictate, or which places her in a position inferior to that of man, are contrary to the great precept of nature, and therefore of no force or authority.

RESOLVED, That woman is man's equal—was intended to be so by the Creator, and the highest good of the race demands that she should be recognized as such.

RESOLVED, That the women of this country ought to be enlightened in regard to the laws under which they live, that they may no longer publish their degradation by declaring themselves satisfied with their present position, nor their ignorance, by asserting that they have all the rights they want.

RESOLVED, That inasmuch as man, while claiming for himself intellectual superiority, does accord to woman moral superiority, it is pre-eminently his duty to encourage her to speak and teach, as she has an opportunity, in all religious assemblies.

RESOLVED, That the same amount of virtue, delicacy, and refinement of behavior that is required of woman in the social state, should also be required of man, and the same transgressions should be visited with equal severity on both man and woman.

RESOLVED, That the objection of indelicacy and impropriety, which is so often brought against woman when she addresses a public audience, comes with a very ill-grace from those who encourage, by their attendance, her appearance on the stage, in the concert, or in feats of the circus.

RESOLVED, That woman has too long rested satisfied in the circumscribed limits which corrupt customs and a perverted application of the Scriptures have marked out for her, and that it is time she should move in the enlarged sphere which her great Creator has assigned her.

RESOLVED, That it is the duty of the women of this country to secure to themselves their sacred right to the elective franchise.

RESOLVED, That the equality of human rights results necessarily from the fact of the identity of the race in capabilities and responsibilities.

RESOLVED, That the speedy success of our cause depends upon the zealous and untiring efforts of both men and women, for the overthrow of the monopoly of the pulpit, and for the securing to woman an equal participation with men in the various trades, professions, and commerce.

RESOLVED, THEREFORE, That being invested by the Creator with the same capabilities, and the same consciousness of responsibility for their exercise, it is demonstrably the right and duty of woman, equally with man, to promote every righteous cause by every righteous means; and especially in regard to the great subjects of morals and religion, it is self-evidently her right to participate with her brother in teaching them, both in private and in public, by writing and by speaking, by instrumentalities proper to be used, and in any assemblies proper to be held; and being a self-evident truth growing out of the divinely implanted principles of human nature, any custom or authority adverse to it, whether modern or wearing the hoary sanction of antiquity, is to be regarded as a self-evident falsehood, and at war with mankind.

Convention on the Political Rights of Women, 1953

The Contracting Parties,

Desiring to implement the principle of equality of rights for men and women contained in the Charter of the United Nations,

Recognizing that everyone has the right to take part in the government of his country, directly or indirectly through freely chosen representatives, and has the right to equal access to public service in his country, and desiring to equalize the status of men and women in the enjoyment and exercise of political rights, in accordance with the provisions of the Charter of the United Nations and the Universal Declaration of Human Rights,

Having resolved to conclude a Convention for this purpose,

Hereby agree as hereinafter provided:

Article I

Women shall be entitled to vote in all elections on equal terms with men without any discrimination.

Article II

Women shall be eligible for election to all publicly elected bodies, established by national law, on equal terms with men, without any discrimination.

Article III

Women shall be entitled to hold public office and to exercise all public functions, established by national law, on equal terms with men, without any discrimination.

Article IV

1. This Convention shall be open for signature on behalf of any Member of the United Nations and also on behalf of any other State to which an invitation has been addressed by the General Assembly.

2. This Convention shall be ratified and the instruments of ratification shall be deposited with the Secretary-General of the United Nations.

Article V

1. This Convention shall be open for accession to all States referred to in paragraph 1 of article IV.

2. Accession shall be effected by the deposit of an instrument of accession with the Secretary-General of the United Nations.

Article VI

1. This Convention shall come into force on the ninetieth day following the date of deposit of the sixth instrument of ratification or accession.

2. For each State ratifying or acceding to the Convention after the deposit of

the sixth instrument of ratification or accession the Convention shall enter into force on the ninetieth day after deposit by such State of its instrument of ratification or accession.

Article VII

In the event that any State submits a reservation to any of the articles of this Convention at the time of signature, ratification or accession, the Secretary-General shall communicate the text of the reservation to all States which are or may become parties to this Convention. Any State which objects to the reservation may, within a period of ninety days from the date of the said communication (or upon the date of its becoming a party to the Convention), notify the Secretary-General that it does not accept it. In such case, the Convention shall not enter into force as between such State and the State making the reservation.

Article VIII

1. Any State may denounce this Convention by written notification to the Secretary-General of the United Nations. Denunciation shall take effect one year after the date of receipt of the notification by the Secretary-General.

2. This Convention shall cease to be in force as from the date when the denunciation which reduces the number of parties to less than six becomes effective.

Article IX

Any dispute which may arise between any two or more Contracting States concerning the interpretation or application of this Convention which is not settled by negotiation, shall at the request of any one of the parties to the dispute be referred to the International Court of Justice for decision, unless they agree to another mode of settlement.

Article X

The Secretary-General of the United Nations shall notify all Members of the United Nations and the non-member States contemplated in paragraph 1 of article IV of this Convention of the following:

(a) Signatures and instruments of ratifications received in accordance with article IV;

(b) Instruments of accession received in accordance with article V;

(c) The date upon which this Convention enters into force in accordance with article VI;

(d) Communications and notifications received in accordance with article VII;

(e) Notifications of denunciation received in accordance with paragraph 1 of article VIII;

(f) Abrogation in accordance with paragraph 2 of article VIII.

Article XI

1. This Convention, of which the Chinese, English, French, Russian and Spanish texts shall be equally authentic, shall be deposited in the archives of the United Nations.

2. The Secretary-General of the United Nations shall transmit a certified copy to all Members of the United Nations and to the non-member States contemplated in paragraph 1 of article IV.

IN FAITH WHEREOF the undersigned, being duly authorized thereto by their respective Governments, have signed the present Convention, opened for signature at New York, on the thirty-first day of March, one thousand nine hundred and fifty-three.

The National Organization for Women's Bill of Rights for Women, 1967

WE DEMAND:

I. That the U.S. Congress immediately pass the Equal Rights Amendment to the Constitution . . . and that such then be immediately ratified by the several States.

II. That equal employment opportunity be guaranteed to all women, as well as men . . .

III. That women be protected by law to ensure their rights to return to their jobs within a reasonable time after childbirth without loss of seniority or other accrued benefits, and be paid maternity leave as a form of social security and/or employee benefit.

IV. Immediate revision of tax laws to permit the deduction of home and child-care expenses for working parents.

V. That child-care facilities be established by law on the same basis as parks, libraries, and public schools, adequate to the needs of children from the pre-school years through adolescence, as a community resource to be used by all citizens from all income levels.

VI. That the right of women to be educated to their full potential equally with men be secured by Federal and State legislation.

VII. The right of women in poverty to secure job training, housing, and family allowances on equal terms with men, but without prejudice to a parent's right to remain at home to care for his or her children; revision of welfare legislation and poverty programs which deny women dignity, privacy, and self-respect.

VIII. The right of women to control their own reproductive lives by removing from the penal codes laws limiting access to contraceptive information and devices, and by repealing penal laws governing abortion.

Reprinted by permission of the National Organization for Women.

The National Women's Conference Plan of Action, 1977

Fifty-six state and territorial conventions forwarded recommendations summarized below for ratification by 2000 delegates gathered in Houston in 1977. Apart from gender, it was the most diverse elected body ever assembled.

1. Arts and Humanities: Equitable representation in management, governance, and decision-making structures in libraries, museums, media and higher education; blind-judging when possible.

2. Battered Women: Elimination of violence in the home through emergency shelters; training and intervention; strengthening and enforcement of laws; legal services for victims.

3. Business: Support for women entrepreneurs through government-related activities and contracts; inclusion of women-owned business in Small Business Administration targeting.

4. Child Abuse: Support for prevention and treatment of abused children including training for public awareness, parent counseling, service and justice agencies.

5. Child Care: Federally supported efforts and legislation at all levels to promote quality child care programs; labor and business support; education for parenthood.

6. Credit: Education and enforcement of the 1974 Federal Equal Credit Opportunity Act.

7. Disabled Women: Enforcement and expansion of legislation on education, employment, housing, and support services recognizing the special needs of disabled women.

8. Education: Enforcement of laws prohibiting discrimination in education; special consideration for physical education, leadership positions, vocation training, elimination of sex and race stereotyping.

9. Elective/Appointive Office: Joint effort by federal and state governments, political parties, and other organizations to increase women in office, policy making positions and judgeships.

10. Employment: A federal full employment policy; enforcement and extension of anti-discrimination laws; efforts by governments, institutions, business, industry and unions to reduce occupational segregation and promote upward mobility; special attention to minority women; amendment of the Veteran's Preference Act; extensions of the labor standards and the right to unionize; support for flextime jobs.

11. Equal Rights Amendment: Ratification of the ERA.

12. Health: Establishment of a national health security program acknowledging the special needs of women; improve community facilities, contraceptive research, reproductive services, substance abuse efforts, representation in professions and on policy boards; increase review of drugs, custodial care, surgical procedures.

13. Homemakers: Revise marital property, social security, and pension laws; in divorce provide for children's needs and sharing of economic burden; support displaced homemaker programs.

14. Insurance: Adoption of Model Regulations to Eliminate Unfair Sex Discrimination amended to cover pregnancy, newborns, policy conversions.

15. International Affairs: Increased participation by women in foreign policy-making roles; enforcement of anti-discrimination laws; improvement of the image of women in the mass media.

16. Media: Increased opportunity for women in professional and policy-making roles; enforcement of anti-discrimination laws; improvement of the image of women in the mass media.

17. Minority Women: Recognition that every Plan recommendation applies to all minority women with recognition of additional burdens through institutionalized bias and inadequate data; enforcement of anti-discrimination laws as they affect education, housing, health, employment; recognition of special needs of American Indian/ Alaskan Native women, Asian Pacific women, Hispanic women, Puerto Rican women, Black women.

18. Offenders: Review of sentencing laws and practices with discriminatory effects on women in penal facilities; address legal, counseling, health, educational needs of women, especially mothers and juveniles.

19. Older Women: Support by governments, public and private institutions of services promoting dignity and security in housing, health services, transportation, education, social security, recognition of the changing image of older women and their capacity to contribute to policy making.

20. Rape: Revise criminal codes to correct inequities against rape victims; rape crisis centers and prevention and self-protection programs; support for the National Center for the Prevention/ Control of Rape; victim compensation.

21. Reproductive Freedom: Support for U.S. Supreme Court decision guaranteeing reproductive freedom; make certain all methods of family planning are available to all women under privately or publicly funded medical services; oppose involuntary sterilization; full access to family planning and education on responsible sexuality for teens, full education programs with child care for teen parents.

22. Rural Women: Rural education policy to meet isolation, poverty and underemployment affecting women; improved data; full ownership rights for farm wives, review conditions affecting plantation/ migratory workers.

23. Sexual Preference: Legislation eliminating discrimination based on sexual preference in employment, housing, public accommodations, credit, public facilities, funding, military, repeal of laws restricting private behavior between consenting adults; evaluation of child custody suits based solely on parenting capacity.

24. Statistics: An analysis of all data collected by the government on the basis of sex and race to assess the impact of programs on women.

25. Welfare and Poverty: Focus on welfare and poverty by federal and state governments as major women's issues compounding inequality of opportunity; support for welfare reform program considering social security, child care, minimum wage, education, job opportunities, health insurance, and legal services; federal floor to ensure an adequate standard of living.

26. Continuing Committee of National Women's Conference: Establishment of a body to consider steps to achieve the Plan and convene a second conference.

Declaration of Sentiments of the National Organization for Women, 1998

On this twelfth day of July, 1998, the delegates of the National Organization for Women gather in convention on the one hundred and fiftieth year of the women's rights movement.

We bring passion, anger, hope, love and perseverance to create this vision for the future:

We envision a world where women's equality and women's empowerment to determine our own destinies is a reality;

We envision a world where women have equal representation in all decision-making structures of our societies;

We envision a world where social and economic justice exist, where all people have the food, housing, clothing, health care and education they need;

We envision a world where there is recognition and respect for each person's intrinsic worth as well as the rich diversity of the various groups among us;

We envision a world where non-violence is the established order;

We envision a world where patriarchal culture and male dominance no longer oppress us or our earth;

We envision a world where women and girls are heard, valued and respected.

Our movement, encompassing many issues and many strategies, directs our love for humanity into action that spans the world and unites women.

But our future requires us to know our past.

One hundred fifty years ago the women's rights movement grew out of the fight to abolish slavery. Angered by their exclusion from leadership and public speaking at abolitionist conventions and inspired by the power of the Iroquois women, a small dedicated group of women and men built a movement. After its inception, the movement was fractured by race. Our history is full of struggle against common bonds of oppression and a painful reality of separation. Nevertheless, these activists created a political force that achieved revolutionary change. They won property rights for married women; opened the doors of higher education for women; and garnered suffrage in 1920.

In 1923, on the seventy-fifth anniversary of the historic Seneca Falls convention, feminists led the demand for constitutional equality for women to win full justice under the law in order to end economic, educational, and political inequality.

Our foremothers—the first wave of feminists—ran underground railroads, lobbied, marched, and picketed. They were jailed and force fed, lynched and raped. But they prevailed. They started with a handful of activists, and today, the feminist movement involves millions of people every day.

Standing on their shoulders, we launched the National Organization for Women in 1966, the largest and strongest organization of feminists in the world today. A devoutly grassroots, action-oriented organization, we have sued, boycotted, picketed, lobbied, demonstrated, marched, and engaged in non-violent civil disobedience. We have won in the courts and in the legislatures; and we have negotiated with the largest corporations in the world, winning unparalleled rights for women.

The National Organization for Women and our modern day movement have profoundly changed the lives of women, men and children. We have raised public consciousness about the plight of women to such an extent that today the majority of people support equality for women.

In the past 32 years, women have advanced farther than in any previous generation. Yet still we do not have full equality.

We have moved more feminists than ever before into positions of power in all of the institutions that shape our society. We have achieved some measure of power to effect change in these institutions from within; yet still we are far from full equality in decision-making. We demand an equal share of power in our families and religions, in law, science and technology, the arts and humanities, sports, education, the trades and professions, labor and management, the media, corporations and small businesses as well as government. In no sphere of life should women be silenced, underrepresented, or devalued.

Today, we reaffirm our demand for Constitutional equality for women and girls. Simultaneously, we are working with sister organizations to develop and pass a national women's equality act for the twenty-first century. And we participate in and advance a global movement for women and demand that the United States join the overwhelming majority of nations of the world in ratifying the

United Nations Convention on the Elimination of All Forms of Discrimination Against Women without reservations, declarations, or understandings that would weaken this commitment.

We reaffirm our commitment to the power of grassroots activism, to a multi-issue, multi-tactical strategy.

We are committed to a feminist ideology and reaffirm our historic commitment to gaining equality for women, assuring safe, legal and accessible abortion and full reproductive freedom, combating racism, stopping violence against women, ending bigotry and discrimination based on sexual orientation and on color, ethnicity, national origin, women's status, age, disability, size, childbearing capacity or choices, or parental or marital status.

We will not trade off the rights of one woman for the advancement of another. We will not be divided. We will unite with all women who seek freedom and join hands with all of the great movements of our time and all time, seeking equality, empowerment and justice.

We commit to continue the mentoring, training, and leadership development of young and new activists of all ages who will continue our struggle. We will work to invoke enthusiasm for our goals and to expand ownership in this movement for current and future generations.

We commit to continue building a mass movement where we are leaders, not followers, of public opinion. We will continue to move feminist ideals into the mainstream thought, and we will build our media and new technology capabilities to control our own image and message.

How long and hard a struggle it was to win the right for women to vote. Today, we fight the same reactionary forces: the perversion of religion to subjugate women; corporate greed that seeks to exploit women and children as a cheap labor force; and their apologists in public office who seek to do through law what terrorists seek to accomplish through bullets and bombs. We will not submit, nor will we be intimidated. But we will keep moving forward.

Those who carried the struggle for women's suffrage through to its end were not there at the start; those who started the struggle did not live to see the victory. Like those strong feminist activists, we will not let ourselves be dispirited or discouraged. Even when progress seems most elusive, we will maintain our conviction that the work itself is important. For it is the work that enriches our lives; it is the work that unites us; it is the work that will propel us into the next century. We know that our struggle has made a difference, and we reaffirm our faith that it will continue to make a difference for women's lives.

Today, we dedicate ourselves to the sheer joy of moving forward and fighting back.

Reprinted by permission of the National Organization for Women.

Woman Suffrage

Women's rights advocates began calling for the right to vote in the 1848 Declaration of Sentiments and Resolutions. Following ratification of the Fourteenth Amendment, guaranteeing citizenship to former slaves, and of the Fifteenth Amendment, establishing their voting rights, suffrage supporters began seeking alternatives to a woman suffrage amendment. Several women attempted to vote, or voted, in the 1872 presidential elections, some arguing that the Fourteenth Amendment gave them the right, others arguing that as citizens they had the right. Suffrage leader Susan B. Anthony was among the women who voted in that year's election, an act that resulted in her being charged, tried, and convicted of voting. In her 1873 speech, she explained the reasoning that led her to believe that she had the right to vote.

Both sides of the woman suffrage debate had women and men in their ranks. Manufacturers and distributors of alcoholic beverages opposed woman suffrage because they believed that women would vote to outlaw liquor, a concern bolstered by women active in the temperance movement. Kate Gannett Wells in her letter and Jeannette L. Gilder in her article emphasize that some women could be prudent and informed voters, but they insist that the benefits of those women casting votes are outweighed by the costs to society.

In 1915, Carrie Chapman Catt, president of the National American Woman Suffrage Association, presented what she called her Winning Plan to pass the Nineteenth Amendment and gain suffrage rights for women. In August 1920, Tennessee became the thirty-sixth state to ratify the amendment.

Speech after Being Convicted of Voting in the 1872 Presidential Election, Susan B. Anthony, 1873

Friends and fellow citizens: I stand before you tonight under indictment for the alleged crime of having voted at the last presidential election, without having a lawful right to vote. It shall be my work this evening to prove to you that in thus voting, I not only committed no crime, but, instead, simply exercised my citizen's rights, guaranteed to me and all United States citizens by the National Constitution, beyond the power of any state to deny.

The preamble of the Federal Constitution says: "We, the people of the United States, in order to form a more perfect union, establish justice, insure domestic tranquility, provide for the common defense, promote the general welfare, and secure the blessings of liberty to ourselves and our posterity, do ordain and establish this Constitution for the United States of America."

It was we, the people; not we, the white male citizens; nor yet we, the male citizens; but we, the whole people, who formed the Union. And we formed it, not to give the blessings of liberty, but to secure them; not to the half of ourselves and the half of our posterity, but to the whole people—women as well as men. And it is a downright mockery to talk to women of their enjoyment of the blessings of liberty while they are denied the use of the only means of securing them provided by this democratic-republican government—the ballot.

For any state to make sex a qualification that must ever result in the disfranchisement of one entire half of the people, is to pass a bill of attainder, or, an ex post facto law, and is therefore a violation of the supreme law of the land. By it the blessings of liberty are forever withheld from women and their female posterity.

To them this government has no just powers derived from the consent of the governed. To them this government is not a democracy. It is not a republic. It is an odious aristocracy; a hateful oligarchy of sex; the most hateful aristocracy ever established on the face of the globe; an oligarchy of wealth, where the rich govern the poor. An oligarchy of learning, where the educated govern the ignorant, or even an oligarchy of race, where the Saxon rules the African, might be endured; but this oligarchy of sex, which makes father, brothers, husband, sons, the oligarchs over the mother and sisters, the wife and daughters, of every household—which ordains all men sovereigns, all women subjects, carries dissension, discord, and rebellion into every home of the nation.

Webster, Worcester, and Bouvier all define a citizen to be a person in the United States, entitled to vote and hold office.

The only question left to be settled now is: Are women persons? And I hardly believe any of our opponents will have the hardihood to say they are not. Being persons, then, women are citizens; and no state has a right to make any law, or to enforce any old law, that shall abridge their privileges or immunities. Hence, every discrimination against women in the constitutions and laws of the several states is today null and void, precisely as is every one against Negroes.

An Argument against Woman Suffrage, Kate Gannett Wells, 1884

I have not come here with any hope of refuting in ten minutes all the arguments of our pro-suffrage friends, nor is it necessary that I should even try to do so, for repeated discussion of the subject has made us all familiar with our own convictions and those of our contrary-minded neighbors. Still less have I come in any unfriendly spirit to the pro-suffragists, for I know many of them too well not to acknowledge that they are working, heart and soul, for what they believe is one of the necessary, if not the most necessary, factors in human progress.

The anti-suffrage women are women so busy in their own homes, so occupied in charities and plans for the poor and ignorant, that they never have had time, more than that, they never have had the wish to come before the public, even in this Green Room. More than that, they do not think it is woman's place to argue or to refute statements in the arena of politics. For years they were silent, passive; their convictions strengthening all the while, they expressing them only as social intercourse demanded. But a year or two ago reproaches were heaped upon them for their passivity, which was called cowardice. They are not cowards, but they are women, and as such they prefer to stay at home and do their part through their home. There are but few of us trained to the public work of addressing you. Those few the distance of many miles keeps from us, but there are thousands of women who feel that if their silence is attributed to fear or to small numbers, they must summon courage to speak, and therefore have they asked me to come and speak as best I may for them.

I stand here because we anti-suffragists believe that the time has come for us to declare that our intellectual judgments, our moral convictions, and our belief in right expediency as one of the grounds on which governmental and constitutional changes should be made, are entirely opposed to the doctrine of female suffrage.

It is said that the casting of a vote is a slight duty, quickly performed. If it were that simple mechanical act, we might not object to such action, but to cast a vote ought to mean to cast it intelligently and honestly; and how can we gain that accurate intelligence except by attending caucuses, primaries, nominating conventions, and supplementing general knowledge as far as possible by personal acquaintance with candidates? Even if some women have time and ability for such work, most of us have not; and even if we all had the time, is it desirable that the presence and co-work of unintelligent and depraved women should be added to the already jarring factions of political life? Every woman knows that all women cannot purify politics; and if a good woman can vote, so can a bad woman! Therefore, gentlemen, we say that to permit us to vote is to permit us to do many impossible things, which, nevertheless, we ought to do as patriotic women. The point in question is a vexed one between the pro and anti-suffragists. They say we have no right to prevent their doing what they consider to be right, and also that we need not vote because they do. We say that their demand for extension of the suffrage does involve us, and therefore we are put on the defensive against them. Party questions and reform measures of all kinds will arise; we may hold convictions different from theirs, and as we also care as much for our country's welfare as they do, when we see some measure we deem unwise likely to succeed, then, to save our country or State, we must vote; therefore do we beseech you not to grant female suffrage. And if it is replied that women will only vote and legislate rightly, I answer that I utterly disagree with such a statement. Women, as a rule, will vote on the side of pure moral issues, but they will also vote for illogical, inexpedient measures to secure some narrow, present good, which should be outweighed by the larger issues of legal stability, validity of order, constitutional and States' rights, which are also involved in the immediate settlement of any question.

What, then, is our general position?

1. That suffrage is not a *natural* right; if it were, no restriction of age; property, or education could be put upon it such as now exists.

2. That the essence of republicanism does not depend upon *every one's* voting, independent of qualification, but that it is the sovereign people, and not a monarchical power, who shall decide what persons may vote and under what restrictions.

3. That to be deprived of a vote is not to be deprived of one's personality; we are persons whether we are voters or not, and as persons should demand and receive careful legislation in all that concerns our interests.

4. Our opponents have rendered it useless for us to reaffirm that an intelligent woman is as capable of casting an intelligent vote as an intelligent man, or that some form of restricted suffrage might perhaps be desirable, for they demand unrestricted, universal female suffrage. They claim that suffrage is an educating power. We "anti" women grant that it may be, but we add that as the country is already so heavily weighted with an ignorant population, and that as our naturalization laws admit foreigners to vote before they have become Americanized, therefore we, as true patriots, will not burden our country with a great class of women to be educated.

We anti-suffragists will not yield one iota to the pro-suffragists in our belief in woman's capacity for advancement in every direction; in her right to receive the highest education, to demand equal wages with men, to work as physician, lawyer, minister, lecturer, or in any occupation she wishes. We also demand of our legislature that they erase from the statutes laws which discriminate unjustly against woman. We also believe that she should serve on school committees, on

State boards of charities, and on all kindred institutions, so that we wish to effect no curtailment of a woman's sphere except in the direction of suffrage.

And why do we wish that she should not enter upon that? Because most women are not fitted for it. We do not say that they never will be, but that they are not now, and will not be for some generations to come. Because I am a woman, because I care for woman's advancement, because I believe that though a large number of women are already fitted to vote, an infinitely greater number of women are not fitted for it, do I—do we—implore you not to give to all what at least most of us are not able to use rightly. You cannot give us suffrage without letting loose influences akin to those which have already debased politics and given rise to words of doubtful morality like wire-pulling, bribery, log-rolling, etc. If you give suffrage to all, you will speedily find that women are adepts in political measures, and will no more shrink at trying all means to secure their ends than do men; though on the other hand many men do, and many women would, employ only honorable means.

It is not necessary that women should vote in order to have the laws more favorable for them. The changes that have already taken place in them are due to the great progress of modern civilization within the last fifty years, and have had nothing to do with suffrage.

There is an opinion in some minds that the State should more and more assume a paternal relation to its population; that it should provide whatever is asked, and that by the making of laws, oppression and poverty will cease. It is also supposed that women can legislate best for themselves. Gentlemen, those who assume either of these opinions are asking the State and the power of suffrage to do the work of personal righteousness. If women can best legislate for themselves, why should not minors, both girls and boys, ask to have themselves qualified before the present legal age? And why should not one class of women legislate for themselves, and still another class for themselves? That there are still unfair and degrading laws is granted, but if we ask for woman suffrage in order to rectify them, we open the way for increased private, class, and personal legislation of all kinds. Is woman suffrage going to cure the evils that come from one's own misdoings? Will a brutal, an intemperate husband be any less brutal or intemperate because his wife has the power to vote? Will trustees cease to speculate with their clients' money because those clients can vote? Again, it is personal righteousness that must do the work which so often is expected from legislation and suffrage.

It is woman's ignorance more than man's wickedness, or the law's injustice, which brings about the evils for which our sympathy is craved. Suffrage is not needed to beget self-respect, or a knowledge of contracts, investments, and the workings of the law, which if carefully studied before action is begun, would save later needless misery. Lastly, it is argued against us that for various reasons we need not fear that the unintelligent will vote. This must remain a matter of opinion between us and those who differ from us. I can only say that my experience has led me to the contrary conclusion. I had occasion one winter to be connected with some work at the North End. The women were too careless and wretched in their lives and in their dress to be here described. They talked with each other in little groups; many a one spoke of the time when she could vote, as the only vengeance left her to exercise upon the wealthy classes. Woman suffrage, they said, would give the unskilled workwomen more ample wages, for they could vote themselves what they needed. Again, I was in a house where workingmen came for their daily dinner. The men were also talking of this subject, and said that the women must vote, "for we want the eight-hour law, and can get it THROUGH the women. They must make the State give us work. The women must see to it that we have work and only work for eight hours." These are but two instances, though I think they could be multiplied a hundred-fold; yet are they not indications of the way in which woman suffrage may be urged to forward some special party measure? Once let the great mass of uneducated women be added to the great mass of already uneducated men voters, and the State will slowly but surely be shaken under the varying demands made upon it for bread, work, money, leisure, and all kinds of laws to favor all kinds of persons. When those times come, there will be more bitter animosities of women against women, of secret warfare, of despicable wire-pulling, and of exercise of the power of personal charms as a weapon of persuasion, than now exists among men.

One word more. Even if in itself suffrage may be based upon the fundamental principle of justice, it does not follow that it should be applied when great injustice must be done. No wise government deals in abstract justice without considering the expediency of the steps necessary to remove justice from an abstract principle into a concrete action. Therefore, if in close argument I should be forced (which I could not be) to surrender all my assumed positions against woman suffrage, I could never be driven from this position, that in the present constitution of events, of facts,—physiological, social, financial, moral, and political,—it is inexpedient for government to grant universal female suffrage.

Inexpedient! Yes, forever inexpedient, until the highest type of morality and the clearest sense of justice and the widest reaches of law in its theoretical and practical applications are reached by all women. Women now do generous, wise, and lofty deeds, and women now do mean, foolish, despicable actions,—oh, how mean! how bad!

So finally we beseech you, gentlemen, to rectify all unjust laws against women; to strengthen the hands of good women all over the land in raising the fallen, in teaching self-respect and self-support to the ignorant, in bringing more happiness into every one's life; and to withhold from us the duty, necessity, right of suffrage, whichever it may be called, until you can have only *noble, honest* women for your voters and legislators.

Printed by the Massachusetts Association opposed to the Extension of Suffrage to Women. Courtesy of the Sophia Smith Collection, Smith College.

Why I Am Opposed to Woman Suffrage, Jeannette Gilder, 1894

It has been quite a shock to people who do not know me, but who thought they did, to find me opposed to woman's suffrage. Because I have been for so many years a working-woman, and because the profession I chose is, or was at the time I entered it, supposed to be entirely a man's profession, they thought I wanted all the privileges of men. But I don't. You could have counted the women journalists on the fingers of one hand at the time I entered the ranks. Nowadays you could not find fingers enough in a regiment to count them on. There are now certain branches of journalistic work that are almost entirely given over to women, and women not only edit mere departments of daily papers, but there are those who edit the Sunday editions of some of the biggest dailies.

I am a great believer in the mental equality of the sexes, but I deny the physical equality. I believe in putting men's work and women's work of the same kind side by side, and judging them not as sex work, but simply as work. To have a "Woman's Building" at the World's Fair did not seem to me a compliment to the sex, but I believe some good reasons were advanced for it. Even some of its staunchest advocates, however, doubt if there will ever be such another building at such another show. I do not believe in sex in literature or art. Every book should be compared with all other books of its kind, and so with every picture, statue, or musical composition. There are few trades or professions that I do not think women fairly well equipped for, or capable of being prepared for. I cannot say that I quite like the idea of a woman preacher, but that may be a mere prejudice; nor do I think that I would retain a woman lawyer. But this is neither here nor there.

In politics I do not think that women have any place. The life is too public, too wearing, and too unfitted to the nature of women. It is bad enough for men—so bad, that some of the best of them keep out of it; and it would be worse for women. Many of the women who are enthusiastic in the cause of suffrage seem to think that if they are once given the power to vote, every vexed question will be settled, every wrong righted. By dropping their ballots in the box they believe that they can set in motion the machinery of an earthly paradise. I wish I could think so. It is my opinion that it *would let loose the wheels of purgatory.* If the ballot were the end, that would be one thing, but it is only the beginning. If women vote they must hold office, they must attend primaries, they must sit on juries. We shall have women "heelers" and women "bosses"; there will be the "girls" of the Fourth Ward (when it comes to New York) as well as the "boys."

What will become of home life, I should like to know, if the mother and the father both are at the "primary" or the convention? Who will look after the children? Hired mothers? But can every woman with political ambitions afford to pay for a "resident" or a "visiting" mother? And even if she can, will such a one take the place of the real mother? I think not. Cannot a woman find a sufficiently engrossing "sphere" in the very important work of training her children? If there are any sons among them, she can mould them into good citizens; if there are any daughters, she can guide their footsteps along any path they may choose, for all paths but the political are open to them. I do not think that to be a good housewife should be the end and aim of every woman's ambition, but I do think that it should be some part of it; for I am old-fashioned enough to be a pious believer in the influence of a mother's training upon her children. Read the life of any great man, and you will see how much of his greatness he owed to his mother. It seems to me that it is a bigger feather in a woman's cap—a brighter jewel in her crown—to be the mother of a George Washington than to be a member of Congress from the Thirty-second District.

From the day Adam and Eve were created to the present year of grace men and women have been different in all important respects. They were made to fill different roles. It was intended by nature that men should work, and that women should share in the disposition and enjoyment of the fruits of their labor. Circumstances alter cases, and women are often—alas! too often—driven out into the world to make their own way. Would they find it any easier if they had the ballot! Do men find it so easy to get work? If they do, why are there so many thousands of the clamoring unemployed?

It is said that the laws are unfair to women. Then call the attention of the law-makers to the fact, and see how soon they will be amended. I think that men want to be fair to women, and a petition will work wonders with a Congressman. Will women always be fair to women? That is a serious question. They may on some points, but the question of chivalry never comes into consideration between women. It does between men and women, and the latter profit by it.

I speak from experience when I say that I don't see how women can cultivate home life and enter the political arena. Circumstances forced me to go out into the world to earn my own bread and a part of that of others. When my mother was living, she made the home, and all went well. But after that, after marriages and deaths, a family of four small children came to me for a home. I don't mean for support, for they had a father living, but for a home. I had to take, as far as possible, the place of my sister, their mother. To do my duty by them and by my work was the most difficult task I ever undertook. I had to go to my office every day and leave them to the care of others. Sometimes the plan worked well, but oftener it worked ill—very ill indeed. I had seven people doing, or attempting to do, what I and two others could have done had I been able to be at home and look after things myself. Suppose that politics had been added to my other cares? Suppose that I had had meetings to attend and candidates to elect, perhaps to be elected myself? What would have been the result? Even direr disaster! We cannot worship God and Mammon; neither can we be politicians and women. It is against nature, against reason. Give woman everything she wants, but not the ballot. Open every field of learning, every avenue of industry to her, but keep her out of politics. The ballot cannot help her, but it can hurt her. She thinks it a simple piece of paper, but it is a bomb—one that may go off in her own hands, and work a mischief that she little dreams of.

From Harper's Bazaar, *May 19, 1894. Courtesy of the Sophia Smith Collection, Smith College.*

The Winning Plan, Carrie Chapman Catt, 1915

. . . National Boards must be selected hereafter for one chief qualification—the ability to lead the national fight. There should be a mobilization of at least thirty-six state armies [after congressional approval an amendment needed the approval of three quarters of the states—or thirty-six states], and these armies should move under the direction of the national officers. They should be disciplined and obedient to the national officers in all matters concerning the national campaign. This great army with its thirty-six, and let us hope, forty-eight divisions, should move on Congress with precision, and a will. . . . More, those who enter on this task, should go prepared to give their lives and fortunes for success, and any pusillanimous coward among us who dares to call retreat, should be courtmartialled.

Any other policy than this is weak, inefficient, illogical, silly, inane, and ridiculous! Any other policy would fail of success. . . .

When a general is about to make an attack upon the enemy at a fortified point, he often begins to feint elsewhere in order to draw off attention and forces. If we decide to train up some states into preparedness for campaign, the best help which can be given them is to keep so much "suffrage noise" going all over the country that neither the enemy nor friends will discover where the real battle is. . . .

We should win, if it is possible to do so, a few more states before the Federal Amendment gets up to the legislatures.

. . . A southern state should be selected and made ready for a campaign, and the solid front of the "anti" south broken as soon as possible.

Some break in the solid "anti" East should be made too. If New York wins in 1917 the backbone of the opposition will be largely bent if not broken. . . .

By 1920, when the next national party platforms will be adopted, we should have won Iowa, South Dakota, North Dakota, Nebraska, New York, Maine and a southern state. We should have secured the Illinois law in a number of other states.

With these victories to our credit and the tremendous increase of momentum given the whole movement, we should be able to secure planks in all platforms favoring the Federal Amendment (if it has not passed before that time) and to secure its passage in the December term of the 1920 Congress.

It should then go to the legislatures of thirty-nine states which meet in 1921, and the remaining states would have the opportunity to ratify the amendment in 1922. If thirty-six states had ratified in these two years, the end of our struggle would come by April 1, 1922, six years hence. . . .

Equal Rights Amendment

The Equal Rights Amendment to the United States Constitution was first conceived by National Woman's Party leader Alice Paul and was first introduced in Congress in 1923. Her 1943 article in the Congressional Digest *outlines the National Woman's Party's rationale for demanding a constitutional amendment for women's equality. Congress passed a somewhat different version of the amendment in March 1972, but it had the same purpose: to guarantee women's equality with men. The resolution for the amendment included a seven-year limit for ratification that was extended for two years.*

Rep. Shirley Chisholm (D-NY)'s comments to the House of Representatives in 1969 outline the reasons she believed that the amendment was necessary. As an African American woman, she compared the racial discrimination and the sexual discrimination that she had experienced.

Ruth Bader Ginsburg, writing before her appointment to the U.S. Supreme Court, provides a legal context for supporting the amendment. Discussing opinions of the Court on which she later served, Ginsburg's 1977 article outlines several Supreme Court decisions related to gender discrimination and the need for the Equal Rights Amendment.

The amendment failed to be ratified by the required thirty-eight states and died on 30 June 1982. Stop ERA founder and leader Phyllis Schlafly, who was the person most responsible for defeating the amendment, recollected her followers' celebration on the day of the defeat in a 1997 article in George *magazine. Amendment supporters, however, continued to believe in the importance of equality and sought other avenues to end discrimination against women, including the passage of state constitutional amendments.*

Should Congress Approve the Proposed Equal Rights Amendment to the Constitution? Alice Paul, 1943

The National Woman's Party is striving to remove every handicap placed upon women by law and by custom. In order to remove those handicaps which the law can touch, it is endeavoring to secure the adoption of an Equal Rights Amendment to the United States Constitution.

The Woman's Party advocates such an Amendment for the following reasons:

1. *A national amendment is the most effective way to establish equality of rights for men and women throughout the country.*

The amendment would, at one stroke, compel both Federal and State governments to observe the principle of Equal Rights since the Federal Constitution is the supreme law of the land. The amendment would override all existing legislation which denies women Equal Rights with men and it would prevent any such legislation in the future.

2. *A national amendment is the most permanent way to establish equality of rights for men and women throughout the country.*

An amendment to the National Constitution would establish the principle of Equal Rights permanently in our country insofar as anything can be established permanently by law. Equal Rights laws passed by legislative bodies, on the other hand, are subject to reversal by later legislative bodies.

3. *A national amendment is the most dignified way to establish equality of rights for men and women throughout the country.*

The principle of Equal Rights for men and women is so important that it should be written into the National Constitution as one of the basic principles upon which our government is founded. The matter is too important to our Nation's welfare and honor to leave it to the States for favorable or unfavorable action, or for complete neglect, as they may see fit.

At this moment when the United States is engaged in a war with the avowed purpose of establishing freedom and equality for the whole world, the United States should hasten to set its house in order by granting freedom and equality to its own women. For the sake of a new and better world, as well as in justice to women themselves, we ask the immediate adoption of the Equal Rights Amendment.

From Congressional Digest *(April 1943). Reprinted by permission.*

Equal Rights for Women, Rep. Shirley Chisholm, 1969

Mr. Speaker, when a young woman graduates from college and starts looking for a job, she is likely to have a frustrating and even demeaning experience ahead of her. If she walks into an office for an interview, the first question she will be asked is, "Do you type?"

There is a calculated system of prejudice that lies unspoken behind that question. Why is it acceptable for women to be secretaries, librarians, and teachers, but totally unacceptable for them to be managers, administrators, doctors, lawyers, and Members of Congress?

The unspoken assumption is that women are different. They do not have executive ability, orderly minds, stability, leadership skills, and they are too emotional.

It has been observed before, that society for a long time discriminated against another minority, the blacks, on the same basis—that they were different and inferior. The happy little homemaker and the contented "old darkey" on the plantation were both produced by prejudice.

As a black person, I am no stranger to race prejudice. But the truth is that in the political world I have been far oftener discriminated against because I am a woman than because I am black.

Prejudice against blacks is becoming unacceptable although it will take years to eliminate it. But it is doomed because, slowly, white America is beginning to admit that it exists. Prejudice against women is still acceptable. There is very little understanding yet of the immorality involved in double pay scales and the classification of most of the better jobs as "for men only."

More than half of the population of the United States is female. But women occupy only 2 percent of the managerial positions. They have not even reached the level of tokenism yet. No women sit on the AFL-CIO council or Supreme Court. There have been only two women who have held Cabinet rank, and at present there are none. Only two women now hold ambassadorial rank in the diplomatic corps. In Congress, we are down to one senator and ten representatives.

Considering that there are about 3 1/2 million more women in the United States than men, this situation is outrageous.

It is true that part of the problem has been that women have not been aggressive in demanding their rights. This was also true of the black population for many years. They submitted to oppression and even cooperated with it. Women have done the same thing. But now there is an awareness of this situation particularly among the younger segment of the population.

As in the field of equal rights for blacks, Spanish-Americans, the Indians, and other groups, laws will not change such deep-seated problems overnight. But they can be used to provide protection for those who are most abused, and to begin the process of evolutionary change by compelling the insensitive majority to reexamine its unconscious attitudes.

It is for this reason that I wish to introduce today a proposal that has been before every Congress for the last 40 years and that sooner or later must become part of the basic law of the land—the equal rights amendment.

Let me note and try to refute two of the commonest arguments that are offered against this amendment. One is that women are already protected under the law and do not need legislation. Existing laws are not adequate to secure equal rights for women. Sufficient proof of this is the concentration of women in lower paying, menial, unrewarding jobs and their incredible scarcity in the upper level jobs. If women are already equal, why is it such an event whenever one happens to be elected to Congress?

It is obvious that discrimination exists. Women do not have the opportunities that men do. And women that do not conform to the system, who try to break with the accepted patterns, are stigmatized as "odd" and "unfeminine." The fact is that a woman who aspires to be chairman of the board, or a member of the House, does so for exactly the same reasons as any man. Basically, these are that she thinks she can do the job and she wants to try.

A second argument often heard against the equal rights amendment is that it would eliminate legislation that many states and the federal government have enacted giving special protection to women and that it would throw the marriage and divorce laws into chaos.

As for the marriage laws, they are due for a sweeping reform, and an excellent beginning would be to wipe the existing ones off the books. Regarding special protection for working women, I cannot understand why it should be needed. Women need no protection that men do not need. What we need are laws to protect working people, to guarantee them fair pay, safe working conditions, protection against sickness and layoffs, and provision for dignified, comfortable retirement. Men and women need these things equally. That one sex needs protection more than the other is a male supremacist myth as ridiculous and unworthy of respect as the white supremacist myths that society is trying to cure itself of at this time.

Let's Have ERA as a Signal, Ruth Bader Ginsburg, 1977

Last year we celebrated the two hundredth anniversary of the Declaration of Independence, but for most American women it's more important to look at four questions that relate to the present decade of the 1970s. First, how have jurists treated official line drawing by gender before the present decade? Second, how has the judicial response altered in the current decade? Third, what is the purpose and function of the equal rights amendment to the federal Constitution? And finally, how may the presence (or absence) of the equal rights amendment affect Supreme Court precedent?

The State of the Art to 1971

"Anything goes" seems to be a fair summary of the Supreme Court's decisions until 1971. The Court consistently had affirmed governmental authority to classify by gender, as a trilogy of cases illustrates—*Muller* v. *Oregon,* 208 U.S. 412 (1908); *Goesaert* v. *Cleary,* 335 U.S. 464 (1948); and *Hoyt* v. *Florida,* 368 U.S. 57 (1961).

In 1905, in the now long-discredited *Lochner* v. *New York,* 198 U.S. 45, the Court rebuffed a state's attempt to enact protective labor legislation for all workers, men and women alike. But in 1908 in *Muller* the Court upheld a ten-hour day for women only. The decision reflects themes first sounded in nineteenth century decisions—first, that women's place in a world controlled by men is divinely ordained (a thought Justice Bradley expressed in his concurring opinion in *Bradwell* v. *Illinois,* 16 Wall. 130 [1873]); and second, that while men can fend for themselves, women must "rest upon and look to [men] for protection." Somewhat inconsistently, the Court added in *Muller* that women require the aid of the law "to protect her from the greed as well as the passion of man."

Next in the trilogy, *Goesaert* illustrates the danger lurking behind "protective" labels. This decision upheld a Michigan statute that allowed women to work as waitresses in taverns but barred them from the more lucrative job of bartender. The law protects women, said the state, while male bartenders plus their union joined in a chivalrous chorus.

One of the plaintiffs was a female bar owner whose daughter, a coplaintiff, assisted in operating the business. The state had protected away mother's and daughter's right to compete with male bar owners. If the Goesaerts would not pay a man to do a job the two women were fully capable of doing themselves, they would have to close up shop. The Supreme Court opinion in *Goesaert* declares and proceeds from this premise: "Michigan could, beyond question, forbid all women from working behind a bar."

Increasingly, as this century has worn on, women who needed jobs to support themselves and in many cases their families became skeptical of this kind of "protection" from the law. From their vantage point, restrictive labor laws operate less to protect women than to protect men's jobs from women's competition.

In the last in the series, *Hoyt,* a unanimous Supreme Court held it permissible to limit women's jury service to those who volunteered. This system yielded the result that lay participation in the administration of justice was virtually all male.

By the late 1960s a revived and burgeoning feminist movement spotlighted the altered life patterns of women. Two factors contributed in particular to this changed atmosphere—the virtual disappearance of food and goods cultivated or produced at home and the access to more effective means of birth control. The Equal Pay Act of 1963 (29 U.S.C. § 206(d)) and Title VII of the Civil Rights Act of 1964 (42 U.S.C. § 2000 (e) *et seq.)* began to focus national attention on the adversely discriminatory treatment that women encountered in the labor market.

The Judicial Response after 1971

The United States Court of Appeals for the District of Columbia Circuit in 1974 summarized the post-1971 developments this way: Supreme Court precedent with respect to gender-based discrimination is "still evolving," "rapidly changing, and variously interpreted" (509 F. 2d 508, 510). In the same year in an article in the *New York University Law Review* Prof. John Johnston, Jr., commented that the courts are "not certain what constitutes sex discrimination, how virulent this form of discrimination is or how it should be analyzed in terms of due process and equal protection." My own appraisal, expressed in an article in *The Supreme Court Review, 1975,* is that the Supreme Court had taken a few remarkable steps in a new direction, but it had shied away from doctrinal development and had left open avenues of retreat.

The first break from the "anything goes" pattern was *Reed* v. *Reed,* 404 U.S. 71, in which the Supreme Court declared unconstitutional an Idaho law providing that as between persons "equally entitled" to administer a decedent's estate, "males must be preferred to females." A year and a half later, in *Frontiero v. Richardson,* 411 U.S. 677 (1973), married women in the uniformed services were held entitled to the same fringe benefits as married men. Under the law that the Supreme Court declared unconstitutional, married men automatically received a housing allowance and medical care for their wives, while married women received these benefits only if they supplied all their own support and more than half of their husband's.

In 1974 the Supreme Court retrenched, first in *Kahn* v. *Shevin,* 416 U.S. 351, a decision upholding exclusion of widowers from the Florida statute that grants widows a real property tax exemption. This exemption saved the real-property-owning widow the grand sum of fifteen dollars annually. A benign favor for (widowed) women? The Supreme Court said the fifteen dollar saving compensated women for past economic disadvantage. Florida gave three classes this little tax break: the blind, the totally and permanently disabled, and widows.

Later in 1974 the Court returned a decision impossible to rationalize as a favor to women. In *Geduldig* v. *Aiello,* 417 U.S. 484, the Court upheld a California statute that excluded women disabled by pregnancy from a workers' income protection disability insurance plan. On the other hand, the Supreme Court has held that school teachers may not be dismissed or placed on involuntary leave arbitrarily at a fixed stage in pregnancy (414 U.S. 632 [1974]) and that pregnant women ready and willing to work may not be denied unemployment compensation (423 U.S. 44 [1975]).

Absence of a consistent, comprehensible approach to this issue was further indicated last month. In *General Electric Company* v. *Gilbert,* 45 U.S.L.W. 4031 (December 7, 1976), the Court confronted an employer's plan providing nonoccupational sickness and accident benefits to all employees, save only those with disabilities arising from pregnancy. Construing Title VII of the Civil Rights Act of 1964, the Court declared this exclusion entailed no gender-based discrimination at all!

With no pregnant problems on its calendar, 1975 brought the Supreme Court back to the 1971–73 track. In *Taylor* v. *Louisiana,* 419 U.S. 522, the Court overturned its 1961 *Hoyt* women's jury service decision and declared unconstitutional a Louisiana provision that restricted jury service by women to volunteers. In *Stanton* v. *Stanton,* 421 U.S. 7, the Court declared unconstitutional a Utah law that required parents to support a son until he is twenty-one but a daughter only until she is eighteen. And in *Weinberger* v. *Wiesenfeld,* 420 U.S. 636, the Court struck down one of a series of Social Security sex lines. It held a widowed father to be entitled to the same benefits to care for his child that a widowed mother receives.

Is *Wiesenfeld* a men's rights case? Only derivatively. The discrimination started with Paula Wiesenfeld, a wage-earning woman. When she died, her social insurance provided less protection for her family than the social insurance of a wage-earning man. Paula Wiesenfeld paid social security taxes without any discount. But the payout to her survivors, husband Stephen and son Jason Paul, was subject to a drastic discount.

Do We Need the E.R.A.?

The key to the Supreme Court's performance in the 1970s is not so much the specific results of decided cases but how those results were reached. The justices so far have avoided articulating general principles and have shown a tendency to deal with each case as an isolated instance in a narrow frame. No opinion attracting five votes acknowledges a clear perception of what computer runs or federal and state statutes so plainly reveal—that the particular statutes presented to the Supreme Court are part of a pervasive design, a design reflecting distinctly nonneutral notions about "the way women (or men) are."

Why does the Court shy away from doctrinal development? For an altogether understandable reason. Justice Powell explained the problem in his *Frontiero* concurring opinion. The Court must act with particular circumspection, he said, in the dim zone between constitutional interpretation (a proper judicial task) and constitutional amendment (a job for federal and state legislatures).

But the equal protection guarantee exists for all persons, and the Supreme Court has indeed acknowledged that women are "persons" within the meaning of the Fourteenth Amendment. Why, then, the reluctance to interpret the equal protection principle dynamically in this area? Because it is historic fact that neither the founding fathers nor the Reconstruction Congress had women's emancipation on the agenda. When the Thirteenth, Fourteenth, and Fifteenth amendments were added to the Constitution, women were denied the vote, the most basic right of adult citizens. If they were married, in many states they could not contract, hold property, or litigate on their own behalf. Courts are sensitive to that history.

Race discrimination decisions may be anchored with some security to the design of those who drafted the Constitution. Indeed, in the 1872 *Slaughter-House Cases,* 16 Wall. 36, the Court said that the Fourteenth Amendment's equal protection clause is so clearly a provision for the black race that the Court doubted whether any other form of official discrimination would ever be held to come within its purview.

Recognition of women as "persons" occurred in the Supreme Court's 1874 *Minor* v. *Happersett,* 21 Wall. 162, opinion, a decision rejecting a woman's claim to the franchise. Beyond doubt women are "persons" and may be "citizens" within the meaning of the Fourteenth Amendment, the Court said. So are children, it went on to explain, and no one would suggest children have a constitutional right to the franchise.

The adoption of the equal rights amendment would relieve the Court's uneasiness in the gray zone between interpretation and amendment of the Constitution. It would remove the historical impediment—the absence of any intention by eighteenth and nineteenth century Constitution makers to deal with gender-based discrimination. It would add to our fundamental instrument of government a principle under which the judiciary may develop the coherent opinion pattern lacking up to now. It also should end the legislative inertia that retards social change by keeping obsolete discriminatory laws on the books. And, as Justice Stevens observed in his confirmation hearings, the amendment would have symbolic importance. It would serve as a forthright statement of our moral and legal commitment to a system in which neither sons nor daughters are pigeonholed by government because of their sex. Rather, so far as laws and officialdom are concerned, males and females will be free to grow, develop, and aspire in accordance with their individual talents, preferences, and capacities.

What Are the Consequences?

What are the consequences of the High Court's unwillingness to articulate a principle of general application governing legislative line drawing by gender?

A look at the Court's docket for this current term indicates the situation. First, Oklahoma's 3.2 beer law is before the Court (No. 75–628). This is a "protective" statute with an unusual twist in that it permits girls to buy 3.2 beer or work in a beer parlor at the age of eighteen, while boys must wait until they are twenty-one. The plaintiff, Carolyn Whitener, is an entrepreneur who sells 3.2 beer, and her coplaintiff is an apparently thirsty young man. It is an embarrassment that a law of this kind is retained by a legislature and must occupy the attention of the highest court in the nation.

Second, there is another Social Security Act challenge (No. 75–699). W, a wage earner, dies. H, her spouse, is not himself covered under social security. H seeks survivors' benefits under W's account. The law says H is not entitled unless W outearned H three to one. For a spouse to qualify under a female wage earner's account, the female must provide all her own support, plus half of his—in other words, three fourths of the total family support.

If the situation were the other way around—if a male were the covered worker, a female the survivor—the survivor would qualify for benefits without regard to H's and W's respective contributions to family income. Women are put on a par with men for social security contribution purposes, but the payout under a woman's account is less than the payout under a man's.

That very same gender differential was declared unconstitutional in *Frontiero* v. *Richardson,* the 1973 military fringe benefits case. And *Weinberger* v. *Wiesenfeld,* the 1975 social security case, overturned a differential that the solicitor general described as "closely analogous." Yet despite a unanimous decision in *Wiesenfeld* and a near unanimous (eight-to-one) judgment in *Frontiero,* the Court did not deem it appropriate to affirm summarily. And the solicitor general argues, with some justification, that each precedent in the 1970s was written for one case and one day alone.

With the ERA on the books, we may expect Congress and state legislatures to undertake in earnest, systematically and pervasively, the law revision so long deferred. History should teach that the entire job is not likely to be done until the ERA supplies the signal. In the event of legislative default, the courts will be guided by a constitutional text clearly and cleanly in point.

Without the ERA, the judiciary will continue to be plagued with a succession of cases challenging laws and official practices that belong on history's scrap heap. The Supreme Court will confront again and again the need for principled decisions to guide the lower courts and the difficulty of anchoring those decisions to the text of eighteenth and nineteenth century draftsmen.

The American Bar Association endorsed the equal rights amendment in August of 1974. The resolution aroused scant opposition. No one spoke against it in the House of Delegates; only a dozen or so "nay" votes were audible. The resolution included a commitment to work for ratification by the number of states required to write the amendment into the Constitution.

That commitment is hardly fulfilled. It is my hope that the Association, as a reasoned voice for the profession, will move swiftly this year to carry out its 1974 undertaking and its pledge to play an active role in educating the public. For the American Bar Association, perhaps more than any other professional organization, has the capacity and resources to dispel misunderstanding on this issue and to explain why the ERA is the way for a society that believes in the essential human dignity and interdependence of each man and each woman.

Reprinted from the American Bar Association Journal, *63 (January 1977), 70–73, with permission from Supreme Court Justice Ruth Bader Ginsburg.*

Eyewitness: Beating the Bra Burners, Phyllis Schlafly, 1997

A giant rainbow of balloons hovered high over the dais in the Omni Shoreham ballroom in Washington, D.C. Some 1,400 battle-weary but triumphant Stop ERA volunteers gathered to savor their victory when the proposed equal rights amendment died at midnight on June 30, 1982.

Amid the clamor, a hotel security guard rushed toward the emcee, Representative Bob Dornan of California, with urgent news: The hotel had received a phone call that a bomb had been planted in the ballroom. But the Stop ERA revelers just had to laugh. No need to evacuate. We anticipated that a bomb threat would be the radical feminists' last insult, and police dogs had already sniffed out the room.

It was the last day of a ten-year David-and-Goliath struggle waged across America. A little band of women, headquartered in the kitchen of my home on the bluffs of the Mississippi in Alton, Illinois, had defeated the big guns. The odds against us could not have been greater. The ERA drew the support of presidents (Richard Nixon, Gerald Ford, and Jimmy Carter), would-be presidents of all political stripes (from Ted Kennedy to George Wallace), all members of Congress except eight in the Senate and 24 in the House, all the pushy women's organizations, a consortium of 35 women's magazines, and what seemed like 99 percent of the media.

In March 1972, Congress sent ERA to the states for their legislatures to approve, and its ratification by the necessary three-fourths of the 50 states seemed inevitable. But the unstoppable was stopped by our unflappable ladies in red. They descended on state capitols wearing their octagonal STOP ERA buttons. They treated legislators to home-baked bread. And they sweetly and persistently made their case that ERA was a fraud: It would actually *take away* legal rights that women possessed, such as the right of an 18-year-old girl to be exempt from the military draft and the right of a wife to be supported by her husband.

Pro-ERA advocates argued that women wanted absolute equality anyway. That line didn't sell in Middle America. A noisy tax-funded national women's confab in November 1977 had showcased ERA's hidden agenda: abortion funding and same-sex unions. The noose around ERA was tightening.

The war over these ideas included annual clashes in key states. But the decisive battle (*i.e.,* what Midway was to World War II) took place in Springfield, Illinois, on June 18, 1980. If we could win in this northern industrial state, then we could triumph in pro-ERA territory, and other states might swing our way. President Carter rang up Democratic legislators, in my view luring votes for ERA with talk of new federal housing projects for their districts. Back in 1978, Governor James Thompson phoned Republican legislators, reportedly promising "jobs, roads, and bridges" for a yes vote. Later, Chicago pols rallied their lawmakers to ERA's side, allegedly under threat of seeing their relatives and friends lose city patronage jobs. Some ERA supporters even offered cash bribes for votes. But in 1980, ERA failed once again.

After the votes were tallied, ABC's *Nightline* caught Eleanor Smeal, president of the National Organization for Women, in the Illinois House gallery. "There is something very powerful out against us," she said. "And certainly it isn't people." The Stop ERAers knew the source of their power: prayer and the truth.

ERA activists persisted in desperate tactics at that crucial statehouse. In May and June of 1982, an excommunicated Mormon, Sonia Johnson, led a hunger strike in the rotunda, while upstairs other pro-ERAers chained themselves to the door of the Senate chamber. On June 25, ERA supporters went to a slaughterhouse, purchased plastic bags of pigs' blood, and used it to spell out the names of the legislators they hated most on the capitol's marble floor. The lawmakers found these tactics, well, unpersuasive. Victory was sealed on June 30, 1982, and many politicians paid tribute. But the day's heroes were the women who came from the 15 states that never ratified ERA and from the 5 states that bravely rescinded their previous ratifications.

That evening, singers Bill and Prudence Fields sang the appropriate themes: "The Impossible Dream" and "Great Day."

From George *Magazine, June, 1997. Reprinted with permission.*

Women, Campaigns, and Political Parties

Women have sought political power by working in their parties and by running for office since the 1870s, long before women had voting rights. The first woman to actively seek the presidency was Victoria Woodhull, a newspaper publisher and owner of a stock brokerage firm, who announced her candidacy in the New York Herald *in 1870. Other women followed Woodhull, but it would be more than ninety years before a woman sought a major party's nomination. The first was Senator Margaret Chase Smith, who sought the Republican Party's presidential nomination in 1964. Eight years later, Rep. Shirley Chisholm (D-NY) became a candidate for the Democratic Party's presidential nomination. She examined the meaning of her candidacy in a speech before the National Women's Political Caucus in 1973. Republican Elizabeth Dole, former Secretary of Labor and former Secretary of Transportation, sought to be her party's nominee in the year 2000 elections.*

The televised and widely reported Republican and Democratic national conventions, held to select each party's presidential nominees, provide the parties with a national stage that they use to attract supporters. Party leaders carefully choose keynote speakers and party activists seek to be one of the keynoters. At the 1976 Democratic national convention, Rep. Barbara Jordan (D-TX) was the first African American woman to keynote a national party convention, captivating the audience with her powerful message.

By the late 1990s, Republican party leaders had become aware of the gender gap that existed between the two major parties. Women tended to favor the Democratic Party and its candidates over the Republican Party and its candidates, a factor that helped elect President Bill Clinton in 1992 and 1996. During the 1996 elections, Rep. Jennifer Dunn (R-WA) sought to convince women that the Republican Party was addressing their concerns when she addressed groups on behalf of male Republican congressional candidates.

I Announce Myself as a Candidate for the Presidency, Victoria Woodhull, 1870

As I happen to be the most prominent representative of the only unrepresented class in the republic, and perhaps the most practical exponent of the principles of equality, I request the favor of being permitted to address the public through the *Herald.* While others of my sex devoted themselves to a crusade against the laws that shackle the women of the country, I asserted my individual independence; while others prayed for the good time coming, I worked for it; while others argued the equality of woman with man, I proved it by successfully engaging in business; while others sought to show that there was no valid reason why women should be treated, socially and politically, as being inferior to man, I boldly entered the arena of politics and business and exercised the rights I already possessed. I therefore claim the right to speak for the unenfranchised women of the country, and believing as I do that the prejudices which still exist in the popular mind against women in public life will soon disappear, I now announce myself as a candidate for the Presidency.

. . . The present position of political parties is anomalous. They are not inspired by any great principles of policy or economy; there is no live issue up for discussion. A great national question is wanted. . . . That question exists in the issue, whether woman shall . . . be elevated to all the political rights enjoyed by man. The simple issue whether woman should not have this complete political equality . . . is the only one to be tried, and none more important is likely to arise before the Presidential election.

Printed in the New York Herald, *April 2, 1870.*

Women in Politics, Rep. Shirley Chisholm, 1973

When it was arranged that I should speak to you today, Liz Carpenter wrote me a note and suggested my speech should be, "Can a Woman Become President?" Knowing Liz, she probably thought this would be a wonderful occasion for me to exhort an audience of potential candidates to plan their own onslaughts on the pinnacle of elective office.

As I look back on the past year and a half, I think my campaign did help to break the barrier against women seeking the presidency and other elective offices, but my experiences also made me acutely aware of some of the problems women candidates face as well as particular problems which the women's movement, and especially the National Women's Political Caucus, must face up to.

One of my biggest problems was that my campaign was viewed as a symbolic gesture. While I realized that my campaign was an important rallying symbol for women and that my presence in the race forced the other candidates to deal with issues relating to women, my primary objective was to force people to accept me as a real viable candidate.

Although many have compared my race to that of Victoria Woodhull, I specifically rejected that comparison. Mrs. Woodhull was a feminist candidate running on a feminist party platform. I specifically rejected this feminist candidacy as I did the projection of myself into a black candidacy or an antiwar candidacy. I chose to run for the nomination of one of the major national parties.

I did this because I feel that the time for tokenism and symbolic gestures is past. Women need to plunge into the world of politics and battle it out toe to toe on the same ground as their male counterparts. If they do not do this, they will not succeed as a presidential candidate or in any other campaign for political office.

First and foremost, it is essential that you believe in yourself and your ability to handle the job you are seeking. If you don't, it is difficult to persuade others to support you. While pretty obvious to anyone who has run for office, I found that the press, the public, and even those in the women's movement found it difficult to understand this key point. Over and over in the campaign, I was asked, "But why are you running, Mrs. Chisholm?" Over and over I would reply, "Because I think I can do the job," "Because I think I am better than the rest of the candidates in the field."

One of the stumbling blocks I encountered was the fact that many people, including feminists, thought that since I "didn't have a chance" it was foolish to work for me.

For those who genuinely preferred another candidate, one can have no quarrel. But for those who thought I was the best candidate but chose to work for someone else because they viewed my campaign as hopeless, they will need to re-examine their thinking for truly, no woman will ever achieve the presidency as long as their potential supporters hold this view.

As the effect of the Wallace phenomenon in this last election points out, a campaign becomes truly effective when those who believe in their candidate pull out all the stops.

One of the other most difficult problems I faced was that many of my wonderful women's movement supporters did not understand that I both wanted and needed to talk about issues other than equal rights, abortion and child care. As you know, I am a strong supporter of all of these issues but in a campaign, there is a great deal of other ground to cover. Senior citizens don't really give a hang about abortion and homosexuals are more concerned with their own situation than the status of the Equal Rights Amendment.

Further, and this is critical to the discussion we will enter into at this convention, different women view different segments of the women's movement agenda as priority items.

The movement has, for the most part, been led by educated white middle-class women. There is nothing unusual about this. Reform as movements are usually led by the better educated and better off. But, if the women's movement is to be successful you must recognize the broad variety of women there are and the depth and range of their interests and concerns. To black and Chicano women, picketing a restricted club or insisting on the title Ms. are not burning issues. They are more concerned about bread-and-butter items such as the extension of minimum wage, welfare reform and day care.

Further, they are not only women but women of color and thus are subject to additional and sometimes different pressures.

For example, the black experience in America has not been one of unbridled success for black men. Indeed, there have been times when discrimination and the economic situation were such that it was easier for a black woman to get a job than her husband. Because of this, anything that might be construed as anti-male will be viewed skeptically by a black woman.

Indeed this is a problem not only for black women but most women.

If this caucus is to have a real impact, we must have a broad base and appeal to the average woman.

Unfortunately, the movement is currently perceived as anti-male, anti-child, and anti-family.

Part of this is bad press. The media does not concentrate on the blue-haired lady in pearls testifying on behalf of the equal employment opportunities bill. It trains its eyes on the young girl shaking her fist and screaming obscenities at an abortion rally.

Part of it is that many of the leaders of the movement have down-graded traditional roles in their attempts to show abuses and to affirm the right of a woman to have a choice of roles to play.

Finally, there have been excesses. Not all sexual advances are sexist. Children are more than a pile of dirty diapers, and families while they have often restricted women, have also provided warmth, security, and love.

If we are to succeed in uniting ourselves and in attracting the typical woman who is likely to be a housewife and mother who likes living in suburbia, we are going to have to make a concerted effort to articulate issues so that everyone will want to be identified with and active in the movement.

Address delivered before the National Women's Political Caucus Convention, Houston, February 9, 1973. Reprinted by permission.

Exploratory Committee Announcement Speech, Elizabeth Dole, 1999

Hello. Thank you for tuning in.

I know your life is busy: so many things you need to do and not enough time for what you want to do, so, thanks for choosing to spend a few minutes with me. I promise to be brief. But I have some thoughts I'm eager to share with you about the future of our country. And I'd like to talk a little about my own sense of obligation as a citizen of the freest land on earth.

As you know, I have been thinking about running for President.

Since I left the American Red Cross, January 15th, I've been traveling around the country, and I've been humbled by the response. It's been inspiring to appear before overflow crowds in such places as New Hampshire, Iowa, Colorado, Florida, and Texas. It's been that way everywhere, but I don't think I'm the cause. I think the crowds and the enthusiasm are evidence of a great American yearning to make our nation a better place.

Yes, I've seen many Presidential campaigns up close. I know what they entail. And I know a run for the Presidency should be undertaken only if you believe in something so strongly that its accomplishment makes everything worthwhile.

And if I run, this will be why: I believe our people are looking for leaders who will call America to her better nature. Yes, we've been let down—and by people we should have been able to look up to. But it's not just that. Politics and the politics of governing have become so negative, so paralyzed by special interests, that as a people we're beginning to lose faith in our own institutions. It's only a short step to losing faith in ourselves, and then we would be lost.

When I entered public service as a young woman, it was considered a noble thing to do. Today, too many of our young men and women can't see the wondrous possibilities of public life for the ugliness of politics. And they turn away from public service.

We must rekindle a spirit in our hearts—something very American, something still alive but buried beneath a thickening layer of skepticism and doubt. We must renew faith in the goodness of our nation, and a sense in ourselves that each one of us can make a difference—no matter how large the challenge. For both are true.

Restoring a national belief in the power of the individual and the need for acceptance of personal responsibility is, I believe, at the center of our challenge today as a nation.

What does a woman like me have to offer the country? I'm not a politician, and frankly today I think that may be a plus. But I have spent a lifetime as a servant of the public. I have served in the administrations of five Presidents. Some of those jobs have included Federal Trade Commissioner, Ronald Reagan's White House staff, and the Reagan and Bush cabinets as Secretary of Transportation and Secretary of Labor. Working with committed teams of public servants and volunteers, I oversaw the largest privatization in government history when we sold the government freight railroad, Conrail; I led the massive safety overhaul of our nation's airline inspection system and placed special emphasis on ensuring passenger safety in the age of deregulation; worked to untangle years of suspicion and mistrust in ending a crippling coal strike while at the Department of Labor; and, as President of the Red Cross, a $2.2 billion dollar corporation—transformed the manner in which half our nation's blood supply is collected, tested and distributed, creating a new gold standard for safety and reliability.

I mention all this to point out that if there is an overriding theme to my thirty-plus years in public life—and I think there is—it lies in placing service over politics, consensus over confrontation and a constant recognition of the desire of my fellow countrymen to do what is right.

If today's politics seem irrelevant, it falls to us—all of us—to make them more relevant. If public life is lacking in civility, then it is our common task to help civilize it.

But what are the issues we want our leaders to address? I'm proud to have served as a lieutenant in Ronald Reagan's army. He was sure of his mission and his policies revolutionized our economy.

And I can well remember when President Reagan asked the telling question: "Are you better off today than you were four years ago?" Perhaps the question we should be asking today is: Are we better? Are our families stronger? Are our public schools committed first to excellence? Are our children safe from drugs? Do we assume responsibility for our culture and our choices? And have we shouldered the burden incumbent on each generation of Americans to man and maintain a national defense with the wherewithal to keep us free?

Today our taxes have reached the highest percentage of gross domestic product in 50 years. The average American family spends 40 percent of its income just paying the tax bill. According to the Tax Foundation, that means the family spent more than 5 months in 1998 working for the government—in federal, state and local taxes combined.

And today, defense spending has reached its lowest percentage of gross domestic product in 50 years.

The readiness of our troops is in question and a whole generation of outdated military equipment is waiting to be replaced. The military has been downsized so far, many of our best people are leaving, and all this at a time when North Korea is building nuclear bombs that could be ready to strike us within a year according to the Secretary of Defense, and Iraq is manufacturing biological weapons that could terrorize the world.

Today the United States reigns as the world's only superpower. But rogue nations and terrorists still threaten our people, our freedom and our way of life. I believe there is an urgent need to refurbish our military and resolve to develop and deploy a strategic missile defense system at the earliest possible date.

Another menace to our way of life lurks within our borders: the cancer of drug abuse. It was recently reported that the head of the Drug Enforcement Agency said, "The nation has neither the will nor the resources to win the drug war" and "Curbing drug use is not a high enough priority with the American people."

People tell me the polls show that drug abuse is not a priority issue. I believe we should make it one. My passion doesn't come from polling. I have a vision of an America free of drugs. Like you, I'm appalled that marijuana and cocaine use by teenagers tripled in recent years. . . . And together I know we can change that. But first we have to recognize that it's not enough to urge foreign countries to reduce the supply. Let's be honest. There wouldn't be a supply if there wasn't a demand. Can we stand by and allow the great United States of America to be consumed by an insatiable appetite for this devastating addiction?

Of course not. America needs a President who will use the bully pulpit, and from it speak out loudly and clearly and often about the dangers of drugs with the unmistakable message that drugs are not cool. They kill. The Federal Government must do a better job of supporting the hundreds of local anti-drug coalitions. And, yes, we must strengthen our interdiction efforts to stop illegal drugs before they reach our borders. At this moment when the number of Americans behind bars—most on drug-related charges—has never been greater, we must make absolutely clear that drugs are a personal and national evil that threatens us all.

But the challenges today to public education pose perhaps the greatest test of our citizenship. I regard public education as one of the glories of American democracy. Which is precisely why the number one priority of any education reform must be this: To restore our public schools to greatness.

I count as one of the most rewarding experiences of my life, teaching in a public school near Boston while I was earning a graduate degree in education. I learned in the classroom what a noble profession teaching really is.

And ever since then, I have refused to join those who often find it expedient to turn teachers into rhetorical punching bags. Yes, we should expect the best out of our teachers. Yes, we should reward outstanding performance. No, we should not be expected to put up with incompetence. But let us never forget that the true heroes of our society are not to be found on a movie screen or a football field— they are to be found in our classrooms.

I doubt any of us remembers which federal official had primary responsibility for education when we graduated from high school. But I bet each and every one of us can remember the teacher who awakened in us a love of history or a fascination with words.

It was at the Department of Labor when education truly became more than an interest for me—it became a passion. Improving the skills of America's current and future workforce was for me a top priority.

Across the board, employers were insisting—and are insisting—on higher skills and a better educated workforce.

And, I was hearing from employers that the preparation students were receiving in our classrooms was inadequate to meet the needs of our workplace. From one corporate leader, I learned that four out of every five job applicants in his company had recently flunked entry level employment exams requiring seventh grade English skills, and fifth grade math.

We are the richest nation in the world. We can afford safer, newer classrooms with smaller classes. Places where real knowledge is transferred by better-trained, more accountable teachers. Where orderly, disciplined students stay in class more hours during more days. If we take up this challenge across America, our public schools will become again places where America's separating classes can melt together, because rich and poor alike will freely choose them for their children.

There are many ideas to restore to local school districts, funds taken in taxes by the Federal Government. We should do this, because local districts know best what their schools need. Maybe it's hiring more teachers, or raising their salaries or fixing up falling down buildings. But the ultimate test of our resolve is not how much money Washington gives to school districts. It's how much control Washington gives back to parents and teachers.

By all means, let's put a computer in every classroom. But let's make sure to put parents in every classroom as well. Parents will do what the government has not: ensure a zero tolerance for incompetence. We should test and track and act on the results, holding teachers and principals and schools accountable for the success of the children in their care. But if a child is trapped in an unsafe, failing school, we must provide other answers, like a voucher to help parents select another school.

And I believe we must return teaching to the heart of the educational enterprise.

Teaching needs to be supported, not only by rewarding excellence in teaching, but by placing the training of teachers at the center of our higher education system. I will be revealing nothing by saying that some of our schools of education have not demanded nearly enough of their students, nor have they been accorded the attention and support they would have in a properly constituted educational order. If teaching is to become a prestigious profession, teachers must undergo rigorous training and hold prestigious degrees.

As we raise the regard for teachers, perhaps we can also reinstate regard for public service. Because service to others—be it in the classroom, in government, or at the local Red Cross—can and does bring out the best in ourselves.

In my eight years at the American Red Cross, I saw things that will haunt me the rest of my life—the dim eyes of starving children in Somalia, the paralyzing grief of parents in Oklahoma City, the despair of those family members who lost loved ones and everything they owned to a tornado's 260-mile-per-hour, terrifying violence.

But I also saw the power of the human heart—of America's heart: neighbors helping neighbors after hurricanes, earthquakes and floods; Americans willing to go to the other side of the globe to help those they didn't know, and would never see again—the victims of war and natural disaster.

As I travel this country, I am buoyed by the goodness of our citizens, the clarity of your vision and the strength of your values. Which is why I am ready to take the next step. This week, I have filed papers to form an exploratory committee. I will be reaching out to you. I want to listen, to hear your hopes and understand your concerns—people to people. And I would like to ask for your support and the support of people all across our country, as I explore a Presidential candidacy. I hope to see you soon on one of my next visits. You may also contact me through my exploratory committee website, www.edole2000.org.

Like you, I love my country. And like you, I want to do whatever I can to make it better. I believe the road ahead beckons to every American, for whom the untraveled world is a place of limitless possibility. God willing, we will travel it together, with courage, confidence, and conviction, leaving no one behind, knowing that the future is our friend.

Thank you. God bless you. And may God bless America.

Reprinted with permission from the Elizabeth Dole campaign.

A New Beginning: A New Dedication, Rep. Barbara Jordan, 1976

One hundred and forty-four years ago, members of the Democratic party first met in convention to select a presidential candidate. Since that time, Democrats have continued to convene once every four years and draft a party platform and nominate a presidential candidate. And our meeting this week is a continuation of that tradition.

But there is something different about tonight. There is something special about tonight. What is different? What is special? I, Barbara Jordan, am a keynote speaker.

A lot of years passed since 1832, and during that time it would have been most unusual for any national political party to ask that a Barbara Jordan deliver a keynote address . . . but tonight here I am. And I feel that notwithstanding the past that my presence here is one additional bit of evidence that the American Dream need not forever be deferred.

Now that I have this grand distinction what in the world am I supposed to say?

I could easily spend this time praising the accomplishments of this party and attacking the Republicans but I don't choose to do that.

I could list the many problems which Americans have. I could list the problems which cause people to feel cynical, angry, frustrated: problems which include lack of integrity in government; the feeling that the individual no longer counts; the reality of material and spiritual poverty; the feeling that the grand American experiment is failing or has failed. I could recite these problems and then I could sit down and offer no solutions. But I don't choose to do that either.

The citizens of America expect more. They deserve and they want more than a recital of problems.

We are a people in a quandary about the present. We are a people in search of our future. We are a people in search of a national community.

We are a people trying not only to solve the problems of the present: unemployment, inflation . . . but we are attempting on a larger scale to fulfill the promise of America. We are attempting to fulfill our national purpose; to create and sustain a society in which all of us are equal.

Throughout our history, when people have looked for new ways to solve their problems, and to uphold the principles of this nation, many times they have turned to political parties. They have often turned to the Democratic party.

What is it, what is it about the Democratic party that makes it the instrument that people use when they search for ways to shape their future? Well I believe the answer to that question lies in our concept of governing. Our concept of governing is derived from our view of people. It is a concept deeply rooted in a set of beliefs firmly etched in the national conscience, of all of us.

Now what are these beliefs?

First, we believe in equality for all and privileges for none. This is a belief that each American regardless of background has equal standing in the public forum, all of us. Because we believe this idea so firmly, we are an inclusive rather than an exclusive party. Let everybody come.

I think it no accident that most of those emigrating to America in the nineteenth century identified with the Democratic party. We are a heterogeneous party made up of Americans of diverse backgrounds.

We believe that the people are the source of all governmental power; that the authority of the people is to be extended, not restricted. This can be accomplished only by providing each citizen with every opportunity to participate in the management of the government. They must have that.

We believe that the government which represents the authority of all the people, not just one interest group, but all the people, has an obligation to actively underscore, actively seek to remove those obstacles which would block individual achievement ... obstacles emanating from race, sex, economic condition. The government must seek to remove them.

We are a party of innovation. We do not reject our traditions, but we are willing to adapt to changing circumstances, when change we must. We are willing to suffer the discomfort of change in order to achieve a better future.

We have a positive vision of the future founded on the belief that the gap between the promise and reality of America can one day be finally closed. We believe that.

This, my friends, is the bedrock of our concept of governing. This is a part of the reason why Americans have turned to the Democratic party. These are the foundations upon which a national community can be built.

Let's all understand that these guiding principles cannot be discarded for short-term political gains. They represent what this country is all about. They are indigenous to the American idea. And these are principles which are not negotiable.

In other times, I could stand here and give this kind of exposition on the beliefs of the Democratic party and that would be enough. But today that is not enough. People want more. That is not sufficient reason for the majority of the people of this country to vote Democratic. We have made mistakes. In our haste to do all things for all people, we did not foresee the full consequences of our actions. And when the people raised their voices, we didn't hear. But our deafness was only a temporary condition, and not an irreversible condition.

Even as I stand here and admit that we have made mistakes I still believe that as the people of America sit in judgment on each party, they will recognize that our mistakes were mistakes of the heart. They'll recognize that.

And now we must look to the future. Let us heed the voice of the people and recognize their common sense. If we do not, we not only blaspheme our political heritage, we ignore the common ties that bind all Americans.

Many fear the future. Many are distrustful of their leaders, and believe that their voices are never heard. Many seek only to satisfy their private work wants. To satisfy private interests.

But this is the great danger America faces. That we will cease to be one nation and become instead a collection of interest groups; city against suburb, region against region, individual against individual. Each seeking to satisfy private wants.

If that happens, who then will speak for America?

Who then will speak for the common good?

This is the question which must be answered in 1976.

Are we to be one people bound together by common spirit sharing in a common endeavor or will we become a divided nation?

For all of its uncertainty, we cannot flee the future. We must not become the new puritans and reject our society. We must address and master the future together. It can be done if we restore the belief that we share a sense of national community, that we share a common national endeavor. It can be done.

There is no executive order; there is no law that can require the American people to form a national community. This we must do as individuals and if we do it as individuals, there is no President of the United States who can veto that decision.

As a first step, we must restore our belief in ourselves. We are a generous people so why can't we be generous with each other? We need to take to heart the words spoken by Thomas Jefferson: "Let us restore to social intercourse that harmony and that affection without which liberty and even life are but dreary things."

A nation is formed by the willingness of each of us to share in the responsibility for upholding the common good.

A government is invigorated when each of us is willing to participate in shaping the future of this nation.

In this election year we must define the common good and begin again to shape a common good and begin again to shape a common future. Let each person do his or her part. If one citizen is unwilling to participate, all of us are going to suffer. For the American idea, though it is shared by all of us, is realized in each one of us.

And now, what are those of us who are elected public officials supposed to do? We call ourselves public servants but I'll tell you this: we as public servants must set an example for the rest of the nation. It is hypocritical for the public official to admonish and exhort the people to uphold the common good if we are derelict in upholding the common good. More is required of public officials than slogans and handshakes and press releases. More is required. We must hold ourselves strictly accountable. We must provide the people with a vision of the future.

If we promise as public officials, we must deliver. If we as public officials propose, we must produce. If we say to the American people it is time for you to be sacrificial; sacrifice. If the public official says that, we (public officials) must be the first to give. We must be. And again, if we make mistakes, we must be willing to admit them. We have to do that. What we have to do is strike a balance between the idea that government should do everything and the idea, the belief, that government ought to do nothing. Strike a balance.

Let there be no illusions about the difficulty of forming this kind of a national community. It's tough, difficult, not easy. But a spirit of harmony will survive in America only if each of us remembers that we share a common destiny. If each of us remembers when self-interest and bitterness seem to prevail, that we share a common destiny.

I have confidence that we can form this kind of national community.

I have confidence that the Democratic party can lead the way. I have that confidence. We cannot improve on the system of government handed down to us by the founders of the Republic, there is no way to improve upon that. But what we can do is to find new ways to implement that system and realize our destiny.

Now, I began this speech by commenting to you on the uniqueness of a Barbara Jordan making the keynote address. Well I am going to close my speech by quoting a Republican President and I ask you that as you listen to these words of Abraham Lincoln, relate them to the concept of a national community in which every last one of us participates: "As I would not be a slave, so I would not be a master."

This expresses my idea of Democracy. Whatever differs from this, to the extent of the difference is no democracy.

Delivered to the National Democratic Convention, July 12, 1976. Reprinted by permission of the Barbara Jordan Archives, Texas Southern University.

What the GOP Has Done for Women, Rep. Jennifer Dunn, 1996

When women back home in my district talk to me about what this Congress is doing these days, I tell them that Congress is dealing with the very problems that women are concerned about.

Well, what is it that we women care about?

We want opportunity for ourselves and our families.

We want some sense that there will be a retirement system we can count on.

We want a healthy environment.

We want a good education for our children.

We want personal safety.

We want health care security.

We want the folks who really need help in our society to get that help.

We want homemaker IRAs, because we know that the work done inside the home is every bit as important, if not more important, as the work done outside the home.

What has the Republican Congress done to answer these needs?

This Congress has indeed been supportive of women and the family. We passed a $500 per child tax credit; we passed marriage penalty tax relief; we passed tougher laws on sexual predators and stalkers; we are supporting employees having the option of selecting either time-off or cash instead of overtime wages. For too long parents have had to choose between work and spending time with their children. A working mother may prefer to see her daughter in a school play rather than be paid time and a half for staying at her job. She should have that choice.

And women care about their families. Much of what we care about concerns the family. Don't let the media fool you when they say this isn't a "family friendly" Congress. It may not seem so to those of us who spend hour after hour, day after day, month after month fighting the battles in the Congress! But it truly is friendly to families.

We increased day care money and child support enforcement provisions in our welfare reform plan—$4.5 billion more dollars than the current welfare system.

We support funding for the "Violence Against Women Act"—which will help state and local governments to focus tax dollars on preventing crimes targeted toward women, like domestic violence.

We support tax credits for couples who choose to adopt a child.

We support tax credits to help families care for elderly parents and grandparents in a loving home as long as they can stay there.

We passed the "Domestic Violence Insurance Protection Act"—which forbids insurance companies from treating domestic violence victims as having a pre-existing condition.

We passed steps to amend Medicare regulations to include the treatment of breast cancer with a proven cancer-stopping drug.

We support increased funding for women's health care research—given how hard this Congress has worked to balance the budget, an increase illustrates our high level of commitment to women's health issues.

And we have passed a bi-partisan "Safe Drinking Water Act" that has been heralded by environmentalists.

Please don't believe the rhetoric—rather, look at our record and look at what we've done.

For instance, take a look at our record on small business—the real engine that creates new jobs and energizes the economy. Small business built this country. Today, more people are employed by women-owned small business than by Fortune 500 companies. And according to the SBA, women are starting businesses at twice the rate of men. It is anticipated that women will own 50 percent of the small businesses in America in the 21st Century.

What are these women small business owners and workers interested in?

Growth and prosperity, less regulation and lower taxes, common-sense laws, and health insurance deductibility for the self-employed. Women small business owners can be assured that their concerns are in sync with the Republican Congress' work on behalf of small business.

Look at what we've passed:
- regulatory relief
- paperwork reduction and elimination
- health care deductibility for the self employed
- we ensured the solvency of the principal lending programs at SBA
- we made tax compliance for "S" Corporations less complicated
- we provided small businesses the ability to quickly write-off the money they spend on practical things like computers and office furniture

In fact, if Congress gets its way—and President Clinton keeps his veto pen in his pocket—women business owners can expect sustained growth, more jobs and better wages . . . sounds a bit like the American Dream, doesn't it?

I've found that my women friends at home in Washington state care about the very same things that this Republican Congress does: helping families keep more of their paychecks so they can decide how to do more for their families and their communities; saving Medicare for our parents and welfare for the folks who are truly in need, and encouraging local answers as we solve the problems of increasing crime, and declining education and protecting the environment.

Our solutions are not complicated. Our solutions do not require Congressional studies, or committee hearings or "expert" testimony.

Our solution is to listen.

I've have found that if you listen to the American woman and respect her advice, the answers are all right there.

According to Representative Dunn's office this speech was given dozens of times during the 1996 campaign on behalf of male Republican Congressional candidates. Reprinted by permission.

Women of Sovereign Nations

Americans live in a culture so dominated by European traditions and laws that it is often difficult to recognize the ways in which other cultures coexist with American life. It is important to realize that while some women in the United States struggled for the vote and equality with men, Native American women have participated in their own political systems, often on equal terms with men, and have ruled their sovereign nations.

At this book goes to press, the United States has not had a woman president, but a sovereign nation that was annexed by it once had a queen. The Hawaiian Islands, sovereign until 1895, were ruled by Queen Liliuokalani from 1891 to 1893, years when colonial interests competed with the throne for power and for control over the islands. Confronted with a provisional government and threats of violence, Queen Liliuokalani sought a strategy that would avoid the loss of life and preserve the option of maintaining her country's sovereignty. She sought assistance from President Grover Cleveland, but ultimately her attempt failed and led to her abdication from the throne in 1895.

Native American Zitkala-Ša, a Yankton Sioux also known as Gertrude Simmons Bonnin, was a leader in the Society of American Indians in the 1910s and was the founder and president of the National Council of American Indians from 1926 to 1938. Dedicated to Native American self-determination, she worked to find a balance between "Americanizing" her people and preserving Native American culture and tradition. Bonnin's convictions emerged from her childhood experiences in a mission school, as described in her article.

In the last decades of the twentieth century, Native American women have established themselves as national leaders with compelling agendas. Anishinabe Winona LaDuke has focused her efforts on the synergy between environmental and women's issues; she ran for Vice President of the United States on the Green Party ticket in 1996. Ada Deer, the first woman to direct the Bureau of Indian Affairs, testified in Congress about proposed amendments to the Indian Child Welfare Act of 1978, which recognized the harm done to Native American children when they were removed from their communities and acknowledged the right of tribal governments to determine tribal membership and to serve the best interests of their children.

Appeal to President Grover Cleveland, Queen Liliuokalani, 1893

I, Liliuokalani, by the Grace of God and under the Constitution of the Hawaiian Kingdom, Queen, do hereby solemnly protest against any and all acts done against myself and the Constitutional Government of the Hawaiian Kingdom by certain persons claiming to have established a Provisional Government of and for this Kingdom.

That I yield to the superior force of the United States of America whose Minister Plenipotentiary, His Excellency John L. Stevens, has caused United States troops to be landed at Honolulu and declared that he would support the Provisional Government.

Now to avoid any collision of armed forces, and perhaps the loss of life, I do this under protest and impelled by said force yield my authority until such time as the Government of the United States shall, upon facts being presented to it, undo the action of its representatives and reinstate me in the authority which I claim as the Constitutional Sovereign of the Hawaiian Islands.

The School Days of an Indian Girl, Zitkala-Ša, 1900

The first turning away from the easy, natural flow of my life occurred in an early spring. It was in my eighth year; in the month of March, I afterward learned. At this age I knew but one language, and that was my mother's native tongue.

From some of my playmates I heard that two paleface missionaries were in our village. They were from that class of white men who wore big hats and carried large hearts, they said. Running direct to my mother, I began to question her why these two strangers were among us. She told me, after I had teased much, that they had come to take away Indian boys and girls to the East. My mother did not seem to want me to talk about them. But in a day or two, I gleaned many wonderful stories from my playfellows concerning the strangers.

"Mother, my friend Judéwin is going home with the missionaries. She is going to a more beautiful country than ours; the palefaces told her so!" I said wistfully, wishing in my heart that I too might go.

Mother sat in a chair, and I was hanging on her knee. Within the last two seasons my big brother Dawée had returned from a three years' education in the East, and his coming back influenced my mother to take a farther step from her native way of living. First it was a change from the buffalo skin to the white man's canvas that covered our wigwam. Now she had given up her wigwam of slender poles, to live, a foreigner, in a home of clumsy logs.

Judéwin had told me of the great tree where grew red, red apples; and how we could reach out our hands and pick all the red apples we could eat. I had never seen apple trees. I had never tasted more than a dozen red apples in my life; and when I heard of the orchards of the East, I was eager to roam among them. The missionaries smiled into my eyes, and patted my head. I wondered how mother could say such hard words against them.

"Mother, ask them if little girls may have all the red apples they want, when they go East," I whispered aloud, in my excitement.

The interpreter heard me, and answered: "Yes, little girl, the nice red apples are for those who pick them; and you will have a ride on the iron horse if you go with these good people."

I had never seen a train, and he knew it.

"Mother, I'm going East! I like big red apples, and I want to ride on the iron horse! Mother, say yes!" I pleaded.

My mother said nothing. The missionaries waited in silence; and my eyes began to blur with tears, though I struggled to choke them back. The corners of my mouth twitched, and my mother saw me.

"I am not ready to give you any word," she said to them. "Tomorrow I shall send you my answer by my son."

With this they left us. Alone with my mother, I yielded to my tears, and cried aloud shaking my head so as not to hear what she was saying to me. This was the first time I had ever been so unwilling to give up my own desire that I refused to harken to my mother's voice.

There was a solemn silence in our home that night. Before I went to bed I begged the Great Spirit to make my mother willing I should go with the missionaries.

The next morning came, and my mother called me to her side. "My daughter, do you still persist in wishing to leave your mother?" she asked.

"Oh, mother, it is not that I wish to leave you, but I want to see the wonderful Eastern land," I answered.

. . . My brother Dawée came for mother's decision. I dropped my play, and crept close to my aunt.

"Yes, Dawée, my daughter, though she does not understand what it all means, is anxious to go. She will need an education when she is grown, for then there will be fewer real Dakotas, and many more palefaces. This tearing her away, so young, from her mother is necessary, if I would have her an educated woman. The palefaces, who owe us a large debt for stolen lands, have begun to pay a tardy justice in offering some education to our children. But I know my daughter must suffer keenly in this experiment. For her sake, I dread to tell you my reply to the missionaries. Go, tell them that they may take my little daughter, and that the Great Spirit shall not fail to reward them according to their hearts."

Wrapped in my heavy blanket, I walked with my mother to the carriage that was soon to take us to the iron horse. I was happy. I met my playmates, who were also wearing their best thick blankets. We showed one another our new beaded moccasins, and the width of the belts that girdled our new dresses. Soon we were being drawn rapidly away by the white man's horses. When I saw the lonely figure of my mother vanish in the distance, a sense of regret settled heavily upon me. I felt suddenly weak, as if I might fall limp to the ground. I was in the hands of strangers whom my mother did not fully trust. I no longer felt free to be myself, or to voice my own feelings. The tears trickled down my cheeks, and I buried my face in the folds of my blanket. Now the first step, parting me from my mother, was taken, and all my belated tears availed nothing.

Having driven thirty miles to the ferryboat, we crossed the Missouri in the evening. Then riding again a few miles eastward, we stopped before a massive brick building. I looked at it in amazement, and with a vague misgiving, for in our village I had never seen so large a house. Trembling with fear and distrust of the palefaces, my teeth chattering from the chilly ride, I crept noiselessly in my soft moccasins along the narrow hall, keeping very close to the bare wall. I was as frightened and bewildered as the captured young of a wild creature.

The first day in the land of apples was a bitter-cold one; for the snow still covered the ground, and the trees were bare. A large bell rang for breakfast, its loud metallic voice crashing through the belfry overhead and into our sensitive ears. The annoying clatter of shoes on bare floors gave us no peace. The constant clash of harsh noises, with an undercurrent of many voices murmuring an unknown tongue, made a bedlam within which I was securely tied. And though my spirit tore itself in struggling for its lost freedom, all was useless.

A paleface woman, with white hair, came up after us. We were placed in a line of girls who were marching into the dining room. These were Indian girls, in stiff shoes and closely clinging dresses. The small girls wore sleeved aprons and shingled hair. As I walked noiselessly in my soft moccasins, I felt like sinking to the floor, for my blanket had been stripped from my shoulders. I looked hard at the Indian girls, who seemed not to care that they were even more immodestly dressed than I, in their tightly fitting clothes. While we marched in, the boys entered at an opposite door. I watched for the three young braves who came in our party. I spied them in the rear ranks, looking as uncomfortable as I felt . . .

. . . Late in the morning, my friend Judéwin gave me a terrible warning. Judéwin knew a few words of English; and she had overheard the paleface woman talk about cutting our long, heavy hair. Our mothers had taught us that only un-skilled warriors who were captured had their hair shingled by the enemy. Among our people, short hair was worn by mourners, and shingled hair by cowards!

We discussed our fate some moments, and when Judéwin said, "We have to submit, because they are strong," I rebelled.

"No, I will not submit! I will struggle first!" I answered.

I watched my chance, and when no one noticed I disappeared. I crept up the stairs as quietly as I could in my squeaking shoes,—my moccasins had been ex-changed for shoes. Along the hall I passed, without knowing whither I was going. Turning aside to an open door, I found a large room with three white beds in it. The windows were covered with dark green curtains, which made the room very dim. Thankful that no one was there, I directed my steps toward the corner far-thest from the door. On my hands and knees I crawled under the bed, and cud-dled myself in the dark corner.

From my hiding place I peered out, shuddering with fear whenever I heard footsteps near by. Though in the hall loud voices were calling my name, and I knew that even Judéwin was searching for me, I did not open my mouth to an swer. Then the steps were quickened and the voices became excited. The sounds came nearer and nearer. Women and girls entered the room. I held my breath, and watched them open closet doors and peep behind large trunks. Some one threw up the curtains, and the room was filled with sudden light. What caused them to stoop and look under the bed I do not know. I remember being dragged out, though I resisted by kicking and scratching wildly. In spite of myself, I was car-ried downstairs and tied fast in a chair.

I cried aloud, shaking my head all the while until I felt the cold blades of the scissors against my neck, and heard them gnaw off one of my thick braids. Then I lost my spirit. Since the day I was taken from my mother I had suffered extreme indignities. People had stared at me. I had been tossed about in the air like a wooden puppet. And now my long hair was shingled like a coward's! In my an-guish I moaned for my mother, but no one came to comfort me. Not a soul rea-soned quietly with me, as my own mother used to do; for now I was only one of many little animals driven by a herder. . . .

. . . Now, as I look back upon the recent past, I see it from a distance, as a whole. I remember how, from morning till evening, many specimens of civilized people visited the Indian school. The city folks with canes and eyeglasses, the country men with sunburnt cheeks and clumsy feet, forgot their relative social ranks in an ignorant curiosity. Both sorts of these Christian palefaces were alike astounded at seeing the children of savage warriors so docile and industrious.

As answers to their shallow inquiries they received the students' sample work to look upon. Examining the neatly figured pages, and gazing upon the In-dian girls and boys bending over their books, the white visitors walked out of the schoolhouse well satisfied: they were educating the children of the red man! They were paying a liberal fee to the government employees in whose able hands lay the small forest of Indian timber.

In this fashion many have passed idly through the Indian schools during the last decade, afterward to boast of their charity to the North American Indian. But few there are who have paused to question whether real life or long-lasting death lies beneath this semblance of civilization.

Excerpted from "Impressions of an Indian Childhood," "The School Days of an Indian Girl," and "An Indian Teacher among Indians" by Zitkala-Ša, Atlantic Monthly 85 (January, February, and March 1900):45–47, 186–187, and 386.

The Indigenous Women's Network: Our Future, Our Responsibility, Winona LaDuke, 1995

I am from the Mississippi Band of Anishinabeg of the White Earth reservation in northern Minnesota, one of approximately 250,000 Anishinabeg people who inhabit the great lakes region of the North American continent. Aniin indinawaymugnitok. Me gweich Chi-iwewag, Megwetch Ogitchi taikwewag. Nindizhinikaz, Beenaysayikwe, Makwa nin dodaem. Megwetch indinawaymugunitok.

I am greeting you in my language and thanking you, my sisters, for the honor of speaking with you today about the challenges facing women as we approach the 21st century.

A primary and central challenge impacting women as we approach the 21st century will be the distance we collectively as women and societies have artificially placed ourselves from our Mother the Earth, and the inherent environmental, social, health and psychological consequences of colonialism, and subsequently rapid industrialization, on our bodies and our nations. A centerpiece of this problem is the increasing lack of control we have over ourselves, and our long term security. This situation must be rectified through the laws of international institutions, such as the United Nations, but as well, the policies, laws and practices of our nations, our communities, our states, and ourselves.

The situation of Indigenous women, as a part of Indigenous peoples, we believe is a magnified version of the critical juncture we find ourselves in as peoples, and the problems facing all women and our future generations as we struggle for a better world. Security, militarism, the globalization of the economy, the further marginalization of women, increasing intolerance and the forced commodification and homogenization of culture through the media.

The Earth is our Mother. From her we get our life and our ability to live. It is our responsibility to care for our mother, and in caring for our Mother, we care for ourselves. Women, all females are the manifestation of Mother Earth in human form. We are her daughters and in my cultural instructions: Minobimaatisiiwin, we are to care for her. I am taught to live in respect for Mother Earth. In Indigenous societies, we are told that Natural Law is the highest law, higher than the law made by nations, states, municipalities and the World Bank. That one would do well to live in accordance with Natural Law, with those of our Mother. And in respect for our Mother Earth of our relations—indinawaymuguni took.

One hundred years ago, one of our Great Leaders, Chief Seattle, stated "What befalls the Earth, befalls the People of the Earth." And that is the reality of today, and the situation of the status of women, and the status of Indigenous women and Indigenous peoples.

While I am from one nation of Indigenous peoples, there are millions of Indigenous people worldwide. An estimated 500 million people are in the world today. We are in the Cordillera, the Maori of New Zealand, we are in East Timor, we are the Wara Wara of Australia, the Lakota, the Tibetans, the peoples of Hawaii, New Caledonia and many other nations of Indigenous peoples. Indigenous peoples. We are not populations, not minority groups, we are peoples, we are nations of peoples. Under international law we meet the criteria of nation states, having common economic system, language, territory, history, culture and governing institutions. Despite this fact, Indigenous Nations are not allowed to participate at the United Nations.

Nations of Indigenous people are not, by and large, represented at the United Nations. Most decisions today are made by the 180 or so member states to the United Nations. Those states, by and large, have been in existence for only 200 years or less, while most Nations of Indigenous peoples, with few exceptions, have been in existence for thousands of years. Ironically, there would likely be little argument in this room, that most decisions made in the world today are actually made by some of the 47 transnational corporations and their international financiers whose annual income is larger than the gross national product for many countries of the world.

This is a centerpiece of the problem. Decisionmaking is not made by those who are affected by those decisions, people who live on the land, but corporations, with an interest which is entirely different than that of the land, and the people, or the women of the land. This brings forth a fundamental question. What gives these corporations like Conoco, Shell, Exxon, Diashawa, ITT, Rio Tinto Zinc, and the World Bank, a right which supercedes or is superior to my human right to live on my land, or that of my family, my community, my nation, our nations, and us as women. What law gives that right to them; not any law of the Creator, or of Mother Earth. Is that right contained within their wealth? Is that right contained within their wealth, which is historically acquired immorally, unethically, through colonialism, imperialism, and paid for with the lives of millions of people, or species of plants and entire ecosystems? They should have no such right, that right of self determination, and to determine our destiny, and that of our future generations.

The origins of this problem lie with the predator/prey relationship industrial society has developed with the Earth, and subsequently, the people of the Earth. This same relationship exists vis-a-vis women. We collectively find that we are often in the role of the prey to a predator society, whether for sexual discrimination, exploitation, sterilization, absence of control over our bodies, or being the subjects of repressive laws and legislation in which we have no voice. This occurs on an individual level, but equally and more significantly, on a societal level. It is also critical to point out at this time that most matrilineal societies, societies in which governance and decisionmaking are largely controlled by women, have been obliterated from the face of the Earth by colonialism and subsequently industrialism. The only matrilineal societies which exist in the world today are those of Indigenous nations. We are the remaining matrilineal societies, yet we also face obliteration.

On a worldwide scale and in North America, Indigenous societies historically, and today, remain in a prey/predator relationship with industrial society, and prior to that, colonialism and imperialism. We are the peoples with the land—land and natural resources required for someone else's development program and the amassing of wealth. The wealth of the United States, that nation which today determines much of world policy, easily expropriated from our lands. Similarly the wealth of Indigenous peoples of South Africa, Central and South American countries, and Asia was taken for the industrial development of Europe, and later for settler states which came to occupy those lands. That relationship between development and underdevelopment adversely affected the status of our Indigenous societies, and the status of Indigenous women.

Eduardo Galeano, the Latin American writer and scholar, has said: "In the colonial to neocolonial alchemy, gold changes to scrap metal and food to poison; we have become painfully aware of the mortality of wealth which nature bestows and imperialism appropriates."

Today, on a worldwide scale, we remain in the same situation as one hundred years ago, only with less land, and fewer people. Today, on a worldwide scale, 50 million Indigenous peoples live in the world rainforests, a million Indigenous peoples are slated to be relocated for dam projects in the next decade (thanks to the World Bank, from the Narmada Project in India, to the Three Gorges Dam Project, here in China, to the Jasmes Bay Hydro Electric Project in northern Canada). Almost all atomic weapons which have been detonated in the world are also detonated on the lands or waters of the Indigenous, like the proposal to detonate atomic weapons this upcoming month. This situation is mimicked in the North American context. Today, over 50 percent of our remaining lands are forested, and both Canada and the United States continue aggressive clearcutting policies on our land. Over two thirds of the uranium resources in the United States, and similar figures for Canada, are on Indigenous lands, as is one third of all low-sulfur coal resources. We have huge oil reserves on our reservations, and we have the dubious honor of being the most highly bombed nation in the world, the Western Shoshone Nation, on which over 650 atomic weapons have been detonated. We also have two separate accelerated proposals to dump nuclear waste on our reservation lands, and similarly over 100 separate proposals to dump toxic waste on our reservation lands. We understand clearly the relationship between development for someone else, and our own underdevelopment. We also understand clearly the relationship between the environmental impacts of types of development on our lands, and the environmental and subsequent health impacts in our bodies as women. That is the cause of the problems.

We also understand clearly that the analysis of North versus South is an erroneous analysis. There is, from our perspective, not a problem of the North dictating the economic policies of the South, and subsequently consuming the South. Instead, there is a problem of the Middle consuming both the North and the South. That is our situation. Let me explain.

The rate of deforestation in the Brazilian Amazon is one acre every nine seconds. Incidentally, the rate of extinction of Indigenous peoples in the Amazon is one nation of Indigenous peoples per year. The rate of deforestation of the boreal forest of Canada is one acre every twelve seconds. Siberia, thanks to American corporations like Weyerhauser, is not far behind. In all cases, Indigenous peoples are endangered. And there is frankly no difference between the impact in the North and the South.

Uranium mining has devastated a number of Indigenous communities in North America. Uranium mining in northern Canada has left over 120 million tons of radioactive waste. This amount represents enough material to cover the trans-Canada highway two meters deep across the country. Present production of uranium waste from Saskatchewan alone occurs at the rate of over 1 million tons annually. Since 1975, hospitalization for cancer, birth defects, and circulatory illnesses in that area have increased dramatically—between 123 and 600 percent in that region. In other areas impacted by uranium mining, cancers and birth defects have increased to, in some cases, eight times the national average. The subsequent increases in radiation exposure to both the local and to the larger North American population are also evidenced in broader incidences of cancer, such as breast cancer in North American women, which is significantly on the rise. There is not a distinction in this problem caused by radiation whether it is in the Dene of northern Canada, the Laguna Pueblo people of New Mexico, or the people of Namibia.

The rapid increase in dioxin, organichlorides, PCBs (poly-chlorinated byphenots) chemicals in the world, as a result of industrialization, has a devastating impact on Indigenous peoples, Indigenous women, and other women. Each year, the world's paper industry discharges from 600 to 3,200 grams of dioxin equivalents into water—sludge and paper product—on the United States Environmental Protection agency statistics. This quantity is equal the amount which would cause 58,000 to 294,000 cases of cancer every year, based on the Environmental Protection Agency's estimate of dioxin's carcinogenicity. According to a number of recent studies, this has increased significantly the risk of breast cancer in women. Similarly, heavy metals and PCB contamination of Inuit women of the Hudson Bay region of the Arctic indicates that they have the highest levels of breast milk contamination in the world. In a 1988 study, Inuit women were found to have contamination levels up to 28 times higher than the average of women in Quebec, and ten times higher than that considered "safe" by the government. It is also of great concern to our women, and our peoples, that polar bears in that region of the Arctic have such a high level of contamination from PCBs, that they may be facing total sterility, and forced into extinction by early in the next century. As peoples who consider the Bears to be our relatives, we are concerned also, significantly, about the ability to reproduce, as a consequence of this level of bio-accumulation of toxins. We find that our communities, like those of our relatives, the Bears, are in fact, in danger of extinction. Consequently, it is clear to us that the problems also found in the south like the export of chemicals, and bio-accumulation of toxins, are also very much our problems, and the problems clearly manifested in our women. These are problems which emanate from industrial societies' mistreatment and disrespect for our Mother Earth, and subsequently are reflected in the devastation of the collective health and well being of women.

In summary, I have presented these arguments for a purpose: to illustrate that these are very common issues for women; not only for Indigenous women, but for all women. What befalls our mother Earth, befalls her daughter—the women who are the mothers of our nations. Simply stated, if we can no longer nurse our children, if we can no longer bear children, and if our bodies themselves are wracked with poisons, we will have accomplished little in the way of determining our destiny, or improving our conditions. And, these problems, reflected in our health and well being, are also inherently resulting in a decline of the status of women, and are the result of a long set of historical processes which we as women will need to challenge if we will ultimately be in charge of our own destinies, our own self determination, and the future of our Earth our Mother.

The reality is that all of these conditions, those emanating from the military and industrial devastation of our Mother the Earth, and subsequently, our own bodies, and the land on which we live are mimicked in social and development policies which affect women.

It is our belief, at Indigenous Women's Network, the following:

1) Women should not have to trade their ecosystem for running water, basic housing, health care, and basic human rights.

2) Development projects, whether in the North or in the South, whether financed by the World Bank, or by the coffers of Rio Tinto Zinc and Exxon, often replicate patriarchy and sexism, and by and large cause the destruction of matrilineal governance structure, land tenure, and cause a decline in the status of women. By denying us the basic land on which we live, and the clean food and streams from which to eat, and instead offering us a wage economy, in which privilege is often dictated by class, sex, and race, Indigenous women are frequently moved from a central role in their societies to the margins and refugee status of industrial society.

3) The intellectual knowledge systems today often negate or deny the existence of inherent property rights of Indigenous people to our cultural and intellectual knowledge, by supplanting our knowledge systems with industrial knowledge systems, calling us "primitive," while our medical knowledge, plants, and even genetic material are stolen (as in the Human Genome Project) by transnational corporations and international agencies. This situation affects Indigenous women, as a part of our communities, but on a larger scale, has affected most women.

4) Subsequently, our women find that the basic rights to control our bodies are impacted by all of the above, through development policies aimed at non-consensual or forced sterilization, medical testing, invasive genetic sampling, and absence of basic facilities and services which would guarantee us the right and ability to control the size of our families safely and willingly. These same development policies often are based on tourism which commodifies our bodies and cultures (the Pacific and Native America as prime examples), and cause the same with women internationally.

Collectively, we must challenge this paradigm, and this international arena. I call on you to support the struggle of Indigenous peoples of the world for recognition, and to recognize that until all peoples have self determination, no one will truly be free, free of the predator, and free to control our destiny. I ask you to look into the charter of the United Nations, Part One, Article Three, which provides that "All peoples have right to self determination. By virtue of that right they may freely determine their political status and freely pursue their economic, social, and political development."

All peoples should be construed to mean Indigenous peoples have that right to self determination. And, by virtue of that right, they may freely determine their political status and freely pursue their economic, social, and political development. Accord us the same rights as all other nations of peoples. And through that process, allow us to protect our ecosystems, their inherent biodiversity, human cultural diversity, and those matriarchal governments which remain in the world. And with the Unrepresented People's Organization (UNPO), we reaffirm that definition of self determination provided in an article of The International Covenant on Social, Economic, and Cultural Rights, further recognizing that the right to self determination belongs equally to women and to men. We believe that the right of all peoples to self determination cannot be realized while women continue to be marginalized and prevented from becoming full participants in their respective societies. The human rights of women, like the human rights of Indigenous peoples, and our inherent rights to self determination, are not issues exclusively within the domestic jurisdiction of states. For further discussion of these, please see the international agreements and accords struck by hundreds of Indigenous nations, such as the Karioka document and the Matatua document.

Finally, while we may, here in the commonness of this forum, speak of the common rights of all women, and those fundamental human rights of self determination, it is incumbent upon me to point out the fundamental inequalities of this situation. So long as the predator continues, so long as the middle, the temperate countries of the world continue to drive an increasing level of consumption, and, frankly continue to export both the technologies and drive for this level of consumption to other countries of the world, there will be no safety for the human rights of women, rights of Indigenous peoples, and to basic protection for the Earth, from which we get our life. Consumption causes the commodification of the sacred, the natural world, cultures, and the commodification of children and women.

From the United States's position, consider the following. The United States is the largest energy market in the world. The average American consumes seven times as many wood products per capita as anywhere else in the industrialized world, and overall that country consumes one third of the world's natural resources. In Canada, by comparison, per capita energy consumption is the highest in the world. Levels of consumption in the industrial world drive destruction of the world's rainforests, and the world's boreal forests, drive production of nuclear wastes, and production of PCBs, dioxin, and other lethal chemicals, which devastate the body of our Mother Earth, and our own bodies. Unless we speak and take meaningful action to address the levels of consumption, and subsequently, the exports of these technologies, and levels of consumption to other countries (like the international market for nuclear reactors), we will never have any security for our individual human rights as Indigenous women, and for our security as women.

If we are to seek and struggle for common ground of all women, it is essential to struggle with this issue. For it is not, frankly, that the women of the dominant society in so-called first world countries should have equal pay, and equal status, if that pay and status continues to be based on a consumption model which is not only unsustainable, but causes constant violation of the human rights of women and nations elsewhere in the world. It essential to collectively struggle to recover our status as Daughters of the Earth. In that is our strength, and the security, not in the predator, but in the security of our Mother, for our future generations. In that we can insure our security as the Mothers of our Nations.

This speech was given at the United Nations Fourth World Conference on Women in Beijing, China, August 31, 1995. Reprinted by permission.

Statement before the Joint Hearing of the House Resources Committee and Senate Committee on Indian Affairs, Ada Deer, 1997

Good morning Chairman Campbell, Chairman Young, and Members of the Committees. I am pleased to be here to present the Department of the Interior's views on proposed amendments to the Indian Child Welfare Act (ICWA) of 1978. The Department of the Interior supports, without reservation, H.R. 1082 and its companion bill, S. 569, which have incorporated the consensus-based tribal amendments developed last year by tribal governments and the National Congress of American Indians (NCAI) and the adoption community to improve the Indian Child Welfare Act.

Background Information

Congress passed the Indian Child Welfare Act in 1978 (ICWA), after ten years of study on Indian child custody and placements revealed an alarming high rate of out of home placements and adoptions. The strongest attribute of the ICWA is the premise that an Indian child's tribe is in a better position than a State or Federal court to make decisions or judgments on matters involving the relationship of an Indian child to his or her tribe. The clear intent of Congress was to defer to Indian tribes issues of cultural and social values as such relate to child rearing.

In addition to protecting the best interests of Indian children, the ICWA has also preserved the cultural integrity of Indian tribes because it affirmed tribal authority over Indian child custody matters. As a result the long term benefit is, and will be, the continued existence of Indian tribes.

Implementation of the ICWA

The Indian Child Welfare Act of 1978 is the essence of child welfare in Indian Country and provides the needed protections for Indian children who are neglected. On the whole, the ICWA has fulfilled the objective of giving Indian tribes the opportunity to intervene on behalf of Indian children eligible for tribal membership in a particular tribe.

There have been concerns over certain aspects of the ICWA and the ICWA should be revised to address problem areas and to ensure that the best interests of Indian children are ultimately considered in all voluntary child custody proceedings. Although several high-profile cases were cited to support the introduction last year of ICWA amendments, which would have been detrimental to Indian tribes and families, those cases do not warrant a unilateral and unfettered intrusion on tribal government authority.

Implications of Proposed Amendments to the ICWA

The provisions contained in H.R. 1082 and S. 569 reflect carefully crafted consensus amendments between Indian tribes seeking to protect their children, culture and heritage and the interests of the adoption community seeking greater clarity and certainty in the implementation of the ICWA. First and foremost, the amendments will clarify the applicability of the ICWA to voluntary child custody matters so that there are no ambiguities or uncertainties in the handling of these cases. We know from experience that State courts have not always applied the ICWA to voluntary child custody proceedings.

The amendments will ensure that Indian tribes receive notice of voluntary ICWA proceedings and also clarify what should be included in the notices. Timely and adequate notice to tribes will ensure more appropriate and permanent placement decisions for Indian children. Indian parents will be informed of their rights and their children's rights under the Act, ensuring that they make informed decisions on the adoptive or foster care placement of their children. When tribes and extended family members are allowed to participate in placement decisions, the risk for disruption will be greatly reduced. While the amendments place limitations on when Indian tribes and families may intervene and when birth parents may withdraw their consent to an adoption, they protect the fundamental rights of tribal sovereignty. Furthermore, the amendments will permit open adoptions, when it is in the best interest of an Indian child, even if State law does not so provide. Under an open adoption, Indian children will have access to their natural family and cultural heritage when it is deemed appropriate.

An important consideration is that upon a tribe's decision to intervene in a voluntary child custody proceeding, the tribe must certify the tribal membership status of an Indian child or their eligibility for membership according to tribal law or custom. Thus, there would be no question that a child is Indian under the ICWA and ensures that tribal membership determinations are not made arbitrarily. Lastly, the amendments will provide for criminal sanctions to discourage fraudulent practices by individuals or agencies which knowingly misrepresent or fail to disclose whether a child or the birth parent(s) are Indian to circumvent the application of the ICWA.

In summary, the tribally developed amendments contained in H.R. 1082 and S. 569 clearly address the concerns which led to the introduction of Title III of H.R. 3286 (104th Congress), including time frames for ICWA notifications, timely interventions, and sanctions, definitive schemes for intervention, limitations on the time for biological parents to withdraw consent to adoptive placements, and finality in voluntary proceedings.

Effect of "Existing Indian Family" Concept
Chairman Campbell and Chairman Young, we want to express our grave concern that the objectives of the ICWA continue to be frustrated by State court created judicial exceptions to the ICWA. We are concerned that State court judges who have created the "existing Indian family exception" are delving into the sensitive and complicated areas of Indian cultural values, customs and practices which under existing law have been left exclusively to the judgment of Indian tribes. Legislation introduced last year, including H.R. 3286, sought to ratify the "existing Indian family exception" by amending the ICWA to codify this State-created concept. The Senate Committee on Indian Affairs, in striking Title III from H.R. 3286, made clear its views that the concept of the "existing Indian family exception" is in direct contradiction to existing law. In rejecting the "existing Indian family exception" concept, the Committee stated that "the ICWA recognizes that the Federal trust responsibility and the role of Indian tribes as parens patriae extend to all Indian children involved in all child custody proceedings." [Report 104–335 accompanying S. 1962, 104th Cong., 2nd Session].

Position of the Department of the Interior

The Department of the Interior's position on the emerging "existing Indian family exception" concept is the same as previously stated in the Administration's statement of policy issued on May 9, 1996. We oppose any legislative recognition of the concept.

The Department's position is that the ICWA must continue to provide Federal protections for Indian families, tribes and Indian children involved in any child custody proceeding, regardless of their individual circumstances. Thus, the Department fully concurs with the Senate Committee on Indian Affairs' assessment and rejection of the "existing Indian family exception" concept and all of its manifestations. We share the expressed concerns of tribal leaders and a majority of your Committee members about continuing efforts to amend the ICWA, particularly those bills which would seriously limit and weaken the existing ICWA protections available to Indian tribes and children in voluntary foster care and adoption proceedings.

The United States has a government-to-government relationship with Indian tribal governments. Protection of their sovereign status, including preservation of tribal identity and the determination of Indian tribal membership, is fundamental to this relationship. The Congress, after ten years of study, passed the Indian Child Welfare Act of 1978 (Pub. L. 95–608) as a means to remedy the many years of widespread separation of Indian children from their families. The ICWA established a successful dual system that establishes exclusive tribal jurisdiction over Indian Child Welfare cases arising in Indian Country, and presumes tribal jurisdiction in the cases involving Indian children, yet allows concurrent State jurisdiction in Indian child adoption and child custody proceedings where good cause exists. This system, which authorizes tribal involvement and referral to tribal courts, has been successful in protecting the interests of Indian tribal governments, Indian children and Indian families for the past eighteen years.

Because the proposed amendments contained in H.R. 1082 and S. 569 will strengthen the Act and continue to protect the lives and future of Indian children, the Department fully embraces the provisions of H.R. 1082 and S. 569.

In closing, we appreciate the good faith efforts of tribal governments in addressing the ICWA-specific concerns raised by certain members of the Congress and in developing tribally acceptable legislative amendments toward resolving these issues within the past year. I would like to thank Chairman Campbell, Chairman Young, and the Committee members for all their hard work and heartfelt assistance to tribes in shepherding the tribal amendments through the legislative process. This Administration will endeavor to ensure that tribal sovereignty will not be compromised, specifically, the right of tribal governments to determine tribal membership and the right of tribal courts to determine internal tribal relations.

This concludes my prepared statement. I will be pleased to answer any questions the Committees may have.

Confronting Racism and Discrimination

Americans have long battled a wide range of prejudices that have included discrimination on the basis of sex, race, religion, country of origin, sexual orientation, and skin color. Viewing racism and discrimination through the eyes of women who have experienced it provides an invaluable perspective for understanding the indignities the targets of these prejudices have endured and the strength required to persevere in the face of them.

In the 1890s, Mary Church Terrell emerged as a leader in the African American women's club movement and served as the first president of the National Association of Colored Women. Through her description of discrimination in the early 1900s, she shares her frustration with the practice and she compels the reader to join her in her resistance to it. In the 1940s, she was a leader in the movement to end discrimination in Washington, D.C.'s restaurants, hotels, and other public accommodations.

Rep. Patsy Mink (D-HI) offers another perspective on race relations, that of a Japanese American. In her 1971 speech to the Los Angeles Japanese-American Citizens League, she outlines discriminatory actions and sentiments. She also discusses generational differences between older Japanese Americans and their children, who may have adopted the dominant cultures in ways that confuse their elders.

Senator Carol Moseley-Braun (D-IL), the first African American elected to the United States Senate, attracted national attention for her opposition to what observers initially thought was a noncontroversial matter. In July 1993, the Senate debated renewing a patent on the Daughters of the Confederacy's flag. Moseley-Braun's arguments against the measure led to its defeat.

In the 1980s and 1990s, gays and lesbians responded in increasingly public ways to the legal, verbal, and physical attacks directed at them. Asserting their humanity, their dignity, and their desire to be recognized as citizens possessing the same civil rights as other Americans, gays and lesbians called on each other and on all Americans to join them in their crusade. In her 1993 speech to the March on Washington, Urvashi Vaid challenged her listeners to join the struggle to end violence, discrimination, and homophobia. She frames her arguments in the context of the civil rights and feminist movements, describing the gay rights movement as "an integral part of the American promise of freedom."

A Black Woman Describes Prejudice in the Nation's Capital, Mary Church Terrell, 1900

For fifteen years I have resided in Washington, and while it was far from being a paradise for colored people when I first touched these shores it has been doing its level best ever since to make conditions for us intolerable. As a colored woman I might enter Washington any night, a stranger in a strange land, and walk miles without finding a place to lay my head. Unless I happened to know colored people who live here or ran across a chance acquaintance who could recommend a colored boarding-house to me, I should be obliged to spend the entire night wandering about . . .

As a colored woman I may walk from the Capitol to the White House, ravenously hungry and abundantly supplied with money with which to purchase a meal, without finding a single restaurant in which I would be permitted to take a morsel of food, if it was patronized by white people, unless I were willing to sit behind a screen. As a colored woman I cannot visit the tomb of the Father of this country which owes its very existence to the love of freedom in the human heart and which stands for equal opportunity to all, without being forced to sit in the Jim Crow section of an electric car which starts from the very heart of the city—midway between the Capitol and the White House. If I refuse thus to be humiliated, I am cast into jail and forced to pay a fine for violating the Virginia laws. Every hour in the day Jim Crow cars filled with colored people, many of whom are intelligent and well to do, enter and leave the national capital . . .

Unless I am willing to engage in a few menial occupations, in which the pay for my services would be very poor, there is no way for me to earn an honest living, if I am not a trained nurse or a dressmaker or can secure a position as teacher in the public schools, which is exceedingly difficult to do. It matters not what my intellectual attainments may be or how great is the need of the services of a competent person, if I try to enter many of the numerous vocations in which my white sisters are allowed to engage, the door is shut in my face . . .

Some time ago a young woman who had already attracted some attention in the literary world by her volume of short stories answered an advertisement which appeared in a Washington newspaper, which called for the services of a skilled stenographer and expert typewriter. It is unnecessary to state the reasons why a young woman whose literary ability was so great as that possessed by the one referred to should decide to earn money in this way. The applicants were requested to send specimens of their work and answer certain questions concerning their experience and their speed before they called in person. In reply to her application the young colored woman, who, by the way, is very fair and attractive indeed, received a letter from the firm stating that her references and experience were the most satisfactory that had been sent and requesting her to call. When she presented herself there was some doubt in the mind of the man to whom she was directed concerning her [race], so he asked her point-blank whether she was colored or white. When she confessed the truth the merchant expressed great sorrow and deep regret that he could not avail himself of the services of so competent a person, but frankly admitted that employing a colored woman in his establishment in any except a menial position was simply out of the question . . .

And so I might go on citing instance after instance to show the variety of ways in which our people are sacrificed on the altar of prejudice in the Capital of the United States and how almost insurmountable are the obstacles which block his path to success. Early in life many a colored youth is so appalled by the helplessness and the hopelessness of his situation in this country that in a sort of stoical despair he resigns himself to his fate. "What is the good of our trying to acquire an education? We can't all be preachers, teachers, doctors, and lawyers. Besides those professions there is almost nothing for colored people to do but engage in the most menial occupations, and we do not need an education for that." More than once such remarks, uttered by young men and women in our public schools who possess brilliant intellects, have wrung my heart.

Reprinted from "What It Means to Be Colored in the Capital of the United States," The Independent, LXII (Jan. 24, 1907), pp. 181–182, 185.

Seeking a Link with the Past, Rep. Patsy T. Mink, 1971

I would like to thank President Kanegai and the other officers and members of the West Los Angeles Japanese-American Citizens League for this opportunity to be with you at your thirtieth anniversary banquet and installation. I am delighted to participate in this memorable occasion.

It must be difficult to look back thirty years to 1941 and relive the pains and agonies that were inflicted upon you as citizens, unloved and unwanted in their own country of their birth. Loving this land as much as any other citizen, it is difficult to fathom the despair and fury which many must have felt, yet who fought back and within a few years had reestablished their lives and their futures. Most of us remember these years vividly. Our faith in justice was tested many times over. Our patriotism was proven by blood of our sons upon the battlefields.

Yet today, thirty years later to many even in this room, it is only a part of our history. Our children, thirty years old and younger, cannot follow with us these memories of the forties. They tire of our stories of the past. Their life is now, today . . . tomorrow. Their youthful fervor was poured into the symbolism of the repeal of Title II of the Internal Security Act of 1950, portrayed by its title, Emergency Detention Act. That Act became law nearly ten years *after* the Japanese were evacuated from the West Coast into "relocation camps." Yet, it stood as a reminder of what could happen again. Of course, despite the successful repeal, it could happen again, as it did indeed to the Japanese-Americans who were rounded up without any statutory authority whatsoever. It was not until 1950 that Title II became law.

It is quite evident that I am standing before an affluent group whose surface appearance does not reveal the years of struggle and doubt that have ridden behind you.

Sociologists have generally described the Japanese-Americans as an easily acculturated people who quickly assimilated the ways of their surroundings. This has always been in my view a friendly sort of jab at our cultural background, for what it has come to mean for me is a description of a conformist which I hope I am not!

I still dream that I shall be able to be a real participant in the changing scenario of opportunity for all of America. In this respect, I share the deep frustration and anguish of our youth as I see so much around us that cries out for our attention and that we continue to neglect.

Many factors have contributed towards a deepening sense of frustration about our inability to solve our problems of poverty and racial prejudice. Undoubtedly the prolonged, unending involvement in Vietnam has contributed to this sense of hopelessness. At least for our youth who must bear the ultimate burden of this war, it seems unfair that they should be asked to serve their country in this way when there are so many more important ways in which their youth and energy can be directed to meet the urgent needs at home. They view our Government as impotent to deal with these basic issues.

It is true that Congress has passed a great many civil rights laws. The fact that new, extra laws were found necessary to make it easier for some people to realize their constitutional guarantees is a sad enough commentary on the American society, but what is even worse is the fact that the majority of our people are still unready, personally, to extend these guarantees to all despite the Constitution and all the civil rights laws, and despite their protestations to the contrary.

Certainly, no one will admit his bigotry and prejudice—yet we always find ways to clothe such feelings in more presentable forms—and few will openly advocate suppression or oppression of other men, but nevertheless, it exists.

Although Congress has repealed the Emergency Detention Act, the fight for freedom is not over. We now see a new witch hunt proclaimed in which all Government employees will be examined for their memberships and organizations. It seems that we have not yet succeeded in expunging the notion that dangerous persons can be identified by class or group relationships and punished accordingly.

I believe that nobody can find safety in numbers—by huddling with the larger mass in hopes of being overlooked. Those who seek to suppress will always find ways to single out others. Instead, we must change the basic attitude that all must conform or be classed as renegades and radicals. Our nation was founded on the idealistic belief in individualism and pioneering spirit, and it would be tragic for our own generation to forswear that ideal for the false security of instant assimilation.

It seems to me that our society is large enough to accept a wide diversity of types and opinions, and that no group should be forced to try to conform to the image of the population as a whole. I sometimes wonder if our goal as Japanese-Americans is to be so like the White Anglo-Saxon population as to be indistinguishable from it. If so, we will obviously never succeed!

There has been and continues to be prejudice in this country against Asians. The basis of this is the belief that the Oriental is "inscrutable." Having such base feelings, it is simple to stir up public outrage against the recognition of the People's Republic of China in the United Nations, for instance, even though reasoned judgment dictates otherwise, unless of course a Yellow Communist is really worse than a Red one!

The World War II detention overnight reduced the entire population of one national origin to an enemy, stripped of property, rights of citizenship, human dignity, and due process of law, without so much as even a stifled voice of conscience among our leading scholars or civil libertarians. More recently, the Vietnam war has reinforced the view of Orientals as something less than fully human. All Vietnamese stooping in the rice fields are pictured as the enemy, subhuman without emotions, and for whom life is less valuable than for us.

During the trial of Lieutenant Calley, we were told about "MGR," the "Mere Gook Rule," which was the underlying basis for Calley's mindless assertion that the slaughter of defenseless women and children, our prisoners of war, was "no big thing." The "Mere Gook Rule" holds that life is less important, less valuable to an Oriental.

Laws that protect other human beings do not apply to "gooks." One reporter noted before the verdict became known that the essence of the Calley case was to determine the validity of this rule. He described it as the "unspoken issue" at the trial.

The issue was not as unspoken as most would prefer to believe. The indictment drawn up by the Army against Lieutenant Calley stated in six separate charges that he did at My Lai murder four "Oriental human beings" . . . murder not less than thirty "Oriental human beings" . . . murder three "Oriental human beings" . . . murder an unknown number of "Oriental human beings" not less than seventy . . . and so on numbering 102. Thus, the Army did not charge him with the murder of human beings as presumably would have been the case had Caucasians been involved, but instead charged the apparently lesser offense of killing mere "Oriental human beings."

The Army's definition of the crime is hardly surprising inasmuch as the Army itself could have been construed as on trial along with Calley for directing a genocide against the Vietnamese. Indeed, the Lieutenant pleaded he was only doing what he thought the Army wanted. It seems clear to me that the Army recognized the "Mere Gook Rule" officially by distinguishing between the murder of human beings and "Oriental human beings." When Calley was convicted, the resulting thunder of criticism verified that many in the public also went along with the concept of differing scales of humanity.

Somehow, we must put into perspective Dean Rusk's dread of the "yellow peril" expressed as justification for a massive antiballistics missile system on the one hand, and on the other, a quest for improved relations with Peking. This latter event could have a great meaning in our own lives as Japanese-Americans. We could help this country begin to deal with Asians as people. Just the other day in a beauty parlor, I heard a congressional secretary discuss China and say, "An Asian is different, you can never figure out what he's really thinking. He has so little value for life!"

Instead of seeking refuge, we should seek to identify as Asians, and begin to serve America as the means by which she can come to understand the problems of the East. Our talents have not been used in American diplomacy, I suspect, largely because we are still not trusted enough.

We must teach our country that life is no less valuable, and human dignity no less precious, in Asia than elsewhere. Our detractors point to the large-scale killings that have occurred in China, Vietnam, Pakistan, and elsewhere in Asia, but we hear remarkably few references to the mass-slaughter of six million Jews in Nazi gas chambers in World War II—that was done by Aryans, not Asians, and the total far exceeds the loss of life in the Orient that has been used to justify the debasement of "mere gooks." I am not trying to compare one group against another, but merely to point out that a lack of appreciation for the value of human life can occur wherever totalitarian government exists. This makes it more than vital for us to oppose such influences within our own country wherever they may occur. The war in Vietnam has lasted for seven years. If Americans believed there was the same worth in the life of an Asian, this war would have ended long ago. If Americans were willing to concede that the Asian mind was no different than his, a peace would have been forged in Paris long ago. I am convinced that racism is at the heart of this immoral policy.

I know that many of you are puzzled and even dismayed by actions of some of your sons and daughters who have insisted on a more aggressive role in combating the war and other evils that exist in our society. I plead with you for understanding of this Third World movement in which not only young Japanese-Americans but many minority groups are so deeply involved.

We are confronted with what seem to be many different revolutions taking place all over the world . . . the black revolution, the revolution of emerging nations, the youth revolution here and in other countries as well—and something that was even more unheard of, the priests challenging the Vatican on the most basic issues of celibacy and birth control. It is no accident that these things are all happening at the same time, for they all stem from the same great idea that has somehow been rekindled in the world, and that is the idea that the individual is important.

All of the systems of the world today have this in common: for they are mainly concerned with industrialization, efficiency, and gross national product; the value of Man is forgotten.

The children of some of you here tonight are involved in the great protests of today—are they chronic malcontents and subversives? I think not—I think they are probably fairly well-educated, thoughtful people who see certain conditions they don't like and are trying to do something about it. I'm not sure they know exactly what they want to do. I do know they are clearly dissatisfied with the way their world has been run in the past.

So, the problem is not what to do about dissent among our young people— the problem is what to do about the causes of this dissent. The question is not "how to suppress the dissent" but how to make it meaningful . . . how to make it productive of a better society which truly places high value on individual human beings as human beings and not merely as so many cogs in the great, cold and impersonal machinery of an industrialized society.

I, for one, believe that the grievances of our youth are real and that they are important. Merely because the majority of students are not involved . . . merely because the dissidents are few . . . should not minimize the need for serious efforts to effectuate change. Our eighteen-year-olds now have the right to vote. Whether we like it or not, we will have to take better account of their wishes. Their acceptance as adults will bring into policy making eleven million new voters next year. Their cause for identity must be encouraged.

Our sons and daughters seek to establish a link with the past. They want to discover who they are, why they are here, and where their destinies are to take them. So many of our children are growing up in complete isolation in a society that places a premium on conformity, in middle-class homes where parents still want to play down their differences, and prefer to homogenize with society. Some of these children are rebelling and are seeking ways to preserve their uniqueness and their special heritage. I see pride and strength in this.

One of the most promising avenues for this renewed search for one's heritage is in our school systems—the logical place for instructing children in the knowledge they need. Programs of Ethnic Heritage Studies are needed in our schools. I feel that this would be particularly valuable in Hawaii, California, and other areas where there are large numbers of children of Oriental descent.

It seems to me that we as Asians have a large stake in encouraging and promoting such a program. We cannot and must not presume knowledge about Asia merely because we are Asians. This requires concentrated study and dedicated determination. Of course, we do not need to become scholars cloistered in the ivory tower of some campus. We need to become aware of the enormous history of Asia and through our daily lives, regardless of what our profession, translate it to all the people with whom we deal. We have not fully met our responsibility to educate the public about Asia and its people.

I hope that all Japanese-American organizations and others with strong beliefs in the magnificent history and culture of the Orient will now help lead the way to a more enlightened America. We have an immense story to tell, for as I have said the public at large too often assumes that all civilization is Western and no worth is given to the human values of the East. As long as this belief persists, we will have future Vietnams. The way to counteract it is to build public knowledge, through school courses, travel, and dedicated emphasis on increased communications, so that our people will know and appreciate all that is Asian.

Last Thursday night in a display of utter ignorance and contempt for diversity, the House of Representatives killed the ethnic heritage studies program by a vote of 200 ayes to 159 noes. And so you see, I speak of an urgent matter. We are so few and they who do not care to understand us are so numerous.

It is fine for all citizens to pursue the good life and worldly goods on which our society places such emphasis, but there is increasing recognition that all will be ashes in our mouths unless our place as individuals is preserved. This is what the young are seeking—and I am among those who would rejoice in their goals.

They need the guidance and support of their parents to succeed, but in any event with or without us, they are trying. It behooves us to do all we can to accept their aspirations, if not all of their actions, in the hope that this new generation will be able to find a special role for themselves in America, to help build her character, to define her morality, to give her a depth in soul, and to make her realize the beauty of our diverse society with many races and cultures of which we are one small minority.

This address was delivered before the West Los Angeles Japanese-American Citizens League in Playa Del Rey, California, November 6, 1971. Reprinted by permission.

Getting Beyond Racism, Sen. Carol Moseley-Braun, 1993

Madam President, I really had not wanted to have to do this because in my remarks I believe that I was restrained and tempered. I talked about the committee procedure. I talked about the lack of germaneness of this amendment. I talked about how it was not necessary for this organization to receive the design patent extension, which was an extraordinary extension of an extraordinary act to begin with.

What I did not talk about and what I am constrained now to talk about with no small degree of emotion is the symbolism of what this vote . . . That is what this vote really means.

I started off—maybe—I do not know—it is just my day to get to talk about race. Maybe I am just lucky about that today.

I have to tell you this vote is about race. It is about racial symbolism. It is about racial symbols, the racial past, and the single most painful episode in American history.

I have just gone through—in fact in committee yesterday I leaned over to my colleague Dianne Feinstein and I said, "You know, Dianne, I am stunned about how often and how much race comes up in conversation and debate in this general assembly." Did not I say that? . . .

So I turned to my colleague, Dianne Feinstein. You know, I am really stunned by how often and how much the issue of race, the subject of racism, comes up in this U.S. Senate, comes up in this body and how I have to, on many occasions, as the only African-American here, constrain myself to be calm, to be laid back, to talk about these issues in very intellectual, nonemotional terms, and that is what I do on a regular basis, Madam President. That is part and parcel of my daily existence.

But at the same time, when the issue of the design patent extension for the United Daughters of the Confederacy first came up, I looked at it. I did not make a big deal of it. It came as part of the work of the Judiciary Committee. I looked at it, and I said, well, I am not going to vote for that.

When I announced I was not going to vote for it, the chairman, as is his due, began to poll the members. We talked about it, and I found myself getting drawn into a debate that I frankly never expected.

Who would have expected a design patent for the Confederate flag? And there are those in this body who say this really is not the Confederate flag. The other thing we did know was a Confederate flag.

I did my research, and I looked it up as I am wont to do, and guess what? That is the real Confederate flag. The thing we see all the time and are accustomed to is the battle flag. In fact, there is some history on this issue. I would like to read the following quote from the *Flag Book of the United States.*

The real flower in the southern flag began in November 1860, when the election of Lincoln to the Presidency caused widespread fear the federal government will try to make changes in the institution of slavery. The winter of 1860 to 1861, rallies and speeches were held throughout the South and, frankly, the United States flag was replaced by a local banner.

This flag is the real flag of the Confederacy. If there is anybody in this chamber, anybody, indeed anybody in this world, that has a doubt that the Confederate effort was around preserving the institution of slavery, I am prepared and I believe history is prepared to dispute them to the nth. There is no question but that battle was fought to try to preserve our nation, to keep the states from separating themselves over the issue of whether or not my ancestors could be held as property, as chattel, as objects of commerce and trade in this country.

And people died. More Americans died in the Civil War than any war they have ever gone through since. People died over the proposition that indeed these United States stood for the proposition that every person was created equal without regard to race, that we are all American citizens.

I am sorry, Madam President. I will lower my voice. I am getting excited, because, quite frankly, that is the very issue. The issue is whether or not Americans, such as myself, who believe in the promise of this country, who feel strongly and who are patriots in this country, will have to suffer the indignity of being reminded time and time again, that at one point in this country's history we were human chattel. We were property. We could be traded, bought, and sold.

Now, to suggest as a matter of revisionist history that this flag is not about slavery flies in the face of history, Madam President.

I was not going to get inflammatory. In fact, my staff brought me this little thing earlier, and it has been sitting here. I do not know if you noticed it sitting here during the earlier debate in which I was dispassionate and tried my level best not to be emotional and lawyering about and not get into calling names and talking about race and racism. I did not use it to begin with. I do want to share it now. It is a speech by the Vice President of the Confederate States of America, March 21, 1861, in Savannah, GA.

"Slavery, the Cornerstone of the Confederacy." And this man goes on to say:

"The new Confederate constitution has put to rest forever all agitating questions relating to our peculiar 'institution,' which is what they called it, African slavery as it exists among us, the proper status of a negro in our form of civilization. This was the immediate cause of the late rupture and present revolution.

The prevailing ideas entertained by Thomas Jefferson and most of the leading statesmen at the time of the formation of the old Constitution were that the enslavement of the African was in violation of the laws of nature, that it was wrong in principle, socially; morally; and politically."

And then he goes on to say:

"Our new government is founded upon exactly the opposite idea. Its foundations are laid, its cornerstone rests upon the great truth that the negro is not equal to the white man, that slavery, subordination to the superior race is his natural and moral condition."

This was a statement by the Vice President of the Confederate States of America.

Madam President, across the room on the other side is the flag. I say to you it is outrageous. It is an absolute outrage that this body would adopt as an amendment to this legislation a symbol of this point of view and, Madam President, I say to you that it is an important issue. It is a symbolic issue up there. There is no way you can get around it.

The reason for my emotion—I have been here almost 7 months now, and my colleagues will tell you there is not a more congenial, laid back, even person in this entire body who makes it a point to try to get along with everybody. I make it a point to try to talk to my colleagues and get beyond controversy and conflict, to try to find consensus on issues.

But I say to you, Madam President, on this issue there can be no consensus. It is an outrage. It is an insult. It is absolutely unacceptable to me and to millions of Americans, black or white, that we would put the imprimatur of the United States Senate on a symbol of this kind of idea. And that is what is at stake with this amendment, Madam President.

I am going to continue—I am going to continue because I am going to call it like I see it, as I always do. I was appalled, appalled at a segment of my own Democratic Party that would go take a walk and vote for something like this.

I am going to talk for a minute first about my brethren, my close-in brethren and then talk about the other side of the aisle and the responsibility of the Republican Party.

The reason the Republican Party got run out on a rail the last time is the American people sensed intolerance in that party. The American people, African-Americans sensed there was not room for them in that party. Folks took a look at the convention and said, "My God, what are these people standing for? This is not America." And they turned around and voted for change. They elected Bill Clinton president and the rest of us to this chamber. The changes they were speaking out for was a change that said we have to get past racism, we have to get past sexism, the many issues that divide us as Americans, and come together as Americans so we can make this country be what it can be in the 21st century.

That is the real reason, Madam President, that I am here today. My state has less than 12 percent African-Americans in it, but the people of Illinois had no problem voting for a candidate that was African-American because they thought they were doing the same thing.

Similarly, the state of California sent two women, two women to the U.S.

Senate, breaking a gender barrier, as did the state of Washington. Why? Because they felt that it was time to get past the barriers that said that women had no place in the conduct of our business.

And so, just as our country is moving forward, Madam President, to have this kind of symbol shoved in your face, shoved in my face, shoved in the faces of all the Americans who want to see a change for us to get beyond racism, is singularly inappropriate.

I say to you, Madam President, that this is no small matter. This is not a matter of little old ladies walking around doing good deeds. There is no reason why these little old ladies cannot do good deeds anyway. If they choose to wave the Confederate flag, that certainly is their right. Because I care about the fact that this is a free country. Free speech is the cornerstone of democracy. People are supposed to be able to say what they want to say. They are supposed to be able to join associations and organizations that express their views.

But I daresay, Madam President, that following the Civil War, and following the victory of the United States and the coming together of our country, that that peculiar institution was put to rest for once and for all; that the division in our nation, the North versus the South, was put to rest once and for all. And the people of this country do not want to see a day in which flags like that are underwritten, underscored, adopted, approved by this U.S. Senate.

That is what this vote is about. That is what this vote is about.

I say to you, Madam President, I do not know—I do not want to yield the floor right now because I do not know what will happen next.

I will yield momentarily to my colleague from California, Madam President, because I think that this is an issue that I am not going—if I have to stand here until this room freezes over, I am not going to see this amendment put on this legislation which has to do with national service. . . . If I have to stand here until this room freezes over, Madam President, I am going to do so. Because I will tell you, this is something that has no place in our modern times. It has no place in this body. It has no place in the Senate. It has no place in our society.

And the fact is, Madam President, that I would encourage my colleagues on both sides of the aisle—Republican and Democrat; those who thought, "Well, we are just going to do this, you know, because it is no big deal"—to understand what a very big deal indeed it is—that the imprimatur that is being sought here today sends a sign out to the rest of this country that that peculiar institution has not been put to bed for once and for all; that, indeed, like Dracula, it has come back to haunt us time and time and time again; and that, in spite of the fact that we have made strides forward, the fact of the matter is that there are those who would keep us slipping back into the darkness of division, into the snake pit of racial hatred, of racial antagonism and of support for symbols—symbols of the struggle to keep African-Americans, Americans of African descent, in bondage.

Speech at the March on Washington, Urvashi Vaid, 1993

Hello lesbian and gay Americans. I am proud to stand before you as a lesbian today. With hearts full of love and the abiding faith in justice, we have come to Washington to speak to America. We have come to speak the truth of our lives and silence the liars. We have come to challenge the cowardly Congress to end its paralysis and exercise moral leadership. We have come to defend our honor and win our equality. But most of all we have come in peace and with courage to say, "America, this day marks the end from exile of the gay and lesbian people. We are banished no more. We wander the wilderness of despair no more. We are afraid no more. For on this day, with love in our hearts, we have come out, and we have come out across America to build a bridge of understanding, a bridge of progress, a bridge as solid as steel, a bridge to a land where no one suffers prejudice because of their sexual orientation, their race, their gender, their religion, or their human difference."

I have been asked by the March organizers to speak in five minutes about the far right, the far right which threatens the construction of that bridge. The extreme right which has targeted every one of you and me for extinction. The supremacist right which seeks to redefine the very meaning of democracy. Language itself fails in this task, my friends, for to call our opponents "The Right," states a profound untruth. They are wrong—they are wrong morally, they are wrong spiritually, and they are wrong politically.

The Christian supremacists are wrong spiritually when they demonize us. They are wrong when they reduce the complexity and beauty of our spirit into a freak show. They are wrong spiritually, because, if we are the untouchables of America—if we are the untouchables—then we are, as Mahatma Gandhi said, children of God. And as God's children we know that the gods of our understanding, the gods of goodness and love and righteousness, march right here with us today.

The supremacists who lead the anti-gay crusade are wrong morally. They are wrong because justice is moral, and prejudice is evil; because truth is moral and the lie of the closet is the real sin; because the claim of morality is a subtle sort of subterfuge, a stratagem which hides the real aim which is much more secular. Christian supremacist leaders like Bill Bennett and Pat Robertson, Lou Sheldon and Pat Buchanan, supremacists like Phyllis Schlafly, Ralph Reid, Bill Bristol, R.J. Rushoodie—the supremacists don't care about morality, they care about power. They care about social control. And their goal, my friends, is the reconstruction of American Democracy into American Theocracy.

We who are gathered here today must prove the religious right wrong politically and we can do it. That is our challenge. You know they have made us into the communists of the nineties. And they say they have declared cultural war against us. It's war all right. It's a war about values. On one side are the values that everyone here stands for. Do you know what those values are? Traditional American values of democracy and pluralism. On the other side are those who want to turn the Christian church into government, those whose value is monotheism.

We believe in democracy, in many voices co-existing in peace, and people of all faiths living together in harmony under a common civil framework known as the United States Constitution. Our opponents believe in monotheism. One way, theirs. One god, theirs. One law, the Old Testament. One nation supreme, the Christian Right one. Let's name it. Democracy battles theism in Oregon, in Colorado, in Florida, in Maine, in Arizona, in Michigan, in Ohio, in Idaho, in Washington, in Montana, in every state where my brothers and sisters are leading the fight to oppose the Right and to defend the United States Constitution. We won the anti-gay measure in Oregon, but today 33 counties—33 counties and municipalities face local versions of that ordinance today. The fight has just begun. We lost the big fight in Colorado, but, thanks to the hard work of all the people of Colorado, the Boycott Colorado movement is working and we are strong. And we are going to win our freedom there eventually.

To defeat the Right politically, my friends, is our challenge when we leave this March. How can we do it? We've got to march from Washington into action at home. I challenge every one of you, straight or gay, who can hear my voice, to join the national gay and lesbian movement. I challenge you to join NGLTF to fight the Right. We have got to match the power of the Christian supremacists, member for member, vote for vote, dollar for dollar. I challenge each of you, not just buy a T-shirt, but get involved in your movement. Get involved! Volunteer! Volunteer! Every local organization in this country needs you. Every clinic, every hotline, every youth program needs you, needs your time and your love.

And I also challenge our straight liberal allies, liberals and libertarians, independent and conservative, republican or radical. I challenge and invite you to open your eyes and embrace us without fear. The gay rights movement is not a party. It is not lifestyle. It is not a hair style. It is not a fad or a fringe or a sickness. It is not about sin or salvation. The gay rights movement is an integral part of the American promise of freedom.

We, you and I, each of us, we are the descendants of a proud tradition of people asserting our dignity. It is fitting that the Holocaust Museum was dedicated the same weekend as this March, for not only were gay people persecuted by the Nazi state, but gay people are indebted to the struggle of the Jewish people against bigotry and intolerance. It is fitting that the NAACP marches with us, that feminist leaders march with us, because we are indebted to those movements.

When all of us who believe in freedom and diversity see this gathering, we see beauty and power. When our enemies see this gathering, they see the millennium. Perhaps the Right is right about something. We call for the end of the world as we know it. We call for the end of racism and sexism and bigotry as we know it. For the end of violence and discrimination and homophobia as we know it. For the end of sexism as we know it. We stand for freedom as we have yet to know it, and we will not be denied.

This speech was given at the march on Washington, April 25, 1993. Reprinted by permission.

Women's Reproductive Lives

A persistently controversial issue in the twentieth century has been women's reproductive lives. Initially, the issue was women's access to contraceptive methods, including information about birth control and methods and devices for it. The state and federal Comstock Laws, the first of which was passed in 1873, classified information about birth control as obscene material. Birth control leader Margaret Sanger began her crusade against the Comstock Laws in the 1910s. Sanger placed birth control in the context of women freeing themselves from the bondage of unwanted pregnancies that threatened their health or that reduced them to poverty.

In 1965, the U.S. Supreme Court overturned a Connecticut law prohibiting the dissemination and use of contraceptives. In deciding the case, Griswold v. Connecticut, *the Court found that a right to privacy was implied in the Constitution, providing the basis for its 1973 decision in* Roe v. Wade, *the landmark case that legalized abortion in the United States. For the balance of the twentieth century, abortion, limitations on it, access to the procedure, and other nuances of the issue led to the creation of new organizations, stirred political debates, and played a significant role in deciding numerous elections.*

Faye Wattleton, president of Planned Parenthood Federation of America, in her speech to employees of the Esprit corporation in 1990, points to the importance of protecting and preserving the right to abortion and other liberties. Feminists have been among the most adamant groups to advocate reproductive freedom, often arguing that it is a matter of a woman being able to control her own life. Some feminists, however, disagree and have aligned themselves with Feminists for Life of America (FFLA), a prolife, feminist organization. Former vice president of FFLA Frederica Mathewes-Green's feminist beliefs led her to becoming a prolife activist.

Since the U.S. Supreme Court's decision in Roe v. Wade, *prolife advocates have sought to limit access to abortion by requiring waiting periods, requiring minors to obtain their parents' permission, and other measures. In the 1990s, attempts to ban a specific abortion procedure known as partial-birth abortion became a volatile political issue. Rep. Helen Chenoweth (R-ID) supports the ban, as she explained to FFLA in 1997. Gloria Feldt, current president of Planned Parenthood Federation of America, discusses how some of those attempts to limit access to abortion impact women's health care in a larger context.*

Birth Control—A Parents' Problem or Woman's? Margaret Sanger, 1920

The problem of birth control has arisen directly from the effort of the feminine spirit to free itself from bondage. Woman herself has wrought that bondage through her reproductive powers and while enslaving herself has enslaved the world. The physical suffering to be relieved is chiefly woman's. Hers, too, is the love life that dies first under the blight of too prolific breeding. Within her is wrapped up the future of the race—it is hers to make or mar. All of these considerations point unmistakably to one fact—it is woman's duty as well as her privilege to lay hold of the means of freedom. Whatever men may do, she cannot escape the responsibility. For ages she has been deprived of the opportunity to meet this obligation. She is now emerging from her helplessness. Even as no one can share the suffering of the overburdened mother, so no one can do this work for her. Others may help, but she and she alone can free herself.

The basic freedom of the world is woman's freedom. A free race cannot be born of slave mothers. A woman enchained cannot choose but give a measure of that bondage to her sons and daughters. No woman can call herself free who does not own and control her body. No woman can call herself free until she can choose consciously whether she will or will not be a mother.

It does not greatly alter the case that some women call themselves free because they earn their own livings, while others profess freedom because they defy the conventions of sex relationship. She who earns her own living gains a sort of freedom that is not to be undervalued, but in quality and in quantity it is of little account beside the untrammeled choice of mating or not mating, of being a mother or not being a mother. She gains food and clothing and shelter, at least, without submitting to the charity of her companion, but the earning of her own living does not give her the development of her inner sex urge, far deeper and more powerful in its outworkings than any of these externals. In order to have that development, she must still meet and solve the problem of motherhood.

With the so-called "free" woman, who chooses a mate in defiance of convention, freedom is largely a question of character and audacity. If she does attain to an unrestricted choice of a mate, she is still in a position to be enslaved through her reproductive powers. Indeed, the pressure of law and custom upon the woman not legally married is likely to make her more of a slave than the woman fortunate enough to marry the man of her choice.

Look at it from any standpoint you will, suggest any solution you will, conventional or unconventional, sanctioned by law or in defiance of law, woman is in the same position, fundamentally, until she is able to determine for herself whether she will be a mother and to fix the number of her offspring. This unavoidable situation is alone enough to make birth control, first of all, a woman's problem. On the very face of the matter, voluntary motherhood is chiefly the concern of the woman.

It is persistently urged, however, that since sex expression is the act of two, the responsibility of controlling the results should not be placed upon woman alone. Is it fair, it is asked, to give her, instead of the man, the task of protecting herself when she is, perhaps, less rugged in physique than her mate, and has, at all events, the normal, periodic inconveniences of her sex?

We must examine this phase of her problem in two lights—that of the ideal, and of the conditions working toward the ideal. In an ideal society, no doubt, birth control would become the concern of the man as well as the woman. The hard, inescapable fact which we encounter to-day is that man has not only refused any such responsibility, but has individually and collectively sought to prevent woman from obtaining knowledge by which she could assume this responsibility for herself. She is still in the position of a dependent to-day because her mate has refused to consider her as an individual apart from his needs. She is still bound because she has in the past left the solution of the problem to him. Having left it to him, she finds that instead of rights, she has only such privileges as she has gained by petitioning, coaxing and cozening. Having left it to him, she is exploited, driven and enslaved to his desires.

While it is true that he suffers many evils as the consequence of this situation, she suffers vastly more. While it is true that he should be awakened to the cause of these evils, we know that they come home to her with crushing force every day. It is she who has the long burden of carrying, bearing and rearing the unwanted children. . . . It is her heart that the sight of the deformed, the sub-normal, the undernourished, the overworked child smites first and oftenest and hardest. It is *her* love life that dies first in the fear of undesired pregnancy. It is her opportunity for self expression that perishes first and most hopelessly because of it.

Conditions, rather than theories, facts, rather than dreams, govern the problem. They place it squarely upon the shoulders of woman. She has learned that whatever the moral responsibility of the man in this direction may be, he does not discharge it. She has learned that, lovable and considerate as the individual husband may be, she has nothing to expect from men in the mass, when they make laws and decree customs. She knows that regardless of what ought to be, the brutal, unavoidable fact is that she will never receive her freedom until she takes it for herself.

Having learned this much, she has yet something more to learn. Women are too much inclined to follow in the footsteps of men, to try to think as men think, to try to solve the general problems of life as men solve them. If after attaining their freedom, women accept conditions in the spheres of government, industry, art, morals and religion as they find them, they will be but taking a leaf out of man's book. The woman is not needed to do man's work. She is not needed to think man's thoughts. She need not fear that the masculine mind, almost universally dominant, will fail to take care of its own. Her mission is not to enhance the masculine spirit, but to express the feminine; hers is not to preserve a man-made world, but to create a human world by the infusion of the feminine element into all of its activities.

Woman must not accept; she must challenge. She must not be awed by that which has been built up around her; she must reverence that within her which struggles for expression. Her eyes must be less upon what is and more clearly upon what should be. She must listen only with a frankly questioning attitude to the dogmatized opinions of man-made society. When she chooses her new, free course of action, it must be in the light of her own opinion—of her own intuition. Only so can she give play to the feminine spirit. Only thus can she free her mate from the bondage which he wrought for himself when he wrought hers. Only thus can she restore to him that of which he robbed himself in restricting her. Only thus can she remake the world. . . .

Woman must have her freedom—the fundamental freedom of choosing whether or not she shall be a mother and how many children she will have. Regardless of what man's attitude may be, that problem is hers—and before it can be his, it is hers alone.

She goes through the vale of death alone, each time a babe is born. As it is the right neither of man nor the state to coerce her into this ordeal, so it is her right to decide whether she will endure it. That right to decide imposes upon her the duty of clearing the way to knowledge by which she may make and carry out the decision.

Birth control is woman's problem. The quicker she accepts it as hers and hers alone, the quicker will society respect motherhood. The quicker, too, will the world be made a fit place for her children to live.

From Margaret Sanger, *Woman and the New Race (New York: Brentano,* *1920), pp. 93–100.*

Reproductive Freedom: Fundamental to All Human Rights, Faye Wattleton, 1990

I love to visit northern California, everyone here is so health-conscious and out-doorsy. I've heard that's especially true of Esprit people, so I think you'll appreciate a sports tidbit I read recently. *Bicycling* magazine polled its readers and learned that 84% daydream about sex while they're cycling. Somehow I wasn't surprised. But then I read that 20% daydream about cycling while they're having sex!

Well, I won't ask for a show of hands here, but I think it's safe to say that sex is important to most of us! Whatever our age or circumstances, we all make sexual decisions—and we cherish the freedom to make those decisions privately, without meddling or coercion.

The freedom to chart our reproductive destinies is a more recent acquisition than you might think. As late as 1965, contraception was still illegal in most of the U.S. Before then, biology was still destiny. Women were economically deprived and socially dependent. And men suffered too, saddled with children they could not feed or clothe.

In this day and age, control over our reproduction is a given. Women and men can plan our futures because we can plan our child-bearing. This dramatic advance is just one of the many steps forward our nation has made in recent decades, including enormous progress in human rights, women's rights, civil rights, children's rights.

But today we look down the road toward the future and we see warning signs: "Danger ahead!" The danger isn't limited to our reproductive liberty, either; we see threats to our very progress as a democratic, pluralistic society. A tyrannical minority is determined to reverse the changes that were achieved in my generation. They want to tell us which forms of speech are censored, which books we may read, which music and art we may enjoy, even which God to pray to. Armed with Puritanical moralism, they have set out to control everything they view as obscene.

This crackdown on free expression will have a cataclysmic impact on our fundamental rights. This is not the America I know and love!

Around the world, nations are steering toward greater freedom for all citizens, holding our constitutional ideals as their compass—while here at home, we fight not to lose ideals. Is this the America we want to see as we end the 20th century?

The framers of our Constitution established the ideal of fundamental freedoms, freedoms that would endure in an ever-changing society, freedoms far removed from the reach of politicians. The Bill of Rights plainly states that "the enumeration [in] the Constitution of certain rights shall not be construed to deny or disparage others retained by the people." In plain talk, that is, the framers didn't want to spell out every one of our liberties. They didn't want to limit our freedoms to their day and age, with no room for expansion!

Given how different life was in those days, I'm glad! Let's remember that Washington and Jefferson owned slaves! Their wives didn't vote! For all we know, they weren't even convinced the world was really round!

With few exceptions, rights have been expanded for the disenfranchised: women, minorities, children, the disabled. Americans have come to take it for granted that our right to decide when and if to reproduce is as fundamental as our right to free speech or to assemble in this room! Nine out of 10 Americans believe that right is constitutionally guaranteed. For 18 years, since the *Roe v. Wade* decision, we've counted on constitutional protection for our right to control our fertility.

But today, we are fighting to hold onto these most basic freedoms. The Reagan-dominated Supreme Court has thrown these rights into chaos.

First, women's access to abortion was restricted in the case called *Webster,* in July 1989. A year later, the court handed down the *Ohio* and *Hodgson* rulings, which allowed states to require parental notification for teens seeking abortions. All three rulings have created more restrictive standards by which all abortion laws will be judged. And though they target the most vulnerable women, the young and the poor, these rulings threaten all women.

I want to focus briefly on the teen cases, and the dangerous idea of legislating family communication. Parents should be involved in teens' important decisions, and their sexual decisions are no exception. I can personally identify with this. My daughter Felicia and I always discuss sexuality issues openly, only these days, *I'm* the one asking most of the questions! But compulsory communication is no joke. Besides, it doesn't work. It only disrupts families, forces young women to lie, and destroys young lives.

Instead of legislating family behavior, we should spend more time and resources on helping families communicate better. Laws should be aimed at giving our young people greater opportunities, not on treating them like property. If Felicia ever became pregnant and felt she couldn't involve me, I'd be hurt and saddened. But she's lived with me for 15 years. She knows me a little better than government regulators. If she couldn't come to me, the last thing I'd want is the government coming to her!

The government has no business telling any of us what to do with our private lives or our family lives! Teen or adult, rich or poor, black, brown, or white, any female able to become pregnant must be able to prevent pregnancy and to choose whether or not to end pregnancy. The government should stay out of it.

No human right is more basic than our right to reproductive freedom. And no human right is so gravely threatened. The late Supreme Court Justice Louis Brandeis once wrote that "the greatest dangers to liberty lurk in insidious encroachment by men of zeal—well-meaning, but without understanding." When it comes to the anti-choice extremists, that description may be overly charitable!

This isn't really a struggle over abortion. It's over controlling women and controlling our sexuality. Otherwise, why would the extremists be intent on eliminating sexuality education and contraception?

The most damaging evidence of their true agenda is their attack on Title X, the federal family planning program that helps prevent 516,000 abortions each year. This attack comes in the form of a so-called gag rule imposed by President Reagan in 1988. The gag rule says that publicly funded clinics can't give a pregnant woman any information on abortion, even if continuing the pregnancy threatens her health! If one of you were a patient in one of these clinics, the staff wouldn't be able to tell you abortion is an option! They couldn't refer you to someone who would tell you! They couldn't even lend you the "Yellow Pages" so you could look up an abortion provider on your own!

This is bald censorship. The gag rule turns doctors into indoctrinators, and patients into pawns. Planned Parenthood argued against the gag rule in the Supreme Court last month. It remains to be seen if the Court will show common sense and compassion, and overturn this obvious ploy to disrupt family planning programs.

It's frightening that the end of the 20th century so closely resembles the beginning. Seventy-five years ago, the founders of the family planning movement had to battle repressive crusades begun in the 19th century, crusades like that of Anthony Comstock, the one-man vice squad who, in 1873, persuaded Congress to label birth control "obscene." In the first year the Comstock statute was in effect, Comstock himself confiscated 200,000 pictures and photos, 100,000 books, 5,000 decks of playing cards, 30,000 boxes of aphrodisiacs, and more than 60,000 of what were then referred to as "rubber articles." I wonder how he fit all that into his night table drawer!

Today, 120 years after his heyday, Comstock is back to haunt us, in the form of Jesse Helms! In 18 years in the Senate, Mr. Helms has tried to erode personal privacy almost as the Comstock statute did in 92 years!

The Supreme Court encouraged busybodies like Senator Helms. When it handed down the *Webster* case, the court invited state legislators to make our private decisions for us. The court declared that it doesn't trust women with our own choices. But legislators soon found themselves facing an angry American majority, who want the government off the backs and out of the wombs of women! And in case some politicians were still missing the point, pro-choice America spelled it out for them last month on election day. Across the country, we remembered who our friends are! We remembered to promote our values by voting our values, the universal values of diversity, pluralism, and independence.

However proud we are of our election day victories, reproductive issues should never make it to the ballot box in the first place. Abortion, contraception, privacy, these are fundamental freedoms that should be off limits to lawmakers. And we, the pro-choice majority, have the power to turn this debate around, to remove it from the political arena. We must renew our determination to fight for permanent protection for our freedoms, whatever it takes, for as long as it takes.

Your activism can help make that goal a reality. In fact, you can be more influential than many people, because you're fortunate enough to work for a company that values activism. I was so impressed to learn about the policy on volunteerism here at Esprit. For an employer to take social change so seriously that they encourage you to be activists on company time, that is truly extraordinary.

So I urge you, become activists on behalf of reproductive freedom, for yourselves, for your loved ones, and for the millions of less fortunate women and men who have no one else to speak on their behalf.

Now is the time to improve family communication about sexuality. Start with your family! Now is the time to call for comprehensive sexuality education in the schools, to help teach young people how to live healthy, responsible lives. Now is the time to improve access to contraception for those who need it most, the young and poor. Now is the time to insist on expanded research for better birth control. The National Academy of Sciences reports that the U.S. lags decades behind other nations in this area, with fewer options available, and no concerted commitment to develop new ones.

Above all, now is the time to demand that our government leaders stay out of our private matters. We must not rest until they recognize that the right to make personal reproductive decisions is fundamental, inalienable, and non-negotiable. It is not contingent on age or circumstances or geography. It is not a "single issue." And it is not open to partisan debate!

America's lawmakers must stop meddling in the lives of women and families. Surely they have more important things to do, like housing the homeless, feeding the hungry, and educating the ignorant. Like showing concern and compassion for the children already born. And like waging war on the root causes of abortion, unintended pregnancy.

Reproductive freedom is in crisis. But realistic solutions are within our reach, if we all work together. I know you may sometimes wonder how much difference one person's efforts can make. Consider the phenomenon that meteorologists call the "Butterfly Effect": A single butterfly stirs, deep in a forest. The motion of its wings makes tiny air currents. At just that moment, a passing swirl of air happens to pick up those tiny currents, and they become a puff of breeze. Then a momentary gust picks up that breeze and it becomes a gentle wind—and so on, and so on, until, weeks later, the movement of that one butterfly at that one moment changed the course of a tornado on the other side of the globe!

All of us in the universe are linked, over time, and over distance. One butterfly, one person, can make a difference. A big difference. So take wing, today. And remember what Queen Victoria once said: "We are not interested in the possibilities of defeat!"

Delivered to an audience of 200–250 employees of Esprit de Corp, San Francisco, California, December 11, 1990. Reprinted by permission.

Abortion and Women's Rights, Frederica Mathewes-Green

The abortion debate seems like an unresolvable conflict of rights: the right of women to control their own bodies, the right of children to be born. Can one both support women's rights and oppose abortion?

Truly supporting women's rights must involve telling the truth about abortion and working for it to cease. Many years ago I felt differently; in college I advocated the repeal of abortion laws, and supported my friends who traveled for out-of-state abortions. In those early days of feminism, women faced daunting obstacles. The typical woman was thought to be charmingly silly, prone to having parking lot fender-benders and then consoling herself with a new hat. Certainly not someone who should run a corporation—perhaps someone who should not even vote.

But the hurdles were not only political; we felt physically vulnerable, as rape statistics rose and women's bodies were exploited in advertising and entertainment. The external world's disparagement of our abilities was compounded by the extra cruelty that our bodies were at risk as well, from violence without and invasion within. For an unplanned pregnancy felt like an invader, an evil alien bent on colonizing one's body and destroying one's plans. The first right must be to keep one's body safe, private, and healthy: without that, all other rights are meaningless.

It is because I still believe so strongly in the right of a woman to protect her body that I now oppose abortion. That right must begin when her body begins, and it must be hers no matter where she lives—even if she lives in her mother's womb. The same holds true for her brother.

The average woman does not gain, but loses, when she has an abortion. She loses, first, the hundreds of dollars in cash she must pay to receive the surgery. Secondly, she must undergo a humiliating procedure, an invasion deeper than rape, as the interior of her uterus is crudely vacuumed to remove every scrap of life. Thirdly, she can lose her health. A woman's body is a delicately balanced ecology, not meant to have its natural, healthy processes disrupted by invasive machinery.

The most devastating loss of all is the loss of her own child. Abortion rhetoric paints the unborn as a parasite, a lump. But it is in fact her own child, as much like her as any child she will ever have, sharing her appearance, talents, and family tree. In abortion, she offers her own child as a sacrifice for the right to continue her life, and it is a sacrifice that will haunt her. Many women grieve silently after abortion, their sorrow ignored by a society that expects them to be grateful for the "freedom' to abort. A man who saw his wife gradually disintegrate after her abortion asks, "What kind of trade-off is that: gain control of your body, lose control of your mind?"

For all these losses, women gain nothing but the right to run in place. Abortion doesn't cure any illness; it doesn't win any woman a raise. But in a culture that treats pregnancy and child-rearing as impediments, it surgically adapts the woman to fit in. If women are an oppressed group, they are the only such group to require surgery in order to be equal. In Greek mythology, Procrustes was an exacting host: if you were the wrong size for his bed, he would stretch or chop you to fit. The abortion table is modern feminism's Procrustean bed, one that, in a hideous twist, the victims actually march in the streets to demand.

If we were to imagine a society that supports and respects women, we would have to begin with preventing these unplanned pregnancies. Contraceptives fail, and half of all aborting women admit they weren't using them anyway. Thus, preventing unplanned pregnancies will involve a return to sexual responsibility. This means either avoiding sex in situations where a child cannot be welcomed, or being willing to be responsible for lives unintentionally conceived, perhaps by making an adoption plan, entering a marriage, or making faithful child-support payments. Using contraceptives is no substitute for this responsibility, any more than wearing a seat belt entitles one to speed.

Secondly, we need to make continuing a pregnancy and raising a child less of a burden. Most agree that women should play a part in the public life of our society; their talents and abilities are as valuable as men's, and there is no reason to restrict them from the employment sphere. But during the years that her children are young, mother and child usually prefer to be together. If women are to be free to take off these years in the middle of a career, they must have faithful, responsible men who will support them. Both parents can also benefit from more flexibility in the workplace: allowing parents of school-age children to set their hours to coincide with the school day, for example, or enabling more workers to escape the expenses of office, commute, and child care by working from home. We also must welcome women back into the work force when they want to return, accounting their years at home as valuable training in management, education, and negotiation skills.

Women's rights are not in conflict with their own children's rights; the appearance of such a conflict is a sign that something is wrong in society. When women have the sexual respect and employment flexibility they need, they will no longer seek as a substitute the bloody injustice of abortion.

From Sisterlife, *the magazine of Feminists for Life. Reprinted by permission.*

Statement to Feminists for Life of America, Rep. Helen Chenoweth, 1997

Thank you for inviting me to the 25th anniversary of Feminists for Life of America. This truly is a special evening.

I would like to take this opportunity to congratulate this group for their efforts to seek true equality for all human beings. Your mission has been clear and consistent and your voice is critical in our communities.

Twenty-three years ago, the Supreme Court removed a God-given, unalienable right from unborn babies, a right it has the duty to secure and protect. In doing so, it elevated a "judge-made" right, the right of a person's privacy, above the God-given right to life.

It has always been my belief that unborn children should be cherished, and abortion for the convenience of the mother is contrary to convictions that mean a great deal. I believe the life of an unborn child is to be respected as truly as the life of a new born.

As you know, our system of laws is based on the idea that people have certain God-given rights. Those rights are life, liberty, and the pursuit of happiness. Those rights existed before laws were established. We must never forget this.

I believe that if the Supreme Court continues to uphold the wrong decision made in *Roe v. Wade,* Congress should enact laws that would disallow abortion, except in very extreme circumstances. At the very least, Congress should prohibit the government from funding abortion. However, before we can pass laws forbidding abortion, we must change the dynamic of the debate by educating the American public to favor the protection of life at its natural beginning—the point of conception. I think that when all Americans, including many women who are confused about this issue, begin to realize the serious ramifications of abortion, they will strongly support the need to protect the sanctity of life.

I am happy to report that the House passed and I supported H.R. 1122, legislation to ban a specific abortion procedure used in the second and third trimesters of pregnancy. The vote to ban so-called partial-birth abortions was 295–136—more than the two-thirds needed to override a promised veto from President Clinton, and more than the bill garnered in three separate votes in 1995 and 1996. H.R. 1122 has exposed to the general public just what abortion is all about—the blatant disregard and brutal destruction of human life—and it's now up to the Senate.

Partial-birth abortion is cold, grizzly murder. This type of procedure has been used on babies who are four-and-a-half months in the womb.

Partial-birth is not a legitimate medical procedure. Doctors at the Metropolitan Medical clinic in New Jersey say that only a minuscule amount of the 1,500 partial-birth abortions they perform are for medical reasons.

As you may know leading abortion-rights advocates lied during debate over "partial-birth abortions." Ron Fitzsimmons, the executive director of the National Coalition of Abortion Providers, intentionally misled the public. He admittedly "lied through his teeth" in a November 1995 interview for ABC's "Nightline." Ron Fitzsimmons felt that the truth about this gruesome procedure would hinder the abortion rights campaign.

Since 1993, abortion supporters and opponents have been engaged in a vicious public relations war over the procedure, with abortion foes using grisly illustrations to tap Americans' general discomfort with late term abortions.

My position in representing the people of Idaho has been guided by the conviction that abortion is wrong and should only be considered in cases of criminal rape, incest, or when the mother's life is in imminent danger. I am committed do all I can to protect our unborn children.

We must continue to stand firm and ensure justice and equality for all human beings.

Again, thank you for this opportunity. This truly is an honor for me to be here with you all this evening.

Address to the Feminists for Life of America 25th anniversary conference, April 26, 1997. Reprinted by permission.

So Much We Can Do: A Nation of Leaders, Gloria Feldt, 1998

"So much we can do" is today's theme. I've subtitled my remarks: "A nation of leaders," because leaders are what we must be. All of us.

What is a leader?

Years ago, when I was in my first grown-up leadership role, a mentor of mine defined the concept for me. She told me that a leader is anyone who gets things done. All of us are leaders—each in our own way—if we get things done. Of course, some leaders stand out.

Time magazine recently named Planned Parenthood founder Margaret Sanger one of the 20 revolutionary leaders of the century.[1] What made Sanger a revolutionary was her vision that women should have the opportunity to shape the course and quality of their lives by choosing when and if they become parents.

Some Americans weren't ready for Sanger's vision.

Philosopher Arnold Schopenhauer observed that all truth goes through three stages: First, it's ridiculed, then it's violently opposed, then it's accepted as a given. Sound familiar?

Today, 90 percent of American voters support family planning—it has become one of our most cherished and supported ideals.[2] Sanger pioneered a revolution in reproductive health care. It's time for the revolution to surge into the new millennium.

We must be the leaders who will raise awareness that reproductive health is fundamental to women's health, and that women's health is essential to the health of families, communities, even nations. I want to talk about barriers to that awareness, highlighting approaches that enhance women's health in the U.S. and worldwide.

Why the emphasis on women's health? Women are more than half the population; they're the nation's largest consumers of health care; and they spend 68 percent more in out-of-pocket health expenses than men do, primarily for reproductive health care—such as birth control—that isn't covered by their insurance plans. Yet women traditionally have been marginalized by the legal, political, as well as medical mainstream.

Such institutional neglect poses significant health risks to women—and by extension, to millions of children and families who rely on women as primary caregivers.

In contrast, Planned Parenthood and most institutional providers of reproductive health care have always taken a more holistic, patient-centered approach to women's health. We're guided by the belief that women's health is determined by the social, political, and economic context of their lives.

Certainly this belief was behind Sanger's initial efforts to legalize birth control. And we've all reaped the benefits—a sharp reduction in pregnancy related deaths in the U.S. and substantially lowered rates of maternal and infant mortality wherever people have access to family planning.

Moreover, the field of reproductive health has served as a harbinger of what would occur in health care. Indeed, today's vision of managed care—a system that would provide coordinated care and emphasize prevention, self-care, education, and consistent quality—is what reproductive health centers have been practicing since their inception.

In the search for new cost-effective health care, the lessons learned from Sanger and our movement can help us to identify the barriers to a better future and further define what we can do to overcome them.

Barrier 1: Politics

Put simply, women's health cannot be separated from its political context. Despite the legal right to make childbearing choices, women still confront legislative barriers to exercising that right. Mandatory delays, restrictions on minors' access—these restrictions are most devastating for those least able to fight back:

The young and the poor;

The geographically isolated;

Those uneducated about family planning;

And those whose local hospital just merged with the Catholic-run system and no longer provides family planning or abortion.

If health care leaders and elected officials are serious about improving women's health, they must become more public in their support of reproductive freedom. They must affirm—in unison and individually—the importance of family planning, sex education, and reproductive choice. Their mission statements, policies, and procedures must say so. Most of all, they must say so as professionals who know what they're talking about, and as responsible citizens.

Barrier 2: Censorship

The media bombards us with sex, yet most television stations refuse to air contraceptive advertisements. Legislators champion "abstinence-only" programs, but deny adequate funding for responsible, age-appropriate sex education. Even some health care providers are reluctant to openly discuss sexual health issues with their patients.

Young people, especially, suffer the consequences of these mixed messages. They learn from popular culture that it's glamorous to have sex. They aren't learning that it's smart to plan for sex. PPFA has developed a remarkable video kit for parents called "Talking About Sex." It's won a dozen national and even international awards. But it's being subtly censored—not a single major catalogue or video store will carry it.

No wonder the U.S. has the highest rates of teen pregnancy and sexually transmitted infections in the developed world.

Educators, providers, and politicians need to take a leadership role in promoting open and honest discussions about sexual issues. We must stop censoring ourselves because we fear controversy. What are we afraid of? Honest, responsible sex education in schools is supported by 82 percent of American voters.[3]

We must help parents fulfill their role as the primary sex educators for their children. People of all ages who seek reproductive health care should be encouraged to ask questions and should expect honest answers.

Barrier 3: Access

For too many Americans, access to reproductive health options is subject to gender, age, income, and geography. Here too, there is so much we can do.

Through our services and our advocacy, we can ensure greater access to all reproductive health options. We can create and promote new options that will improve the health and well being of women, men, and their families. The health care community can demonstrate its unified support for the nation's family planning program, Title X, without debilitating amendments.

Each year, Title X funding helps to prevent 1.3 million pregnancies and more than 600,000 abortions.[4] And it saves money to boot! But year after year, Title X is a favorite target of anti-choice forces that work relentlessly to eliminate it.

We can promote emergency contraception. Widespread use of emergency contraception could prevent up to 2.5 million unintended pregnancies and a million abortions each year.[5] But many women don't know enough about emergency contraception to request it. Practitioners are unfamiliar with it and do not discuss it with their patients. Your committed advocacy and service provision can change that.

We can advocate for increased funding for reproductive health-related research and clinical trials, including those for new methods of contraception. Research funding for women's health is generally inadequate, but funding for reproductive health is abysmal. Indeed, despite bipartisan support in Congress for doubling funding to the National Institutes of Health, NIH funding for contraceptive research has remained flat, at $8 million, for a decade. By way of comparison, of NIH's current budget of more than $15 billion, more than $300 million goes to diabetes research, more than $850 million is allocated for research on heart disease, and $50 million is being spent to study alternative medicine.[6]

We can educate health care providers about early medical and early surgical abortion procedures and encourage greater use of them. These procedures can give women more privacy and control over their decision, and they can be safer and less stress-inducing experiences for women who choose to terminate an unintended pregnancy.

But access to services depends on the availability of providers, which brings me to …

Barrier 4: Training

Many primary caregivers do not receive adequate training in the prevention or management of unintended pregnancies and other reproductive health care needs:

Only 12 percent of ob/gyn residency programs routinely provide training for first-trimester abortions.[7]

86 percent of U.S. counties have no abortion services at all.[8]

As older abortion providers retire—the average age is 60—the pool of younger physicians to replace them becomes smaller and smaller.

The training gap extends to patient education services. One-third of women at risk for an unplanned pregnancy say that their doctors never mentioned birth control during their most recent visit. And half the women polled in a recent survey assume that they're screened for sexually transmitted infections, when in fact testing is optional and must be requested.

Clearly, what's needed is better training for practitioners, with curricula that emphasize all facets of reproductive health care. At the same time, practicing health care providers must have opportunities to update their skills.

Politics. Censorship. Access. Training. There's so much we can do to overcome each of these barriers. But there's a fifth barrier that encompasses all the others ... I alluded to it at the start of my talk.

Barrier 5

The stubborn perception of women as a "special population" when it comes to health care. This distinction only contributes to segregation and diminishment. It must be abandoned! Doing so will require a major attitude shift in the way the American people think about, treat, and value women and children.

The health care community can take the first step by acknowledging that women's leadership can improve the way we provide health care in this country, just as Sanger did so many years ago.

We need more women appointed to positions of authority. Women comprise more than 40 percent of all medical school students, less than 5 percent of academic chairs. And only one-fourth of all medical school faculty are women.[9]

We can further bolster women's empowerment by encouraging their full participation in decisions about their reproductive health. Providing girls especially with the information they need to make their own decisions and live their own lives will help develop the next generation of women leaders.

Each of you leaders can facilitate the process by working toward a world in which reproductive health care needs of all women and their families are met.

Together, we can overcome the five barriers. And we can use them as opportunities for building a world in which all women are acknowledged as moral decision-makers for their reproductive choices. A world in which all women and men have access to the reproductive health care they need to make healthy, responsible choices. And in which all children are welcomed joyfully by parents prepared to care for them.

This was the world that birth control revolutionary Margaret Sanger envisioned. The final transformation of that vision into reality is our challenge as a nation of leaders in reproductive health. Let it also be our destiny.

Thank you.

Address to the Planned Parenthood of Maryland Women's Health Conference, April 22, 1998. Copyright © 1999 Planned Parenthood Federation of America. Reprinted by permission.

[1]Isaacson, W. "Our Century and the Next One." *Time Magazine*, April 13, 1998. p.70.

[2]Lake Sosin Perry poll conducted for Planned Parenthood Federation of America, Inc. 1996.

[3]Lake Sosin Perry poll conducted for Planned Parenthood Federation of America, Inc. 1997.

[4]Kaeser, L. "Title X and the U.S. Family Planning Effort." *Issues in Brief*, The Alan Guttmacher Institute, 1997.

[5]Glasier, A. & Baird, D. "The Effects of Self-Administering Emergency Contraception." *The New England Journal of Medicine* 359, no. 1, July 2, 1998, p.1–4.

[6]Havemann, J., "Crusading for Cash; Patient Groups Compete for Bigger Shares of NIH's Research Funding." *Washington Post*, Dec. 15, 1998, p.Z10; Recer, Z. "Which Diseases Get Studied? Report Suggests Vocal Interest Groups Get Funding." *Houston Chronicle,* July 9, 1998. p. 4.

[7]MacKay, H.T. & Mackay, A.P. "Abortion Training in Obstetrics and Gynecology Residency Programs, in the United States." *Family Planning Perspectives* 27, no. 3, May/June 1995, pp.112–115.

[8]Henshaw, S.K. "Abortion Incidence and Services in the United States." *Family Planning Perspectives* 30, no. 6, Nov./Dec. 1998, pp.263–270 & 287.

[9]American Academy of Medical Colleges. "Increasing Women's Leadership in Academic Medicine." *Academic Medicine* 71, no. 7, 1996, pp.799–811.

Perspectives on Family and Community

Women's roles as wives and mothers and the limits those roles placed on pursuing careers and other opportunities emerged as one of the issues that women began questioning in the 1960s. Betty Friedan identified the frustration many women felt and labeled it "The Problem That Has No Name" in her 1963 book The Feminine Mystique. *Many women, including Friedan, argued that women should not have to choose between having a family and having a career and that married partners could share parenting responsibilities and support each other as they developed their work lives.*

Some women have not had the luxury of making the choices that suburban housewives have had. Instead, cultural, economic, or other constraints have limited their options and have demanded other decisions. The workshop resolutions of the first National Chicana Conference articulate the limits that have been placed on Chicanas by religious dogma and by the roles assigned to Chicana women within their families and their communities. The resolutions call for a greater recognition of Chicana's full humanity as sexual beings, as partners in marriage, and as participants in the community.

African American Marian Wright Edelman, founder of the Children's Defense Fund, has been one of the most outspoken and respected advocates for children since the 1970s. Her leadership has contributed to the passage of federal legislation to benefit children and to the development of private programs for them. She believes that the African American community must support its families and children, as she explained in her 1987 speech to the Congressional Black Caucus.

For the balance of the twentieth century, women's roles in their families have been an issue for both feminists and conservatives. Conservative leaders in the 1980s and 1990s sought to define the American family as a married man and woman and their children, assigning responsibility for the family's financial support to the husband and the sustenance of the family to the wife. As the result of divorce, economic necessity, and other factors, fewer and fewer families fit conservatives' definition of family. One group of families in particular does not conform to the definition: same sex partnerships with children. Gay couples and lesbian couples with children seek to have their partnerships and the families they create recognized, respected, and honored in the same ways that other kinds of families are. Kate Kendall explains the ways her family and others like it are changing the definition of family.

The Problem That Has No Name, Betty Friedan, 1963

The problem lay buried, unspoken, for many years in the minds of American women. It was a strange stirring, a sense of dissatisfaction, a yearning that women suffered in the middle of the twentieth century in the United States. Each suburban wife struggled with it alone. As she made the beds, shopped for groceries, matched slipcover material, ate peanut butter sandwiches with her children, chauffeured Cub Scouts and Brownies, lay beside her husband at night—she was afraid to ask even of herself the silent question—"Is this all?"

For over fifteen years there was no word of this yearning in the millions of words written about women, for women, in all the columns, books and articles by experts telling women their role was to seek fulfillment as wives and mothers.

Over and over women heard in voices of tradition and of Freudian sophistication that they could desire no greater destiny than to glory in their own femininity. Experts told them how to catch a man and keep him, how to breastfeed children and handle their toilet training, how to cope with sibling rivalry and adolescent rebellion; how to buy a dishwasher, bake bread, cook gourmet snails, and build a swimming pool with their own hands; how to dress, look, and act more feminine and make marriage more exciting; how to keep their husbands from dying young and their sons from growing into delinquents. They were taught to pity the neurotic, unfeminine, unhappy women who wanted to be poets or physicists or presidents. They learned that truly feminine women do not want careers, higher education, political rights—the independence and the opportunities that the old-fashioned feminists fought for. Some women, in their forties and fifties, still remembered painfully giving up those dreams, but most of the younger women no longer even thought about them. A thousand expert voices applauded their femininity, their adjustment, their new maturity. All they had to do was devote their lives from earliest girlhood to finding a husband and bearing children.

By the end of the nineteen-fifties the average marriage age of women in America dropped to 20, and was still dropping, into the teens. Fourteen million girls were engaged by 17. The proportion of women attending college in comparison with men dropped from 47 per cent in 1920 to 35 per cent in 1958. A century earlier, women had fought for higher education; now girls went to college to get a husband. By the mid-fifties, 60 per cent dropped out of college to marry, or because they were afraid too much education would be a marriage bar. Colleges built dormitories for "married students," but the students were almost always the husbands. A new degree was instituted for the wives—"Ph.T." (Putting Husband Through).

Then American girls began getting married in high school. And the women's magazines, deploring the unhappy statistics about these young marriages, urged that courses on marriage, and marriage counselors, be installed in the high schools. Girls started going steady at twelve and thirteen, in junior high. Manufacturers put out brassieres with false bosoms of foam rubber for little girls of ten. And an advertisement for a child's dress, size 3–6x, in the *New York Times* in the fall of 1960, said: "She Too Can Join the Man-Trap Set."

By the end of the fifties, the United States birthrate was overtaking India's. The birth-control movement, renamed Planned Parenthood, was asked to find a method whereby women who had been advised that a third or fourth baby would be born dead or defective might have it anyhow. Statisticians were especially astounded at the fantastic increase in the number of babies among college women. Where once they had two children, now they had four, five, six. Women who had once wanted careers were now making careers out of having babies. So rejoiced *Life* magazine in a 1956 paean to the movement of American women back to the home.

In a New York hospital, a woman had a nervous breakdown when she found she could not breastfeed her baby. In other hospitals, women dying of cancer refused a drug which research had proved might save their lives: its side effects were said to be unfeminine. "If I have only one life, let me live it as a blonde," a larger-than-life-sized picture of a pretty, vacuous woman proclaimed from newspaper, magazine, and drugstore ads. And across America, three out of every ten women dyed their hair blonde. They ate a chalk called Metrecal, instead of food, to shrink to the size of the thin young models. Department store buyers reported that American women, since 1939, had become three and four sizes smaller. "Women are out to fit the clothes, instead of vice-versa," one buyer said.

Interior decorators were designing kitchens with mosaic murals and original paintings, for kitchens were once again the center of women's lives. Home sewing became a million-dollar industry. Many women no longer left their homes, except to shop, chauffeur their children, or attend a social engagement with their husbands. Girls were growing up in America without ever having jobs outside the home. In the late fifties, a sociological phenomenon was suddenly remarked: a third of American women now worked, but most were no longer young and very few were pursuing careers. They were married women who held part-time jobs, selling or secretarial, to put their husbands through school, their sons through college, or to help pay the mortgage. Or they were widows supporting families. Fewer and fewer women were entering professional work. The shortages in the nursing, social work, and teaching professions caused crises in almost every American city. Concerned over the Soviet Union's lead in the space race, scientists noted that America's greatest source of unused brainpower was women. But girls would not study physics: it was "unfeminine." A girl refused a science fellowship at Johns Hopkins to take a job in a real-estate office. All she wanted, she said, was what every other American girl wanted—to get married, have four children and live in a nice house in a nice suburb.

The suburban housewife—she was the dream image of the young American women and the envy, it was said, of women all over the world. The American housewife—freed by science and labor-saving appliances from the drudgery, the dangers of childbirth and the illnesses of her grandmother. She was healthy, beautiful, educated, concerned only about her husband, her children, her home. She had found true feminine fulfillment. As a housewife and mother, she was respected as a full and equal partner to man in his world. She was free to choose automobiles, clothes, appliances, supermarkets; she had everything that women ever dreamed of.

In the fifteen years after World War II, this mystique of feminine fulfillment became the cherished and self-perpetuating core of contemporary American culture. Millions of women lived their lives in the image of those pretty pictures of the American suburban housewife, kissing their husbands goodbye in front of the picture window, depositing their station-wagonsful of children at school, and smiling as they ran the new electric waxer over the spotless kitchen floor. They baked their own bread, sewed their own and their children's clothes, kept their new washing machines and dryers running all day. They changed the sheets on the beds twice a week instead of once, took the rug-hooking class in adult education, and pitied their poor frustrated mothers, who had dreamed of having a career. Their only dream was to be perfect wives and mothers; their highest ambition to have five children and a beautiful house, their only fight to get and keep their husbands. They had no thought for the unfeminine problems of the world outside the home; they wanted the men to make the major decisions. They gloried in their role as women, and wrote proudly on the census blank: "Occupation: housewife."

For over fifteen years, the words written for women, and the words women used when they talked to each other, while their husbands sat on the other side of the room and talked shop or politics or septic tanks, were about problems with their children, or how to keep their husbands happy, or improve their children's school, or cook chicken or make slipcovers. Nobody argued whether women were inferior or superior to men; they were simply different. Words like "emancipation" and "career" sounded strange and embarrassing; no one had used them for years. When a Frenchwoman named Simone de Beauvoir wrote a book called *The Second Sex*, an American critic commented that she obviously "didn't know what life was all about," and besides she was talking about French women. The "woman problem" in America no longer existed.

If a woman had a problem in the 1950's and 1960's she knew that something must be wrong with her marriage, or with herself. Other women were satisfied with their lives, she thought. What kind of a woman was she if she did not feel this mysterious fulfillment waxing the kitchen floor? She was so ashamed to admit her dissatisfaction that she never knew how many other women shared it. If she tried to tell her husband, he didn't understand what she was talking about. She did not really understand it herself. For over fifteen years women in America found it harder to talk about this problem than about sex. Even the psychoanalysts had no name for it. When a woman went to a psychiatrist for help, as many women did, she would say, "I'm so ashamed," or "I must be hopelessly neurotic." "I don't know what's wrong with women today," a suburban psychiatrist said uneasily. "I only know something is wrong because most of my patients happen to be women. And their problem isn't sexual." Most women with this problem did not go to see a psychoanalyst, however. "There's nothing wrong really," they kept telling themselves. "There isn't any problem."

. . . It is no longer possible to ignore that voice, to dismiss the desperation of so many American women. This is not what being a woman means, no matter what the experts say. For human suffering there is a reason; perhaps the reason has not been found because the right questions have not been asked, or pressed far enough. I do not accept the answer that there is no problem because American women have luxuries that women in other times and lands never dreamed of; part of the strange newness of the problem is that it cannot be understood in terms of the age-old material problems of man: poverty, sickness, hunger, cold. The women who suffer this problem have a hunger that food cannot fill.

. . . If I am right, the problem that has no name stirring in the minds of so many American women today is not a matter of loss of femininity or too much education, or the demands of domesticity. It is far more important than anyone recognizes. It is the key to these other new and old problems which have been torturing women and their husband and children, and puzzling their doctors and educators for years. It may well be the key to our future as nation and a culture. We can no longer ignore that voice within women that says: "I want something more than my husband and my children and my home."

From The Feminine Mystique *by Betty Friedan. Copyright © 1983, 1974, 1973, 1963 by Betty Friedan. Reprinted by permission of W. W. Norton & Company, Inc.*

Workshop Resolutions—First National Chicana Conference, 1971

Sex and the Chicana

We feel that in order to provide an effective measure to correct the many sexual hangups facing the Chicano community the following resolutions should be implemented:

I. Sex is good and healthy for both Chicanos and Chicanas and we must develop this attitude.

II. We should destroy the myth that religion and culture control our sexual lives.

III. We recognize that we have been oppressed by religion and that the religious writing was done by *men* and interpreted by *men*. Therefore, for those who desire religion, they should interpret their Bible, or Catholic rulings according to their own feelings, what they think is right, without any guilt complexes.

IV. Mothers should teach their sons to respect women as human beings who are equal in every respect. *No double standard.*

V. Women should go back to the communities and form discussion and action groups concerning sex education.

VI. Free, legal abortions and birth control for the Chicano community, controlled by *Chicanas*. As Chicanas we have the right to control our own bodies.

VII. Make use of church centers, neighborhood centers and any other place available.

"Liberate your mind and the body will follow. . . ."

"*A quitarnos todos nuestros complejos sexuales para tener una vida mejor y feliz*" (Let's cast off all our sexual complexes to have a better and happier life).

Marriage—Chicana Style

Reaffirmation that Chicano marriages are the beginnings of Chicano families which perpetuate our culture and are the foundation of the movement.

Points brought up in the workshop:

1. Chicano marriages are individual and intimate and solutions to problems must be primarily handled on an individual basis.

2. A woman must educate and acquaint herself with outside issues and personal problems (sexual hangups, etc.).

3. It is the responsibility of Chicanas with families to educate their sons and thus change the attitudes of future generations.

4. Chicanas should understand that Chicanos face oppression and discrimination, but this does not mean that the Chicana should be a scapegoat for the man's frustrations.

5. With involvement in the movement, marriages must change. Traditional roles for Chicanas are not acceptable or applicable.

Resolutions:

I. We, as *mujeres de La Raza,* recognize the Catholic Church as an oppressive institution and do hereby resolve to break away and not go to it to bless our unions.

II. Whereas: Unwanted pregnancies are the basis of many social problems, and

Whereas: The role of Mexican-American women has traditionally been limited to the home, and

Whereas: The need for self-determination and the right to govern their own bodies is a necessity for the freedom of all people, therefore,

Be It Resolved: That the National Chicana Conference go on record as supporting free family planning and free and legal abortions for all women who want or need them.

III. Whereas: Due to socio-economic and cultural conditions, Chicanas are often heads of households, i.e., widows, divorcees, unwed mothers, or deserted mothers, or must work to supplement family income, and

Whereas: Chicana motherhood should not preclude educational, political, social, and economic advancement, and

Whereas: There is a critical need for a 24-hour child-care center in Chicano communities, therefore,

Be It Resolved: That the National Chicana Conference go on record as recommending that every Chicano community promote and set up 24-hour day-care facilities, and that it be further resolved that these facilities will reflect the concept of La Raza as the united family, and on the basis of brotherhood (La Raza), so that men, women, young and old assume the responsibility for the love, care, education, and orientation of all the children of Aztlan.

IV. Whereas: Dr. Goldzieher of SWRF has conducted an experiment on Chicana women of westside San Antonio, Texas, using a new birth control drug, and

Whereas: No human being should be used for experimental purposes, therefore,

Be It Resolved: That this Conference send telegrams to the American Medical Association condemning this act. Let it also be resolved that each Chicana women's group and each Chicana present at the conference begin a letter writing campaign to:

Dr. Joseph Goldzieher c/o SW Foundation for Research and Education, San Antonio, Texas, and Director, SW Foundation for Research and Education, San Antonio, Texas.

Religion

I. Recognize the *Plan de Aztlan*

II. Take over already existing Church resources for community use, i.e., health, Chicano awareness-public information of its resources, etc.

III. Oppose any institutionalized religion.

IV. Revolutionary change of Catholic Church or for it to get out of the way.

V. Establish communication with the barrio and implement programs of awareness to the Chicano movement.

From Chicanas Speak Out. Women: New Voices of La Raza *by Mirta Vidal (1971). Copyright © 1971 by Pathfinder Press. Reprinted by permission.*

Educating the Black Child: Our Past and Our Future, Marian Wright Edelman, 1987

For many of you sitting in this room, it is the best of times. Black per capita income is at an all-time high and many of you have moved up the corporate ladder even if the ladders you are on frequently don't reach towards the pinnacle of corporate power. Black purchasing power, now at $200 billion, exceeds the gross national product of Australia and New Zealand combined. But it has not yet been translated into commensurate black economic influence and benefit. Black elected officials are more numerous than ever (6,681 in 1987, a 350 percent increase since 1970). But white economic power still controls our city tax bases. The amassing of committee and subcommittee chairmanships (8 full House Committee chairs including the Select Committee, and 18 Subcommittee chairs) by members of this Congressional Black Caucus is impressive by any standard, although the main political game in town is cutting the budget deficit. Spelman

College, my alma mater, looks towards its future with a stronger endowment and student body than ever before while many other black colleges are struggling mightily to survive.

Bill Cosby is America's favorite Daddy and Michael Jackson and Whitney Houston dot the top ten charts. Black leadership has permeated a range of mainstream institutions. Bill Gray chairs the House Budget Committee, Frank Thomas heads the Ford Foundation, and Cliff Wharton heads TIAA-CREF. A. Barry Rand is in charge of marketing at Xerox. Anita De Frantz is America's representative to the Olympic Committee, and Richard Knight is the city manager of Dallas.

I am proud of these and many similar accomplishments and applaud the black middle class for whom the times are good tonight. We've worked hard to get where we are. However, we have to work harder still to stay there and to move ahead.

But there is another black community that is not riding high tonight and that is going down and under. If you and I don't build a bridge back to them and throw out some strong lifelines to our children and youths and families whom poverty and unemployment and hopelessness are engulfing, they're going to drown, pull many of us down with them, and undermine the black future that our forebears dreamed, struggled, and died for.

I am grateful, therefore, that the Congressional Black Caucus has focused attention this year on Educating the Black Child. Just as Martin Luther King, Jr., and others accepted the challenge of their time, so the challenge of our time is educating all of our children in mind, in body, and in soul if we are to preserve and strengthen the black future.

It is the worst of times for poor black babies born within a mile of this hotel and in many inner cities around the country who have less of a chance of living to the first year of life than a baby born in Costa Rica. Black babies are still twice as likely to die in the first year of life than white babies.

It is the worst of times for black youth and young adults trying to form families without decent skills or jobs and without a strong value base. Young marriages have essentially stopped in the black community. Sixty percent of all black babies today are born to never married single mothers; 90 percent of those born to black teens are born to unmarried mothers. One out of two children in a female-headed household is poor. Two out of three (67.1 percent) children in black female-headed households are poor. If that household is headed by a mother younger than 25, three out of four are poor. Even when teen pregnancy results in marriage, young two-parent families are almost three times as likely to be poor as those with parents 25 to 44 years of age.

A significant cause of this black family problem lies in young black men's eroding employment and wage base. Only 26.5 percent of all black male teens were employed in 1986 and 61.3 percent of those 20 to 24 years old. And even when they are lucky enough to work they frequently can't earn enough to lift a family out of poverty. Between 1973 and 1984, the average real (inflation-adjusted) annual earnings among males ages 20 through 24 fell by nearly 30 percent (from $11,572 to $8,072 in 1984 dollars). This sharp drop affected virtually all groups of young adult males—whether white, black, or Hispanic although young black men suffered the most severe losses (nearly 50 percent). So the links between teen pregnancy and poverty are related not just to age and single parenthood but also to the poor skills and employment experience young parents seek to bring to the work force and to the lower wages young workers are paid.

To combat the poverty which is engulfing half of the black babies born today—half of our future as a black community—we must all work to prevent too early sexual activity and pregnancy and encourage our boys and girls to wait until they have the education and economic stability to form lasting families. If the share of single births in the black community grows at the rate of the last decade, by the year 2000, only one black baby in five will be born to a married woman. And if you don't care about these babies unselfishly you'd better care selfishly, for the future black voting and economic base upon which much of our leadership status rests resides in the health and education of the black child and the strength of the black family.

Not only are too many black babies and youths fighting poverty and sickness and homelessness and too little early childhood stimulation and weak basic skills preparation, they are also fighting AIDS and other sexually transmitted diseases; drug, tobacco, and alcohol addiction and crime which hopelessness and the absence of constructive alternatives and support systems in their lives leave them prey to. A black baby is seven or eight times more likely to be an AIDS victim than a white baby and minority teens (15 to 19) are the highest risk group for a range of sexually transmitted diseases. A black youth is five times more likely than a white youth to end up in an institution and is nearly as likely to be in prison as he is to be in college. Between 1979 and 1985 the number of black youth in juvenile detention facilities rose by 40 percent while the number of black youth entering college immediately after high school graduation fell by four percent. More black males go to prison each year than go to college. There are more black drug addicts than there are black doctors or lawyers.

Now some of you sitting here will ask what this has to do with you. You struggled and beat the odds and those folks who haven't made it could do the same. Others of you will rightfully say you're already doing your bit for the race by achieving yourself and by contributing to black organizations. Still others place the blame for growing black family poverty and weakening community bonds and support systems on urbanization and the continuing racial discrimination in national life which devalues black talent and curbs black opportunity.

As many nuggets of truth as each of these views may contain, I will simply say that unless the black middle class begins to exert more effective and sustained leadership with and without the black community on behalf of black children and families both as personal role models and value instillers and as persistent advocates for national, state and local policies—funded policies—that assure our children the health and child care, education, housing, and jobs they need to grow up into self sufficient adults, to form healthy families, and to carry on the black tradition of achievement, then all of our Mercedes and Halston frocks will not hide our essential failure as a generation of black haves who did not protect the black future during our watch.

Just as our nation is committing moral and economic suicide by permitting one in four of its preschool children to be poor, one in five to be at risk of being a teen parent, one in six to have no health insurance, and one in seven to face dropping out of school at a time when the pool of available young people to support an aging population and form a strong workforce is shrinking, so we are committing racial suicide by not sounding the alarm and protecting our own children from the poverty that ravages their dreams. For America will not treat our children fairly unless we make it.

We must recapture and care about our lost children and help them gain the confidence, self-esteem, values, and real world opportunities—education, jobs, and higher education which they need to be strong future guardians of the black community's heritage.

How do we do this? There are nine steps we must take if we are to help our children.

The first step is to remember and teach them that black folk have never been able to take anything for granted in America and we had better not start in these waning Reagan years of budget deficits and looming economic recession. Frederick Douglass put it bluntly: "Men may not get all they pay for in this world, but they must certainly pay for all they get." So you make sure that you are ready to do your part to help yourself and black children and to hold public and private sector officials accountable for doing their part in fostering health, education, and fair employment policies that are essential to black family survival.

Tell our children they're not going to jive their way up the career ladder. They've got to work their way up—hard and continuously. Too many young people want a fast elevator straight to the top floor and resist walking up the stairs or stopping on the floors of achievement between the bottom and the top. Tell them do their homework, pay attention to detail, and take care and pride in their work. People who are sloppy in little things tend to be sloppy in big things. Tell them to be reliable, to stick with something until they finish and resist jumping from pillar to post. And tell them to take the initiative in creating their own opportunity. They can't wait around for other people to discover them or to do them a favor.

The second step is to teach them the importance of getting a good education. While not a guarantee of success, education is a precondition to survival in America today. At a time when a smaller proportion of black high school graduates go on to college than ten years ago, we need to tell all of our children that college pays. In 1986, the average unemployment rate among black college graduates under 25 was 13.2 percent—more than one in every eight. Among young black high school graduates, it was 26.6 percent—more than one in four. College doubles their chance of getting a job. And we need to insist that they get a liberal education and learn how to think so that they can navigate an ever changing job market.

The third step is to tell them that forming families is serious business and requires a measure of thoughtful planning and economic stability. In 1986, one in every five black families with children under 18 had someone unemployed. Of those 44 percent were single parents with no one at work. Among black married couples with children, only 18 percent had no one working.

That is the crucial point. Education alone, although of enormous value in itself, cannot guarantee a young black adult the income needed to raise children in economic safety today. But two black adults, both working, have the safety net of the second income when unemployment strikes. Remember, that's the only safety net President Reagan hasn't found a way to cut yet.

All these figures are from 1986, the fourth year of a long period of economic recovery. When the next recession arrives—and it will—the black unemployment rates will soar. Since this recession will come at a time when we have an extraordinary budget deficit, there is a great danger that the American voters will buy the argument that we must cut government spending in order to reduce interest rates and stimulate the economy. If this happens, there will be many unemployed teachers, nurses, employment counselors, and government workers of all sorts.

There is a warning here that relates to steps one and two. Just as black penetration into civil and social service professional jobs occurs, the growth and security of such jobs fall. Just as blacks rise to senior ranks in industrial and industrial union jobs, steel and auto manufacturing industries enter a steep decline. The economic goal posts keep shifting. How, then, do we work towards a full share in the power to set the goals in place, and not just the right to run the race?

The fourth step is to set goals and work quietly and systematically towards them. So often we feel we have to talk loud rather than act effectively. So often we get bogged down in our ego needs and lose sight of our broader community goals. T. S. Eliot in his play "The Cocktail Party" said that "half the harm that is done in this world is due to people who want to feel important." Wanting to feel important is good, but not at the expense of *doing* important deeds—even if we don't get the credit. You can get a mighty lot done in this world if you don't mind doing the work and letting other people take the credit. You know what you do and the Lord knows what you do and that's all that matters.

The fifth step is knowing the difference between substance and style. Too many of us think success is a Saks Fifth Avenue charge card or a "bad" set of wheels or coming to this Black Caucus dinner. Now these are things to enjoy, but they are *not* life goals. I was watching one of President Johnson's inaugural balls on television with a black college president's wife in Mississippi when Mrs. Hamer, that great lady of the Mississippi civil rights movement who lacked a college degree, but certainly not intelligence or clear purpose, came onto the screen. The college president's wife moaned: "Oh my, there's Miz Hamer at the President's ball and she doesn't even have a long dress." My response was: "That's alright. Mrs. Hamer with no long gown is there and you and I with our long gowns are not." So often we miss the real point—we buy BMWs and fur coats before we think about whether where we're going to drive and wear them is worthwhile. Nobody ever asks about what kind of car Ralph Bunche drove or designer suit Martin Luther King, Jr., bought. Don't confuse style with meaning. Get your insides in order and your direction clear first and then worry about your clothes and your wheels. You may need them less.

The sixth step is valuing family life. We must build on the strong black tradition of family and teach our children to delay family formation until they are economically and emotionally stable and ready to raise the new generation of black children and leaders. Black and white men must support their children as best they can and not have them until they are ready to take responsibility for them. We must strengthen family rituals: prayers if we are religious, regular family meals, and participation in school work and in non-school activities. Our children need constructive alternatives to the street. We must *do* things with our children. Listen to them. Be moral examples for them. If we cut corners, they will too. If we lie, they will too. If we spend all our money on our backs and wheels and tithe no portion of it for our colleges, churches, and civic causes, they won't either.

We must join together as an entire community to establish an ethic of achievement and self-esteem in poor and middle class black children. They can do science and math as well as basketball and football, computers as well as cotillions, reading along with reggae. If we expect these accomplishments of them, support them in their learning processes, and help them in setting priorities. They need strong consistent adult buffers to withstand the negative messages of the external world that values them less than white or middle class children.

When I, like many of you, was growing up in my small segregated southern town, the whole outside world, the law of the land, local officials, the media, almost everybody outside our own community told black children we weren't worth much or were second rate. But we didn't believe it because our parents said it wasn't so. Our preachers said it wasn't so. Our caring teachers said it wasn't so. And they nurtured us as a community, shielded us against the constant psychological battery of our daily environment and made us understand that we could make it—had to make it—but in order to do so, we had to struggle to make our own opportunities in order to help change America. And we went on to college—poor and black—and tried to carry out their other lesson to give some of what they gave us back in service to others left behind. Service, they taught, is the rent you pay for living. Where is our buffer today for the black and poor children who are daily wounded by a national administration who would rather judge than help the poor? Where are the strong local officials and community voices and hands shielding and fighting for the poor children in our city streets against the ravages of drugs and crime? Where are the role modelling, mentoring, and tutoring programs that help black children overcome the pernicious undercurrents of many, even our purported friends, who really think black children lack the potential of other children? What activities are your churches and sororities and fraternities sponsoring to keep children busy and off the streets?

The seventh step is to vote and use our political and economic power. Only 51 percent of all voting age blacks voted in the 1980 election and only 56 percent in the 1984 election. Seventy percent of 18- to 25-year-old black youths did not vote in the last election. People who do not vote have no line of credit with people who are elected and pose no threat to those who act against our interests. Don't even pretend that you care about the black community, about poor children, about your nation, even about your own future, if you don't exercise the political leverage Medgar Evers and others died to make sure we had. And run for political office. And when you win don't forget that you are the means to serve others well and not the end.

No one running for president or any office should get black community support unless they have a well thought-out set of policies designed to lift the black child and family. Similarly, we need to use our economic power for the benefit of black families, particularly in industries where we constitute a large market share.

Two last steps and I'm done.

Remember your roots, your history, and the forebears' shoulders on which you stand. And pass them on to your children and to other black children whose parents may not be able to. As a black community today there is no greater priority than assuring the rootedness of all our children—poor, middle class, and Ivy League. Young people who do not know where they come from and the struggle it took to get them where they are now will not know where they are going or what to do for anyone besides themselves if and when they finally arrive somewhere. And if they run into bad weather on the way, they will not have the protective clothing to withstand the wind and the rain, lightning and thunder that have characterized the black sojourn in America. They need the anchor and rightful pride of a great people that produced a Harriet Tubman and Sojourner Truth and Frederick Douglass from slavery, a Benjamin Mays and Martin Luther King, Jr., and Fannie Lou Hamer from segregation, people second to none in helping transform America from a theoretical to a more living democracy.

The last step is to keep dreaming and aiming high. At a time when so many in public and private life seem to be seeking the lowest common denominator of public and personal conduct, I hope you will dream and set new examples of service and courage.

Dr. Benjamin Mays, a former president of Morehouse College and role model for me said: "It must be borne in mind that the tragedy of life doesn't lie in not reaching your goal. The tragedy lies in having no goal to reach. It is not a calamity to die with dreams unfulfilled, but it is a calamity not to dream. It is not a disaster to be unable to capture your ideal, but it is a disaster to have no ideal to capture. It is not a disgrace not to reach the stars, but it is a disgrace to have no stars to reach for. Not failure, but low aim, is sin." We must aim high for our children and teach them to aim high.

Address to the Congressional Black Caucus 17th annual legislative weekend banquet at the Washington Hilton Hotel, September 26, 1987. Reprinted by permission.

It's the Family, Stupid! Kate Kendall, 1999

My life experienced a significant intersection in the past few weeks. On June 27 1996, my partner Sandy, gave birth to our son, Julian Lucas. And, as first Legal Director and now Executive Director at the National Center for Lesbian Rights I have the honor of working daily on ground-breaking litigation on behalf of families of lesbians and gay men. The personal is political.

After years of being marginalized, raving, fringe dwelling, sex addicts, lesbians and gay men are finally emerging in an image which embodies the Radical Right's worst nightmare: family. Yes, after being seen as only uniformly depraved we are now increasingly portrayed as what many of us are—fine, tax-paying citizens, pushing baby strollers or park swings. I am convinced that as long as we could be successfully characterized as the "other," we posed little threat to middle America and her so-called "family values." But what is a gay-baiting, homophobe to do when we look like him? When our kids attend school with hers? We hit too close for comfort. For if we, the disgusting, are so much like she, the pious, maybe she could be we? No wonder we have become the universal symbol for evil.

Now of course this is not to say that we all should get married and have children. In fact many of us should never do either. But after years of the existence of our families being denied or ignored it now is impossible to do either, and that has our enemies apoplectic with fear. The high ground on "family values" becomes decidedly more crowded when we stand there as well and, in fact, teach them a thing or two about true values, such as acceptance, tolerance, diversity and self-empowerment.

It is no coincidence that issues of lesbian and gay equality have hit their zenith at the same time more lesbians and gay men are having children, creating families and fighting for equal marriage rights. These are mainstream issues coming from a community that for decades has been viewed as a bunch of pedophiles incapable of commitment. Many of us who bought into that image as well have altered our own perceptions and recognized that being a lesbian or gay parent is not an oxymoron. Family is in. From Children of Lesbians and Gays Everywhere (COLAGE), to Parents and Friends of Lesbians and Gays (PFLAG), to the Alternative Family Project to the National Center for Lesbian Rights (NCLR)—the family is the thing, we all came from one and we can have one of our own creation if we so choose.

For me perhaps the most exciting growing trend I observe is the increasing number of gay men who are choosing to parent. Who are overcoming substantial biological obstacles in order to make real their desire to have and raise children. I love the gay male parents I know. They blast sex roles, they dismantle patriarchy, and they really do a mind trip on our enemies. To those enemies gay fathers are seen as predatory child abusers, lesbian mothers as castigating, man-hating child manipulators. Yet with each family, with each child, with each parent, those myths are dying, slowly but surely from sheer lack of credibility or any shred of truth. We are changing perceptions because we are not, nor have we ever been, guilty as stereotyped. We didn't believe the hype and in fact have defied the hype.

It is clear that our families are making their mark. Not only are we more visible and our opposition more vitriolic, but we are now in court more often—fighting each other. Now it may be odd of me to celebrate this fact, which I don't, but the fact is when we are in court as a family, fighting among ourselves for custody or visitation or paternity, we force the courts to deal with us—to see us. As disheartening to me as inter-community battles are, they do send the clear message that we are here. Such battles do force the legal system—often our foe—to adjust, even imperceptibly, to our needs. Real change happens in maddeningly slow increments.

The best news is that a generation is now being raised by us in numbers sufficient to make a difference—to force change. These kids, our kids, will know the truth, and will be able to unmask the lies and fear-mongering perpetuated by the Radical Right. We will raise our families, we will fight the good fight, we will continue to do battle, and just when we are too weary to continue we will prevail. I pray for my family, and yours, that this will be so.

Fron the National Center for Lesbian Rights website. Reprinted by permission.

Women and Work

Women have endured unsafe workplaces, discrimination, low pay, and sexual harassment. For more than a century, women have identified, challenged, and sought to change these and other conditions. In the 1890s, social reformers began seeking ways to end employment practices that kept laborers in poverty and required workers to labor for long hours. They also fought to require employers to provide safe and healthy work environments. One of the more notable crusaders was Florence Kelley whose reform efforts included ending child labor. In her 1905 speech to the National American Woman Suffrage Association, she argued that voting rights would allow women to end child labor.

Dolores Huerta has dedicated her life to improving the working conditions of Mexican-American agricultural laborers. A cofounder with César Chávez of the United Farm Workers of America, she has led grape and strawberry boycotts, organized laborers, picketed growers, and negotiated labor contracts. Her dedication to agricultural laborers has helped end some of the worst abuses of workers and has helped improve their lives through increased wages, by implementing safeguards against exposure to agricultural chemicals, and by insisting on educational opportunities for laborers' children. Her narrative provides perspectives on her work and the work of the laborers she has served since the late 1950s.

Sexual harassment has long plagued women's work lives, but it only gained wide public attention in 1991, when law professor Anita Hill accused Supreme Court nominee Clarence Thomas of sexually harassing her. Hill's allegations led to the Senate Judiciary Committee reopening Thomas's confirmation hearings and to a national debate on the topic. Thomas was confirmed, but the debate continued.

Until passage of the Equal Pay Act of 1963, it was legal to pay women less than men holding the same job with the same responsibilities. After passage of the measure, however, women continued to earn less than men. AFL-CIO vice president Linda Chavez-Thompson focused on the enduring problem of the wage gap between women earners and men earners in her statement on Equal Pay Day in 1998.

Child Labor and Woman Suffrage, Florence Kelley, 1905

We have, in this country, two million children under the age of sixteen years who are earning their bread. They vary in age from six and seven years (in the cotton mills of Georgia) and eight, nine and ten years (in the coal-breakers of Pennsylvania), to fourteen, fifteen and sixteen years in more enlightened States.

No other portion of the wage earning class increased so rapidly from decade to decade as the young girls from fourteen to twenty years. Men increase, women increase, youth increase, boys increase in the ranks of the breadwinners; but no contingent so doubles from census period to census period (both by percent and by count of heads), as does the contingent of girls between twelve and twenty years of age. They are in commerce, in offices, in manufacture.

To-night while we sleep, several thousand little girls will be working in textile mills, all the night through, in the deafening noise of the spindles and the looms spinning and weaving cotton and woolen, silks and ribbons for us to buy.

In Alabama the law provides that a child under sixteen years of age shall not work in a cotton mill at night longer than eight hours, and Alabama does better in this respect than any other Southern State. North and South Carolina and

Georgia place no restriction upon the work of children at night; and while we sleep little white girls will be working to-night in the mills in those States, working eleven hours at night.

In Georgia there is no restriction whatever! A girl of six or seven years, just tall enough to reach the bobbins, may work eleven hours by day or by night. And they will do so to-night, while we sleep.

Nor is it only in the South that these things occur. Alabama does better than New Jersey. For Alabama limits the children's work at night to eight hours, while New Jersey permits it all night long. Last year New Jersey took a long backward step. A good law was repealed which had required women and [children] to stop work at six in the evening and at noon on Friday. Now, therefore, in New Jersey, boys and girls, after the 14th birthday, enjoy the pitiful privilege of working all night long.

In Pennsylvania, until last May it was lawful for children, 13 years of age, to work twelve hours at night. A little girl, on her thirteenth birthday, could start away from her home at half past five in the afternoon, carrying her pail of midnight luncheon as happier people carry their midday luncheon, and could work in the mill from six at night until six in the morning, without violating any law of the Commonwealth.

If the mothers and the teachers in Georgia could vote, would the Georgia Legislature have refused at every session for the last three years to stop the work in the mills of children under twelve years of age?

Would the New Jersey Legislature have passed that shameful repeal bill enabling girls of fourteen years to work all night, if the mothers in New Jersey were enfranchised? Until the mothers in the great industrial States are enfranchised, we shall none of us be able to free our consciences from participation in this great evil. No one in this room to-night can feel free from such participation. The children make our shoes in the shoe factories; they knit our stockings, our knitted underwear in the knitting factories. They spin and weave our cotton underwear in the cotton mills. Children braid straw for our hats, they spin and weave the silk and velvet wherewith we trim our hats. They stamp buckles and metal ornaments of all kinds, as well as pins and hat-pins. Under the sweating system, tiny children make artificial flowers and neckwear for us to buy. They carry bundles of garments from the factories to the tenements, little beasts of burden, robbed of school life that they may work for us.

We do not wish this. We prefer to have our work done by men and women. But we are almost powerless. Not wholly powerless, however, are citizens who enjoy the right of petition. For myself, I shall use this power in every possible way until the right to the ballot is granted, and then I shall continue to use both.

What can we do to free our consciences? There is one line of action by which we can do much. We can enlist the workingmen on behalf of our enfranchisement just in proportion as we strive with them to free the children. No labor organization in this country ever fails to respond to an appeal for help in the freeing of the children.

For the sake of the children, for the Republic in which these children will vote after we are dead, and for the sake of our cause, we should enlist the workingmen voters, with us, in this task of freeing the children from toil.

Dolores Huerta Talks, Dolores Huerta, 1972

My family goes way back to the 1600s in New Mexico. My father was a migrant worker who used to travel from New Mexico to Wyoming, following the work, living in little shacks. My mother was a very ambitious woman. She got a little lunch counter together, then she got a bigger restaurant, and when the war came she got a hotel. That's how I was able to go to school and how I got a more affluent background than the other kids.

When my dad and my mom divorced, he stayed in New Mexico and she came to California. I would beg my mother to let me go to the fields when I was little, but she would not let me. My brothers used to go pick tomatoes in Stockton, but my mother wasn't going to let *her* daughter go work in any field. So when I was fourteen, I went to work in the packing sheds instead, which were just as bad.

I was a little bit luckier than most Chicanos because I was raised in an integrated neighborhood. All the Chicanos who went to school where I did are all making it. We grew up in Stockton but we weren't in a ghetto. In our school, there was the Mexican, black, white, Indian, Italian; we were all thrown in together. We had all of the old-guard teachers who treated everybody very mean. But they didn't discriminate against one or the other. They treated us all equally mean. So we all hated the teachers, but we didn't hate each other. We didn't have a whole bunch of hang-ups, like hating Anglos, or hating blacks.

When I got into high school, then it was really segregated. There was the real rich and the real poor. We were poor too, and I got hit with a lot of racial discrimination. My four years in high school hit me very hard and it took me a long time to get over it.

When I was in high school I got straight A's in all of my compositions. I can't write any more, but I used to be able to write really nice, poetry and everything. But the teacher told me at the end of the year that she couldn't give me an A because she knew that somebody was writing my papers for me. That really discouraged me, because I used to stay up all night and think, and try to make every paper different, and try to put words in there that I thought were nice. Well, it just kind of crushed me.

I couldn't be active in college though, because it was just too early. I was the only Chicano at Stockton Junior College. At that time, there was just a handful of us that you might call liberals.

I was frustrated. I had a fantastic complex because I seemed to be out of step with everybody and everything. You're trying to go to school and yet you see all of these injustices. It was just such a complex!

Then my mother took me to Mexico City when I was about seventeen. She had never been there either. It was our first trip. But that opened my eyes to the fact that there was nothing wrong with Chicanos. I felt inside that [in the United States] everybody was wrong and I was right. They were wrong in beating the people up in the streets and all of the things they did to people. I felt I had all of these frustrations inside of me, so I started joining different Chicano organizations—El Comité Honorífico, Women's Club, all of these organizations that didn't do anything but give dances and celebrate the Fiestas Patrias.

By the time I was twenty-five years old, I had been married and gotten a divorce. I was still living in Stockton when Fred Ross came into town and he started telling us about forming this organization, the Community Service Organization.

And he told us about how in Los Angeles they had sent these policemen to San Quentin and Fred had organized it.

When Fred started telling us that if we got together we could register voters, elect Spanish-speaking representatives, and turn everything around, I just didn't believe it. He showed us how they had gotten these clinics in San Jose and he told us about César Chávez. He showed me all these pictures of big meetings with one hundred to two hundred people together. Well, I thought he was telling me a fairy tale.

I thought he was a Communist, so I went to the FBI and had him checked out. I really did that. I used to work for the Sheriff's Department. See how middle-class I was. In fact, I was a registered Republican at the time. I don't think I was ever a real cop-out, though, because I had always been real close to a lot of the people. My mother even used to tell me all the time that all my friends were either ex-cons or pachucos [zoot-suiters].

But I always thank the day that I met Fred. I always hated injustice and I always wanted to do something to change things. Fred opened a door for me. He changed my whole life. If it weren't for Fred, I'd probably just be in some stupid suburb somewhere.

Anyway, I started my first job getting people to register to vote. Eventually, some of the people started paying attention to us. So then we started fighting the Police Department and we got them to stop searching and harassing people arbitrarily. Then we had a big fight with the County Hospital and we turned that around. But it was just like magic. You start registering people to vote and all of these things start happening.

I was actually in the organization for two years before I got to talk to César [Chávez]. I met him once, but he was very shy. He wouldn't talk to anybody except the people he was organizing. But I heard him speak one time at a board meeting and I was really impressed. Well, after a big voter registration drive in 1960 where we registered one hundred and fifty thousand people, César got this bright idea to send me to Sacramento.

So I went to Sacramento and we got all these bills passed. I headed up the legislative program in 1961 when we fought for the old-age pension for the noncitizens, for *los viejitos* [the little old people]. I lobbied the welfare bill through so that the parents could stay in the home. César and I and the rest of us worked to get the right to register voters door to door, and the right for people to take their driver's license exams in Spanish, and disability insurance for farm workers, and the right for people to get surplus commodities. And, of course, we were the ones who ended the bracero program. I have a lot of experience in legislation, and I guess I've become sort of a trouble-shooter in the union.

I guess because I'm articulate, I came to the forefront. A lot of people who do a lot of hard work in the union are not mentioned anywhere. "Son los soldados razos del movimiento" [We are the common soldiers of the movement]. And that's what I consider myself—just a person working at what I'm supposed to be doing. The fact that I get publicity is sort of a by-product of the union. But there's an awful lot of people who have worked continuously since the union started, a lot of women, for example, who nobody even knows.

There's been no reaction from the farm workers to my role as a woman within the union. They will appreciate anybody who will come in to help them.

In terms of the leadership itself I get very little friction from anybody, really. Anyone who can do the job is welcome to come in and share the suffering.

There are a lot of other women in the union besides me and they share some of my problems. But I think it's mostly a personal conflict and it depends how much you let it hang you up in terms of what you're doing. If you let it bug you when people say that you're not being a good mother because you're not with your kids twenty-four hours a day, well then of course it will deter you from what you're doing. In the union, you know, everybody cooperates to take care of your kids.

The idea of the communal family is not new and progressive. It's really kind of old-fashioned. Remember when you were little you always had your uncles, your aunts, your grandmother, and your comrades around. As a child in the Mexican culture you identified with a lot of people, not just your mother and father like they do in the middle-class homes. When people are poor their main interest is family relationships. A baptism or a wedding is a big thing. In middle-class homes you start getting away from that and people become more materialistic. When you have relatives come to visit it's a nuisance instead of a great big occasion.

While I was in jail some of my kids came down to Delano to see me, but my little girl, Angela, didn't come. She wrote me a little note which said, "Dear Mom. I love you very much, but I can't come because the people need me. I've got to go door-knocking this weekend and I can't leave my job." I think that's really great because she puts her priorities on the work she has to do instead of coming down to see me.

The time I spend with my kids is very limited. This year I was in Washington, D.C., for almost two months, then I was in Arizona for another six weeks, then I was in Los Angeles working on the McGovern campaign for another two weeks. So this year I've spent very little time with my children. Since August twenty-seventh I've seen them twice for visits for about an hour.

Sure, it's a hardship for me, but I know that my kids are all working in the union itself. They have to grow up with the responsibility of their work, but they have fun too. Probably the problems they have is like the kind of schools that they go to which are very reactionary.

I think it's important for the children to be fed and clothed, which they are. When I first started working with César I had this problem worrying about whether my kids were going to eat or not, because at the time I started working for the union I was making pretty good money, and I knew I was going to start working without any money, and I wondered how I could do it. But the kids have never gone hungry. We've had some rough times, particularly in Delano during the strike, because my kids went without fresh milk for two years. They just had powdered milk we got through donations. It's made them understand what hardship is, and this is good because you can't really relate to suffering unless you've had a little bit of it yourself. But the main thing is that they have their dignity and identity.

My family used to criticize me a lot. They thought that I was a traitor to my Raza, to my family and to everybody else. But I think they finally realized that what I'm doing is important and they're starting to appreciate it now. They thought that I was just neglecting my children and that what I was doing was just for selfish reasons.

The criticism came mostly from my dad and other relatives, but my brothers are very understanding. My mother was a very active woman, and I just followed her. She's dead now, but she always got the prizes for registering the most voters, and she raised us without any hang-ups about things like that.

You could expect that I would get a lot of criticisms from the farm workers themselves, but it mostly comes from middle-class people. They're more hung-up about these things than the poor people are, because the poor people have to haul their kids around from school to school, and the women have to go out and work and they've got to either leave their kids or take them out to the fields with them. So they sympathize a lot more with my problem in terms of my children. Sometimes I think it's bad for people to shelter their kids too much. Giving kids clothes and food is one thing, you know, but it's much more important to teach them that other people besides themselves are important, and that the best thing they can do with their lives is to use it in the service of other people. So my kids know that the way that we live is poor, materially speaking, but it's rich in a lot of other ways. They get to meet a lot of people and their experiences are varied.

I know people who work like fools just to give their kids more material goods. They're depriving their family of themselves, for what? At least my kids know why I'm not home. They know that I'm doing this for something in which we're all working—it makes a whole different thing. My children don't have a lot of material things but they work hard for what they do get, just like everybody else, and that makes them really self-sufficient. They make their own arrangements when they go places. They all have a lot of friends and they don't get all hung-up about having a lot of goodies. I think my kids are very healthy both mentally and physically. All the women in the union have similar problems. They don't have to leave their families for as long as I do. But everybody shares everything, we share the work.

The way we do the work is we do whatever is needed regardless of what we'd really like to do. You have a problem when you develop into a kind of personality like César because that really takes you away from the work that has to be done with the farm workers in education and development of leadership. That's what I'd really like to do. I'd just like to keep working down there with the ranch committees and the farm workers themselves because they have to take over the union. I can put my experience there. César would much rather be organizing than anything. He loves to organize because it's really creative. But he can't do it because right now he has to go around speaking, as I am doing also. I'd rather be working on the strike.

It's hard when you learn how to do something but you have to do something else. But they've kept us on the run. We had been successful in organizing farm workers so in order to try to stop the union they introduced this bill, AB-964. This bill was just exactly like Proposition 22 and they thought they could get it through the legislature. Well, we mobilized and were able to stop it. Thousands of farm workers' supporters went to Sacramento to stop it. That was 1971. They tried it again in 1972 but the bill didn't really go very far. We had been involved with the lettuce negotiation all of last year, after we stopped the boycott. Then they got the bright idea in the Nixon administration to try to take the boycott away from us in the federal courts. What they were using as an argument was that we were covered by the National Labor Relations Law (NLRB) so that we couldn't boycott.

They took us to federal court in Fresno saying we were part of the NLRB. Well, this is ridiculous because we've never been part of it. So what this means is that it's strictly a political issue and logic and justice, none of these factors, have anything to do with it.

We went to Washington and started putting heat on the Republican party all over the country. We picketed people like Bañuelos [U.S. Treasurer Romana Bañuelos] and Senators Tower, Percy, and Hatfield. I was in Washington talking to the Republicans and the Democrats trying to stop this thing, kind of coordinating it.

In a way they might win by keeping us on the run but in a way they lose. Arizona is a good example, I was there for about two months before César went out there. They passed a proposition in the legislature similar to Proposition 22 here. So I called César up to ask him to come to a rally. I said "The governor's going to sign the bill but maybe if you come we can at least make a good protest." So we called the governor's office to tell him that César was going to be coming, and would he please give us the courtesy of meeting with us before he signed it. We thought we still might have a chance to stop it. Well, the governor knew that we were having this noon-time rally so he signed the bill at nine o'clock in the morning without even meeting with us. So what's happening now is we're getting everybody registered to vote, we're going to recall the governor and turn the state upside down. We organized the whole state just because the governor signed the stupid bill. So you might say that they win because they make us come out to the cities, but maybe while we're here, we're organizing too. Every time they try to do something against the union it works in our favor.

The main thing they keep us from doing is working with the farm workers. We'd be going after other growers and going to other states but we can't do that right now. But maybe that's the way it's supposed to happen. It's like this letter that this farm worker wrote me. "Dice que parece que estamos siguiendo un mandamiento de Dios" [They say that it seems that we are following a command from God]. We see these things as bad things that are happening to us right now but maybe they're good things and we can't see them that way because God wants us to do them. Every time we had some problem that kept us from ending the grape strike, I'd always tell César it's because God wants us to organize something else before the grape strike is over.

We've been working more and more with the Democratic party, because it's been the more liberal of the two parties. We depended on the Democrats to pass all those bills I told you about. You hardly ever get Republicans to vote for you. We live in a practical world, in a world of survival. And when the Democrats do us dirt, "también los atacamos a ellos" [we'll attack them also], although on an individual basis. So we maintain a certain amount of independence because our first responsibility is to the farm workers.

It's not true that both parties are just as bad for Chicanos, because the few benefits that we have gotten have come through the Democratic party. The only thing I have to say to people who attack the Democrats is that they should attack the Republicans. They should be going after Nixon, after Secretary of Agriculture Butz, after Reagan and all of these Republicans in the valley who vote against us every single time. That's who they should be going after, not after the guys who are trying to help us.

On the other hand, if anybody needs straightening up in the Democratic party, we straighten them up. We went after certain guys, like Alex García who's a Mexican, and we almost got him defeated. He won by two hundred votes, and if it wouldn't have been for the fast in Arizona and our work on the McGovern campaign, we would have beaten Alex García, and Alex knows it.

I think that if people are dissatisfied with the Democratic party they should get involved and take it over. I've told Assemblyman Moretti that he can make a decision either for or against the poor people, and that if he's against us we're going to fight him. But you can't go saying this to Reagan. He won't even meet with us.

There were some problems at the Democratic Convention. It was really unfortunate because there was a little clique that was trying to put down McGovern. The rumor was going around that McGovern wouldn't talk to Chicanos. Well, this was ridiculous because in East Los Angeles McGovern would go to every little place Chicanos wanted him to go, and speak to them. But there were people who were spreading this rumor around. I think they were part of the Nixon sabotage squad! . . .

I know that the farm worker issue is not the only Chicano issue. But in terms of the visibility of the Chicano issues, I think first of all there wasn't an agreement among the Chicanos themselves on what the issues were. Some people talked about bilingual education, other people talked about something else. I don't know, there just wasn't that much of a consensus on what we wanted to make public. So, I talked to Senator McGovern's staff, Frank Mankiewicz and some other people, and I told them that Chicanos wanted more visibility there. Naturally, they turned to me and said they wanted me to make a seconding speech for Eagleton or somebody. And I told them that I didn't want to be in the limelight, that other Chicanos wanted the focus. So that's when they had Mondragón make the speech he made.

I would say the Chicanos were disorganized. They had a platform with a lot of Chicano issues which they wanted to submit. But it was put together kind of fast, I think. You didn't have a kind of cohesiveness. But that's not unusual, you see, because in the black caucus you had the same kind of divisions.

Understanding that Chicanos have to come from all walks of life, from different experiences and different communities, you're not always going to get everybody to think the same. I think the Chicano caucus they had in San Jose is a good idea, where you can get Chicanos to decide the two or three priorities we want for California and get everybody to push together on them. But again, you got too many factions going. Everybody wants their own thing.

We're just now reaching a level where we can get mature political participation. We're going to get it as people get more interested in politics and make it a life-long thing, like Art Flores who ran against Alex García in East Los Angeles. Art really likes politics and he wants to do the right thing and he's not afraid to tell a guy he's an s.o.b. Then there's Peter Chacón, who's an assemblyman, "pero es muy cobarde" [but he is very cowardly]. When people are doing something against Chicanos he's afraid to tell them so, because he says he has to rely on a lot of white votes. So he lets them tell *him* what to do. But if we would have had fifteen Chicanos in California who were really involved in politics, "pero que no fueran miedosos" [but who were not afraid], the whole McGovern campaign would have been run by Chicanos. But we didn't have enough guys who had the political savvy.

But that's all going to change. If you ever get a chance, go down to Parlier. Chicanos turned around the whole city council there. So when the farm workers set up a picket line in Parlier, the cops wouldn't even come near us. There's a whole change in the picture because those people exercised their political power, they participated in democracy.

The worst thing that I see is guys who say, "Man, they don't have no Chicanos up there and they're not doing this or that for Chicanos." But the "vatos" are just criticizing and they're not in there working to make sure that it happens. We criticize and separate ourselves from the process. We've got to jump right in there with both feet.

Most of the people doing the work for us are *gabachillos* [nice Anglos]. When we get Chicano volunteers it's really great. But the Chicanos who come down to work with the farm workers have some hang-ups, especially the guys that come out of college. "En primer lugar, le tienen miedo a la gente" [in the first place, they are afraid of the people]. Unless they come out of the farm worker communities themselves, they get down there and they're afraid of the people. I don't know why it happens, but they're afraid to deal with them. But you have to deal with them like people, not like they were saints. The Chicano guys who come down here have a very tough time adjusting. They don't want to relate to the poor farm workers anymore. They tried so hard to get away from that scene and they don't want to go back to it.

We have a lot of wonderful people working with us. But we need a lot more because we have a whole country to organize. If the people can learn to organize within the union, they can go back to their own communities and organize. We have to organize La Raza in East Los Angeles. We have to do it. We have one thousand farm workers in there right now organizing for the boycott. In the future, we would very much like to organize around an issue that isn't a farm worker issue. But we just can't because we just don't have the time.

Maybe some day we can finish organizing the farm workers, but it's going so slow because of all the fights we have to get into. We'll have a better idea of where we're at once the lettuce boycott is won. See, there's about two hundred to three hundred growers involved in the lettuce boycott. The same growers who grow lettuce grow vegetables like artichokes and broccoli. So if we get that out of the way we'll have about one third of the state of California organized. That's a big chunk. From there, hopefully, we can move on to the citrus and get that out of the way. We have to move into other states, like we did into Arizona.

It would seem that with the Republicans in for another four years, though, we'll have a lot of obstacles. Their strategy was to get Chicanos into the Republican party. But we refuse to meet with, for example, Henry Ramírez [chairman of the President's Cabinet Committee on Opportunities for the Spanish-Speaking]. He went around and said a lot of terrible things about us at the campuses back east. He thought that we didn't have any friends back there. But we do, and they wrote us back and told us that he was saying that the farm workers didn't want the union, that César was a Communist, and just a lot of stupid things. This is supposed to be a responsible man.

Then there is Philip Sánchez [National director of the Office of Economic Opportunity]. I went to his home in Fresno once when a labor contractor shot this farm worker. I was trying to get the D.A.'s office to file a complaint against the labor contractor. So I went to see Philip Sánchez to see if he could help me. But the guy wouldn't help me. Later when the growers got this group of labor contractors together to form a company union against us, Sánchez went and spoke to their meeting. It came out in the paper that he was supporting their organization. As far as I'm concerned, Philip Sánchez has already come out against the farm workers.

It's really funny. Some of the *Puerto Riqueños* who are in the President's Committee for the Spanish-speaking, man, they *tell* the administration what the Puerto Ricans need. "Se pelean con ellos" [They fight with them]. But the Chicanos don't. They're caught. They just become captives.

I spoke to a lot of the guys in Washington who were in these different poverty programs. Some of the Chicanos had been dropped in their positions of leadership. They put [other] guys over [the Chicanos]. . . . they put watchdogs on them to make sure that they don't do anything that really helps the farm workers. The guys are really afraid because there's just a few jobs and they can be easily replaced. They're worse off than the farm workers, you see. The farm workers at least have the will to fight. They're not afraid to go out on strike and lose their jobs. But the guy who has a nice fat job and is afraid to go out and fight, well, they've made him a worse slave than the farm worker.

An ex-priest told me one time that César should really be afraid somebody might write a book to expose him. I said, "Don't even kid yourself that César is afraid of anybody because he's not. The only ones who might scare him are God and his wife, Helen. But besides them he's not afraid of anyone."

He's got so much damn courage, "y así come es él" [and he is as he is]. That's the way the farm workers are. They have this incredible strength. I feel like a big phony because I'm over here talking and they're out there in the streets right now, walking around in the rain getting people to vote. "Son tan dispuestos a sufrir" [They are so ready to suffer], and they take whatever they have to take because they have no escape hatch.

Being poor and not having anything just gives an incredible strength to people. The farm workers seem to be able to see around the corner, and César has that quality because he comes out of that environment. César's family were migrant workers. It was kind of the reverse of mine because they started with a farm in Yuma but lost it during the depression. They had to migrate all over the state to earn a living, and they had some really horrible times, worse than anything we ever suffered. So there was a lot more hardship in his background. But his family had a lot of luck. His mom and dad were really together all the time.

César always teases me. He says I'm a liberal. When he wants to get me mad he says, "You're not a Mexican," because he says I have a lot of liberal hang-ups in my head. And I know it's true. I am a logical person. I went to school and you learn that you have to weigh both sides and look at things objectively. But the farm workers know that wrong is wrong. They know that there's evil in the world and that you have to fight evil. They call it like it is.

When I first went to work in the fields after I had met Fred Ross, the first thing that happened was that I was propositioned by a farmer. People who work in the fields have to take this every day of their lives, but I didn't know how to handle it. So I wondered if I should be there at all, because I had gone to college. I had gone to college to get out of hard labor. Then all of a sudden there I was doing it again.

I feel glad now that I was able to do it. It's good my kids have done field work now, too, because they understand what it all means. I feel very humble with the farm workers. I think I've learned more from them than they would ever learn from me.

From La Voz del Pueblo *(November–December 1972). Reprinted by permission.*

Sexual Harassment: The Nature of the Beast, Anita Hill, 1992

The response to my Senate Judiciary Committee testimony has been at once heartwarming and heart-wrenching. In learning that I am not alone in experiencing harassment, I am also learning that there are far too many women who have experienced a range of inexcusable and illegal activities—from sexist jokes to sexual assault—on the job.

"The Nature of the Beast" describes the existence of sexual harassment, which is alive and well. A harmful, dangerous thing that can confront a woman at any time.

What we know about harassment, sizing up the beast:

Sexual harassment is pervasive . . .

1. It occurs today at an alarming rate. Statistics show that anywhere from 42% to 90% of women will experience some form of harassment during their employed lives.

2. It has been occurring for years.

3. Harassment crosses lines of race and class.

We know that harassment all too often goes unreported for a variety of reasons . . .

1. Unwillingness (for good reason) to deal with the expected consequences.

2. Self-blame.

3. Threats or blackmail by co-workers or employers.

4. What it boils down to in many cases is a sense of powerlessness that we experience in the workplace, and our acceptance of a certain level of inability to control our careers and professional destinies.

That harassment is treated like a woman's "dirty secret" is well known. We also know what happens when we "tell." We know that when harassment is reported the common reaction is disbelief or worse . . .

1. Women who "tell" lose their jobs.

2. Women who "tell" become emotionally wasted.

3. Women who "tell" are not always supported by other women.

What we are learning about harassment requires recognizing this beast when we encounter it, and more. It requires looking the beast in the eye.

We are learning painfully that simply having laws against harassment on the books is not enough. The law, as it was conceived, was to provide a shield of protection for us. Yet the shield is failing us: many fear reporting, others feel it would do no good. The result is that less than 5% of women victims file claims of harassment.

As we are learning, enforcing the law alone won't terminate the problem. What we are seeking is equality of treatment in the workplace. Equality requires an expansion of our attitudes toward workers. Sexual harassment denies our treatment as equals and replaces it with treatment of women as objects of ego or power gratification.

We are learning that women are angry. The reasons for the anger are various and perhaps all too obvious . . .

1. We are angry because this awful thing called harassment exists in terribly harsh, ugly, demeaning, and even debilitating ways.

2. We are angry because for a brief moment we believed that if the law allowed for women to be hired in the workplace, and if we worked hard for our educations and on the job, equality would be achieved. We believed we would be respected as equals. Now we are realizing this is not true. The reality is that this powerful beast is used to perpetuate a sense of inequality, to keep women in their place, notwithstanding our increasing presence in the workplace.

What we have yet to explore about harassment is vast. It is what will enable us to slay the beast.

How do we capture the rage and turn it into positive energy? Through the power of women working together, whether it be in the political arena, or in the context of a lawsuit, or in community service. This issue goes well beyond partisan politics. Making the workplace a safer, more productive place for ourselves and our daughters should be on the agenda for each of us. It is something we can do for ourselves. It is a tribute, as well, to our mothers—and indeed a contribution we can make to the entire population.

I wish that I could take each of you on the journey that I've been on during all these weeks since the hearing. I wish that every one of you could experience the heartache and triumphs of each of those who have shared with me their experiences. I leave you with but a brief glimpse of what I've seen. I hope it is enough to encourage you to begin—or continue and persist with—your own exploration.

Reprinted by permission of the Southern California Law Review, *65 S. Cal L Rev. 1445–1449 (1992).*

Statement on Equal Pay Day, Linda Chavez-Thompson, 1998

Last September, the AFL-CIO—which with 5 1/2 million women members is the largest organization of working women in the country—asked working women in every kind of job—in every part of the country—to tell us about the biggest problem they face at work.

Ninety-nine percent said a top concern is equal pay.

And most women told us that despite the economic good times, it is just as hard now as it was five years ago to make ends meet. . . . or it's become even harder.

The truth is that working women need and deserve equal pay.

The wage gap between women and men is huge.

If it is not changed, the average 25-year-old working woman can expect to lose $523,000 over the course of her work life.

That's enough to make a world of difference for most working families.

It can mean decent health care . . . a college education for the kids . . . a secure retirement . . . and simply being able to pay the monthly bills on time.

That is what the wage gap now takes from working women.

It's the price of unequal pay.

Patricia Hoersten knows what that's about.

Pat served lunch and dinner at a diner in Lima, Ohio. She got paid half of what the male servers got paid—because her supervisor thought she only needed extra money, not money to live on.

The tragedy is that there are millions of women who are experiencing the very same injustice.

Is this a women's issue?

It is—but it's also a family issue, because women's wages are essential to their families.

Most working women contribute half or more of their household's income.

So when working women lose out, working families lose out.

The good news is that working women are joining together to fight for equal pay.

I've been able to hear from many of them.

One is Maria Olivas. She's a clerical worker at Columbia University.

Maria worked with her union to make sure that her employer disclosed how much it paid men and women for the same job. They found out that men were paid $1,500 more than women for the same job. After a long struggle, they were able to win equal pay.

There are lots more like her.

Grocery store clerks at Publix Supermarkets won $80 million in back pay because they were not getting equal pay and promotions.

But no woman should have to fight by herself for equal pay.

That's why the AFL-CIO has launched a nationwide grassroots campaign to fight for women's wages.

That's why the union movement is making equal pay one of the main goals of our 1998 Agenda for Working Families.

And that's why the AFL-CIO applauds, supports, and will work to enact the legislation being introduced by Senator Tom Daschle and Representative Rosa DeLauro.

This legislation will give women an important weapon to battle wage discrimination and to help close the wage gap. It's about time.

Reprinted by permission of the AFL-CIO.

Appendix 2: Facts and Statistics

Table A.1 Number of Women in Congress[A]

Congress	House of Representatives	Senate
65th (1917–1919)	1 (0D, 1R)	0 (0D, 0R)
66th (1919–1921)	0 (0D, 0R)	0 (0D, 0R)
67th (1921–1923)	3 (0D, 3R)	1 (1D, 0R)
68th (1923–1925)	1 (0D, 1R)	0 (0D, 0R)
69th (1925–1927)	3 (1D, 2R)	0 (0D, 0R)
70th (1927–1929)	5 (2D, 3R)	0 (0D, 0R)
71st (1929–1931)	9 (5D, 4R)	0 (0D, 0R)
72nd (1931–1933)	7 (5D, 2R)	1 (1D, 0R)
73rd (1933–1935)	7 (4D, 3R)	1 (1D, 0R)
74th (1935–1937)	6 (4D, 2R)	2 (2D, 0R)
75th (1937–1939)	6 (5D, 1R)	2 (1D, 1R)
76th (1939–1941)	8 (4D, 4R)	1 (1D, 0R)
77th (1941–1943)	9 (4D, 5R)	1 (1D, 0R)
78th (1943–1945)	8 (2D, 6R)	1 (1D, 0R)
79th (1945–1947)	11 (6D, 5R)	0 (0D, 0R)
80th (1947–1949)	7 (3D, 4R)	1 (0D, 1R)
81st (1949–1951)	9 (5D, 4R)	1 (0D, 1R)
82nd (1951–1953)	10 (4D, 6R)	1 (0D, 1R)
83rd (1953–1955)	11 (5D, 6R)	2 (0D, 2R)
84th (1955–1957)	16 (10D, 6R)	1 (0D, 1R)
85th (1957–1959)	15 (9D, 6R)	1 (0D, 1R)
86th (1959–1961)	17 (9D, 8R)	2 (1D, 1R)
87th (1961–1963)	18 (11D, 7R)	2 (1D, 1R)
88th (1963–1965)	12 (6D, 6R)	2 (1D, 1R)
89th (1965–1967)	11 (7D, 4R)	2 (1D, 1R)
90th (1967–1969)	11 (6D, 5R)	1 (0D, 1R)

Table A.1 Number of Women in Congress *(continued)*

Congress	House of Representatives	Senate
91st (1969–1971)	10 (6D, 4R)	1 (0D, 1R)
92nd (1971–1973)	13 (10D, 3R)	2 (1D, 1R)
93rd (1973–1975)	16 (14D, 2R)	0 (0D, 0R)
94th (1975–1977)	19 (14D, 5R)	0 (0D, 0R)
95th (1977–1979)	18 (13D, 5R)	2 (2D, 0R)
96th (1979–1981)	16 (11D, 5R)	1 (0D, 1R)
97th (1981–1983)	21 (11D, 10R)	2 (0D, 2R)
98th (1983–1985)	22 (13D, 9R)	2 (0D, 2R)
99th (1985–1987)	23 (12D, 11R)	2 (0D, 2R)
100th (1987–1989)	23 (12D, 11R)	2 (1D, 1R)
101st (1989–1991)	29 (16D, 13R)	2 (1D, 1R)
102nd (1991–1993)	28 (19D, 9R)	4 (3D, 1R)
103rd (1993–1995)	47 (35D, 12R)	7 (5D, 2R)
104th (1995–1997)	48 (31D, 17R)	9 (5D, 4R)
105th (1997–1999)	54 (37D, 17R)	9 (6D, 3R)
106th (1999–2001)	56 (39D, 17R)	9 (6D, 3R)

Note: A. This table shows the maximum number of women serving at one time. It does not include delegates from territories or Washington, D.C. Some of the women filled unexpired terms and others were not sworn into office.

Source: Center for the American Woman and Politics, Eagleton Institute of Politics, Rutgers University.

Table A.2 Women of Color in Congress

Congressmember	Heritage	Years Served
Patsy Takemoto Mink (D-HI)	Japanese American	1965–
Shirley Chisholm (D-NY)	African American	1969–1983
Yvonne Burke (D-CA)	African American	1973–1979
Barbara Jordan (D-TX)	African American	1973–1979
Cardiss Collins (D-IL)	African American	1973–1997
Katie Hall (D-IN)	African American	1982–1985
Patricia F. Saiki (D-HI)	Japanese American	1987–1991
Ileana Ros-Lehtinen (R-FL)	Cuban American	1989–
Eleanor Holmes Norton (D-DC)	African American	1991–
Barbara-Rose Collins (D-MI)	African American	1991–1997
Maxine Waters (D-CA)	African American	1991–
Carol Moseley Braun (D-IL)	African American	1993–1999
Corrine Brown (D-FL)	African American	1993–
Carrie Meek (D-FL)	African American	1993–
Cynthia McKinney (D-GA)	African American	1993–
Eva Clayton (D-NC)	African American	1993–
Eddie Bernice Johnson (D-TX)	African American	1993–
Lucille Roybal-Allard (D-CA)	Mexican American	1993–
Nydia Velasquez (D-NY)	Puerto Rican	1993–
Sheila Jackson Lee (D-TX)	African American	1995–
Juanita Millender-McDonald (D-CA)	African American	1996–
Julia Carson (D-IN)	African American	1997–
Donna Christian-Green (D-VI)	Caribbean American	1997–
Carolyn C. Kilpatrick (D-MI)	African American	1997–
Loretta Sanchez (D-CA)	Mexican American	1997–
Barbara Lee (D-CA)	African American	1998–
Stephanie Tubbs-Jones (D-OH)	African American	1998–
Grace Napolitano (D-CA)	Mexican American	1998–

Note: Eleanor Holmes Norton and Donna Christian-Green are delegates from the District of Columbia and the Virgin Islands, respectively.

Source: Martin, *Almanac of Women and Minorities in American Politics* (1999) and Center for the American Woman and Politics, Eagleton Institute of Politics, Rutgers University.

Table A.3 Women in Congressional Leadership Roles

U.S. Senate

106th Congress 1999–2001

Senator Barbara Boxer (D-CA), Deputy Minority Whip

Senator Kay Bailey Hutchison (R-TX), Senate Deputy Majority Whip

Senator Barbara Mikulski (D-MD), Secretary of the Senate Democratic Conference

Senator Olympia Snowe (R-ME), Secretary of the Senate Republican Conference

105th Congress 1997–1999

Senator Kay Bailey Hutchison (R-TX), Senate Deputy Majority Whip

Senator Barbara Mikulski (D-MD), Secretary of the Senate Democratic Conference

Senator Olympia Snowe (R-ME), Secretary of the Senate Republican Conference

104th Congress 1995–1997

Senator Kay Bailey Hutchison (R-TX), Senate Deputy Whip

Senator Barbara Mikulski (D-MD), Secretary of the Senate Democratic Conference

103rd Congress 1993–1995

Senator Barbara Boxer (D-CA), Deputy Majority Whip

Senator Barbara Mikulski (D-MD), Assistant Senate Democratic Floor Leader

U.S. House of Representatives

106th Congress 1999–2001

Representative Barbara Cubin (R-WY), House Deputy Majority Whip

Representative Diana DeGette (D-CO), House Deputy Minority Whip

Representative Rosa DeLauro (D-CT), Assistant to the Democratic Leader

Representative Tillie Fowler (R-FL), Vice Chairman of the House Republican Conference

Representative Kay Granger (R-TX), Assistant Majority Whip

Representative Eddie Bernice Johnson (D-TX), Democratic Deputy Whip

Representative Nita Lowey (D-NY), Minority Whip At-Large

Representative Deborah Pryce (R-OH), House Republican Conference Secretary

Representative Louise Slaughter (D-NY), Minority Whip-At-Large

Representative Lynn Woolsey (D-CA), House Deputy Minority Whip

105th Congress 1997–1999

Representative Eva Clayton (D-NC), Co-chair of the House Democratic Policy Committee

Representative Barbara Cubin (R-WY), House Deputy Majority Whip

Representative Rosa DeLauro (D-CT), House Chief Deputy Minority Whip

Representative Jennifer Dunn (R-WA), Vice Chair of the House Republican Conference

Representative Tillie Fowler (R-FL), House Deputy Majority Whip

Representative Kay Granger (R-TX), Assistant Majority Whip

Representative Barbara Kennelly (D-CT), Vice Chair of the Democratic Caucus

Representative Nita Lowey (D-NY), Minority Whip At-Large

Representative Susan Molinari (R-NY), Vice Chair of the House Republican Conference

104th Congress 1995–1997

Representative Eva Clayton (D-NC), Co-chair of the House Democratic Policy Committee

Representative Barbara Cubin (R-WY), House Deputy Majority Whip

Representative Rosa DeLauro (D-CT), House Chief Deputy Minority Whip

Representative Tillie Fowler (R-FL), House Deputy Majority Whip

Representative Barbara Kennelly (D-CT), Vice Chair of the Democratic Caucus

Representative Nita Lowey (D-NY), Minority Whip At-Large

Representative Susan Molinari (R-NY), Vice Chair of the House Republican Conference

Representative Barbara Vucanovich (R-NV), Secretary of the House Republican Conference

103rd Congress 1993–1995

Representative Nancy L. Johnson (R-CT), Secretary of the Republican Conference

Representative Barbara Kennelly (D-CT), House Democratic Chief Deputy Whip

102nd Congress 1991–1993

Representative Barbara Kennelly (D-CT), House Democratic Chief Deputy Whip

100th Congress 1987–1989

Representative Lynn Martin (R-IL), Vice Chairman of the House Republican Conference

Representative Mary Rose Oakar (D-OH), Vice Chair of the House Democratic Caucus

99th Congress 1985–1987

Representative Lynn Martin (R-IL), Vice Chairman of the House Republican Conference

Representative Mary Rose Oakar (D-OH), Secretary of the House Democratic Caucus

98th Congress 1983–1985

Representative Geraldine Ferraro (D-NY), Secretary of the House Democratic Caucus

97th Congress 1981–1983

Representative Shirley Chisholm (D-NY), Secretary of the House Democratic Caucus

86th to 93rd Congresses 1959–1975

Representative Leonor K. Sullivan (D-MO), Secretary of the Democratic Caucus

83rd, 84th and 88th Congresses 1953–1957 and 1963–1965

Representative Edna F. Kelly (D-NY), Secretary of the Democratic Caucus

81st Congress 1949–1951

Representative Chase G. Woodhouse (D-CT), Secretary of the Democratic Caucus

---

Note: Additional information from Biographical Directory of the United States Congress 1774–1989, U.S. Government Printing Office, Women in the United States Congress, Congressional Research Service and Congressional Women's Websites.

Source: © Copyright 1999. Center for the American Woman and Politics (CAWP). Reprinted by permission.

Table A.4 Women Appointed to Cabinet Positions[1]

Appointee	Position	Appointed By	Dates
Frances Perkins	Secretary of Labor	F. D. Roosevelt (D)	1933–1945
Oveta Culp Hobby	Secretary of Health, Education, and Welfare	Eisenhower (R)	1953–1955
Carla Anderson Hills	Secretary of Housing and Urban Development	Ford (R)	1975–1977
Juanita A. Kreps	Secretary of Commerce	Carter (D)	1977–1979
Patricia R. Harris	Secretary of Housing and Urban Development	Carter (D)	1977–1979
Patricia R. Harris	Secretary of Health and Human Services	Carter (D)	1979–1981
Shirley M. Hufstedler	Secretary of Education	Carter (D)	1979–1981
Jeane J. Kirkpatrick	U.N. Ambassador[2]	Reagan (R)	1981–1985
Margaret M. Heckler	Secretary of Health and Human Services	Reagan (R)	1983–1985
Elizabeth Hanford Dole	Secretary of Transportation	Reagan (R)	1983–1987
Ann Dore McLaughlin	Secretary of Labor	Reagan (R)	1987–1989
Elizabeth Hanford Dole	Secretary of Labor	Bush (R)	1989–1991
Carla Anderson Hills	Special Trade Representative[3]	Bush (R)	1989–1993
Lynn Morley Martin	Secretary of Labor	Bush (R)	1991–1993
Barbara H. Franklin	Secretary of Commerce	Bush (R)	1992–1993
Madeleine K. Albright	U. N. Ambassador[2]	Clinton (D)	1993–1997
Hazel R. O'Leary	Secretary of Energy	Clinton (D)	1993–1997
Alice M. Rivlin	Director, Office of Management and Budget	Clinton (D)	1994–1996
Laura D'Andrea Tyson	Chair, National Economic Council[4]	Clinton (D)	1995–1997
Carol M. Browner	Administrator, Environmenal Protection Agency[5]	Clinton (D)	1993–
Janet Reno	Attorney General	Clinton (D)	1993–
Donna E. Shalala	Secretary of Health and Human Services	Clinton (D)	1993–
Madeleine K. Albright	Secretary of State	Clinton (D)	1997–
Aida Alvarez	Administrator, Small Business Administration[6]	Clinton (D)	1997–

Charlene Barshefsky	U.S. Trade Representative[3]	Clinton (D)	1997–
Alexis Herman	Secretary of Labor	Clinton (D)	1997–
Denice Lachance	Director, Office of Personnel Management[7]	Clinton (D)	1997–
Janet Yellen	Chair, Council of Economic Advisors[8]	Clinton (D)	1997–

Notes: [1]Because each president defines cabinet-level differently, a combined figure for cabinet and cabinet-level positions is unavailable.

[2]The position of U.N. Ambassador was considered cabinet-level during the Reagan and Clinton administrations.

[3]The position of Special Trade Representative was considered cabinet-level during the Bush Administration, as is the U.S. Trade Representative in the Clinton administration.

[4]The position of Chair of the National Economic Council is a cabinet-level in the Clinton administration.

[5]The position of Administrator of the Environmental Protection Agency is a cabinet-level position in the Clinton administration.

[6]The position of Administrator of the Small Business Administration is a cabinet-level position in the Clinton administration.

[7]The position of Director, Office of Personnel Management is a cabinet-level position in the Clinton administration.

[8]The position of Chair, Council of Economic Advisors is a cabinet-level position in the Clinton administration.

Source: © Copyright 1999. Center for the American Woman and Politics (CAWP). Reprinted by permission.

Table A.5 Women in State Legislatures, 1895 to 1999

Year	Number of Women Legislators	Percentage of Total Legislators
1895	3	1.9
1897	6	2.7
1899	8	2.8
1901	1	0.3
1903	2	0.7
1905	0	0
1907	0	0
1909	2	0.6
1911	5	1.5
1913	11	1.9
1915	9	1.0
1917	12	1.1
1919	25	1.9
1921	39	1.0
1923	99	1.4
1925	141	1.9
1927	128	1.7
1929	150	2.0
1931	152	2.0
1933	136	1.8
1935	139	1.8
1937	147	2.0
1939	150	2.0
1941	154	2.1
1943	200	2.7
1945	236	3.2
1947	216	2.9
1949	220	2.9
1951	242	3.2
1953	299	4.0
1955	312	4.1
1957	317	4.2
1959	341	4.4
1961	325	4.2
1963	344	4.4
1965	377	4.8
1967	320	4.2
1969	315	4.1
1971	346	4.5
1973	444	5.9
1975	609	8.1
1977	703	9.3
1979	776	10.4
1981	912	12.2
1983	992	13.3

1985	1,101	14.8
1987	1,171	15.7
1989	1,268	17.0
1991	1,359	18.2
1993	1,527	20.6
1995	1,535	20.7
1997	1,605	21.6
1999	1,661	22.4

Note: Of the women state legislators currently serving, 249 (240D, 9R) or 15 percent are women of color: 171 African American, 49 Latina, 17 Asian American, and 12 Native American. Women of color constitute 3.4 percent of all state legislators.

Source: Cox, *Women State and Territorial Legislators* (1996); Center for the American Woman and Politics, Eagleton Institute of Politics, Rutgers University.

Table A.6 Statewide Elective Executive Women, 1969–1999

Year	Total Women[A]	Total Women Party Breakdown[B,C]	Total Positions	Percent Women
1999	89	45D, 41R, 1RP, 2NP	323	27.6
1998	82	34D, 45R, 3NP	323	25.4
1997	82[D]	34D, 45R, 3NP	323	25.4
1996	80[E, F]	33D, 44R, 3NP	324	25.6
1995	84	36D, 45R, 3NP	324	25.9
1994	73	40D, 30R, 2NP, 1I	324	22.5
1993	72[G]	42D, 27R, 2NP, 1I	324	22.2
1992	60[H]	35D, 22R, 2NP, 1I	324	18.5
1991	59[I, J, K]	34D, 22R, 2NP, 1I	324	18.2
1990	47[L]	34D, 11R, 2NP	323	14.6
1989	46[M]	34D, 11R, 1NP	322	14.3
1988	41[N, O]	32D, 9R	322	12.7
1987	45[P, Q, R]	36D, 9R	323	13.9
1986	45[S]	34D, 11R	323	13.9
1985	43	32D, 11R	323	13.3
1984	38[T]	26D, 12R	323	11.8
1983	34	24D, 10R	324	10.5
1982	34[U, V]	25D, 9R	324	10.5
1981	34[W]	25D, 9R	324	10.5
1980	34[X, Y]	26D, 7R, 1NP	N/A	N/A
1979	35[Z]	28D, 6R, 1NP	327	10.7
1978	32[AA,BB, CC]	25D, 6R, 1NP	N/A	N/A
1977	33[DD]	25D, 7R, 1NP	333	9.9
1976	32	24D, 7R, 1NP	N/A	N/A
1975	33	25D, 7R, 1NP	337	9.8
1974	26	18D, 7R, 1NP	N/A	N/A
1973	26	18D, 7R, 1NP	342	7.6
1972	24	18D, 6R	N/A	N/A
1971	24	18D, 6R	343	7.0
1970	24	15D, 9R	N/A	N/A
1969	23[EE]	14D, 9R	346	6.6

Notes: [A]These figures do not include: officials in appointive state cabinet-level positions (unless the appointment is to an elected position); officials elected to executive posts by the legislature; members of the judicial branch; or elected members of university Boards of Trustees or Boards of Education.

[B]"NP" indicates an officeholder elected in a nonpartisan race; "I" indicates an independent; "RP" indicates Reform Party.

[C]The Minnesota Democratic Farmer-Labor (DFL) Party is included in the Democratic (D) figures; the Minnesota Independent Republican (IR) Party is included in the Republican (R) figures.

[D]Includes Jane Dee Hull (R-AZ), elected as Secretary of State who became governor in 9/97 through constitutional succession; as well as Betsey Bayless (R-AZ) who Hull appointed as Secretary of State in 9/97, and Denise Bode (R-OK) who was appointed to the Public Service Commission in 10/97. Does not include Gloria Tristani (D-NM), who resigned to take a post with the Federal Communications Commission in 11/97.

[E]Does not include Frances Jones Mills (D-KY), who died in office 1/15/96 while serving as State Treasurer.

[F]Does not include Martha Whitehead (D-TX), who abolished her office of State Treasurer 10/20/96, thereby fulfilling a campaign promise.

[G]Does not include Mary Sue Terry (D-VA), who resigned as Attorney General 1/28/93 to run for governor, or Kay Bailey Hutchison (R-TX), who resigned as State Treasurer 6/14/93 after she won a special election to the U.S. Senate. Does include Martha Whitehead (D-TX), who was appointed State Treasurer and took office 7/6/93; and Kim Robak (D-NE), who was appointed Lieutenant Governor and took office on 10/4/93.

[H]Does not include Lena Guerrero (D-TX), who resigned as Railroad Commissioner 9/25/92.

[I]Includes Lena Guerrero (D-TX), who was appointed to the Railroad Commission and took office 1/23/91.

[J]Includes Susan Loving (D-OK), who was appointed Attorney General and took office 6/21/91.

[K]Does not include Mary Stallcup (D-AR), who was appointed Attorney General 1/1/91 and, who left office 1/14/91.

[L]Includes Norma Paulus (NP-OR), who was appointed Superintendent of Public Instruction 10/1/90.

[M]Includes Clarine Nardie Riddle (D-CT), who was appointed Attorney General and took office 10/27/89.

[N]Does not include Clarine Nardie Riddle (D-CT), who was appointed acting Attorney General 12/22/88.

[O]Includes Rose Mofford (D-AZ), who became Governor 4/5/88 following the impeachment and conviction of Governor Evan Mecham (R). She had been serving as Secretary of State when she became Governor by constitutional succession.

[P]Includes Mary Landrieu (D-LA), who was elected State Treasurer in November 1987. Voters cast two ballots; one to finish an unexpired term for which she took office 11/30/87; the other for her own four year term which began 3/14/88.

[Q]Does not include Mary Evelyn Parker (D-LA), who retired as State Treasurer 1/15/87.

[R]Does not include Ruth Meiers (D-ND), who died in office 3/19/87 while serving as Lieutenant Governor.

[S]Includes M. K. Heidi Heitkamp (D-ND), who was appointed Tax Commissioner and took office 2/2/86.

[T]Includes Margaret Kelly (R-MO), who was appointed State Auditor and took office 5/30/84.

[U]Does not include Barbara Kennelly (D-CT), who left her position as Secretary of State 1/12/82 to assume her seat in the U.S. House of Representatives.

[V]Includes Maura Melley (D-CT), who was appointed Secretary of State and took office 1/29/82.

[W]Includes Kay Orr (R-NE), who was appointed State Treasurer and took office 6/15/81.

[X]Does not include Juanita McDaniel (D-AL), who resigned as Public Service Commissioner 2/80.

[Y]Includes Mary Jane Odell (R-IA), who was appointed Secretary of State 11/3/80.

[Z]Does not include Paula Hawkins (R-FL), who resigned as Public Service Commissioner 3/21/79.

[AA]Does not include Elwill Shanahan (R-KS), who retired as Secretary of State 5/10/78.

[BB]Does not include Melba Till Allen (D-AL), who left office as State Treasurer 6/78.

[CC]Includes Annie Laurie Gunter (D-AL), who was appointed State Treasurer 6/78.

[DD]Includes Rose Mofford (D-AZ), who was appointed Secretary of State and took office 10/20/77.

[EE]Does not include Sarah Folsom (R-AZ), who died in office 6/11/69 while serving as Superintendent of Public Instruction.

Source: © Copyright 1999. Center for the American Woman and Politics (CAWP). Reprinted by permission.

Fact Sheet 1 The Gender Gap
Voting Choices, Party Identification, and Presidential Performance Ratings

The "gender gap" refers to differences between women and men in political attitudes and voting choices. Although the gender gap has historical roots, political differences between women and men have increased in scope and shown greater persistence in recent years. A gender gap has been apparent in voting behavior, party identification, evaluations of performances of recent presidents, and attitudes toward various public policy issues.

Voting Choices in Recent Presidential Elections

The 1996 presidential election was marked by an 11 point gender gap, the largest ever recorded, with women favoring Bill Clinton and men preferring Bob Dole. In 1992, the gender gap was 4 points. In both 1996 and 1992, women were less likely than men to vote for Ross Perot. All three presidential elections held during the 1980s showed notable gender gaps. In each of these elections, fewer women than men voted for the victorious Republican candidate (by 6–9 percentage points).

Presidential Candidates *Voter News Service**

	Women	Men
1996		
Bill Clinton	54%	43%
Bob Dole	38%	44%
Ross Perot	7%	10%
1992		
Bill Clinton	45%	41%
George Bush	37%	38%
Ross Perot	17%	21%

Voter News Service is the service which was known as *Voter Research and Surveys* until 1993. It is referred to on this fact sheet by the newer name.

	ABC News/ CBS News/ Washington Post		New York Times		NBC News	
	Women	Men	Women	Men	Women	Men
1988						
George Bush	50%	57%	50%	57%	51%	57%
Michael Dukakis	49%	42%	49%	41%	49%	43%
1984						
Ronald Reagan	54%	62%	56%	62%	55%	64%
Walter Mondale	46%	38%	44%	37%	45%	36%
1980						
Ronald Reagan	47%	53%	46%	54%	47%	56%
Jimmy Carter	42%	35%	45%	37%	45%	36%
John Anderson	9%	9%	7%	7%	8%	8%

Voting Choices in U.S. House Races

In recent elections, women more often than men have voted Democratic in U.S. House races.

Voted for Democrat for U.S. House

	Women	Men	Source
1996	53%	44%	*Voter News Service*
1994	54%	43%	*Voter News Service*
1992	55%	52%	*Voter News Service*
1990	52%	48%	*CBS News/New York Times*
1988	48%	45%	*CBS News/New York Times*
1986	54%	51%	*CBS News/New York Times*
1984	49%	45%	*CBS News/New York Times*
1982	57%	54%	*CBS News/New York Times*

Gender Gap a Factor in a Majority of Races

Elections in the 1990s show that the gender gap, which was evident throughout the 1980s in races around the country at various levels of office, continues to be a factor in a majority of races.

• In 1996, in 38 of the 49 races (78%) where *Voter News Service* (VNS) conducted exit polls on election day, there were gender gaps of at least four percentage points. There were gaps of this magnitude in 6 of 11 gubernatorial races, and in three of four at-large House races studied by VNS. In all but one of the 38 races with gender gaps, female voters were more supportive of Democratic candidates than were male voters.

• In 1994, in 51, or 81% of the 63 races where *Voter News Service* conducted exit polls on election day, there were gender gaps of at least four percentage points. In 49 of the 51 races with gender gaps, female voters were more supportive of the Democratic candidates than were male voters. In one of the two exceptions (the Ohio attorney general's race), women voters supported a female Republican at a greater rate than did male voters.

• Similarly in 1992, in 34, or 67% of the 51 races where *Voter News Service* conducted exit polls on election day, there was a gender gap of at least four percentage points. In 30 of the 34 races, women voters supported Democratic candidates in larger numbers than did male voters. In one of the four exceptions, women voters supported a female Republican candidate at a greater rate than did male voters.

• Likewise in 1990, in 43, or 61% of the 70 races where *Voter News Service* conducted exit polls there was a gender gap of at least four percentage points. In all but four of the 43 races with a gender gap, women voters supported the Democratic candidates in larger numbers than did male voters. In three of the four exceptions, women voters supported Republican women candidates at a greater rate than did male voters.

Races with the Largest Gender Gaps

In 1996, the races with the largest gender gaps (over 12 percentage points) were senatorial races; two were won by Democratic men and one by a Republican woman. In the 1994 election, the races with the largest gender gaps (14 percentage points in each case) were gubernatorial races with male candidates. In the 1992 and 1990 elections, the races with the largest gender gaps (14 to 16 percentage points) tended to be those with Democratic women candidates.

				Voter News Service	
			Women	**Men**	**Results**
1996					
GA	Senate	Max Cleland (D)	56%	41%	Won
		Guy Miller (R)	40%	55%	Lost
ME	Senate	John Brennan (D)	48%	39%	Lost
		Susan Collins (R)	43%	56%	Won
SD	Senate	Tim Johnson (D)	57%	45%	Won
		Larry Pressler (R)	42%	54%	Lost
1994					
AR	Governor	Jim Guy Tucker (D)	66%	52%	Won
		Sheffield Nelson (R)	34%	48%	Lost
KS	Governor	Jim Slattery (D)	43%	29%	Lost
		Bill Graves (R)	57%	71%	Won
MI	Governor	Howard Wolpe (D)	46%	32%	Lost
		John Engler (R)	54%	68%	Won
1992					
CA	Senate	Barbara Boxer (D)	57%	43%	Won
		Bruce Herschensohn (R)	37%	51%	Lost
CA	Senate	Dianne Feinstein (D)	64%	50%	Won
		John Seymour (R)	33%	46%	Lost
OR	Senate	Les AuCoin (D)	56%	40%	Lost
		Bob Packwood (R)	44%	60%	Won
1990					
CA	Governor	Dianne Feinstein (D)	58%	42%	Lost
		Pete Wilson (R)	42%	58%	Won
OR	Governor	Barbara Roberts (D)	56%	40%	Won
		Dave Frohnmayer (R)	29%	45%	Lost
TX	Governor	Ann Richards (D)	59%	44%	Won
		Clayton Williams (R)	41%	56%	Lost

Senate and Gubernatorial Races Where Women's Votes Provided the Margin of Victory

Below are U.S. Senate and gubernatorial winners from the past seven election cycles where election day voter polls indicated that women provided the margin of victory for winning candidates. In all but one of these races, women more often than men voted for the Democratic candidate. (In the 1990 Connecticut gubernatorial race, women favored the third party candidate.) In the races marked with an asterisk, men's votes were about evenly divided (within the margin of sampling error), while the women voters showed a clear preference for the Democratic candidate.

			Women	Men	Source
1996					
GA	Senate	Max Cleland (D)	56%	41%	*Voter News Service*
LA	Senate	Mary Landrieu (D)	54%	45%	*Voter News Service*
MT	Senate	Max Baucus (D)	52%	46%	*Voter News Service*
SD	Senate	Tim Johnson (D)	57%	45%	*Voter News Service*
IA*	Senate	Tom Harkin (D)	55%	49%	*Voter News Service*
MA*	Senate	John Kerry (D)	56%	47%	*Voter News Service*
MN*	Senate	Paul Wellstone (D)	55%	46%	*Voter News Service*
NC*	Senate	James H. Hunt (D)	61%	50%	*Voter News Service*
1994					
CA	Senate	Dianne Feinstein (D)	52%	41%	*Voter News Service*
NE*	Senate	Bob Kerrey (D)	59%	51%	*Voter News Service*
NJ	Senate	Frank Lautenberg (D)	55%	44%	*Voter News Service*
NM*	Senate	Jeff Bingaman (D)	59%	50%	*Voter News Service*
NV*	Senate	Richard H. Bryan (D)	54%	48%	*Voter News Service*
VA	Senate	Charles S. Robb (D)	50%	40%	*Voter News Service*
FL	Governor	Lawton Chiles (D)	55%	46%	*Voter News Service*
MD	Governor	Parris N. Glendening (D)	57%	44%	*Voter News Service*
OR*	Governor	John Kitzhaber (D)	57%	47%	*Voter News Service*
1992					
CA	Senate	Barbara Boxer (D)	57%	43%	*Voter News Service*
IL*	Senate	Carol Moseley-Braun (D)	58%	51%	*Voter News Service*
WA*	Senate	Patty Murray (D)	58%	51%	*Voter News Service*
WA	Governor	Mike Lowry (D)	57%	50%	*Voter News Service*
1990					
MN	Senate	Paul Wellstone (D)	52%	46%	*Voter News Service*
NJ	Senate	Bill Bradley (D)	54%	49%	*Voter News Service*
CT	Governor	Lowell Weicker (ACP)	42%	38%	*Voter News Service*
OR	Governor	Barbara Roberts (D)	56%	40%	*Voter News Service*
TX	Governor	Ann Richards (D)	59%	44%	*Voter News Service*
1988					
CT	Senate	Joseph Lieberman (D)	51%	48%	*CBS News/NY Times*
NJ	Senate	Frank Lautenberg (D)	51%	44%	*CBS News/NY Times*
NV	Senate	Richard Bryan (D)	56%	43%	*CBS News/NY Times*
WI	Senate	Herbert Kohl (D)	54%	50%	*NBC News*
1986					
AL	Senate	Richard Shelby* (D)	50%	47%	*CBS News/NY Times*
CA	Senate	Alan Cranston (D)	53%	47%	*CBS News/NY Times*
CO	Senate	Timothy Wirth (D)	53%	48%	*CBS News/NY Times*
GA	Senate	Wyche Fowler, Jr.(D)	50%	46%	*CBS News/NY Times*
LA	Senate	John Breaux (D)	56%	49%	*CBS News/NY Times*
NV	Senate	Harry Reid (D)	54%	45%	*CBS News/NY Times*
NC	Senate	Terry Sanford (D)	53%	49%	*CBS News/NY Times*
ND	Senate	Kent Conrad (D)	53%	45%	*CBS News/NY Times*
WA	Senate	Brock Adams (D)	52%	47%	*CBS News/NY Times*
PA	Governor	Bob Casey (D)	52%	48%	*CBS News/NY Times*

*Senator Shelby won his 1986 and 1992 races as a Democrat; he switched parties to become a Republican in 1994.

			Women	Men	Source
1984					
IL	Senate	Paul Simon (D)	55%	46%	*CBS News/NY Times*
IA	Senate	Tom Harkin (D)	53%	49%	*ABC News/*
					Washington Post
MI	Senate	Carl Levin (D)	52%	47%	*CBS News/NY Times*
VT	Governor	Madeleine Kunin (D)	1%	42%	*CBS News/NY Times*
1982					
MI	Governor	James Blanchard (D)	56%	47%	*NBC News*
NY	Governor	Mario Cuomo (D)	56%	48%	*NBC News*
TX	Governor	Mark White (D)	57%	50%	*NBC News*

Party Identification

Larger proportions of women than of men are Democrats.

	Democrats		Republicans		
	Women	Men	Women	Men	Source
April 1997	36%	26%	26%	31%	*Gallup Report/CNN*
June 1996	44%	33%	26%	29%	*CBS News/New York Times*
June 1995	31%	25%	29%	36%	*CBS News/New York Times*
June 1994	38%	34%	25%	29%	*CBS News/New York Times*
June 1993	38%	30%	28%	30%	*CBS News/New York Times*
June 1992	36%	29%	32%	34%	*CBS News/New York Times*
May 1991	38%	26%	28%	31%	*CBS News/New York Times*
May 1990	38%	28%	30%	32%	*CBS News/New York Times*
June 1989	36%	32%	31%	31%	*CBS News/New York Times*
May 1988	41%	32%	29%	31%	*CBS News/New York Times*
May 1987	44%	35%	30%	31%	*CBS News/New York Times*
June 1986	40%	35%	29%	28%	*CBS News/New York Times*
May 1985	38%	30%	31%	28%	*CBS News/New York Times*
April 1984	40%	37%	28%	31%	*CBS News/New York Times*
June 1983	43%	32%	21%	25%	*CBS News/New York Times*

A significant gender gap is also evident among the youngest voters (ages 18-24). Among those voters who identify with a party, a larger proportion of women identify themselves as Democrats and a larger proportion of men identify themselves as Republicans.

Democrats		Republicans		Independents	
Women	Men	Women	Men	Women	Men
38%	23%	24%	35%	35%	39%

Source: The Public Perspective, June/July 1996 (drawn from Gallup)

Presidential Performance Ratings

Throughout Bill Clinton's term in office, a gender gap has sometimes been apparent, with women more likely than men to support Clinton. At other times no gender gap has been evident.

Approve of the way Clinton is handling his job as President

	Women	Men	Source
April 1997	59%	50%	*Gallup Report*
March 1996	57%	47%	*Gallup Report*
December 1995	53%	49%	*Gallup Report*
May 1995	53%	48%	*Gallup Report*
January 1995	51%	43%	*Gallup Report*
July 1994	43%	42%	*Gallup Report*
June 1994	49%	42%	*Gallup Report*
April 1994	48%	48%	*Gallup Report*
November 1993	49%	46%	*Gallup Report*
July 1993	45%	38%	*Gallup Report*
February 1993	61%	57%	*Gallup Report*

Women were less likely to approve of George Bush's and Ronald Reagan's performances as President.

Approve of the way Bush is handling his job as President

	Women	Men	Source
July 1992	30%	33%	*Gallup Report*
July 1991	69%	72%	*Gallup Report*
July 1990	61%	66%	*allup Report*
July 1989	61%	72%	*Gallup Report*

Approve of the way Reagan is handling his job as President

	Women	Men	Source
July 1988	43%	59%	*Gallup Report*
July 1987	44%	54%	*Gallup Report*
July 1986	58%	69%	*Gallup Report*
July 1985	60%	65%	*Gallup Report*
July 1984	49%	59%	*Gallup Report*
July 1983	34%	51%	*Gallup Report*
July 1982	38%	48%	*Gallup Report*
July 1981	55%	63%	*Gallup Report*

Source: © Copyright 1997. Center for the American Woman and Politics (CAWP). Reprinted by permission.

In 72% (47 of 65) races where Voter News Service (VNS) conducted exit polls on election day, there were gender gaps of at least four percentage points - that is, a difference of at least four percentage points between the proportion of women's and men's votes garnered by the winner. There were gender gaps of this magnitude in 70% (23 of 33) gubernatorial races and in 75% (24 of 32) senatorial races. (See table entitled "Election 1998: Exit Poll Results by Gender in Races Where Voter News Service Conducted Exit Polls.") In all but 3 of the 47 races with gender gaps, female voters were more supportive of Democratic candidates than were male voters.

Outcomes Affected by Gender Gaps

There were thirteen races where a majority of women voted for a different candidate than did the majority of men. Five Democratic candidates owe their victories to women and eight victorious Republicans to men. (See table entitled "1998 Races Where Female and Male Voters Made a Different Voting Choices.")

VNS reports an average margin of error of four percentage points for its statewide polls. Using this standard, there are an additional six races where the votes of one sex were about evenly divided between the candidates while the votes of the other sex more clearly favored one candidate over the other. Among those races, there were four where men were about evenly divided and the Democratic candidates preferred by women won; there were two races where women were about evenly divided and the Republican candidates preferred by men won. (See table entitled "1998 Races Where Female and Male Voters May Have Made Different Voting Choices.")

Races with the Largest Gender Gaps

In fourteen races, the gender gaps exceeded ten percentage points. In three of those races, women's votes determined the winners: Senate races in New York and North Carolina where Charles Schumer (D) and John Edwards (D) won, and the gubernatorial race in Maryland, where Parris Glendening (D) won. In four gubernatorial races with large gender gaps, men's votes determined the winners: Bill Owens (R-CO); Jeb Bush (R-FL); A. Paul Cellucci (R-MA); and Robert Taft (R-OH). In the other seven races with gender gaps larger than ten percentage points, majorities of women and men favored the same candidates but by widely divergent margins. Those contests included the Senate races of: John Breaux (D-LA); Ben Nighthorse Campbell (R-CO); Christopher Dodd (D-CT); Byron Dorgan (D-ND); Barbara Mikulski (D-MD); and two gubernatorial races: John Kitzhaber (D-OR); Jeanne Shaheen (D-NH).

Women Candidates

VNS conducted exit polls in nine of the ten Senate races involving women candidates.(VNS did not poll in Hawaii.) In eight of these races, there were gender gaps. Women voters were more supportive of Democratic women candidates in five races: Barbara Boxer (D-CA); Blanche Lincoln (D-AR); Barbara Mikulski (D-MD); Carol Moseley-Braun (D-IL); and Patty Murray (D-WA). All of these candidates except Moseley-Braun won their Senate races. In two races with Republican women candidates (ND and WA), women voters were more likely than men to support the Democratic candidates.

VNS conducted exit polls in nine of the ten gubernatorial races involving women candidates. There were gender gaps in six of those races: Colorado, Connecticut, Maryland, Nevada, New Hampshire and Oklahoma. Women voted for women gubernatorial nominees in Arizona, Colorado, Nevada and New Hampshire. In three races, the majority of women voters favored the Democratic male candidate: Maryland, Rhode Island and Vermont.

*The data used for this article are from Voter News Service (VNS) which conducted exit polls in 65 races. VNS reports an average margin of error of four percentage points for its statewide polls; the margin of error for part of the sample (e.g. female or male voters) may be greater.

Source: © Copyright 1999. Center for the American Woman and Politics (CAWP). Reprinted by permission.

Chronology

1638	The General Court of Massachusetts Bay banishes Anne Hutchinson.
1648	Margaret Brent unsuccessfully seeks to have two votes in the Maryland Assembly.
1769	The Daughters of Liberty begin supporting the Nonimportation Agreement.
1776	Abigail Adams tells John Adams to remember the ladies and limit their husbands' power over them.
	New Jersey grants women the right to vote in its state constitution.
1777	New York defines voters as free, white, male citizens.
1780	Massachusetts defines voters as free, white, male citizens.
1783	New Jersey grants women suffrage rights.
1784	New Hampshire defines voters as free, white, male citizens.
1792	*A Vindication of the Rights of Woman* by Mary Wollstonecraft is published in the United States.
1807	The New Jersey legislature disenfranchises women.
1821	Connecticut makes abortion after quickening illegal.
	The first women's college-level institution, Troy Female Seminary, opens.
1826	The American Society for the Promotion of Temperance is founded.
1829	Fanny Wright becomes the first female speaker in the United States.
1833	Lydia Maria Child publishes *An Appeal in Favor of That Class of*

1833 cont.	*Americans Called Africans,* the first antislavery book by a northern abolitionist calling for the immediate emancipation of the nation's 2 million slaves.
	The Female Anti-Slavery Society of Philadelphia is founded.
1834	Lowell mill girls strike.
1839	Mississippi passes the first married women's property law in the nation.
1848	The first women's rights convention is held in Seneca Falls, New York.
1849	Amelia Bloomer starts publishing the *Lily,* a temperance newspaper and the first newspaper in the United States owned, edited, and published by a woman.
1850	Harriet Tubman begins leading slaves to freedom.
	The first national women's rights convention is held in Worcester, Massachusetts.
1851	Sojourner Truth addresses a women's rights convention in Akron, Ohio, making what becomes known as her "Ain't I a Woman" speech.
1853	Lucy Stone keeps her own name after marriage; other women who keep their names are known as Lucy Stoners.
1859	The American Medical Association announces its opposition to abortion.
	Kansas territory grants women the right to vote in school elections.
1860	Connecticut becomes the first state to prohibit all abortions.
1866	The Fourteenth Amendment is passed by Congress, defining citizens as male for the first time.
	The American Equal Rights Association is founded. It is the first organization in the United States to advocate national woman suffrage.
	Elizabeth Cady Stanton is the first woman to run for a seat in the U.S. House of Representatives, running as an independent. No woman, including herself, could vote for her.
1868	Sorosis, the first professional women's club, is founded.
	Susan B. Anthony and Elizabeth Cady Stanton begin publishing *The Revolution.*
1869	The National Woman Suffrage Association is founded.
	The American Woman Suffrage Association is founded.
	Wyoming Territory grants women the rights to vote and to hold public office.
1870	The American Woman Suffrage Association begins publishing *The Woman's Journal.*

The Fifteenth Amendment is added to the Constitution. It does not specifically exclude women from voting, and several women attempt to vote.

Utah Territory grants women suffrage.

1872   Victoria Claflin Woodhull becomes the first woman presidential candidate.

Susan B. Anthony and fourteen other women register and vote, testing whether or not the Fourteenth Amendment can be interpreted as protecting women's rights.

Congress passes a law to give female federal employees equal pay for equal work.

1873   In *Bradwell v. Illinois,* the U.S. Supreme Court decides that states can restrict women from practicing any profession in the interest of "preserv[ing] family harmony and uphold[ing] the law of the Creator."

Congress passes the Comstock law, defining contraceptive information as obscene material.

1874   The Woman's Christian Temperance Union is founded.

1875   In *Minor v. Happersett,* the U.S. Supreme Court rejects the argument that the Fourteenth Amendment grants women voting rights.

1878   The woman suffrage amendment, known as the Susan B. Anthony Amendment, is introduced in the U.S. Congress for the first time.

1879   Belva Lockwood successfully lobbies Congress to pass legislation permitting women to practice before the U.S. Supreme Court. She becomes the first woman admitted to practice before the Court.

1884   Belva Lockwood, presidential candidate of the National Equal Rights Party, becomes the first woman to receive votes in a presidential election.

1887   The U.S. Senate debates and defeats the woman suffrage amendment.

Utah women lose the suffrage rights granted them in 1870.

1889   Jane Addams opens Hull House in Chicago.

1890   The National American Woman Suffrage Association is formed by the merger of the National Woman Suffrage Association and the American Woman Suffrage Association.

The General Federation of Women's Clubs is founded.

Wyoming becomes a state with woman suffrage.

1893   The National Council of Jewish Women is founded.

Colorado women gain suffrage rights.

Mary Elizabeth Lease is the first female candidate for the U.S. Senate, running on the Populist Party ticket.

1893 cont.	Laura J. Eisenhuth becomes the first woman elected to statewide office by male and female voters when she is elected North Dakota's superintendent of public instruction.
1894	Clara Cressingham, Carrie C. Holly, and Frances Klock, all Republican, are elected to serve in the Colorado House of Representatives, the first women elected to serve in a state legislature.
1895	The National Federation of Afro-American Women is founded.
1896	The National Association of Colored Women is founded.
	Idaho women gain suffrage rights.
	Utah reinstates woman suffrage.
	The first woman state senator in the nation, Martha Hughes, is elected to the Utah legislature.
1899	The National Consumers League is founded.
1900	The first official women delegates (one each) attend the Democratic National Convention and Republican National Convention.
1907	The Women's Trade Union League is founded.
	Kate Barnard is the first woman elected to statewide office by male-only voters when she becomes commissioner of charities and collections in Oklahoma.
1908	The Alpha Kappa Alpha Sorority is founded.
	The U.S. Supreme Court decides that "sex is a valid basis for classification" in employment and that protective legislation is constitutional in *Muller v. Oregon.*
1909	The National Association for the Advancement of Colored People is founded.
1910	Washington state grants women suffrage.
1911	The Triangle Shirtwaist Company fire in New York City takes 145 women employees' lives and leads to the state legislature limiting the workweek to fifty-four hours and enacting a new industrial code.
	California grants women suffrage.
1912	Congress creates the Children's Bureau, and as its first director, Julia C. Lathrop is the first woman to head a major federal bureau.
	Tye Leung is the first Asian American woman to vote in a presidential election, in California, which granted women the right to vote in 1911.
	Kansas, Oregon, and Arizona grant women suffrage.
	The Progressive Party supports woman suffrage.

1913	Alice Paul and Lucy Burns form the Congressional Union, which later becomes the National Woman's Party.
	More than 3,000 suffragists parade in Washington, D.C., on the day of Woodrow Wilson's presidential inauguration, drawing attention away from his arrival. The marchers are mobbed by spectators.
	Ida B. Wells-Barnett founds the Alpha Suffrage Club.
	Illinois women gain presidential suffrage by legislative action.
	Women in the Alaska Territory gain suffrage rights.
	Delta Sigma Theta Sorority is founded.
1914	Annette Abbott Adams is appointed U.S. attorney for the Northern District of California, the highest judicial position ever held by any woman in the world.
	Women in Montana and Nevada gain suffrage rights.
1915	The National Birth Control League is founded.
	The Woman's Peace Party is founded.
	The U.S. House of Representatives votes on woman suffrage for the first time and defeats the measure.
1916	Margaret Sanger and Ethel Byrne open the first American birth control clinic and are arrested ten days after the opening.
	Republicans add support for woman suffrage to their platform.
1917	Jeannette Rankin (R-MT) becomes the first woman to serve in the U.S. Congress.
	Women in New York gain suffrage rights.
	Women in North Dakota, Nebraska, and Rhode Island gain presidential suffrage by legislative action.
	Women in Arkansas gain primary suffrage by legislative action.
1918	Kathryn Sellers becomes the first woman in the U.S. to hold a judgeship as she is named a judge in the juvenile court of Washington, D.C.
	The U.S. House of Representatives passes the federal suffrage amendment.
	The U.S. Senate rejects the federal suffrage amendment by two votes.
	President Woodrow Wilson declares his support for woman suffrage.
	Women in Michigan, Oklahoma, and South Dakota gain suffrage rights.
	Women in Texas gain presidential suffrage by legislative action.
1919	The Democratic National Committee creates the position of associate member for women.

1919 cont.	The U.S. Senate again rejects the federal suffrage amendment. President Woodrow Wilson pressures the Senate into passing the amendment. On 4 June, the federal suffrage amendment passes and goes to states for ratification.

The League of Women Voters is founded.

The National Federation of Business and Professional Women is founded.

Women in Indiana, Maine, Missouri, Iowa, Minnesota, Ohio, Wisconsin, and Tennessee gain presidential suffrage by legislative acts.

1920 Congress establishes the Women's Bureau of the U.S. Department of Labor, and Mary Anderson becomes its first director.

Annette Abbott Adams is appointed the first female U.S. assistant attorney general.

The Democratic National Committee adopts the fifty-fifty plan and replaces associate members with national committeewomen.

The Nineteenth Amendment to the United States Constitution, granting women full suffrage rights, is ratified on 18 August and signed on 26 August.

1921 Margaret Sanger organizes the American Birth Control League.

Representative Alice Mary Robertson (R-OK) becomes the first woman to preside over a session of the U.S. House of Representatives.

The Women's International League for Peace and Freedom is founded.

The American Association of University Women is formed.

The Sheppard-Towner bill for maternal and infant health education is passed by Congress.

1922 Emily Newell Blair becomes the first woman vice chair of the Democratic National Committee.

Rebecca Latimer Felton (D-GA) becomes the first woman sworn in to the U.S. Senate, an appointment that lasts only two days.

Florence Ellinwood Allen becomes the first woman to serve on a state supreme court when she is elected associate justice in Ohio.

Alice Brown Davis beomes the first woman tribal chief when she is appointed chief of the Seminole Nation by President Warren G. Harding.

The first Cable Act passes, giving married women citizenship independent of their husband's citizenship.

1923 Representative Mae E. Nolan becomes the first woman to chair a standing congressional committee, the House Committee on Expenditures in the Post Office Department.

The U.S. Supreme Court decides in *Adkins v. Children's Hospital* that a minimum wage for women and children is unconstitutional.

The first congressional hearings are held on a federal Equal Rights Amendment.

1924   Cora Reynolds Anderson is the first Native American woman elected to a state legislature when she enters Michigan's House of Representatives.

The National League of Colored Republican Women is founded.

1925   Democrat Nellie Tayloe Ross becomes governor of Wyoming, the first woman sworn in as a governor in the nation.

Fifteen days after Governor Ross is sworn in, Democrat Miriam Ferguson becomes governor of Texas.

Republican Cora Belle Reynolds Anderson, a La Pointe Band Chippewa, enters the Michigan House of Representatives, the first Native American woman elected to a state legislature.

1926   Bertha Knight Landes is the first woman elected mayor of a large city, in Seattle, Washington.

Gertrude Bonnin organizes the National Council of American Indians and becomes its founding president.

1927   Minnie Buckingham-Harper becomes the first African American woman to serve in a state legislature when she is appointed by the West Virginia governor to fill her deceased husband's seat.

1928   Republican Minnie Buckingham Harper becomes the first African American woman to serve in a state legislature when West Virginia's governor appoints her to the state's House of Delegates.

Genevieve Cline of Ohio becomes the first female federal judge as a judge for the U.S. Customs Court.

1930   The Association of Southern Women for the Prevention of Lynching is founded.

1931   Democrat Fedelina Lucero Gallegos and Republican Porfirria H. Saiz enter the New Mexico House of Representatives, the first Hispanic American women elected to a state legislature.

Jane Addams becomes the first woman to receive the Nobel Peace Prize.

1932   Senator Hattie Wyatt Caraway, appointed to the U.S. Senate in 1931, becomes the first woman elected to serve in the body.

The National Recovery Act includes a provision that allows only one family member to hold a government job. Many women lose their jobs.

1933   Frances Perkins becomes the first woman to serve in a president's cabinet, when Franklin D. Roosevelt appoints her secretary of labor.

1933 cont.	Democrat Miriam Ferguson begins her second term as governor of Texas.
	Republican Minnie D. Craig of North Dakota becomes the first woman speaker of a state House of Representatives.
	Ruth Bryan Owen (Rohde) is appointed head of a U.S. diplomatic mission to Denmark, making her the first woman to hold the position of Envoy Extraordinary and Minister Plenipotentiary.
1935	Sadie Tanner Mosell Alexander helps write Pennsylvania's 1935 public accommodations law prohibiting racial segregation.
	Mary McLeod Bethune becomes director of Negro Affairs in the National Youth Administration, appointed by President Franklin D. Roosevelt, making her the first African American woman to hold a major federal appointment. She also founds the National Council of Negro Women.
1936	A court case, *United States v. One Package of Japanese Pessaries,* finds that birth control information is not obscene and that contraceptive devices can be legally imported into the United States.
1937	Representative Mary Teresa Norton becomes the first woman to chair a major congressional committee, the Labor Committee.
1938	Democrat Crystal Bird Fauset becomes the first African American woman elected to a state legislature, the Pennsylvania legislature.
	The National Federation of Republican Women is founded.
1939	Marian Anderson sings at the Lincoln Memorial.
	Jane M. Brolin becomes the first African American woman to hold a judgeship in the United States when she is appointed to New York City's Court of Domestic Relations.
	The Birth Control Federation of America, which later becomes Planned Parenthood Federation of America, is founded.
1940	The Republican Party is the first major party to include the Equal Rights Amendment in its platform.
1941	Concha Ortiz y Pino becomes the first Hispanic woman to hold a leadership position in a state legislature as the house majority whip in New Mexico.
1944	The National Committee to Defeat the UnEqual Rights Amendment is organized.
1946	Eleanor Roosevelt is the first female delegate to the United Nations, appointed by President Harry S. Truman.
1948	In *Goesaert v. Cleary,* the U.S. Supreme Court concludes that state laws can allow discrimination in employment on the basis of sex.
1949	Eugenie Moore Anderson is appointed the first female U.S. ambassador.

Georgia Neese Clark becomes the first woman treasurer of the United States and the first woman whose signature appears on U.S. currency.

Senator Margaret Chase Smith becomes the first woman elected to the U.S. Senate for a six-year term whose husband did not precede her in the Senate.

1951   Ambassador Eugenie Moore Anderson becomes the first woman to sign a treaty between the United States and another nation.

1952   Progressive Party vice presidential nominee Charlotta Spears Bass becomes the first African American woman to have her name appear on the national presidential ballot.

Cora M. Brown becomes the first African American woman elected to a state Senate, the Michigan Senate.

1953   Oveta Culp Hobby is appointed secretary of health, education, and welfare by President Dwight Eisenhower.

The Second Sex by French feminist Simone de Beauvoir is published in the United States.

1955   African American Rosa Parks refuses to relinquish her seat on a Montgomery, Alabama, city bus, is arrested, and launches a boycott of the city's buses.

The Daughters of Bilitis is founded by Del Martin, Phyllis Lyons, and six other women.

1957   Patsy Takemoto Mink enters Hawaii's territorial legislature, the first Asian American woman elected to a territorial or state legislature.

Daisy Bates helps integrate Central High School in Little Rock, Arkansas.

1960   Ella Baker helps organize the Student Nonviolent Coordinating Committee.

1961   Elizabeth Gurley Flynn becomes the first woman chair of the Communist Party/USA.

Women Strike for Peace is founded.

In *Hoyt v. Florida,* the U.S. Supreme Court decides that an all-male jury does not violate an accused woman's Fourteenth Amendment rights.

President John F. Kennedy creates the President's Commission on the Status of Women.

1962   Dolores Huerta and Cesar Chavez found the United Farm Workers of America.

Rachel Carson publishes *Silent Spring* and helps launch the environmental movement.

1963   Betty Friedan publishes *The Feminine Mystique* and launches the modern feminist movement.

| 1963 | The Equal Pay Act of 1963 makes it illegal to have different rates of pay |
| cont. | for women and men who do the same work. |

The President's Commission on the Status of Women issues its report, *American Women*.

1964   Congress passes the 1964 Civil Rights Act, including Title VII, which prohibits discrimination on the basis of sex, race, creed, and national origin in employment.

Republican Margaret Chase Smith becomes the first woman to run for the presidential nomination of a major party.

Fannie Lou Hamer founds the Mississippi Freedom Democratic Party.

1965   In *Griswold v. Connecticut,* the U.S. Supreme Court overturns state laws prohibiting the prescription and use of contraceptives by married couples.

Representative Patsy Mink (D-HI) becomes the first Asian American woman to serve in the U.S. Congress.

Patricia Roberts Harris becomes the first African American woman appointed as a U.S. ambassador.

Lorna Lockwood is the first female chief justice of a state supreme court, in Arizona.

President Lyndon Johnson's Executive Order 11246 requires federal agencies and federal contractors to take affirmative action to overcome employment discrimination. The measure does not include women.

1966   Constance Baker Motley becomes the first African American woman appointed as a federal judge.

Olga Madar becomes the first woman member of the International Executive Board of the United Auto Workers.

The National Organization for Women is founded.

1967   Democrat Lurleen Wallace becomes governor of Alabama.

The Chicago Women's Liberation Group organizes.

The Day Care Council of American is founded.

New York Radical Women is founded.

The National Welfare Rights Organization is founded.

Executive Order 11375 amends Executive Order 11246 and prohibits sex discrimination in employment by the federal government and its contractors.

The federal Civil Service Commission creates the Federal Women's Program.

California becomes the first state to legalize abortion.

1968   Barbara Watson becomes the first woman and the first African American appointed to an undersecretary position in the Department of State when President Lyndon Johnson names her assistant secretary of state.

Federally Employed Women is founded.

The first national Women's Liberation Conference is held.

The Women's Equity Action League is founded.

New York Radical Women gains media attention for the women's movement when its members protest the Miss America Pageant in Atlantic City, New Jersey. The group also begins using consciousness raising as a tool.

The Equal Employment Opportunity Commission rules that sex-segregated, help-wanted newspaper advertising is illegal unless there is a bona fide occupational qualification.

1969   Representative Shirley Chisholm (D-NY) becomes the first African American woman to serve in Congress.

In *Bowe v. Colgate-Palmolive Company* the U.S. Supreme Court rules that women meeting the physical requirements can work in many jobs that had been for men only.

A federal appeals court finds that sex is not a bona fide occupational qualification for the job of switchman in *Weeks v. Southern Bell Telephone and Telegraph Company.*

The National Abortion and Reproductive Rights Action League is founded.

The National Association of Commissions for Women is founded.

1970   LaDonna Harris founds Americans for Indian Opportunity.

Comisión Feminil Mexicana Nacional is founded.

Betty Friedan organizes the first Women's Equality Day in recognition of the fiftieth anniversary of woman suffrage.

The Equal Rights Amendment is reintroduced in Congress.

California passes the first no-fault divorce law in the nation.

1971   Anne L. Armstrong becomes the first woman national cochair of the Republican National Committee.

Romana Acosta Banuelos becomes the first Hispanic American U.S. treasurer.

The National Women's Political Caucus is founded.

Ms. magazine is founded.

The Center for the American Woman and Politics is founded.

1971
cont.

New York Radical Feminists hold speak-outs and a conference on rape and women's treatment by the criminal justice system.

In *Phillips v. Martin Marietta,* the U.S. Supreme Court decides its first gender discrimination case under Title VII of the Civil Rights Act of 1964.

In *Reed v. Reed,* the U.S. Supreme Court creates an intermediate level of scrutiny that applies only to sex discrimination cases.

A federal appeals court finds that being female is not a bona fide occupational qualification for a flight attendant in *Diaz v. Pan American World Airways, Inc.*

1972

Representative Shirley Chisholm (D-NY) becomes the first African American woman to run for president and has her name formally placed in nomination at the Democratic National Convention.

Patsy Mink is the first Asian American woman to run for the Democratic presidential nomination, in the Oregon primary.

Jean Westwood becomes chair of the Democratic National Committee, the first woman to chair either of the two major parties.

Republican Anne L. Armstrong becomes the first woman to deliver a keynote address at a major party national convention.

Stop ERA is founded by Phyllis Schlafly.

Feminists for Life of America is founded.

The Ms. Foundation for Women is founded.

Ms. magazine begins publication.

In *Eisenstadt v. Baird* the U.S. Supreme Court rules that the right to privacy includes an unmarried person's right to use contraceptives.

Congress passes Title IX of the Education Amendments of 1972, outlawing sex discrimination in education in programs receiving federal financial assistance.

Congress passes the Equal Opportunity Act, giving the Equal Employment Opportunity Commission authority to take legal action to enforce its rulings.

On 22 March, Congress passes the federal Equal Rights Amendment and sends it to the states for ratification. By the end of the year, twenty-two of the necessary thirty-eight states ratify it.

1973

Anne Armstrong becomes the first woman counselor to the president, appointed by President Richard M. Nixon.

Representative Leonor K. Sullivan (D-MO) becomes chair of the House Committee on Merchant Marine and Fisheries.

9to5, National Association of Working Women is founded.

The Children's Defense Fund is founded.

Catholics for a Free Choice is founded.

The National Right to Life Committee is founded.

The Religious Coalition for Reproductive Choice is founded.

Congress passes the Women's Educational Equity Act.

In *Roe v. Wade*, the U.S. Supreme Court establishes a woman's right to abortion. *Doe v. Bolton* is decided at the same time.

The U.S. Supreme Court decides that family members of females in the armed services have the same rights to benefits as family members of males in the armed services in *Frontiero v. Richardson*.

Eight more states ratify the federal Equal Rights Amendment.

1974   Mary Louise Smith becomes chair of the Republican National Committee, the first woman to hold the post.

The first Filipina American women are elected to a state legislature, Democrat Thelma Garcia Buchholdt to the Alaska legislature and Republican Velma M. Santos to the Hawaii legislature.

March Fong becomes the first Asian American woman elected to a statewide position when she is elected California's secretary of state.

Lilai Smith becomes the first African American woman to be elected mayor, in Taft, Oklahoma.

Elaine Brown becomes the first woman chair of the Black Panther Party.

Elaine Noble becomes the first open lesbian elected to a state office when she wins her race for a seat in the Massachusetts legislature.

The Women's Campaign Fund is founded.

The Alliance of Displaced Homemakers is founded.

The Coalition of Labor Union Women is founded.

In *Cleveland Board of Education v. LaFleur*, the U.S. Supreme Court finds that some mandatory maternity leave policies violate the due process clause of the Fourteenth Amendment.

The U.S. Supreme Court decides the first equal pay case, *Corning Glass v. Brennan*.

In *Geduldig v. Aiello*, the U.S. Supreme Court rejects an employed woman's claim that her Fourteenth Amendment rights have been violated because California's disability insurance program does not cover pregnancy.

The Fair Housing Act of 1968 is extended to prohibit discrimination on the basis of sex.

| 1974 | The Equal Credit Opportunity Act prohibits sex discrimination in all |
| cont. | consumer credit practices. |

The Women's Educational Equity Act funds the development of nonsexist teaching materials and model programs, nondiscriminatory career counseling, sports education, and related programs.

Three more states ratify the federal Equal Rights Amendment.

1975   Carla Hills is appointed secretary of housing and urban development by President Gerald Ford.

Democrat Ella Grasso becomes governor of Connecticut.

Susan Brownmiller publishes *Against Our Will,* a book that contributes to changes in rape legislation.

The Eagle Forum is founded.

MANA, a National Latina Organization, is founded.

The National Commission on the Observance of International Women's Year is established.

In *Taylor v. Louisiana,* the U.S. Supreme Court decides that Louisiana's exemptions from jury service violate the Sixth and Fourteenth Amendments.

In *Weinberger v. Wiesenfeld,* the U.S. Supreme Court decides that denying Social Security benefits to a widower and the children of a deceased worker that would have been available to a widow and the children of a deceased worker violates the due process clause.

California passes the nation's first Displaced Homemaker Act.

One more state ratifies the federal Equal Rights Amendment.

1976   Representative Barbara Jordan (D-TX) becomes the first woman and first African American to deliver a keynote speech at a Democratic National Convention.

Representative Corinne Claiborne (Lindy) Boggs (D-LA) becomes the first woman chair of a Democratic National Convention.

ERAmerica is founded to serve as a national bipartisan political organization to coordinate ratification of the federal Equal Rights Amendment.

In *Craig v. Boren,* the U.S. Supreme Court finds unconstitutional Oklahoma's law establishing different ages for men and women to legally purchase beer.

In *Planned Parenthood of Central Missouri v. Danforth,* the U.S. Supreme Court rejects parts and accepts parts of a Missouri abortion law.

The U.S. Supreme Court decides in *Bellotti v. Baird* that in some circumstances states may require a minor woman to obtain parental consent before having an abortion.

The U.S. Supreme Court finds in *General Electric v. Gilbert* that excluding pregnancy from a disability plan does not violate Title VII of the Civil Rights Act of 1964.

1977   Patricia Roberts Harris is appointed secretary of housing and urban development and becomes the first African American woman to hold a federal cabinet position.

Juanita Kreps is appointed secretary of commerce by President Jimmy Carter.

Democrat Dixy Lee Ray becomes governor of Washington.

Margaret (Midge) Costanza becomes the first woman assistant to the president.

Eleanor Holmes Norton becomes the first woman to chair the Equal Employment Opportunity Commission.

Mari-Luci Jaramillo is the first Hispanic American woman to serve as a U.S. ambassador, appointed by President Jimmy Carter.

Patsy Takemoto Mink becomes the first Asian American woman to serve as assistant secretary of state, appointed by President Jimmy Carter.

The Congressional Caucus for Women's Issues is founded as the Congresswomen's Caucus.

The National Women's Conference is held in Houston, Texas.

In *Dothard v. Rawlinson,* the U.S. Supreme Court considers bona fide occupational qualifications and applies the disparate impact standard to sex discrimination.

In *Nashville Gas Company v. Satty,* the U.S. Supreme Court decides that denying seniority to women returning to work after a forced pregnancy leave violates Title VII of the Civil Rights Act of 1964.

In *Beal v. Doe,* the U.S. Supreme Court decides that Pennsylvania's Medicaid program does not have to pay for nontherapeutic abortions.

In *Poelker v. Doe,* the U.S. Supreme Court decides that hospitals owned by cities have no constitutional obligation to perform nontherapeutic abortions.

In *Carey v. Population Services International,* the U.S. Supreme Court rejects New York's law limiting access to contraceptives.

The U.S. Supreme Court finds constitutional a Connecticut regulation limiting Medicaid payments for first-trimester abortions to those considered medically necessary, in *Maher v. Roe.*

One more state ratifies the federal Equal Rights Amendment.

1978   Carolyn Robertson Payton becomes the first woman and first African American to head the U.S. Peace Corps, appointed by President Jimmy Carter.

1978
cont.

Jean Sadako King becomes the first Asian American woman elected lieutenant governor in the United States.

The National Coalition Against Domestic Violence is founded.

The Older Women's League is founded.

The National Women's Conference Committee is organized.

Concerned Women for America is founded.

In *Bakke v. Regents of the University of California,* the U.S. Supreme Court upholds the constitutionality of affirmative action plans.

Congress passes the Pregnancy Discrimination Act.

President Jimmy Carter establishes the National Advisory Committee for Women.

An extension for the ratification of the Equal Rights Amendment passes Congress.

Concerned Women for America is founded.

1979

Patricia Roberts Harris is appointed secretary of health and human services by President Jimmy Carter.

The American Life League is founded.

Polly Baca becomes the first Hispanic American woman to serve in a state Senate when she is elected in Colorado.

Suffragist Susan B. Anthony becomes the first woman depicted on an American coin.

In *Orr v. Orr,* the U.S. Supreme Court finds that Alabama divorce laws providing that husbands, but not wives, may be required to pay alimony are unconstitutional.

In *Personnel Administrator of the Commonwealth of Massachusetts v. Feeney,* the U.S. Supreme Court finds Massachusetts's veterans preference law constitutional.

In *Colautti v. Franklin,* the U.S. Supreme Court finds unconstitutionally vague a Pennsylvania law requiring physicians performing abortions to use the method most likely to preserve the life and health of a fetus thought to be viable.

1980

Shirley Hufstedler is appointed secretary of education by President Jimmy Carter.

Eunice Sato becomes the first Asian American woman elected mayor of a large city, Long Beach, California.

The gender gap appears in presidential elections when fewer women than men vote for Republican Ronald Reagan.

In *Harris v. McRae* the U.S. Supreme Court decides that states are not required to pay for medically necessary abortions under their Medicaid plans.

In *Williams v. Zbaraz*, the U.S. Supreme Court finds that states are not required to pay for medically necessary abortions that are not covered by Medicaid.

In *McCarty v. McCarty*, the U.S. Supreme Court finds that military retirement pay is the personal entitlement of the retiree and that states cannot allocate it to former spouses as part of a divorce settlement.

1981   Jeane J. Kirkpatrick is appointed ambassador to the United Nations by President Ronald Reagan.

Sandra Day O'Connor is appointed to the United States Supreme Court by President Ronald Reagan and becomes the first woman appointed to the Court.

Katherine D. Ortega becomes U.S. treasurer.

The National Coalition of 100 Black Women is founded.

In *Kirchberg v. Feenstra*, the U.S. Supreme Court invalidates a Louisiana law designating a husband head and master having unilateral control of property jointly owned with his wife.

In *Washington County, Oregon v. Gunther*, the U.S. Supreme Court decides that workers can make claims of undercompensation, even though the jobs are not the same.

The U.S. Supreme Court decides in *County of Washington, Oregon v. Gunther* that employees can claim they have been undercompensated when compared to other employees, even though they do not do the same work.

The Congressional Caucus for Women's Issues introduces the Economic Equity Act.

1982   Roy M. Vesta serves as governor of New Hampshire from 29 December 1982 to 6 January 1983.

Loretta Glickman becomes the first African American woman elected mayor of a large city, Pasadena, California.

In *Mississippi University for Women v. Hogan*, the U.S. Supreme Court decides that a state law excluding men from a state-supported nursing school violates the Fourteenth Amendment.

The extension for ratification of the federal Equal Rights Amendment expires. Three more states were needed for the amendment to be included in the U.S. Constitution.

1983   Margaret Heckler is appointed secretary of health and human services and Elizabeth Dole is appointed secretary of transportation.

In *Planned Parenthood Association of Kansas City, Mo. v. Ashcroft*, the U.S. Supreme Court rejects some parts and accepts some parts of a Missouri abortion law.

In *Akron v. Akron Center for Reproductive Health*, the U.S. Supreme

Court finds unconstitutional the several provisions of a city ordinance related to abortion, including the requirements that physicians tell patients seeking an abortion that life begins at conception, and that minor women seeking abortions had to obtain parental consent.

1984   Democrat Geraldine Ferraro becomes the first woman nominated by a major party for vice president.

Democrat Martha Layne Collins becomes governor of Kentucky.

Katherine D. Ortega, U.S. treasurer, becomes the first Hispanic American to keynote a national convention of a major political party at the Republican National Convention.

Valerie Terrigno becomes the first openly lesbian mayor in the United States when she is elected in West Hollywood, California.

The National Political Congress of Black Women is founded by Shirley Chisholm.

In *Grove City v. Bell*, the U.S. Supreme Court decides that Title IX of the Education Amendments of 1972 applies only to the program within an educational institution receiving federal funds and not to the entire institution.

In *Hishon v. King and Spalding*, the U.S. Supreme Court decides that Title VII of the Civil Rights Act of 1964 covers partners in a partnership.

In *H. L. v. Matheson*, the U.S. Supreme Court decides that a Utah law requiring a minor woman to notify her parents before obtaining an abortion is constitutional.

1985   Democrat Madeleine Kunin becomes governor of Vermont.

Wilma Mankiller becomes the first woman elected principal chief of a major Native American tribe.

The Council of Presidents is formed.

The National Organization of Black Elected Legislative Women is founded.

EMILY's List is founded to elect prochoice Democratic women candidates.

1986   In *Meritor Savings Bank v. Vinson*, the U.S. Supreme Court makes its first decision regarding sexual harassment and concurs with the Equal Employment Opportunity Commission's definition of a hostile work environment and that sexual harassment is a form of sexual discrimination.

In *Thornburgh v. American College of Obstetrics and Gynecology*, the U.S. Supreme Court rejects provisions of a Pennsylvania abortion law.

The U.S. Supreme Court finds constitutional a Georgia law categorizing sodomy as a criminal act in *Bowers v. Hardwick*.

Operation Rescue is founded.

1987   Ann Dore McLaughlin is appointed secretary of labor by President Ronald Reagan.

Republican Kay Orr becomes governor of Nebraska, the first Republican woman governor in the nation.

Dorothy Comstock Rile of Michigan becomes the first Hispanic female chief justice of a state supreme court.

Joy Cherian becomes the first Asian American to sit on the Equal Employment Opportunity Commission, appointed by President Ronald Reagan.

The Feminist Majority is founded.

Susan Estrich is the first woman to head a major presidential campaign, for Democrat Michael Dukakis.

In *California Savings and Loan v. Guerra*, the U.S. Supreme Court decides that California's law for disability leave for pregnant workers does not conflict with Title VII of the Civil Rights Act of 1964.

In *Johnson v. Transportation Agency, Santa Clara County*, the U.S. Supreme Court finds constitutional an affirmative action plan for women.

An appeals court finds constitutional the Democratic Party's equal division rule, designed to promote greater representation of women and minorities in state delegations to national party conventions, in *Bachur v. Democratic National Committee*.

1988   Democrat Rose Mofford becomes governor of Arizona.

Susan Estrich becomes the first woman to head a major presidential campaign when Democratic presidential nominee Michael Dukakis chooses her for the position.

Lenora Fulani of New York is the first African American woman to appear on the presidential ballot in all fifty states, on the National Alliance Party ticket.

Elaine Chao becomes the first Asian American woman to chair a federal commission, the Federal Maritime Commission, appointed by President Ronald Reagan.

Juanita Kidd Stout of Pennsylvania becomes the first African American woman appointed to a state supreme court.

National Gender Balance Project USA is founded.

The Civil Rights Restoration Act of 1988 overturns the U.S. Supreme Court decision in *Grove City v. Bell*.

1989   Carla Anderson Hills is appointed special trade representative, and Elizabeth Hanford Dole is appointed secretary of labor, by President George Bush.

1989 cont.	Representative Ileana Ros-Lehtinen (R-FL) becomes the first Hispanic American woman to serve in the U.S. House of Representatives.

Joyce Kennard becomes the first Asian American woman to sit on a state supreme court when she is appointed in California.

Julia Chang Bloch becomes the first Asian American woman U.S. ambassador, appointed by President George Bush.

The Christian Coalition is founded.

In a sex discrimination case, *Price Waterhouse v. Hopkins,* the U.S. Supreme Court decides that when an employer considers sex in employment, it is not in violation of Title VII of the Civil Rights Act of 1964, if the employer would make the same decision without considering the employee's sex.

In *Webster v. Reproductive Health Services,* the U.S. Supreme Court affirms the rights of states to deny public funding for abortions and to prohibit public hospitals from performing abortions.

1990   Antonia Novello becomes the first woman and the first Hispanic American U.S. surgeon general.

In *Hodgson v. Minnesota* the U.S. Supreme Court upholds the requirement that a minor woman notify both of her parents or obtain a judicial waiver before having an abortion.

In *Ohio v. Akron Center,* the U.S. Supreme Court decides that an Ohio law requiring a physician to notify the parents of a minor woman before performing an abortion is constitutional.

The Court rejects a parental notification measure that did not have the judicial bypass procedure.

The Women's Health Equity Act is introduced.

1991   Democrat Joan Finney becomes governor of Kansas.

Democrat Ann Richards becomes governor of Texas.

Democrat Barbara Roberts becomes governor of Oregon.

Lynn Morley Martin is appointed secretary of labor by President George Bush.

Patricia Saiki is appointed by President Geoge Bush as head of the Small Business Administration, making her the first Asian American woman to head that department.

Anita Hill alleges that U.S. Supreme Court nominee Clarence Thomas sexually harassed her, leading to the Senate Judiciary Committee reopening the confirmation hearings. Sexual harassment receives public attention.

Minnesota becomes the first state to have a majority of female supreme court justices, with four out of seven justices being women.

874   *Chronology*

In *Rust v. Sullivan,* the U.S. Supreme Court finds permissible regulations that forbid the discussion of abortion as an option at family planning centers that receive federal family planning funds.

In *UAW v. Johnson Controls,* the U.S. Supreme Court decides that refusing to hire women for certain jobs to protect them from workplace hazards violates the Pregnancy Discrimination Act of 1978.

Congress passes the Civil Rights Act of 1991, part of which overturns *Price Waterhouse v. Hopkins* (1989).

The Congressional Caucus for Women's Issues introduces the Health Equity Act.

For the first time, at least one woman serves in every state legislature in the nation.

1992   Barbara H. Franklin is appointed secretary of commerce by President George Bush.

Democrat Georgianna Lincoln, an Athabascan, becomes the first Native American woman elected to a state Senate, the Alaska Senate.

Leah Sears-Collins becomes the first African American woman elected to a state supreme court when she wins a seat in Georgia.

Irma Gonzalez, Lourdes Baird, and Sonia Sotomayor beome the first female Hispanic Americans appointed as federal judges, in California and New York, respectively.

In *Planned Parenthood of Southeastern Pennsylvania v. Casey,* the U.S. Supreme Court discards the trimester framework that it established in *Roe v. Wade.*

1993   Ruth Bader Ginsburg is appointed to the U.S. Supreme Court by President Bill Clinton.

California becomes the first state to have two female U.S. senators serving simultaneously, Dianne Feinstein and Barbara Boxer.

Carol Moseley-Braun is the first African American woman sworn in to the U.S. Senate.

Sheila Widnall becomes the first woman secretary of the Air Force.

Joycelyn Elders becomes the first African American woman U.S. surgeon general.

Alice Rivlin is appointed director of the Office of Management and Budget, Carol M. Browner is appointed administrator of the Environmental Protection Agency, Donna Shalala is appointed secretary of health and human services, African American Hazel O'Leary is appointed secretary of energy, and Janet Reno is appointed U.S. attorney general by President Bill Clinton.

Native American Ada Deer becomes the first woman assistant secretary for Indian affairs in the U.S. Department of the Interior.

1993
cont.
Roberta Achtenberg is the first open lesbian to serve in a subcabinet position, as assistant secretary in the U.S. Department of Housing and Urban Development, appointed by President Bill Clinton.

In *Bray v. Alexandria Clinic,* the U.S. Supreme Court finds that the Civil Rights Acts of 1871 does not cover protest actions at abortion clinics.

In *Harris v. Forklift Systems,* the U.S. Supreme Court decides that an employee does not need to show serious psychological damage or other injury to prove sexual harassment.

President Bill Clinton signs the Family and Medical Leave Act.

For the first time, at least one woman serves in both chambers of every state legislature and in Nebraska's unicameral legislature.

1994
Christine Todd Whitman becomes governor of New Jersey.

Alaska is the first state to have both legislative chambers headed by women, with Gail Phillips as speaker of the House and Drue Pearce as Senate president pro tem.

Deborah Batts is the first openly lesbian federal judge appointed, in the U.S. District Court in New York.

Marcy Kahn becomes the first openly lesbian state supreme court justice in the United States when she is elected to New York's supreme court.

In *NOW v. Scheidler,* the U.S. Supreme Court decides that the Racketeer Influenced and Corrupt Organizations Statute applies to anti-abortion groups.

The Violence Against Women Act funds services for victims of rape and domestic violence, allows women to seek civil rights remedies for gender-related crimes, provides training to increase police and court officials' sensitivity, and funds a national twenty-four-hour hotline for battered women.

Congress passes the Freedom of Access to Clinic Entrances Act.

1995
Laura D'Andrea Tyson is appointed chair of the National Economic Council by President Bill Clinton.

Women's Policy, Inc. is founded.

1996
In *United States v. Virginia,* the U.S. Supreme Court decides that the male-only admissions policy of Virginia Military Institute violates the Fourteenth Amendment.

1997
Aida Alvarez is appointed administrator of the Small Business Administration, Charlene Barshefsky is appointed U.S. trade representative, Alexis M. Herman is appointed secretary of labor, and Madeleine Albright is appointed secretary of state, the first woman to hold the position, by President Bill Clinton.

Jeanne Shaheen becomes governor of New Hampshire.

Jane Dee Hull becomes governor of Arizona.

In *Clinton v. Jones,* the U.S. Supreme Court decides that the Constitution does not prohibit a private citizen from suing a sitting president for acts committed before becoming president.

1998   Arizona becomes the first state with an all-female executive cabinet (governor, secretary of state, attorney general, treasurer, and superintendent of public instruction).

1999   Representative Tammy Baldwin (D-WI) becomes the first open lesbian to serve in the U.S. House of Representatives.

Bibliography

Addams, Jane. *Twenty Years at Hull-House.* New York: Macmillan, 1911.

Allen, Helena G. *The Betrayal of Liliuokalani: Last Queen of Hawaii, 1838–1917.* Glendale, CA: The Arthur H. Clark Company, 1982.

Alonso, Harriet Hyman. "Nobel Peace Laureates, Jane Addams and Emily Greene Balch." *Journal of Women's History* 7, no. 2 (Summer 1995): 6–26.

———. *Peace as a Women's Issue: A History of the U.S. Movement for World Peace and Women's Rights.* Syracuse, NY: Syracuse University Press, 1993.

Altschuler, Bruce E. "State ERAs: What Have They Done?" *State Government* 56, no. 4 (1983): 134–137.

American Jurisprudence. 2nd ed. Vol. 15. Rochester, NY: The Lawyers Co-operative Publishing Co., 1976.

Anderson, Kathryn. "Practicing Feminist Politics: Emily Newell Blair and U.S. Women's Political Choices in the Early Twentieth Century." *Journal of Women's History* 9, no. 3 (Autumn 1997): 50–72.

———. "Steps to Political Equality: Woman Suffrage and Electoral Politics in the Lives of Emily Newell Blair, Anne Henrietta Martin, and Jeannette Rankin." *Frontiers* 18, no. 1 (1997): 101–121.

Anderson, Marian. *My Lord, What a Morning.* New York: Viking Press, 1956.

Anderson, Mary. *Woman at Work.* Minneapolis: University of Minnesota Press, 1951.

Andrews, Deborah, ed. *The Annual Obituary 1990.* Chicago: St. James Press, 1991.

Baca, Polly. "Seasons of a Life." In *True to Ourselves.* Ed. Nancy M. Neuman. San Francisco: Jossey-Bass Publishers, 1998.

Bacon, Margaret Hope. *Valiant Friend: The Life of Lucretia Mott.* New York: Walker and Company, 1980.

Baer, Judith A. *The Chains of Protection: The Judicial Response to Women's Labor Legislation.* Westport, CT: Greenwood Press, 1978.

———. *Women in American Law: The Struggle toward Equality from the New Deal to the Present.* 2nd ed. New York: Homes and Meier, 1996.

"Barbara Hackman Franklin, Secretary of Commerce, Advocate for U.S. Business." *Business America* (9 March 1992): 13–14.

"Barbara Lee, D-Calif." *Congressional Quarterly Weekly Report* 56 (11 April 1998): 949.

Barnett, Bernice McNair. "Black Women's Collectivist Movement Organizations: Their Struggles during the 'Doldrums.'" In *Feminist Organizations: Harvest of the New Women's Movement.* Ed. Myra Marx Ferree and Patricia Yancey Martin. Philadelphia: Temple University Press, 1995.

Barry, Kathleen. *Susan B. Anthony: A Biography of a Singular Feminist.* New York: New York University Press, 1988.

Barthel, Joan. "Mary Frances Berry." *Ms.* (January 1987): 68, 70, 95, 96.

Bataille, Gretchen, ed. *Native American Women: A Biographical Dictionary.* New York: Garland Publishing, 1993.

Bates, Daisy. *The Long Shadow of Little Rock: A Memoir.* New York: David McKay, 1962.

Beard, Patricia. *Growing Up Republican: Christie Whitman: The Politics of Character.* New York: HarperCollins, 1996.

Becker, Mary E. "Prince Charming: Abstract Equality." In *The Supreme Court Review 1987.* Ed. Philip Kurland, Gerhard Casper, and Dennis J. Hutchinson. Chicago: University of Chicago Press, 1988.

Bell, Tina. "Operation Rescue." *The Human Life Review* 14, no. 3 (Summer 1988): 37–52.

Berry, Dawn Bradley. *The 50 Most Influential Women in American Law.* Los Angeles: Lowell House, 1996.

Berry, Mary Frances. *Why the ERA Failed: Politics, Women's Rights, and the Amending Process of the Constitution.* Bloomington: Indiana University Press, 1986.

Bigelow, Barbara Carlisle. *Contemporary Black Biography: Profiles from the International Black Community.* Vol. 7. Detroit: Gale Research, 1994.

Bingham, Clara. *Women on the Hill: Challenging the Culture of Congress.* New York: Times Books, 1997.

Bird, Caroline. *What Women Want: From the Official Report to the President, the Congress, and the People of the United States.* New York: Simon and Schuster, 1979.

Birtel, Marc. "New Member Profile: Mary Bono." *Congressional Quarterly Weekly Report* (11 April 1998): 948.

Blair, Emily Newell. "Putting Women into Politics." *Woman's Journal* 16 (March 1931): 14–15, 29.

Blanchard, Dallas A. *The Anti-Abortion Movement and the Rise of the Religious Right: From Polite to Fiery Protest.* New York: Twayne Publishers, 1994.

"Blanche Lincoln." *Congressional Quarterly Weekly Report* 56 (7 November 1998): 3005.

Blood, Thomas. *Madam Secretary: A Biography of Madeleine Albright.* New York: St. Martin's Press, 1997.

Boggs, Lindy, with Katherine Hatch. *Washington through a Purple Veil: Memoirs of a Southern Woman.* New York: Harcourt Brace, 1994.

Boles, Janet. "Building Support for the ERA: A Case of 'Too Much, Too Late.'" *PS* 15 (Fall 1982): 572–577.

———. "The Equal Rights Movement as a Non-Zero-Sum Game." In *Rights of Passage: The Past and Future of the ERA*. Ed. Joan Hoff-Wilson. Bloomington: Indiana University Press, 1986.

Bouton, Katherine. "Marian Wright Edelman." *Ms.* (July–August 1987): 98–100, 204, 205.

Boxer, Barbara. *Strangers in the Senate: Politics and the New Revolution of Women in America.* Washington, DC: National Press Books, 1994.

Boyle, Mary T. "Affirmative Action in the Democratic Party: An Analysis of the Equal Division Rule." *The Journal of Law and Politics* 7 no. 3 (Spring 1991): 559–590.

Braden, Maria. *Women Politicians and the Media.* Lexington: University of Kentucky Press, 1996.

Bradley, Craig M. "*NOW v. Scheidler:* RICO Meets the First Amendment." In *1994 The Supreme Court Review.* Ed. Dennis J. Hutchinson, David A. Strauss, and Geoffrey Stone. Chicago: University of Chicago Press, 1995.

Breckenridge, Sophonisba. *Women in the Twentieth Century: A Study of Their Political, Social and Economic Activities.* New York: McGraw-Hill, 1933.

Bredbenner, Candace Lewis. *A Nationality of Her Own: Women, Marriage, and the Law of Citizenship.* Berkeley: University of California Press, 1998.

Brill, Alida. "Freedom, Fantasy, Foes, and Feminism: The Debate around Pornography." In *Women, Politics, and Change.* Ed. Louise A. Tilley and Patricia Gurin. New York: Russell Sage Foundation, 1990.

Brooks, Paul. *Rachel Carson at Work: The House of Life.* Boston: G. K. Hall, 1985.

Brown, Dorothy M. *American Women in the 1920s: Setting a Course.* Boston: Twayne Publishers, 1987.

———. *Mabel Walker Willebrandt: A Study of Power, Loyalty, and Law.* Knoxville: University of Tennessee Press, 1984.

Brown, Elaine. *A Taste of Power: A Black Woman's Story.* New York: Pantheon Books, 1992.

Brownmiller, Susan. *Against Our Will: Men, Women, and Rape.* New York: Simon and Schuster, 1975.

Bryant, Keith L., Jr. "Kate Barnard, Organized Labor, and Social Justice in Oklahoma during the Progressive Era." *Journal of Social History* 35, no. 2 (May 1969): 154–164.

Buell, Janet W. "Alva Belmont: From Socialite to Feminist." *The Historian* 52, no. 2 (February 1990): 219–241.

Burgess, Patricia., ed. *The Annual Obituary 1986.* Chicago: St. James Press, 1989.

———. *The Annual Obituary 1987.* Chicago: St. James Press, 1990.

Burkett, Elinor. *The Right Women: A Journey through the Heart of Conservative America.* New York: Scribner, 1998.

Burrell, Barbara C. *A Woman's Place Is in the House: Campaigning for Congress in the Feminist Era.* Ann Arbor: University of Michigan Press, 1994.

Bush, Barbara. *Barbara Bush: A Memoir.* New York: Charles Scribner's Sons, 1994.

Cameron, Jean. *Anne Hutchinson, Guilty or Not? A Closer Look at Her Trials.* New York: Peter Lang, 1994.

Camp, Helen C. *Iron in Her Soul: Elizabeth Gurley Flynn and the American Left.* Pullman: Washington State University Press, 1995.

Carabillo, Toni, Judith Meuli, and June Bundy Csida. *Feminist Chronicles: 1953–1993*. Los Angeles: Women's Graphics, 1993.

Carleton, Francis. "Women in the Workplace and Sex Discrimination Law: A Feminist Analysis of Federal Jurisprudence." *Women and Politics* 13, no. 2 (1993): 1–25.

Caroli, Betty Boyd. "Jacqueline Kennedy." In *America's First Ladies: Their Lives and Their Legacies.* Ed. Lewis L. Gould. New York: Garland Publishing, 1996.

Carroll, Berenice A. "Direct Action and Constitutional Rights: The Case of the ERA." In *Rights of Passage: The Past and Future of the ERA.* Ed. Joan Hoff-Wilson. Bloomington: Indiana University Press, 1986.

Carter, Rosalynn. *First Lady from Plains.* Boston: Houghton Mifflin, 1984.

Catlin, Robert A. "Organizational Effectiveness and Black Political Participation: The Case of Katie Hall." *Phylon* 46, no. 3 (Fall 1985): 179–192.

Cavin, Susan. "The Invisible Army of Women: Lesbian Social Protests, 1969–1988." In *Women and Social Protest.* Ed. Guida West and Rhoda Lois Blumberg. New York: Oxford University Press, 1990.

Chamberlin, Hope. *A Minority of Members.* New York: Praeger Publishers, 1973.

Chaudhuri, Molly, and Kathleen Daly. "Do Restraining Orders Help? Battered Women's Experience with Male Violence and Legal Process." In *Domestic Violence: The Changing Criminal Justice Response.* Ed. Eve S. Buzawa and Carl G. Buzawa. Westport, CT: Auburn House, 1992.

Chen, Constance M. *"The Sex Side of Life": Mary Ware Dennett's Pioneering Battle for Birth Control and Sex Education.* New York: New Press, 1996.

Chipley, Ann W., comp. *AAUW: Historic Principles, 1881–1989.* Washington, DC: AAUW, 1989.

Clark, Septima, with Cynthia Stokes Brown. *Ready from Within: Septima Clark and the Civil Rights Movement.* Navarro, CA: Wild Trees Press, 1986.

Clifford, Deborah Pickman. *Crusader for Freedom: A Life of Lydia Maria Child.* Boston: Beacon Press, 1992.

Collins, Gail. "The Fall and Rise of Mary Matalin." *Working Woman* (August 1994): 34–37, 74.

Collins, Louise Mooney, ed. *Newsmakers: 1994 Cumulation.* Detroit: Gale Research, 1994.

Collins, Louise Mooney, and Lorna Mpho Mabunda, eds. *The Annual Obituary 1993.* Chicago: St. James Press, 1994.

Collins, Louise Mooney, and Geri J. Speace, eds. *Newsmakers: 1995 Cumulation.* Detroit: Gale Research, 1995.

Congressional Quarterly. *Cabinets and Counselors: The President and the Executive Branch.* 2nd ed. Washington, DC: Congressional Quarterly, 1997.

———. *Congressional Quarterly Almanac, 87th Congress, 2nd Session . . . 1962.* Vol. 18. Washington, DC: Congressional Quarterly, 1962.

———. *Congressional Quarterly Almanac, 88th Congress, 1st Session . . . 1963.* Vol. 19. Washington, DC: Congressional Quarterly, 1964.

———. *Congressional Quarterly Almanac, 88th Congress, 2nd Session . . . 1964.* Vol. 20. Washington, DC: Congressional Quarterly, 1965.

———. *Congressional Quarterly, Almanac 89th Congress, 1st Session . . . 1965.* Washington, DC: Congressional Quarterly, 1966.

————. *Congressional Quarterly Almanac, 91st Congress, 2nd Session . . . 1970.* Washington, DC: Congressional Quarterly, 1970.

————. *Congressional Quarterly Almanac, 92nd Congress, 1st Session . . . 1971.* Washington, DC: Congressional Quarterly, 1972.

————. *Congressional Quarterly Almanac, 92nd Congress, 2nd Session . . . 1972.* Vol. 28. Washington, DC: Congressional Quarterly, 1972.

————. *Congressional Quarterly Almanac, 93rd Congress, 1st Session . . . 1973.* Vol. 29 Washington, DC: Congressional Quarterly, 1974.

————. *Congressional Quarterly Almanac, 95th Congress, 1st Session . . . 1977.* Vol. 33. Washington, DC: Congressional Quarterly, 1977.

————. *Congressional Quarterly Almanac, 95th Congress, 2nd Session . . . 1978.* Vol. 34. Washington, DC: Congressional Quarterly, 1979.

————. *Congressional Quarterly Almanac, 97th Congress, 1st Session . . . 1981.* Vol. 37. Washington, DC: Congressional Quarterly, 1982.

————. *Congressional Quarterly Almanac, 97th Congress, 2nd Session . . . 1982.* Vol. 38. Washington, DC: Congressional Quarterly, 1983.

————. *Congressional Quarterly Almanac, 98th Congress, 1st Session . . . 1983.* Vol. 39. Washington, DC: Congressional Quarterly, 1984.

————. *Congressional Quarterly Almanac, 98th Congress, 2nd Session . . . 1984.* Vol. 40. Washington, DC: Congressional Quarterly, 1985.

————. *Congressional Quarterly Almanac, 100th Congress, 2nd Session . . . 1988.* Vol. 44. Washington, DC: Congressional Quarterly, 1989.

————. *Congressional Quarterly Almanac, 101st Congress, 2nd Session . . . 1990.* Vol. 46. Washington, DC: Congressional Quarterly, 1991.

————. *Congressional Quarterly Almanac, 102nd Congress, 1st Session . . . 1991.* Vol. 47. Washington, DC: Congressional Quarterly, 1992.

————. *Congressional Quarterly Almanac, 102nd Congress, 2nd Session . . . 1992.* Vol. 48. Washington, DC: Congressional Quarterly, 1993.

————. *Congressional Quarterly Almanac, 103rd Congress, 1st Session . . . 1993.* Vol. 49. Washington, DC: Congressional Quarterly, 1994.

————. *Congressional Quarterly Almanac, 103rd Congress, 2nd Session . . . 1994.* Vol. 50. Washington, DC: Congressional Quarterly, 1995.

————. *Congressional Quarterly Almanac, 104th Congress, 1st Session . . . 1995.* Vol. 51. Washington, DC: Congressional Quarterly, 1996.

————. *Congressional Quarterly Almanac, 104th Congress, 2nd Session . . . 1996.* Vol. 51. Washington, DC: Congressional Quarterly, 1997.

————. *Congressional Quarterly's Federal PACs Directory, 1998–1999.* Washington, DC: Congressional Quarterly, 1998.

————. *Politics in America 1984.* Washington, DC: CQ Press, 1983.

————. *Politics in America: The 100th Congress.* Washington, DC: CQ Press, 1987.

————. *Politics in America 1992.* Washington, DC: CQ Press, 1991.

————. *Politics in America 1994: The 103rd Congress.* Washington, DC: Congressional Quarterly, 1993.

————. *Politics in America 1996.* Washington, DC: CQ Press, 1995.

————. *Politics in America 1998.* Washington, DC: CQ Press, 1997.

Cook, Blanche Wiesen, ed. *Crystal Eastman on Women and Revolution.* New York: Oxford University Press, 1978.

————. *Eleanor Roosevelt.* Vol. 1: *1884–1933.* New York: Viking Press, 1992.

Costain, Anne N. "Lobbying for Equal Credit." In *Women Organizing: An Anthology*. Ed. Bernice Cummings and Victoria Schuck. Metuchen, NJ: Scarecrow Press, 1979.

Cott, Nancy F. "Feminist Politics in the 1920s: The National Woman's Party." *Journal of American History* 71, no. 1 (June 1984): 43–68.

Cowan, Gloria. "Pornography: Conflict among Feminists." In *Women: A Feminist Perspective*. 5th ed. Ed. Jo Freeman. Mountain View, CA: Mayfield Publishing, 1995.

Cox, Elizabeth. *Women State and Territorial Legislators, 1895–1995: A State-by-State Analysis, with Rosters of 6,000 Women*. Jefferson, NC: McFarland and Co., 1996

Crawford, Ann Fears, and Crystal Sasse Ragsdale. *Women in Texas: Their Lives, Their Experiences, Their Accomplishments*. Austin, TX: State House Press, 1992.

Crawford, Vicki L., Jacqueline Anne Rouse, and Barbara Woods, eds. *Women in the Civil Rights Movement: Trailblazers and Torchbearers, 1941–1965*. Bloomington: Indiana University Press, 1993.

Crisp, Mary Dent. "My Journey to Feminism." In *True to Ourselves*. Ed. Nancy M. Neuman. San Francisco: Jossey-Bass Publishers, 1998.

Crocker, Elvira Valenzuela. *MANA: One Dream, Many Voices*. San Antonio, TX: DagenBela Graphics, 1991.

"Current Programs." *Congressional Digest* 74, nos. 6–7 (June–July 1995): 166–167.

Daniels, Arlene. "W.E.A.L.: The Growth of a Feminist Organization." In *Women Organizing: An Anthology*. Ed. Bernice Cummings and Victoria Schuck. Metuchen, NJ: Scarecrow Press, 1979.

Davis, Flora. *Moving the Mountain: The Women's Movement in America since 1960*. New York: Simon and Schuster, 1991.

DeLeon, David, ed. *Leaders from the 1960s: A Biographical Sourcebook of American Activism*. Westport, CT: Greenwood Press, 1994.

Devilbiss, M. C. *Women and Military Service: A History, Analysis, and Overview of Key Issues*. Maxwell Air Force Base, AL: Air University Press, 1990.

Devine, Elizabeth, ed. *The Annual Obituary 1983*. Chicago: St. James Press, 1984.

Dinkin, Robert J. *Before Equal Suffrage: Women in Partisan Politics from Colonial Times to 1920*. Westport, CT: Greenwood Press, 1995.

Doherty, Carroll J. "Surface Racial Harmony on Hill Hides Simmering Tensions." *Congressional Quarterly Weekly Report* 56, no. 12 (21 March 1998): 715–720.

Dole, Bob, and Elizabeth Dole, with Richard Norton Smith and Kerry Tymchuk. *Unlimited Partners: Our American Story*. New York: Simon and Schuster, 1996.

Donaldson, Lee. "The First Woman Governor." *The Woman Citizen* (November 1926): 7–9, 48, 49.

Douglas, Helen Gahagan. *A Full Life*. Garden City, NY: Doubleday, 1982.

DuBois, Ellen Carol. *Harriot Stanton Blatch and the Winning of Woman Suffrage*. New Haven, CT: Yale University Press, 1997.

———. *Woman Suffrage and Women's Rights*. New York: New York University Press, 1998.

Dunn, Charles W., and David J. Woodward, *The Conservative Tradition in America*. Lanham, MD: Rowman and Littlefield, 1996.

East, Catherine. *American Women: 1963 1983 2003*. Washington, DC: National Federation of Business and Professional Women's Clubs, 1983.

Echols, Alice. *Daring to Be Bad: Radical Feminism in America, 1967–1975.* Minneapolis: University of Minnesota Press, 1989.

Eckhardt, Celia Morris. *Fanny Wright: Rebel in America.* Cambridge: Harvard University Press, 1984.

Edwards, India. *Pulling No Punches: Memoirs of a Woman in Politics.* New York: G. P. Putnam's Sons, 1977.

Eisenhower, Julie Nixon. *Pat Nixon: The Untold Story.* New York: Simon and Schuster, 1986.

Elders, Joycelyn, and David Chanoff. *Joycelyn Elders, M.D.: From Sharecropper's Daughter to Surgeon General of the United States of America.* New York: William Morrow, 1996.

"Election '96: Deciding the Vote." *Outlook* (Spring 1997): 6–8.

Engelbarts, Rudolf. *Women in the United States Congress, 1917–1972.* Littleton, CO: Libraries Unlimited, 1974.

Evans, Sara M. *Born for Liberty: A History of Women in America.* New York: Free Press, 1989.

———. *Personal Politics: The Roots of Women's Liberation in the Civil Rights Movement and the New Left.* New York: Alfred A. Knopf, 1979.

Evory, Ann, and Peter M. Gareffa, eds. *Contemporary Newsmakers, 1985.* Detroit: Gale Research, 1985.

"Ex-Rep. Lincoln to Seek Bumpers' Senate Seat." *Congressional Quarterly Weekly Report* 55 (2 August 1997): 1887.

Fallon, Richard H., Jr. "Sexual Harassment, Content, Neutrality, and the First Amendment Dog That Didn't Bark." In *The Supreme Court Review 1994.* Ed. Dennis J. Hutchinson, David A. Strauss, and Geoffrey R. Stone. Chicago: University of Chicago Press, 1995.

Feit, Rona F. "Organizing for Political Power: The National Women's Political Caucus." In *Women Organizing: An Anthology.* Ed. Bernice Cummings and Victoria Schuck. Metuchen, NJ: Scarecrow Press, 1979.

Felner, Julie. "Dolores Huerta." *Ms.* (January–February 1998): 46–49.

Felsenthal, Carol. *The Biography of Phyllis Schlafly: The Sweetheart of the Silent Majority.* Chicago: Regnery Gateway, 1981.

Ferraro, Geraldine A., with Linda Bird Francke. *Ferraro: My Story.* New York: Bantam Books, 1985.

Ferree, Myra Marx, and Beth B. Hess. *Controversy and Coalition: The New Feminist Movement across Three Decades of Change.* Boston: Twayne Publishers, 1994.

Fitzgerald, Tracey A. *The National Council of Negro Women and the Feminist Movement, 1935–1975.* Washington, DC: Georgetown University Press, 1985.

Flexner, Eleanor, and Ellen Fitzpatrick. *Century of Struggle: The Woman's Rights Movement in the United States.* Enlarged ed. Cambridge: Belknap Press at Harvard University, 1996.

Foerstel, Karen, and Herbert N. Foerstel. *Climbing the Hill: Gender Conflict in Congress.* Westport, CT: Praeger, 1996.

Foner, Eric, and John A. Garraty, eds. *The Reader's Companion to American History* Boston: Houghton Mifflin, 1991.

Foner, Philip. *Women and the American Labor Movement: From the First Trade Unions to the Present.* New York: Free Press, 1982.

Foner, Philip S., ed. *Frederick Douglass on Women's Rights.* New York: Da Capo Press, 1992.

Ford, Betty, with Chris Chase. *Betty: A Glad Awakening.* Garden City, NY: Doubleday, 1987.

———. *The Times of My Life.* New York: Harper and Row, 1978.

Forest, Jim. *Love Is the Measure: A Biography of Dorothy Day.* New York: Paulist Press, 1986.

"Former Rep. Oakar Sentenced in Campaign Finance Case." *Congressional Quarterly Weekly Report* 56 (24 January 1998): 178.

Francis, Claude, and Fernande Gontier. *Simone de Beauvoir: A Life . . . A Love Story.* New York: St. Martin's Press, 1987.

Franke, Linda Bird. *Ground Zero: The Gender Wars in the Military.* New York: Simon and Schuster, 1997.

Freeman, Jo. "Feminism vs. Family Values: Women at the 1992 Democratic and Republican Conventions." *Off Our Backs* 23, no. 1 (January 1995): 2–3, 10–17.

———. "From Protection to Equal Opportunity: The Revolution in Women's Legal Status." In *Women, Politics, and Change.* Ed. Louise A. Tilley and Patricia Gurin. New York: Russell Sage Foundation, 1990.

———. "How 'Sex' Got Into Title VII. Persistent Opportunism as a Maker of Public Policy." *Law and Inequality: A Journal of Theory and Practice* 9 (March 1991): 163–184.

———. "The Legal Basis of the Sexual Caste System." *Valparaiso University Law Review* 5, no. 2 (1971): 203–236.

———. *The Politics of Women's Liberation: The New Feminist Movement across Three Decades of Change.* New York: David McKay, 1975.

———. "Who You Know vs. Who You Represent: Feminist Influence in the Democratic and Republican Parties." In *The Women's Movement of the United States and Western Europe: Feminist Consciousness, Political Opportunity and Public Policy.* Ed. Mary Katzenstein and Carol Mueller. Philadelphia: Temple University Press, 1987.

———. "Women and Public Policy: An Overview." In *Women, Power and Policy.* Ed. Ellen Bonepath. New York: Pergamon Press, 1982.

———. "Women at the 1988 Democratic Convention." *PS: Political Science and Politics* 21, no. 4 (Fall 1988): 875–881.

Friedan, Betty. *The Feminine Mystique.* New York: Norton, 1963.

Friedman, Jane M. *America's First Woman Lawyer: The Biography of Myra Bradwell.* Buffalo, NY: Prometheus Books, 1993.

Gabin, Nancy F. *Feminism in the Labor Movement: Women and the United Auto Workers, 1935–1975.* Ithaca, NY: Cornell University Press, 1990.

Gaer, Emily. "A Study of the Activities of Women in Congress with Special Reference to the Careers of Margaret Chase Smith, Mary T. Norton, and Edith Nourse Rogers." Master's thesis, Bowling Green State University, 1952.

Garcia, Richard A. "Dolores Huerta: Woman, Organizer, and Symbol." *California History* 72, no. 1 (Spring 1993): 56–72.

Gareffa, Peter M., ed. *Contemporary Newsmakers.* Detroit: Gale Research, 1986.

———. *Newsmakers: 1989 Cumulation.* Detroit: Gale Research, 1990.

Garraty, John A., and Mark C. Carnes. *American National Biography.* 24 vols. New York: Oxford University Press, 1999.

George, Emily. *Martha W. Griffiths*. Washington, DC: University Press of America, 1982.

Getman, Julius G. "The Emerging Constitutional Principle of Sexual Equality." In *1972 The Supreme Court Review*. Ed. Philip B. Kurland. Chicago: University of Chicago Press, 1973.

Giddings, Paula. *In Search of Sisterhood: Delta Sigma Theta and the Challenge of the Black Sorority Movement*. New York: William Morrow, 1988.

———. *When and Where I Enter: The Impact of Black Women on Race and Sex in America*. New York: William Morrow, 1984.

Gill, LaVerne McCain. *African American Women in Congress: Forming and Transforming History*. New Brunswick, NJ: Rutgers University Press, 1997.

Ginsburg, Ruth Bader. "Gender in the Supreme Court: The 1973 and 1974 Terms." In *1975 The Supreme Court Review*. Ed. Philip Kurland. Chicago: University of Chicago Press, 1976.

Gollaher, David. *Voice for the Mad: The Life of Dorothea Dix*. New York: Free Press, 1995.

Gould, Lewis L. "First Lady as Catalyst: Lady Bird Johnson and Highway Beautification in the 1960s." *Environmental Review* 10, no. 2 (Summer 1986): 77–92.

"Grace F. Napolitano." *Congressional Quarterly Weekly Report* 56 (7 November 1998): 3012.

Graham, Sara Hunter. *Woman Suffrage and the New Democracy*. New Haven, CT: Yale University Press, 1996.

Grant, Joanne. *Ella Baker: Freedom Bound*. New York: Wiley, 1998.

Griffith, Elisabeth. *In Her Own Right: The Life of Elizabeth Cady Stanton*. New York: Oxford University Press, 1984.

Gruenwald, Juliana. "Women in the Military: Mission in Progress." *Congressional Quarterly Weekly Report* 55, no. 33 (16 August 1997): 1962–1966.

Gurko, Miriam. *The Ladies of Seneca Falls: The Birth of the Woman's Rights Movement*. New York: Macmillan, 1974.

H. W. Wilson. *Current Biography 1940*. New York: H. W. Wilson, 1940.

———. *Current Biography: Who's News and Why, 1942*. New York: H. W. Wilson, 1942.

———. *Current Biography: Who's News and Why, 1943*. New York: H. W. Wilson, 1943.

———. *Current Biography: Who's News and Why, 1944*. New York: H. W. Wilson, 1944.

———. *Current Biography: Who's News and Why, 1945*. New York: H. W. Wilson, 1945.

———. *Current Biography: Who's News and Why, 1946*. New York: H. W. Wilson, 1946.

———. *Current Biography: Who's News and Why, 1947*. New York: H. W. Wilson, 1947.

———. *Current Biography: Who's News and Why, 1949*. New York: H. W. Wilson, 1949.

———. *Current Biography: Who's News and Why, 1950*. New York: H. W. Wilson, 1950.

———. *Current Biography: Who's News and Why, 1953*. New York: H. W. Wilson, 1953.

———. *Current Biography Yearbook, 1959.* New York: H. W. Wilson, 1959.

———. *Current Biography Yearbook, 1961.* New York: H. W. Wilson, 1961.

———. *Current Biography Yearbook, 1962.* New York: H. W. Wilson, 1962.

———. *Current Biography Yearbook, 1964.* New York: H. W. Wilson, 1964.

———. *Current Biography Yearbook, 1965.* New York: H. W. Wilson, 1965.

———. *Current Biography Yearbook, 1969.* New York: H. W. Wilson, 1969.

———. *Current Biography Yearbook, 1971.* New York: H. W. Wilson, 1972.

———. *Current Biography Yearbook, 1974.* New York: H. W. Wilson, 1974.

———. *Current Biography Yearbook, 1975.* New York: H. W. Wilson, 1975.

———. *Current Biography Yearbook, 1978.* New York: H. W. Wilson, 1978.

———. *Current Biography Yearbook, 1979.* New York: H. W. Wilson, 1979.

———. *Current Biography Yearbook, 1980.* New York: H. W. Wilson, 1980.

———. *Current Biography Yearbook, 1981.* New York: H. W. Wilson, 1981.

———. *Current Biography Yearbook, 1982.* New York: H. W. Wilson, 1982.

———. *Current Biography Yearbook, 1983.* New York: H. W. Wilson, 1983.

———. *Current Biography Yearbook, 1984.* New York: H. W. Wilson, 1984.

———. *Current Biography Yearbook, 1985.* New York: H. W. Wilson, 1985.

———. *Current Biography Yearbook, 1986.* New York: H. W. Wilson, 1986.

———. *Current Biography Yearbook, 1987.* New York: H. W. Wilson, 1988.

———. *Current Biography Yearbook, 1988.* New York: H. W. Wilson, 1988.

———. *Current Biography Yearbook, 1989.* New York: H. W. Wilson, 1989.

———. *Current Biography Yearbook, 1990.* New York: H. W. Wilson, 1990.

———. *Current Biography Yearbook, 1991.* New York: H. W. Wilson, 1991.

———. *Current Biography Yearbook, 1992.* New York: H. W. Wilson, 1992.

———. *Current Biography Yearbook, 1993.* New York: H. W. Wilson, 1993.

———. *Current Biography Yearbook, 1994.* New York: H. W. Wilson, 1994.

———. *Current Biography Yearbook, 1995.* New York: H. W. Wilson, 1995.

———. *Current Biography Yearbook, 1996.* New York: H. W. Wilson, 1996.

———. *Current Biography Yearbook, 1997.* New York: H. W. Wilson, 1997.

———. *Current Biography Yearbook, 1998.* New York: H. W. Wilson, 1998.

Haarsager, Sandra. *Bertha Knight Landes of Seattle: Big-City Mayor.* Norman: University of Oklahoma Press, 1994.

Hall, Jacquelyn Dowd. *Revolt against Chivalry: Jessie Daniel Ames and the Women's Campaign against Lynching.* New York: Columbia University Press, 1979.

Halsted, James B. "Domestic Violence: Its Legal Definition." In *Domestic Violence: The Changing Criminal Justice Response.* Ed. Eve S. Buzawa and Carl G. Buzawa. Westport, CT: Auburn House, 1992.

Hankerson, Mark. "Courts Have Extended Sex Bias Law's Reach." *Congressional Quarterly Weekly Report* (27 March 1999): 747.

Hardy, Gayle J. *American Women Civil Rights Activists: Biobibliographies of 68 Leaders, 1825–1992.* Jefferson, NC: McFarland, 1993.

Harrison, Cynthia. *On Account of Sex: The Politics of Women's Issues, 1945–1968.* Berkeley: University of California Press, 1988.

Harrison, Maureen, and Steve Gilbert, eds. *Abortion Decisions of the United States Supreme Court: The 1970s.* Beverly Hills, CA: Excellent Books, 1993.

———. *Abortion Decisions of the United States Supreme Court: The 1980s.* Beverly Hills, CA: Excellent Books, 1993.

————. *Abortion Decisions of the United States Supreme Court: The 1990s.* Beverly Hills, CA: Excellent Books, 1993.

Hartmann, Susan M. *The Home Front and Beyond: American Women in the 1940s.* Boston: Twayne Publishers, 1982.

Hayden, Casey, and Mary King. "Sex and Caste: A Kind of Memo from Casey Hayden and Mary King to a Number of Other Women in the Peace and Freedom Movements." *Liberation* (April 1966): 35–36.

"Heather Wilson, R-N.M. (1)." *Congressional Quarterly Weekly Report* 56 (27 June 1998): 1752.

Heilbrun, Carolyn G. *The Education of a Woman: The Life of Gloria Steinem.* New York: Ballantine Books, 1996.

Higginbotham, Evelyn Brooks. "In Politics to Stay: Black Women Leaders and Party Politics in the 1920s." In *Women, Politics and Change.* Ed. Louise A. Tilly and Patricia Gurin. New York: Russell Sage Foundation, 1990.

Hill, Anita. *Speaking Truth to Power.* New York: Doubleday, 1997.

Hine, Darlene Clark, ed. *Black Women in America: An Historical Encyclopedia.* Brooklyn, NY: Carlson Publishing, 1993.

Hine, Darlene Clark, and Kathleen Thompson. *A Shining Thread of Hope: The History of Black Women in America.* New York: Broadway Books, 1998.

Hoff, Joan. *Law, Gender, and Injustice: A Legal History of U.S. Women.* New York: New York University Press, 1991.

Hoff-Wilson, Joan. "The Unfinished Revolution: Changing Legal Status of U.S. Women." *Signs* 13, no. 1 (Autumn 1987): 7–36.

Holtzman, Elizabeth, with Cynthia L. Cooper. *Who Said It Would Be Easy? One Woman's Life in the Political Arena.* New York: Arcade Publishing, 1996.

hooks, bell, with Tanya Mckinnon. "Sisterhood: Beyond Public and Private." *Signs* 21, no. 4 (1996): 814–829.

"House Ends Investigation of Sanchez's Election." *Congressional Quarterly Weekly Report* 56 (14 February 1998): 376.

Ireland, Patricia. *What Women Want.* New York: Dutton, 1996.

James, Edward T., ed. *Notable American Women, 1607–1950: A Biographical Dictionary.* Cambridge, MA: Belknap Press of Harvard University Press, 1971.

"Jan Schakowsky." *Congressional Quarterly Weekly Report* 56 (7 November 1998): 3015.

Jensen, Joan M. "Annette Abbott Adams, Politician." *Pacific Historical Review* 35, no. 2 (May 1966): 185–201.

Johnson, David L., and Raymond Wilson. "Gertrude Simmons Bonnin, 1876–1938: 'Americanize the First Americans.'" *American Indian Quarterly* 12 (Winter 1988): 27–40.

Johnson, John W. *Historic U.S. Court Cases 1690–1990: An Encyclopedia.* New York: Garland Publishing, 1992.

Jones, Beverly Washington. *Quest for Equality: The Life and Writings of Mary Eliza Church Terrell, 1863–1954.* Brooklyn, NY: Carlson Publishing, 1990.

Jordan, Barbara, and Shelby Hearon. *Barbara Jordan: A Self-Portrait.* Garden City, NY: Doubleday, 1979.

"Judy Biggert." *Congressional Quarterly Weekly Report* 56 (7 November 1998): 3015.

Kanellos, Nicolas. *The Hispanic-American Almanac.* Detroit: Gale Research, 1993.

Kaptur, Marcy. *Women of Congress: A Twentieth-Century Odyssey.* Washington, DC: Congressional Quarterly, 1996.

Kendrick, Ruby M. "'They Also Serve': The National Association of Colored Women, Inc." In *Black Women in American History: The Twentieth Century.* Vol. 3. Ed. Darlene Clark Hine. Brooklyn, NY: Carlson Publishing, 1990.

Kennedy, David M. *Birth Control in America: The Career of Margaret Sanger.* New Haven, CT: Yale University Press, 1970.

Kennedy, Flo. *Color Me Flo: My Hard Life and Good Times.* Englewood Cliffs, NJ: Prentice-Hall, 1976.

Kerr, Andrea Moore. *Lucy Stone: Speaking Out for Equality.* New Brunswick, NJ: Rutgers University Press, 1992.

Kinyon, Jeannette, and Jean Walz. *The Incredible Gladys Pyle.* Vermillion, SD: Dakota Press, 1985.

Klapper, Zina. "Activist Lawyer." *Ms.* (November 1985): 67–69.

Kunin, Madeleine. *Living a Political Life.* New York: Alfred A. Knopf, 1994.

Kyvig, David E. "Women against Prohibition." *American Quarterly* 28, no. 4 (Fall 1976): 465–482.

LaBlanc, Michael, ed. *Contemporary Black Biography: Profiles from the International Black Community.* Vol. 1. Detroit: Gale Research, 1992.

"Lack of Evidence Brings Probe of Senate Election to an End." *Congressional Quarterly Weekly Report* 55 (4 October 1997): 2376.

"Lady from Nebraska." *Newsweek* (20 December 1954): 20.

Lamson, Peggy. *In the Vanguard: Six American Women in Public Life.* Boston: Houghton Mifflin, 1979.

Lane, Ann J. *To Herland and Beyond: The Life and Work of Charlotte Perkins Gilman.* New York: Meridian Books, 1991.

Lasch, Christopher, ed. *The Social Thought of Jane Addams.* Indianapolis: Bobbs-Merrill Company, 1965.

Lash, Joseph P. *Eleanor: The Years Alone.* New York: W. W. Norton, 1972.

Layton, Stanford J. "Ivy Baker Priest, Treasurer of the United States." In *Worth Their Salt: Notable but Often Unnoted Women of Utah.* Ed. Colleen Whitley. Logan: Utah State University Press, 1996.

Lee, Richard W. *"Do Everything" Reform: The Oratory of Frances E. Willard.* New York: Greenwood Press, 1992.

Lehrer, Susan. *Origins of Protective Labor Legislation for Women, 1905–1925.* Albany: State University of New York Press, 1987.

Lemons, J. Stanley. *The Woman Citizen: Social Feminism in the 1920s.* Urbana: University of Illinois Press, 1973.

Lerner, Gerda. *The Feminist Thought of Sarah Grimké.* New York: Oxford University Press, 1998.

Levin, Phyllis Lee. *Abigail Adams: A Biography.* New York: St. Martin's Press, 1987.

Levine, Susan. *Degrees of Equality: The American Association of University Women and the Challenge of Twentieth-Century Feminism.* Philadelphia: Temple University Press, 1995.

Levy, Anne, and Michele Paludi. *Workplace Sexual Harassment.* Upper Saddle River, NJ: Prentice Hall, 1997.

Linden-Ward, Blanche, and Carol Hurd Green. *American Women in the 1960s: Changing the Future.* New York: Twayne Publishers, 1993.

Lindenmeyer, Kriste. *"A Right to Childhood": The U.S. Children's Bureau and Child Welfare, 1912–1946.* Urbana: University of Illinois Press, 1997.

Linkugel, Wil A., and Martha Solomon. *Anna Howard Shaw: Suffrage Orator and Social Reformer.* New York: Greenwood Press, 1991.

"Lois Capps, D-California." *Congressional Quarterly Weekly Report* 56 (14 March 1998): 687.

Louchheim, Katie. *By the Political Sea.* Garden City, NY: Doubleday, 1970.

Lunardini, Christine A. *From Equal Suffrage to Equal Rights: Alice Paul and the National Woman's Party.* New York: New York University Press, 1986.

Mabunda, L. Mpho, ed. *Contemporary Black Biography: Profiles from the International Black Community.* Vol. 8. Detroit: Gale Research, 1995.

———. *Contemporary Black Biography: Profiles from the International Black Community.* Vol. 9. Detroit: Gale Research, 1995.

———. *Contemporary Black Biography: Profiles from the International Black Community.* Vol. 10. Detroit: Gale Research, 1996.

Malone, David. *Hattie and Huey: An Arkansas Tour.* Fayetteville: University of Arkansas Press, 1989.

Mankiller, Wilma, and Michael Wallis. *Mankiller: A Chief and Her People.* New York: St. Martin's Press, 1993.

Margolies-Mezvinsky, Marjorie, with Barbara Feinman. *A Woman's Place . . . the Freshmen Women Who Changed the Face of Congress.* New York: Crown Publishers, 1994.

Markoff, Helene S. "The Federal Women's Program." *Public Administration Review* 32, no. 2 (March–April 1972): 144–151.

Martin, George. *Madam Secretary Frances Perkins.* Boston: Houghton Mifflin, 1976.

Matthews, Glenna. *The Rise of Public Woman: Woman's Power and Woman's Place in the United States, 1630–1970.* New York: Oxford University Press, 1992.

Matthews, Jean W. *Women's Struggle for Equality: The First Phase, 1828–1876.* Chicago: Ivan R. Dee, 1997.

McClure, Sandy. *Christie Whitman: A Political Biography for the People.* Amherst, MA: Prometheus Books, 1996.

McFeely, William S. *Frederick Douglass.* New York: W. W. Norton, 1991.

Mead, Margaret, and Frances Bagley Kaplan, eds. *American Women: The Report of the President's Commission on the Status of Women and Other Publications of the Commission.* New York: Charles Scribner's Sons, 1965.

Melich, Tanya. *The Republican War against Women: An Insider's Report from Behind the Lines.* New York: Bantam Books, 1996.

Miller, Kathleen Atkinson. "The Ladies and the Lynchers: A Look at the Association of Southern Women for the Prevention of Lynching." *Southern Studies* 17 (Fall 1978): 221–240.

Miller, Kristie. *Ruth Hanna McCormick: A Life in Politics 1880–1944.* Albuquerque: University of New Mexico Press, 1992.

Miller, Sally M. *From Prairie to Prison: The Life of Social Activist Kate Richards O'Hare.* Columbia: University of Missouri Press, 1993.

Mills, Kay. "Maxine Waters: The Sassy Legislator Who Knows There's More Than

One Way to Make a Political Statement." *Governing* 1, no. 6 (March 1988): 26–33.

———. *This Little Light of Mine: The Life of Fannie Lou Hamer.* New York: Dutton, 1993.

———. "Women Standing for Women: The Early Political Career of Mary T. Norton." *New Jersey History* 96, nos. 1–2 (Spring/Summer 1978): 27–42.

Molinari, Susan, with Elinor Burkett. *Representative Mom: Balancing Budgets, Bill, and Baby in the U.S. Congress.* New York: Doubleday, 1998.

Mooney, Louise, ed. *Newsmakers: 1990 Cumulation.* Detroit: Gale Research, 1990.

———. *Newsmakers: 1993 Cumulation.* Detroit: Gale Research, 1993.

Morello, Karen Berger. *The Woman Lawyer in America: 1638 to the Present.* Boston: Beacon Press, 1986.

Morgan, Georgia Cook. "India Edwards: Distaff Politician of the Truman Era." *Missouri Historical Review* 78 (April 1984): 293–310.

Morris, Sylvia Jukes. *Rage for Fame: The Ascent of Clare Boothe Luce.* New York: Random House, 1997.

Motley, Constance Baker. *Equal Justice under Law: An Autobiography.* New York: Farrar, Straus & Giroux, 1998.

Moynihan, Ruth Barnes. *Rebel for Rights: Abigail Scott Duniway.* New Haven: Yale University Press, 1983.

Mullaney, Marie Marmo. *Biographical Directory of the Governors of the United States 1983–1988.* Westport, CT: Meckler Publishing, 1989.

———. *Biographical Directory of the Governors of the United States 1988–1994.* Westport, CT: Greenwood Press, 1994.

Murray, Pauli. *Song in a Weary Throat: An American Pilgrimage.* New York: Harper and Row, 1987.

National Consumers League. *Roots of the Consumer Movement: A Chronicle of Consumer History in the Twentieth Century.* Washington, DC: National Consumers League, 1979.

National Women's Political Caucus. *Democratic Women Are Wonderful: A History of Women at Democratic National Conventions.* Washington, DC: National Women's Political Caucus, 1980.

———. *National Directory of Women Elected Officials 1995.* Washington, DC: National Women's Political Caucus, 1995.

"NFRW: Fifty Years of Leadership, 1938–1988." Washington, DC: National Federation of Republican Women, 1987.

Norton, Mary Beth. *Liberty's Daughters: The Revolutionary Experience of American Women 1750–1800.* Glenview, IL: Scott, Foresman, 1980.

Noun, Louise. "Amelia Bloomer, A Biography: Part I, the Lily of Seneca Falls." *The Annals of Iowa* 47, no. 7 (Winter 1985): 575–617.

———. "Amelia Bloomer: Part II, The Suffragist of Council Bluffs." *The Annals of Iowa* 47, no. 8 (Spring 1985): 575–621.

Office of the Historian, U.S. House of Representatives. *Women in Congress, 1917–1990.* Washington, DC: U.S. Government Printing Office, 1991.

Orleck, Annelise. *Common Sense and a Little Fire: Women and Working-Class Politics in the United States, 1900–1965.* Chapel Hill: University of North Carolina Press, 1995.

Painter, Nell Irvin. *Sojourner Truth: A Life, a Symbol.* New York: W. W. Norton, 1996.

Park, Maud Wood. *The Front Door Lobby.* Ed. Edna Lamprey Stantial. Boston: Beacon Press, 1960.

Parks, Rosa, with Gregory J. Reed. *Quiet Strength: The Faith, the Hope, and the Heart of a Woman Who Changed a Nation.* Grand Rapids, MI: Zondervan Publishing House, 1994.

Paul, Sonay, and Robert Perkinson. "Winona LaDuke." *Progressive* 59 (October 1995): 36–39.

Perkins, Carol O. "The Pragmatic Idealism of Mary McLeod Bethune. " *Sage* 5, no. 2 (Fall 1988): 30–36.

Perry, Elisabeth Israels. *Belle Moskowitz: Feminine Politics and the Exercise of Power in the Age of Alfred E. Smith.* New York: Oxford University Press, 1987.

Phelps, Shirelle, ed. *Contemporary Black Biography: Profiles from the International Black Community.* Vol. 12. Detroit: Gale Research, 1996.

———. *Contemporary Black Biography: Profiles from the International Black Community.* Vol. 13. Detroit: Gale Research, 1997.

Podell, Janet, ed. *The Annual Obituary 1981.* New York: St. Martin's Press, 1982.

Raimo, John W., ed. *Biographical Directory of the Governors of the United States 1978–1983.* Westport, CT: Meckler Publishing, 1985.

Randall, Mercedes M., ed. *Beyond Nationalism: The Social Thought of Emily Greene Balch.* New York: Twayne Publishers, 1972.

Ravitch, Diane, ed. *The American Reader: Words That Moved a Nation.* New York: HarperCollins, 1990.

Reagan, Nancy, with William Novak. *My Turn: The Memoirs of Nancy Reagan.* New York: Random House, 1989.

"Representative Pearl Peden Oldfield." *The Democratic Bulletin* 4, no. 4 (April 1929): 10.

Richards, Ann, with Peter Knobler. *Straight from the Heart: My Life in Politics and Other Places.* New York: Simon and Schuster, 1989.

Richardson, Marilyn, ed. *Maria W. Stewart, America's First Black Woman Political Writer: Essays and Speeches.* Bloomington: Indiana University Press, 1987.

Riley, Glenda. *Divorce: An American Tradition.* New York: Oxford University Press, 1991.

Roberts, Barbara. "Coloring Outside the Lines." In *True to Ourselves.* Ed. Nancy M. Neuman. San Francisco: Jossey-Bass Publishers, 1998.

Roberts, Cokie, and Steve Roberts. "When Working Mothers Make the Laws." *USA Weekend* (9–11 May 1997): 4–6.

Roberts, Jerry. *Dianne Feinstein: Never Let Them See You Cry.* New York: Harper-Collins West, 1994.

Rogers, Mary Beth. *Barbara Jordan: American Hero.* New York: Bantam Books, 1998.

Rogow, Faith. *Gone to Another Meeting: The National Council of Jewish Women, 1893–1993.* Tuscaloosa: University of Alabama Press, 1993.

Roosevelt, Eleanor, and Lorena A. Hickok. *Ladies of Courage.* New York: Putnam, 1954.

Rosenberg, Rina. "Representing Women at the State and Local Levels: Commissions on the Status of Women." In *Women, Power and Public Policy.* Ed. Ellen Bonepath. New York: Pergamon Press, 1982.

Rymph, Catherine E. "Marion Martin and the Problem of Republican Feminism, 1937–1947." University of Iowa, 1996. Unpublished paper.

Sachs, Albie, and Joan Hoff Wilson. *Sexism and the Law: A Study of Male Beliefs and Legal Bias in Britain and the United States.* New York: Free Press, 1978.

Salem, Dorothy. *To Better Our World: Black Women in Organized Reform, 1890–1920.* Brooklyn, NY: Carlson Publishing, 1990.

Sample, Herbert A. "California's Newest 'New Democrat.'" *California Journal* (March 1997): 48–50.

Schneir, Miriam, ed. *Feminism in Our Time: The Essential Writings, World War II to the Present.* New York: Vintage Books, 1994.

Schoenebaum, Eleanora, ed. *Political Profiles: The Eisenhower Years.* New York: Facts on File, 1977.

———. *Political Profiles: The Nixon/Ford Years.* New York: Facts on File, 1979.

———. *Political Profiles: The Truman Years.* New York: Facts on File, 1978.

Schroeder, Pat. *24 Years of House Work . . . and the Place Is Still a Mess: My Life in Politics.* Kansas City, MO: Andrews & McMeel Publishing, 1998.

Schroeder, Pat, with Andrea Camp and Robyn Lipner. *Champion of the Great American Family.* New York: Random House, 1989.

Schweber, Claudine A. "But Some Were Less Equal . . . the Fight for Women Jurors." In *Women Organizing: An Anthology.* Ed. Bernice Cummings and Victoria Schuck. Metuchen, NJ: Scarecrow Press, 1979.

Scott, John Anthony. *Woman against Slavery: The Story of Harriet Beecher Stowe.* New York: Thomas Y. Crowell, 1978.

"Sheila Frahm, R-Kansas." *Congressional Quarterly Weekly Report* (25 May 1996): 1480.

"Shelley Berkley." *Congressional Quarterly Weekly Report* (7 November 1998): 3018.

Sicherman, Barbara, and Carol Hurd Green, eds. *Notable American Women: The Modern Period.* Cambridge, MA: Belknap Press of Harvard University, 1980.

Sklar, Kathryn Kish. *Florence Kelley and the Nation's Work: The Rise of Women's Political Culture, 1830–1900.* New Haven, CT: Yale University Press, 1995.

Slavin, Sarah, ed. *U.S. Women's Interest Groups: Institutional Profiles.* Westport, CT: Greenwood Press, 1995.

Smith, Jessie Carney, ed. *Epic Lives: One Hundred Black Women Who Made a Difference* Detroit: Visible Ink, 1993.

———. *Notable Black American Women.* Detroit: Gale Research, 1991.

———. *Notable Black American Women, Book 2.* Detroit: Gale Research, 1996.

———. *Powerful Black Women.* Detroit: Visible Ink, 1996.

Smith, Sally Bedell. *Reflected Glory: The Life of Pamela Churchill Harriman.* New York: Touchstone Books, 1997.

Solomon, Martha. *Emma Goldman.* Boston: Twayne Publishers, 1987.

Spender, Dale, ed. *Feminist Theorists: Three Centuries of Key Women Thinkers.* New York: Pantheon Books, 1983.

Spritzer, Lorraine Nelson. *The Belle of Ashby Street: Helen Douglas Mankin and Georgia Politics.* Athens: University of Georgia Press, 1982.

Stan, Adele M. "Frances Kissling: Making the Vatican Sweat." *Ms.* (September–October 1995): 40–43.

Stanley, Ruth Moore. "Alice M. Robertson, Oklahoma's First Congresswoman." *Chronicles of Oklahoma* 45 (Autumn 1967): 259–289.

"Stephanie Tubbs Jones." *Congressional Quarterly Weekly Report* 56 (7 November 1998): 3021.

"Still on the Front Line." *Ebony* (July 1990): 58–59.

Stimpson, Catharine, ed. *Women and the "Equal Rights" Amendment: Senate Subcommittee Hearings on the Constitutional Amendment, 91st Congress.* New York: R. R. Bowker, 1972.

Stineman, Esther. *American Political Women: Contemporary and Historical Profiles.* Littleton, CO: Libraries Unlimited, 1980.

Strakosh, Avery. "A Woman in Law." *The Saturday Evening Post* (24 September 1927): 17, 190, 192.

Süllwold, Corliss. "Nebraska's Virginia": A Study of Former Congresswoman Virginia Dodd Smith." Master's thesis, University of Nebraska, 1993.

"Tammy Baldwin." *Congressional Quarterly Weekly Report* 56 (7 November 1998): 3024.

Taylor, Bron Raymond. *Affirmative Action at Work: Law, Politics, and Ethics.* Pittsburgh: University of Pittsburgh Press, 1991.

Telgen, Diane, and Jim Kamp, eds. *Notable Hispanic American Women.* Detroit: Gale Research, 1993.

Thomas, Sue. *How Women Legislate.* New York: Oxford University Press, 1994.

Tilly, Louise A., and Patricia Gurin, eds. *Women, Politics and Change.* New York: Russell Sage Foundation, 1990.

Tolchin, Susan. *Women in Congress: 1917–1976.* Washington, DC: Government Printing Office, 1976.

Tomlinson, Barbara J. "Making Their Way: A Study of New Jersey Congresswomen, 1924–1994." Ph.D. diss., Rutgers University, 1996.

Trattner, Walter I. *Crusade for the Children: A History of the National Child Labor Committee and Child Labor Reform in America.* Chicago: Quadrangle Books, 1970.

Treese, Joel D., ed. *Biographical Directory of the American Congress 1774–1996.* Alexandria, VA: CQ Staff Directories, 1997.

Turner, Roland, ed. *The Annual Obituary 1980.* New York: St. Martin's Press, 1981.

Underhill, Lois Beachy. *The Woman Who Ran for President: The Many Lives of Victoria Woodhull.* Bridgehampton, NY: Bridge Works, 1995.

Upton, Harriet Taylor. "The Machine and the Woman." *The Ladies Home Journal* (October 1922): 13, 159.

Van Sickel, Robert. *Not a Particularly Different Voice: The Jurisprudence of Sandra Day O'Connor.* New York: Peter Lang, 1998.

Van Voris, Jacqueline. *Carrie Chapman Catt: A Public Life.* New York: Feminist Press, 1987.

Viorst, Judith. "The Woman behind the First Lady." *Redbook* (June 1993): 64–66, 68.

Von Mehren, Joan. *Minerva and the Muse: A Life of Margaret Fuller.* Amherst: University of Massachusetts Press, 1994.

Wallace, Patricia Ward. *Politics of Conscience: A Biography of Margaret Chase Smith.* Westport, CT: Praeger, 1995.

Wandersee, Winifred D. *On the Move: American Women in the 1970s.* Boston: Twayne Publishers, 1988.

Ware, Susan. *Partner and I: Molly Dewson, Feminism, and New Deal Politics.* New Haven, CT: Yale University Press, 1987.

Warshaw, Shirley Anne. *Powersharing: White House–Cabinet Relations in the Modern Presidency.* New York: State University of New York Press, 1996.

Weaver, Judith L. "Edith Bolling Wilson as First Lady: A Study in the Power of Personality, 1919–1920." *Presidential Studies Quarterly* 15, no. 1 (Winter 1985): 51–76.

Weddington, Sarah. *A Question of Choice.* New York: G. P. Putnam's Sons, 1992.

"Welfare Overview." *Congressional Digest* 74, nos. 6–7 (June–July 1995): 163–165, 192.

Wells-Barnett, Ida B. *Crusade for Justice: The Autobiography of Ida B. Wells.* Ed. Alfreda M. Duster. Chicago: University of Chicago Press, 1970.

Wertheimer, Barbara M. *We Were There: The Story of Working Women in America.* New York: Pantheon Books, 1977.

Whitman, Alden, ed. *American Reformers: An H. W. Wilson Biographical Dictionary.* New York: H. W. Wilson, 1985.

Williams, Clare B., comp. *The History of the Founding and Development of the National Federation of Republican Women.* Washington, DC: Women's Division, Republican National Committee, 1963.

Wood, James E. "The Religious Coalition for Abortion Rights: An Analysis of Its Role in the Pro-Choice Movement." Master's thesis, Baylor University, 1990.

Yelverton, Mildred Griffin. *They Also Served: Twenty-Five Remarkable Alabama Women.* Dothan, AL: Ampersand Publishing, 1993.

Young, Louise M. *In the Public Interest: The League of Women Voters 1920–1970.* Westport, CT: Greenwood Press, 1989.

Zia, Helen, and Susan B. Gall, eds. *Notable Asian Americans.* Detroit: Gale Research, 1995.

Internet Sources

http://allpolitics.com/1998/03/31abzug/

http://baez.woz.org

http://clerkweb.house.gov

http://copper.ucs.indiana.edu/~ljray/lifelink/plfem.html

http://dol.gov/dol/opa/public/media/press/wb/wb96066.htm

http://feminist.com

http://fix.net/sldoc/lois-bio.html

http://nwpc.org

http://orgs.womenconnect.com

http://plato.divanet.com/mansco/qnn/1997/oct/qnn-97-10-01%20 articles%2010.1.97.3html

http://redbud.lbjlib.utexas.edu/eisenhower/fa7317.txt

http://secretary.state.gov/www/albright.html

http://secretary.state.gov/www/iacw/

http://supct.law.cornell.edu/supct/html/89-1215.zo.html

http://supct.law.cornell.edu/supct/justices.bio.html

http://tamusbor.tamu.edu/Biographies/ala.htm

http://wp5.washingtonpost.com/wpsrv/politics/campaign/keyraces98/stories/ ca040698.htm

www.aauw.org
www.abanet.org
www.acf.dhhs.gov
www.aclu.org
www.af.mil
www.aflcio.org
www.aflcio.org/profile/chavez.htm
www.all.org
www.basenet.net
www.biggert.com
www.bog.frb.fed.us
www.bpwusa.org
www.businessweek.com
www.businessweek.com/1997/09/b3516111.htm
www.cath4choice.org
www.cc.org
www.cdc.gov
www.childrensdefense.org
www.civilrights.org
www.cluw.org
www.crlp.org
www.cwfa.org
www.doi.gov/adabio.html
www.dol.gov
www.dol.gov/dol/asp/public/programs/handbook/fmla.htm
www.dol.gov/dol/wb/public/edu/gallery.htm
www.dol.gov/dol/wb/public/programs
www.dst1913.org
www.eagleforum.org
www.eagleforum.org/mics/descript/html
www.ed.gov
www.edc.org
www.edc.org/WomensEquity/weeainfo/index.html
www.eeoc.gov
www.eeoc.gov/facts/fs-preg.html
www.emilyslist.org
www-eshoo.house.gov/bio/html
www.feminist.com.
www.feminist.com/nwpc.htm
www.feminist.org
www.few.org
www.gfwc.org
www.gis.net
www.gis.net/~dismith/dob1.html
www.governor.state.az
www.governor.state.az.us/news/html
www.greens.org
www.hhs.gov

www.house.gov/carson/bio1.htm
www.house.gov/chenoweth/chenbio.htm
www.house.gov/christensen/dcgbio.htm
www.house.gov/clayton/bio.htm
www.house.gov/degette/BIOLAST.htm
www.house.gov/delauro/bio.html
www.house.gov/dunn/bio.htm
www.house.gov/ebjohnson/bio.htm
www.house.gov/emerson/bio.htm
www.house.gov/fowler/bio_fowler.html.
www.house.gov/furse/efbio2.htm
www.house.gov/granger/bio.htm
www.house.gov/harman/
www.house.gov/hooley
www.house.gov/jacksonlee/bio
www.house.gov/kaptur/bio_oh09.htm
www.house.gov/kennelly/bio.htm
www.house.gov/lindasmith/bio.htm
www.house.gov/lofgren/bio_lofgren.html
www.house.gov/lowey/bio./htm
www.house.gov/lowey/caucus.htm
www.house.gov/maloney/
www.house.gov/mckinney/biograph.html
www.house.gov/meek/bio.htm
www.house.gov/molinari/bio.htm
www.house.gov/myrick/bio.htm
www.house.gov/northrup/bio.htm
www.house.gov/norton/bio.htm
www.house.gov/pelosi.bio_pel.htm
www.house.gov/pryce/prycebio.htm
www.house.gov/rivers/bio.htm
www.house.gov/ros-lehtinen/bio.htm
www.house.gov/royball-allard/biography.htm.
www.house.gov/slaughter/bio.htm
www.house.gov/stabenow/about
wwwhouse. gov/suekelly/bio.htm
www.house.gov/tauscher.biograph.htm
www.house.gov/thurman/about.htm
www.house.gov/velazquez/bio.htm
www.house.gov/wilson/biography/index.htm
www.house.gov/woolsey/bio.htm
www.iwf.org
www.lbjlib.utexas.edu/ford/library/faintro/armstro1.htm
www.lwv.org
www.medill.nwu.edu
www.medill.nwu.edu/people/cook
www.ms.foundation.org
www.naacp.org

www.nacw.org

www.nara.gov/fedreg/eo1963k.html

www.naral.org

www.ncadv.org

www.nclnet.org

www.ncnw.com

www.nfrw.org

www.njcw.org

www.now.org

www.npcbw.org

www.pbs.org

www.pbs.org/newshour/

www.plannedparenthood.org

www.rci.rutgers.edu/~cawp

www.rci.rutgers.edu/~cawp/fed/cab97.html

www.rcrc.org.

www.rfc-pac.org

www.sba.gov/alvarez/

www.seminoletribe.com

www.senate.gov/boxer/~#alphbio/committees

www.senate.gov/~feinstein/dfbio.html

www.senate.gov/~hutchison/bio.htm

www.senate.gov/~mikulski/bio.htm

www.senate.gov/~moseley-braun/bio.htm

www.senate.gov/~murray/bio2.html

www.senate.gov/~snowe/bio.htm

www.serve.com/fem4life

www.shelleyberkley.com

www.ssa.gov

www.state.nh.us/governor/bio.html

www.tammybaldwin.com

www.thewishlist.org

www.usccr.gov

www.usda.gov

www.usda.gov/agencies/gallery/thompson.htm

www.usdoj.gov

www.usdoj.gov/bios/jreno.html

www.usdoj.gov.vawo/bcbio.htm

www.usdoj.gov.vawo/vawafct.htm

www.usdoj.gov/vawo/vawofct.htm

www.ustr.gov/people/Ambassador/barshefsky.html

www.wctu.org

www.whitehouse.gov

www.whitehouse.gov/wh/eop/cea/html/yellen.html

www.whitehouse.gov/wh/eop/first_lady/html/hillary_bio.html

www.whitehouse.gov/wh/glimpse/firstladies/html/rc39.html.

www.wilpf.org

www.womenconnect.com

www.womenconnect.com/ncbw/history.htm
www.womenwork.org
www.ywca.org
www4.od.nih.gov/orwh/overview.html

Laws Cited

Adkins v. Children's Hospital, 261 U.S. 525 (1923)

Bachur v. Democratic National Committee, 836 F.2d 837 (4th Cir. 1987)

Beal v. Doe, 432 U.S. 438 (1977)

Bellotti v. Baird, 428 U.S. 132 (1976)

Bellotti v. Baird, 443 U.S. 622 (1979)

Bowe v. Colgate-Palmolive Company, 416 F.2d 711 (1969)

Bowers v. Hardwick, 478 U.S. 186 (1986)

Bray v. Alexandria Clinic, 506 U.S. 263 (1993)

California Savings and Loan Assn. v. Guerra, 479 U.S. 272 (1987)

Carey v. Population Services International, 431 U.S. 678 (1977)

City of Akron v. Akron Center for Reproductive Health, 462 U.S. 416 (1983)

Cleveland Board of Education v. LaFleur, 414 U.S. 632 (1974)

Clinton v. Jones, No. 95-1853 (1997).

Colautti v. Franklin, 439 U.S. 379 (1979)

Corning Glass Works v. Brennan, 417 U.S. 188 (1974)

County of Washington, Oregon v. Gunther, 452 U.S. 161 (1981)

Craig v. Boren, 429 U.S. 190 (1976)

Diaz v. Pan American World Airways, Inc., 442 F.2d 385 (1971)

Doe v. Bolton, 410 U.S. 179 (1973)

Dothard v. Rawlinson, 433 U.S. 321 (1977)

Eisenstadt v. Baird, 405 U.S. 438 (1972)

Frontiero v. Richardson, 411 U.S. 677 (1973)

Geduldig v. Aiello, 417 U.S. 484 (1974)

General Electric v. Gilbert, 429 U.S. 125 (1976)

Goesaert v. Cleary, 335 U.S. 464 (1948)

Griswold v. Connecticut, 381 U.S. 479 (1965)

Grove City College v. Bell, 465 U.S. 555 (1984)

H. L. v. Matheson, 450 U.S. 398 (1981)

Harris v. McRae, 448 U.S. 297 (1980)

Hishon v. King and Spalding, 467 U.S. 69 (1984)

Hodgson v. Minnesota, 497 U.S. 417 (1990)

Hoyt v. Florida, 368 U.S. 57 (1961)

Johnson v. Transportation Agency, 480 U.S. 616 (1987)

Kirchberg v. Feenstra, 450 U.S. 455 (1981)

Maher v. Roe, 432 U.S. 464 (1977)

McCarty v. McCarty, 453 U.S. 210 (1981)

Meritor Savings Bank v. Vinson, 477 U.S. 57 (1986)

Mississippi University for Women v. Hogan, 458 U.S. 718 (1982)

Muller v. Oregon, 208 U.S. 412 (1908)

Nashville Gas Co. v. Satty, 434 U.S. 136 (1977)

Ohio v. Akron Center, 497 U.S. 502 (1990)

Orr v. Orr, 440 U.S. 268 (1979)

Personnel Administrator of the Commonwealth of Massachusetts v. Feeney, 442 U.S. 256 (1979)

Phillips v. Martin Marietta, 400 U.S. 542 (1971)

Planned Parenthood Association of Kansas City, Mo. v. Ashcroft, 462 U.S. 476 (1983)

Planned Parenthood of Central Missouri v. Danforth, 428 U.S. 52 (1976)

Planned Parenthood of Southeastern Pennsylvania v. Casey, 505 U.S. 833 (1992)

Poelker v. Doe, 432 U.S. 519 (1977)

Price Waterhouse v. Hopkins, 490 U.S. 228 (1989)

Reed v. Reed, 404 U.S. 71 (1971)

Rust v. Sullivan, 500 U.S. 173 (1991)

Taylor v. Louisiana, 419 U.S. 522 (1975)

Thornburgh v. American College of Obstetrics and Gynecology, 476 U.S. 747 (1986)

UAW v. Johnson Controls, 499 U.S. 187 (1991)

United States v. Virginia, 518 U.S. 515 (1996)

Webster v. Reproductive Health Services, 492 U.S. 490 (1989)

Weeks v. Southern Bell Telephone and Telegraph Company, 408 F.2d 228 (1969)

Weinberger v. Wiesenfeld, 420 U.S. 636 (1975)

Williams v. Zbaraz, 448 U.S. 358 (1980)

Index

Equal division rule. *See* Democratic Party

Equal Employment Opportunity Act (1972), 19, **234**, 235

Equal Employment Opportunity Commission (EEOC), xlii, 142, 144, 230, **234–236**, 305, 484, 504–505, 528, 550. *See also* Civil Rights acts; Sex discrimination; Sexual harassment

Equal Employment Opportunity Program, 257

Equal Pay Act (1963), 143, 173, 175, 208, 213, 230, 234, **236–237**, 305, 528
  support for, 28, 105, 301, 305, 507, 534

Equal Rights Amendment (ERA), xli, xliii, 116, **237–245**, 276, 417, 437, 461, 479, 484, 485, 496, 596, 626, 633, 710, 748–756
  in Democratic Party, 191–192, 193, 194
  groups opposing, 162–163, 215, 237, 242, 291, 395, 461, 475–476, 485, 543, 646, 717
  groups supporting, 28, 105, 143, 162, 167–168, 246–247, 291, 395, 417, 461, 479, 484–485, 496, 710
  individuals opposing, 240, 601–602, 655
  individuals supporting, 116, 238, 276, 437, 543, 596, 626, 633
  movement preceding, 217–218, 489–491, 524, 527
  passage of, 237–244, 246, 305–306, 546
  and protective legislation, 35, 36, 192, 237, 383, 395, 475–476, 491, 533–534, 543, 655, 708, 715
  ratification attempts, 240, 242–244, 326, 486, 494, 602, 621, 642
  in Republican Party, 178, 572, 573
  text of, 240

Equal rights amendments, state, **245–246**

Equal Rights Party, 542, 721

Equality League of Self-Supporting Women (ELSSW), 75, 717

ERA. *See* Equal Rights Amendment

ERA Action Committee, 242

ERAmerica, 105, 117, 118, 243, **246–247**

Ervin, Sam J., Jr., 240

Eshoo, Anna, **247–248**

Eslick, Willa, **248**

Estrich, Susan, **248–249**

Evers-Williams, Myrlie, **249–250**

Executive Order 10925 (1961), 19

Executive Order 10980 (1961), **250**, 542

Executive Order 11126 (1963), 142, **250–251**, 544

Executive Order 11246 (1965), 19, **251**, 257

Executive Order 11375 (1967), 19, 222, **251**, 257, 258, 485

Executive Order 11478 (1969), 257

Executive Order 11832 (1975), 473

Executive Order 12050 (1978), 457

Extended Voting Rights Act (1975), 365

Fair Employment Practices Commission, 189

Fair Housing Rights Act (1968), 470

Fair Labor Standards Act (1938), 237, 507, 531, 544, 709

Fair Pay Act, 105

Family and Medical Leave Act (1993), xliv, 95, **253–254**
  support for, 105, 166, 168, 395, 444, 447, 501, 510, 588, 604

Family cap, 570

Family, Liberty, and God, 242

Family planning. *See* Abortion; Contraception; Reproductive rights

Family policies. *See* Child day care; Domestic violence; Family and Medical Leave Act

Family Stability and Work Act (1995), 444

Family Support Act (1988), 134–135, 588

Family Violence Prevention and Services Act (1984), 206

Farenthold, Frances (Sissy), 193, **254–255**, 316–317, 542, 642

Farrington, Mary Elizabeth, **255–256**

Fauset, Crystal, **256–257**, 638

Federal Contract Compliance, Office of, 19

Federal Women's Program (FWP), 251, **257**, 258

Federally Employed Women (FEW), **257–258**

Feigen, Brenda, 642

Feinstein, Dianne, 166, **258–260**

Feldt, Gloria, 803

Felton, Rebecca, **260–261**

Female Anti-Slavery Convention, 453

Females Opposed to Equality, 242

Feminine Mystique, The (Friedan), **261–262**

Feminism/feminist movement, xlii, 194, 261–262, **263–265**, 339, 352, 413, 456–457, 523, 626, 715–716
  first/second wave, 263–265
  individuals in, 46–47, 61–62, 280–282, 339, 413–414, 441–442, 640–643
  and lesbians, 442, 486, 558, 642
  and men, 282
  precursors of, 283–285, 291–293, 307
  See also Radical feminism; Spider Web

Feminist Majority Foundation, 263

Feminist Majority, The, **262–263**, 345

Nader, Ralph, 302
Napolitano, Grace, **456**
Nash, Diane, 148
Nashville Gas Co. v. Satty, 231, **465–466**
National Abortion Rights Action League (NARAL), **466**
National Advisory Committee for Women (NACW), 11, **467**, 475, 494, 495
National Afro-American Council, 694
National Alliance against Racist and Political Oppression, 183
National American Woman Suffrage Association (NAWSA), 16, 26, 63, 72, 74, 123–125, **467–469**, 650–652, 653
    Congressional Committee of, 169–170, 429, 525, 526, 651, 675
    individuals in, 16, 63, 72, 74, 123–125, 195, 429, 521, 613–614, 637–638, 646
    Winning Plan of, 123, 125, 468–469, 651–652, 746
National Association for the Advancement of Colored People (NAACP), **469–471**
    individuals in, 50–51, 249–250, 347, 372–373, 388–389, 451–452, 522, 618, 657, 660, 693–694
    issues supported by, 43, 146, 147
National Association of Colored Women (NACW), 146, 160, 290, **471–472**, 479, 481, 483, 592, 653
    individuals in, 70, 388–389, 657, 660, 661, 693
National Association of Commissions for Women (NACW), 161, **472**, 483
National Association Opposed to Woman Suffrage, 631
National Birth Control League (NBCL), 195
National Child Labor Committee, 373, 683
National Coalition Against Domestic Violence (NCADV), **473**
National Coalition of 100 Black Women (NCBW), 426, **473**
National Colored Women's League (NCWL), 471
National Commission on the Observance of International Women's Year, **473–475**, 495, 621, 643
National Committee on Federal Legislation for Birth Control (NCFLBC), 599
National Committee on Pay Equity, **475**, 528
National Committee on the Cause and Cure of War, 126
National Committee on the Status of Women, 476

National Committee to Defeat the Un-Equal Rights Amendment (NC-DURA), 238, **475–476**
National Conference of Puerto Rican Women, 174
National Congress of Mothers, 714
National Consumers League (NCL), 196, 237, 372, 458, 475, **476–478**, 550, 714
National Council of Catholic Women, 476
National Council of Jewish Women (NCJW), **478–479**, 714
National Council of Negro Women (NCNW), 70, 146, 174, 326, 327, 472, 476, **479–481**
National Council on Indian Opportunity, 321
National Day of Commitment to Eliminate Racism, 727
National Displaced Homemakers Network, 707
National Education Association, 216, 286, 384
National Farm Workers Association (NFWA), 343
National Federation of Afro-American Women (NFAAW), 160, 290, 471, **481**, 592, 661
National Federation of Independent Business, 253
National Federation of Republican Women (NFRW), 424, **481–483**, 570, 572, 625, 692
National Gender Balance Project USA (NGBP), **483**
National Institute of Public Affairs, 703
National Institutes of Health (NIH), 712
National League of Republican Colored Women (NLRCW), **483–484**
National Organization for Women (NOW), xlii, 216, 282, 329–330, 351–353, 375–376, 422, 460, **484–486**, 545, 735, 737
    and ERA, 239, 242, 243, 244, 246
    issues supported by, 8, 46, 113, 140, 233, 235, 270, 509, 518, 541
    Legal Defense and Education Fund, 485
    and lesbianism, 398, 486, 558
National Organization of Black Elected Legislative Women (NOBEL), **486–487**
National Plan of Action (NWC), 493, 494, 495, 735
National Political Congress of Black Women (NPCBW), 140, **487–488**
National Republican Coalition for Choice, 178
National Retail Federation, 253

Peace movement, 53–54, 75, 217, 341, 436, **529**, 560, 705–707, 713–714.
See also Nonviolence; Nuclear arms testing

Pelosi, Nancy, **529–530**

People's Party, 396

Perkins, Frances, 109, 110, 191, 197, 507, **530–532**, 666

Personal Responsibility and Work Opportunity Reconciliation Act (1996), xliv, 135, 173, **532**, 588, 693

Personnel Administrator of the Commonwealth of Massachusetts v. Feeney, **533**

Peterson, Elly, 572

Peterson, Esther, 236, 305, **533–534**, 543

Pettis Roberson, Shirley, **534–535**

Pfost, Gracie, **535**

Phillips v. Martin Marietta Corporation, 231, **535**

Phillips, Wendell, 649

Planned Parenthood Association of Kansas City, Mo. v. Ashcroft, **536**

Planned Parenthood Federation of America (PPFA), 113, **536–537**, 599, 687–688, 797, 803

Planned Parenthood of Central Missouri v. Danforth, **537**

Planned Parenthood of Southeastern Pennsylvania v. Casey, **538**, 664

Poelker v. Doe, **538**

Political leadership education, 126–127, 168, 174, 393–396, 486, 716, 728.
See also Women's officeholding; Women's status, commissions on

Pollution, 119–121

Populist Party, 396

Pornography, 212–213, 298, 413–414, **539**

Poverty, children in, 532

Poverty, women in, 265–266

Pratt, Eliza Jane, **539–540**

Pratt, Ruth, **540–541**

Pregnancy, 162, 510, 532
male, 641
in military, 335, 439
teenage, 8–9, 227, 265, 532, 537, 567
See also Abortion; Contraception; Reproductive rights

Pregnancy discrimination, courts on, 112–113, 152–153, 289–290, 465–466, 510, 673

Pregnancy Discrimination Act (1978), 112–113, 231, 288, 290, 395, 496, **541**, 604, 673

Presidential appointments, xxii

Presidential campaign management, 248, 450–451

Presidential candidates/nominees, 138, 140, 404, 428, **541–542**, 562, 624, 636, 720, 721, 757, 758, 760

Presidential commissions, 160–161, 250.
See also Women's status, commissions on

Presidential orders. *See individual executive orders*

President's Advisory Committee for Women, 467

President's Commission on the Status of Women (PCSW), xlii, 142, 160, 236, 239, 250, 251, 476, **542–545**, 709
individuals on, 216, 301, 459, 460, 534, 586

President's Interagency Council on Women, **545**

President's Task Force on Women Business Owners, 695

President's Task Force on Women's Rights and Responsibilities, **545–547**

Presidents' wives, xxvi

Price Waterhouse v. Hopkins, 145, 232, **547–548**

Priest, Ivy Baker, 87, **548**, 572

Prison reform, 56, 355, 700–701, 705, 715

Privacy rights, 88, 308, 313, 581, 582

Prochoice advocates, 5. *See also* Abortion; Reproductive rights

Progressive Party, 58, 542, **548–549**

Prohibition (1919–1933), 660, 700

Prohibition Party, 699

Pro-life Action League (PLAL), 509, 518, **549**

Prolife advocates, 5. *See also* Abortion; Conservatism; Reproductive rights

Property rights, 31, 38, 92, 142, 176–177, 421–422, 544, 606, 635

Protective legislation, xli, 217–218, 234, 372–373, 476, **550**, 560, 719
courts on, 173, 457–458, 477–478, 690–691
and ERA, 35, 36, 192, 237, 383, 395, 476, 491, 533–534, 655, 708, 715
See also Bona fide occupational qualification; Child labor; Sex discrimination; Work hours; Workplace conditions

Pryce, Deborah, **550–551**

Public accomodations laws, 23, 143, 546, 662–663

Public defenders, 699–701

Public office, women elected to, xliii, **551–553**, 573, 608, 711, 725
financing campaigns for, 164, 552, 709
See also Congress; Gender balance; Political leadership education; State legislatures

World Women's Congress for a Healthy
    Planet, 12
Wright, Frances (Fanny), xl, 4, 553,
    723–724
Wright, Mary A., 638

Year of the Woman (1992), **725**

Yellen, Janet, 110, **725–726**
Yorkin, Peg, 263
Young Women's Christian Association
    (YWCA), 104, 132, 174, 326–327,
    726–728

Zonta International, 144

Suzanne O'Dea Schenken is an independent scholar specializing in politics, feminism, and the political history of Iowa. Her published works include *Legislators and Politicians: Iowa's Women Lawmakers,* and her columns have appeared in the *Sioux City Journal.*